THE JOHN HOTSON MEMORIAL SERIES

MELTDOWN

MONEY, DEBT AND THE WEALTH OF NATIONS

How zero inflation is leading the world's monetary and economic systems to collapse

Volume 3 of an anthology of articles from the Journal of the Committee on Monetary and Economic Reform, 2002–2003

William Krehm, Editor

ISBN 978-0-9680681-4-4

Printed and bound in Canada.

COMER Publications
245 Carlaw Street, Suite 107
Toronto, ON M4M 2S6
Telephone: 416-924-3964
Fax: 416-466-5827

Look for COMER online on the World Wide Web at www.comer.org.

Typesetting and design: Tony Koch, Pagecraft Computer Services
Set in Minion and Frutiger.

Printing: Maracle Press Limited, Oshawa, Ontario, Canada

CONTENTS

INTRODUCTION

AT THIS POINT in the 1990 decade the processes of deregulation and globalization surrendered the world of economics to the tyrannical domain of the infinite. Our first contact with it had been the atomic bombs the brought the Japanese surrender in World War II. But that initial encounter of man and the infinite could be considered a matter of strictly military technology. There had been no time for it to flower into philosophy or theology. By the 1990s we had further proof of a relationship that had already been covered by Marshall Macluhan's *The Medium is the Message*, or by my own realization some decades later that even great thinkers unconsciously end up influenced in their thinking by the prevailing industrial technology. Thus Marx growing up in the railway-building age, developed a corresponding view of society's development predetermined by rails of steel leading from stop to stop at fixed intervals until reaching the ultimate grand terminal, where we can all descend in near-inevitable beatitude, provided, of course, that there have been no derailments.

In a similar sense the 1990s were the period when the mathematics of the infinite took command of economics. But in university economics courses there is a basic ignorance of the essence of exponential growth or development. and even of exponential development that has its philosophical and social implications. I remember a highly dedicated and fine economist of our own tendency filling a whole blackboard of a study class illustrating how compound interest grows in a devouring way, in the belief that this was exponential growth.

With that view often goes the popular example, that if the Virgin Mary had bought for the Infant Jesus a bond yielding 3%, there would not be enough silver in the world today to pay the interest earned. But the Infant Jesus, had he not been crucified, would have had to wait 2008 years to reach that situation. The atomic bomb dropped on Hiroshima, on the other hand, flattened the city in a matter of seconds. "Exponential" means not "very, very, big, big," but is a very precisely structured growth rate so that the rate of growth of the rate of growth – the acceleration, and the rate of growth of the acceleration to infinity all move up to equal the value attained by the base expression itself. Since reproducing that by computer taxes my command of that beast, I refer the reader to the nearest maths textbook covering exponential development.

During the 1990s the meddling of economists with the concept of infinite growth took place by several different paths. First came the relaxation or outright removal of the restrictions against banks acquiring interests in the other "financial pillars" – stock brokerages, insurance and mortgage firms. The Rooseveltian ban on such takeovers was well-based: each of these "other pillars" had its own cash reserves needed for its own business. Allow banks to take over these reserves, and they will use them as the cash base on which to apply the bank multiplier. The latter, basic to banking, is the multiple of the

cash in the banks' vaults that the banks lend out, under formally organized "fractional-reserve banking." Remove such restraints and you open the door to a skyscraper of restructuring of the bank-credit supply with the same procedure of factional reserve banking repeated at each floor, and an elevator designed only to move upward. Moving downward would be a holocaust of credit destruction, a run on the banks of the land, that is the equivalent of a lethal epidemic.

This effect is heightened by the simplification of the original controls to protect the economy against this giddy process. Under the Rooseveltian banking reform, that became in a general way an international model, these controls of interest and bank credit for good reason were double – for so much wealth and power would come with entrusting this to a single policy device and hence to a single social group. That would concentrate too much power in bankers' hands. One such control that had been avoided had been the benchmark interest rate that one bank may charge another for overnight borrowing – not from the central bank, but from another bank. In the US this is known as the "federal funds rate" and the central bank does not lend such moneys to banks, but only sets the rate. The reason for that is that – particularly today when the world is off the gold or any other metallic standard – loans from the central banks are the only legal tender in existence and therefore must be kept undefiled by subprime assets whose market value may not be available. There is in the US another rate – the discount rate – where the central bank actually lends out the money to a bank in distress, but at a considerably higher rate. Banks make use of it only when no other choice is open to them and, in addition, the fact that a bank would borrow at the discount window at a higher interest rates, and subject to careful approval, would advertise that the borrowing bank is under stress, the equivalent in the banking world to a synthesis of HIV and leprosy.

First, as the banks recovered from their gambling binges due to the stern prohibition of their acquiring interests in other "financial pillars" – to wit, at the time, stock brokerages, insurance, and mortgage companies, being relaxed, and then largely overridden. And the banks used the access acquired to the cash reserves held by such non-banking "financial pillars" as base money for the application of the banking multiplier, that is, of the essence of fractional reserve banking.

It began with the mathematics of derivatives of rates of growth or shrinkage to various degrees being applied to almost anything in the economy: to quantities of whatever goods produced, profits made, interest rate increases. Insurance against an undesired outcome – say a loss occurring on a particular deal. The latter is known as a "swap," because it swaps quite the opposite happening against which an investor might wish to obtain protection. But this is not in the least necessarily connected with the real producing economy. The swap insurance may outrun by say 50 or 100 times the stake of the buyers of such in the real economy, It may be there to protect a against a real risk or it can be entirely independent of any economic position taken. That means that the insurer who insures against the undesired happening is vastly exposed and may himself disappear when the time comes for him to pay off a vast lost bet. Such swaps can readily entail 100 times the actual exposure of anyone to a position in the real economy.

In fact the Holy Scriptures could, if need arose, be rewritten as one grand Swap with the Lord or the Devil. Or even partly with either. We have shaken the dust of the earthly economy from our hands and hearts and entered a metaphysical world. And to complete the miracles, the anointed must add a few digits to the stakes to emphasize our transition into the metaphysical.

William Krehm

Privatization Strikes Back

AS IN THE DRIFT APART of once-united continents, there is a growing distance between what reigning ideologies profess and their hidden agenda. Education and science are becoming acceptable only when on a leash. That brings to centre stage a brand of know-nothing politician who scoffs at learning and appeals wholly to "common sense." Often their own indifferent experience with schools and books leads them to take joy in standing teachers in the corner, putting them on severe rations, and even submitting them to "requalification" tests.

Of all that Mike Harris, the retiring premier of Ontario, Canada's wealthiest province, is a textbook example. His very manner suggests the schoolyard bully, quicker with fists than mind. Throw your opponent off-balance with a blow to the midriff. Push through a volume of "reforms" while the going is good, without you yourself realizing what you're up to.

In this way Harris's hasty budget cuts and privatization brought on fatal E. coli outbreaks in smaller municipalities. With poll ratings parallelling the stock market meltdown, Harris has opted for retirement. But in departing, he has made a point of slamming the door in a way that will not be soon forgotten. He is rushing through the privatization of the public power system established a century ago by his own party and that served as an international model. And this at a time when power deregulation and privatization have led to disaster not only in California, but for Enron Corp., the main promoter of power and other privatizations and futures trading internationally. And when September eleventh has resulted in considerable rethinking of privatization even in the United States.

Elsewhere in this issue, we note Enron had risen to dizzy market valuations by a variety of accounting devices for keeping liabilities off its balance sheets. This not only involved complex derivatives, but undisclosed partnerships with its own Chief Financial Officer. Similar shifts off-balance-sheet are taking over in other fields – in the historical record, economic theory, political control, and society itself. Lack of adequate timely disclosure guarantees nasty surprises eventually turning up in the sacred "bottom line" itself. And with that "the maximizing of shareholder equity" – the maxim that had gone far to replace public morality in our time – also takes a mortal hit. Crucial sections of laws on our books seem to have been rewritten in invisible ink. We seem prone to cut out key chapters of our history much as little girls do paper dolls. Each vital bit of information shifted "off balance-sheet" begets still others. Before long not only accounting, but democracy itself has been reduced to figurehead status, a *roi fainéant* crowned with a jester's cap to be trotted out for ceremonial occasions. And throughout it all, the back-room boys decide basic policy according to private interests. Bothersome exponents of seditious ideas or even with excessively good memories are rendered non-existent.

Let us begin with some off-balance-sheet history.

When Harris was elected seven years ago, the federal Liberal government had already slashed its grants to the provinces, to recoup the added debt taken on in bailing out the chartered banks from their immense losses in speculative oil and real estate flings during eighties.

Under its Conservative predecessor in Ottawa a revision of the Bank Act had been slipped through parliament without debate or press release phasing out the cash reserves that the banks had to put up with the Bank of Canada. These had served as a token backing for the deposits of the public that they held, and also provided an alternative to the use of interest rates to help stimulate or cool the economy as the need arose. They earned the banks no interest. When held by the Bank of Canada federal debt is practically an interest-free loan, since the interest paid on it reverts to the central government almost entirely as dividends. For the sole shareholder of the central bank is the Canadian government. When chartered banks hold the same debt, that interest stays with them. With the end of the reserves in Canada around the end of 1993, our banks were able to take on a further $80 billion of federal debt. This amounted to an entitlement of somewhere between $5-7 billion a year, depending on how high the Bank of Canada had set the interest rate.

Converted into a perpetual bond, it would have a value of about $100 billion – more than 30% of the existing federal debt at the time.

Mr. Martin's Big Secret

That is the big unspeakable secret behind the current mantra of our Finance Minister: "We've got to balance the budget." At the end of WW2 the federal debt had amounted to 144.9% of the Gross Domestic Product. By 1975 it had been reduced to 22.1%. By 1993 the federal debt had risen again to 58.8% of the GDP, nothing to panic about, but indicating the cost of subsidizing our banks in the new casino plays that deregulation allowed them. In 1975 the Bank of Canada had held 20.8% of the federal debt; by 1993 that had been reduced to 5.8%. Meanwhile, the sky-high interest rates imposed "to lick inflation" and attract the hot money to finance the debt of all levels of government had shrivelled the tax-base and pushed up the debt. The portion held by non-residents outside Canada rose during the same period from 4.2% to 26.3%. This has played a key part in the weakening of our dollar. And that in turn has been a major argument of a pressure group for our adoption of the US currency.

With an increasing amount of key history kept off the nation's balance-sheet, one thing always leads to another. Today, the real financial state of many public companies becomes available to the investing public only when they file for bankruptcy – that is, when the clock stands at midnight.

There are still more big secrets kept off the nation's balance-sheet. that have a bearing on the deficit that has our Finance Minister, Paul Martin, so preoccupied. Over the past forty years four royal commissions had recommended the introduction into the government's books of accrual accountancy. To no effect. A couple of years ago the Auditor General of Canada dug in his heels and refused to give unconditional approval to the government's books, the federal liberal government finally agreed to it. It is slated to come into effect in 2002. Also known as "capital budgeting," accrual accountancy has always been used by private firms. It treats investments in buildings or equipment that will be useful for many years as long-term assets to be written off gradually over the period of their usefulness. Most governments, including that of the US up to 1996, wrote or write them off in a single year.

The net effect of this is to exaggerate the burden of the debt, by ignoring the undepreciated capital assets – land, building, equipment that part of that debt had contributed to buy. It was like calculating your net worth by noting that you owed the amount of the mortgage that you contracted to buy your home, but omitting the value of the house itself. And even the Auditor General has still not proposed that the public investment in human capital such as education, health and social services, be depreciated and amortized the debt to finance them in a similar way. And yet economists have long recognized – in footnotes but not in their models – that the most productive of all investments is in humans.

Keynes's Forgotten Advice

John Maynard Keynes had handled the issue with clarity. He proposed a double budget – an "operational budget" which should always be balanced; and a "capital budget" which should be balanced when the economy is approaching its full physical capacity, but should invest more than its current revenues and amortization when the private sector is depressed. Underlying this proposal, was Keynes's concept of the "liquidity trap." This occurs when confidence of investors and consumers has been undermined and everybody is too frightened to lend or borrow, because of the accumulated unsold inventories and bad debt. Then, argued Keynes, in the very name of prudence, the government must step in to catch up with essential investments so that the total investment – private and public – be restored to previous levels. This explains why near zero – interest rates haven't lifted the Japanese economy out of its depression in a decade, and why the US Fed's repeated interest-rate cuts, rather than effective, have suggested the stuttering of someone in a blue funk. Alone they will not restore the US and Canadian economies.

The trouble, too, is that by keeping the details of the 1991 bank bailout off-balance-sheet, the government is preparing for an encore, as the Enron and countless other failed financial high jinx catch up with our financial institutions. A period of government surpluses or even balanced budgets is an ideal time for putting an end to the GST which is not only an unjust tax on the most vulnerable members of society, but on those who have suffered most from the slashing of social programs. Putting an end to the GST is the surest way of reviving consumer demand. The article on Kalecki elsewhere in this issue emphasizes his

point that workers spend essentially all their income (certainly over their life-span) whereas non-workers are far less likely to. In such times middle and upper class people would be far more likely to use tax-cuts not to increase their consumption but to pay off existing debt.

When Privatization Becomes a Racket

But there is another important by-product of the fixation on debt reduction, while keeping both the origin of much of our federal debt and the functions of federal debt off-balance-sheet. The most irresponsible and indeed anti-social way of continuing debt reduction is by privatization. Unless they are incorporated as separate Crown Corporations, such assets appear on government books – in the absence of capital budgeting – with a token value of one dollar. Even in the case of crown corporations the government may have covered large losses over the years to build up services viewed as socially necessary. Selling them even at a fraction of their worth will appear as a profit that can be applied to create a budgetary surplus for the year which is usually politicians' immediate goal. And then the asset can be incorporated as a private company listed on the stock market, the prices of its services reassessed at market value, and the resulting profits real or imagined, capitalized into the remote future. That may assure fat capital gains for the promoters, and at times for the purchasers of stock under the Initial Public Offering (IPO). With the stock market in headlong drop, it is scarcely an ideal time for privatizations from the public point of view. Since capital budgetting has been adopted by the federal government, it would make sense for provincial governments to consider its adoption as well where it does not exist. That in turn would underline advisability of delaying privatization, even when it might be wise, until the true capital value of the assets to be sold were ascertained and entered into the government books.

There are other considerations affecting the possible profit prospect of a privatized asset. Few public assets in developed countries were developed just to yield a profit to the government. Most had the original purpose of providing a public service that was either not available, or available at an unacceptable cost. Privatizing it and transforming into just a commercial company, usually means dropping this aspect of its original function. In the instance of the Canadian National Railways that was put together early in the century from bankrupt smaller lines that brought railway services to many otherwise inaccessible communities. Privatization may make it a more efficient commercial operation if that is measured by its rate of profit, but less efficient in providing society with essential services.

Harris's Hydro Privatization at First Glance

The outstanding consideration in Harris's announcement of the privatization of Hydro One would seem to be to come to the rescue of Bay St. when its prospects hung low. What is involved is the transmission of facilities to bring up to a possible $200 million of fees to brokerage and other financial houses, which are mostly controlled by our large banks. It could be seen in fact, as the first installment from the provincial government on the next bank bailout. That bailout, indeed, is likely to be of such proportions that it will be necessary for all levels of government to contribute towards it. And the "off-balance-sheet" arrangement lowers transparency in enough areas to make that possible. At an expected $5 billion it is forecast (G&M, 13/12, "Ontario utility IPO seen setting fee record" by Jacquie McNish and Andrew Willis) that brokerage houses stand to earn $200 million if their fees are at standard rates, but in any case no less than half that amount.

The G&M (14/12, "Utility sale seen hurting users" by Martin Mittelstaedt) reports: "The privatization of Hydro One Inc. will lead to economic pain for consumers in the form of higher electricity rates according to the industry group representing Ontario's largest power users, the Association of Major Power Users says that all users – large and small – will be paying more because of the way the province is selling its transmission utility: the choice of an Initial Public Offering of the shares of a company controlling 90% of lines that deliver power to consumers. To move the largest IPO on record (over twice the amount of the next largest) 'underwriters will want major price concessions.'

"The Association of Major Power Consumers in Ontario that offered this criticism includes such firms as General Motors of Canada Ltd., and Dofasco Inc., the steelmaker, both of which consume vast amounts of power. Transmission costs account for typically 15% of the final cost of electricity. The rest of the bill goes to the power generator, the local utility that actually delivers the energy to customers, and a special charge to retire the debt of Ontario Hydro, the forerunner to Hydro One. Almost all the components of electricity bills in Ontario are under upward pressure, and Dofasco, the province's largest single user, said that when the province opens its market to competition next spring rates could rise by 20 to 40%. David Goldsmith, vice chairman of the AMPCO remarked, 'Turning Hydro One into a non-profit operation, the other option under consideration, could have allowed the province to cut rates by about 15% by eliminating the Ontario Hydro debt retirement. A conversion to a debt-funded non-profit would have yielded twice as much money for the province, allowing the debt charge to be removed. The charge would have gone to zero immediately.'"

William Krehm

A Systems View: Stress and Priorities

FROM TIME TO TIME we all meet with challenges that demand some adaptive response. If we are lucky, these demands will not be beyond our capacities and we will have time to mobilize resources, so that we may solve the problems and meet the needs. However we now live in a world where the pace of change is itself a problem. Challenges often come faster than they can be disposed of. The time required to respond and regroup may be too great to accommodate the demands, and disorders accumulate in the lives of individuals and societies across the world.

At the level of the biological organism, in addition to the specific effects of a damaging agent (for example, an injury or infection), there are non-specific effects associated with the general mobilization of defences. There is a call on resources to repair the damage and restore the conditions of equilibrium necessary for continuing life and for readiness to meet future challenges. Among such reactions, which may include responses to threat or danger in the absence of any actual injury, there may be various kinds of overreaction and misplaced responses. These may in turn be the source of further damage. In the individual such maladaptive reactions may lead to high blood pressure, peptic ulcers, and many other diseases.

Similar system principles operate in societies. Since the assault on New York on September 11, there have been several calls to national alertness, said to be necessitated by circumstances. Yet it is simply not possible for any individual or society to maintain a state of maximum alertness for any prolonged period of time, and the effort to do this produces increasingly dangerous overload and exhaustion. Under such circumstances judgment suffers, attention tends to be occupied by what is less important, while more serious and complex problems go unregarded. Moreover there may be a sense that those responsible for policy, in alerting the public to dangers which cannot be specified, are trying to offload their responsibilities, not knowing what else to do. Political leaders have mostly been elected because they know how to protect vested interests, but the time when those were adequate skills is quickly passing. And so we may lose confidence in leadership.

We tend to cling to what we know, which can be a danger when circumstances have changed. This kind of problem is a recurrent theme and source of tragedy in human affairs. When in 1845 the Franklin expedition became trapped in the ice of the Northwest passage they apparently tried to save their silverware and other precious goods, and thus encumbered went to their death. If they had abandoned what was not necessary and tried to live off the land they might have had a better chance.

The evidence suggests that most of our leaders in government, practical men and women though they may be, have few or no serious strategies for the management of complexities. As a result, we have in Canada the offloading of responsibilities by those who have the power onto those who face the actual responsibilities – and of course the latter cannot refuse. In addition, at the level of social systems – federal, provincial and municipal – signs of overload and generalized stress reactions are also in evidence. Political leaders not only keep things simple for the people, they tend to oversimplify the problems for themselves. The consequences are downloaded, to be reflected in personal stress, high levels of indebtedness, family breakdown and divorce, etc. To add to the impositions, in a bizarre twist our leaders tell us that consumers must spend in order to increase business activity!

As a society we are like a ship sinking lower in the water, perhaps close to our rated weight limits. Since we have no measure of such limits. we do not know how long we can stay afloat. Various specific demands may be reasonable in themselves, but demands may pile up an unreasonable numbers. Resources may then be inadequate for meeting even important needs, such as those in education, health care and transportation, as well as disease prevention and public safety. Under such circumstances, valuations that support business activity at the expense of human life must come into question.

At the very least we need a better discussion of options and tradeoffs. A lack of coherent strategy invites systemic breakdown whether at the level of the biological organism, the human mind, the family, group or society. We need to ask more of our leaders, whose responsibilities go beyond protecting themselves from criticism.

No Sure Answers to Existential Problems

There are no sure or certain answers to such existential problems, but there are methods which may be useful in rendering the complexities more manageable.

The first requirement is to reduce confusions by being clear about values and priorities, making the kinds of choices and commitments required not just to simplify and bring order our of chaotic events but to focus upon what matters most. Of course, any specific commitment involves risk. The values given priority, the actual choices made, will have their own particular consequences. Now the choice of an absolute fundamentalism, which by definition does not allow for correction of errors or for learning, is a dead end. (In this sense all fundamentalists are of the same mold despite cultural or religious differences.)

The management of stressful insecurity almost always requires attention to long-term values, on the goals required to sustain life. Among the values competing in the world today are many which reflect fear and narrow self-interest, ignorance, anger and frustration, and the evils of terrorism and destruction. There is not space here to summarize the values and assumptions which can distract and overload our leaders, which threaten and confuse us into an inability to set any priorities at all. And unfortunately the realization of what is important in life is not easy, and often depends upon the experience of some major personal tragedy.

But on behalf of society we fortunately have some farsighted thinkers who have pointed the way. These include Hazel Henderson[1] and Donella Meadows[2] as well as many others. These intellectual leaders point to the necessity of an adequate vision for the organizing of a sustainable world, for values in terms of

which we can reduce the confusions which threaten to overwhelm our capacities for responsible thought and democratic governance. It is essential to pursue the values associated with the requirements of life, so that the values associated with economic goods can be seen in perspective.

Values on behalf of life, while anticipated in many traditions as a matter of faith, are also grounded in the realities of biology and in systems science. In such lights, the attempt to avoid the resolution of a life-threatening conflict is to court breakdown – including physical disorders and incapacities, mental disorders (denial, evasion, anxiety displaced into irrelevant preoccupation and imaginary worlds, delusions of omnipotence and/or paranoia), and social breakdown (starvation, crime, corruption, terrorism). Strategies to deal with such problems must clearly deal with fundamentals.

It is possible for many to become relatively insulated from such matters – to maintain illusions – for considerable periods of time. When the Black Death ravaged Europe it was possible for some of the elite to live a temporary life of quarantine in their castles. But there can be nowhere to escape such realities for long.

In our time attempts at social isolation assume many forms. Wealthy elites can live in enclaves and employ private guards. But perhaps the most pernicious isolation is that of transnational corporations which can ride above the vicissitudes of particular regions and problems, to exploit opportunities to which they can respond and avoid other responsibilities (economic "externalities") whenever possible. Attempts to rationalize irresponsibility in this regard – claims that "the fad for corporate social responsibility is doing real harm"[3] are driven by self-interest and ideological blinkers, in disregard of the foundational requirements for life.

The values of the free market cannot for long be given more weight than those values which sustain the world on which all life depends. To understand the need for changed priorities it is necessary to abandon illusions. This is also the key to strategies against terrorist delusions. Unfortunately it is a fact of life that changes in values and priorities so often must depend upon felt occasions of grief and loss. And yet, if they do not give full sway to animal instincts of fear and hate, these feelings can open the way to new possibilities for learning and development.

Bruce Buchanan

1. Henderson, Hazel (1996). *Building a Win-Win World: Life Beyond Global Economic Warfare* (p. 4). Bettett-Koehler Publishers.
2. Meadows et al (1992). *Beyond the Limits: Confronting Global Collapse & Envisioning a Sustainable Future.* Chelsea Green.
3. Curse of the ethical executive. (2001, Nov. 17). *The Economist*, p. 70.

REVIEW OF A BOOK BY MALCOLM C. SAWYER, MACMILLAN, LONDON, 1985

The Economics of Michal Kalecki

IN A NEW BOOK OF MINE now in the hands of the printers, there occurs this paragraph in the chapter on John Maynard Keynes: "Anything that smacks of Keynes's teachings, real or imagined, is blocked and buried. Government constitutions have been rewritten with special provisions to ensure that he stay demurely under his tombstone. As much as his doctrines, his personality accounted for the spell he cast. For in sheer analytical power, there were others who got to the core of things a bit sooner and a bit deeper. But Keynes was the one bred at the very heart of orthodoxy who could scoff at the pious in their own accents to challenge their suicidal greed. He charted a way of manicuring capitalism's claws, and rendering it housebroken. He mocked the very philosophy that drove its futile bustle, and endorsed the views of his Bloomsbury friends about the ultimate ends of living. And while doing all this, he showed a more commanding familiarity with the system's nuts and bolts than its choirboys."

Amongst these "others" who may have said it before Keynes and perhaps even better, probably the most prominent is Michal Kalecki. A self-taught Polish socialist, most of Kalecki's seminal work was done in Poland and in Polish. With a Marxist-Ricardian background, he lacked just about all of Keynes's advantages of circumstance.

Sitting at table well above the salt with the mighty of this world, Keynes could always count on an awed hearing. Yet Robert Sidelsky writes of the obstacles that even Keynes encountered in having his ideas translated into policy. He suggests that Roy Harrod, Keynes' first biographer, omitted mention of Keynes's early homosexuality and his registration as a conscientious objector in the First World War to avoid challenges to Keynesian economics based on objections to Keynes as a person. He omits, too, any mention of Keynes's late sympathy with the labour theory of value expressed in his *General Theory* (1936) – a sharp change of position since his dismissal of it as "unscientific" just a decade earlier. Malcom C. Sawyer observes, "The resistance to the ideas of Kalecki, involving a sharper challenge to capitalism, would have been much stronger (p. 204). Not only did Kalecki not expect to seduce those in the saddle, but developed a laconic style that stopped short of even trying to.

There is a reason why I should be devoting so much attention to a technical analysis of Kalecki's writings. It has to do with the key importance I attribute to the Tinbergen Counting Rule that emphasizes matching the number of independent variables in any proposed solution to that in the problem addressed. Evaluating the relative achievement of Keynes and Kalecki can best be done in the light of the Tinbergen Test.

Keynes's aberrant brilliance, in a country renowned for eccentrics, was relatively easy to put up with. But a Polish-Jewish, self-taught, socialist economist might as well have arrived as a stowaway from another planet.

This contrast in their origins also had its influence on their respective methodologies, Sawyer notes the contrast in their respective choices of significant variables, and in what statistics they disaggregate or fail to. The reader will note that the Tinbergen Rule imposes a high degree of disaggregation to be able to come up with the number of variables in the proposed solution to match those in the problem.

The labour theory of Ricardo and Marx held that wages represented the cost of labour power, i.e., just enough for the worker to survive and reproduce. Slightly reworked, this provides Kalecki's basic maxim: "workers spend what they earn, whereas capitalists save what they spend." Keynes does not even break up consumer spending into the two constituents of workers' and capitalists' outlays. Instead he deals merely with the aggregate "consumer expenditures," a function of disposable private sector income."

Sawyer makes little of the fact that Keynes sees price as a derivative – where the rate of profit (i.e., increase in value) on the last unit sold is zero – an equilibrium point.

An Economy of Derivatives

With Kalecki it is the actual cost function not its rate of increase on the last unit marketed. Writing 15 years before the flowering and implosion of the New Economy it would be too much to demand of Sawyer to appreciate the dazzling progeny of marginal price theory that arose as financial derivatives. These in fact have made possible the boom and bust of the "New Economy." Kalecki hews rigorously to real values and costs in the Ricardo-Marxian tradition, and is proof against mistaking derivatives of any order – marginal utility or financial derivatives – with the core determinants of the economy.

Sawyer writes: "To illustrate our point we take the model of the National Institute of Economic and Social Research (London), which has often been described as a Keynesian approach. This description may be a suitable one if the intention is to distinguish their approach from a monetarist one." However, a comparison leads Sawyer to the conclusion: that this and other macroeconometric models are more in tune with the views of Kalecki than with the views of Keynes.

In Keynes's writing expectations about the future play a great role in determining current economic behaviour Yet, given the essential unknowability of the future, the basis of those expectations is flimsy. In short the basic subjectivity of marginal utility value – like that of the stock market – is an evanescent thing that invites manipulation.

"In contrast, Kalecki relies on 'objective' rather than 'subjective' factors. His approach leads to relatively stable relationships which can be estimated. There is, however, a *caveat* to that in an essay of his comparing econometric models and historical materialism. Essentially, he argued that an econometric model was based on unchanging relationships between the variables involved in their earlier values. 'Historical materialism considers the process of the development of a society as that of productive forces and productive relations [the base] which shape all the other social phenomena…[the superstructure]….' The thrust of that paper appears to be that econometric models are useful provided that the assumptions of what is taken as unchanging are clearly borne in mind, and that at times 'the path of economic developments will alter abruptly.'"

Keynes' criticism of econometrics was far more realistic. Interventionism on the market and the non-market sectors of the economy has been ongoing. That will in itself undermine assumptions based on the past performance of the favoured variables and thus the coordinates chosen for the best fit with those variables.

What is of particular interest today is that the further disaggregations may provide the necessary variables to match the variables in our proposed solutions to those in the problems they address. They furnish the additional options we have need of to orchestrate solutions that will address all the independent variables of the problem.

Foreseeing Political Business Cycle

Reflecting his background, Kalecki was particularly sensitive to the class structures of society, and their effects on policy.[1] That was perhaps most obvious in his notion of a "political business cycle" that he foresaw. "The maintenance of full employment would entail substantial government intervention in capitalist economies, and would generate substantial social and political changes. He organized his discussion of the opposition to full employment under three headings: (a) the dislike of government interference; (b) the dislike of the direction of government spending (public investment and subsidizing consumption); (c) the dislike of the social and political changes resulting from the maintenance of full employment.

"Under *laissez-faire* capitalism, the level of employment strongly depends on the 'state of confidence.' If confidence falters, then so does investment, and thereby output and employment. Confidence is a fragile flower that needs great care, i.e., policies industrial leaders approve of. The use of public expenditure to maintain the level of demand is seen to 'remove considerable power from capitalists, whose threats not to invest if confidence is harmed becomes less potent. When a government is prepared to use public expenditure to ensure full employment, investment, the control [of investors] loses its power over the level of employment.'

"The argument against public expenditure will be wrapped in semi-moralistic arguments on the need to balance the budget, not to spend more than one's means, etc. And the need for 'sound finance.' But the 'social function' of the doctrine of 'sound finance' is to make the level of employment dependent on the 'state of confidence.'

"Kalecki forecasted that there would be the argument that by subsidising consumption, the Government would not be embarking on any sort of 'enterprise.' In recent years this argument has re-emerged, as [the claim] that public expenditure is not wealth-creating and the public sector lives on the back of the wealth-creating private sector. Secondly there is a 'moral' principle of the highest importance at stake: 'You shall earn your bread in sweat – unless you have private means.'

"However, these arguments against public investment do not apply against expenditure for armaments.

"It is worthwhile to quote Kalecki's views on the political and social changes inherent in the maintenance of full employment. 'Under the maintenance of full employment, "the sack" would cease to play a role as a disciplinary measure. The social position of the boss would be undermined and the self-assurance of the working class would grow. But 'discipline in the factories' and 'political stability' are more appreciated by business leaders than profits. Their class instinct tells them that lasting full employment is unsound from their point of view and that unemployment is an integral part of the normal capitalist system.

"He predicted that as a result of these contradictory pressures, a political business cycle would develop. Popular pressure for full employment would reach its height at or near elections, leading to government-induced pre-election booms. But between elections, unemployment would be allowed to rise to prevent the political and social changes which would result from continuous full employment."

This was first published by Kalecki in 1971, and anticipated the "natural rate of unemployment" "zero inflation" and other features that were to grace the eighties and nineties. It introduced politics into economic policy to an extent that had not existed before. Keynes appealed to the ruling class in a purely rational way. His appeal was to the "national" interest as though in fact nations were units. Kalecki's point of departure was the existence of conflicts of interest. His theories were designed to bridge such conflicts with compromise, rather than ignore them. No sound bridge can be designed unless the engineer is completely familiar with the extent of the gap to be spanned.

W.K.

1. "Kalecki was born in 1899 into a Polish-Jewish family in Lodz, Poland. He finished school in 1917 and then studied at the Polytechnic of Warsaw (1917-19) and at the Polytechnic of Gdansk (1921-23). His studies were interrupted by military service and were brought to an end by his father's unemployment. He was forced to find work to support the family. Kalecki's studies were in engineering which meant that his mathematical knowledge was considerable. He was influenced by the work of Marx, which meant that his background was different from that of most American and British economists." That was not helpful in obtaining a hearing from the body of economists in the West.

A Bankruptcy Court for Economic Theory?

THE SAGA OF ENRON teaches us that to find out what is afoot in such overly dynamic companies, we have to await their filings in bankruptcy court. Too often their success is due to their innovations in manipulating the demand for their output. The flowering of such talents under Deregulation and Globalization today would have been unthinkable without the introduction of marginal utility a century ago to drop a curtain over the seamier aspects of capitalism. That identified value with price of the last transaction on a supposedly self-balancing market.

Everything about that invites manipulation. The moment of truth comes when corporations have to file hard facts on their sales, debt, and assets under the bankruptcy laws. That, however, is a bit late in the day. It is largely for the convenience of the vulture capitalists moving in for basement bargains confirmed by information hidden from investors who financed the original enterprise. The mantra of our age – "the maximization of shareholder equity" – bites the dust.

In a desperate attempt to make up for shrivelling advertising income our better newspapers are beefing up their investigative reporting to win readers. We are thus getting very different readings on yesterday's sensational stock favourites whose market capitalizations have suddenly dropped by as much as 90% within months or even completely gone through the floor. There are enough fired executives turned whistle-blowers to provide a gush of information that would have been worth trillions had it been available at the proper time.

Thus the *Toronto Star* (8-9/12, "How a Giant fell to Earth" by Robert Criss and Tyler Hamilton) pieces together the real facts of the Nortel Networks that at its peak accounted for 36% of the total capitalization of the Toronto Stock Exchange. A half year earlier the writing was already on the wall, but the CEO John Roth, his eyes on the stars, failed to read it. Instead he went right on gobbling up other companies, paying for them with Nortel shares and options at inflated multiples of their revenue in the absence of profit.

A Voracious Chain of Predators

All this was largely the product of manipulation by a voracious chain of predators that included Nortel itself, its underwriters, and analysts.

"By the time Roth had [completed his shopping] there were 50% more Nortel shares trading in the market.

"'People confuse good technology with profitability, 'says Leo de Bever, senior vice-president of research and economics of the Ontario Teachers' Pension Plan Board, the largest single pension fund with C$73 billion invested. That pension fund pension board lost more than $600 million in 2000 through its Nortel investments.

"Likewise, by its year-end of March 31, 2001, the $7 billion Canadian Pension Plan had lost $872 million, much of it directly related to Nortel." So much for the carefully orchestrated plan to make more of the official pension money available for "growing on the stock market."

Asked about Nortel's board of directors – charged with overseeing corporate strategy and protecting the interests of investors – Roth was succinct, "I was in the process of retiring. so I was stepping back to give the new fellow room to grow." The main consideration seems to have been shaping the career of the top chap, whoever he might be.

"By the end of the summer 2000, the large business media were all reporting difficulties ahead for the telecommunications market and an uncertain future for suppliers including Nortel.

"At Cisco, Nortel's main competitor, CEO Chambers warned his sales staff that the market was getting murky.

"In mid-September, Roth was still denying signs of an industry slowdown. He told reporters at a corporate event in California that sales in its optical division could be as high as $12 billion (US) up from his original prediction of $10 billion. A day later Nortel shares jumped 6% to $99.25 on the TSE.

"While many analysts base their reports on information from the companies, these same companies base their forecasts on the analysts' reports. 'It's a revolving, cycling kind of mess where they feed on each other,' says one insider, who used to work with Nortel's business strategy and intelligence group." The mirror image, in fact, of the "peer approval" in academia.

"Paul Sagawa, an analyst with Wall St. firm Sanford C. Bernstein, started asking questions. 'Nortel was announcing "outrageous" improvements every quarter, while its biggest customers were showing signs of slowdown and the industry's smaller, less established players were accumulating enormous debt in their rush to build high-speed networks in an already saturated market. That was the red flag.

"Sagawa spent two months interviewing 59 of Nortel's customers in North America and Europe. He combed through balance sheets. Only four of these companies had positive cash flow. The rest were spending more than they were taking in. On September 28, 2000, he released a report that 'described a sharp deceleration in the telecommunications market and an uncertain future for suppliers including Nortel. Sagawa was dubbed 'Chicken Little' and dismissed by his colleagues and Nortel.

"But by October, another of Nortel's largest rivals, Lucent Technologies had already announced two profit warnings in addition to an earlier caution in July.

"In response Lucent's stock was severely battered, plunging from to $20 from $60 US in mid-July. Its CEO Richard McGinn, fired that month, blamed much of the fall on a risky strategy called 'vendor financing.' To land sales with customers who can't pay, suppliers like Nortel and Cisco loan them billions of dollars. It is a common practice that can amount to suppliers buying their own equipment to pad sales figures."

Indeed, since high-technology is driven to early obsolescence by the same desperate situation, the equipment "sold" makes poor collateral.

"'The focus is to gain as much market share at any price, so you can announce that you dominate the industry,' says Richard Woo, an analyst with Thomson Kernaghan & Co. in Montreal."

Destruction of Money Supply on the Stock Market

Meanwhile, many times the money supply created by all this sleight of hand and morality is bound to become bad debt even if one or two companies might finally achieve profitable "market dominance." What these fellows are ultimately gambling on, given the scale of their operations, is the solvency of the economy as a whole. In all the outburst of belated investigative reporting, the aspect of creation of and eventual destruction of money supply on the stock market is overlooked. When Chairman Greenspan vaguely alluded to it as early as 1996, he got his knuckles rapped by Wall St. types and he didn't return to that theme until it was far too late.

"In 2000 alone Nortel had committed more than US $5 billion in multi-year loans to customers more than double the previous year's amount and much of it to service providers headed for bankruptcy.

"In months to come a string of companies indebted to Nortel (Nettel Communications Inc., Cannect Communications Inc. and Axxent Corp., ICG Communications of Englewood Colo., Pathnet Telecommunications Inc. of Reston, VA, and Net2000 Communications of Herndon, VA) would meet similar fates.

"On October 24 Roth told analysts: 'Right now the issue is installing as fast as we can ship. The market is continuing to gain steam.' But the market had lost some of its blind faith. The next day the stock fell from $96.10 to $71.55, costing the company about $83 billion US.

"Every time the stock fell, brokers across the country got calls from clients asking, 'Is now a good time to buy Nortel?' The prevailing answer was 'Yes!'"

Taking value to depend entirely on the demand-supply ratio on the market leads to mistaking stock market manipulation for wealth production. It blurs the line separating bad theory from criminal practice.

In the *WSJ* (13/12, "When Bad Stocks Happen to Good Mutual Funds: Enron Could Spark New Attention to Accounting"), Aaron Lucchetti writes: "Janus Fund, American Century Ultra Fund, Alliance Premier Growth Fund. What do these huge mutual funds have in common? Besides having tens of billions of dollars in assets and the highly paid stock pickers of major money-management firms at their disposal, all three earlier this year had outside positions in Enron Corp., the Houston energy-trading firm now seeking bankruptcy-court protection.

"How could these funds – and numerous others – blunder like this? Turns out it is not an isolated incident. Mutual-fund companies, which manage money for millions of investors, held large stakes in just about every broken stock of the past few years from Cedant Corp. and Waste Management Inc. to Lucent Technologies Inc. The frequency with which funds have been caught holding stocks that plummet amid accounting problems raises two questions: "What are the fund managers missing as they evaluate stocks? And is there anything they can do about it?"

Since the question is asked in *WSJ's* August columns, we will provide a clue to the required answer.

The true state of an increasing number of transnationals becomes accessible only when they file for bankruptcy. Our accountancy merely echoes the economic model that is drummed into the heads of economists and the public. What is lacking is an institution which will play a similar a role in the fundamental matters of economic theory and policies that is filled by bankruptcy court when individual firms collapse. Today it is the system itself that has imploded.

William Krehm

An Evasion of the Key Issue of our Times

INTERBREEDING DISASTERS strain our ability to keep track of their progeny. Economic and monetary theory, budgetary policy, accountancy, and much else have been shaken to their moral foundations. For moral footings each of these must have if society is not to be plunged headlong into the chasm. Quite literally headlong, since it was our minds that failed us first.

Our economists operate with a model that sees mankind's future depending on absolute freedom for the movements of speculative capital and little else. So long as the stock market continued on its way up, we were assured it "worked." But now that the stock market has collapsed in clouds of corruption, long overdue reassessments have been sidetracked by piercing martial bugles.

Lewis H. Lapham in *Harpers* ("Notebook American Jihad") starting from a different port, arrives at a similar conclusion: "Three months ago I thought we'd been given a chance for a conversation about the future of the American political idea, the attacks on the Pentagon and the World Trade Center providing an impressive occasion for timely remarks on the topics of our foreign and domestic policy: informed argument about why America had come to be perceived as a dissolute empire, instructive doubts on the supposed omniscience of the global capital markets, sustained questioning of the way in which we divide the country's wealth.

"By December I knew that I'd been barking at the moon. The conversation maybe had a chance of taking place in magazines of small circulation or possibly somewhere in the distant reaches of C-SPAN, but not in the chambers of Congress, not under the circus tents of the big-time news and entertainment media.

"The Editor of *The New Republic,* outraged by the noise of protest in the streets, wrote: 'The nation is now at war. And in such an environment, domestic political dissent is immoral without a prior statement of national solidarity, a choosing of sides…. Caught up in the memory of a tale told by Homer or Rudyard Kipling, the keepers of the nation's conscience gladly smother the peepings of dissent and quickly learn to stuff a sock in the mouth of an impiety. Show them a cruise missile or a map, and they become more ferocious than the generals. The eagerness to enlarge the theater of military operations – a strategy endorsed not only by the regimental commanders at Fox News but also by Newt Gingrich, Henry Kissinger, and Senator John McCain – seemed as senseless as the elevation of Osama bin Ladin to a world figure.'"

The declaration of war in fact was an evasion of crucial issues that have clearly fuelled blind terrorism. It sidestepped serious assessment by transforming a clueless President overnight into a Commander-in-Chief who must be saluted rather than questioned. The greatest debt default ever in the Argentine is just the latest sign that the combination of financial deregulation with the privatization of the sovereign powers of money creation is arriving at the road's end. During a full decade the mésalliance of its peso with the US dollar, the Argentine had been held up as the role model for emerging and even developed countries like Canada. Declaring war against a private band of terrorists was seizing opportunity by the forelock. Continued long enough, the state of war, shifting to other "rogue states" of Washington's choosing is the ultimate ducking of Washington own dilemma. Not only will "military Keynesianism" (for which Keynes of course bears no responsibility) revive the economy, but gag any serious questioning of the official line. By now that line is in an extremely dotted condition, calling for signing rather than analysis. Since the demise of the Soviet Union the American administration has sorely missed a rival superpower. That is clear from its rush to declare war on a faceless enemy lacking even a fixed address. That leaves a convenient blank for the enemy country to be filled in at Washington's pleasure. That could keep the economy purring so long as victories, virtually bloodless for the victors, roll in. But it won't make US better loved internationally.

Instead of our focusing on the core problem of our times, we are left talking about a host of issues, trivial or important, but powerless to really do much about. That is because the core problem, discussion of which is taboo, guarantees that the resources for dealing with them will be preempted for unavaowable goals, and government treasuries will always appear as bare as Mother Hubbard's cupboard. That certainly takes care of child poverty with a bang. What is needed is public debate on our core problem, that makes all other problems derivative.

Historical Precedents

There is plenty of historic precedent for this concept of a "core problem" that literally paralyzed society from doing anything about its survival. The Great Depression of the Thirties was a case in point. The private sector had gambled itself into bankruptcy by 1929, and the breadlines circled city blocks. People starved while the government was ever further from its goal of balancing its budget. Its answer was cutting public services, which increased unemployment and added to the government deficit. Even when Keynes and others finally formulated the answer to this core dilemma, its adoption was blocked – by the concern of growing deficits leading to a replay of the hyperinflation in Germany of 1923. What was lost from sight was that the German hyperinflation was the result of a lost war, the occupation of the Ruhr industrial heartland by the French and Belgian armies, a general strike throughout Germany that both the Left and the Right supported, and virtual civil war. In the official telling any rise of the price level would lead to hyperinflation of the German sort. The nonsense of such fears could have been exposed by playing the scenario in reverse: if Germany in the early thirties had balanced its budget, it somehow would not have lost the war, the Ruhr would not have been occupied by the French, its Foreign minister would not have been assassinated, there would have been no virtual civil war. But it suited the interests and the prejudices of a powerful minority to stick to the official version: those who had money rather than debts never had it better than when prices dropped by 25% across the board.

The misread experience of the hyperinflation lives on to this day. It has been enshrined in the constitution of the European Union, where member countries had to reduce their budgetary deficit below 3% of their GDP before qualifying for membership of the European Union. By a bit of creative accountancy Italy did so by using off-balance-sheet derivatives to move some of the government liabilities into the following year's accounts when it would already have achieved entry into the monetary union.

In our day the core issue, key to practically all our economic problems, is avoiding the use of central banks to finance necessary public investment *within the limits of real economic capacity and the available foreign exchange.*

Identifying that core issue served Japan brilliantly in 1931 when the yen went off gold. And again after WWII when a crushed Japan proceeded to plan the public infrastructure for future industries. Key to its policy was applying its limited supply of foreign credits to create the infrastructures that would make possible the development of export industries to net it the greatest net foreign exchange earnings – after paying for the imports that they would require. In that way Japan replaced its position as the world's most aggressive textile exporter before WWII with a similar position in automobiles.

No country – First, Third or Emerging World – need forgo essential public investments – health education or physical infrastructures – *within the above-mentioned constraints.*

A Crisis of Globalization and Deregulation

For "fiscal responsibility" to make sense, the double budget proposed by John Maynard Keynes and others must be introduced – an operational budget that should always be balanced, and a capital budget covering investments (physical and human) that will be amortized over the term of their usefulness. The capital budget must step up its investments when the private sector lapses into recession.

Countries receiving aid could be closely audited by appropriate international organizations on which debtor as well as creditor nations would be represented to ensure that the loans are directed to their intended goals. In the light of the accountancy and other scams being revealed as major factors in the late Wall St. boom, the private financial sector lacks credentials for sitting in judgment on the public sector of any country. What is needed is transparency and periodic assessment of policy results in both sectors – especially where bailouts of private corporations by governments have taken place. That includes every major country, since bank bailouts have been occurring

regularly throughout the world once every 7 to 10 years.

In this perspective the Argentine crisis must be considered in its implications for an assessment of Deregulation and Globalization, rather than just an Argentinian problem.

The notion of a crucial core problem that must be addressed to resolve major crises is not unfamiliar to historians. In 1917, for example, the Bolsheviks were a small fraction of the Russian Democratic Socialist Party, and Lenin, in Swiss exile, had limited influence in Russia. But the Eastern front had become a vast slaughter house for troops ill-trained and ill-equipped by a regime that had already shown its hopeless incompetence in the Crimean and Japanese Wars. Foot soldiers went into battle sans rifles, with orders to pick up the gun of the soldier ahead when he fell. The Bolsheviks addressed the indispensable need before all other problems could be dealt with – to get Russia out of the senseless war. That, to their own surprise, hoisted them to power.

The Nazis picked up power in 1933, when during the Great Depression all other traditional parties – including the Socialists – refused to even consider the government incurring debt to provide jobs and survival to the growing army of jobless.

Today we have entered a similar stage where everything depends on restoring the functions of our central banks to their original purpose.

That will make possible the funding of all the derivative problems essential for society's survival.

William Krehm

A Letter to the CBC

Mr. Robert Rabinovitch
President and CEO
Canadian Broadcasting Corporation

I am editor of *Economic Reform*, a monthly publication now in its 14th year.

Last Friday, I received a phone call from Dianne Kalen, of the CBC's *Counterspin* program, asking me whether I would appear on a program on January 14 devoted to Employment Insurance. She mentioned the name of a highly respected official of the CAW as having recommended me. I assumed it was on the panel and I agreed. But I did point out that revisions of the EI, as necessary as they may be, could not possibly deal with the present deflationary emergency that is engulfing us. To pretend that they could, would be an evasion rather than a serious treatment of the subject.

I explained that we have reached a depth of crisis that prompted the founding of the Bank of Canada in 1935. That made it possible for the Canadian Government to create the funds to finance 16% of its spending during WWII and to undertake the public investments to catch up with the neglect of a decade of depression and almost six years of war. These articles in the BoC that make this possible, though little used, are still there intact in the *Bank of Canada Act* (Preamble, articles 14,

17 and 18). Because the federal government (article 14 is sole shareholder of the BoC) interest paid on federal debt held by it results in a substantially interest-free loan. I offered to bring along a copy of the *BoC Act* for the briefest mention to alert the audience that an alternative to complete reliance on EI does exist. She encouraged me to do so, I mentioned that as late as the mid-1970s over 22% of the federal debt was held by the BoC. Currently it is close to 5%. Obviously, on a program devoted to EI, it would be impossible to explain fully the technicalities of money creation involved. But it would be important and possible to alert the public that options do exist.

On arriving at the CBC an hour before the program was scheduled to start, I found out that I was to be a member of the audience not the panel.

I decided nonetheless to remain in the expectation of being able to ask a question of the panel. That was prearranged not to be. Before the show went on, the audience was instructed on procedure and invited to express brief opinions, which were carefully noted. I made the point that EI was not designed to cope with crises of the sort we are experiencing. The economy has again landed us in the 1930s in what Keynes called a "Liquidity Trap," in which borrowers are too frightened to borrow, and lenders to lend. At such junctures only the government, with the credit of the nation behind it, can create the credit through the central bank for catch-up in attacking the great backlog of necessary investments in human and physical capital. A young lady took careful note of opinions expressed. There was certainly no discrimination against people who expressed passionate doubts about capitalism in the abstract. But there was no tolerance for any reference to what the Bank of Canada was able to do in the past and what it is failing to do today.

Friends who have followed the program for some time, summed it up. "They sat you in the 'pea gallery' where nobody is ever given a chance to ask a question." Apparently the routine is systematically practised to enlist the presence of critics in the audience to create the semblance of free discussion that is in fact being artfully excluded.

These days the financial press is full of the scam of off-balance-sheet liabilities that created much of our recent stock market bubble and our current unemployment. The *CounterSpin* program reminds us that that such off-balance-sheet accounting is rife in the information industry as well. Much of our history is being suppressed precisely when we need it most.

We know that CBC has more than its fair share of budgetary problems, yet it is sad that the corporation has sunk to such shoddy compliance. It makes it difficult for its friends to defend it, and vulnerable to those who would destroy it.

This letter will be carried in *Economic Reform* and on its website, www.comer.org. We are reserving like space for your reply should you wish to make it.

Yours truly,

William Krehm

A Bit of Glasnost in Ottawa?

ON THE VERY DAY of his appointment, our new "junior finance minister" John McCallum, not so long ago a highly reputable economics professor at McGill and passingly chief economist of the Royal Bank, has done something worthy of applause. "Banks are charging vastly inflated interest rates on credit-card debt, says John McCallum, 'I think they look grotesquely high at this time of economic slowdown – and I think they should lower them,' he told reporters yesterday while heading into his first cabinet meeting" (*The Globe and Mail*, 17/1,"Minister blasts banks over credit-card rates" by Steven Chase).

Notable was his choice of the word "inflated," For a couple of decades Canadians have had their pockets picked with high interest rates in the name of "fighting inflation." Now we learn from a high official source that the cure itself is "inflationary."

That imposes a chain of other questions. But we cannot expect McCallum to carry the ball alone. All of us must pitch in and direct the follow-up questions to Ottawa. How do the banks dare pull such a scam against some of the most vulnerable members of our society? Especially since only a decade ago the banks themselves were bailed out at a staggering cost to the taxpayers from their gambling losses.

Their bailout of 1991 was slipped through Parliament without debate or press release. It phased out the cash reserve that the banks had previously left with the Bank of Canada as a token backing for the public deposits they held. These reserves earned them no interest. Shortly before the Bank for International Settlements in Switzerland had issued the *Risk-Based Capital Requirements* for Banks declared the debt of OECD countries risk-free requiring that banks put up none of their own capital to acquire. That enabled the banks to take on another $60 billion of federal debt – three times what they are already held. That amounted to an annual entitlement of at least $5 billion annually. When a year later COMER finally dug up what had happened and blew the whistle, both the banks and the government replied in chorus: "It was an unjust tax on the banks – the banks' competition, the trust companies don't have to pay it." Most of the trust companies of any size have since been gobbled up by the banks.

That "defense" misrepresented the surrender to the banks of the bulk of the sovereign powers of money-creation – the modern version of the monarch's monopoly of coining precious metals that goes back to before the Norman Conquest. That triggered an identity crisis of our banks. They came to believe that only their own hard-earned money was really involved. They lost all sense of the need for at least some quid pro quo towards the public. They screwed up fees, cut down services, closed branches, stepped up their lobbying with enough success to enable them to swallow brokerage houses, credit-card operations, merchant banking, derivative shops. They hurled themselves into highly speculative ventures that not so long banks would not have allowed even their clients to engage in. And in pushing for their right to merge, they clobbered the facts. They even argued that unless that were to be allowed to merge and further deregulate, they couldn't compete with the mammoth Japanese banks. At the time, however, the large Japanese banks were out of the loan business completely: they had already lost most or more than all their capital in the speculative eurodollar businesses that our banks lusted after.

Unless the details of the 1991-93 bank bailout are brought to light, Canadians will never understand the origins of the slashing of federal grants to the provinces, who passed on the courtesy to the municipalities. The banks had simply shoved ahead of the unemployed, the single mothers on the public welfare line. But why raise all this past history? Simply because everything is poised for it to happen again.

That is the news out of the Argentine, where the Bank of Nova Scotia acquired one of the large banks now threatened with bankruptcy. That would entail a likely loss of about $250 million US on this single investment. Canadian banks – particularly Nova Scotia – have been ridiculed in the American financial press as the fall guys buying into "securitization" of the iffiest loan deals put together by the large US banks. After pocketing their fees, the originating banks often sell much of their own participation to provincial yokels bitten by "get big quick" bug. Just an old American tradition.

I doubt that it will make Canadians proud to learn that the CBIC put up practically the only real money in a skyscraper of dissimulation thrown up to deceive investors by Enron. Enron currently is being investigated by umpteen official panels for its ingenious scams in the process of organizing a trading empire that aspired to have no real assets. Only credits running every which way. The only trouble is that only real assets with real earnings can serve as collateral to support credits. So Enron did some fabulous improvising along their way.

The Wall Street Journal (17/01, "A blockbuster Deal Shows how Enron Overplayed its Hand" by Rebecca Smith) reports: "When Enron Corp. and Blockbuster Inc. joined forces in mid-2000, it looked like they were onto something big. The companies announced they would soon be allowing consumers across America to choose from thousands of movies, including hot new features, sent via telephone lines to their TVs.

"Announcing the partnership in July 2000, Enron Chairman Kenneth Lay called it the 'killer app' for the entertainment industry' Blockbuster Chairman John Antico and Oracle Corp. Chairman Larry Ellison committed his private company, nCube Corp for critical computer hardware and $2 million.

"It looked like another brilliant move by Enron, already a Wall St. hero originally specializing in gas and energy trading. The 20-year deal would bring traffic to Enron's fledgling fiber-optic telecommunications network. Within eight months of the launch the partners had split but Blockbuster didn't know the half of it. Only when Enron filed for bankruptcy – the largest on record – did the extent of Enron's sleight of hand emerge in conjuring up assets where they didn't exist and hiding liabilities in other companies' books. And in the midst of all this, who provides the cash to keep the magic going, but the third largest Canadian bank, the CIBC. "Within months of inking the deal, Enron had set up a an affiliated partnership, code-named Project Braveheart, an apparent allusion to the 1995 Mel Gib-

son movie. Enron obtained a US $115.2 million investment in the partnership from the CIBC World Markets, the investment-banking arm of Canadian Imperial Bank of Commerce in Toronto.

"The partnership had no separate staff and no assets other than Enron's stake in the venture with Blockbuster, which was merely getting off the ground in late 2000. Still Enron claimed $110.9 million in profits from Braveheart in the fourth quarter of 2000 and the first quarter of 2001.

"At its peak, in March 2001 the venture with Blockbuster provided around 1,000 test customers with movies in four US cities. Many customers didn't even pay.

"Braveheart was one of dozens of outside partnerships that Enron officials created to burnish the company's financial results. These would then justify its soaring stock price. One of the reasons Enron began sliding towards bankruptcy court last fall was the abandonment of some of these accounting maneuvers, which resulted in huge losses and the collapse of its stock."

Our Banks Play the Village Idiots among the Big Boys at Our Taxpayers Expense

What interest did Canadian taxpayers have not only to bail out our chartered banks in the early nineties but at the same time deregulating them so that they could play the village idiots amongst the really big boys? Our government owes us an answer.

This game has gone on long enough and with such incredibly high leverage – 377:1 in total bank assets to the cash in their possession as of last September – that a 4% drop in the value of the C$1.6 trillion banks' total assets would gobble up all the cash in the banks' possession. Add the footnote that most of the banks' securities are held at the original rather than market value, and it emerges that there is a high probability that taken as a group, our chartered banks may already have lost much or all their capital, and are well on the way for their next bailout by the government.

That is not surprising, since bank bailouts across the globe have averaged more frequently in every country than once a decade. The Argentine, for example, spent half its GDP a few years back on its previous bank bailout.

Unless we bring into the open (1) the details of the last bailout; (2) the use that our banks have been allowed to make of their annual entitlement resulting from that bailout; (3) their current liquidity; (4) whether the firewall between banking and stock-market and other speculative activity should be re-established.

Failing such investigation, we will be letting ourselves in for some brutal surprises. Repeating the type of bailout our banks that took place in 1991 would be a giant step for Canada towards the plight that has overtaken Argentina.

William Krehm

A Systems View: An Open Letter to *The Economist*

THE EDITORS of *The Economist* may be wise in many things, but are not all wise, and there are many indications in a supplement, "The World in 2002," that some important factors and trends are misunderstood and misrepresented. It is worthwhile to consider some of these.

In describing the economic consequences of terror, Clive Cook notes, "The issue is confidence – American's greatest economic vulnerability." "The 2002 redefinition of economic policy – which renders the orthodox expertise of economists almost redundant – is only one of the ways in which, after September 11th, the world has changed." "The front line will not be in finance ministries, but in public confidence" (p. 15).

Let us recognize that in a democratic society public confidence has roots deeper than merely a willingness to spend money.

The article on "Civil Society," which in contrast might have shed light on developments in relation to public confidence, betrays an unwillingness to come to grips with the actualities involved. John Grimmond writes: "There is no definition [of Civil Society]. It is tempting, therefore, to dismiss the entire idea as a woolly expression for woolly-minded people. That, however, would be too charitable." Grimmond delivers his verdict that civic society includes "assorted busybodies and do-gooders, self-appointed but unelected" (p. 18).

Now, to maintain that the validity of all electoral processes and the integrity of all elected officials must remain beyond doubt is to fly in the face of the evidence. And to deny by innuendo the potential usefulness of contributions from the grass roots seems to indicate a mind closed by ideology, able only to repeat what is familiar, a frightening limitation in today's world.

Of course Grimmond is not alone; he represents a widely shared view. Martin Wolf, writing in the *Financial Times*, argued that "the claims of NGOs to represent civil society as a whole, and to possess legitimacy…is outrageous."[1] Such arguments overgeneralize to make debating points while ignoring the realities of daily life.

A little elementary research might have led to work such as that of Hazel Henderson. That the growing volume of such work is ignored is itself a problem. She writes: "Input from citizens is an essential form of expertise…. Civic Society Organizations (CSOs), sometimes still called Non-Governmental Organizations (NGOs), also went global. They incorporated the expertise of a broad range of new experts under-represented in conventional science. Such citizen groups soon learned that addressing purely local issues on a fragmented basis too often left them blind-sided by powerful global corporations and financial players." "Civic society is the primary source of social innovation" (p. 22).

In many areas of life civil society organizations are attempting to identify and address major problems. In such activities they have often found themselves at crossed purposes with multinational corporations (who so often have special leverage over governmental policies), who are also sometimes included under the rubric of Non-Governmental Organizations (NGOs). To distinguish CSOs from corporate interests is clear and useful, confusing only to those who wish to blur roles and responsibilities.

As the late Nobel prize-winner Jonas Salk said, "We are the first generation in human history in which large numbers of ordinary people are taking personal responsibility for the future of the entire species" (Henderson, p. 23).

Globalization that Bypasses the Planet

Insofar as terms such as "globalization" are based upon perspectives that do not include the planet Earth and its diversity of life forms they imply relationships which may be unsustainable. A more appropriate design of these systems, institutions and processes is a prerequisite for all efforts to rebalance our societies for sustainable development. This requires including at all levels the missing feedback from nature, planetary and local ecosystems, as well as the human beings marginalized by current forms of globalization. Such a systems approach requires distinctions among levels, including (1) the Global system, (2) the international system, (3) the Nation-State, (4) Corporate systems, (5) provincial and local systems, (6) the Civic Society (e.g., voluntary and non-profit groups, to whom governments habitually appeal), and (7) the Family and individuals – vital ingredients. All of these distinctions are useful and important, and the health of all these systems is vital to the future of mankind.

To deal with these complex realities and relationships with a policy of denial and obfuscation is intellectually irresponsible. Yet the arbitrary intrusion of ideology by *The Economist* is not new. A recent example is the special attention given by *The Economist* (August 2, 2001) to the ideas of the *Skeptical Environmentalist*,[2] the statistical analyses of which have been largely rejected by more informed commentators, including the editors and contributors to the *Scientific American*.[3] It is only human to have blind spots, but habitually to deny the possibility of blind spots is to risk disaster.

A number of writers[4] have described some features of capitalism as similar to a cancer on the fabric of societies and ecosystems. A diagnosis of possible cancer is serious business, not to be dealt with by mere rhetorical put-downs.

The concepts and processes involved in cancerous types of disorder require careful research and analysis if they are to be understood. In such work everything depends upon an adequate grasp of ideas and methods. Cancer implies such processes as the lack of nutrients for basic needs, the diversion of energies to useless activities, declining health of multiple systems and the subversion of goals by substituting feedback signals that support waste, the corruption of healthy processes and the accumulation of various toxic residues.

Healthy systems, in contrast, require accurate and timely signals and feedback loops as these are needed to support life processes. Systems of governance include a civil society which depends very much on sound information which reflect both the structures within which we must work and the realities with which we must deal. To subvert such systems with misleading information can only lead to disaster. *The Economist* is a leader in providing accurate and timely information but some of the conclusions it promulgates raise questions concerning the ends it has in view.

For example, readers of *The Economist* might have benefited from some editorial perspective on the article by Robert B. Zoellick, US trade representative – presumably an example of the wisdom of elected officials. He writes: "By moving forward with trade liberalization we signal that there is an international coalition for openness and growth that respects core values… openness, appreciation of differences, opportunity, integration, freedom of choice, governance through agreed rules and a hope for the improvement of life for all peoples."[5] It is far beyond the scope of this column to try to analyze what these grand phrases have meant in terms of disappointment to many peoples and countries in the recent past, and what, on the basis of that experience, many peoples fear for the future (see 9).

Zoellick goes on: "At the dawn of this new century, we have a choice of ideas. Which ones will triumph: those of fear, destruction and dwindling dreams, or those of humankind's untapped potential and the creative energy of free peoples seeking better lives?" Presumably this kind of message is what our duly elected officials want people to believe, although it is doubtful that competent officials who are in touch with the problems of the modern world base actual policies on such remote and problematic simplicities, designed as they are to benumb and persuade rather than inform.

Such statements provide yet more evidence that there is a vital role for an independent citizenry. Few people can really believe that the creative energies of peoples will find fulfilment in the paths of life envisaged by the propagandists for corporate interests.

Bruce Buchanan

1. As quoted in Henderson, Hazel (1999). *Beyond Globalization: Shaping a Sustainable Global Economy* (p. 21). Kumarian Press.

2. Lomborg, Bjorn (2000). *The Skeptical Environmentalist*. Cambridge U. Press.

3. "Answering the Skeptical Environmentalist," in *Scientific American*, January 2002, p. 61.

4. For example: McMurtry, John. *The Cancer Stage of Capitalism*; Korten, David. Globalizing *Civil Society: Reclaiming Our Right to Power*; Henderson, Hazel. *Paradigms in Progress: Life Beyond Economics*.

5. Zoellick, Robert. "Trading is good for you" in *The World in 2002*, p. 30.

Entering into our Ex-Soviet Heritage

WHEN PAUL TELLIER, former top-tier Canadian civil servant, took over the Canadian National Railway, it was as though we had come into the heritage of the ex-Soviet countries. There too top commissars, with an inside knowledge of where the corpses were buried and where goodies were to be found, had an immense advantage over outsiders in acquiring government assets for a song. CNR had been a Crown Corporation for close to 80 years so that it was not carried on the books for a token $1 as was the case with other privatized federal and provincial assets. But even so there was no accounting in its books for billions of dollars of public money that had been poured into the bankrupt railway companies reorganized into the CNR and into the CNR itself. Impossible to calculate the extent of the real worth of all that? Exactly. That is why high government officials should have been ineligible to enter the bidding, for, say, at least five years after leaving office.

All such government investment, of course, was considered "inefficiencies" because it earns nobody a profit, simply serving the nation instead. And by selling off money-losing lines, Tellier was able to sextuple the market value of the reorganized stock in two or three years. With these sales and the merger he negotiated with the Burlington Northern he would have succeeded in turning the east-and west axis of the CNR system to a north-and-south one, had the US competition bureau not disallowed the merger. So we are depending upon the US competition regulators to preserve the tattered remnants of our sovereignty. O Canada, bless the Lord that someone stands on guard for thee!

Remains the question: were those lines that he sold off just "inefficiencies" or part of the bone structure of a sovereign nation called Canada? If you don't take the latter view, you must assess Canada itself as a whopping inefficiency. The Fathers of Confederation in that perspective should have headed not to Charlottetown but to Washington for their chats.

That in fact is the conclusion that Mr. Tellier seems to have reached. There is this about stock market coups based on privatizations. The market value attained by customary hype assumes that the rate of "value enhancement" reached can be continued into the indefinite future They are accordingly under the constraint of continuing along the same aggressive path. Their ambitions for more of the same are never sated. Accordingly they almost inevitably switch track onto a new standard of public morality gathering speed as they go along.

Thus *The Globe and Mail* (15/12, "CN Boss predicts common currency with US") reports "Canadian National Railway Co. CEO Paul Tellier said yesterday that Canada is destined to share a common currency with the US, and called for a national debate on 'the very sensitive' issue of a closer economic ties with our bigger trading partner.

"The Canadian dollar has fallen to historic lows, around 62 cents US, from a value of $1.05 in the mid-1970s, and in the process Canada has retained the nominal – with nominal underlined three times – ability to set its own monetary policy. 'But what is it costing Canada to maintain a separate dollar?,' Mr. Tellier [asked] in a speech to a rail industry group. 'So what is the Canadian dollar costing Canada's ability to attract the brightest and the best people from around the world?'

"'My own view is that, eventually Canada and its biggest trading partner will move to a common currency. But the broader point is that we must have a discussion on this now.'

"He told reporters afterwards that he personally believes a common currency – likely the American Greenback – is in the cards, but that he doesn't know when it might be appropriate and that he isn't advocating it now. All I'm saying is that we need a debate."

I thought in fact that we have been having such a debate over the past few years, with a recent poll showing that Canadians in their majority are not willing to surrender their currency, though – significantly enough – they were of the opinion that eventually we nevertheless will." Undoubtedly the paradox reflected their view of where our democracy is heading.

Mr. Tellier apparently believes that a discussion is not a discussion unless the public is bamboozled into taking his view in advance.

There seems to have been no mention of the sorry state of the Argentine, which not too long ago was cited (along with Panama!) as the key argument for our adopting the US currency. In a world overwhelmed with deflation, the Argentine had surrendered its option of devaluating its currency to keep up with competition on the world markets.

The low exchange value of the Canadian currency to the US dollar is due to the crisis in the Deregulation and Globalization program which has caused the a mass flight to the US as the seemingly best refuge. Also the September 11th attacks in New York has had its part in the flight to the dollar that led to the weakening of our looney. The US $1.05 figure for the looney in the mid-seventies cited by Mr. Tellier reflected the state of the US economy as a result of its involvement in Vietnam. Surely the only sensible course is for Canada to keep as many options open as possible to protect its interests in the present world mess.

To justify the CNR privatization, the immense subsidies to keep it going were made much of. But is that not also the case with our highways? But highways too are high on the list of privatizations. With the crowding of our highways with needless trailer-truck traffic unleashed by NAFTA, toll highways avoiding metropolitan areas are booming. "The Ontario government under Mike Harris built the world's first electronic toll highway for $1.5 billion and sold it as a tidy profit of $1.6 billion in May 1999," according to Mr. Harris (*The Globe and Mail*, 10/01, "Taxpayers got good deal on the sale of 407, Harris Says" by Graeme Smith). Mr. Harris didn't specify how the value of the farmland expropriated for the purpose was estimated. "An Australian investment bank, Macquarie Infrastructure Group, produced an analysis of the highway in September when it bought part of the Spanish company that owns a majority stake in the road. The bank paid four times the highway's original equity price – the amount the buyers paid in cash – putting a value of $6.3 billion on the project, which the province sold

for $3.1 billion. "The *G&M* incorrectly reported yesterday that the bank's analysis valued the road at four times the sale price." "'That doesn't mean the province was shortchanged, Mr. Harris said, only that the road has been improved.'"

"But critics say taxpayers and drivers are starting to look like the losers as tolls continue to rise and financial statements suggest that the new owners are reaping massive rewards."

But could the province have afforded holding onto the toll road? The answer is to be found in the *Bank of Canada Act*, article 18(c): "[The Bank may] buy and sell securities issued or guaranteed by Canada or any province." "Buy and sell" includes its ability to "hold." And since the federal government is the sole shareholder of the central bank, the interest paid on securities of the province or guaranteed by the province for building the toll highway and held by the BoC would substantially have ended up as dividends paid to the federal treasury. That would have provided an opening for an arrangement between the two levels of government for restoring part of the federal grants to the province slashed to help finance the bailout of our chartered banks in 1991.

There are more options for financing public assets on our law books than our political leaders, federal or provincial, choose to remember. At present the $5 billion Hydro One privatization that is being rushed through to rescue Bay Street financial houses with fat underwriting fees. This will apparently result in 20% increases in power costs to consumers. Ottawa and Queen's Park should be reminded that privatization scams should be stopped before the assets privatized are brought onto the balance sheet at reasonable values. At present they are off-balance-sheet – exactly like the private deals done by Enron executives that are currently causing such commotion in the White House.

William Krehm

Could bin Laden be Hiding Somewhere in the White House?

MUCH contemporary economic theory is an effort at doubling bottom lines by confusing wealth with its absence.

It is decades since physicists discovered the realm of antimatter where the matter known to us has a mirror image: a negatively charged proton and positive electrons. Since Einstein identified mass with energy, potential differences are what count. Anti-matter turned up as a negative term in the solution of an equation long before its discovery in a particle accelerator. Physicists, however, went to the trouble of building accelerators and studying what they revealed before changing their model of physical reality.

That distinguishes them from the economists who legitimized our economic policy. Duplicating the wealth concept by raising non-wealth and even anti-wealth (debt) to similar and even superior status to that of actual wealth is not really a mirror image. It suffers from the asymmetry that separates the real and the bogus. It is more akin to the art of the counterfeiter.

The more debt came to serve as money, the greater the need for oversight of our economic theory, our money creation, and our accountancy. But it hasn't worked in that way. Though dialogue and debate became an ever greater need to help us pick our way through this unexplored field, less and less of it has been tolerated. Private speculative interests, under the alias of an "all-wise" market took over and brought the world to its present plight. Like high finance, information increasingly became "off the books."

Accountancy Becomes Obsolescent

Every time the banks had to be bailed out by government, the more they were deregulated, the sketchier the whole notion of wealth became. High technology was taken to have made accountancy obsolescent.

Increasingly, the approval even of the largest accounting firms is coming to have its price. Physical assets came to be seen as something for dunces. Thus *The Wall Street Journal* (15/01, "From the Ashes: Enron Lessons: Firms Need to Have Assets, and Auditors Oversight") gives us the crux of the lesson that is costing us so dearly: "Like many of his dot.com counterparts, former Enron CEO Jeffery Skilling argued that a company didn't need a lot of hard assets to thrive. Information, not a physical presence in the form of power plants or pipelines was the key to dominating energy markets. Hard assets, Mr. Skilling said, tied up cash that could be more profitably employed trading. He emphasized divesting 'big iron' and instead putting the money to work trading everything from electricity to broadwidth, from memory chips to advertising space."

But while the talk was about "information" replacing physical assets, the walk was keeping more and more key information off the books, by complex derivative hedgings, where the counterparty – also "light" on physical collateral could

evaporate overnight, and by private partnerships with high Enron executives having an undeclared interest. What was in increasingly short supply was collateral that would not disappear overnight.

This strikes at the heart of policy-making. It is not confined to the New Economy but pervades the Old Economy as well. It stems from the basic marginal utility theory that reduced the very notion of value with a derivative of price increase "on the margin" reflecting the imbalance of supply and demand. Everybody including workers was seen as traders comparing the satisfactions of the wages offered for working with the satisfactions of leisure in their parlours. What went on in the factories or society at large was deemed an externality. That is where we have to start to pick up the train of manipulated disaster that has subverted not only our accountancy, but basic morality on which trust is based.

The Wall Street Journal (2/01/02, "Despite the Recession Americans Continue to be Avid Borrowers" by Jathon Sapsford and Patrick Barta) tells an incredible tale: "Ten months into the current recession consumer credit defaults and payment delinquencies are as high as they have been since the last recession a decade ago. This time around, however, lenders, who were quick to reduce the flow of credit during past recessions, have left the tap wide open. That's allowed Americans to continue borrowing to pay for homes, cars and other big-ticket items, bolstering the weakened economy. But the resulting growth in consumer credit – to a record $7.5 trillion at the end of the third quarter of 2001 – also has exposed a potential new economic fault line.

"Rising consumer debt is typically a sign of robust spending. In the short term, consumer spending stimulated the economy. That's clearly what the Federal Reserve had in mind over the past year as it repeatedly lowered interest rates. But the unusual growth in consumer borrowing during the current recession also poses a danger: that at some point the consumers will have to divert more and more of their income away from spending on goods and services towards repaying their debt.

"Such a shift would slow the economy, reducing the chances of a speedy recovery. So far, easy credit has helped soften the downturn, and despite months of dire predictions, there has been little sign of a reckoning. Lenders' charge-off rates for bad credit-card debt, for example, were at 5.35% at the end of the third quarter, up from 4.22% at the end of the last recession. But even if that number abruptly shoots higher, most lenders today are far better capitalized than ever before, and thus better positioned to [deal with] their losses."

But are they really? The structures of negative wealth as Enron or the optic-fiber giants weave their way throughout our financial institutions but have still not been remotely totted up. They are not likely to be for years to come. Corresponding to the negative wealth, a negative accountancy has sprung up to fill a powerful market need, and a negative morality to enable that negative accountancy to operate. Not only our economic, but our social life has been radically restructured in ways that we are just beginning to learn. All this is not irrelevant to the plague of terrorism disguised as religion. George Orwell wrote in what may turn out to have been an age of relative innocence.

"Much of the growth in consumer debt, particularly in the mortgage market, reflects consumers' desire to take advantage of the historically low interest rates engineered by the Fed. But many economists worry that by buying now what they would otherwise be buying tomorrow, consumers are dulling one of the few major benefits of a recession. Though painful, recessions usually purge the economy, as lenders reduce the availability of credit to compensate for the higher risk that their loans will go bad."

"During the first two quarter of the early 1990s recession, the average American household reacted to those tighter credit conditions by paring his debt by an inflation-adjusted $410, says Mark Zandl, chief economist of Economy.com, a consulting firm in West Chester, PA. That helped leave consumers in shape to borrow anew when the economy ultimately turned the corner. By contrast, Mr. Zandl says that during the first two quarters of the current recession, which began in March, the average US household took on $1,420 of new debt."

"Thus far, low interest rates have helped keep consumers' debt payments relatively manageable. But when rates rise, as they inevitably will, lots of debt pegged to fluctuating rates – including many credit cards and mortgages – will require higher payments, further stretching household budgets."

"And if the economy takes a turn for the worse, outsized debt levels and rising lay-offs could cause far more personal bankruptcies, and add a new layer to the debt debacle already affecting corporations in sectors from telecommunications to energy. The total number of personal bankruptcies for 2001 appears likely to top the record of 1.4 million set in 1998.

"Companies of all stripes are feeding the current debt frenzy. Auto makers have bolstered their sales amid the recession by offering zero-rate financing. Retailers such as Sears, Roebuck & Co., Home Depot Inc., and Dell Computer Corp. are offering similar financing deals. Despite the surge in layoffs accompanying the current downturn, credit-card companies, led by Capital One Financial Corp. and MBNA Corp., are likely to have mailed out a record five million new credit-card solicitations in the year just ended, up from 3.5 billion in 2000.

"Credit counsellors say they are busier than ever, because many people don't realize the dangers of the credit available to them. They say many consumers know that they are acting irrationally, but are convinced that the rules of the game have somehow changed to keep them out of trouble."

You might think that is crazy. But isn't that what our Nobel economics laureate, who ran the Long Term Capital Fund into near bankruptcy, believed, so why not the ordinary Joe at the sucker's end of the advertising stick? You might wonder why credit counseling should be becoming a major profession. But if we have swimming instructors to teach people not to drown, why shouldn't our school system explain to kids the dangers at consumers' credit to lure people into ruinous debt.

"In the short run, the continued availability of credit – and consumers' willingness to use it – is one reason the current recession seems less painful than past downturns. Auto sales surged to an all-time high in October, thanks to those aggressive financing deals, and 2001 is expected to be the second-best year for US home sales.

"But those purchases take a heavy toll on the family budget,. American households spend nearly 14% of their disposable income in servicing debt. Everybody's telling people to spend, spend, spend, but it's going to be difficult for them if they're hounded by collection agencies."

Is Our Economy Subprime?

"Some corporations have already been burned by the recent growth of consumer debt, largely in the riskier or 'subprime' corner of the market, which focuses on consumers with marginal credit histories. In August, Bank of America Corp. said it was taking a $1.25 billion charge to shut down its subprime lending operations. In October, shares of Providian Financial Corp., the fastest-growing company in the consumer-finance industry, sank 59% in a single day after the company announced losses in its subprime loan portfolio." That was about consumer subprime debt. If you add that to the producer and financial subprime debt – like Enron and the high-tech companies – the inevitable conclusion is that our economy itself is 'subprime.'

"In December Ford announced it would report a large fourth-quarter loss, in part because of a sudden rise in soured auto loans. Despite the current economic downturn, the average credit limit during the third quarter of 2001 was up 16% from a year earlier. That's partly because the Fed's low interest-rate policy has helped reduce, at least for now, the risks lenders face from deteriorating credit quality. But a new technology and other factors have also played a role, transforming the way lenders design, market and manage their credit products.

"Over the past decade, lenders have been boosting their capital reserves, and they have learned to manage their risks more effectively by selling some of the loans in their portfolios, in the form of tradable securities. Those sales shift the lenders' risk to pools of outside investors."

That's one way of looking at it. Another – more relevant – is that of spreading a deadly epidemic like AIDS or small-pox.

"At the same time, powerful computers have enabled banks and other financial institutions to automate the process of assessing their credit risks and approving borrowers. In some cases, automation has shortened the waiting period to a matter of minutes for everything from credit cards to car loans and mortgages."

Pushing applicants for old-fashioned bank loans into the pool of credit-card or other high-risk debt shifts some of the banks' screening costs onto their shoulders – and to the economy as a whole. Such is the wisdom of the deregulated market.

"The government is exhorting consumers to keep spending – and thus borrowing – as a patriotic duty in the wake of September 11 officials from the Bush administration visited Detroit immediately after the attacks and pushed car makers to come up with ways to keep consumers spending. GM officials say that visit was one reason behind the industry's much-publicized zero-financing offers."

There are moments when you wonder whether Bin Laden has not hunkered down somewhere in the White House.

William Krehm

The Pump Runs Dry in the Global Village — Washington Writes Off Argentina

A S MASS LOOTING of stores in Buenos Aires was put down with a toll of 29 dead, Washington washed its hands of Argentina's problems. And even before reaching for a towel Treasury Secretary Paul O'Neill practically flung the dirty basin water into Buenos Aires's face. *The Wall Street Journal* (21/12, "White House Says No to Argentina Aid" by Michelle Wallin and Pamela Druckerman) quoted Mr. O'Neill verbatim. "The notion that the rioting, which catalyzed the resignation of President Fernando de la Rua yesterday, might justify more aid from the US or from the IMF, in which the US is the largest shareholder, suggests that we should accept the responsibility for how they run their country, which is inappropriate to me.'

And yet Washington has had more than a little input into how Argentine ran its affairs over some decades. It supported and even instigated military coups throughout Latin America

But most relevant to Argentina's present difficulties was the pegging of its currency to the US dollar a decade ago. This arrangement was upheld as an example to be followed from Ecuador to Canada. Most of the countries of Latin America are still suffering from the consequences of the US Federal Reserve's ballistic interest rates in the early eighties imposed "to lick inflation." The debt incurred at the time has never been repaid or cancelled. Its periodic restructurings provided the IMF with the leverage for imposing the American view on how the world ought to be run. High priorities were the removal of all road bumps that might impede the flow of short-term money, the scaling down of tariffs, and privatizations. But above all there was the pledge never, ever to use the domestic central bank to finance infrastructures and industries that would lessen the countries' dependence on hot money.

And yet when domestic labour and materials were available for a necessary project, there was no reason for the financing to have to come from abroad.

Canada has never been at the mercies of the IMF. Yet the proposal of replacing the Canadian dollar with the American, though repudiated by every Canadian economist unattached to a corporation, has not been allowed to die.

However, the Argentine was nailed to a cross by such "dollarization" of its economy. It has been deprived of all other options for dealing with its problems – e.g., deflating its currency to compete with competitors on a shrinking world market. On the other hand its powerful neighbour Brazil has refined currency devaluation to a fine art. The Argentine had to have a US dollar in its vaults before it could issue the equivalent in pesos. If it devalues its currency today, $132 billion of debt denominated in dollars will explode in terms of its domestic money, with catastrophic effect for the government, corporations, and households. If it suspends servicing its debt, it will have the dubious distinction of having pulled off the greatest default in the history of the planet. And yet unless it can cheapen its exports,

its unemployment will continue growing. It is around 20% at the moment. And this in a country with full-employment traditions.

A Too-fragile Solution

Because of the facile convertibility solution resorted to a decade ago rather than price controls, the country has nowhere to turn. All this has been considerably worsened by a dollar become muscle-bound *vis-à-vis* all other currencies in the world. Reeling under the chaos caused in large part by the collapse of Deregulization and Globalization, money has been pouring into the US as the safest parking place until the mounting financial storms are spent. In part Argentine's dilemma is the reverse side of the indebtedness of the US itself.

Until very recently the Argentine along with Panama were the two countries cited by the propaganda blowing into Canada from south of the border for the abandonment of the looney for the US dollar. They are a most unlikely pair. Panama owed its independence from Colombia entirely to a "revolution" cooked up by a French agent of the US, to get around what Washington considered too high a rent asked by Colombia for the route of the canal the US was planning. In that revolution the Panamanians themselves had no part – its only casualty was a Chinese restaurateur. On the other hand almost a century earlier, the gaucho armies from the Argentine criss-crossed the Andes to meet with Bolivar's Venezuelan *llaneros* in Peru after liberating all Spanish South America. Mentioning the Argentine and Panama in a single breath as models for the surrender of a core feature of sovereignty is an insult to the Argentines. Panama did not adopt convertibility. From the moment of its "independence" it had no currency of its own.

A century ago Argentina seemed to have a most promising future. In 1870, 3 million people had occupied most of the vast land. One third of its three million square kilometers was practically uninhabited. Producing meat and grain for Europe, its population by 1914 had grown to 8 million, and doubled once more by 1947.

The source of that wealth gave rise to a peculiar social structure. The fertile pampas needed much of its labour only during harvest time, and the huge haciendas that covered most of the country were not available for settling a small peasantry. Instead, its labour shortfalls dovetailed with the population excess of mountainous regions of Italy. The small peasants deeply attached to their near-vertical plots had to migrate for several months each year to support their families. They provided most of the stone masons and construction crews who built the grand buildings in St. Petersburg and just about every European capital.[1] Many of them made an annual two-way trip across the South Atlantic to work on the Argentinian pampas, and became known as golondrinas, "swallows." In their baggage they brought some of the political passions of Garibaldi's Italy. They helped build the railways, ports and other infrastructures to serve the vast empty land. Those who did stay on in the Argentine, gravitated to the capital. Buenos Aires that became one of the largest cities in the world and the residence of as much as 30% of the country's total population. Violent strikes were a characteristic feature of Argentine life. In the early twenties the army put down a strike of Patagonian farm workers with hundreds of fatalities.

The industries that arose served two distinct markets. Luxury products were largely imported from Britain as a quid pro quo for the market that it provided for Argentinian meat and grain. Until Britain ran out of foreign currency as a result of WWII, the Argentine was considered her "Sixth Dominion," an intimate relationship that had been somewhat chilled with the promotion of "Imperial Preference" in the mid-1930s. Simple industrial products for the bulk of the people enjoyed generous tariff protection and subsidies.

Child labour was common, but money wages were higher than in Europe. Speculation in urban land was shameless. But educational facilities even for the children of poor immigrants were available and contributed to Argentina's rich cultural life. Let no US political leader, no matter how sincere his ignorance, dismiss the Argentine, even down on its luck, as just another beggar.

Less Forbidding Wall between Oppressed and Oppressors

Military dictatorships were endemic throughout Latin America. As often as not after WWII they enjoyed the high regard of Washington as potential allies in the Cold War. But in the Argentine where the poor were mostly of European immigrant stock rather than American Indian or blacks, the wall of inhibitions separating the oppressed and oppressors was less forbidding. Those in power – whether elected politicians or military dictators – tended to lapse into the role of intermediaries between the upper and lower classes who were more equally balanced than in other parts of Latin America. In some respects Juan Peron conformed to the European model of strongman that used to be referred to as "Bonapartist" – a term originally applied to Napoleon III in France. Peron and some of his successors introduced social legislation, largely rhetorical, but occasionally of some substance.[2]

"From the mid-1940s full employment became a reality in the Argentine and was maintained until the end of the 1980s. During these forty years unemployment cropped up largely as a theoretic concern in polemics, except for recession years in specific regions."[3]

Even as a theoretical norm, "full employment" ran counter to the official ideology that took over internationally in the seventies and gave us "zero inflation," and the "natural rate of unemployment."

"In 1943 Michal Kalecki arrived at the conclusion that full employment raises problems that lead from economics into politics, because they may encroach on the ability of entrepreneurs to maintain discipline they consider essential in their industries. Kalecki opposed the conventional view that the main consideration for employers is to maximize their profits, and held entrepreneurs may be ready to accept a recession to create enough unemployment to strengthen their control of labour."[4]

This goes far to explain why Argentinian entrepreneurs were so prepared to do deals with corrupt anti-democratic regimes.

Equally fateful for democracy, was the government manipu-lation of the trade-union movement under Peron (1946-1955). In the years after his fall (1955-58) the unions were persecuted and restructured by the government. When dictatorial state power is combined with the control of organized labour, communication between opposing social forces is distorted. We see something of this today when Muslim militant fundamentalism fills the vacuum in social services left by politically-administered mega-debt. Something similar happened in the Argentine with the Peronista control of CGT (Confederacion General de Trabajo). Combined with the goal of full employment it was an endless source of turbulence. Part of the "natural" resolution of such problems is to be found in economic growth, but structure and circumstances of Argentinian industry ruled this out. Argentina operated with antiquated, often second-hand equipment bought during the war to fill demand on a protected domestic market.

And while the rest of the world was adapting to the post-war, politics in Argentine focused on the new division of the national product developed during the boom years of War II. Between 1940 and 1948 it is estimated that agricultural workers had increased their share of the national income by 50% and skilled workers by 30% After the war readjustment of labour's income took place throughout the world. But the leading countries had had price controls during the war, and when these were lifted labour's share moved upward. Expanding, modernized economies made that possible. In the Argentine the adjustment was downward. Industry was in no position to expand on an increasingly competitive market. Its historic outlet – Great Britain – was curtailing hard-currency purchases.

The resulting deadlock fuelled an inflation that averaged 25% in the years between 1955 and 1975, and reached a maximum of 100%. Real wages between 1955 and 1965 remained constant, but jumped forward again in 1972 with the return of Peronism to power. Under the murderously oppressive and corrupt military regime that succeeded it, wages were violently pushed back That was compounded by usury and speculation made possible by the IMF. Frustrated on the domestic front, the army led the country into the Falkland Islands adventure. That cured the country, temporarily in any case, of looking to military saviours.

During their brief return to power (1972-74) the Peronistas drove full employment to its limits. This climaxed in an explosion of inflation in which prices increased in the month of July 1975 by 100%. Over the subsequent fifteen years prices continued their average rise at 300% annually. This played a very similar role as the 1923 hyperinflation did in Germany in slamming the public mind shut to any suggestion of stimulating the economy with deficit financing – even in the depth of the Depression. In the Argentine, budgetary deficits soared especially during the ballistically high interest rates imposed under Paul Volcker's watch at the US Federal Reserve. Real wages could not possibly keep up with such prices.

The dollar-convertibility of the Argentinian peso had for years been cited as a model for the abandonment of the Canadian dollar. With quite the same logic, the bruising German 1923 hyper-inflation in Germany served central banks as bogeyman to frighten the unwary into the belief that any price increase above zero must expand into something similar. Not dissimilarly, the highly special experience that produced the Argentinian super-inflation led to the country grasping convertibility with the dollar in despair.

During the period of dollar-peso convertibility the nation's foreign money reserves were squandered on luxury imports of consumer goods and corruption. As we go to press, the Argentine has a dual exchange rate – for official transactions at 1.40 pesos to the dollar and a free market as high as 1.95.

The consequences of the convertibility failure are a first-hand social disaster. It has reversed the historic flow of immigration from Spain and Italy to the Argentine. Native Argentinians of Spanish and Italian extraction are lining up outside the Spanish and Italian consulates for visas to migrate to the land of their forefathers. The Spanish banking system that invested heavily in Argentinian banks is likely to be shaken.

"Wholesale privatization of state enterprises was supposed to raise efficiency, while providing the means for cleaning up government finances. Between 1991 and 1994, state enterprises worth US$24 billion were privatized. Import tariffs have been reduced by an average 50% to a uniform 10% and non-tariff trade barriers substantially done away with."

As in Canada, the absence of capital budgeting, has left the government itself in the dark as to the real worth of the state agencies being privatized, since they are carried on the books at a token $1. Capital budgeting is slated to be brought into the Canadian federal books in 2002. One of the key lessons from the Argentine, is not to privatize until you have introduced a level of accountancy that gives you some idea of the value of the public assets being sold. Without that, privatization is bad for public morality as it is for the fiscal health that is supposed to be the goal of the exercise.

William Krehm

1. Sella, Domenica (1973). Au dossier des migrations montagnardes : l'exemple de la Lombardie au XVIIe siècle. In *Melanges en l'Honneur de Fernand Braudel*. Edouard Privat, Toulouse, writes, "A factory for the production of men for the use of others: that is the incisive formula by which Braudel defined the mountainous Mediterranean regions at the beginning of modern times."

2. "During his long reign, Peron liked to boast that, like Uncle Scrooge, he could walk on the gold bars in the Treasury House; once he had fled there was no gold left to walk on and Peron appeared on international financial lists as one of the richest men in the world. After Peron, the thefts continued and increased" (*The Globe and Mail*, 27/12, "No Money, No Vision, No Faith" by Alberto Manguel).

3. Schvarzer, Jorge (1997). Das System der Lohnregulierung im modernen Argentinien. Eine Annaeherung an seine globalen Bedingungen. In Sevilla, Rafael, & Zimmerling, Ruth (Eds.), *Argentinien – Land der Peripherie* (pp. 215-263). Bad Honnef, Germany: Laenderseminare Horlemann.

4. Messner, Dirk (1997). Wirtschaft und Entwicklung in Argentinien in den neunziger Jahren: ein schwieriger Neuanfang. In Sevilla & Zimmerling, p. 215.

REVIEW OF A BOOK BY BY ROBERT E. WOOD, UNIVERSITY OF CALIFORNIA PRESS, BERKELEY, 1986.

From Marshall Plan to Debt Crisis — Foreign Aid and Development Choices in the World Economy

"IN 1955, ex-US State Department official Joseph Jones [remarked], 'The experience of the Marshall Plan's creation suggested 'not the limits but the infinite possibilities of influencing the politics, attitudes and actions of other countries by statesmanship in Washington.' By the 1980s, popular disenchantment with aid was such that one survey found the US public's desire to reduce foreign aid outranked its fear of nuclear war' (Editorial, *The New York Times*, 31/10/83).

As a sociologist, Wood excuses himself for "tackling a subject generally the preserve of economists, and to a lesser extent of political scientists. I have not felt that I have left my sociologist's craft behind. It has become apparent to me that foreign aid plays a significant role in shaping those aspects of the world that sociologists look at: social equality, class structure, politics, gender relations, rural-urban relations, and so forth. My training as a sociologist has made me sensitive to structures behind processes that on the surface seem without 'rhyme or reason.' It is time that economists availed themselves of help from other disciplines to tidy up the mess in their workshop.

"This book documents the system of aid provision, of structured access to concessional external financing. The central focus is on how this structure has changed over time and shaped development options in the Third World. Although the debt crisis has other roots as well, this book elucidates an important set of determinants generally overlooked. It seeks to show that the debt crisis defines a new era, not only a set of extraordinary events between, say, Mexico's request for rescheduling in August 1982 and Argentina's coming to terms with the International Monetary Fund in September 1984. The legacy of debt will continue to be a central focus of international relations for years to come."

Wood begins by examining the original agenda of the Marshall Plan. "For one thing, the activity financed by aid may not be the true measure of aid's impact because the recipient government might have carried out such activity in the absence of aid. This problem is usually referred to as 'fungibility' or 'substitutability.' The real impact of aid may be to finance some alternative government activity or simply to underwrite higher domestic (often luxury) consumption."

The Truth about the Marshall Plan

"The Marshall Plan has come to symbolize boldness and success. Whenever new directions in US foreign aid programs have been proposed, the theme of 'a new Marshall Plan' has been pressed into service. Officially known as the European Recovery Program (ERP), the Marshall Plan dispensed over $13 billion between 1948 and 1952 to Western European countries constituted as the Organization for European Economic Cooperation (OEEC). Over 90% of this aid was in the form of grants.

"These statements are misleading. Very few [of its original] goals had been achieved by the end of 1951; indeed, the Marshall Plan was in a deep crisis that was resolved only through rearmament and the expanded aid of its successor, the Mutual Security Agency. In reality, the Marshall Plan's uniqueness was that it addressed the breakdown of the prewar economic order. The real success of the Marshall Plan lay in its contribution to the construction of a new international order, not in the quantity of capital and raw material it provided Western Europe.

"Five sets of changes in the world economy created the dollar shortage in the postwar.

"First, the breakdown of trade between Eastern and Western Europe. In 1948 Western European exports to Eastern Europe were less than half the prewar level. Imports from Eastern Europe were only one third. And this trade declined over the next five years. European countries had to rely on imports from the US for needs formerly met by trade with Eastern Europe.

"Second there was the loss of important colonial sources of dollars. Vietnam was in rebellion. So was the Netherlands' major dollar earner, Indonesia. Guerrilla insurgency was increasing in Britain's most profitable colony, Malaysia. In addition the European powers bore the costs of fighting the liberation movements. France had 110,000 troops in Indochina, and the Netherlands had 130,000 in Indonesia. Britain had 1.4 million troops around the world. South Africa took its gold sales out of the sterling area dollar pool.

"Third, there was Europe's loss of earnings on foreign investments. Continued sale of these investments was a condition of lend-lease aid during the war. For both France and Britain, overseas investment earnings had long helped offset trade deficits.

"In addition, Britain had run up $13.7 billion in debts, known as sterling balances, to other sterling area countries, particularly India. These countries now clamored for the right to use the balances to finance their development plans.

"Fourth, many of the European countries and their overseas territories were hit with deteriorating terms of trade. 'Had the price of gold and rubber gone up as those of other items traded did, the same exports to the US during the five years following the war would have earned an additional $3.5 billion for the sterling area. Total Marshall Plan aid to Great Britain came to $2.7 billion. Without such declining terms of trade, some countries would not have had a dollar deficit at all.

"Finally, the European countries found themselves dependent on the US as never before. This left them susceptible to small fluctuations in the US while no new mechanisms had yet evolved to provide the international liquidity that sterling once provided. Britain's need for aid after the war was partly rooted in US aid policies during the war. It was official US policy to administer lend-lease in such a way that the UK's gold and dollar balances would not fall below $600 million or rise above $1 billion. This was secured by altering what the British were expected to pay for in dollars and what would be included in lend-lease. The US reasoning was that reserves less than $600 million would force Britain to resort to the kind of economic controls the US was dedicated to prevent, whereas over $1 billion would leave Britain too independent of postwar US influence."

Largely domestic concerns prompted Washington to begin preparing the Marshall Plan long before the Cold War cast its shadow and was fully exploited to get the Marshall through Congress. "Americans believed that their prosperity was due to rearmament and war and feared a postwar depression. A 1941 survey of the American Economic Association found 80% of its members predicting a postwar depression."

The Errors in the Marshall Plan

It early became evident that Europe's dollar-earning capacity would not solve the US's problem in exporting enough to keep their economy from relapsing into depression. "US imports from Europe constituted only 0.33% of US GNP. Politically untouchable tariff walls made increasing most European imports impossible. US policymakers looked instead to the overseas territories of European countries to bail out their colonial masters. In a triangular trade model, dollars would flow into European hands indirectly through their colonies. The basic idea of triangular trade was reiterated again and again throughout the Marshall Plan."

Its most fateful error was that it overlooked the powerful movements throughout the colonial territories to cut their ties with the imperial powers. It imparted an incoherence to Washington's policies *vis-à-vis* the colonial insurgencies – encouraging them at times, but at other times supporting the imperial powers' efforts to suppress them. Arms sales were not an unimportant factor in this ambiguity.

"Marshall reported in 1949: 'When we reached the problem of increasing the security of Europe, I found the French troops of any quality were all out in Indochina, and the Dutch troops of any quality were all out in Indochina, and the one place where they were not was in Western Europe.'" The colonial wars had to be resolved.

No Marshall Plan for Latin America

The brutality with which Latin America was told that Marshall plans were not in the cards for them contributed to the riots that marred the Bogota Conference of 1948. Instead, Latin America would be dependent on private investment. The unspoken footnote was that the CIA and the American military were already mobilized to guarantee that the region would be wide open to American corporate investment on its terms.

But even with this restriction, bridging the dollar gap with the rest of the world – the initial goal of the Marshall Plan – was not doing well. "Most of the progress had been achieved by discrimination against dollar imports. In 1951 the dollar gap was the worst since 1948. It was feared that the inflationary impact of the Korean War would lead to 'a retreat to autarkical policies.' However, the [Marshall Plan] came to be a success partly through a redefinition of goals. At the end of the Marshall Plan, conservative social forces had greatly strengthened their political control in all Western Europe. European resistance to rearmament had been overcome. In the popular mind, the Marshall Plan had prevented Europe from 'going communist.'

"In this context of deep pessimism about the dollar gap by 1952 rearmament emerged as the only practical solution. Adoption of a critical National Security Council document (NSC-68) committed the Truman administration to a massive military build-up months before the Korean war. One State Department document observed that Congress was more favorably disposed to military aid than to aid for economic recovery. It added, 'The distinction between aid in support of foreign military effort abroad and aid for economic recovery is largely artificial.'" There was the added advantage to military Keynesianism abroad, that it ensured a sustainable relationship with Europe by tying it to American military hardware, whereas purely economic aid might prepare the recipients for uniting to assert their autonomy from the US.

"The Marshall Plan created a body of operating principles and procedures that remain an integral part of the aid regime. From its beginning, aid has been as much about the nature as about the pace of economic growth. Although aid's use to block socialism has been well understood, its role in limiting national capitalism extends beyond the Marshall Plan period." The hammer to achieve this goal has been debt.

"Over one-fifth of US aid between 1948 and 1952 went directly to the underdeveloped areas. Specific procedures and techniques were devised that subsequently became diffused in the aid regime. The use of counterpart funds (money to be advanced, but held back as security for the fulfilling of specified conditions), became a method of expanding the leverage of aid."

The Proliferation of the Aid Regime

"Economic assistance to the Third World during the Marshall Plan period essentially involved a single country and a single agency: the US and its Economic Cooperation Administration (ECA). By the 1980s, however, the aid picture had become enormously complex. Separate aid programs were now administered by all sixteen countries of the Development Assistance Committee (DAS); by at least eight communist and ten OPEC countries, by approximately twenty multilateral organizations in addition to various components of the United Nations system, by hundreds of private organizations. Aid programs had even been initiated by Third World countries.

"The 1950s were a period of the dominance and diversification of bilateral aid programs of the advanced capitalist countries – a state of affairs, ironically, assured by the advent of smaller Soviet and Chinese aid programs. The 1960s were marked by the emergence of new forms of multilateralism, largely either under the auspices of, or modeled after, the World Bank. The 1970s witnessed the sudden emergence of Middle Eastern oil-producing countries as major aid donors, as well as an expansion of the World Bank that consolidated its position as leading aid institution. In the mid-to-late 1970s, the expansion of non-concessional private bank lending in lieu of official

financing came to constitute a fundamental challenge to the functioning of the aid regime, a challenge culminating in the debt crisis.

"The specter of communist aid led the US to press the OEEC countries (constituted in 1961 as the Organization for Economic Cooperation and Development [OECD], with an expanded membership including Canada and Japan) to initiate or expand their own aid programs."

Khrushchev even suggested that the Western aid programs be credited to the Soviets, for without the Soviet programs the West would never have spent all that money.

New multilateral institutions accounted for 40% of multilateral aid in 1970, and 50% by 1980.

"The institutions emerged largely in response to Third World pressure, but they represented a defeat of the effort of Third World countries to establish a UN institution providing capital assistance over which they would have control. Instead the underdeveloped countries got a soft-loan window at the World Bank (the International Development Association) and a series of regional development banks closely modelled on the World Bank itself.

"The most unexpected institutional development during the 1970s was the explosion of aid flows from the major oil-producing countries of the Middle East, members of the Organization of Petroleum-Exporting Countries (OPEC). By far the greatest proportion of their dollar reserves was deposited with commercial banks in the advanced countries, but some was lent directly to Third World countries at concessional rates. From 5% of official financing in 1972, in 1975 and 1976 OPEC accounted for 25% of official financing.

"Marshall Plan aid was overwhelmingly grants, but aid to the Third World in the later 1950s and 1960s was increasingly loaned. The most striking innovations in external financing in the mid-to-late 1970s occurred not in the aid regime but in the practices of private commercial banks. The late 1970s showed a partial return to the situation of the mid 1950s, when private flows were about equal to official flows. But whereas in the 1950s they consisted almost entirely of direct private investment, in the later 1970s lending by private commercial banks far surpassed direct private investment."

This could not be attributed to an improvement in the creditworthiness of the Third World countries – except for those with oil to export. Rather it had to do with the growth of the Eurodollar market. This refers to the offshore markets for loans in any strong currency. The offshore venue of such loans not only kept them free of taxation and other restrictions in the home countries. Those who lent on the eurodollar market, in effect created their own notional money supply, which was effectively off their balance sheet so long as contractual obligations were honored. It was off-balance in a several respects – not only by-passing home-based restrictions and controls, but ideally equipped to circumvent invasions of privacy. Benjamin Cohen has remarked that it constituted a privatization of liquidity. Liquidity refers to short-term lending, rather than to brick and mortar investments. And unless repatriated, it has a tenuous connection with the real economy.

The Third World thus became entangled with the wrong end of the credit spectrum. Its finances became exposed to every wiggle in short-term funds. That in itself would tend to repel productive investors.

The oil price increases in 1973-4, resulted in OPEC countries placing $22 billion in Eurocurrency deposits in 1974. But the expansion of the banks' financing of the Third World began earlier. Between 1965 and 1976, the number of US banks with foreign branches rose from 13 to 125 and the number of branches from 211 to 731. Faced with stagflation at home, the banks of the First World turned to the Third World for expansion. Making multimillion dollar loans to a single minister or dictator, rather than having to deal with thousands of small borrowers at home was seen as an "economy of scale." Besides, the buzzword of the day was the risklessness of "sovereign debt," i.e., loans to governments. Corruption took care of any remaining doubts. Much of the money lent to Third World lands stayed in special accounts in the US as undeclared commissions. Morality took a beating.

Regime or Jungle?

"External financing for underdeveloped countries has become highly differentiated. The types of flows have grown in number, the number of bilateral donors has increased, and multilateral institutions have proliferated. No formal coordination exists. The United Nations has virtually no influence over bilateral aid programs, or over the multilateral institutions officially affiliated with it, such as the IMF and the World Bank. The multilateral banks consult regularly, but guard their decision-making autonomy jealously. The advanced capitalist countries have banded together in the Development Assistance League, but they have been careful to give it no power over themselves."

Wood draws on the work of political scientists "interested in how international relations must be regulated even in the absence of formal management and authority."

A random sample of this analysis is his commentary on the statement of high officials of the World Bank (Chauncey F. Dewey and Harinder S. Kohli's "Market Factors in Large Industrial Development Projects): "Departures from international market prices are treated as 'distortions' and industrial projects depending on protective tariffs, subsidized interest rates, or other types of government support are rejected as uneconomic. The notion that international market prices may themselves be distorted is not entertained in these analyses."

William Krehm

Ragtime on the Mighty Wurlizer

THE DISCLOSURES in the bankruptcy filings of Enron, Global Crossings, and countless other former mega concerns have been making the American New Economy a promising nominee for a literary prize in fiction. And now it seems that the US government itself, concerned as always about a high standard of competition, is entering the race.

A Washington dispatch in the Toronto *Globe and Mail* by John Ibbitson (21/02, "Pentagon's false-news plan sets off alarm bells") informs us: "Defence and media experts were alarmed yesterday by a report that a little-known Pentagon office wants to plant false stories in the international media to bolster support for the US war on terrorism.

"*The New York Times* said that the Office of Strategic Influence which was established after September 11, is proposing to plant news stories – some of which may be deliberately false – with foreign media, using outside agencies to cover the sources of the information.

"'We shouldn't be in that business. Leave the propaganda leaks to the CIA, the spooks,' one defence official said.

"'The proposal has not been finalized,' sources in the Pentagon and the State Department said. Nor has the idea of deliberately misinforming media outlets been submitted to US Defence Secretary Donald Rumsfeld for approval.

"But although there was little detailed information about the new office available to the media, an official confirmed that its activities could include 'black' disinformation, which the *Times* said could include false reports e-mailed to foreign journalists, government officials and civic leaders.

"The return address will probably be a dot-com, not a dot-mil,' the official was quoted as saying.

"The Central Intelligence Agency has long used covert disinformation campaigns in unfriendly countries. However, those cooperations require presidential approval and may not target US citizens."

That *The New York Times* should for a moment believe that suggests how much the US public have been victimized by just such manipulated news.

In my book, *Towards a Post-Autistic Economy – a Place for Society at the Table*, which will be available this month, I refer to the revelations of the Church and Pike Congressional Committees in 1975 and 1976 of the vast counterfeiting enterprise of the CIA. One of its techniques was offering media reporters genuine news scoops in exchange for their sending out fraudulent material prepared by a CIA agency. Entering the arrangement could assure a journalist instant celebrity. Genuine news scoops thus became currency for corrupting the media at home and abroad. In this way disinformation plants ended up incorporated into standard literature that scholars might innocently launder for posterity. Nothing like it had been seen since Joe Stalin rewrote the history of the Russian revolution according to whom he had shot the week before.

In addition, the CIA organized the Congress for Intellectual Freedom in Berlin involving writers of the stature of Arthur Koestler – celebrated for unmasking similar hoaxes of the Soviets. Only in 1967 when the CIA funding was disclosed was it disbanded. The CIA referred to its disinformation machine as its "Mighty Wurlitzer."

It takes only a passing glance at the financial pages of our press to realize that not only truth but accountancy has had its throat slit in North America. And that is what Washington is imposing upon the world as a model to be blindly followed. None of that could possibly have happened if economic theory had not been systematically devastated in our universities and the media. Peer reviews of the economists' profession could well fly the banner: "Peer you may, but not tell." What gets published on John Maynard Keynes in the media is more likely to deal with his bisexuality than with his ideas.

Nor is it wise for Washington to assume that its growing impotence through corruption is lost on the countries that President Bush has proclaimed "the axis of terror." They, too, are not unendowed with the human talent for concentrating on the mote in their opponents' eye.

Long before the Muslim faith came to Iran the Zoroastran fire worshippers identified speaking the truth with cleansing fire. Traditions like that will survive even changes of religion. In the hands of philosophers and musicians, Zarathustra fascinated late 19th century Europe. The Three supreme virtues were riding well, shooting straight, and speaking the truth. Of the first two Washington is certainly supreme master. But speaking the truth – even without the latest contrivance in the works – is a different matter.

In the interests of its own defence and the well-being of the world, Washington must restore that ancient Iranian virtue at home.

William Krehm

Smoke Screens are Being Laid on the Health Care Issue

TO PENETRATE THE FOG of disinformation surrounding health care, we have to go back a couple of decades when the achievements of the first three postwar decades began to be dismantled. New Zealand, suffering from a passing exchange problem, was chosen as guinea pig. What commended it for the role was the advanced nature of both its democracy and its high degree of social justice. Had exchange controls not been ruled out by the new fundamentalism, the exchange problem could have been handled without destroying the entire social structure of the country. In 1993, reviewing the political factors that made such structural adjustments possible the convenor of the Washington-based Institute for International Economics, John Williamson remarked: "When a major crisis occurs within the existing system, it creates new opportunities for actors until then prevented from taking the initiative. Where a crisis does not occur 'naturally,' it might make sense to provoke one. The most effective time to act is the honeymoon stage immediately after taking power, when the need for, and the costs of reform can be blamed on previous governments. The problem of sustaining the changes might be overcome by deliberately creating beneficiaries likely to fight to protect the reforms."[1]

Williamson's wisdom – refined in hundreds of coordinated think-tanks across the world – was applied to the letter in NZ. Jane Kelsey quotes B. Easton of the new regime, "In each case the lightning strike involved a goal attained following a surprise announcement and a very rapid implementation. Opponents were always on the defensive debating last week's reforms." Meanwhile new ones in new areas had already been heaped on their heads. The strategy was brilliant. The only trouble [with] this rapid encirclement in many policy areas, is that the new regime is clueless about the real effects of the massive policy putsch. That is how the Walkerton, Ontario, E. coli tragedy occurred in Canada leaving a trail of dead and thousands of seriously ill citizens in a small rural community. The supervision of the water tests had been privatized and the budgets cut for more "efficiency." But even though Premier Harris on the heels of the investigation issued an apology for the responsibility of his government in the disaster, and was not running for a third term, he was one of the leaders of the aggressive move to undermine the Canadian health system at the Vancouver policy premiers' summit.

Language is taken over like a fortress. In New Zealand a neo-conservative leader came up with the inspired term "retroactive consensus" to cover the tactic: the election is won with promises of the vaguest benefits with no reference to the costs and for whom – "health care is to be delivered more efficiently." Then when the election is won and legislation is brought in, it turns out that the project is essentially shifting the costs of the health program from those who can to those who cannot afford to pay the user fees and will have to make do with less. But the emphasis will be on the electoral majority which is presented as having approved a program that at no time had been spelled out.

Meanwhile, the public system must cope with the defects, the growing delays, in an increase in stresses on public health from increased unemployment, inadequate housing, overcrowded schools, rising criminality.

And the drum-roll of panic over costs serves a specific purpose in Canada today. The meeting of the provincial premiers in Vancouver in the last week of January, simply could not wait for the federal report on health care by a federal commission under former Saskatchewan premier Roy Romanov due in September. They agreed to give the federal government 90 more days to come up with a mechanism to resolve disputes between the federal government and a province over violations of the *Canada Health Act*. At present Ottawa can withhold funds unilaterally from provinces that infringe the Act.

The wealthier provinces are the most vocal in calling for a dual health delivery system and all of them, are feeling the effects of the deepening recession. Less affluent provinces, such as Saskatchewan, Manitoba, Nova Scotia and Newfoundland are friendlier to conserving a single-tier system. All, however, are united in demanding that Ottawa restore the cuts in its contribution to the provinces for health care of the early nineties. But the anti-federal front was maintained largely by keeping that issue of user fees from surfacing in public. When Saskatchewan premier Lorne Calvert criticized Alberta's Ralph Klein for advancing controversial ideas for changing medicaid, he was reportedly told by Premier Klein of Alberta to "butt out" from his province's affairs. "As long as we abide by the principles of the *Canada Health Act*, it is entirely up to the province to determine how it is going to deliver health care services." But lurking in the background is the itch of BC, Ontario, and Alberta to open the field to private investment.

The exaggerations are unconscionable. Thus Dr. Gordon Guyatt of the Medical Reform Group "trudged out his numbers last week when provincial premiers sang panicky choruses about costs out of control. Health spending represented 10% of GDP in 1992; currently it is 9.4%. The amount spent on health is distorted because the total amount of government expenditure has been reduced from 18% to 14% of GDP.[2]

Health Spending Looks Bigger in a Shrivelled Budget

The federal government, however, has itself to blame for much of the confusion. Its slashing of grants to the provinces for health care, education and social services, followed closely after the bailing-out of our banks from their speculative losses in the eighties This took the form of discontinuing the reserve requirements of the banks that allowed them to load up with some $60 billions of additional federal loans without putting up any of their own money, and pocketing the interest paid on this additional debt. The interest on federal debt held by the Bank of Canada comes back to Ottawa. Held by the chartered banks, it stays with them. In essence Ottawa cut its grants to the provinces because it had spent them to bail out the banks.

On top of that it acceded to their lobbying for deregulation that allowed them to take over stock market activities. A dark secret, kept from the public despite its crucial relevance to the debate, is that investment in human capital – spending on public health, along that on education, social services, is the most productive of all investments. That was proved by economists after WWII. It won a Nobel prize for Theodore Schultz in the sixties. He developed that view when he served on teams of economists assigned to forecasting the time that devastated Japan and Germany would require to rebuild their economies. The misfire of their forecasts led him to that conclusion. Were this incorporated even in the current debate on the health system, it would swing the argument powerfully in favour of public health care. However, these parties in this place great store in not questioning the dogmas of the financial community.

Equally underpublicized, is the bill passed by the federal parliament in mid-2000 introducing "accrual accountancy" (capital budgeting), ending the practice of the federal government and most of the provinces of writing off physical investments such as buildings, land and equipment as investments in a single year and carrying them on the books at a token $1. This gave rise to the bizarre situation that while Enron and many other private corporations carried their *debts* off balance sheet, central governments like Ottawa carried its *physical capital* off their balance-sheet.

When you privatize the government health assets carried on its books at a token $1, you can practically give them away and book a misleading profit. This would happen if the provinces privatized hospitals and other facilities. They would then be reorganized as private companies, charge user fees, and be listed on the stock market for profits to the promoters. That has happened with Highway 407 in Ontario. The need for such privatizations is felt particularly acutely at present because of the collapse of the stock market in clouds of corruption. By giving away public assets for a fraction of their value, the government is made to look more provident for reducing its debt.

That situation in fact, makes the whole matter of the bank bailout of a decade ago a land mine waiting to blow up in Ottawa's face. Unless we catch up with our knowledge of their bailout in the early nineties, we and our health system will be well en route to a replay of the slashing of vital services that took place in the early nineties. That would be a major step to the break-down of our society.

William Krehm

1. Quoted by Jane Kelsey in *Economic Fundamentalism* (Pluto Press, 1995).
2. Valpy, Michael (24/01). One group goes to the ramparts for health care. *The Globe and Mail.*

The Senate of Canada and Health Care

Early in 2001 the Senate of Canada adopted an Order of Reference authorizing its Standing Committee on Special Affairs, Science and Technology to examine the state of health care in Canada. At the end of October the Committee sat for two days in Toronto to hear prearranged submissions. No notice of the hearing was published in the local press. However, an alert member of COMER became aware of the event, and notified fellow member Robert Campbell, who also attended. As is usual in such cases, the latter was permitted to make a brief statement as a member of the public at the conclusion of the hearing. He subsequently filed a written submission with the Committee. The following are some excerpts from this.

Basis of the Canadian Health Care System

The basis of the Canadian health care system is the Canadian *Health Act*, enacted unanimously by Parliament in 1984. Its five principles – accessibility, universality, comprehensiveness, public administration and portability – are the essential elements of the system. Developed through many struggles, beginning in the aftermath of WWII, health care has long been regarded as a defining attribute of the Canadian way of life.

Notwithstanding this, constant erosion of public health care continues to take place.

Health Care as a Right

The majority of Canadians believe that Canada, as a modern country in the 21st century ought to embody in its governmental structures the means for the attaining a better future for those fortunate enough to live in this country. This conviction has for so long been an accepted proposition that it is curious the question should again be the subject of debate. The issue may indeed become the subject of litigation. It is to be hoped that in this event the courts will conclude that health care, as the most basic of human needs, is by implication indeed a right under the Charter.

The Economy and Health Care

The adoption of fiscal conservatism and monetarist policies by successive federal governments have resulted in cutbacks for social programs damaging to the health care system since the mid-1970s:

1. The Bank of Canada

Not the Bank of Canada in itself, but the distortion of its role:

• To the attempted control of inflation almost solely through manipulation of interest rates. This resulted in high unemployment and planned economic recession.

• Progressive reduction of reserves required to be maintained with the Bank of Canada, with the abandonment of such reserves beginning in 1991, a subsidization of the private banks and a major factor in the creation of a speculative economy.

• Continuous reduction of the Bank's injection of debt-free

money into the economy and instead looking to the private banking system to create interest-bearing debt-money through loans, factors which contribute to a diminished but inflationary economy.

• Abandonment of the statutory power of the Bank of Canada to finance the government's fiscal requirements as provided in the *Bank of Canada Act*, at nominal interest rates, and instead borrowing at market rates from the chartered banks.

2. The adoption of deliberately regressive tax policies characterized by:

• Shrinkage of the tax base by transfer of the tax burden from corporations and recipients of high income to the middle and lower income groups.

• The imposition of a consumption tax in the form of the GST:

The combined effects of these policies have resulted in large deficits and growth of the debt. These were used to justify reduced funding for health care and other social programs, despite evidence that such costs have remained relatively stable. A 1991 StatsCan study has shown:

• That half the deficit is due to excessive interest charges,

• That only 6% is attributable to government spending, and

• That the remaining 44% is the result of tax expenditures, that is, tax concessions and allowances.

3. The economic assault reached a new level in the federal budget of 1995, imposed on Canada by its own government on instructions of the International Monetary Fund. This was effectively a structural adjustment program based on the Washington Consensus of the type required of Third World countries borrowing from the World Bank and the IMF. In that budget, government spending was slashed by $25 billion over three years, 45,000 public service workers were to be discharged, Canadian National Railways and Petro Canada privatized, $4.5 billion cut from social programs, including health care, over three years.

4. Contrary to their publicized effects, the Canada/US Free Trade Agreement and the NAFTA, free trade as defined in them have had profoundly adverse effects on Canada's economy. The FTA was introduced into an economy already saturated with foreign control. It was to create thousands of jobs, result in prosperity, lower consumer prices and end American trade harassment. It failed to achieve any of these. It led to a frenzy of foreign and domestic takeovers, buyouts and plant closures and massive unemployment. Consumer prices did not fall.

In the FTA, Canada surrendered export price or other trade controls of its energy supplies, including oil, gas, coal, uranium and electricity, and agreed to share with its trading partner any shortage in its domestic supply, based on export levels over the preceding 36 months. The prospect is of virtually uncontrollable depletion of non-renewable resources in one of the world's harshest climates.

NAFTA is a far-reaching reworking of FTA, including Mexico as well as Canada and the US, but with sweeping additions, including deregulations and opening Canadian telecommunications to foreign investment, a comprehensive code of intellectual property monopoly rights, and continentalization of land transportation which brought American trucking industry into Canada. Chapter 11, on investment, gives American corporations the right to "national treatment," "most favoured nation treatment," and rights greater than those enjoyed by domestic corporations.

The economic effects of these agreements is obscured by the increased volume of goods traversing the border. Much of this "trade" under the pacts is intra-corporational transfers between subsidiaries of the same transnational corporation or its head office. This is not trade in the real sense. It is characterized by an artificial regime of transfer pricing, designed to minimize taxes to the corporation, bringing little or no revenue to this country. There are lengthy tax holidays granted as inducements to establish business in Canada, subsidies, loan guarantees, and sale of government-owned lands and assets to foreign businesses at distress prices.

Of crucial importance for Canada's survival is withdrawal from negotiations for the Free Trade Area of the Americas (FTAA), the extension of FTA and NAFTA.

Free Trade and Canada's Health Care

NAFTA opened Canada to the American for-profit health care industry. The FTA and NAFTA were models for the WTO and a proliferation of "rules-based" agreements, all designed to eliminate the capacity of national governments to resist penetration of their economies by transnational, corporations. This has led to the persistent encroachment and takeover of segments of the system by American health care corporations. This is wrong. No country ought to be subjected to a hostile and unfair trading and investment regime to dismantle its fundamental institutions.

Public opinion in this country is that health care is not, never has been and ought never to become a "market," but rather is public service for the general good.

Free Trade and Foreign Ownership

The degree of foreign ownership in the Canadian economy is one of the highest, if not the highest, of the developed countries. It used to be referred to in Europe as "the Canadian disease" not to be tolerated there. Since then foreign ownership has increased as a result of FTA, particularly in more industrialized provinces. The process has often been accomplished by takeovers and buyouts, not infrequently financed by Canadian commercial banks, with little infusion of foreign capital.

The trade agreements are in reality investment agreements. They will lead to complete ownership of the Canadian economy, very much as happened in New Zealand beginning in 1984. Canadians will become tenants in their own country.

The first step in reclaiming control of our destiny and the restoration of some degree of sovereignty is the abrogation of FTA and NAFTA. Each of these agreements provides for withdrawal of a contracting party on the giving of six months' notice.

About a further consequence of NAFTA there is no doubt. That is the potential irreversibility of steps taken towards privatization of any part of the system, due to the prohibitive costs of reclaiming what has been privatized from public ownership. It doesn't matter how pressing the need, or the strength of popular support for change.

Robert Campbell

Robert Campbell is a member of COMER's board, who retired from private legal practice of many years in downtown Toronto in 1992. This is the first of two instalments of a summary of his submission to the Standing Senate Committee on Social Affairs, Science and Technology.

Finding our Way Out of the Jungle

THE CRISIS engulfing the world doesn't just concern the GDP and our stock markets. It is bringing to the fore issues long banished from public attention. Not least of these is the relationship between high finance and the real economy.

In its remote origins money was essentially a measure of value and a medium of circulation. As such it was a handmaiden of trade. Only later did it become primarily a store of value and occasionally an instrument for speculation. Most recently it has become a highly speculative game in itself, too readily mistaken for the economy. The process that effected this apotheosis was begun in the early 1950s, and received its final touches, when money creation was "privatized" and increasingly removed from the control of central banks. Today, its purpose is to feast upon rather than serve the real economy. The effect on society has been devastating. Just open your morning paper and you will find the economic catastrophe of the world's strongest country pushing its military victories out of the headlines.

Several factors and stages can be identified in the process that eventually led to the Enron phenomenon. An early rule of banking in both the United States and Great Britain, was that banks could properly lend only against the security of "real bills," i.e., drafts and notes of exchange arising out of commercial transactions. It specifically excluded stocks and bonds, because of a conviction that left to their own devices, the banks would misdirect the credit resources of the nation to speculation. Until the 1920s, nationally chartered banks in the US could not lend on the security of real property, though state-chartered banks or trust companies usually were able to do so.

Monetary policy of the government and the role of central banks were essentially passive. The Fed discounted eligible commercial paper brought to its "discount window" to release the banks' capital for further lending. For years even government bonds were not acceptable as collateral for loans from the Federal Reserve. And these were the money-base on which further loans were pyramided. If the Fed bank wanted to do more lending, it lowered its discount rate below the interest rates in the local market. This encouraged business people to increase their volume of transactions. Gold movements also played their part. It was only later that government bonds under normal circumstances were accepted as collateral at the central banks'

"open window."[1]

The "discount window" was passive – it depended upon what discountable paper was brought to it by the banks. But the local Fed banks could play a more active role, seeking out paper to discount through the Fed's Open market Investment Committee. In the early Fed years they were driven to do so to cover their expenses and pay dividends to the banks who held their shares. By then government bonds and bankers' acceptances (paper endorsed by a bank) were the collateral most prized by the banks and the Fed.

All this suggests that commercial banking saw its role as serving the productive economy. In our day the reverse has become true.

Enter the Age of Unreal Bills

A key factor in this transformation was the creation of a short-term money market that was seen as the key mechanism for keeping the economy on an even keel. Over a period of years the Bank of Canada offered a variety of inducements to create a class of jobbers in short-term government debt. It conceived them immaculate, and nursed them from breast and bottle until they took over the entire show. In this way the Bank of Canada brought into existence the "young men in red suspenders" who came to terrorize the business world and the central bank itself and shot down the British pound, the Italian lira, and the Canadian dollar from their high perches in the fall of 1992.[2] In Canada this required a dogged effort on the part of the central bank, though the final result "the money market" has been held up as a masterpiece of nature itself.

Eventually the Bank designed the repossession arrangements by which the securities it accepted as collateral for financing the jobbers' short-term debt inventory could be repurchased from it by the jobbers at a predetermined price. Credit was advanced to them to buy short-term paper at less than market rates.

The emphasis on short-term loans ruled out not only many long-term investments in the private sector when money grew tight, but restricted the ability of the government to finance its own longer term investments through the central bank. When the BoC holds federal debt it is at a near zero-interest rate: over 95% of the interest the government paid on the debt held by the BoC reverts to it as dividends. For since 1938 the federal government has been the sole shareholder of the Bank of Canada. However, today the BoC holds only around 5% of the federal debt. In the mid 1970s that proportion was well over 20%. To bail out our chartered banks from their crushing speculative losses in the 1980s, they were relieved of their obligation to deposit on an interest-free basis an average of around 4% of the public deposits they took in. That, and the deregulation of what they could invest in, allowed them a leverage that has risen from 11:1 in 1946 to as much as 400 to 1 in more recent years. Part of the credit they have created went into financing some of Enron's shadowy partnerships and other such dubious ventures.

With this trend, the ability of banks to service brick-and-mortar investments was curtailed. The surrender of our monetary policy to "the market" inserted a wedge between banking and the real economy.

The Root of the Speculative Takeover

This trend, indeed, reaches back to the adoption of marginal utility theory to replace the value theories based on the real economy well over a century ago. These earlier theories had made a sharp distinction between the latest price fetched by a commodity and some more enduring value. One such value theory, the labour theory of value, that had attained its most refined form in the work of a retired stockbroker, David Ricardo. Relating the value of a good to the amount of "average labour" that entered its production, this had been taken up by Marx and other socialists to support their views for restructuring society in a way that would have curled the hair on Ricardo's head. The labour theory of value had become increasingly unacceptable to the propertied classes at a time when the growing class of factory workers was becoming strident in its opposition to the raw young capitalism of the day. The other popular value theories – espoused, among others, by John Stuart Mill – was the cost of production theory of value. This added up the average costs of entrepreneurs in producing a commodity and topped the total with a reasonable profit for the successful entrepreneur That resembled in broad terms what accountants did in their more conscientious moments.

Marginal utility theory, for its part, does not look beyond the latest market price. It is important to note, however, that:

1. To have their price model taken seriously the founders of marginal utility theory had to restructure society beyond any resemblance to what ever existed in the real world. Everybody, from the unemployed to the most successful bankers, were regarded only as traders, each intent on maximizing their satisfactions in the different ways open to them. The unemployed were idle only because, having compared the satisfactions of accepting work at the wage offered with the delights of leisure in their parlours, they chose the latter. All actors in the economy were of such tiny power and importance, that nothing that they did or failed to do individually could influence price or the economy. That provided the smooth cost and price curves necessary for applying the infinitesimal calculus that the authors of the model mistook for scientific method *per se.*

2. As the volume of production rose, it was assumed that costs per unit rose. This was essential to provide the points of intersection between cost and price curves that yielded the equilibrium points that defined such a "free and perfect" market. That was nonsense when it was first conceived; it is particularly absurd in the age of Bill Gates.

3. Were value simply a matter of increasing demand over available supply to raise prices, then the allurements of marketing could take care of enhancing wealth. Contriving enough demand to push up prices would be enough to assure a glowing future for a firm, and by heroic extension, for society itself. The reader will note that the word "marginal" in "marginal utility" refers to the *rate of growth*. And when the second *derivative*, the change in the rate of growth, the acceleration equals zero the supply-demand curves reach a maximum or minimum – i.e., an equilibrium point. In short, the derivative of official value theory is blood cousin to the *derivatives* that gave wings to the late stock market boom and made inevitable the subsequent

bust. They are not in themselves securities or money but the rate of change in the quantity of these or any combinations of them.

This not only condemns speculations relying on the model for eliminating risk. The number of massive misfires of these should long since have alerted society to reexamine the basic price model in use. Until that is done society will be helpless to work its way out of its current cave.

The spectacular failure of the globalization and deregulation was in a sense predetermined by marginal price theory. For that is the genome that reduced the very concept of prosperity to how much demand could be drummed up to overwhelm available supply. Even more than the Old, the New Economy was launched into the stratosphere of make-believe, replacing actual market demand with artificial projections of market shares achieved by selling below cost, giving the stuff away, and/or simply diddling the public corporations' books.

The Economy Goes into Orbit

Economic theory has ever been a hybrid of a would-be science and advocacy. With the giant strides in information technology, however, the advocacy component has completely taken over. The economists most quoted on the mass media are those who avoid mentioning basic issues deemed unmentionable. For example, the destruction of the firewall put up in the 1930s between banking and financial speculation, which somehow came to be mistaken for the financial equivalent of the Berlin Wall – something to be demolished. Banks have taken over brokerage firms, and have become underwriters, merchant bankers, derivative boutiques, and are prominent in speculations as principals and financing their clients' mega-gambles. That suggests a medical doctor merging with the local undertaking establishment. In a book of mine currently in the printers' hands[3] I describe the resulting situation: "As it approaches omnipotence, power sprouts pretensions to spirituality. Today a new mysticism is creeping into economic discourse. French sociologists have been more nimble in picking up the resulting oddities. Thus Jean Baudrillard has written, with just the tip of his tongue in his cheek, 'Marx did not foresee that it would be possible for capital, faced with the imminent threat to its existence, to launch itself into an orbit beyond the relations of production and political contradictions, to make itself autonomous in a free-floating, ecstatic and haphazard form, and thus to totalize the world in its own image. Capital can henceforth function independently of its former aims, and absolutely without reference to any aims whatsoever. Money is now the only genuine artificial satellite. A pure artifact, it enjoys a truly astral mobility. It has now found its proper place, far more wondrous than the stock exchange: the orbit in which it rises and sets like some artificial sun.'"[4]

Baudrillard reviews the contemporary cultural scene and finds all symbols of human existence – art, sex, the economy – denatured, endlessly reduplicated, and sent into outer space beyond the critical faculties or indeed any relationship with the needs or decisions of the individual. By increasing the magnitude of the menace, it is downgraded to the status of a "virtual menace" ever overhead but somehow neutralized in our thinking. Thus an oversupply of atomic bombs becomes a guarantee of peace.

If you have any doubt, consider this passage from *The Wall Street Journal* (Kessler, 19/7/99): "You can sell products at or below cost and still make money. Amazon.com has created a great business selling books and other stuff for a lot lower margins than traditional traders who pay rent. In a flash market share is taken [instead of earnings for appraising the stock] and billions in market value are created. In a further flash, the next wave emerges: on-line companies sell product at zero margin or (gulp) negative gross margin. Can they make money? Sure. Buy.com in Aliso Viejo, Calif., and Onsale in Mountain View, Calif., figure they can leverage the increased volume by selling ad space, marking up shipping, selling warranties, and getting kickbacks from manufacturers. They can do Visa kiting by collecting credit-card payments in three days and paying vendors in 90. Once you get the model perfected, it becomes a dangerous weapon."

Thus *The Wall Street Journal* (15/01, "From the Ashes: Enron Lessens Firms' Need to Have Assets, and Auditors Oversight") gives us the crux of the lesson that is costing us so dearly: "Like many of his dot-com counterparts, former Enron CEO Jeffery Skilling argued that a company didn't need a lot of hard assets to thrive. Information, not a physical presence in the form of power plants or pipelines, was the key to dominating energy markets. Hard assets, Mr. Skilling said, tied up cash that could be more profitably employed trading. He emphasized divesting 'big iron' and instead putting the money to work trading everything from electricity to broadwidth, from memory chips to advertising space."

Baudrillard was anything but completely mad. Had they listened to the high executives of Enron with as attentive an ear, our financial chieftains would have grasped the confession in Enron's boast. Since credit depends upon collateral, and CEO Skilling proclaimed his goal of carrying as few physical assets as possible, what collateral would be left to back the pyramiding of leverage?

Eliminating Use–Value

But there is a deeper factor that steps in to prevent such questions being asked. The father of modern linguistic theory, the Swiss Ferdinand de Saussure (1857-1913) held that our grasp of reality "revolved around our use of verbal signs." The concepts we use are (in part) creation of the language we speak. He compared the terms of language to coins that can be exchanged for other coins or bills, but in another dimension can be traded for some good of use-value. "The first type of relationship corresponds to the structural aspect of language; the second to its functional purpose. Baudrillard held these two dimensions to be distinct but articulated, i.e., they work together and cohere. At this 'classical' stage of configuration, there is a complete parallel with the system of exchange value in material production as Marx described it. Use-value functions as the original goal of exchange value: it refers to the role of the commodity in being consumed. Exchange value, on the other hand, relates to the interchangeability of all commodities under the law of equivalence."

In the [New Economy] revolution the two aspects of value which used to be thought of as internally linked have become disarticulated. "Gone are all references to production, signification, affect, substance, history, and the whole equations of 'real' contents that anchor it with a burden of utility. In a commodity, the relation of word to image or meaning and referent is broken and restructured so that its force is directed not to the referent of use value or utility, but to desire." The misapplied mathematics of marginal utility is the genetic code that made possible – even inevitable – the explosion of the financial sector.

The concept, of course, rubs shoulders with Marshall McLuhan's "The medium is the message."

I was still pondering Baudrillard's powerful symbol of entire areas of our social existence being blasted into an orbit of hyperreality, when I opened *The Wall Street Journal* (19/7/1999, "Defense Firms Mull Trans-Atlantic Deals" by Anne Marie Squeo and Jeff Cole). At the time the bickering over Kosovo within NATO lay sultry in the air. The members of the European Union were squabbling over mergers of transnationals even unrelated to defense. But with so much fur flying, the *WSJ* pops the surprising question: "Is the US ready for a wave of mergers between its own defense giants and those of Europe?"

"It should be soon, say the aerospace unit of Daimler-Chrysler executives, experts and some members of Congress. Recent encouragement from top Pentagon brass such as Undersecretary of Defense Jacques Gansler has touched off a new round of industry maneuver aimed at major trans-Atlantic mergers in the months and years ahead."

"The aerospace unit of Daimler-Chrysler AG of Germany is moving quickly towards a small deal. Its board has been expected to vote soon on a purchase of about a 12% stake in US space-shuttle contractor Spacehab Inc. of Washington for about 12 million. In other steps to expand its US presence, the company is exploring a possible US public offering and more frequent high-level sessions at the Pentagon." That would help build up an American constituency in obtaining approval of larger mergers and military orders.

Note that this was some three years prior to the Twin Tower attack and the declaration of war against a faceless enemy of no postal or other address. Are we not reduced to Baudrillard's phrase about "the relation of word to image or meaning and referent being broken and restructured so that its force is directed not to the referent of use value, but to desire." The desire, of course, is for Himalayan stock market values ever ascending on a scale not seen since very continents collided head on. Once that takes over, other details shrivel into footnotes printed in illegible type in fading ink. For example, what assurance would we have that on the board of one of the Daimler-Benz subsidiaries – cloned across the world and all ravishingly hungry for high-tech orders, bin Laden might not be seated disguised with a shave and a haircut? Might the US ambassador to the local government be lobbying it for a high-tech order to Daimler-Chrysler in return for turning over to it some of the latest high-tech?

Lower the cost of advanced armament exports means that more will be have to be produced and sold cheap to reap the same benefits for the US – and relaunching the stock market and keeping it going is an important motive both in mergers and armament sales. Otherwise expressed, since the cost of killing a man will come down with the increased efficiency from the merger, more men will have to be killed, if the merged company is not to bomb on the stock market rather than just in the Third World countries being liberated.

The *WSJ* item adds, "Senator John McCain, R-Arizona, who heads the Commerce Committee, has expressed concern about maintaining competition in the event of major trans-Atlantic mergers. But he says that US economic health is closely tied to the free-flow of goods and services between countries: You may find this irrelevant to advanced military technology – to say nothing of the actual trade policy of Washington – for example in lumber, steel, and much else. But remember we are in "virtual territory."

You can pick up the frayed threads of logic so hopelessly entangled at countless points. That sends us back to de Saussure's distinction between the structural and functional dimensions of language. The functional dimension has to do with the use of words as symbols to evoke important non-verbal relationships. The structural one deals with the degree of autonomy be taken over by language itself. There are fields when this can unleash imaginative creativity – notably in the case of the poet and the scientist striving to understand unfamiliar areas of reality. But it can also take on purely predatory forms. That is particularly the case when quantification is cut loose from what is being quantified.

That provides us with the necessary compass to find our way out of the resulting chaos. In rapid succession the entire structure of Globalization and Deregulation has caved in under the sheer weight of false assumptions. Accountancy is becoming a cover-up. The bursting of the stock market bubble mistaken for the economy followed suit. The banking system was bailed out by allowing it to pipe into the public treasury in the early nineties, and deregulated at the same time to make full use of its new entitlements as a platform for launching its speculations. In the inspired confusion ensuing, high executives are too often feathering their private nests at the expense of their employees and even their shareholders. The crisis of our economy has become a crisis of morality.

We must start groping our way back by reclaiming the invaluable heritage of economic thought that is still to be found on our library shelves, indeed, even in the *Bank of Canada Act*. Above all, we must restore dialogue. There is no other way out of this jungle.

William Krehm

1. Mayer, Martin (2001). *The Fed – The Inside Story of How the World's Most Powerful Financial Institution Drives the Markets* (p. 148). New York, The Free Press.
2. "For several years the Bank, in trading treasury bills, had progressively widened the spread between its buying and selling levels to create an incentive for the chartered banks to look elsewhere for buyers. These efforts had little success and in early 1953 a number of new steps were taken. The objective was to broaden the market for treasury bills and other short-term paper by encouraging some of the larger investment dealers to act as 'jobbers,' i.e., to hold an inventory of short-term securities and stand ready to buy or sell. The Bank of Canada undertook to provide investment dealers prepared to take a jobber position with an alternative means of financing inventories of short-term Government securities through the Purchase and Resale Agreements (PRA) The Bank would provide dealers with short-term accommodation by purchasing treasury bills and/or short-term Government bonds under an arrangement to resell the securities at a pre-determined cost to them. Initially these facilities were made available to 'approved' dealers at a rate lower than that charged by the banks for call loans, but it was hoped that a true call loan market would develop and that the Bank would become a lender of the last resort" (Watts, George S. (1993). In Rymes, Thomas K. (Ed.). *The Bank of Canada – Origins and Early History*. Ottawa: Carleton University Press). That in itself widened the gap between the real and the speculative economy. What is most vital for the real economy is the availability of long-term financing. Speculators, however, are interested in quick sorties for predatory profits.
3. Krehm, William (2002). *Towards a Non-Autistic Economy – A Place at the Table for Society* (p. 66). Toronto: COMER Publications.
4. Baudrillard, Jean (1993). *The Transparency of Evil* (James Benedict, Trans., pp. 11-13). New York: Verso.

The Americans will Dictate our Military Role

US DEFENCE SECRETARY Donald Rumsfeld's proposal for an "Americas command" structure deserves much more thoughtful analysis than it has been given to date. The fact that our Defence Department seems willing, even anxious, to be part of such a command structure should engage the minds of all interested Canadians.

Is such a command needed? It is inconceivable that any power on Earth would attempt to attack the US with conventional military force. No one has the capacity to do it. And if the proposal is an outgrowth of the "war on terrorism," it would appear to be significant overkill.

The more plausible explanation for such a scheme is to rationalize the hodgepodge of US continental command structures so that the US army, navy and air force are all subject to a single, commander. This is a problem that Canada addressed in the 1960s when I was defence minister but we abandoned it a decade or so later. A good case can be made for the Americans putting their military house in order on their side of the border and for us doing the same on ours.

But in appearing to support the idea of an "Americas Command," Canadian vice-chief of defence staff Lieutenant-General George MacDonald said expanded collaboration by the two countries' armies and navies could be modelled on the North American Defence Command, where a single, bi-national command directs war planes from both countries in the defence of

North America.

The analogy as well as the advice of senior officers is suspect. One of the reasons the air force was always so gung-ho on NORAD is because it provided a job for one additional three-star general with a large supporting staff. NORAD postings were considered cushy jobs with their mountain views, beautiful skiing and foreign expense allowances.

If the navy and army were to be similarly assigned to Colorado's mountains, each would claim an additional three-star general with staff. The ratio of senior officers to operational troops would get further out of line than it is already.

NORAD made sense at the time it was established, but less so now. A good case could be made for Canadian withdrawal, but such a move would rock the American boat too much. So we have to stay the course.

It is worrisome, however, to hear Canada's senior airman publicly espousing Canada's participation in the US national missile defence. Informed opinion in this country has been almost universally critical of such a scheme, and apart from the questionable efficacy of the proposed system, and the false sense of security it may engender, it is not a Canadian priority. Canada should spend any available defence dollars on helicopters that are safe to fly and transport planes capable of carrying equipment in support of our troops.

The biggest deception of all, however, is the notion that NORAD is, and that an "American Command" would be, a shared command. The American Commander-in-Chief of NORAD is American. His deputy may be Canadian but he does not enjoy full power to act in his commander's absence.

The US command was given pre-authorization by both the President of the US and Canada's Prime Minister to use nuclear weapons in the event of a Soviet attack. The Canadian deputy was never given similar power. So when Gen. MacDonald says he is afraid Canada could be marginalized if we don't participate in an "American Command," I would argue that the opposite is true. We have already been marginalized and signing up two more of our services would only compound the problem.

Far more worrisome, however, is the proposed mandate for the new command. A senior US official said last week: "It's not going to be just a homeland defence command, It's going to be a command that has responsibility beyond homeland defence."

Does that mean that an American commander will be able to commit Canadian troops to the next Vietnam War, wherever it may be? This is clearly unacceptable!

It is one thing for Canada to commit a battalion to work or fight alongside the Americans in Afghanistan. And I can certainly understand why our troops are so anxious to go. They have been so vilified that they cherish the opportunity to prove to their fellow Canadians what most of the world already knows – that soldier for soldier they are as good as any.

But their engagement was Canada's choice and a power that we don't want to lose. So when Defence Minister Art Eggleton says that we would not be giving up one ounce of sovereignty by turning our troops over to an "Americas Command," he takes the prize for naivete. What is proposed here is nothing less than the biggest surrender of sovereignty since Canada gained its independence from Britain.

And for all of that we would get nothing, while losing the ability to deploy our troops where and when we want, and where they might be of the most use for peace and security.

Paul Hellyer

Paul Hellyer, a former Assistant Prime Minister of Canada is head of the Party of Canadian Action, and long-time member of COMER. The above article was first published in The Globe and Mail *(4/02).*

The Sociology of the Grand Bust-Up

FAITH CAN BE as elastic as a lady-of-the-night's garters. And there is no lack of resourcefulness as the official profits of the New Economy avoid any too disturbing conclusions from the endless series of major bankruptcies. On the oped page of *The Wall Street Journal* (11/01, "A Corporate Crime Wave?"), George Gilder provides as usual a brilliant example: "Politicians must stop tinkering with the structure of law and regulation under which entrepreneurial plans play out. Businesses find themselves operating amid the turbulence of constant legal and monetary change. In extremis, caught in a baffling web of often conflicting bankruptcy, tax, regulatory, and securities laws, many executives make decisions that in retrospect can be interpreted as incriminating.

"Bankruptcy, however, is not a crime but a punishment. Virtually no one plans for its concussive effects or expects them at all. The real source of the 'crime wave' is the undulation of policy and the babel of alibis from politicians and bureaucrats searching for scapegoats."

But for a more earthbound summary of the facts let's retreat to the reporting pages of the same publication (21/01/02, "Murky Waters: A Primer on Enron Partnerships" by John R. Emshwiller and Rebecca Smith): "With names such as Martin and Rawhide, Braveheart and Raptor, [the Enron partnerships] sound like fancy bar drinks or maybe top-secret military missions.

"They are, in fact, a few of the myriad entities that Enron Corp. helped set up over the past decade and that now find themselves at the heart of one of the biggest corporate scandals in history. Government investigators are sifting through the complex financial structures of these partnerships, limited-liability companies and other affiliates to determine what, if any, accounting rules and laws have been violated.

"The partnerships – which Enron told investors little or nothing about – hid hundreds of millions of dollars of losses and debt from public view.

"Why did Enron create the limited partnerships? By setting them up, Enron could draw in capital from outside investors, such as banks, insurance companies, pension funds and even wealthy individuals. If structured properly, including at least 3% of their equity from outside investors, the partnerships could be kept off the company's balance sheet. This was an important consideration for a fast-growing energy-trading company that feared that much debt would damage its credit rating. Another, more personal incentive arose over time as Enron executives headed and partly owned some of the partnerships, they provided a lucrative source of outside income for those involved. Enron's former chief financial officer, Andrew Fastow, made more than $30 million from partnerships he ran."

Enron's Limited Partnership Scams

"In all Enron had about 3,500 subsidiaries and affiliates, many of them limited partnerships and limited-liability companies. In the partnerships' simplest form, Enron and outside partners would each put up money to invest in specific projects, such as a pipelines or a power plant, and then split any profits when the partnership ended. In some of these Enron parked assets that were troubled and falling in value, such as certain overseas energy facilities or stock in companies that had been spun off to the public by Enron. That hid losses that Enron would have had to report. In some cases Enron promised to compensate partnership investors, often by issuing Enron stock to them. Compounding the problem was the stock-market retreat of last year.

"The company says that it set up safeguards that required top company officers and the board to review and approve deals between Enron and the partnerships. But there are some questions as to whether the executive-run partnerships received favored treatment. For example, internal documents from the LJM2 partnership indicate that at least on one occasion, the partnership renegotiated a deal that saved it millions of dollars, seemingly at Enron's expense. Public attention started focussing on these partnerships in October; it opened concerns about a raft of problems buried in their complex web. With all this attention, investor confidence in Enron collapsed, and by December it was forced to file for bankruptcy-court protection.

"Arthur Anderson, as Enron's accounting firm from 1985 forward, was intimately involved in the company's strategy. As auditor, it was entrusted to make sure Enron's reports fairly represented the company's financial condition. But Anderson itself was potentially conflicted since it operated as inside accountant, outside auditor and consultant to Enron, reaping tens of millions of dollars a year in fees."

And here we enter upon an unexplored area – the sociology of corporate capitalism of our day. Not only is it unexplored but pre-empted by the marginalist value theory that identifies a highly idealized market model of the economy. This not only excludes all other subsystems of our mixed economy as "externalities" – the public sector, the household economy, the ecology, and so forth – but assumes a perfectly self-balancing market.

On this fairness and inevitability are assured by the assumption that all factors on it are of inconsequential size. Nothing that any of them does or leaves undone can influence price or anything else on the market. The derivatives marshalled to "manage risk" (and incidentally to keep debts and other awkward details "off balance sheet") are, more often than not,

without serious basis. Their consoling higher mathematics are not only irrelevant but misleading. If it worked despite the clash between the premises of the theory and the reality around us, it would be a miracle, fit to be ascribed to a saint or heaven. But, of course, it hasn't worked.

Yet there are enough choruses of PhDs in the employ of both universities and brokerage houses to assure that the public that it will. And boom markets achieved by some highly inventive and muscular interventions of Enron-like corporations relieve participants from worrying too much about the ethics involved. Such economic theory was as reassuring as a papal indulgence in medieval times.

Doing business according to the laws and even the rule book has immense advantages. Not least of which is an unburdened conscience, not having to remember your lies, and the risk of being caught, burned and shamed. There must be some powerful driving force – akin to a magnetic field – that causes such an outburst of mega-scams in high places. Undoubtedly it has something to do with the compulsion of maximising shareholder value which instantaneously capitalizes the achieved rate of growth, real or imagined and the rate of improvement of that rate of growth into the indefinite future, and incorporates that into the current market price. That puts CEOs under compulsion to achieve exponential growth or a convincing semblance of it. Non-growth is not an option. And the quickest way of achieving ongoing growth is to merge, preferably with a minimum of legal tender changing hands. On a buoyant market, this is likely to increase the prices of the shares of the merging companies, and provide the credit base for further acquisitions. Obviously the bonanza tends to spill over to the firm's accountants and auditors. They are likely to be in the big league themselves, listed on the stock market under growth compulsions not unlike those of their clients. Imperceptibly they tend to become of one flesh.

Let the *WSJ* survey take up tale: "Ties between Enron and Arthur Andersen, its auditors, became particularly close in 1993 when Enron hired the accounting firm to undertake its internal audit. While that made some Enron employees uneasy, they became even more troubled by the hiring of Andersen employees, among them Enron's chief accounting officer and the company's chief financial officer.

"Andersen's Houston office, which employs some 1,400 people out of the firm's total of 85,000 world-wide, was a sort of farm club for Enron. The Andersen employees wore Enron gold shirts and decorated their desks with Enron knick-knacks.

"The hiring between Andersen and Enron worked both ways. In 1993, when Andersen took over Enron's internal audit operation, 40 people moved from the company's payroll to Andersen. Also in the early 1990s Enron's Thomas Chambers, the energy trader's vice president of internal audit, left Enron to run the Andersen group assigned to Enron's internal audit."

Surely the various investigative panels that are springing up within governments and without, must not neglect these aspects. The sociology of Globalization and Deregulation must not be taken for granted. While the bubble was in ascent, the accepted economic theory and the proclaimed "inevitabilities" of Deregulation and Globalization extended a sweeping indulgence over all excesses. Morality was dismissed as a built-in service provided by "the market." The only concern of the CEOs of our huge corporations was to "maximize shareholder equity." Obviously the model is not working, when so many shareholders have been taken to the cleaners. Under these circumstances, any enquiry that does not take in Globalization and Deregulation and marginal utility price theory will be an evasion.

William Krehm

Greenspan Re-evaluated

CHAIRMAN ALAN GREENSPAN is a man of few words, and those he speaks are wondrously convoluted. Time was when he openly espoused monetarism, the dogma that the price level in the long run reflects the amount of money in existence and little else. Believe that and you will accept as a minor swallow that all that is needed to lick "inflation" is to turn the screws on the money supply, by driving up interest rates. Of course, the resulting scarcity of credit does push firms over the cliff, and send workers to the food banks. But you will consider that just a passing discomfort, that will eventually benefit everybody – including the broken families, those who lost their homes and the suicides.

In 1987, as newly baked chairman of the Fed, Mr. Greenspan helped bring on the greatest crash since 1929 by shoving up interest rates as monetarism dictated. After that, Mr. Greenspan started riding the learning curve on the job – a striking example of education at the public expense. Rarely if ever since has he mentioned the money supply – the equivalent of Taliban not allowing the Prophet's name to cross its lips. Instead, he has concentrated on such miscellaneities as productivity, carloadings, inventories, delivery times. That was shrewd because in our deregulated economy nobody has a clue what the money supply might be. For our banks are free to engage in just about every aspect of gambling, and their winnings are near-money[1] supply, while their losses are money destroyed and missing. The only clear rule today in banking is that the central bank must not lend money to the government, because if it did, over 95% of the interest charged on the loan would find its way back to the government and that would be unfair competition with the private lenders. When banks are bailed out from their gambling losses that is seen as just a law of nature.

In Canada and the UK this recovery of interest paid on federal debt held by the central bank occurs because the state is its sole shareholder. However, in the United States the Fed., though owned by private banks, remits about the same proportion of its profits to the federal government. That is an extension of the sovereign state's traditional monopoly of coining precious metals, *seigniorage*.

What Mr. Greenspan fell back on, when his monetarist faith was gone, was a swap deal with Wall St. They declared him the prophet with 20-20 foresight, and he abided by the immensely complicated needs of the deregulated banks. These had acquired brokerage houses, underwriters, merchant bankers, derivative boutiques, credit cards and other risky Wall St. ventures, and that ruled out high-interest rates as a panacea for the economy's ills. However, in the inspired prophecy business, there is more than a single risk and as early as 1996 Mr. Greenspan warned publicly about the "irrational exuberance" of the stock market. At once he was told in no uncertain terms by Wall St. types to concern himself only with commodity inflation and leave stock prices alone. He got the point. Only when it was far too late did he start delivering discount rate cuts as though by machine-gun. And with crash of Wall St. Mr. Greenspan was brought down from Mt. Olympus and reclaimed for the human race.

Dissent within Fed

And in that capacity he is meeting a growing degree of harassment within the Fed itself. The story is told in *The Wall Street Journal* (28/12/01, "Did Greenspan Push High Tech Optimism on Growth too Far?" by Greg Ip and Jacob M. Schlesinger): "Today, Fed policy makers are debating whether they went too far. The answer could help determine whether the current recession marks a temporary aberration in an era of growth, or whether the rapid growth of the late 1990s itself was the aberration.

"Mr. Greenspan hasn't lost the faith. 'New capital investment, especially the high tech type, will continue where it left off,' he declared in a speech last Monday at Rice University in Houston. He ignored the collapse of so many symbols of the 1990 boom, including Enron Corp., the sponsor of the 'distinguished public service' award he was receiving that evening. 'The long-term outlook for productivity growth, as far as I'm concerned, remains substantially undiminished, the Fed Chairman asserted.

"But others in the central bank have now re-embraced a less sanguine view. During 2001, the Fed's research staff has steadily marked down its estimate of the rate at which the economy can grow during the next two years without sparking inflation. The economic aftermath of Sept. 11 has only darkened the picture further, as companies *shift the sources away from boosting efficiency and toward improving security* [our emphasis]. Fed Gov. Laurence Meyer, in a relatively downbeat speech in St. Louis just two weeks after Mr. Greenspan's sunny comments in Houston, stressed the 'frenzied pace of investment in high-tech equipment [in the later 1990s]. That now appears to have been unsustainable.'

"The key to this whole discussion is productivity, which economists define as a worker's – or nation's output, divided by the relevant hours of labour. As far back as 1993, Mr. Greenspan noted a surprising surge in capital-goods orders. He speculated that companies were enjoying unusual gains in productivity. He concluded that greater productivity would permit the economy to grow faster without demand getting out of sync with supply. The Fed could hold back on raising interest rates without fear of inflation."

These quotations give us a bird's eye view of the confusion of the model that leads the world by the nose. How could the efficiency of the economy increase *without* looking after its security? Could an increasingly insecure economy possibly be more efficient? Especially since the spread of the deregulated market is undermining the traditional social systems across the world, and congesting supply lines. Modern technology has unleashed a population explosion with damaging consequences for both our political systems and the environment. Right there you have an indictment not only of the official model but of the accountancy supposed to keep track of its "efficiency." The media have been full of the boldness of the accountancy scams that contributed so greatly to the recent boom. From the *WSJ* article it is clear that the model itself is excessively cooked to deprive it of any serious relevance.

You need only glance at your war news out of Afghanistan alongside speculations about which country will be next for the US's anti-terror campaign, the default of the Argentine debt, with its inevitable consequences throughout the world, the menace of a nuclear encounter between India and Pakistan. The very dependence on military expenditures for the revival of the world economy, speaks to the mindlessness of rating the economy's efficiency without considering the growing danger of the whole boodle blowing up.

"The Fed staff forecast prepared for the December 2000 policy meeting predicted that consumer spending would slow because of falling stock-market wealth. But businesses' fixed investment, notably, outlays for equipment and software, was projected to remain relatively robust,' according to the minutes. Mr. Greenspan himself was taken aback in October 2000 by a chart in *WSJ* showing a huge gap between the rapid growth of fiber-optic capacity and the much slower growth of demand for the technology, a discrepancy that soon led to the collapse of a raft of start-up broadband companies.

"Early this year, the Fed was cutting interest rates in an effort to keep growth from stalling, while still issuing upbeat statements about the New Economy. 'To date there is little evidence to suggest that the associated gains in productivity are abating,' the central bank's policy makers said after the first rate cut in early January. 'Virtually no one, official or outside [the Fed} was talking about the fact that high stock prices were essentially generating too much investment by industries in high-tech gear,' says Stephen Cechhetti, head of research at the Federal Reserve Bank of New York from 1997 to1999 and now an economics professor at Ohio State University."

Essentially, the Fed moved with the deregulated banks in espousing the stock market as part of the holy family. As long as it continued soaring everything was assumed fine with the world.

William Krehm

1. "Near-money" is government credit that earns interest. Legal tender – whether gold or silver coins or government notes – does not.

Columbus was a Piker, Crossing but a Single Ocean

THE WORLD of high finance had just begun reeling from the disclosures of Enron's fictions, when a second explosion of revelation came to interrupt Washington's self-congratulations on its Afghan victory. In ingenuity the Global Crossing collapse ceded nothing to Enron.

The Wall Street Journal (29/1, "Winnick's Lavish Ways Matched His Big Ambitions for Global Crossing" by Deborah Solomon and Anna Wilde Mathews) sketches the corporation and its creator: "Gary Winnick's dreams for Global Crossing knew no boundaries in 1997 at the ecom upstart's first sales meeting. The company he co-founded was selling capacity on its trans-Atlantic fiber. As he watched the eager reaction, Mr. Winnick took a piece of yellow legal paper, taped it to the wall, and scrawled on it a globe with lines connecting the various continents.

"Global Crossing would offer fiber throughout the world." No preliminary research of effective demand, costs, timing were required. The difference between future and present had simply been erased. Balance sheets had been parted, as the Lord himself had the land and the waters, the night and day. Future assets lit up the company's balance sheets, while liabilities crouched demurely under the table.

With Enron it was mostly partnerships, off-balance-sheet, that turned out to be private fiefs operated by Enron officials. By the time GC filed for bankruptcy early in February/02, its stock had fallen from a $64 high in 1999 to 30 cents a share. As a by-product of the bankruptcy procedure for the first time the truth of how GC's financial wizardry was achieved emerged.

In the *WSJ* of 13/2 ("Optical Illusion: Global Crossing Used Swaps to Enhance Its Revenue: It Wasn't The Only One" by Dennis K. Berman and Deborah Solomon) delivered some details: "Analysts are scrambling to decipher accounting practices of scores of telecom companies to figure out whether other bombshells are lurking.

"'It raises the question whether companies are creating real economic revenue or sham transactions,' says Lynn Turner, former chief accountant at the Securities and Exchange Commission between 1990 and 2001. At the center of the debate is a type of lease known as an Indefensible Right of Use. Pioneered decades ago when AT&T Corp. was still a monopoly, such leases allowed competitors to gain access to the costly undersea cables that only Ma Bell could afford to build.

"Today, so-called IRUs allow a telecom carrier to buy all types of telecom capacity and gear at low rates, typically for periods of 20 or 25 years. Since IRUs are technically rights to a physical part of an underground cable, they can be considered an asset. That means their cost isn't part of a company's operating results, but of the property, plant, and equipment line listed on a firm's balance sheet.

"The transactions under scrutiny work like this: Company A sells an IRU to Company B, and books the incoming cash as revenue. Meanwhile, Company A buys a different IRU from the same Company B, and treats the transaction as an asset purchase, which doesn't affect financial results that excluded interest, taxes, depreciation or amortization and, in some cases were used to secure debt financing. But some accounting experts now question that approach, saying many such transactions would more properly be recorded as straight exchanges of assets, which restrict a company's ability to book revenue.

"Several telecom companies have acknowledged booking revenue through capacity swaps – often through deals with Global Crossing, Qwest Communications International Inc and 360 Networks Inc. For instance, both sold assets to vendors from which they also bought assets during the past few years." One such transaction was treated as investment, the other, though identical, as income. What it received over the years for what it sold could be discounted for present value to show more net worth and as collateral for loans.

"Among the most aggressive was Qwest which booked revenue from the swaps up front. For the first nine months of 2001, Qwest sold $870 million worth of network capacity to vendors from which it also bought $868 million of capacity in separate transactions."

Trading Future Profits for Present Cash

"Many observers say that CEO Winnick's insatiable thirst for growth was GC's undoing. Since the Initial Public Offering in 1998, Mr. Winnick, GC's largest shareholder, has sold shares in the company for combined proceeds of $600 million. One of his biggest paydays came in May last when Pacific Capital Group, the investment firm he controls, generated $123 million, enough through a complex transaction known as a collar. The collar lets Pacific Capital receive a portion of future price increases in GC stock, while receiving proceeds from the sale immediately."

A common feature of all great intercom scams is trading a cut of the unknown future for present gains and thus creating fictional money-supply. With Nortel it was sales of intercom equipment financed under the table by Nortel itself, thus creating the mirage of demand. Such sleight of hand would be impossible without marginal utility theory which sees no other value than the excess in the *rate of increase* of demand over that of supply "on the margin" – i.e., the last transaction on an idealized market of inconsequentially small traders that never existed. The black arts of advertising and accountancy make it possible for ingenious chaps to do whatever they wish in manipulating the latest sales on the market.

The operator knows the bunny is in the hat, because he put it there. It is the bucket shop writ big, operated in the shadow of technological revolutions.

Of course, considerable money does change hands: "Global Crossing zoomed to the top tier of corporate campaign donors during the 2000 election campaign, providing $2.8 billion in donations 58% to Democrats, according to the Center for Responsive Politics, a non-partisan Research group. The amount made GC the leading donor among telecom-services companies. Its contributions even exceeded those of Enron Corp., which gave $2.4 million during the period."

In *Economic Reform* we have long emphasized the juggling

of time and space by stock market analysts and even by some economists.

Capital Budgeting, for example has not existed in the government accounts of our federal and most provincial governments. In contrast to the optic fiber capacity swaps of GC, governments ignore their own investments, both physical and in human capital. Globalization and Deregulation achieves similar results: it keeps off the economy's balance-sheet the cost of greater wear-and tear on human and physical infrastructures and the environment, while puffing up the GDP by capitalizing the cost savings of transferring many simpler manufacturing processes to the Third World. To a large extent this is possible because, amongst much else, because of such things as urbanization without adequate urban services. Obviously a basic rethinking is overdue not only of the accountancy of our high-flying corporations but of society at large.

Meanwhile the biased accountancy of Enron and Global Crossing and other high-tech companies are likely to have a disastrous effect on the solvency of our banking system. *The Globe and Mail* (31/1/02, "CIBC shares slide after disclosure" by John Partridge) informs us: "Canadian Imperial Bank of Commerce shares took a beating yesterday – dealing a glancing blow to other bank stocks – as several analysts reduced their earning forecasts following the company's revelation that it is boosting loan-loss provisions because of exposure to Enron Corp. and Global Crossing Ltd. These factors all helped hammer US banks Tuesday as regulators forced PNC Financial Services Group Inc. of Pittsburgh to restate its earnings in connection with loans it had sold into the secondary market, a practice most heavily used in Canada by CIBC and Bank of Nova Scotia. CIBC's shares fell as far as $52.60 – down $2.50 from Tuesday's close.

"Analysts said that although CIBC disclosed its exposure to GC ($386 million) only on Tuesday, the Bermuda telecommunications company's troubles had been obvious for months.

"CIBC said that, as a result of its loans to GC and Enron, it is boosting its loan-loss provisions forecast for fiscal 2002 to the $1.25 to $1.35 billion range from an initial estimate of $1.2 billion. Michael Overvelde of UBS Warburg Inc. said CIBC may be in a better position than its competition to reduce provisions when the economy recovers, and added that those related to GC a are only 'a tiny fraction' of the merchant banking gains it [previously] made in the now moribund company."

It is disturbing that our banks who were bailed out from their risky ventures in the 1980s should be using the resulting entitlement to engage in highly speculative gambles. The merchant banking gains they made by unloading much of their interest in GC at a profit would be at the expense of their clients to whom those securities were sold. If our banks used their deposits and money-creation powers to fund a profitable visit to the gambling tables at Vegas, it would still be necessary to ask whether that was a fitting investment for Canadian banks to whom the Bank of Canada has assigned almost all its money (credit) creation. Even if they come out of the GC encounter with a profit, our banks have no business in the role of Typhoid Mary.

William Krehm

For Lack of a Twig in the Sand

YOU MAY HAVE BELIEVED that the merry pranks of Enron emptying pockets and retirement funds across the globe was just a lone tale of introverted Robin Hoods. That is the impression that governments and central bankers are spreading. Nor is it just that someone in Lower Manhattan has reinvented perpetual motion – actually perpetual *acceleration* rather than just simple *motion*. Innocently, without knowing what it was up to, Wall St. had stumbled onto the mathematics of the atomic bomb. That is what Enron set up as norm for the ultimate maximization of shareholder value.

Even while mouthing the usual placebos that fundamentals are sound, the financial press is starting to realize that they are anything but. The focus has shifted from business hyper-scams to "accountancy." Listen to *The Wall Street Journal* (30/01/02, "Stocks Take a Beating as Accounting Worries Spread Beyond Enron" by E.S. Browning and Jonathan Weil): "It's not the economy anymore, stupid. It's the accounting. Yesterday was the day that the smoldering corporate accounting scandal, which started with Enron Corp. and quickly spread to Arthur Andersen LLP, engulfed the rest of the stock market. Shares tumbled to their lowest levels in nearly three months as accounting problems surfaced at several new companies, stoking fears that other mini-Enrons could be lurking.

"Investors fled any company with even a whiff of an accounting question. Stocks in the banking industry, for instance, fell sharply following word that PNC Financial Services Corp., a Pittsburgh-based banking group, was restating its 2001 results. Analysts immediately fretted that many other banks could be hit."

For well over a decade we have been warning that banks internationally having taken over every variety of stock market gamble, having been deregulated at the very time that they had elbowed their way to the head of the public welfare list. We predicted a bigger and better banking crisis that will dwarf that of the early nineties. That prediction, unfortunately, is being realized.

Should Accountants be Allowed to Regulate Themselves?

That is the significance of the frequency with which companies are restating their previous corporate results. "The fundamentals of the accounting profession have been called into question. Where two decades ago, accountants were still held in high esteem, now they rank in public opinion polls below politicians and even journalists. Investors also suspect that organizations assigned to make the rules, like the Financial Accounting Standards Board, often act more like protectors of the industry they watch. That, in part, is why Enron, like so many other companies, was allowed to exploit lax rules for 'special purpose entities' that [kept] tens of billion dollars of debt off its balance sheets. This contributed to Enron's abrupt downfall. Politicians are openly questioning whether the accounting industry should be allowed to continue regulating itself."

When stock markets are surging, almost everything goes.

Who is Moses to question the Burning Bush? But when that turns into an Australian bush fire, everything changes overnight. "Companies like Tyco which had relied on high-priced acquisitions with its own stock to fuel their growth, no longer have [this substitute] currency to keep buying other companies. But that is like stopping a missile in its course while going into orbit. While investors and analysts often are willing to let things slide during good times, they want real answers when stocks are going down and wiping out their portfolios.

"But Enron has added a new dimension. What many investors are starting to recognize is that they don't understand the financial statements of many other companies in which they hold big stakes. Neither, they fear, do the agencies ranking the quality of their debt or the Wall St. analysts and brokers who are recommending their stocks. The real surprise among Wall St. veterans is that it has taken this long for aggressive accounting to become a mainstream concern. Restatements [of company results] have been on the rise for more than a decade, and the SEC has more accounting-fraud cases on its hands than ever before. There were 157 financial restatements by companies in 2000, compared with 207 in 1999 and 100 in 1998. The three-year total of 464 was higher than in the previous 10 years combined.

"Enron exposed the degree to which hundreds of other companies' accountancy practices are similar in certain ways to Enron's. The large accounting firms, such as Andersen, say the problem is not with their conduct but with weaknesses in generally accepted accounting principles themselves. Likewise, they say, if only they could be delegated the job of fixing the system, then it could be fixed."

It depends, of course, entirely on how you define "fix."

The United States has only five really big accountancy firms – the exact number as Canada has really large banks. Increasingly, Andersen's colleagues in this elite are beset with problems not unlike those of Andersen with respect to Enron. *The WSJ* (31/01, "Ernst & Young faces queries over role in PNC accounting" by Carrick Mollenkamp, Susan Pulliam, and Paul Beckett) reported, "Yesterday [it] confirmed that it had played an unusual dual role in the accounting problems that this week plagued PNC Financial Group. On Tuesday [the latter] said it would have to restate its financial results because of the way it accounted for three companies it set up with insurance company American International Group."

Since Andersen and other large accountancy firms are publicly traded, they must strive to maintain the idealized future that has already been incorporated into their stock market price. Remorselessly, they are enlisted on the tread-mill in the sky on which all public companies are supposed to maximize their shareholder's stake. Like their clients, they are driven to exponential ambitions. And that requires acting out on human bodies and souls what the wise Greek mathematicians managed to do with a stick in the sand – the classic *reductio ad absurdum* proof. They assumed a hypothesis true and then step by step traced the implications of that assumption. If it led to the opposite result, – they had proved in the most rigorous way that the proposition is false. To the best of my knowledge, there is not a single instance of an economist using the "reduction to absurdity" method.

Nevertheless, the present meltdown can only be seen as a *reductio ad absurdum* proof – of the unsustainability of the exponential growth on which Deregulation and Globalization has launched the world.

Our economy has been forced to act out the reduction to absurdity test of the "self-balancing market in real life rather than with a pencil and paper." Deregulation and Globalization, the "maximization of shareholder value" and the rest of the orthodox decalogue. That helped set the stage for the enormous crimes of the bin Ladens, big and small. The ultimate answer is likely to be found not in Guantanamo but on Wall St. and on the Harvard campus.

William Krehm

A Laser-Beam on Accountancy and Beyond

IN THE PREFACE to my new book *Towards a Non-Autistic Economy – A Place at the Table for Society,* I observed that the World Trade Center was not the first diabolically plotted catastrophe to hit Lower Manhattan. Previous months had witnessed the implosion of an incredibly rigged stock market which had been passed off as the economy. "Everything we had learned about keeping the market system from falling apart in chaos had been buried. The universities, the media, textbooks had been purged of references to the great debates of the thirties. For infernal cunning and the number of its victims, Manhattan #1 and the destruction of meaningful economic thinking took no backseat to the crime of the Twin Towers."

A declaration of war against an enemy of no known address was Washington's response to Manhattan #2. "War," however, provides a better setting for cover-up than for analysis. And as the progress on the Grand Alliance against Terror proceeds, the whole underlying problem is getting dreadfully out of focus. Moreover, the factors contributing to Manhattan #1 and #2 intertwine. The stench of oil, the throttling of society by debt, a circus of accountancy acrobatics compound the confusion.

Yet, a forward step of some significance is being made. From the profiteers at the head of the growing number of bankrupt transnationals, attention has shifted to the accountants who approved and even helped design the strategy of much malfeasance. Even a touch of philosophical reflection on the origins and nature of accountancy has begun turning up (*The Wall Street Journal,* 14/03/02, "Depreciated – Did You hear the One about the Accountant? How a Decade of Greed Undid the Proud Respectability of a very Old Profession" by Ianthe Jeanne Dugan). The report reaches back to Sumeria, Florence and Goethe for a sense of the fall of that once awesome profession.

However, only when we are offered similar reflections on economic theory will the Enron scandal be seriously addressed.

But back to the *WSJ* and Enron's accountants.

"During 25 years at Ernst & Young's office in Buffalo, auditor C. Anthony Rider put his imprimatur on thousands of pristine financial statements. But that wasn't enough.

"A few years ago, Mr. Rider says, E&Y set a quota for him: $3 million more a year in revenue from clients whose books he policed. He joined more than 2,000 fellow partners in rigorous training on how to sell consulting services on law, insurance, partnerships – 'anything under the sun,' the 50-year-old accountant says.

"'It was like telling a reporter to sell subscriptions,' he says, 'I couldn't do it, if I knew my clients didn't really need it.'

"In 1999, his $300,000 salary was cut 10%. Then in early 2000 Mr. Rider was fired.

"E&Y won't comment on Mr. Rider's case. 'Our partners' compensation is based on how well the firm does in any given year and how well the partners serve their individual clients within specialty areas,' says spokesman Les Zuke."

From Watchdogs to Lapdogs

"Mr. Rider's experience is essential to understanding how accountants 'morphed from 'watchdogs to lapdogs,' as the evolution was described during recent congressional hearings. [So many things in the world have changed beyond recognition in recent years, that the term 'morph' has been coined to cope with them.] Yesterday Arthur Andersen was bracing for the government to file criminal obstruction charges against it as potential suitors' interests in a merger waned.

"Long before AA's document-shredding hogged the headlines, accountants, the pinstriped paragons of rectitude, found themselves under pressure from many directions to alter their centuries-old practices. Over the past two decades, innovations in computer technology rendered obsolete many of the old-fashioned auditors' functions, prodding accountants to find other ways to bring in revenue. Companies' desire to produce ever rosier results for an ever-larger and savvier shareholding public compelled accountants to find ways to put the best possible spin on clients' financial reports.

"And there was simple greed. In the eighties the savings-and-loan crisis raised questions about how accountants could have let things get so bad."

Salivating over their Clients' Books

The sagging morality of the accounting profession derived from what was happening to those of their clients who were becoming the "dominant revenue" in society. The "dominant revenue" is a concept of the late French economist François Perroux, referring to the power position of a class whose prosperity is identified with the well-being of society as a whole. Once such a view takes hold, anything that contributes to the established system is regarded acceptable. And accountants found it harder to avoid salivating as they did the books of the stocks and bonds trade. That proved to the chosen that eventually the overbrimming bonanza would reach even the impoverished of the world and thus assure the compliant a reward in heaven as well. It is difficult to resist such officially approved certainties. There is even dwindling reason for trying to do so.

"The Big Five accounting firms – PricewaterhouseCoopers, Deloitte & Touche, Ernest & Young, AA and KPMG – collectively doubled their revenue in less than a decade to $26.1 billion last year. But most of that increase went to consultants and hard-sell accountants, not to the likes of Mr. Rider.

"Now accountants wallow at the bottom of professions in public-opinion polls they topped 20 years ago. The business is drawing fewer top students, more government scrutiny and bad jokes. 'We just got a message from Saddam Hussein,' President George W. Bush chortled recently. 'The good news is that he's willing to have his nuclear, biological, and chemical weapons counted. The bad news is he wants Arthur Andersen to do it.'"

"Accountancy," continues the *WSJ* article, "was formed as a vessel of trust, originating 10,000 years ago with stone counters in Jericho. In ancient Sumerian cities of what is now Iraq, book-keepers documented wealth by pressing the ends of sticks into damp clay tablets that hardened into permanent clay records.

"'What would Lucas Pacioli think?' asks Larry Crumbley, an accounting professor at Louisiana State University in Baton Rouge. Mr. Crumbley is referring to a Franciscan friar considered the father of accounting for his 1494 *Summa de Arithmetica, Geometria, Proportioni et Proportionalita (Everything about Arithmetic, Geometry and Proportions)*. The treatise described double-entry bookkeeping – for every credit entered into a ledger there must be a debit. That concept was created by Florentine merchants and hailed by Goethe as 'one of the most beautiful discoveries of the human spirit.'"

Until about a century ago the beauty of double-entry book-keeping hailed by Goethe hovered over economic theory as well. This took the form of one of two theories that distinguished more lasting value in commodities from the price in the last market trade. One of these value theories – used notably by John Stuart Mill – mirrored the computations of the accountant – the cost of production theory of value added up costs and topped them with a reasonable profit for the producer. The other referred to the amount of "average human labour" that had entered the production of a commodity.

The mid and latter 1800s was a period of ghastly conditions in Europe's factories – described by Charles Dickens in Britain and Emile Zola in France. The workshops had become infernos of exploitation of men, women and children. However, the workers were becoming increasingly literate, and drawn to revolution. A need arose for a less provocative theory than the labour theory of value with its strong overtones of double-entry bookkeeping in human toil.

That need was filled with marginal theory that identified value with the price attained in the most recent trade, and cast all actors in the economy as simple traders on a level playing field – from the unemployed to industrialists and bankers. All were deemed of such infinitesimal size as to be powerless to affect the market. This was done to be able to apply infinitesimal calculus which was confused with scientific method. The stern beauty of double-entry bookkeeping was scrapped. What remained was the manipulation of desire. The black magic of advertising, psychology and the power to misinform, developed to virtuosity in this age of "information," did the rest. All players on the market, from the unemployed to the banking tycoon, were seen as just maximizing their satisfactions. If they had no job it was simply because they found greater satisfaction in the joys of leisure in their parlours than in the wages offered. How much more level a playing field could you possibly expect?

Price – i.e., the only recognized value – was seen as the result of the balancing of market supply and demand. The "pure and perfect market" looked after social justice.

In more recent years when financial institutions took over the helm of the economy, this was in fact improved on. The driving force in the economy today is the supposed "Maximization of Shareholder Value." That dictates that the company continue growing in girth and profit at the rate already attained. For that is already transformed into present value and incorporated into the price of the stock. If foreseen profits even falter from this schedule, the value of the stock and the mountainous credit based upon it caves in. Only accountants can approve and even help design the tricks to avoid this. To reinforce their loyalties they were rewarded amply for consultant work as well as for auditing – two incompatible functions.

Until the double-entry principle is brought back to our economic thinking, the official enquiries on the Enron-AA scam will lead the world nowhere – even if the commissions of enquiry set up run into the hundreds. With theory that declares anything not bought and sold an "externality" – i.e., "off the balance sheet" – we have ended up with an increasing number of mega-corporations keeping a portion of their liability off the books. Significantly the public sector does just that with most of its capital assets. At this point you are up against the power structure that has profited from such arrangement. To deal with that will call for an immense amount of public education. That has been our goal ever since our first issue fourteen years ago. But never has the need been so great.

The Editor

Genetic Engineering Self-Refuted? A Multiple Lesson for Economists

THE FEBRUARY ISSUE of *Harper's Magazine* carries a report "Unraveling the DNA Myth" by Barry Commoner that has great implications for economic theory and practice. Commoner is senior scientist at the Center for the Biology of Natural Systems at Queens College, City University of New York and heads the Critical Genetics Project. Since we are the humblest of laymen in the field, we will confine ourselves to quotations of key statements, and limit our own words to some striking analogies with what brought the world its current economic grief.

"Today biology, armed with the power of genetics, has replaced physics as the activist science: it stands poised to assume godlike powers of creation, calling forth artificial forms of life rather than undiscovered elements and subatomic particles. Pigs now carry a gene for bovine growth hormone and show significant improvement in weight, feed, efficiency, and reduced fat. Most soy-bean plants in the US have been genetically engineered to survive powerful herbicides."

"Our leading scientists and scientific entrepreneurs (two labels increasingly interchangeable) assure us that these feats, though complex, are nonetheless safe and reliable. Conveniently ignored, or in some instances simply suppressed, are the caveats, the fine print, the flaws and spontaneous abortions. Most clones exhibit developmental failures before or soon after birth, and even apparently normal clones often suffered from kidney or brain malformations.

"The wonders of genetic science are all founded on the discovery of the DNA double helix – by Francis Crick and James Watson in 1953 – and they proceed from the premise that this molecular structure is the exclusive agent of inheritance in all living things. Known to molecular biologists as 'the central dogma,' the premise assumes that an organism's genome – its total complement of DNA genes – should fully account for its characteristic assemblage of inherited traits.

"The premise, unhappily, is false. Tested between 1990 and 2001, in one of the largest and most highly publicized scientific undertakings of our time, the Human Genome Project, the theory collapsed under the weight of fact. *There are too few human genes to account for the complexity of our inherited traits or for the vast inherited differences between plants, say, and people* [our emphasis]. By any reasonable measure, the finding (published last February) signaled the downfall of the central dogma; it also destroyed the scientific foundation of genetic engineering and the validity of the biotechnology industry's widely advertised claim that its methods of genetically modified food crops are 'specific, precise, and predictable,' and therefore safe. In short, the most dramatic achievement to date of the $3 billion Human Genome Project is the refutation of its own scientific rationale."

A Dogma Disproved

"Forty-four years ago Crick advanced the central dogma to reduce inheritance, something that only living things possess, to molecular dimensions. He saw as its agent deoxyribonuclear acid, a 'very long, linear molecule, tightly coiled within the cell's nucleus.' It is composed of four subunits or nucleotides, joined in each gene in a particular sequence. By molecular processes segments of DNA constitute the genes that determine our inherited characteristics.

"With this concept Crick hoped to catalogue the entire inventory of genes in the human body. In 1990 he elaborated the sequence of the three billion nucleotides involved. He proclaimed that it held the entire information determining 'if you have life as a fly, carrot or man.' This posited a 'clear-cut chain of molecular processes from a single DNA gene to a specific inherited trait, that the DNA genes have unique, absolute, and universal control of the totality of inheritance in all life forms.'"

Crick recognized that for this genes would have to "govern the synthesis of protein, since proteins form the cell's internal structures and, as enzymes, catalyze the chemical events that produce specific inherited traits. The ability of DNA to govern the synthesis of protein is facilitated by their similar structures – both are linear molecules composed of specific sequences of subunits. A gene is distinguished by the precise linear sequence of the four different nucleotides that appear in its DNA. Similarly, a protein is distinguished by the specific sequence of the twenty different kinds of amino acids of which it is made.

"Crick's 'sequence hypothesis' neatly links the gene to the protein: the sequence of the nucleotides in a gene. It is a simple code for the amino acid sequence of a particular protein." It follows that *in each living thing there should be a one-to-one correspondence between the total number of genes and the total number of proteins* [our emphasis]. The entire array of human genes – i.e., the genome – must therefore represent the whole of a person's inheritance, which distinguishes a person from a fly, and from anyone else. Finally, because DNA is made of the same four nucleotides in every living thing, the genetic code is universal, The gene should be capable of producing its particular protein wherever it happens to find itself, even in a different species.

"Crick's theory includes a second doctrine: 'Once (sequential) information has passed into protein it cannot get out again.' This means that genetic information originates in the DNA sequence and terminates, unchanged, in the protein amino acid sequence.' This endows the gene with undiluted control over the identity of the protein and the inherited trait the protein creates. Crick was aware of the brashness of his bet, for it was known that in living cells proteins come into promiscuous molecular contact with numerous other proteins and with molecules of DNA and RNA. His insistence that these interactions are genetically chaste was designed to protect DNA's genetic message – the gene's nucleotide sequence – from molecular intruders that might change the sequence or add new ones that might change the sequence as it was transferred, step by step, from gene to protein and thus destroy the system's elegant simplicity.

"Last February the journals *Nature* and *Science* reported the results of the work of the two genome research teams – in essence a defeat for Crick's gamble. Instead of 100,000 or more genes for the expected number of human proteins, the gene count was about 30,000, or about twice as genetically endowed as a fruit fly or a primitive worm. That contradicted Crick's central dogma. If the human gene count does not suffice to match the number of proteins and the inherited traits they engender, it cannot explain the vast inherited difference between a weed and a person. There must be more than the genes alone to hold the ultimate code of life.

"Scientists and journalists somehow failed to notice what had happened. The discovery that the human genome is not much different from the earthworm's led Dr. Eric Lander, one of the leaders of the project, to declare that humanity should learn 'a lesson in humility.' In *The New York Times,* Nicholas Wade merely observed that 'human self-esteem may be in for further blows from future genome analyses, which had already found that the genes of mice and men are very similar."

That certainly confirms the passionate attachment of scientists to their paradigm. "The reports offered little to explain the shortfall in the gene count. One of the possible explanations for why the gene count is so discordant with our predictions 'was described, in full, last February in *Science* as follows: 'nearly 40% of human genes are alternatively spliced.'

"Alternative splicing is a startling departure from the orderly design of the central dogma, in which the distinctive nucleotide sequence of a single gene encodes the amino acid sequence of a single protein. According to Crick's sequence hypothesis, the gene's nucleotide sequence (i.e., its 'genetic information') is transmitted altered in form but not in content, through RNA intermediation, to the distinctive amino acid sequence of a particular protein. In alternative splicing, however, the gene's original nucleotide sequence is split into fragments that are then recombined in different ways to encode a multiplicity of proteins, each of them different in their amino acid sequence from each other and from the sequence that the original gene, if left intact would encode."

The first lesson: neither the manufacturers, nor any one else have sure knowledge of what undesirable consequences may ensue from the genetically engineered products they are peddling. The cartoon accompanying the *Harper's* article shows human shoulders from which an elephant's trunk emerges rather than a neck and a head, and from the trunk a stalk of cereal. Panic-mongering? No more than the probabilities suggested by the statistics of alternative splicing.

We have witnessed the tragedies that can result from keeping facts concerning profits, losses, and money creation off the balance sheet. But in making false claims, genetic engineering is misrepresenting the secrets of the Lord's kitchen as they have begun to emerge, and marketing the false claim of having in hand His entire recipe book. There is simply no ceiling on the irreparable damage that can ensue.

There is another no less important, if less sensational lesson. Our readers will note the importance that we have assigned to the Tinbergen Test based on nothing more complicated than the solving of simultaneous equations that we learned in our first year of high school – the number of independent variables in any proposed solution must equal in number those in the problem. That is what turns up in the need to match the available genes with the number of inheritance traits, and the alarm over the discrepancy between the two. What we are encountering here is, under another form, the schoolboy blunder of our central bankers in applying their "one blunt tool" – higher interest rates – to solve society's teeming economic problems.

William Krehm

The Senate of Canada and Health Care

THERE ARE AT LEAST three separate bodies, two federal and one provincial that have been charged with examining the Canadian health care system. FIRST, the Commission on the Future of Health Care in Canada, established by the Parliament of Canada and headed by the Honourable Roy Romanow, former premier of Saskatchewan. It is required to report to the Prime Minister by November. SECOND, in Alberta, a premier's advisory council, led by Don Mazankowski, a former minister of finance in the federal Progressive Conservative government of Brian Mulroney. Its report was released early in January. THIRD, the Senate of Canada, which has ordered its Standing Committee on Social Affairs, Science and Technology to examine and report on the state of the health care system in Canada by June 30.

The Romanow Commission issued an interim report in February which came to no definite conclusions and has been criticized for vagueness. It did conclude that medicare needs more money, but did not decide whether this should be borne by the government, or by the public through user fees.

The Mazankowski report recommended increased participation by the private sector, funded at public expense, increased health premiums to pay for insured services, and medical savings accounts. It was hailed by the Canadian Alliance and the Canadian Taxpayers Federation and condemned by the Canadian Health Coalition

The Alberta report could be seen as an attempt to force the hand of the federal government, as premier Klein has promised immediate implementation of its recommendations on the basis of urgency and his contention that health care is in a state of crisis. This view is in stark contrast to that of public interest advocates who say that the system is not broke and does not need to be fixed, beyond straightforward adjustments and resumption of adequate and stable funding.

The Senate Standing Committee's hearings may also be designed to preempt the field in assessing the state of health care, as its final report in June will occupy public attention months before Romanow reports in November. Its chair, Senator Michael Kirby, has been an outspoken advocate of user fees. He is also a board member of Extendicare Inc., one of Canada's largest operators of retirement and nursing homes. Conflict of interest does not appear to bother the senator or his colleagues.

In the final analysis the Romanow commission ought to be the definitive assessment, but in the meantime, the Senate Committee has provided an opportunity to examine what the 'reformers' of health care are advocating. That is a more privatized and corporate system that will begin to resemble the American one.

Robert Campbell

The Template of Official Thinking

LIKE A BAD DREAM, the "recession" and its problems are now officially behind us. That is the impression left by a front-page *Wall Street Journal* article (4/03, "Lessons of Expansion are Helping Economy Beat Recession. New Flexibility in Inventory, Debt and the Work Force May Soften Booms, Busts").

Remarkably, the reappearance of symptoms of the underlying disease is taken for recovery.

The writers themselves do have their fingers crossed, but their doubts do not appear in the headlines crafted by other hands. "A robust rebound would be all the more extraordinary considering the shocks the economy has sustained in the last two years: the bursting of one of the biggest speculative stock bubbles in US history, a spike in energy prices, the terrorist attacks of Sept. 11 and the collapses of giant Enron Corp., and Argentina, Latin America's third-largest economy."

But these are all secondary factors in the world's great illness. The basic one is the unrelenting drive towards exponential growth of stock market prices, no matter what the cost to society (a.k.a. "maximizing shareholder value"). It is like an alcoholics' clinic hailing as the sign of a cure the ability of the their patients to sparkle socially again after a few gulps of the "right stuff."

"The US economy's ability so far to absorb those traumas and apparently escape with only a mild recession suggested that a fundamental change could be under way. At the heart of the argument is a belief that the economy has become more flexible. Manufacturers are quicker to adjust their inventories and the labor force to sales fluctuations. Financial markets are better able to parcel out risk. And policy makers were faster to cut interest rates and taxes in an effort to prevent recessions. This could mean that while the business cycle – the wave of alternating booms and busts – isn't dead, it has become easier for business executives and economic officials to tame."

And the writers quote Fed chairman Alan Greenspan telling Congress the previous week: "The recuperative powers of the US economy have been remarkable." He attributed the performance to the economy's "apparent increased flexibility and resiliency, especially in the financial markets and in companies' access to timelier data such as sales and inventories."

On reading this, you have to pinch yourself to make sure that you are not dreaming. From the congressional hearings on Enron, Global Crossing, and myriad other stars of the boom, it would seem that the distinction between real sales of those companies and what was off-balance sheet inventory was kept hidden not only from the shareholders but from the institutions that peddled their overpriced securities.

Mr. Greenspan as usual balances between the two views: "there are still 'ample reasons' to assume the recovery will be tepid. The forecast of Fed policymakers is for the economy to expand at just a 2.5%-to-3% rate over the course of the year, too slow to keep unemployment from rising." The new flexibility so gleefully hailed would not apply to the growing number of unemployed. These must be seen as impaired consumers unable to contribute to recovery.

The writers continue, "For a look at the economy's new flexibility, consider the auto industry. Vehicle sales clocked a remarkably strong annual rate of 16.7 million units in February, defying expectations of a bigger drop after last fall's record pace. A big reason has been the exceptionally generous manufacturers' incentives put in place after Sept. 11, including zero-percent financing on many models.

"In the old days, such offers might have been difficult since all three of Detroit's major auto makers had their credit ratings slashed last year because of slumping profits. That would have impaired their access to the bond and commercial paper markets and thus their ability to finance low-cost loans to buyers."

The Flexibility of Broken Reeds

"But the downgrades last year didn't present a major constraint – in part because auto makers have increasingly turned to the growing market for asset-backed securities to finance sales. [Today] investors are more willing to buy the pools of consumer auto loans, which carry high credit ratings, than the debt of the automakers themselves. Last year, finance companies – including the finance arms of auto makers – securitized 32% of auto loans and leases in this way, compared with 15% in 1990, according to Federal Reserve data."

The thing about securitized loans is that an appraisal of the individual debtor's creditworthiness is skipped. And equally notable, the profit position of the manufacturer is also ignored. And yet unexpectedly it may force its way onto the screen. Manufacturers with low profit margins are likely to dump their leased cars on the market at the end of the lease. And that will affect the value of the collateral backing the securitized no-interest loans. Their value will also be affected negatively by any increase in market rates. And with growing unemployment, many of the purchasers are likely to default.

What we have then rather than increased flexibility is simple deferment. The basic ailment of our economy is that it gorges on a future that is not only unknown to mortals but like toothsome taffy is stretched to the breaking point.

Something similar can be said of President Bush's tax cuts. "In January consumer spending grew at a surprisingly brisk 0.4% rate unadjusted for inflation [over that in December], the Commerce Department said. One striking factor: last year's tax cut, which helped boost disposable income 1.6%. That strength may not be sustained. The University of Michigan said Friday that the index of consumer sentiment slipped for the first time in five months.

"But there were stronger signs of growth elsewhere: In February, the purchasing managers' index maintained by the Institute for Supply Management, shot from 49.9 in January to 54.7. That indicates an expanding industrial sector for the first time in 19 months.

"[This] increased flexibility has been an important source of resilience for the overall economy. In the last decade, manufacturers have tightened their control of inventories, often with supply-chain management software that closely tracks parts, materials and customer inventory, helping the companies to reduce waste, interest expenses and lead times."

But this is poppycock when the top management of Enron, Global Crossing, etc., kept their shareholders in the dark about what was a real sale and what was make-believe. And against the economies of capitalizing what might or might not happen in the future, we must place the cost of retaining battalions of lawyers to straighten out the muddle.

These things, however, are treated as "externalities" – i.e., off-balance-sheet. That is strictly after the model of our official economic theory's handling of the environment, public education and health, and on other non-marketed but vital services.

Possibly the point would register more easily if we dropped the term "off balance sheet" for undeclared debts, options, and whatever, and used "externality" instead. Then economists might realize that one such group of "externalities" leads to other externalities. That is the essence of the Enron and Global Crossing scandals.

Like the Efficiency of Cancelling Fire Insurance

Of course, stripping inventories to the bare minimum with the aid of "supply-chain management software," would be the purest efficiency if the software could alert management to when the economy will turn around and everybody will scurry to build up their inventories to get in on "the good thing." The fact that it doesn't will give back some of the supposed efficiencies: prices will shoot up, delivery times lengthen. You might as well cancel your fire insurance in the name of greater "efficiency."

The same holds for the growing dependence on temporary workers, "who are among the first [to be let go]when business slows." Temporary employees account for 2% of employment, but they represent more than a third of the net loss of jobs since the end of 2000.

"Perhaps no part of the economy has shown as much increased flexibility as the financial markets. None was as critical in helping the economy survive its slump as the migration from banks to the capital markets. Asset-backed securities and more exotic derivatives have proliferated.

"As the markets have become more sophisticated, they have become quicker to respond to new information, indeed, as fast as the Fed was to respond to the slowing of the economy by starting to cut rates in January of 2001." But at no time have the Fed, the Bank of Canada, or the Bank for International Settlements abandoned their dogma that "inflation" must be combatted by raising interest rates. This almost destroyed the economy in the early eighties and once again in 1987. In fact a rising price level may not be due to real "inflation," but to disasters forcing attention to some of the neglected "externalities" – the environment, public health, education, social security. Such "externalities," in fact, are essential public investments whose costs must turn up eventually in a deeper layer of taxation in the price level. Yet our central banks ignore not only the depression that has overtaken the world, but the alternative to interest rates as a means of controlling real inflation when it exists – for example

by the simple device of increasing the reserve requirements that banks must deposit with the central bank as a proportion of their public deposits. This was abolished in Canada in 1991-93 to increase the amount of federal debt the banks could hold without having to put up cash or capital of their own. If the Fed was "fast to respond to the slowing of the economy" it was not that it or the market had become more sophisticated, but that our banks had taken over every aspect of stock market activity. High interest rates no longer served their interests as when they were first and foremost lenders. Rising interest rates are poison to almost every aspect of stock market activities. As for the sophistication shown by their interest in financial instruments in more exotic derivatives, Enron and Global Crossing showed again that derivatives are essentially a gambling device. Too often they are beyond the understanding of the "experts" who sell or use them. Too frequently their purpose is to con rather than to clarify. Too often the gaps in their supposed hedging for purposes of risk management is filled by little more than the dogma of the "self-balancing market." The highly unbalanced state of the world today is overwhelming evidence that the deregulated market is anything but self-balancing.

Globalization is Shrinking the World

The important phenomenon that commentators shut their eyes to is that the virtuous empire is shrinking steadily. The Third World has never recovered from its massive losses caused by the carnivorous interest rates of the early 1980s. Its debts were simply restructured. The effects of the East Asian meltdown of 1987 knocked out a goodly part of East Asia, as did the Russian partial default on its debt in 1998. More money has been pulled out of the Third World in the past decade that has gone back into it. Now the Argentine, once a promising First World Country, is a basket case as is Japan, its banks crammed with assets that have become pure fiction with the collapse of its stock markets and real estate values. Globalization and Deregulation has removed all fire walls against the spread of deflation. At the very time that the Americans are whistling in the dark as only Washington can, obscure items in their financial press are telling of the spread of the "Japanese disease" – really the "American" – to the heart of Europe. Thus, *The Wall Street Journal* (12/03, "Telecom Debt Gets Tougher to Pare Down" by Almar Latour) informs us: "Since the beginning of 2000, France Telecom's shares have fallen 85% and Deutsche Telekom's more than 80%. This sharp decline is a pressing issue all across the European industry, prompting operators to consider writing down investments such as costly new wireless technology licenses that in some cases have so far gone unused. But no major operator has done so yet. For example, Telefonica SA of Spain stated recently that it has no plan to write down investments in Group 3G, the German venture with Finland's Sonera Corp. that many observers consider valueless.

"The ratios of debt to market capitalization of France Telecom and Deutsche Telekom are, respectively 160 and slightly more than 100%, the first and third-highest in Europe: KPN NV of the Nederlands is No. 2 with a ratio of 156%."

There are several further shoes waiting to drop. And with Globalization this will not stop at the shores of the Atlantic. A good part of the revival spirit that has taken over Wall Street is sheer hysteria – the hysteria of fear about what has yet to happen.

William Krehm

A Systems View: "Wealth" versus Life

IN HER IMPRESSIVE BOOK, The Divine Right of Capital,[1] Marjorie Kelly provides much food for thought as well as a rational program for social and economic action. Rich in insights and profound in its radical conservatism – going to the roots of problems that stem from ancient traditions of aristocratic privilege – Kelly points to an agenda that we cannot afford to ignore. She reminds us that, even in an age of respect for science and its methods, many of our societal arrangements carry damaging remnants of the past, including assumptions and habits surrounding wealth and its legitimacy.

Notions of rights and privilege vested in ownership and property involve beliefs steeped in traditions that still live on. To escape the bonds of conditioned thought we need to distinguish more clearly between excellence of character and performance, on the one hand, and social status due to possessions on the other. Respect for excellence is certainly deserved where this is earned, whether through Olympic achievements or in less celebrated forms, as in academia, the professions, business and the workplace. But rights of ownership and privileges in perpetuity are not easily justified.

A clear distinction is essential between recognition and rewards due to talent and productive effort, on the one hand, and access to inherited and otherwise unearned wealth on the other, including income streams that require no responsibility. Most of us recognize that great wealth now brings many rights and privileges which cannot withstand reasonable analysis in terms of justice or freedom. The legitimacy of arrangements which support special privileges are now being seen as in need of special justification.

Kelly's analysis plumbs the foundations of political and economic history, and of the history of ideas. She describes the way in which the divine right of kings was replaced by the rights of the land-owning nobility. (Those lacking property have been largely out of luck ever since.) She extends the point made by Hazel Henderson, that "Economics is politics in disguise",[2] and recounts the history of legal fictions based upon the notion that "The Prince is not subject to laws: He himself is the animate Law on earth." She shows the continuity of this idea with the modern doctrine that stockholders, in effect, can do no wrong. Due to the doctrine of limited liability, stockholder owners bear no continuing responsibility for what the corporation may do, no matter how disastrous. Such corporate fictions, like those which surrounded kings, serve the overriding purpose of protecting current power arrangements.

Historically, of course, these doctrines allowed the Crown's business representatives to engage in piracy as well as unconscionable exploitation of peoples in remote regions, the "heart of darkness" being out of sight and out of mind. A wilful and convenient ignorance is still among the privileges of ownership.

Kelly accepts as valid the observation that the world is evolving in the direction of a kind of capitalism. But she also emphasizes that capitalism itself is evolving, toward new structures which she describes in some detail, including "economic democracy." Today's free enterprise is only the middle chapter is a history of sovereignty that still contains possibilities of economic liberty and justice for all. However the final chapters have yet to be written.

Waking to New Ideas

As she explains, one of the first and most difficult steps is that of waking up to new ideas, of updating the maps by which we interpret our world – in terms of politics and economics, certainly, but also in terms of more systemic values. It is also the case that our assumptions of how the world works, of what is possible to change, are key to our receptiveness to new ideas. Our views on political and economic security will depend on the perceived risks to our own place in society and to the welfare of our families, on our own personal needs and values. For we are human beings and vulnerable, and all in this together.

Enlightenment is about seeing things differently, for change begins in the mind. And there can be no social change without knowledge. New language and mental maps are being developed for practical use. Kelly follows Hazel Henderson in describing a variety of indices in terms of which the costs and production of corporations and societies may be better calculated. We now have opportunities to refine our language and describe trends more precisely, e.g., in terms of Productivity Reports for Employees and Stockholders, as well as of a Market Efficiency Audit, an assessment of the full cost of the products being sold.

Among the principles of a new economic democracy, Kelly deals with sovereignty as well as democracy, justice and the public good. A major principle is that corporate wealth belongs to those who create it, and community wealth belongs to all. Putting up the original money, or subsequent speculations in the global casino, are a small part of the story.

Appropriate feedback is a vital systems principle. Organizational effectiveness is best served when gains go to those who actually do create the wealth. As Thomas Jefferson put it, the "artificial aristocracy founded on wealth" must make room for the "natural aristocracy" of talent and industry.

One of our greatest societal needs is for wise leadership, and there are still large numbers of people who are inordinately impressed by what they see as the superiority of the wealthy, people who continue to hope for some quality of character in addition to the power that wealth can obviously buy. Such attitudes run very deep. Indeed it is important to distinguish excellence of performance from the self-serving ideology of power attached to the possession of wealth as such. And certainly government by opinion surveys and spin doctors may make this difficult.

Moreover, to doubt the arrangements under which we presently live is difficult, an anxiety-provoking challenge inconceivable for many. It may take many disappointments before the realization dawns that the emperor may really be a very ordinary person, or worse.

Yet it is likely that we have reached a point in history where large numbers of educated citizens are reaching a critical mass – the so-called "cultural creatives"[3] – for whom the problems associated with doubt and accepting personal responsibility have become less fearsome than the prospects of being railroaded by incompetents serving world systems bent on exploitation and bankruptcy.

Market principles, at their best, are about self-reliance, hard work and competition.

It makes little sense, according to Kelly, for corporate law to remain feudal, with stockholders owning the firm's assets and everything these create, but with limited or no responsibilities. Without the needed feedback, our lords and masters may, like the Enron aristocrats, steer the juggernaut into a deadly whirlpool, all the while being unable to account for the manifest turbulence. Yet markets are also about creative destruction, and it is past time for a little creative destruction of the privileges of destructive wealth.

Kelly quotes Jefferson: "A little rebellion now and then is a good thing, and as necessary in the political world as storms in the physical."[4] It was and is the right of the people to establish government. John Locke, the English political theorist, wrote that governance rights can be forfeited when the ruler delivers "the people into the subjection of a foreign power."[5] The intrusion of multinational corporations into national sovereignty may mark such a "dissolution of government" which leaves the people free to make new arrangements. What is required is that the people assert this right.

On the basis of such established principles, Kelly holds, citizens have the right to alter or abolish such corporations as presume to govern the world but do not serve its peoples.

Bruce Buchanan

1. Kelly, Marjorie (2001). *The Divine Right of Capital: Dethroning the Corporate Aristocracy*. Berrett-Koehler.
2. Henderson, Hazel (1996). *Building a Win–Win World: Life Beyond Global Economic Warfare*. Berrett-Koehler.
3. Ray, P. & Anderson, S. (2001). *The Cultural Creatives: How 50 Million People Are Changing the World*. Three Rivers Press.
4. Kelly, p. 173.
5. Kelly, p. 123.

Behind the Present Crisis of Globalization Yet Another Possibly Greater One is Shaping

THE WORLD is absorbed in the "War against Terror" and America's unceasing promotion of Globalization in the midst of spreading monetary collapse from previous efforts in the field. And meanwhile new menaces are appearing on the horizon.

Basically Globalization was imposed on the world by Washington with a simple rationale. By getting simpler manufacturing processes done in Third World, the US would benefit by lower labour costs to keep the price of the end product low. "Inflation" could thus be tamed by exporting less skilled jobs rather than by raising interest rates. High interest rates at home are increasingly unacceptable to the financial elite that have come to dominate the American scene. For Deregulation has involved banks and other financial institutions in every aspect of the stock market and thus makes them vulnerable to high interest rates. The export of simpler industrial processes has helped at least temporarily to overcome some of the foreign exchange crises that that have afflicted the Third World since the seventies.

A further attractive feature of the Globalization scheme for American transnationals was the constant possibility of seeking a more wretched country with still lower wages if workers in the initial host land grew demanding. The investors always had a foot out the door and a further list of accommodations available in other countries.

The costs and destructive aspects of the Globalization program were evident from the beginning. They destroyed extensive portions of the subsistence economies of the host lands, created a further need for expensive infrastructures that were not met, since tax concessions were usually the part of the inducement package that attracted the investment. Playing off one wretched country against the other was a core part of the scheme.

But the entry of China into this picture has dramatically changed the topography of the game. American massive investment in China may contribute to China heading towards a technical competence that will eventually convert it into a formidable competitor not only of Third World countries, but of the US itself.

The Wall Street Journal (14/03, "China's Secret Weapon: Smart Cheap Labor for High-Tech Goods" by Peter Wonacott) wrote, "All over the factories along this stretch of China's southeastern coast the same extraordinary scenario is unfolding: workers move into more and more sophisticated jobs, while their pay stays relatively low. It's not what's happening in other developing nations, as pay jumps as workers get smarter – driving employers away to nations with cheaper labor. But China's population is so vast that that it can stay smart and cheap – a formula that's making it a new superpower in high-tech manufacturing.

"It's also key to China's challenge to modernize and still keep social unrest to a minimum. As worker protests become more common in creaky state-run industries, Beijing moves toward a free-market economy that has produced years of double-digit growth and an increasingly mobile, ambitious and better-educated work force. For many, the opportunities in coastal areas favored by foreign investors are a step up no matter how low the wages."

China a Future High-tech Land?

"The result: other countries are increasingly ceding high-tech industries to China as well as low-tech ones. That spells trouble for impoverished garment producers in Pakistan and for software developers in Japan. Foreign direct investment in China last year totaled $46.8 billion, according to the UN Conference on Trade & Development. That was a 15% gain over 2000, the highest FDI total the country has seen yet and the most received among developing countries. The comparable figure declines last year for South Korea, the Philippines and Malaysia. Taiwan stayed about the same, and Indonesia saw some divestment.

"'I tell my customers that we don't have to worry about China for the next ten years,' says Ash Bhardwaj, president for the Asia-Pacific region for Flextronics. The Singapore-based company, the world's biggest contract manufacturer, makes phones, circuit-boards and other gear for a long list of electronics companies. 'There's enough talent in the poor interior that prices will stay really low.'

"Flextronics has become a leading investor among a belt of factories around Zhuhai largely because of the low labor costs. These plants have tapped not only cut-rate engineers, but also some of the cheapest unskilled workers in the industrialized world. Mr. Bhardwaj compares the rate of 60 cents an hour for unskilled labor in China to $2.50 in Malaysia, $5 in Singapore and $25 in Japan. Flextronics has slashed jobs in places such as Singapore while expanding its campus just outside Zhuhai. Next month it starts construction on a $100 million plant in Shanghai.

"The phenomenon of persistently low wages amid fast growth defies the laws of economics. It begins with farmers who abandon farming or menial jobs in small towns and provide a constant stream of cheap factory labor. Vocational schools have responded to the rise in tech jobs by offering more engineering classes. So have universities, where 37% of the graduates in 2000 were engineers, compared with about 6% in the US."

China, in the area of education at least, does not disregard the importance of human investment as is happening in the US. Given China's huge population and motivation, Washington is making a bad mistake to be relying on starwar hardware to keep ahead of the high-tech technological giant that China may become.

"More than two decades of reforms have relaxed Chinese residence-permits, left from the days when the communists wanted farmers rooted in the land and workers welded to state factories. Flextronics head-hunters now drop by struggling state enterprises in the north and travel west to top-flight universities that turn out more engineers than local industries can absorb. As a result, starting salaries at Flextronics have barely budged in three years.

"The Flextronics plant has gone from making simple mobile-phone chargers to advanced miniature printed circuit boards. The workers electronically design the boards now and cut them with lasers, underlining the shift to skilled labor at toy-assembly prices. Flextronics might even start producing Microsoft Corp.'s sophisticated games console, Xbox. If it does, employees boast they'll make it more cheaply than plants in Mexico can.

"Last year, China's high-tech exports, including goods made by foreign-owned plants, accounted for 17.5% of total exports, compared with 5% in 1985. China is also outpacing other East Asian countries, according to Shahid Yusuf, head of research for development economics at the World Bank. Between 1985 and 1998, China's high-tech exports grew 43% a year on average compared with 18% to 28% for other East Asian countries

"As other countries feel pressure to match China's low wages, there's risk that wage stagnation will spread to Malaysia, Mexico and elsewhere. But there is a downside for China, too: low pay breeds disenchantment. For two decades exports have fueled China's growth while a repressive leadership has quelled potential labor unrest. But with 18 million people coming into the work force each year, and economists predicting that unemployment and the wage gap will continue to grow for the next 10 years, tensions could increase. Few see the government lifting wages. The Communist Party is now the development party. Their whole legitimacy is built on economic development."

A Source of Unrest at Home and Abroad?

That guarantees continued political, social and political unrest with the destruction of subsistence agriculture and protected local industries that previously provided some elementary defences. These have been ripped to tatters by Globalization and Development. Washington's most visible preparations for the emergencies that are bound to result is building up its high-tech – land-borne military gear to quell local unrest throughout more and more of the world, and planning high-tech stuff in the skies to confront a major challenge that may emerge from China's mighty industrialization on the cheap.

The entire Third World program of the Western powers from the IMF to Globalization and Deregulation was oriented towards preventing the Third World from accumulating the capital to industrialize. China seems to have devised a means of overcoming these barriers. Whether it will succeed in achieving a First World status before its internal problems close in on it, remains to be seen. But it appears to be winning the current round against Washington's strategists.

W.K.

Global Crossing — A Canadian Bank's Adventures in Wonderland

THE SUCCESSES as well as the failures of our banks are leaving some bank executives wondering what banking is about.

The Globe and Mail (8/03, "CIBC's billion dollar stock bonanza" by Jacquie McNish) tells an incredible tale: "In February, 2000, the Canadian Imperial Bank of Commerce blessed a select team of New York bank executives with a billion-dollar fortune in Global Crossing shares. In addition to the NY team's mother lode, CIBC expects to earn more than C$2.6 billion in pretax profits through direct or pre-hedged sales of Global Crossing shares.

"To some the CIBC's lottery-sized win on GC is one of the starkest illustrations of the dysfunctional economics of the technology sector's boom and bust. Intermediaries such as CIBC reaped the lion's share of the rewards from risky ventures, while most investors were wiped out."

But what has been so good for the bank's bottom line is becoming a nightmare for its public relations. There was a day when banks, secure in their fake Greek temples, were the very soul of conservatism. Now they have sold off their Greek temples, but still use what is left of that austere image to lure investors into the riskiest promotions. Little more than a decade ago Canadian banks were bailed out of previous speculations at enormous cost to the nation. The cost – $5 to $7 billion a year, or the equivalent of a $100 billion permanent bond was about 30% of the federal debt at the time. It was also of a magnitude suggestively similar to that of the reduction of Ottawa's grants to the provincial governments which occurred shortly afterwards. The banks appeared to have nudged out the needy in the welfare lines. Still more amazing, the banks were additionally rewarded by being deregulated,

Off to Vegas with the Bailout Money

They were allowed to enter just about every type of activity connected with the stock market, as principals or intermediaries. This set the scene for the high adventures of the CBIC in Global Crossing stock.

"How did Canada's second-largest bank become entangled in one of the messiest corporate breakdowns in US history?"

You get a good whiff of the answer by noting the new associates it at once sought out in its new career after its latest bailout. It was like the village parson, after a drunken binge, joining the big town's motorcycle gang.

Gary Winnick had been a convertible bond salesman at Drexel Burnham Lambert Inc., sitting at a desk only a few feet away from the junk bond genius Michael Milken who left his mark on an epoch of US financial history before ending up in jail. "Winnick invested $15 million US in Pacific Island Capital Group, a Cayman Island company, but he needed hundreds of millions of dollars to build the undersea fiber optic network un-

der the Atlantic. One of the first people he called was a former Drexel colleague Bruce Raben who joined CIBC when the bank acquired Argosy Partners LP. Raben alerted CIBC about Winnick's global network strategy, because the junk bond expertise it had acquired would allow the bank to break into the top tier of the junk bond market."

CIBC and the banking system as a whole were taking a giant step into Michael Milken's huge shoes left so sadly empty.

"Knowing how much CIBC needed the junk bond firm and its connections, Argosy's partners asked for the moon. The bank paid very little up front for the firm and agreed instead to a so-called 'earn-out' agreement. This allowed the partners during their first few years at the bank, to keep more than 50% of the profit generated on the junk bond deals." The bank was to learn that there were still other ways of money creation than government bailouts.

"As part of the agreement, the Argosy partners were also entitled to a share of the equity in ventures financed by the junk bond unit – at the same initial cost paid by the bank. A number of CIBC's old guard bankers, including then chairman Al Flood, had reservations about the generous compensation plan. Mr. Flood could not be reached for comment.

"Argosy's partners would bag huge profits if their deals were successful, senior bankers warned, while CIBC risked its capital by underwriting, investing in junk bonds and lending money to support the group's transactions."

The lordly banks, turned gamblers, were embarking on a new chapter of their partnership with the government – the government would share the losses in the form of future bailouts, and the banks would pass on half the winnings to the hardened speculators who had become their mentors. This is what the boasted "intermediation" of the banks had become.

"CIBC's Mr. Capatides said the Argosy group's compensation was key to 'retaining the type of employees capable of identifying opportunities such as Global Crossing.'

"If Argosy partners struck it rich, supporters of the deal such as Mr. John Hunkin, currently chairman of the CIBC, argued, the bank would earn a share of the profits. And a bigger presence in the US merchant banking field.

"The bank had been pitching itself in the US, as a 'complete solution' for all corporative needs, and GC was one of its earliest successes at providing multiple services to a corporation." This was at the very time that retail customers were being pushed outside the bank to stand in line before ATMs, or by the half hour to get at the few remaining live tellers.

"As part of the package of financial support, CIBC invested hundreds of million dollars to help launch GC's predecessor company in the Cayman Islands. It paid $41.2 million for a 45% equity interest in GC (Cayman)." That amounted to about 30 cents a share. Within weeks of acquiring the GC stock, CIBC sold some of its stake to other investors reducing its stake to 34%.

"CIBC's financial package to GC's predecessor in March, 1997 included a $482 million loan and the purchase of $250 million in senior notes and preferred shares. Portions of the loans and securities were later syndicated or sold to other financial institutions or investors.

"Like most merchant bankers CIBC hoped to score on its GC investments through what industry players call a 'liquidity event' – the moment when a startup has enough revenue and prospects to attract investors prepared to pay 'big bucks' for securities that it has bought for pennies.

"GC's 'liquidity event' came to pass on August 13, 1998. By then the Cayman Islands holding company had become transformed into a Bermuda operating company that began building the underwater networks. At the end of the first day the GC shares had jumped by 34%. By May, 1999, the CBIC stake was worth $4.5 billion.

"The CIBC's New York operators thought this was just the start of bliss, but in Toronto the bank chairman at the time, Mr. Flood, viewed the miracle with a jaundiced credit manager's eye: 'We've made enough money.'

"In hindsight, Mr. Flood's decision easily ranks as one of the best banking calls of all times." CIBC was left with billions in profit, but with a moral dilemma that bankers had rarely if ever faced. The CBIC – like other banks – rose to the occasion.

A Morality Implant

Bankers in Canada, were mutating into a new breed. And this was at the very time when the Government was responding to COMER's disclosures about the phasing out of reserves by arguing in unison with the banks: "Rightly so, the statutory reserves were an unjust tax on the banks." In fact it was a morality implant – the new bank morality was that of Mike Milken who was doing time as guest of his government.

"Several months earlier, CIBC had served as co-lead underwriter of Global Crossing's Initial Public Offering (IPO) and had been allotted 1.3 million shares to sell to its clients. If word got out that the bank was selling or planning to sell its 25% stake in the company, the price would have plunged, damaging the holdings of it its clients and thousands of investors." So after wrestling with its corporate conscience, it had its executives one by one resign from the GC board to clear the way for the sale of its shares.

"But the most controversial move was yet to come. In one of the largest equity hedges ever negotiated in Canada, it locked in its profit on 47 million GC shares at future dates ending in 2003 at fixed prices between $20 and $64 (US) a share."

Such is the miracle of derivatives! You can sell your interest unknown to the world. With banks sitting on a variety of moral chairs at the same time, this is one reason why they love their derivatives so dearly. Despite the complications posed by its many roles at GC, CIBC's Mr. Hunkin said after the annual meeting last week: "I think it's a great strategy and one that we will continue to employ."

Canadians should remember that statement the next time CBIC comes to the government for a bailout.

Our banks should be given the choice of continuing as commercial banks or becoming stock market operators. But they ought not to be allowed to combine the two conflicting functions. For the same reason that doctors on the make are not allowed to acquire undertaking establishments.

William Krehm

The Enron After-shock

IN A FRONT-PAGE ARTICLE with no less than four by-lines (7/03, "Enron Triggers a Slew of Proposed Fixes But What Will Stick?" by Steve Liesman et al.), *The Wall Street Journal* reports, "As more than 10 congressional committees pursue inquiries, 32 Enron-related bills have been introduced to address ills ranging from auditor conflicts of interest to the scams of an unregulated derivatives market. The Securities and Exchange Commission pledges to reform accounting rules, get tough on fraud and overhaul auditor oversight. General Electric Co. says it will issue a disclosure statement the size of a phone book, if that's what investors want." The trouble is that such a phone book, if it reflected the state of economic science in its present gelded form, would omit the phone numbers of all emergency departments, the building inspectors, and notably the university faculties dealing with scientific method.

An exaggeration? By no means. The supposed mathematical foundations of the official model assumes that all actors in the economy are of such tiny size that nothing they do or don't do individually can have the slightest effect on prices, supply, and demand. That assumption turns up in the derivatives that were at the bottom of the supposed "risk management" of big hedging disasters like Enron, Global Crossing, and the celebrated Long Term Capital Fund that almost brought down the international financial system in 1998. That assumption was brought in to set up the fiction of "the level playing field" certainly the most overworked catchword among policy-makers in recent decades. It is supposed to cover the relationship between transnationals and the employees of their subcontractors in Latin America and Asia, of Wall St. and the defenceless temporary workers and the unemployed. It sums up the bottomless gap that has opened up between high finance and the productive economy, between the real state of public corporations and their audited reports issued for public consumption when massive debt has been shifted off the company's balance sheet.

The "level playing field" catch-word distracts attention from the monstrous discrepancy between the accountancy practised by the government in its own books and what the large corporations get away with. The corporations hide their *debts* by keeping them "off-balance-sheet." The government buries its *investments*. The level playing field is the Mother Lie that has birthed the swarm of distortions and untruths that are now crawling out from under every table and from every crack in the walls.

It is gratifying that the media and some of our politicians are starting to recognize some of what *ER* had warned about for many years. But the most basic lie is still protected by the greatest of taboos. It goes on being drummed into freshmen's heads in every country of the world. No Finance Minister can open his mouth without it jumping out at you. The mirage of a self-balancing economy made up of tiny actors that are all powerless individually to affect prices is the "scientific" version of the "level playing field."

That could hardly cover an economy dominated by the Microsofts, General Electric, and the Enrons. Surely you have to deal with that obvious clash between the fine theory and the reality to which it is being applied. You might as well send astronauts to Mars, with instructions based on the assumption that the planet is made of cheese cake.

That the level playing field nonsense goes on being seriously, and is used to justify countries surrendering their sovereignty merely on the basis of this rhetoric, indicates the mighty power structures that run the world. That is why Sylvia Ostry, one of Canada's leading negotiators in the Uruguay Round of negotiations that led to the WTO, has said: "We had no idea at the outset how much sovereignty would be given up." The reason is that this prominent academic had a head full of "the level playing field" mantra. For decades she had been infecting her students with it.

The *WSJ* article refers to this master power mechanism whereby fiction replaces fact: "Now the big question is: How many of these changes will melt away like forgotten New Year's Resolutions and how many will endure? New accounting rules will likely make it harder for companies to conceal some transactions off the books, but they're unlikely to outlaw all the different tricks of the trade. Accountants are likely to lose the ability to reap huge consulting fees from some companies whose books they audit, but the industry is fighting a more sweeping ban.

"Politicians have made more noise than reform in recent business breakdowns. Not much changed in the banking world after the savings-and-loan crisis of the 1980s. The largely unregulated derivatives market has ballooned since the near collapse of the once-huge hedge fund and derivatives player Long-Term Capital Management."

Worse than that, particularly in Canada, the bailout of our chartered banks from their huge speculative losses in oil and real estates ventures, took the form of ending the cash reserves they had to put up as a token backing for the deposits they received from the public. Incongruously, at the very time they were being bailed out once more, there was further sweeping deregulation of activities that they were allowed to engage in. In *Insight* (Feb. 22/02), the publication of Sprott Securities Inc., we read a confirmation of what *ER* has been saying for years: "The accounting practices of Canadian banks are being examined by the OSC, particularly, their disclosures (or lack thereof) of off-balance-sheet derivative transactions. We have always found it appalling how derivative transactions in the trillions of dollars receive such little attention in the financial statements of banks. Those who believe these derivatives are 'perfect hedges' and, therefore, risk-free are living in a dream-world, especially in this post-mania environment where all it takes is for a handful of contracts to go awry and it's all over."

W.K.

REVIEW OF A BOOK BY PAUL T. HELLYER, CHIMO MEDIA INC.

Goodbye Canada

IN DISCUSSING his political prospects Paul Hellyer has been known to describe himself as a "man with baggage." The reference was, of course, this one-time senior Liberal cabinet member leaving the Liberals and seeking the leadership in turn of other parties. But in our topsy-turvy political world, that was a sign not of opportunism but of his constancy to principles. Having come up against the deep rot in our system, he ended up like Diogenes inhabiting a modest political barrel, but ever in search of light and forthrightness.

For historians of Canadian political process this little book is likely to be recognized as mother lode.

Hellyer talks of two levels of government in Canada as elsewhere – "the permanent government – the executives of one hundred of our largest corporations, the big legal firms that do their work, the important public relations and lobbying firms that work on both public and government opinion, and the top mandarins both civil and military." The temporary government is the elected one. Essentially it takes its orders from the permanent one.

He has tales to support this view that should make Canadians hang their heads in shame.

"In the fall of 1968, a time when Central Mortgage and Housing was part of my responsibility, there was a shortage of mortgages to finish out the season. I asked the cabinet for money, knowing pretty well what the response would be. There was no money available. Still, the need was urgent, and I put forward a compromise proposal. I asked for permission to sell $68 million of mortgages from the Corporation's portfolio and invest the money in new housing. [The sale of the mortgages would also tend to bring down interest rates and revive the economy.]

"The Minister of Finance, Ben Benson, agreed, and cabinet approved. Early the following morning I got a call from Bob Bryce, the Deputy Minister of Finance. 'Paul,' he said, 'no deal.' 'But cabinet approved,' I replied. 'No deal,' he responded. 'Your minister was there and he agreed,' I continued. 'Dammit,' Bob exclaimed. 'I don't care what the minister said, there is no deal.' That was the end of it.

"Thirty years later, when I read cabinet minutes in the course of writing my memoirs, I found all reference to the decision had been expunged. The old boys net was so powerful that even cabinet minutes could be doctored to suit the occasion." Such incidents led to Hellyer resigning from the government.

This dual government – the permanent and the temporary one – produced some startling fault lines in Canadian politics. "Mike Wilson as Tory finance critic described the high interest rate policy initiated by Paul Volcker's atomic attack on everything that moved and breathed as 'insane.' Ten years later, as minister of finance, the same Mike Wilson was out on the hustings defending BoC Governor John Crow for invoking a repeat performance of Volcker.

"Brian Mulroney, at the time of the 1983 Conservative leadership campaign said, 'Don't talk to me of free trade. That issue was decided in 1911. Free trade is a danger to Canadian sovereignty.' Signing the FTA was a complete 'volte-face.' There is no doubt that the idea originated south of the border. The American Ambassador at the time has since taken credit. He lobbied members of Canada's permanent government who then began to lobby the 'provisional' one we had elected." Such memories bring Hellyer to his conclusion:

"In my opinion, about twenty-five or thirty men and women have wrecked Canada in the last two decades by giving the governments of the day bad advice. The three epicentres of disaster have been the Bank of Canada, the Department of Finance, and the Department of Trade. Each successive 'loaded' report, be it telecommunications or transportation, provides a fresh invitation to tear down the border. So any new part, if it wants to implement any new controversial policies, will have to screen and fire some of the more obtuse senior officials in Ottawa."

The analysis of our vanishing sovereignty leads to a shrewd political assessment of our moldering political structures which could be preparing the ground for a new party. "It would be internationally oriented rather than protectionist, but it would pursue agreements based on fair rather than free trade – to preserve some capacity to paddle our own canoe.

"It would not be necessary for everyone supporting such a party to agree on every detailed policy. Everyone has his or her own priorities, and each will be required to make compromises. The first and foremost and the only one that is non-negotiable for me, is the abrogation of NAFTA, and refusal to negotiate or sign the FTAA, to get rid of the infamous 'national treatment' provision. Other provisions: Full employment, defined as about 4% unemployed. Protection of the environment to rank equally with job creation. Universal access to first-class health-care and to public education. Maintenance of public ownership and operation of essential services, including sewers, water and roads. Provision of tens of thousands of new units of quality non-profit housing. The use of the Bank of Canada to help finance essential services. Strong support for the arts and the CBC. Working with First Nations and aboriginal people to determine what they want rather than continue the top down approach. Parliamentary and electoral reform including proportional representation, limitations on financial contributions, curbs on the prime minister's near dictatorial power, and an elected Senate. An independent foreign policy appropriate to Canadian ideals.

"Just think what would be possible on the world scene if a future Canadian government went to a meeting of the G8 and actually proposed that the IMF be wound up, the World Bank be converted to an aid agency, the WTO disbanded while new and fairer trading arrangements were devised, and that that Third World debt be paid off by increasing cash reserve requirements for the banks."

The rationale for that is clearly expressed: "In respect to the major global industries, in your country [under the present IMF–World Bank regime] the cost of getting established will be too great to start. The existing transnational companies will squeeze you out of business and your government will not be able to assist you in the early days because that would be considered a subsidy, and subsidies are not allowed. If you break this rule, the WTO will allow foreign countries to punish you by imposing tariffs on your other exports.

"That is what the GATS is about. It is basically designed to prevent effective competition with the world leaders in each area of endeavour. It is probably the most effective form of protectionism, which is the word now used in the pejorative against any small country attempting to give its fledgling and underdog industries a break."

Then Hellyer gives us his views on inflation (p. 107): "For more than a quarter of a century I have argued that the principal cause of the inflation which began to be a problem in Western industrialized economies in the mid-1960s. could be explained by wage increases being out-of-joint with productivity…. The inflation trend line has been determined by the gap between nominal wages and real output."

Semantic Fly Traps

But what is "productivity" when official statistics and economic theory disregard damage to the environment as an "externality," and the deterioration of many other non-market areas essential to the well-being of our society? Even though econometricians construct a ratio of real output to labour costs and call it "labor productivity" that ratio may depend as much on other ignored factors as on labour and its rewards. For example, the finance costs, the technology, the proportion of capacity that the economy is working at, and whether government accountancy recognizes public investment or not. If for example it goes on writing off capital investments, human and physical, entirely in the year in which the government makes them, it will show either higher taxes or a higher deficit than is really warranted. Either of these will under the present economic regulations lead to higher interest rates which will increase the denominator and decrease the ratio still further. But it will not necessarily point to a more monopolist position of labour. It is in fact the type of semantic flytrap that has been set up all over the lot, and against which Hellyer has warned in other connections.

The movement for economic and political renewal to which Hellyer has made so unique a contribution, cannot afford the luxury of orthodoxy. The theory to which Hellyer refers goes back to the writings of Sidney Weintraub a quarter of a century ago. The late John Hotson, the first managing director of COMER, had been a student of his, and John and I used to discuss the implication of Weintraub's income policies based on his price analysis. If my memory serves me, Weintraub went on to suggest that where oligopolic powers of labour contribute to inflation employers who surrendered to the demands of their too powerful trade unions should be penalized with special taxes. In retrospect the effect – certainly not Weintraub's intention – would be to put the unpleasant task of battling out the issue with the unions on the employers' doorstep. The tax penalty would have imparted a sharper edge to the class struggle. It would have enlisted the state to undermine the powers of industrialists to resist the plans of speculators to take them over.

And to complete the picture, none of the tools for identifying the real causes of rising prices had been provided by official economic theory.

To even express an informed opinion on the role of the excessive powers of key trade unions, you would have to understand the growing depth of the layer of taxation in price. This reflects the increase in the public sector (all government levels) in Canada from an estimated 8% before WWII to somewhere in the 40% region today. To imagine that this could be handled with a flat price level is not realistic. In my new book, I establish this by two successive applications of the *reductio ad absurdum* test.[1] But for our present purpose I will mention a detail that should simplify the proof still further. Nobody moving from a town of 5,000 to a metropolis of several million expects his living costs to remain constant. But only economists would try enforcing a flat price level when the world's population makes just such a move. Moreover, to discuss such matters meaningfully, you would have to introduce a system of public accounts that would notch up an environmental debt if the environment were allowed to deteriorate. That would alert us that a balanced budget or a flat price level under such circumstances would mask effective deflation. The same goes for the deterioration of public health, education, the crime situation, etc.

Paul Hellyer has been a valued member of COMER for many years. His contribution in preparing a new economy and a new political system in this country has been immense, and by its very nature, unique. But debate is a necessary feature of such organizations. Public dialogue among the dedicated is a vital element in the renewal of our society. There cannot be too much of it. I am sure that Paul would agree with me on that.

William Krehm

1. *Towards a Non-Autistic Economy – A Place at the Table for Society*, p. 17.

REVIEW OF A BOOK BY WILLIAM KREHM, COMER PUBLICATIONS, 2002

Towards a Non-Autistic Economy — A Place at the Table for Society

POLICY MAKING in relation to economic affairs has become so specialized and remote from common human experience, its consequences so unpredictable yet fateful, its methods so questionable, that democracy itself seems to be in jeopardy. From a common sense perspective it has also become ever more apparent that economics is not a science, but, in the words of Henderson, is "politics in disguise."[1] In this vigorous, wise and graceful work William Krehm contributes for purposes of public debate some of the economic insights needed by an alert citizenry entering the new century.

Among his summary thoughts: "[To] address the heart of our problems we have need of a serious economic theory. What passes for one today is little more than a decoy" (p. 176). While

some books are to be tasted, some chewed and some digested, this is a book to be mined for its nuggets and insights. Krehm offers us the considerable benefits of his experience towards what can only be a communal enterprise. The book should take a worthy place beside works of Hazel Henderson, John McMurtry, David Korten, Marjorie Kelly and selected others.

There can scarcely be a more important subject for the future of society and mankind on earth than the ways in which speculative capital has taken on a self-justifying life of its own – the autism of which Krehm speaks – to exploit peoples, societies and environments. The author addresses his complex subject forthrightly, and necessarily makes demands on the reader for thoughtful attention. In coming to grips with the realities, Krehm recognizes the complexities; he points to the kinds of methods (but requires no specialized knowledge of his readers) – informed by mathematics, systems concepts, economics, finance and political processes – as needed for adequate understanding and the development of realistic strategies.

His audience will include men and women of the civil commons who wish to be more fully aware of the issues now shaping our world, as well as students of politics and economics, those planning careers in leadership, and current teachers of economics and politics. The book should engage the attention of the growing numbers of "cultural creatives," citizens able to ask their intellectual and political leaders for informed commentary on the kinds of questions and suggestions posed by Krehm.

Leaders often deplore a lack of new ideas to stimulate innovative policies. Here are some additions to the arsenal of democratic debate. Krehm does not have all the answers, nor does he make any such claim. But he provides essential background and poses some of the decisive questions. The need is for such ideas to be taken up and advanced in a democratic search for adequate public policies. In the light of his discussions of price, interest, inflation and the public sector, among many other topics, citizens can be better positioned to hold leaders in business and politics accountable.

It is not possible in a short review to capture the content of this book in the kind of detail required to do it justice. It is a kind of research report, and addresses many aspects of economic theory and policy with candid observations – concerning money, capital, deregulation and globalization, unemployment and terrorism – grounded in practical considerations and the quest for understanding of essential relationships. The approach contrasts with current tendencies to fragmentation, which breed opportunism.

As Krehm points out, the gravity of our situation is related to the prevalence of self-serving logic at the very highest levels, illustrated by the debacle of the Long-Term Capital Management Fund (with its Nobel laureate advisors) and many other examples – including Enron. Stable economic plans and structures require foundations in logic and science rather than the sophistries of legal and sales talent in the services of great wealth.

When a writer taps into universal insights he may do so in terms which reveal the paths he has taken. I find Krehm's use of a few selected terms perhaps limiting in this sense, but none the less valid. He speak of "non-autistic" where the term "open" in a Popperian or systems sense might apply; and he makes reference to the Tinbergen counting rule were the cybernetic Principle of Requisite Variety may be an alternative formulation. But such commonalities of concepts simply reinforce the fundamentals which underlie the validity of his insights.

Krehm is a thinker passionately concerned with the practical and moral importance of the problems he addresses, with the intellectual integrity of his methods, and the real world specifics that make them urgent. It is easy for the reader, who is likely to have less mastery of the theory and practice, to be confused by abstractions or to be less certain in questions of detail. Certainly the subject matters are not easy. Yet Krehm is an excellent guide, and a master of vigorous and incisive prose. The challenge faced by the reader is no more than the complexities demand.

There are many gems of observation and suggestions in the book, and, as far as I can judge, few errors. He writes: "…800 French students of economics signed a petition in 2000 asking that instead of the 'autistic mathematical theory' taught them, the curriculum be revised to include something relevant to society and its problems. Distinguished academics supported their request…. The manifesto of the French students received widespread coverage in the French media, some attention in Britain, but did not rate a mention in the North American press…." (p. 16). Whether the general press covered it I do not know, but the French movement has now received public support from students and professors of economics from some 22 nations, and there are now Portuguese and Spanish Sections. The "Kansas City Proposal" (from the University of Missouri) addressed an International Open Letter (Sept. 2001) to all economics departments. which began: "Economics need fundamental reform – and now is the time for change."[2]

Of course there will never be a last word on these matters, and some of the directions in which Krehm points are now being explored, e.g., new theories of complex systems.[3] But Krehm's work merits a place on the bookshelf of anyone concerned for economics as a developing science and professional practice, which includes all economists, business and political leaders, and most especially economic reformers and activists.

Bruce Buchanan

1. Henderson, Hazel (1996). *Building a Win–Win World: Life Beyond Global Economic Warfare* (p. 7). Bettett-Koehler Publishers.
2. See www.paecon.net.
3. For example, see Arthur, W. Brian, Durlauf, Steven & Lane, David (1997). *The Economy as an Evolving Complex System II.* Sante Fe Institute.

Our Walk-in Submission to the Romanow Commission

AT THE END of World War II, Washington sent swarms of economists to Germany and Japan to estimate how long it would take them to rise again from the ashes of their defeat. Years later, one of these economists, Theodore Schultz, expressed amazement at how wide of the mark their forecasts had been.

And he mused on the reason. They had concentrated on the destruction of physical plant and overlooked the key importance of human capital – education, skills, and social structures, that had remained largely intact. Schultz concluded that these had to be society's most productive investment. But once you open your eyes to that, you must accord health equal importance. For it is the vessel in which this priceless human capital is held.[1]

Health care must not be considered as just a current expense, to be written off in the year when made. Its productive effects may go on for generations.

Selma J. Muskin[2] has written, "In a modern economy biological selection is no longer an acceptable method of investing in health, not only because our humanitarian instinct rebels against it, but because it costs too much. In our present economy, brain power and other capabilities and talents are far more important than physical stamina."

For his discovery Schultz was awarded the Nobel Prize in Economics. And yet this lesson of the Second World War has been put out of mind by our policy-makers.

If you regard health care as a current expense, you ignore its capital value in increasing the tax-base of all government levels. Indeed, in Canada – as in Britain, the US and most other countries – even physical facilities like hospitals and equipment delivering health services are carried at a token dollar value on government books. The case of human capital which adds nothing tangible to the public domain that you can rap your knuckles on, is still more elusive. All government capital, unless it is in the form of foreign currency or securities is viewed as an "externality" known to exist, but for matters that count, is disregarded.

That has made possible setting up the government deficit and debt as scarecrows pushing up interest rates. This in turn multiplied the real deficit and the debt in the interest of speculative finance.

The disastrous effects of this have been unlimited. If a publicly owned hospital is written off in a single year and carried on the government books at one dollar, it can be sold for a tenth of its value to report a capital gain for the government of the entire price less that one dollar. Such privatizations made no mean contribution to the late stock market boom. The haste

of three of our provincial governments today to shove forward the privatization of health facilities even before the final report of the Romanow Commission appears next fall has alarming implications for public morality.

A Faustian Deal?

That is particularly so since in mid-2000 the then Auditor General withheld unconditional approval of the government's balance sheet unless it committed itself to bring in accrual accountancy ("capital budgeting") by the year 2002. This will depreciate physical capital over its useful life. Obviously to win his point after tough negotiations that extended over many months, the Auditor General ended up doing a Faustian deal with our Finance Minister. The evidence of this is plentiful. Only Conrad Black's *National Post*, desperate for readers, carried word of this reversal of government policy. Our media have reason to hang their heads in shame on that account. And in his report the AG argued that since the bookkeeping change had brought no new money into Ottawa's coffers, it warranted no increase in spending. However, the distortion of the government deficit and debt in the early nineties had been used to justify the wholesale hacking of grants to the provinces. There is then an obvious asymmetry in the logic that our Finance Minister imposed on the AG as the price of his agreement. It calls to mind Enron's way with their external auditors, Arthur Andersen.

Today the papers are full of shocking reports of how the auditors of Enron, Global Crossing, and many other large corporations in the US colluded with their clients to keep much of their debt off their balance sheets. In our governments' accountancy we have a not unparallel situation, with the shoe on the other foot. The government's auditors had cooperated to distort the significance of the capital assets that are finally to be recognized.

But where would the money come from to restore the cuts to our health and other social programs? That question must be answered with another question: where did the money go? As a native of Saskatchewan and former Premier of that province, Mr. Romanow is aware that when the Bank of Canada was founded in 1935 one of its main immediate purposes was to save Saskatchewan from bankruptcy after a half decade of depression and drought. The first governor of the BoC, Graham Towers, took personal charge of negotiating that rescue. Since there was no lack of idle labour and physical resources in Canada in 1935, it was strictly a matter of organizing the credit to put them to work. The key detail that made that possible, was that the bulk of the interest paid on the loans by the Bank of Canada reverted to the federal government in consequence of the traditional monopoly of the monarch in coining and recoining precious metals. In that way the cost to the federal government of aiding Saskatchewan was nominal. The country recovered far more than its cost through the expanded tax-base that resulted. Without the Bank of Canada's intervention to save Saskatchewan from bankruptcy, that province could never have pioneered public health care in Canada. In a sense our national health program was a by-product of the original purpose for which the Bank of Canada was founded. Why is it not even mentioned in the turbulent debate on the future of health care today? Why has the Bank of Canada not made a loan to the provinces for decades?

After the nationalization of the BoC by the Liberal Government in 1938, roughly the same proportion of the bank's profits were passed on to the Ottawa government as before, but more transparently as dividends.

But was this not "unsound" financing? To even express an opinion on the question you would have to set up a serious system of accountancy.

Up to now, when the government borrows to build some facility, the debt incurred is treated as a current expense and the asset is entered on its books at a token dollar. Noting the debt incurred but ignoring the asset financed distorts the significance of the reported public deficit and the public debt.

A substantial part of the debt of the federal and provincial governments has been due to this bad bookkeeping and the policy of high interest rates to "lick inflation." Carrying so much fictitious net debt on its books without noting the public investments has played havoc with the governments' credit ratings. And those distorted ratings increased further the tribute of interest that our government chose to pay our chartered banks rather than doing much of its financing with the Bank of Canada. In the mid 1970s, over 22% of the federal debt was held by the Bank of Canada. Today it is in the 5% region.

The slashing of the federal grants to the provinces in the early 1990s was the way in which our chartered banks were bailed out from their crushing losses in speculative ventures in real estate and gas and oil. This was achieved by phasing out the statutory reserves that the banks held with the Bank of Canada on an interest-free basis.[3] These reserves had given the central bank an alternative way to high interest rates for controlling the bank credit creation This and other measures made it possible for our banks take on another $60 billion dollars of federal debt, without putting up significant money of their own. Depending upon where interest rates were, this amounted to an annual entitlement of $5-$7 billion dollars. That was no one-shot act of charity, but an entitlement that recurs every year. Translated into a permanent bond its value was of the order of $100 billion – about 30% of the outstanding federal debt at the time and about three times the capital of the chartered banks. To make room for this arrangement, the Bank of Canada reduced its holdings of federal debt in both relative and absolute terms. The federal government undertook to pay interest on what it had received virtually interest-free from the Bank of Canada.[4]

To make matters still worse, the chartered banks were deregulated at the same time to participate in every sort of stock market gamble, brokerage houses, derivative boutiques, credit cards, security underwriting. In effect they were allowed to dictate many of the terms of their bailout. They were in fact launched on orbits that have led them into further trouble.

The provisions that made possible federal funding for substantial increased investment in health education, and other social services, remain intact in the *Bank of Canada Act*, section 18(c) and 18(j).

The Romanow Report would be woefully incomplete if it failed to refer to: (1) the importance of health and education as the most productive of all public investments; (2) the need to extend accrual accountancy to government bookkeeping to recognize human capital as well as physical investments; (3) to stress the importance of postponing further privatization of health care facilities until the bill adopted in 2000 has been fully implemented and the depreciated value of all such facilities appear in the government books;[5] (4) adequate reference to the role of the Bank of Canada in financing the Canadian health system in its early years.

A New Dimension for Negotiation and Compromise

There is a technical detail about central banking that is particularly important in federated countries like Canada. The BoC charter allows it to hold both funded and unfunded debt of the federal and provincial governments and of any entity if the loan is guaranteed by the federal or a provincial government. But over 95% of the interest paid on such loans finds its way as dividends *only to the federal government as the bank's sole shareholder*. This opens up a new dimension for negotiation and compromise between the federal and provincial levels of government.

Much of the current crisis in our public health institutions can in fact be traced to the bailing out of our chartered banks from the loss of much or more than their capital in their speculative venture during the eighties – good examples are Dome Petroleum. Olympia and York's skyscrapers across Canada, New York, London, Robert Campeau's hobby of collecting US department store chains. For the purpose a bill was slipped through parliament in mid-1991 that changed the nature of the county's economy. The statutory non-interest-bearing reserves that banks had to deposit with the BoC as a token backing for the deposits held from the public were phased out by mid-1993. This reserve had for many years before during and after the war been as high or higher than 10%. By 1991 it had already been brought down to 4%.

The annual tribute that resulted was of the same magnitude as the reduction of the federal grants to the provinces that took place during the subsequent years, There was an obvious connection between the two.

And to add to the mindless audacity of the coup, the banks were deregulated with respect to what they can do with the money they received as hidden taxpayers' subsidies. With it, today our banks are engaged in stock market activities that conflict with their banking function. Canadian banks have been prominent in financing off-balance partnerships of bankrupt New Economy corporations like Enron and Global Crossing. The CIBC has been named as one of the nine large banks in a class-action by the University of California for helping to set up the Enron scam. The Bank of Nova Scotia is the proud owner of one of the largest Argentine banks, purchased with the bailout money from our taxpayers and the higher fees and interest rates extorted from modest Canadian bank customers. The suit describes the dual role played by the CIBC and the other Enron bankers as underwriters of a "hall of mirrors inside a house of cards." CIBC has soiled not only its own name but the image of Canada.

We have then a constellation in the financial heavens that opens prospects of resolving the crisis that has overtaken our health system. For over a decade the questioning of the vast change in the structure and purpose of our banking has been suppressed. But now the financial sector has worked itself into such financial and moral opprobrium that their powers of censorship are fading.

This of course has an immense bearing on our health care situation. Privatization clearly can be a scam to revive a thoroughly discredited stock market rather than as a solution of our problems.

"When our deep plots do pall, there's a divinity that shapes our ends. rough-hew them how we will."

We must not fumble the occasion.

W. Krehm

1. "Investment in Human Capital" reproduced in Kiker, R.F. (1971). *Human Capital* (p. 14). Columbia: University of South Carolina Press.

2. Kiker, p. 389.

3. Krehm, William (1993). *A Power Unto Itself, The Bank of Canada* (p. 55). Toronto: Stoddard.

4. At the beginning of 1991 the total capital of our chartered banks amounted to $31,324 million. (*Bank of Canada Review*, March 1991) consisting of $12,966M, of common stock, $4,642 of preferred stock, $262 of contributed surplus and $14,020 retained earnings. By the time the statutory reserves were completely phased out in 1993, the chartered banks held some $80 billion of federal debt well over 250% of their total capital, much if not all of which had disappeared in the meltdown of the investments made by the banks in the 1980s. These figures indicate how desperate the banks were for the government bailout. It also underlines the scandal of the federal government further deregulating the banks so that they might pursue their disastrous gambles of the 1980s in a broader arena. The extent of their losses – financial and moral – have only begun coming in.

5. A similar move had been made in the US at the beginning of 1996 when the Bureau of Economic Analysis under the Secretary of Commerce began depreciating the physical capital assets of the government as investments over their useful life. However, instead of calling them "investments," it has listed them as "savings." This is hardly appropriate because they are not held as cash but as capital assets. However, given the crucial role that "investments" rather than "savings" play in the Keynesian revolution, the designation is tantamount to keeping from the public what was involved. The important thing for President Clinton was to produce a statistic that would help bring down interest rates, without abandoning his hold on the "political center." That stroke of cunning not only contributed to bring about the economic recovery but the unprecedented stock market boom and bust. (Krehm, William (Ed.). (1999). *Meltdown: Money, Debt and the Wealth of Nations* (p. 225). COMER Publications.)

The Collapse of a Great Faith

FOR MILLENNIA Christianity and the other great faiths preached the evangel of salvation by curbing humanity's baser appetites…. The New Economy improved on that. In its view God so loved the world that He spared its inhabitants the inconveniences of having to curb their greed. They would be so reduced in notional power as to regain the innocence of children; and freed from having to rein in their voracity. That was in fact transmuted into a virtue.

The new morality made virtue a matter of scale. And that miracle, believed because of its very absurdity, persisted even when by that very doctrine they grew into transnational corporations that rewarded their chieftains in nine and ten digits.

All this was planned to make it possible to bring in infinitesimal calculus. About mathematics the missionaries of the new dispensation had limited knowledge, believing that instead of just revealing the implications of the assumptions fed into a model, their use was in itself a guarantee of high science. By multiplying the integration signs on a page you could intimidate the doubters.

But what really kept the system going was that it seemed to be working. That, however, is no longer the case.

The Wall Street Journal (28/03, "A Dwindling Supply of Credit Plagues Corporations" by Gregory Zuckerman) gives us the score: "For years, the commercial-paper market has served as the corporate world's automated teller machine, spitting out a seemingly endless supply for businesses at super-low interest rates.

"But now, amid financial jitters caused by Enron Corp.'s collapse, the machine is sputtering, sending a surprising number of companies of all sizes scrambling to find money for their basic needs, from paying salaries to buying office supplies. Some are paying higher interest rates so that they can continue selling paper. But others have turned to raising debt by other, costlier means. These companies include Qwest Communications International Inc., Sprint Corp., Gap Inc., and Computer Associates International Inc.

"Last month, amid investor concerns about accounting at Tyco International Ltd., the conglomerate had to draw on a backup line of credit from its banks to come up with cash it needed. to replace cheap commercial paper with the more expensive bank line. The move will cost Tyco about $400 million in additional after-tax, annual borrowing expenses.

"For an economy still in the tentative stages of a turnaround, the problems in the commercial-paper market underscore the profound effect Enron's collapse on the basic workings of American finance. Increasingly skittish about corporate-accounting practices, the ultra-conservative investors who control the commercial-paper market have cut back on a key source of liquidity. Economists worry that the troubles could put a lid on capital spending, as companies scramble to save cash – a move that could delay or even reverse the recovery.

"For the past 40 years the massive commercial-paper market has been a critical – almost invisible – lubricant for the economy. Through the commercial-paper market, companies issue IOUs for critical short-term financing, lasting for as long as 270 days or as short as one day. The money is used to pay for their most basic, immediate needs, though in recent years it has also covered billion-dollar acquisitions. Commercial paper generally requires no collateral. It is the cheapest source of debt financing, with rates that typically are several percentage points below those of longer-term bonds and loans from banks. That's because it's less risky to lend money for a short period – the chance for an unforeseen downturn is less.

"Like running water, it's only missed when it stops flowing. The market began experiencing difficulties about a year ago, as the economy slowed. Enron's collapse fuelled more worry – it caused credit-rating agencies to become more hawkish. Stung by criticism that both Moody's and Standard & Poor's kept Enron at investment grade until just five days before it filed for bankruptcy, the rating agencies started poring over balance sheets, looking for companies that seemed over-dependent on commercial-paper.

"Sprint, the long-distance and cellular provider, felt the squeeze last month. The company, which had been relying on commercial-paper for $3 billion of its day-to-day expenses, suddenly couldn't convince gun-shy commercial-paper investors to buy its debt. The cash crunch set Sprint shares tumbling, and had credit agencies sending warnings.

"The result: Sprint was forced to take on more expensive debt including a $1 billion new loan and $5 billion in long-term bonds, costing the company almost $200 million in additional borrowing costs each year, according to analysts. Like a home-owner cutting back on spending when his variable-rate mortgage shoots up. Sprint is now slashing its capital spending by $400 million."

"The fears have gotten so bad that Pacific Investment Management Co. (PIMCO), the $250 billion fund company known in the bond market for its aggressive bets, has slashed its holdings of lower-tier commercial-paper to just 4% of its portfolio, down from 25% at the end of 1999.

"Last week Bill Gross, PIMCO's CEO, declared his firm wouldn't even buy commercial-paper from General Electric Co., which had been relying on this market for about half its financing needs."

Credit is an Act of Faith

But more is involved than the nuts and bolts of the credit market. Big or small, commercial credit is an act of faith. Its bottom line is that somebody has to believe in the trustworthiness of his fellow-man. But the creed that vice-writ-big-becomes-virtue has come upon evil times. Even the auditing profession has become the butt of ribald jokes and criminal investigation.

Remember the slick explanation of how the new system worked? CEOs got all those options and fat salaries that translated into massive annual rewards? That was declared necessary to attract and retain these rare talents who alone could "enhance shareholder values." Nobody else knew the secret of that magic.

The New York Times (7/04, "Did Pay Incentives Cut Both Ways?" by David Leonhardt) devotes the greater part of its business section to appraising the relationship between CEO rewards and performance.

"For corporate directors and chief executives, 2001 presented a test: were they really willing, in a down year, to link executive pay to performance?

"Just as the nation's top executives received fat raises during the 1990s boom, those who had tied pay to their companies' results were almost certainly going to receive leaner pay-checks last year, when profits suffered their worst annual decline in decades. But in the clubby culture of the boardroom, many executives knew they could convince their directors to overlook the bottom line and keep the raises coming – if the directors had not taken it upon themselves to look the other way.

"The results were a split decision: companies divided into roughly two equal-sized groups. The first cut the pay of the top executive for the first time in years. The other half, which seems to believe simply in paying a lot, reacted to a year of recession and war by creating the impression they had reduced pay without actually doing so." In short a further round of deception.

"Cisco Systems lost $1 billion, but its CEO, John T. Chambers made $154 million and finished at the top of a pay survey of 200 large companies conducted for Money & Business by Pearl Myer & Partners, a consulting firm in New York.

"Over all, the average compensation for chief executives declined 8% to $15.5 million, as the tough economic conditions wiped out many of the truly enormous paychecks, the survey showed. It was the first decline in nine years.

"But as the largest rewards became smaller, pay for the typical CEO continued to climb. The median compensation rose 7%. Many boards also made up for declining bonuses, which are often linked to results, by awarding more valuable packages of stock options and more shares of stock.

"As a recession weakened the American economy, CEOs oversaw the elimination of many of the one million jobs lost last year. In the weeks after the Sept. 11 attacks, the recession worsened and executives joined policy makers in saying Americans would have to make sacrifices during tough times.

"Over the past few years, executives at some companies released inaccurate earning statements and, before correcting them, sold large amounts of stock at inflated prices. It happened at major technology companies like Oracle and Sun Microsystems. It happened at Guess and Xerox, at Dollar General, a discount retailer, and at Providian Financial, a credit card company"

Sweet Trips to the Merger Mall

Andrew Ross Sorkin ("Those Sweet Trips to the Merger Mall") reviews the case of executive rewards for mergers, not a few of which end up disasters for shareholders.

"William B. Harrison was beaming. Chairman of the Chase Manhattan Corporation, he has designed a deal to buy J.P. Morgan & Company for $30.9 billion and was spinning the deal to shareholders….

"Most important, when we look at the overall transaction two years from now, it should be accretive to the shareholders. Rather than being 'accretive' – i.e., increasing earnings per share – the stock has lost more than one-third of its value in 18 months."

We love the term "accretive." Obviously "maximizing" as in "maximizing shareholders' equity," was recognized as a flat tire that needed changing.

"Mr. Harrison, like many top executives these days, was about to be paid a lot for going shopping. For overseeing the acquisition of J.P. Morgan, which he nonchalantly said took only three weeks, he received a special bonus of $20 million. And that bonus came on top of his $1 million salary and $5 million regular bonuses last year and whatever he receives for this year.

"All told, Chase directors paid the bank's executives more than $50 million for their outing at the bank mall. (They had done a little window-shopping, chatting up Goldman Sachs and Deutsche Bank, before settling on J.P. Morgan.) Mr. Harrison's huge payday is hardly an anomaly in the world of executive compensations. Mergers and acquisitions can be get-rich-quick paths for top corporate managers to get the deal done, no matter what happens to shareholders.

"So-called 'retention bonuses' used to be reserved for executives of companies being acquired, as an incentive to stick around while operations were combined and the buyers generally took control.

"Now, pay experts say executives of the acquiring companies are increasingly asking boards to compensate them simply for overseeing the businesses they buy – in part because they are not getting the same payout as their peers at the acquired companies.

"The trend has outraged some shareholders and academics who say executives are being overpaid for simply doing their jobs.

"A well-known merger lawyer put it this way: 'Publicly, we have to call these things retention bonuses. Privately, sometimes it is the only way we would have got the deal done. It's a kickback. And sometimes it is my job to negotiate the kickback. Unless you want to put me into early retirement, please don't use my name."

We hear – for good enough reason – a lot about the corruption of the business world in places like Indonesia, Africa, and Russia. But here we have on a far greater scale the same corruption.

The time has come to clean out these smelly stables so that we can address society's problems.

William Krehm

A Systems View: Out of Control

MUCH CONCERN is currently being expressed over the ways in which events in the Middle East are spiraling out of control amidst the flames of war. Such metaphors point to events caught up in the destabilizing effects of positive feedback. The issues at stake are vital, and the kinds of metaphors and models we use in framing the problems and deciding upon policy and action are just as crucial. If we want to slow or stop the disorders it is important to understand not only the triggering events but also the complexities of continuance and propagation, some of which are far from obvious.

It is said by many commentators that the sticking point in the impasse between Israel and Palestine is the unwillingness of the latter to admit Israel's right to exist as a Jewish state. If Arafat could agree to this, it is said, the way might be clear for other agreements. Yet the significance of this point is a reflection of the larger context.

In the face of complexity we ordinarily try to keep things simple. But an orientation which is adequate to the difficulties may be essential, and a variety of considerations must be borne in mind.

Such considerations include the following: (1) There is never any single absolute or "correct" version of events which can be known to human beings. (2) Observers who insist that their own version is the only correct one are playing a game in which they are trying to dictate to others what is to be seen as reality. (3) Once disturbances (confusions, recriminations, tit-for-tat responses, etc.) reach a critical degree of momentum and complexity, they become self-propagating. The original events are no longer important except as interpreted in the present e.g., as history and myth. (4) Some individuals may be so altered by the intensity of traumatic experiences as to be both physically and mentally damaged. For such persons, associations with the trauma become "hot button" issues – those which Pavlov identified with "pathological points," i.e., dysfunctional cells in the cerebral cortex – which interfere with normally adaptive thought. (5) A capacity for sustained abstract thought is required to support reason and discussion. Without the intellectual ability and freedom of all participants to consider hypothetical possibilities, negotiations may be subverted for use as strategies for concrete actions, e.g., of delay and deception. (6) In the extreme case, where the unalterable goal for any combatant is the uncompromising destruction of others, there is no recourse for control other than physical force; it is illusory to believe otherwise.

While none of these principles are perhaps surprising, their articulation may help to clarify factors which are ordinarily seen as political and economic realities but which are, relatively speaking, surface phenomena.

Moreover, living systems require capacities for the detection and correction of errors to enable them to make progress towards their goals, and also to reassess goals. Mechanical systems, in contrast, are governed by laws of motion such that an object or force will continue in the same direction unless and until it is acted upon by some other force. A military approach, of course, treats of people as objects to be manipulated. As we know, such methods are alone inadequate and require a larger framework of democratic intent if outcomes are to be desirable. Results achieved will be determined by the means used. Whenever vital factors and needs are ignored these simply gather force and lead potentially to breakdown.

In the natural world, growth and evolution almost never proceed in one line or direction for long. Some kind of natural limit is always reached such that further developments require a change of approach. Opportunities may arise, but only for those who are prepared. Even the most deliberate and carefully planned changes in human affairs are subject to reversals. During the French revolution the ideas of brotherhood gave way to methods of terror, followed by Napoleon and the return of monarchy. The Russian revolution foundered in disaster when the struggles for freedom were exploited in the interests of arbitrary power by unprincipled leaders (Lenin and Stalin).

It is often said that politics is "the art of the possible," a phrase open to various interpretations. What politicians see as possible is often simply limited to what they believe is acceptable to the voters, a view which often limits progress. Of course, in framing political alternatives it is always important to recognize both the role of perception as well as objective conditions. Yet in no case can the objectives of policy be conformance to impossible expectations, and the political leader who walks into such a trap will fail.

So the actual choices will be among real possibilities – those which are better and those which are worse. What is most desired may not be an available option for the near term, but should not be foreclosed for the sake of immediate expediency.

What is possible may be difficult and uncertain of achievement; it may require courage, inconvenience and patience, and may demand sacrifice, perhaps of previous hopes. It was the political genius of Gandhi, Martin Luther King and Nelson Mandela to discern the needed visions, create possibilities and provide leadership.

In grave circumstances, such as Israel's situation at present, when antagonists are locked in a struggle to the death and options are few, progress and even survival may depend upon some kind of intervention that in effect changes in the rules of the game, i.e., raises the level of abstraction within which the conflict is conceived. The system as it presently exists may be better understood if it is seen from the level of the metasystem – which also includes its systems of beliefs and relationships.

Such a change in perspective brings attention to values which may point to creative alternatives and potentialities. Historically, of course, religious prophets have tried to provide the insights and motivation for individual awakening, the overcoming of blind habits and the expansion of life and the wellbeing of peoples. In any case, in whatever guise, the governing principles must reflect a complex world and the whole i.e., the interconnectedness of all life.

Nor are economic systems left untouched by an adequate review. Theories of economics which are remote from the exigencies of life lead to problems. Similarly, we are ill-served by political ideologies which rely upon unrealistic ideas of human nature and individualism, and devalue institutions of public service. Also problematic are priorities which hold societal values hostage to corporate pressures, with the neglect of human needs which lie outside the money economy. To the extent that corporations exploit all situations as opportunities for profit – e.g., seeing communities as no more than markets for tobacco and armaments, etc. – they are part of the problem. Such complexities are very real in their ramifications.

Yet it is disheartening that, while the principles of fairness and justice are essential points of reference, no principles are absolute. Justice is desirable but has a variety of costs, and its attainment may not always be possible. In desperate situations survival may be the priority consideration.

Essential for continuing existence are human capacities for coherent thought, including recognition of error and acceptance of responsibility. For some people this may be expressed most meaningfully in religious terms, e.g., as acknowledgement and forgiveness of sin, and repentance expressed in tangible forms. For others there may be other ways of accepting what must be through grief and reconciliation. But without working through such human dynamics little can be achieved in terms of enduring change in hearts and minds.

At this level of existential concern the standard assumptions of economic and mechanistic models of human action are utterly inadequate. Without forgiveness and commitment to shared values, stable relationships are hardly possible.

Power and prestige have their uses, but another lesson of the ages has to do with the virtue – the inherent strength – involved in a wise humility. Under some conditions survival may require an avidity for information and learning, transparency in service to the common good, and a raised consciousness of values so as to reevaluate one's position and relationships.

A Civilized Response to Terrorism

These considerations bear upon a civilized response to terrorism. The terrorist believes, in effect, that his or her situation is beyond rational thought, requiring action even if blinded by rage. To combat terrorism a tit-for-tat approach which assumes the same playing field must miss the mark. A hopeful approach must give thought to strategy, and, with understanding of the forces at work, will be more likely to fight fire with water than simply pour on more fire.

In any case, an adequate analysis must take into account all sources of grievance, all modes of exploitation which generate problems, with a keen realization that false claims and rationalizations for injustice will not last. And to the extent that political and economic systems promote the exploitation of vulnerable peoples, the foundations for cooperation will crumble. Even if torn out by root and branch, if the soil and seeds for terrorism persist, new growth will arise.

The problems are so serious because they inextricably involve the interconnected whole of the modern world – beliefs, customs and technologies alike. And failure to come to terms with all these fundamentals will impede solutions to the problems of any specific or economic interests and peoples wherever they live.

The challenge of what is really possible for political action in today's world is immense. What is required is a reevaluation commensurate with the risks facing the world – including an assessment of the values governing current economic relationships. This essential task, which may seem impossible to many, will not be as hazardous as trying to sustain civilized life in an unjust world.

Bruce Buchanan

A TALE OF TWO CITIES

"Vive la différence!"

WHILE Wall St. continues in major disarray in all areas from accountancy to morality, Washington doesn't seem to have a doubt in the world – from its reemphasis on nuclear rearmament to its pressure on Canada to enter into a security alliance and a common currency. This latter would mean downsizing what distinguishes us from our neighbour that most of us cherish as sincerely as we do our neighbour itself. That difference enabled us, for example, to give refuge to thousands of refugees from enlistment in the Vietnam War. In the process we not only helped salvage many useful American lives, but tactfully conveyed our view on that war to which many Americans in official circles eventually arrived themselves.

Matters are so disquieting that we are at a loss to say which is the bigger menace – Washington's military certainties or Wall St.'s securities. We find it disturbing that the US ambassador has developed a degree of aggressiveness in telling us what we must do in running our country that has few precedents and should not be encouraged. Nor is the situation helped by having a prominent analyst in the employ of one of the brokerage-banking conglomerates telling her fellow-Canadians why we must surrender our currency and adopt the US dollar. Bay St. analysts would be well advised to concentrate on cleaning up their security analysis act, rather than attempting to broker the surrender of our sovereignty. And this just when dollarization has contributed to reduce the Argentine, once the proudest and wealthiest of Latin American countries, to begging the IMF for bits of additional charity so that they can withdraw money from their bank accounts to buy groceries.

That is why we are introducing this series of notes on the difference between our institutions and those of the US. Hopefully, it will explain why we should cherish our sovereignty and persuade – in the friendliest but firmest of manners – the big elephant that we share most of the continent with – from rolling over.

Since the world is in a shooting mode, let us express ourselves in military metaphor. One of the basic things that have undone our economic theory has been its maximization of "collateral damage." The Washington Consensus has reshaped economic theory to utilize as sole favoured financial "blunt tool" – higher interest rates. That, however, must smash up the entire economy when its avowed target is just inflation. The "inflation" concept is itself similarly unfocussed and productive of "collateral damage" since all price rise can not be traced to too much demand and too little supply. Much of it might be due to the additional taxation needed for greater security, higher urbanization, the need for a better educated population. Nobody moving from a town of say 20,000 to New York City can expect his living expenses not to jump. That is not all "inflation." Much of it is merely the cost of running a huge modern city. Why then would our central bank assume that society can make a similar move into urbanization and keep prices flat? They are in fact dealing with two unrelated problems with a single blunt tool – higher interest rates.

Raise interest rates and you batter the private sector and all three levels of government with "collateral fire," but accentuate the problem by creating more unemployment, more neglect, and more criminality.

Peacetime Collateral Damage

The very political process in the United States is structured to maximize "collateral damage." Take *The Wall Street Journal* (10/04, "Fortune Turns Against 'Greens' on Energy Bill" by John J. Fialka): "As early as today [Alaska Republican] senator Frank Murkowski will make his long-awaited move to add language allowing oil exploration in Alaska's federally protected Arctic National Wildlife Refuge. Yesterday, just 24 hours after Iraq pulled its oil from the world market, Sen. Murkowski rose in the Senate to try to marshal enough votes to quash a likely Democrat-led filibuster against his White-House-backed proposal.

"The sprawling 590-page bill is proving an appealing target for artful lobbying and parochial senators to make impromptu changes and expensive backroom deals. If enacted, the Senate measure would reach into nearly every facet of American life, determining the content of gasoline, the structure of the nation's electricity-transmission and even the performance of pick-up trucks.

"Senate Democrats launched their own version initially as a vehicle to promote a variety of 'green causes' – including renewable energy, energy conservation and ways to combat climate change. But it has been amended to the point where major environmental groups have begun to abandon it. And after two weeks of prior debate, the bill faces about 250 amendments." One ploy in the works could result in an unusual alliance between Democratic Sen. Robert Byrd of West Virginia and Alaska's other GOP senator, Ted Stevens. To entice Sen. Byrd and other steel-state Democrats to vote for opening the Alaska refuge, Sen. Stevens is mulling a multibillion dollar steel-rescue package to the energy bill. The measure, being drafted by West Virginia Democratic Senator Jay Rockefeller, would give some of the nation's biggest steel companies relief from health care for retired workers and from death benefits.

"As the bill stands, its biggest winners are a coalition of farm groups and members of the American Petroleum Institute. In several months of meetings, they helped write a section that, that by mandating a federal gasoline-additive standard, would double the size of the ethanol industry. That industry, which makes a gasoline additive out of corn has potent political support, given its importance to Iowa, home of the fiercest presidential caucuses, where several Democratic candidates are already competing."

Contrast this with the Canadian parliamentary system where the party in power controls the House of Commons, and also the appointments to the Senate. Bills deal with one matter at a time, they are not a crazy quilt put together by lobbyists. Focussing on a single target, there is minimal likelihood of collateral damage.

For the long-overdue revision of economic theory, we have proposed as our point of departure the "Counting Rule" of Jan Tinbergen. That transfers to economics the basic rule we learned in our first-year high-school algebra classes: to solve equations with two independent variables you need two different equations. One won't do. Nor will a single bill dealing with fifty different subjects.

The American political system fails the Tinbergen Test. It maximizes collateral damage, since such a bill will be passed with a vote that does not target a single issue. Not a single of the issues standing alone might command a majority. And with so much depending on frustrating democratic choice it invites corruption.

The Lord knows that under our own parliamentary system politicians and power groups have devised sufficient ways of mocking democratic process. For example, by slipping through legislation without parliamentary debate or press releases – like the bill phasing out the statutory reserves that the banks had to hold with the Bank of Canada in 1991. Or the bill that finally, in semi-stealth, introduced capital budgeting into the federal books in 2002 while misrepresenting the effect on federal finances. But introducing the US presidential system would be a giant regressive step. For generations it made possible such abominations as the introduction and preservation of Jim Crow in the South and much else.

William Krehm

Focus on Options

IT COULD BE a game of button, button, for its sweep of territory, and by how closely the players approach the button's lair without finding it. But then it had been put out of sight with the closest mating of cunning and art short of fraud. And in our turbulent times such boundaries are frail and ever harder to respect.

The creation of money – long a defining trait of sovereignty – has been bestowed on the banks. For its money needs the government itself had been made dependent on the bankers who nevertheless come to it with regularity of planets in the skies when they lose their capital in the gambles allowed them by Deregulation. Not only were they generously afforded the help denied the more deserving needy, but they were freed to do more and more of what they set their hearts on – lending an increasing multiple of the legal tender which in many cases they had already lost. The very Decalogue had been compressed into a single stricture: If money were kept scarce and dear, "fun-

damentals were sound." But the chosen system has collapsed in a miasma of corruption. And now the quest is underway in all the corporate halls for what brought this on. Commissions in blurred number are enquiring how the laws can be reshuffled to prevent its recurrence. But despite all the valiant press releases, the button itself that might keep statesmanly trousers demurely in place has still not turned up.

Inevitably the search has shifted to options, the device by which corporate heads reward themselves by being empowered to buy their corporation's stock years ahead at today's and even yesterday's prices. But let *The Wall Street Journal*, a sheet noted for seeking out indigestible truth in its news columns that it disputes heatedly on its editorial page (26/3, "Perk Police – Stock Options Come Under Fire in Wake of Enron's Collapse" by Greg Hitt and Jacob M. Schlesinger): "One day last month lobbyists from 30 of the nation's biggest companies met in a conference room [in Washington] at the offices of software giant Oracle Corp. Another 30 joined in via speaker phone.

"They represented business as diverse as Citigroup Inc., and Oracle's archrival, Microsoft Corp. In the wake of the Enron Corp. scandal, they were united in a common cause: saving stock options – a goodie widely blamed for fuelling many of the corporate excesses of the 1990s. Their common foe: a broad new coalition of lawmakers from both parties, Federal Reserve Chairman Alan Greenspan, big institutional investors and global accountants.

"Their opponents say options have bred a culture of irresponsible greed showering executives with outlandish paydays that sometimes reach into the tens and hundreds of millions of dollars.

"Last month, when he introduced a bill to rein in the benefits of options, Sen. Carl Levin, a Michigan Democrat, described the cycle this way: Most executive pay packages rely heavily on options, encouraging corporate managers to push accounting rules 'to the limit,' to make their financial statements look better so that their stock prices will go up, 'so that the executives can cash in their options.'

"Options also help companies pump up the earnings they report. Accounting rules don't require companies to treat options as other forms of pay – as an expense that reduces profits. Mr. Levin's bill would deny companies lucrative tax deductions if they don't do that.

"The last serious clash over stock options was in 1994, and the business lobby won it handily. Odds are that it also will prevail this time around, with a pitch that options make the American economy perform better. As Lisa Wolkst, a lobbyist for the International Mass Retail Association, puts it, 'it makes more likely that employees will pick up the gum wrapper in the aisle.'" In the course of the operation, executives, however, pick up a lot more than gum wrappers.

"For years, detractors have complained that options provided executives with obscene returns, but that didn't seem to bother the public so much, as long as other investors prospered too. Then, as the Enron scandal unfolded, the nation learned that top Enron executives had continued to make many millions of dollars by cashing in their options even as they were leading their company toward ruin. Enron Chairman Kenneth Lay realized $123.4 million from exercising stock options in 2000. By contrast, most ordinary shareholders ended losing the bulk of their Enron investments and thousands of Enron workers lost their jobs and much of their retirement savings.

"Testifying before Congress last month, former Enron CEO Jeffrey Skilling conceded that stock options offer an 'egregious way to inflate a company's reported earnings.' 'Essentially what you do is issue your stock options to reduce compensation expense, and therefore increase your profitability,' explained Mr. Skilling, who realized $62.5 million in 2000 by cashing in Enron options.

"Current rules require companies to report the cost of issuing options only as a footnote in their annual reports. Treating stock options as an expense would lower the earnings of nearly every major corporation in the US. Out of the stocks in Standard & Poor's 500, only two companies – Boeing Co. and Winn-Dixie Stores Inc. – have chosen to count stock options as an expense in their financial reports.

"The business lobby is fighting hard to defend options because the stakes are so high. Consider Oracle, which hosted the mid-February strategy session. Oracle CEO Larry Ellison gained $706 million last year from exercising stock options. And according to Bear Stearns, Oracle's operating income was $933M higher for 2001 than if it had given employees cash instead of options.

"Legendary investor Warren Buffet, one of the few business executives who rail against options, makes a simple argument for counting them as a cost: 'If options aren't a form of compensation, what are they? If compensation is not an expense, what is it? And, if expenses shouldn't go into calculations of earnings, where in the world should they go?'

"Accounting-rule writers grappled with the issue as far back as at least 1972. Not only weren't stock options widely used back then, but the challenge of calculating their cost was daunting. So officials decided that options needn't be treated as an expense.

"During the 1980s, however, stock options became increasingly popular, particularly in Silicon Valley. where high-tech startups offered them not only to executives, but to all ranks of employees."

They became in fact a supplement to the official money supply with particular attraction to the payees because of their possibilities of tax evasion or deferment, and even fabulous capital gains. They were like a hybrid of money and a lottery ticket, combining the best of two worlds. In Silicon Valley, even suppliers fought to receive them rather than notes bearing the picture of a long-dead politician. They were a version of the future that eliminated the whole spectrum except for rosy-tinged gold.

"By the early 1980s, there were sophisticated new methods available for projecting the long-term value of stock-option grants. Companies were beginning to use a mathematical model developed by economists Fischer Black and Myron Scholes to tell employees how much their stock options were worth. Mr. Scholes later won a Nobel Prize in economics for the model. The Federal Accounting Standards Board (FASB) reasoned that

if companies could estimate the long-term value of the options to their employees, they could also give shareholders an accounting of the long-term cost of those options.

The Risks of Risk Management

"And so the FASB voted in April 1993 to require companies to treat options as an expense, based on the estimated future value of those options. In 1994, thousands of high-tech workers gathered in Northern California for a raucous pro-options demonstration called 'Rally in the Valley," sporting T-shirts and placards with such slogans as 'Stop FASB' 'Federal Accounting Stops Business.' The high-tech sector circulated studies showing corporate profits falling by 50% and that capital would dry up as a result of the new rule.

"The Clinton Administration weighed in against FASB. So did financial investor groups who said the rule change would muddy financial statements."

Today it is amusing reading these claims in the light of the more recent experience of option-happy Enron, Global Crossing, and a wide swath of investors and employees. The damage has not been confined to any particular group of stakeholders in the companies affected. It undermines the very notion of credibility and trust without which there can be no serious economy. For clearly "Nobel Prize for Economics" or not, the mathematics were just another version of the underlying dogma of the self-balancing market dressed up in mathematics of a quality that would flunk a freshman in a maths or physics course.[1] It was based on the premise that all agents in the economy are so insignificant in size and power that they are helpless to influence prices, salaries or anything that counts. The scientific worth of such "science" is no greater than that of the fabulously rewarded salesmen on Wall St. who peddled Enron and the many other wildly overvalued stocks. You might as well skip the pseudo-mathematical act and award the "Nobel Prize for Economics" to the super-salesmen of the brokerage houses directly.

Their underlying powers of make-believe and cover-up took over economic modelling when marginal utility value theory came in over a century ago. Elsewhere, I have traced its historical roots (1) in the need to present society exclusively as a bunch of traders on a level playing field and nothing else; (2) in the semi-educated belief of the founding fathers of marginal theory that calculus is a guarantee of scientific method. This was the wooden leg mistaken for a soaring wing that was supposed to help economists to fore-knowledge of the future.

Marginal utility theory replaced all objective notion of value with the relative growth rates of supply and demand as the one source of wealth. Desire and appetite nudged out all notions of objective factors essential to nurture life and realize its potentials. Capital accumulation becomes the one criterion of prosperity. And stock options are but a higher derivative of that aberration. Inevitably, since arousing desire and demand is what salesmanship and advertising are about, the name of the game becomes cooking the books, and making a timely getaway to carefully prepared tax havens. It all fits together like a jigsaw puzzle with not a part misplaced. In fact there are parts left over that may be conveniently hidden under the table.

Such a part too many is the *WSJ's* reference to Black and Scholes "sophisticated new methods for projecting the long-term value of stock options that won them their the Nobel Prize in Economics." To begin with it should be made clear that the "Nobel prize for economics" is a hitch-hike on the prestige of the Nobel Prizes for achievement on behalf of Peace, Science and Literature. There is no real connection. The Economics Prize was established, not by Alfred Nobel, but by a Swedish Bank decades later. Most of its awards betray its banker origins. Secondly the Black and Scholes model underlay the ill-fated Long-Term Capital Management Fund that would have brought down the world financial system were it not for the intervention of the US government to save it from bankruptcy.

W.K.

1. Krehm, W. (2002). *Towards a Non-Autistic Economics – A Place for Society at the Table* (Chapter One). Toronto: COMER Publications.

A Genetic Predisposition to Increasing Instability

WHILE CHEERFUL WORDS are heard in high places about the recession having come to a close, or better yet, never even having occurred, a gloomier reality is asserting itself. The reigning variant of capitalism has no rewards for the classical virtues of modesty, stability, so highly prized in chapels and sacred scriptures. For the present system even to stand still and for the stock market not to keel over, they must not only shoot forward, but at an accelerating pace.

To make this capitalized future even plausible, calls for both ongoing technological revolutions and unflinching salesmanship. But launching such ever new ships of hope, does not automatically safeguard the seaworthiness of those already far out at sea. This strange economic system begotten by tumescent greed has an increasing dependence upon trust, evident in the figures of outstanding debt; yet by its very nature trustworthiness is ravaged by ever overweening ambition.

And that contradiction erupts throughout the economy. In this note I am concerned with the model's assumption that as production increases, costs per unit rise rather than fall – "the law of diminishing returns." Without that supposition, the supply curve would not intersect the demand curve that does increase as prices drop, and the market would not be cleared. That would destroy the self-balancing feature that is the purpose of the dogma.

The supposed law of diminishing return in fact contradicts the very dynamics that operates by discounting into present credit an ever accelerating future. That has some sinister implications for our ever credit-hungry economy.

If costs indeed were to rise with the volume produced, it would mean that unsold inventories would tend to increase in value. Existing collateral would accordingly tend to increase in value, debt would be better secured, and lenders would be less likely to call it in. However, as wholesale prices tend to drop or even as they fail to rise, the contrary happens. The unsold inventory shrinks as a proportion of the debt it supports. Matters would even become worse if the inventory became obsolescent because of rapid technological progress.

And a system whose guiding model and relevant reality move in opposite directions is an invitation to unlimited disasters. Were all the "externalities" of the economy assimilated into the price level as they should be, this menacing shrivelling of the value of unsold inventory would lessen. But that is not what is happening. Not only are many infrastructural costs kept off balance-sheet, but the search for ever cheaper labour in countries where more basic costs are kept out of the export prices also contributes to the declining value of inventories.

Wherever we look we encounter this pairing of irreconcilables that assures the deepening instability of the system.

While all this is heading to a gruesome climax as amidst a world-enveloping deflation, the chillingly familiar warnings about incipient inflation go on being emitted by the Bank of Canada. For strictly sanitary reasons, if none other, policies that have repeatedly revealed their bankruptcy, should not be left unburied to litter the minds of our policy-makers.

How deep that trouble is becoming appears from *The Wall Street Journal* (13/03, "Telecom's Troubles Spread from Upstarts to Sector's Leaders. It's Never Been This Bad" by Rebecca Blumenstein and Gregory Zuckerman).

"A perfect storm has hit the telecom business, spreading beyond small upstarts to threaten some of the industry's biggest players. A few months ago, most of the damage seemed confined to overleveraged entrepreneurs competing with Baby Bells and to fiber-optic companies brought low by a spectacular glut of cable. But now, spooked by accounting questions and faltering growth prospects, investors and banks are recoiling from the whole $300-billion-a-year industry. Long-distance carriers, wireless companies and even local phone giants are getting caught up in the turmoil, and many face sharply higher borrowing costs.

"'It's never been this bad, not even close,' says Scott Cleland, chief executive of Precursor Group, an independent research company based in Washington, DC.

"On Monday, WorldCom Inc. and Qwest Communications International Inc., two of the nation's largest phone companies, acknowledged that the Securities and Exchange Commission is investigating their accounting practices. Two congressional committees have joined the SEC in looking into Global Crossing's bookkeeping. All say their accounting is proper, but the news added to fears that accounting issues could cast a shadow over the industry."

"Last month, Sprint Corp. found itself shut out of the commercial paper market, where it raises short-term cash. The nation's No.3 long-distance company was forced to put up its valuable yellow-pages businesses as collateral to borrow $1 billion from banks. Yesterday, big equipment maker Lucent Technologies Inc. told analysts it doesn't expect to return to profitability until 2003.

"Prices are plummeting in the wireless industry as the number of new users slows. AT&T Wireless Services Inc., the nation's third-largest wireless company reduced its projections for 2002 on March 1, in part because the rise in the minutes of use is not enough to compensate for the fall in prices.

"The Dow Jones Global Telecommunications Index is off 11% since the beginning of the year, compared to a 1.5% rise for the Standard & Poor's 500. In the past two years, investors have suffered $2 trillion in paper losses from a 60% drop in the sector's market capitalization, according to Dow Jones Statistics.

"The fortunes of the biggest players have changed with striking speed. Joseph P. Nacchio, Qwest's chief executive, told investors that as new entrants had difficulties, there would be a flight to safety' to the more established companies like Qwest. But when fiber-optic carrier Global Crossing filed for bankruptcy-court protection, the fourth largest bankruptcy in US history, many investors fled. 'People are petrified,' said senior trader John Greco of Credit Suisse First Boston. They've lost so much money so quickly, and they don't want to be in the next land mine.'

"Many of the industry's current problems can be traced to overcapacity, spurred by the *Telecommunications Reform Act* of 1996, which pledged to open the historically regulated industry to competition. The telecom industry went on a building binge. By the time the Internet bubble burst, an estimated 39 million miles of fiber-optic cabled stretched underneath the US – only 10% of which is in use today, according to the latest estimate of Merrill Lynch & Co.

"To pay for it all, telecom companies took on huge debts. Since 1996 telecoms have borrowed more than $1.5 trillion from banks and issued more than $630 billion in bonds, according to Thomson Financial, topping all other industries."

What this amounted to was the monetization of the future, of fairy tales told by promoters and bankers who pocketed their fees and profits and made for the nearest exit. That has left craters in both the credit and the credibility of the system itself.

William Krehm

Enron was Just One of New Kind

IN ENRON'S own fevered imagination, we had not only landed on the moon but settled there and were going on to set up shop on Mars. There was thus no limit on the multiplication of its deals.

Here is how *The Wall Street Journal* is handling the story (3/03, "Enron Rival Used Complex Accounting to Burnish Profile – With Help from Citigroup, Dynegy Inc. Addressed a Cash Flow Concern" by Jason Sapsford and Paul Beckett): "'How does Dynegy make sure its numbers are real?' the company asks on its Web site. And it answers, 'By starting with real assets.'"

The allusion was to the claim of Enron's CEO that the age of "heavy iron" was over and there was no sense tying up capital in real assets when it could be used out there maximizing shareholders' equity by swapping derivatives.

"But in response to a problem that developed in the late 1990s, Dynegy had engaged in some complex accounting at least in part to buff its financial profile. As energy traders typically do, the company had used highly subjective estimates to assign a current value to its contracts to buy and sell natural gas and other commodities in the future. That value had soared in the late 1990s, boosting the company's net income.

"The problem was that Dynegy's cash flow from actual operations wasn't keeping up. And eventually analysts and investors might interpret the discrepancy as suggesting that the contract valuations had been too high."

Devising a Solution

"So Dynegy came up with a solution. Executives called it Project Alpha. Designed primarily by the company's tax division and launched a year ago, it uses bold accounting maneuvers and a complicated system of gas trades to help address the discrepancy between cash flow and net income that has been augmented by rising commodity contract values.

"The project, which relies on a $300 million loan and other help from Citigroup Inc., is designed to operate for another four years, although most of the benefits were realized last year. In 2001, Project Alpha aimed to boost Dynegy's cash flow from operations by $300 million, according to company documents. It also cut Dynegy's tax bill by $80 million, company officials say. Apart from that the project has little impact on the company's net income.

Auditors' Blessing

"Arthur Andersen LLP, Dynegy's auditors until last month, blessed the benefits created by Project Alpha, Dynegy officials say. Andersen is now under federal indictment for shredding Enron-related documents. PricewaterhouseCoopers has since concluded that the accounting and disclosure of Alpha were appropriate. Still, Alpha raises questions about Dynegy's financial pronouncements. Andersen and Pricewaterhouse declined to comment.

"'They are increasing cash flow and then tax losses but not anything of economic value,' says Douglas Carmichael, an accounting professor at Baruch College in New York. 'It doesn't seem to have any other real business purpose.'

"Unlike some of Enron's controversial transactions, there is no indication that Dynegy executives owned any interest in the partnership at the center of Project Alpha. But like some of Enron's dealings, Project Alpha underscores how the nation's top financial institutions and law firms reap big profits from helping corporations set up complex accounting arrangements at least in part for touching up their financial portraits. Dynegy paid a total of $33 million in Project Alpha fees, among others, to Citigroup and Vinson & Elkins, a prominent Houston law firm.

The latter two were involved in Enron deals as well.

"Project Alpha grew at least in part out of the way Dynegy and other trading companies account for 'derivative' contracts they use to buy and sell commodities. Under accounting standards, the companies must record today the value of trades for gas, electricity and other commodities, even though the actual transactions may take place years hence. In 2000, Dynegy and other energy traders were facing criticism from some analysts for assigning overly optimistic current values in their derivatives contracts. Formed in 1985, Dynegy began as a gas marketeer and trader. It grew into one of the largest energy suppliers in the US. It reported net income last year of $648 million, up 29% from 2000. Revenue jumped 43% to $42.2. A discrepancy was developing between the company's net income, as boosted by sharply rising derivative-contract values, and its reported cash flow from trades that actually had been performed."

It is fair to say, not that derivatives *forced* Dynegy to cook its books, but that it practically *instructed* it how it could be done – partly to comply with "accounting standards." And to appreciate the implications of this, we must remember that the entire bureaucracy of world banking – from the Bank for International Settlements to commercial banks – has fiercely resisted introducing controls of derivatives. That made possible a high percentage of the mega-financial scams that have rattled the world in recent years. In the dock today are not only Enron and Dynegy and their innumerable colleagues, but our financial-monetary system.

"There was a catch, however. Net income is the starting point for calculating cash flow from operations. Since the $115 million hadn't actually flowed into the company, Dynegy had to adjust its cash flow figure downward by $115 million. That heightened the discrepancy between cash flow and net income.

"The gap grew again in 2000. That year the company reported unrealized gains of $354 million, again boosting the bottom line by a comparable amount. Dynegy adjusted down its cash flow from operations by a corresponding $354 million.

"Internal, undated Dynegy documents relating to Project Alpha noted that while the company was assigning ever higher values to its derivative contracts, those contracts 'do not generate cash.' The danger was that the disconnect between reported net income and its cash intake could become more obvious to investors. One mechanism for beefing up reported cash flow numbers was Project Alpha, which began on April 1, 2001."

Was the choice of date a Freudian slip? With the air already so thick with symbols, surely they could have shifted the date of its inauguration by a day in either direction.

"The project's goals are made clear in its documents: 'Operating cash will increase by $300 millions in 2001.'"

Gain and Loss

"Alpha relied on a complicated series of financial and accounting steps. Citigroup arranged a loan of roughly $300 million that ended up with a specially created entity that entered a series of gas-trading contracts with a partnership called DMT supply LP. Through a subsidiary, Dynegy held an interest in DMT. During the first nine months of the arrangement, DMT bought gas from the entity at prices below market. DMT then resold the gas into the market at a profit. The $300 million offset the special entity's losses on these trades.

"DMT is required to buy gas at above market prices, generating a series of losses."

Like Einstein, Dynegy and its accountants transformed time into shoe-leather.

"Valued as part of Dynegy's larger portfolio of derivative contracts, the two sets of gas transactions were designed to cancel each other out, according to documents and interviews. They aren't supposed to produce a loss or gain in Dynegy's net income."

The conclusion that emerges from the bankruptcy and other legal proceedings in which Enron, Dynegy, Global Crossing and countless other high-tech corporations are involved is that the entire financial system today has been caught with its morality at half mast. That could have immense consequences. So powerful had the command of our economy, our governments, and our media by high finance become, that serious discourse on economic and monetary policy had become impossible. Now the ball is moving into the court of the critics too long denied a hearing.

W.K.

An Old Routine Fails — Venezuela

AS WE GO TO PRESS we learn of the overthrow of the Venezuelan President Hugo Chavez and his return to power two days later under popular pressure. While the details of this unusual chain of events are still in short supply, the bizarre episode is perfectly understandable in the light of the Latin-American-US background.

It is no accident that the two Latin American republics most prominently in the headlines today should be the Argentine and Venezuela. It was the cowboys from the Argentinian *pampas* – the gauchos and the llaneros from Venezuela's *llanos*, swept over the Andes to meet in Peru, overthrowing Spanish rule en route on the entire continent. Given this unique role that Argentina and Venezuela shared in the liberation of Spanish America, it was inevitable that they should have had a strong sense of their national identity. European union deprived the Argentine of its historic British market for its meat and grains. And a succession of bloodthirsty dictatorships that enjoyed the backing of Washington's Cold Warriors, left it after a supreme military adventure crushed under exchange problems.

An easy short-term highly recommended solution was to use US dollar as its effective currency requiring a US dollar in a special account for every Argentine peso issued. (An arrangement that is being stubbornly promoted in Canada despite its disastrous record the Argentine.) There it deprived the government of any possibility of protecting its foreign exchange balance by lowering the exchange rate of currency to discourage imports and improve the competitiveness of its exports. A "solution" that suited Washington fine.

Venezuela does not have that problem. As the third foreign source of oil of the US, Venezuela's problem has been its overwhelming dependence on oil, which has prevented the development of a better balanced economy that would allow it to leave behind its present semi-colonial economic status. In the latter 1940s the left of centre governments of Romulo Gallegos and Romulo Betancourt, came to power after a democratic revolution in alliance with a sector of the army. That democratic regime was overthrown by a military coup that certainly led to no visible mourning in Washington.

The present regime of President Hugo Chavez was a new assertion of the popular Bolivarian tradition in Venezuela. While still a parachuter in the army, Chavez had headed an unsuccessful attempt at a coup, but on a second legitimate attempt won the presidency by legitimate means. Again in the Bolivarian tradition, rather than joining the United States in its economic boycott of Cuba, he provided it with oil at special reduced rates as a gesture of hemispheric solidarity. What probably annoyed President Bush almost as much was that he refused to plow back the profits of the national oil company in further investment to counter the decline in Venezuela's oil exports. Instead he opted to reinvest enough oil profits in human capital that would provide an economy friendlier both to the environment and society. That brought his regime in head-on clash both with the Bush government and with the management of the national oil company that declared a strike. Four days after Iraq declared a boycott of oil exports to the US in aid of the Palestinian resistance, Chavez was overthrown by a section of the army. At once the incoming government headed by a business leader cancelled the Chavez legislation disliked by the foreign oil companies – very much a Venezuelan version of Trudeau's Canadian Energy Policy that got up the oil companies' noses in the 1970s.

Though Washington had taken no overt part in the anti-Chavez coup, Latin America has seen that act played out so many times, that it could replace the missing text. Mass demonstrations and a decisive portion of the army led to Chavez's return to power. That was not supposed to happen. Security Advisor Condolezza Rice declared that hopefully Chavez had learned his lesson. Probably he realizes more clearly that Bolivar's feat in criss-crossing the Andes to lead a continent to freedom was child's play compared to the goal he has set himself. But the extent of Latin-American poverty does not give it much choice. Rather than become suicide bombers, it is better that they persist in facing even those odds to win a humane future.

William Krehm

The Plight of Academic Economists

A FINE BRITISH ECONOMIST remarked to me in a mixture of relief and despair, "We academic economists are irrelevant."

But is that really so? To accept such a position is certainly not without consequence for society's future. For silence on the part of academic economists can only be interpreted as support for the official dogma. Our universities are supposed to teach the younger generation to use their minds. If an education in so important a field is reduced to scoring the highest marks by making least use of their critical faculties, the only result can be cynicism. It could, of course, be an ideal preparation for a lucrative career on Wall St. promoting bogus stocks. Or in government implementing dubious policies. If you can swallow the most basic premises of recognized economic theory, you can readily accept just about anything that will help your "bottom line."

Certainly no greater nonsense could be devised than assuming in the globalized age of Microsoft and General Electric that all players are of negligible size. But without that assumption it would be impossible to apply calculus and bowl over the impressionable with forests of integration signs. Yet these were the underpinnings of the work on risk management that for which two economists, were awarded the so-called Nobel prize for Economics. They went on to organize the Long-Term Capital Management hedge fund that in 1998 tottered on the brink of so vast a bankruptcy that the US Federal Reserve had to step in to arrange support for it to save the world financial system. Amongst the investors who took a beating in its near-collapse were the legendary Warren Buffet and General Electric.

Were it just a question of understanding, much of the grief that has overtaken the world could have been avoided by the economics staff at our universities correcting what they mistake for mathematics by taking appropriate undergraduate maths courses. The point, however, is that the myth of the self-balancing market has nothing to do with serious mathematics. It is a power position. more desperately defended as its bankruptcy became clear.

However, academic economists are rarely people of independent means: there are usually mortgage payments and families to be looked after. Usually they are in no position to face the consequences of challenging the official dogma. To flourish in their careers they must "publish or perish" and the only publications that count are "peer reviews." In this context, however, that has come to mean "Peer you may, but tell you may not." Universities depend increasingly for their financing on grants from governments that depend on corporate contributions for their election expenses. Or increasingly on the direct largesse of large corporations.

Not all people are born to be martyrs. Heroism, moreover, like hats, comes in different shapes and sizes. Courage tempered with discretion for survival can play a positive social role, as well as the more spectacular variety that is ready to go up in flames for a good cause. It is perfectly understandable therefore that even conscientious economics teachers should at times avoid pursuing a logical train to its ultimate syllogism. There are other ways of helping economics back to being an honest stab at a science rather than a major hindrance. A good grounding in the play of ideas can be developed by a knowledge of the history of economic theory, above all the record of the Great Depression, the financing of WWII, and the quarter of a century of prosperity and reconstruction that followed; the deregulation of our banks and its costs to society. That will prepare the minds of their students to pick their way to further conclusions.

Today the official model has two levers at its disposal: higher interest rates to enforce a near-flat price level, and balanced budgets. Those who work those levers are not supposed to plan a joint strategy though each of these measures will cause collateral damage in areas of the economy quite unrelated to their targeted goals. That restriction is imposed by the so-called independence of the central bank from the government. Nevertheless the budgetary deficits that are supposed to be the main concern of the ministers of finance have grown vastly over the past two decades largely because of the great increase of the commercial banks' holdings of central government debt and the corresponding drop in the portion of that debt held by the central bank.

Most of society's vital interests have been proclaimed "externalities" in the official model that is reared around "the pure and perfect market." That means that any harmful effect on non-market areas – the public sector, the ecology, the household economy is dismissed as "collateral damage." The term, of course, has been borrowed from warfare, but there is this distinction: military action by its nature is temporary, but society and its economic administration are ongoing.

The conclusion that emerges is that instead of dealing in massive statistical blocks in our economic analysis, these should be broken down into significant components that would give us a better idea of the full effects of a given economic policy.

That is the message that has been straining to catch our attention over the past sixty years.

Keynes made a notable contribution to this process by distinguishing Savings from Investment. In economies with a developed credit system, investment must precede savings, rather than the contrary. But in his handling of "effective demand," Keynes made no distinction between the demand resulting from the income of entrepreneurs and that of workers. Michal Kalecki, on the other hand, breaks up the aggregate of earnings to its independent components in his maxim: "Workers spend what they earn; the entrepreneur earns what he spends.' Otherwise expressed, a major portion of the income of entrepreneurs' profits is not spent on personal consumption but reinvested – *if the conditions are favourable for investment.* And that investment in turn increases his profits. The worker has no choice but to spend what he earns for his living expenses whether the times are good or bad.

François Perroux in France carried the notion of disaggregating key statistics much further. He spoke of "the errors connected with the rudimentary procedure that deduces from a small number of matrices applying to past conditions the probable course of the changing technical coefficients of the future. *Surreptitiously* the theory of growth is influenced by Walrasian equilibrium. It has not readily shed the illusion of balanced growth maintained from period to period."[1]

But our economy has become far more complex since the days of Keynes, Perroux and Kalecki. The subsystems of the environment, the household economy, the public sector each operate by their own logic though they do interact. This calls for disaggregation in more dimensions than appeared some decades ago. The Tinbergen Counting Rule fills the bill and leads us directly into systems theory, which conventional economists have shunned like the plague. It holds that for a policy to be effective, it must have as many independent variables as can be identified in the problem. It follows directly from what we learned in our first-year high school classes in the solution of simultaneous linear equations.

The immediate benefit of including such matters in university courses would be to provide vital dialogue which for at least two decades has not been taking place. If the proposals for restructuring of economic theory are invalid, the economic departments of our universities have the duty to refute them in public debate. Ignoring them will not do.

The full resources of the human mind are absolutely indispensable for humanity to face the deepening crisis of our economic system. Anything less is simply not acceptable.

William Krehm

1. Perroux, François (1965). *Les techniques quantitatives de la planification* (p. 74). Paris: Presses Universitaires de France.

The Games Words and Numbers Can Play

WORDS AND NUMBERS become absorbed in lives of their own. Though their purpose is to transmit information they can become taken up with gossiping with one another to the point of forgetting the message that they were entrusted with, or delivering it to the wrong address.[1]

Something parallel happens in the field of economic services and policies. *The Wall Street Journal* (19/04, "Numbers Game – Looking to Improve Your Credit Score? Fair, Isaac Can Help" by Ruth Simon) rolls out an amazing example of this.

"San Rafael, California – Maybe you were forced to put down a big deposit when you got phone service. You may have ended paying extra high rates for auto insurance despite a flawless driving record. Or maybe you suddenly had trouble finding homeowner's insurance.

"In all three cases the reason could well have been the same: your credit score wasn't high enough. These days, that score, calculated from your personal financial data using a secret formula, has more influence over your life than ever before.

"Increasingly, lenders, merchants and even many insurers consider a customer's credit score a critical tool for predicting whether they'll make money on that customer. The scores are based on complex and closely guarded mathematical formulae, many of them written by Fair, Isaac & Co.

"Its scores play an important part in many insurance decisions, a trend that is drawing increasing scrutiny from regulators. Now, Thomas Grudnowski, Fair, Isaac's chief executive since 1999, is leading the company into another potentially controversial business: teaching people how to boost their credit scores and to use them to better advantage.

"Starting this spring, Fair, Isaac plans to launch the first of a new set of services – for a fee. One of the new services, which will draw on the company's insider knowledge of its own credit score formulas, will show consumers how certain key financial variables influence their credit scores. For another additional fee, another service would alert consumers to changes in their scores that might indicate that somebody was stealing their financial identity. Yet another fee-based service would show people who want to refinance their mortgages how to get a better interest rate by timing their refinancing to coincide with an increase in their credit score.

Seeking Sales Growth

"Fair, Isaac's sales growth has slowed in recent years as consolidation in the financial industry has reduced the company's traditional customer base. It thinks selling data to consumers could be a $500 million to $1 billion market for the company within five years. Fair, Isaac had 2001 sales of $329.1 million.

"Ed Mierzwsinki of the US Public Interest Research Group says the company's new services are just another way of charging consumers for something that should rightfully be theirs for free: access to their credit scores.

"The new services put Fair, Isaac in the unusual position of charging consumers for tips on how to better the very scores that Fair, Isaac writes the rules for. But the company doesn't see any conflict in that position. It says its models merely use technology to measure the same kinds of risk factors that a lender would weigh in deciding whether to make a loan.

"It says credit scores based on its flagship FICO formula are a factor in about three-quarters of all mortgages approved in the US.

"Federal laws require the nation's credit-reporting companies, the sources of much of Fair, Isaac's data, to give consumers access to their credit reports for a nominal fee, or, in some cases, free of charge. But those laws don't apply to credit scores.

"Last year, under mounting pressure from legislators and consumers groups, Fair, Isaac launched myfico.com, a Web site that gives consumers access to their personal FICO scores. For a fee of $12.95, a consumer gets 30 days of online access to his FICO report. So far, the company says, more than one million consumers have paid for the service, which it operates as a joint venture with Equifax Inc.

"On the FICO scale, a score of 300 indicates that a consumer is a terrible risk, while a score of 850 denotes an ideal borrower. In addition to their scores, consumers who buy the basic myfico.com service get a copy of their Equifax credit report and a general explanation of the factors that might be holding down their credit scores. Critics say these explanations are too vague to be of much help.

"Partly in response, Fair, Isaac plans to upgrade its $12.95 myfico.com service to include an online calculator that will let consumers see how seven key variables may affect their FICO score. According to a prototype of the new service, a consumer with a 707 score could raise that score by paying down $750 on $2,230 in credit card balances. But the prototype's advice isn't always so straightforward. For example, a consumer with a 707 score could either raise or lower that score by 10 points by obtaining a new charge card with a $3,000 credit limit.

"Fair, Isaac says it plans to market its new consumer-oriented services primarily through lenders and financial Web sites, including Quicken.com and Citibank, a unit of Citigroup Inc.

"Increasingly, credit scores are also being used to make business decisions that don't involve lending money. Fair, Isaac pioneered their use by insurance companies. Now some auto insurers believe that the scores are a better predictor of a client's propensity to file insurance claims than is the client's driving record. The result: if your credit score goes down, your auto insurance may go up – or your insurer might choose to drop you."

Hokus-pokus based on complicated mathematical formulas that nobody quite understands is thus blowing into insurance practices from the mathematics of high finance, where it has already done much damage.

"Critics say the use of credit scores by insurers penalizes poor people, immigrants who often pay their bills with cash and [thus] have no credit histories. Earlier this month, the state of Washington passed a law that would restrict the use of credit-based scores for home and auto insurance. Last week, Utah and Idaho enacted related laws. Credit scoring legislation also has been introduced in more than 20 other states.

"Consider one recent challenge: FICO scores penalized consumers who were constantly applying for credit. But as more consumers began visiting multiple lenders in search of the best auto or home loan, Fair, Isaac Vice-President Michael Rapaport told his team to come up with a way to avoid putting savvy shoppers at a disadvantage. Their solution was to count all the loans requests a consumer makes within a 14-day period as a single loan inquiry.

"Fair, Isaac's complex scoring models can be tough even for the company's executives to decipher. Last year, Mr. Grudnowski, the CEO, who earned more than $800,000, was startled to learn that his FICO score was just 706, worse than 55% of all borrowers. He says he was able to raise his score to 780 by cancelling a bunch of unused credit cards."

Here as in increasing areas of the economy, the theoretic models, even when understood, don't necessarily make sense. But the importance is to have a model with a sufficient show of certainty to inspire the entrepreneurs to go on punching. The wronged parties with sufficient resources will fight back and protect themselves against the most flagrant abuses. It is the vulnerable sections of society that are victimized to contribute to the system grinding on.

W.K.

1. Krehm, William (2002). *Towards a Non-Autistic Economy – A Place at the Table for Society* (p. 90). Toronto: COMER Publications.

Ontario Hydro — Privatization as a Morality Play

W E ARE INDEBTED to two successive Ontario governments for a perfect illustration of how the world got into its present mess. The timing was perfect. The stocks that had soared highest and convinced Wall St. that accountancy had become obsolete, were the ones that plopped most drastically. Commissions as numerous as the fingers on your hands are extracting from the smelly wreckage the chicanery that made it possible. Corporations like Enron kept their real financial condition off their books while their shares were pushed into orbit by brokerage houses become one flesh with our banks. While their companies were losing undeclared billions, high executives were rewarding themselves with kings' ransoms in salaries, options and bonuses. Only when the corporations filed for bankruptcy protection did the public catch a glimpse of the shocking facts. The talk is of criminal charges as well as just civil ones. Never since 1929 had the deregulated market been in such disrepute.

Though it was all done in the name of "maximizing shareholder equity," investors were wondrously minimized as yesterday's star stocks shed as much as 90% of their value. It would be years before the extent of the losses will be ascertained. And who but the government will be there to pick up the bill for all this sport?

The Governor of California has accused the bankrupt trading company Enron of having rigged up power rates to the tune of $20 billion.

You would imagine that at so solemn a moment governments would suspend major corporate restructurings until visibility of the past and future had improved. Yet this was the very moment that the government of Ontario chose to push ahead to sell off the bleeding segments of what was Ontario Hydro. The urgency, beyond a doubt, was that our banks and stock markets simply needed the business and in a big hurry.

For close on to a century after it was set up by a Conservative government, Ontario Hydro had provided reliable and inexpensive power. But at the very time that privatization in California was producing brown-outs, bankruptcies, and stock market scandals not seen since the early 1930s, Ontario's Premier Mike Harris rushed ahead with breaking up Hydro into three corporations – generators, transmission lines, wholesale and retail traders. Each of these was free to trade on its respective market. But no self-respecting promoter will privatize anything – not even his grandmother – to score less than a killing. Our major problems today stem from stock market excesses rather than from problems with our power. And it is because of its own troubles that our financial sector has the capital accumulations in the public sector in its sights – hospitals, jails, schools, roads,

railways, airports, and prince of all, energy systems. The entire Hydro privatization would run into some $10 billion.

Like every electrical utility on the continent Hydro has suffered huge losses – the so-called "stranded debt" amounting to some $26 billion, $4.5 billion of which have been assigned to Hydro One. But that was due less to poor management, than to the costly surprises of nuclear technology. There was not a major private utility in the United States without similar and far worse experiences. They were in fact the first to be hit with it. Remember Three Mile Island near Harrisburg, PA?

From the handling of the Hydro hot potato by Premier Harris's successor, Ernie Eves, it is clear that the government rushed into the privatization without considering the costs of the adventure. Premier Ernie Eves is flying blind in a fog with ideology his only radar.

Bonanza in a Lean Year

When Harris retired, his successor Eves pressed on with the Hydro privatization. when a public storm broke loose. The Initial Public Offering of Hydro One – the transmission lines – had already been arranged. Bay St. was salivating over the commissions in the offing during a very lean year. Private companies were signing up customers at fixed rates well above the current ones. At that point Mr. Justice Arthur Gans of the Ontario Supreme Court ruled that the province had no legal power to privatize the transmission lines. The government beat a ragged retreat. Energy Minister Chris Stanwell, confronted by a hostile audience in London, announced that he was dropping the idea of a sale of the public assets to consider a lease running from 25 to 99 years.

A few days later the Government suffered another set-back when a senior official at the Ontario Energy Board declared that Ontario's *Electricity Act* has no provision for municipalities selling electricity distribution companies they had acquired – a total of 88 local electricity companies had been bought by Hydro One from such municipalities at a cost of $500 million. In the rush to get the Big Deal done, the government had skipped doing its homework.

Meanwhile, the prospectus for the Initial Public Offerings of Hydro One reveals some shocking details of the type of savings we can expect from it. *The Globe and Mail* (15/05, "Hydro One Payouts to be Probed" by Richard Mackie) reports: "The president of Hydro One, Eleanor Clitheroe, was formerly a deputy minister of finance and received payments last year of $1.8 million with $174,000 for cars and $173,000 in vacation pay. This from a company burdened with $5 billion of stranded debt arising from its nuclear plants.

"In the event of the sale of Hydro One, Ms. Clitheroe will receive between $5.4 and $6 million and an annual pension between $700,000 and $1 million as a pension adjusted to inflation."

What does this remind you of? Surely the ex-Commie biggies in the Soviet Union, who put to profitable use their knowledge of where the gems were buried in the public domain and before going private cut themselves a piece of empire to take as a souvenir of their public service. That has become the pattern in Canada as well – notably in the case of the privatization of the CNR by another high official. With rewards like that, what is the message being sent out to other high civil servants? Don't be stupid! Cut yourselves a slice of the public domain and take it onto the stock market. Surely there should be a period of, say, three years during which no high official in the employ of the government and involved in a privatization on that side is allowed to accept an executive position in the privatized company.

The Eves government assures us that they are considering all options.

However, the most logical option of all has not even been mentioned. It is to be found in article 18(c) of the *Bank of Canada Act*: "The Bank may buy and sell securities issued or guaranteed by Canada or any province." That obviously authorizes the BoC to hold Ontario Hydro bonds guaranteed by the province of Ontario.

Were that done, the interest Hydro would pay on them would go almost wholly as dividends to the sole shareholder of the BoC. Since 1938 this happens to be the Government of Canada. In 1938 Ottawa bought out 12,000 private shareholders of the Bank of Canada, founded only three years earlier by a Conservative Government. Since an alleged inability of government agencies to raise capital has been cited as reason for privatizing Hydro, why has the government made no use of the BoC's facilities?

The money spent by Ottawa to buy out private shareholders of the BoC – compounded over 66 years – represents quite a figure. Using that investment to allow Hydro or similar utilities across the country to finance their retirement of the "stranded debt" would be simple justice. Nuclear power was not dreamt up by the management of Ontario Hydro. It was the official policy of Ottawa. Today, indeed, nuclear power is being revived by the G8 powers to cope with possible oil shortages arising from the Near Eastern confrontation. Herb Dhaliwal, Canada's Natural Resources Minister, after the recent G8 meeting, told reporters that he "was a little surprised by the degree of pro-nuclear sentiment from other G8 countries around the table yesterday."

What is needed to deal with such "stranded debt," past and future, is an undertaking by Ottawa to use its power in the Act (14(2)) to instruct the Governor of the BoC to arrange for loans to Ontario Hydro to finance the "stranded debt." This could be amortized over an appropriate term under an arrangement between the federal government and the province of Ontario: a portion of the loan interest reaching the federal government as dividends of BoC would be remitted to the Hydro companies for financing and amortizing the "stranded debt" – the fruit of federal nuclear power policy. Similar arrangements would, of course, be available to the other provinces.

William Krehm

Keeping the Future in the Petty Cash Box

IN A SENSE it flows from the conviction of some Americans that the Lord carries an American passport. Once you arrive at that belief, it is a tiny step to assume that you have access to inside information on the future. Our purpose is not to be unkind, but just to understand what ails the United States. For what ails America, ails the world.

Fortunately for all of us, the United States has its strengths as well as its weaknesses. One of the most important of these is the powerful investigative reporting of part of its business press – in contrast to most of the editorial sections of the same publications. And the disclosures based on the bankruptcy filings of a whole series of recent star companies – Enron, Dynegy, etc., has put Americans before a cruel mirror. It remains only for the economists of academe and the government to be half as valiant as the editors of the news columns of newspapers like *The Wall Street Journal* and *The New York Times*.

In its market valuations, American big business and its accountants have treated the future as small coin that could be held in the familiarity of one's vest pocket. On the data assured by this faith, the formidable multipliers of the deregulated financial system then go to work. In this performance there simply is no reverse gear, no brake. The high interest rates that a quarter of a century ago were elevated to the one blunt tool to "lick inflation" have served as the wrecking ball of the most voracious sector of the system – the financial conglomerates; and on such bargain basement foundations skyscrapers of prognostications of monstrous capital gains are reared.

In the process "market shares" have been enlisted to substitute for non-existent earnings, and reversals are put out of sight by keeping real liabilities off the books, while treating profits that are just a twinkle in the CEO's eye as clinking coin.

The same perception syndrome has an important role in the present crisis of the US steel industry. *The Wall Street Journal* (25/04, "Retiree Cost Drive Big Change in Steel; Retirees are Losers" by Robert Guy Matthews) recounts: "US steelmakers face an estimated $10 billion in cost for health care, life insurance and pensions they promised to retirees, who now far outnumber active workers. These expenses known as legacy costs, make it harder to cope with imports and are a key reason many companies can't earn a profit. In the past four years, 31 have filed for bankruptcy, either to liquidate or reorganize. The liquidating ones have left 125,000 retirees and dependents without the benefits promised."

Steel's Negative Legacies

"These costs deter the consolidation that would normally result from such a severe profit squeeze. That's because any acquirer will inherit these retiree obligations.'

"Now some companies, having failed to get the government to take over their retiree costs, are starting to reshape themselves to either unload the cost burden or survive in spite of it. If their strategies succeed, the companies may well stay alive, and some of their workers stay employed. But their retirees are likely to face the loss of their benefits."

"In one strategy, Bethlehem Steel Corp. is moving to link up with better-financed steelmakers that would operate its plants, leaving Bethlehem just a holding company. It would still have obligations to retirees, but since it's in Chapter 11, they would have to compete for its assets in bankruptcy court – against creditors ahead of them.

"LTV Corp. has gone out of business and sold its assets. The buyer will reopen the operation, recreating LTV under a new name. But the buyer won't have to pay the legacy costs because it didn't buy the company, but simply the carcass.

"At Geneva Steel Holding Corp., an 'integrated' that made steel the traditional way from iron ore, coal and coke, the strategy is to switch to simply melting down scrap. In turning itself into a 'minimill' it will try to get the union to agree to the labor system that the mostly nonunion minimills use – pay linked to plant productivity. It will also seek an agreement reducing its obligations to current retirees.

"Closely watching all this is giant US Steel Corp., which has diligently socked away large sums to cover benefits for its 91,000 retirees and dependents. But if competitors win union concessions on retiree costs, US Steel wants some too. They might conceivably be enough to let US Steel proceed with its longtime hope of taking over ailing National Steel, which US Steel says it won't do so long as a takeover means absorbing National's legacy costs.

"The US is not losing an industry. It is rebuilding an industry,' says Robert W. Crandall, Brookings Institute economist.

"The United Steelworkers of America is in a bind. Should it agree to cut back retiree benefits, which could keep the companies alive and preserve some current jobs? Or should it refuse to bend at all on the retiree benefits, running a risk that the companies go broke and both the jobs and the retiree benefits vanish? The union continues to push the government to take over legacy costs."

An Opportunity for Foreign Firms

"In this mess, producers from China, Brazil, Europe and Canada see opportunity. To them, the US industry's changes and severe need for cash offer possibilities of gaining a foothold in the big US market and avoiding the tariffs the Bush administration recently imposed.

"The seeds of steel's situation were sown a half-century ago. The industry agreed in 1949 to labor contracts that tempered the wage boosts the union wanted by providing it with retiree benefits such as hospital coverage and life insurance. The industry saved cash by agreeing to the benefits, and the union won its members some old age security.

"But steel strikes were endemic, and President Eisenhower ended one particularly severe one in 1952 by brokering a settlement. One result: better retiree benefits. Seven years later, Vice-President Nixon forged settlement to another strike, and the result was another boost to retiree benefits for steelworkers, as well as to their pay, by then the highest of all US manufacturing industries.

"To cover the costs, American steelmakers raised prices, which they could get away with because of their global dominance at the time. But rising US labor costs changed the competitive landscape. In 1955, a ton of US-made steel contained $2.72 of labor cost, compared with 43 cents in Japan. By the mid-1970s that figure was $9.08 in the US and $4.19 in Japan. That spurred both imports and the rise of new production in developing nations.

"American steelmakers began closing plants and dismissing thousands of workers. The more they closed, the more the ratio of active workers to retirees was skewed. At US Steel for every active worker, there are now six retirees and retiree dependents. At Bethlehem that figure is 10. Strapped steelmakers began settling labor-contract talks by offering less in the way of wages and more in retiree benefits.

"The contracts obliged companies to set aside funds to pay these obligations. Many said they couldn't afford to. The leading exception was US Steel. It has built up a fund of more than a half-billion dollars to cover health and life insurance for current and retired workers, plus a pension fund that's $1.2 billion in surplus.

"Its ability to do so has undercut the industry's pleas for a federal bailout.

"Consider LTV. It if had sold its plants while they were still open, any buyer would have had to keep on paying the benefits of 85,000 retirees and dependents – an estimated half-billion dollar obligation. There were no takers. Instead, LTV simply went out of business last year.

"Its plants and other assets were auctioned off. The buyer was W.L. Ross & Co., a private New York investment firm, which said it would restart the plant before summer.

"Since W.L. Ross didn't acquire an ongoing business but merely assets, it doesn't have an obligation to pay the health-care and life-insurance coverage that LTV's labor contracts had promised. That will lower the cost of each ton of steel produced by $20 to $40. That could make the difference between profits and losses.

"Mr. Ross also wants to pay workers a base rate that rises with plant productivity. Such a system is in place at the US industry's most profitable player, Nucor Corporation, a nonunion company that makes steel from scrap rather than iron ore.

"The union says it is pressing Congress to take over some retiree costs, while working with ailing companies to make sure they stay alive. It is supporting a bill just introduced by Sen. Jay Rockefeller of West Virginia that would safeguard the benefits through a federally backed trust that eventually could cost $12 billion.

"Bethlehem is close to a deal with Brazilian steelmaker Companhia Siderurgica Nacionale (CSN). CSN would operate Bethlehem's modern Sparrows Point plant in Maryland, paying fees to Bethlehem for the right. Bethlehem is working on similar deals with other parties to run other steel plants. If the deals go through, Bethlehem will become a holding company in bankruptcy. Bethlehem intends to use the cash from relinquishing day-to-day operation to pay its creditors.

"If the CSN deal goes through, Bethlehem remains alive as a holding company and retains its retiree obligations. But it can't meet them. It is about $2 billion short. The cash from a deal with CSN would go to secured creditors, not to retirees.

"Increasingly, foreign producers are shopping for steel assets in the US to avoid tariffs and get into a large market where steel commands relatively high prices. When LTV was liquidating, the interested parties included Brazil's CSN, China's Shanghai Baosteel Group Corp. and Canada's Dofasco Inc. The world's largest steelmaker, the French-German-Spanish company Arcelor SA, also wants to be a player.

"There is plenty of finger-pointing on all sides. Companies accuse the union USWA of having been greedy and unyielding when they needed steep concessions to stay afloat. The union accuses companies of demanding that workers give up benefits when executives are unwilling to do the same.

"Caught in the middle is Richard Dowdell. He earned $80,000 a year 'with a ton of overtime,' he says, before retiring from LTV's Indiana plant in January after 38 years as a steelworker. While LTV was alive, he paid a total of $260 a month for health care for him and his wife who has a heart problem. Now he pays $1,314 a month for health insurance, plus $100 a month in copayments for the nine medicines his wife takes.

"Mr. Dowdell, 59, can no longer afford life insurance for his wife, a benefit he had under LTV. He will probably not be able to send his 18-year-old son to college next year.

"There is no reason for people to work all their lives and end up with no health insurance. I'm as mad as hell that bankruptcy laws allow a company's employees to end up with nothing."

At a more philosophical level, the deferral of a company's contractual obligations to the mirage of the future is responsible for this mess. As much as it was in the victimization of Enron's staff and investors. The trouble, however, was that the executives of the steelmakers put themselves at the head of the line, as did the financiers. Most of the guys left out in the cold were those who actually made the steel. The end conclusion: even the blessed years of the American economy were not quite as good or fair as the official version claimed. An essential detail of the model of the free self-balancing market, left untold, is that those who actually believe in its justice are left holding the bag.

William Krehm

Equipping Our Libraries to Help the Search for a New Paradigm

THE ROARING MARKETS of Globalization and Deregulation are in collapse. Much of what was supposed to herald a new era, has turned out simple fraud. That much emerges from the filings of once stellar companies for bankruptcy protection. More serious still, is the connivance of some of the largest international accountancy firms in designing the scams. Obviously we must seek the deeper roots of so much rot.

It is not a simple task. The writings of the seminal thinkers, beginning with Adam Smith himself, have been distorted or suppressed. It was to help remedy that situation that COMER and its publication arm, COMER Publications, were founded fourteen years ago. Today there is an urgent need to get its publications into our libraries. That is why we are offering university and public libraries their choice of books that we have published or authored as a gift in return for an official receipt for tax purposes made out to the donor who will pay for the gift. The procedure is simple: the library informs us of what books or *Economic Reform* issues it wishes under the arrangement. We provide the name of the donor. On receipt of the gift, the library issues the official tax receipt to the donor provided by us.

We strongly recommend the following of our publications:

• William H. Hixson, *It's Your Money* (1997). This is a popular introduction to money and banking by a COMER founder. $10.

• William Krehm, *Price in a Mixed Economy – Our Record of Disaster* (1975). This contains a summary of the work of the remarkable French school of economists, most prominent of whom was François Perroux. Perroux not only presented one of the most telling criticisms of marginal utility theory which introduced the notion of an unshackled market. He also developed the notion of the "dominant revenue" that sheds light on the raw power factor that determines the reigning paradigm of any given epoch. Krehm develops the notion of pluralistic price that is indispensable in a pluralistic society. The non-market sectors characteristic of such a society are funded by the state, and that gives rise to a price gradient that has nothing to do with inflation, i.e., an excess of supply over demand. These non-market sectors, i.e., health, education, social security, public infrastructures, the ecology, are essential even for the continued functioning of the market sector itself. $15 paperback; $25 hard cover.

• William Krehm, *Babel's Tower – the Dynamism of Economic Breakdown* (1977). This introduces systems theory to economics, and borrows the entropy concept from physics to help us understand the cannibalizing of one subsystem by another. $10.

• William Krehm, *The Bank of Canada – A Power unto Itself* (1993) – Explains the workings of the Bank of Canada, the Bank for International Settlements, and the abolition of the statutory reserves in 1991-3 which permitted the bailout of the banks from their gambling losses of the 1980s by taking on another $60B of federal debt without putting up any significant amount of their own money. $10.

• William Krehm (Ed.), *Meltdown: Money, Debt and the Wealth of Nations* (1999). An anthology of the first ten years of *Economic Reform*, the monthly publication of COMER. How the ransacking of the public common actually happened. including correspondence with those in power. A rich source for future historians. 385 pages. $25.

• William Krehm, *Towards a Non-Autistic Economics – A Place for Society at the Table* (2002). Some main features of the paradigm that have already emerged with notable policy applications. $20.

• *Economic Reform* subscriptions – $30 per annum. Back numbers of the 150 issues that have already appeared are available at $3 per issue. Where there are no printed copies available (20% or so of the issues) xeroxed copies will be provided.

Postage and handling charges are extra. Send orders to COMER Publications, 245 Carlaw Avenue, Suite 107, Toronto, Ont. M4M 2S6. Telephone: 416-924-3964. ∾

A Missing Footnote in the Great Health Care Discussion?

THE GREAT DEBATE on preserving Canada's health system or sacrifice it to the "American" system rolls on. In it the governments of three provinces are so certain of the superiority of the "free market" in providing health insurance, that they are even reluctant to wait for The Romanow Commission to complete its enquiry and assess the evidence. In this context the front-page article of *The Wall Street Journal* (9/04 "Insurer's Tactic: If You Get Sick, the Premium Rises" by Chad Terhune) is of great interest to Canadians. It poses the question: how much private medical insurance worthy of the name may still survive in the US, and for how long?

"Shaneen and Tom Wahl were paying $417 a month for health insurance when Mrs. Wahl was diagnosed with breast cancer in 1996. Their premiums began rising steadily, and by August 2000, the new rate would be $1,881 a month.

"Mrs. Wahl, whose cancer was in remission, tried to find out why. Unsatisfied with answers they got on the phone, the Port Charlotte, Florida, couple visited the Wisconsin offices of the insurer, American Medical Security Group Inc. There an executive explained why her premium was soaring: 'because of your dread disease.'

"It's called reunderwriting. Normally, companies that sell health insurance to individuals evaluate their medical history just once, at the outset. American Medical reviews customers' health at each annual renewal. If they have developed a chronic disease in the past 12 months, or filed claims that seem to foretell more claims to come, it raises their premiums."

There seems some doubt about who it is being insured against the customer's health risk – the customer or the insurance company.

"This isn't [to be compared with] some types of insurance, such as auto or homeowners' coverage. Drivers who have accidents or get speeding tickets can expect to see their premiums rise. But reunderwriting of individual health insurance faded away in the 1950s, in part because of regulatory pressure. Now, the practice is making a quiet comeback – a sign of how soaring health-care costs are driving some insurers to aggressive practices that can have severe consequences for consumers.

"American Medical, while minimizing price increases for healthy customers, slaps those who are less healthy with double-digit increases year after year. To pay, some squeeze their budgets, cutting out restaurant meals and tuition savings for their children. One Florida woman took out a second mortgage. Others boost their deductible to limit the rate increase, leaving themselves on the hook for more medical expenses."

Lending a Banker's Umbrella

Remember the old adage about your banker lending you an umbrella when the sun is out, and taking it back as soon as it begins to rain? Could it be that with the banks acquiring an increasing prominence in the insurance business, this has come to apply to insurance?

"Policyholders who become aware of reunderwriting say they sometimes hesitate to see a doctor for fear of giving the company reason to raise its rates. Ed Bonsignore, a 59-year-old who had a heart attack four years ago, was notified of a 60% rate increase at his last renewal date. He says that although his doctor told him to go to a hospital if he feels chest pains, he just takes a nitroglycerin tablet and tries to relax. 'I try to ignore the pains. Either I drop dead or it blows over.'

"Rising drug costs, advances in medical technology, an aging population and the retreat from tightly managed care are increasingly pressuring insurers' profits. But American Medical recorded a 56% earnings increase last year. The stock has just hit a 52-week high.

"This fall, an insurance industry group plans to ask state regulators to be more open to individual reunderwriting.

"Some insurers remain opposed, and others are waiting to see how much resistance American Medical faces. Three states have ordered the company to stop reunderwriting. Now Florida is trying to stop American Medical from selling insurance in the state."

"In an administrative complaint, Florida's insurance department accuses American Medical of illegally discriminating against customers based on their health. It also says the company violates unfair-trade-practices law by not warning policyholders that getting sick may drive up rates. In addition, a class-action suit seeks refunds for nearly 12,000 American Medical customers in Florida. The company sells individual policies in 27 states and is reunderwriting in more than half of them.

"American Medical says there is no discrimination because customers who present the same health hazard are treated the same. As for informing them their health could affect future premiums, that's up to the independent agents who sell the policies. It also says it is not covered by many of Florida's rules because of the way it markets to Floridians: they buy through a non-profit association incorporated in Ohio, a state that doesn't regulate health insurance rates.

"Timothy Moore, American Medical's general counsel, says rate increases are 'based on an individual's experience, just like auto or homeowners' insurance. If the risk changes, the premiums change.'

"'Their analogy between auto and health insurance is simply false, It's nonsense,' says Joseph Belth, professor emeritus of insurance at Indiana University.

"At most health insurers, buyers of individual policies are initially charged varying prices, based on medical history. Then all face roughly the same annual percentage increase, reflecting medical inflation and the claims filed by an entire policyholder group."

"About a half-dozen states not only bar reunderwriting, but don't even let companies do individual underwriting when they first sign up customers. These states, including New York and New Jersey, make insurers charge everybody in a certain geographic area the same rates, regardless of health, age, sex, or smoking habits. American Medical avoids those states."

The question then is not whether private health care insurance is more economical than public insurance, but whether private health insurance worthy of the name exists, or is likely to continue existing in any significant sense. To answer that, requires more than a devout belief that the free market will deliver everything more efficiently.

W.K.

A Systems View:
Stupidity in High Places?

TO AVOID being caught off guard or "blind-sided" it may be vital to understand, as fully as possible, all the realities which may bear on one's objectives. Stock market commentary is concerned with little else. Unanticipated problems afflict economic forecasts, but the hazards are multiplied when forecasters are constrained by prejudice. The achievement of an adequate perspective is no easy task; the future will always harbour unknowns. Yet much of what happens may be foreseeable in general terms, even if not by those who choose to remain blind.

In a current best seller, "Stupid White Men," Michael Moore[1] has a field day in pointing out the ways in which political leaders of every kind in the United States have attempted to ignore and falsify many of the realities with which average citizens must deal. His account makes obvious the degree to which those with power to make policies have failed to use common sense; they tend of overlook the kinds of considerations which are part of popular knowledge and concern.

Moore makes his points tellingly by engaging in the broadest kind of satire, and his language is rather unrestrained. As "stupid white men" he points to the Bush family and corporate buddies, but he extends his diatribe to almost all politicians, whether Republican or Democrat. Indeed, Moore finds little in their actual behaviors to distinguish these two parties. He has more respect

for Ralph Nader and his Green party (although disagreeing with Nader on matters of strategy). However the range and variety of Moore's commentary provide many pointers to realities often overlooked. Of special interest is the fact that he has obviously struck a responsive chord in many readers.

My own very selective interpretation of Moore's thrusts (not really a thesis!) runs as follows. The leadership of the most powerful nation on earth is essentially at a loss in dealing with problems of world peace, a shaky economy, energy, job security, health care, education and other societal needs in ways that are either fair or inspire confidence. The average citizen often finds that he or she does not count, that the needs of those who are not wealthy are little regarded by those in power. The economic system, education and political arrangements all discriminate against the average citizen, although information industries mostly disguise this fact. Freedoms of choice in the market as well as in politics and government are being eroded. Income inequalities persist and grow. The prison populations in the US have doubled in the past decade. Squalor, debasement, misery, hatred and death continue to be world problems. Efforts to support corporate globalization appear to be detached from such concerns.

We may ask: to what extent do economic forecasts take such factors into account? Such problems enter into the thinking of citizens and customers who have not bought into all the hopes of marketers for communications technologies and products. To what extent do market forecasters and others mislead us all with an obsessive emphasis on information they can chart and quantify?

While a random summary can point to the extent of the problems, what is really needed is a level of understanding on which coherent policies can be based.

Stupidity Easier to Handle

If the problems were only based upon stupidity, their resolution might be easier.

It adds to the problem that leaders in government and the corporate world are not lacking in intelligence. The real issues are deeper, and relate to political will and values, and those to whom economic and social benefits flow. It may be more accurate to speak not of stupidity but of greed and a broken – écrasé – intellectual center – literally, craziness in high places.

If these observations are not to be left as a mishmash of disconnected items, how may they be seen within a coherent system which offers priorities and provides some strategic purchase or leverage? How may we connect these particulars to the kinds of theorizing – economic and other – which may explain them? In what ways must our ideas and theories be altered if results are to be changed?

There are perhaps three major options around which such thinking may gather. The first is the kind of abstract/theoretical approach of traditional economics. Here the problem is that too much of such theory is not clearly related to the facts of experience. The guidance which it provides is much like guesswork. The second is the approach of Postmodernism, which, as a kind of mirror image or negative of theory, simply denies the possibility of any ideas adequate to provide a coherent understanding of the real world. The third strategy is a systems approach, which emphasizes process and builds on an analysis and specification of target values, and develops the organization required to meet these. Let us consider these three methods as possible ways to go.

(1) Traditional economic abstractions (e.g., general equilibrium theory, etc.) have been less than adequate in managing many of the real problems of the world. An increasing literature attests to the growing dissatisfaction with continuing reliance on such approaches.[2] Such methods are being seen as part of the problem, not of the solution.

(2) However, to reject all abstract ideas or theories as tainted in the same way is an unthinking response – although it may provide a convenient rationalization for a decision maker who wishes to be arbitrary. The influence of Postmodernism and mistaken ideas of relativism leads many to believe that there are no ways of thinking upon which human beings can depend to lead them out of the trap of subjective preference and forward in a common cause.

In a recent article, Varoufakis[3] points out the mistakes and hazards of such a view. While "modern thought" may have marginalized formal religion, it still appears to worship theory, and thereby holds on to an implied transcendence. Economics has pretended to the status of a kind of higher truth. Varoufakis comments: "Economics valiantly attempts to extricate itself with a touching commitment to mathematics but, sadly, it only ends up as a religion with equations." However, some theories are more capable of approaching objectivity than others.

(3) What is required is an approach grounded as objectively as possible in universals reflective of human nature, capacities and needs. Of course human knowledge is relative, but this only means that the frame of reference and perspective requires specification. As we have seen, men are far from god-like in their capacities, and they bring on many troubles when, in the grip of illusions, they fail to recognize what are objectively legitimate human needs.

Such ideas are not new. Indeed they have always been part of human experience.

But their significance has been suppressed under a variety of pretexts in the interests of those with power to influence political decisions in their own favour, regardless of the consequences for others. Only the exercise of such arbitrary powers can account for the disorders in which we find ourselves.

We need a systems approach based upon the analysis of values to be served – the human needs to be met and the priorities required when needs are in conflict.

There is no space here to explore the implications of this idea adequately, but some cautions may be in order. The approach required must link, by means of properly arranged and timed feedback, the progress of events with the objectives and targets to be achieved.

There may be no need, in practice, to distinguish stupidity from cupidity, craziness and/or conspiracies among the powers that be. The remedy is the same – an insistence on full disclosure. Demands by those in power for secrecy with respect to

decision processes and tribunals must always be treated with the utmost skepticism. Trust must be earned, and cannot be demanded. Without the possibility of verification, the presumption of trust cannot be secure. As every educated person is increasingly aware, transparency and accountability are essential in public life.

It is forlorn to hope that those who cling to power can be simply replaced by men who will wield power differently. Real power cannot be simply preempted or replaced. What is required is informed democratic control based upon clear comparisons of promises with outcomes. A freedom of information which amounts to noise obfuscates everything. National and world security must be sought in the arena of more adequately structured processes of public information.

Moore identifies many glaring problems in the public sphere, and it is obvious that he strikes a responsive chord in many readers. Satire and ridicule may be potent in helping arouse public opinion. But we also need to realize that ideas are available, intellectual tools that offer better prospects than those now commonly in use. Such ideas deserve more attention from those who claim the authority of leadership.

Bruce Buchanan

1. Moore, Michael (2001). *Stupid White Men…and Other Sorry Excuses for the State of the Nation!* New York: HarperCollins.
2. *Post-Autistic Economics Review:* www.btinternet.com/~pae_news/review.
3. Varoufakis, Yanis. "Why Critics of Economics Can Ill-afford the 'Postmodern Turn.'" *Post-Autistic Economics Review*, issue no. 13, May 2, 2002, article 1.

Does Corporate America Owe Royalties to Gogol?

WESTERN READERS used to enjoy a double tremor of enjoyment in going through the great classics of Russian literature – they combined a glimpse of Inferno complete with flame, brimstone and the assurance that it couldn't happen here. Outstanding on the list was Nikolai Gogol's *Dead Souls*. Chichikov, an entrepreneurial swindler has struck it rich. He buys up dead souls from landowners who had not yet registered their deaths. By Russian law the worth of an estate was registered and taxed according to the number of serfs that went with it. To more delicate ears, it all did have vaguely familiar ring, since there were tax advantages to the sellers as well as huge capital gains to the buyers. How privileged we in the West where such things were inconceivable!

Once again, the seditious streak in the reporting department of *The Wall Street Journal* (in contrast to the paleolithic editorial and oped pages), strips us of our ultimate illusions. (19/4, "Worker Dies, Firm Profits – Why? Where to Put the Dead Peasants" by Ellen E. Schultz and Theo Francis).

"Felipe M. Tillman loved music – opera, jazz, country. He played keyboards and drums, sang and was choral director at his Tulsa, Okla., church. To make ends meet he worked at record stores. One of those jobs was a brief stint in the early 1990s at a Camelot Music store.

"In 1992, he died of AIDS complications. He never bought life insurance, so his family received no insurance benefit. But CM Holdings Inc., then parent company of Camelot Music, did – $339,302 worth.

"Like hundreds of other large companies, CM Holdings took out life insurance on thousands of its employees, with itself as beneficiary. Most workers covered this way don't know it, nor do their families.

"The practice is as widespread as it is little known. Millions of current and former workers at hundreds of large companies are thus worth a great deal to their employers dead, as well as alive, yielding billions of dollars in tax breaks over the years, as well as a steady stream of tax-free death benefits. Nestle USA has policies covering 18,000 workers, Pitney Bowes Inc. 23,000, and Procter & Gamble 15,000 covered workers, spokespeople of these companies confirm.

"The coverage is called broad-based insurance, or corporate-owned life insurance, usually shortened [suggestively] to COLI. For years, companies could insure only key personnel deemed essential to the business. But a loosening of state rules in the 1980s allowed for an explosion in a new kind of COLI that covers rank-and-file insurance – known in the insurance industry as janitors insurance, or in at least one instance, dead peasant insurance. 'I want a summary sheet that has…the Dead Peasants in the third column,' one of Winn-Dixie Stores Inc.'s insurance consultants wrote in a 1996 memo."

Models from Russion Novels?

We do not know how many executives or insurance consultants even know who N. Gogol might be, but it seems that there is a sermon for us of this high-tech West in this detail of taxonomy the next time we feel the itch of superiority.

"Companies have put millions of dollars into COLI policies. These yield tax-free income as their investment value rises, just like the conventional whole life policies. Companies also borrow against the policies to raise cash. Public Service Co. of New Mexico has noted in public filings in recent years that it once set up life-insurance coverage on hundreds of its managers to raise money to eventually take its nuclear power plants out of service." However, there are a few other problems left stranded in the ingenious arrangement.

"Until 1996, the biggest lure was the tax deductions companies were taking on interest they paid on these loans. But then the Internal Revenue Service began disallowing these deductions, arguing in subsequent disputes that these COLI arrangements served no legitimate business purpose. Now the agency is investigating more than 85 companies that it says took $6 billion in illegal deductions, an IRS spokeswoman confirms.

"Companies can use the death benefits for anything they like. CM Holdings used $168,875 of the death benefit on Mr. Tillman for executive compensation, court documents show. The documents also show that $280 went to the 'Star County Children's Services' to help cover delinquent child-support

payments from a nephew of Camelot Music's founder who was working at the company at the time.

"John Sullivan, chief financial officer of Trans World Entertainment Corp., an Albany, NY, company that acquired CM Holdings in 1999, said he couldn't comment in detail because of a case pending in the US Court of Appeals in Philadelphia. In that case Trans World is seeking to have reinstated some interest-payment tax deductions it took on borrowings against its janitors insurance. Mr. Sullivan says that Trans World 'inherited the policies' from CM Holdings. The policies covered at least 1,400 employees in 1990. Younger workers will generate from about $400,000 to almost $500,000 in death benefits each, while older workers will bring the company about $120,000 to $200,000 each. (Younger workers yield larger payouts because, based on actual calculations, they are less likely to die soon, so the same premium amount buys more coverage for them.)

"Security and Exchange Commission filings provide some clues about the amount of tax dollars at stake. In 2001, American Greetings Corp. recorded a charge of $143 million for potential exposure to disallowed deductions on COLI-loan interest payments. R.R. Donnelly & Son Co., a Chicago printing company agreed this month to pay the IRS $150 million for disputed deductions related to policies covering more than 20,000 workers. And W.R. Grace & Co. indicated in its 2001 filings that it deducted $163 million in interest after 1992 and has current tax exposure of $57 million.

"The courts have tended not to accept companies' rationale for using COLI. 'We do not believe that the purpose of the [plan] was to fund employee benefits,' wrote Judge Robert P. Ruwe in a 1999 federal Tax Court ruling against Winn-Dixie. The supermarket chain brought the case against the IRS, seeking to reinstate deductions it took on COLI policy loans covering 56,000 workers. Judge Ruwe noted that Winn-Dixie had high staff turnover and didn't end up providing retiree medical benefits to most of its workers, while it continued to collect death benefits on those who leave the company before retirement. The judge concluded that the executives 'recognized that it was a tax shelter,' and that ultimately, over the 60-year life of the policies, the company hoped to save $2 billion in taxes.

"While the IRS can find out about COLI policies directly from the companies. disclosure requirements aren't tight, making it hard for others to determine just how much money is squirrelled away in the insurance. Disclosure rules don't require employers to distinguish between executive COLI and janitors COLI. Accounting rules require only that employers report increases in the aggregate cash values of their life insurance policies – and only if the increases are 'material.' Materiality isn't defined.

"Since Congress reined in some of the tax breaks, most employers have nonetheless left their janitors coverage in force. After all, they still enjoy the tax-free build-up of value in the policies, which adds to net income. (This income is referred to in financial statements under generic headings like 'other assets.') And then the death benefits go to the company, tax free. These future death benefits become an 'attractive off-balance sheet asset,' says Albert Schiff, president of the Association for

Advanced Life Underwriting and CEO of NYL Benefits LLC, a leading marketer of executive benefits. 'Companies understand that they have this significant downstream earnings growth. That's why they keep an eye out for the deaths of employees after they have left the company.'"

Given the amount of liabilities off-balance-sheet revealed in recent bankruptcy filings by major US corporations, the very notion of having unspecified growing assets kept off the books has a special allurement for US corporations. It should help the CEO sleep more soundly.

"In some states, including California, Michigan, Ohio, Illinois and Minnesota, companies are required by law to secure employee consent to include them in coverage. In that case, the employer may offer workers an incentive of a modest amount of life insurance without charge."

William Krehm

The Greenhouse Effect and Diesel-Powered Trucks

THE GREENHOUSE EFFECT is a phenomenon which takes place in the atmosphere, and as it is increasing it is causing trouble. So if we eliminate the atmosphere we will eliminate the greenhouse effect. Problem solved! Well not quite, because if we eliminate the atmosphere, as if we could, we would eliminate all life as we know it, including ourselves. Alternately what can we do?

Since the greenhouse effect takes place in the atmosphere and we want to know how and what is happening, let's look at the atmosphere first. In school we were taught that it is composed of 79% nitrogen, 20% oxygen and the remaining 1% is composed of a large number of other gases mostly in minute and very minute quantities. Of that 1%, $1/3$ is carbon dioxide, continuously blazoned as the greenhouse gas, which has increased from under $1/3$ of 1% prior to the industrial revolution to over $1/3$% today. This adds up to 100% and is our air.

What, then, is atmosphere? It's identified in the word itself. "Atmos" is the Greek for mist, moisture, humidity, and water vapour. So atmosphere is air with water in it. How much moisture? The average home is climate-controlled at about 21 degrees Celsius and 50% relative humidity contains about one gallon of water. If that "atmos" were condensed, we would have a gallon of water. That is over and above the 100% air as described above. If the temperature of your home were raised to 33 degrees and the relative humidity held at 50% the water content would increase to 2 gallons. So the amount of water in the atmosphere depends on the temperature of that atmosphere and its relative quantity to the temperature. That is what the term relative humidity means. Atmosphere is then the gaseous envelope of air, with moisture in it, surrounding our planet. Some scientists have done a lot of guestimating to come up with the figure that if all the moisture were suddenly to drop out of that envelope the levels of planet earth's oceans would rise by $1/3$

inch. That is a lot of water.

Now let's go on to the greenhouse effect. First let's examine a typical old-fashioned greenhouse. It has a wooden frame with a glass roof and glass walls. It is warmed with the rays from the sun. Our sun is a great, big ball of very hot fire. It emits tremendous amounts of all sorts of energy in all directions all the time. Two energies we are keenly interested in, or should be, are heat and light. These two come to us in very small invisible energy packages called rays travelling in straight lines and taking about 8 minutes to travel from the sun to our greenhouse. Glass is a very unique material. If you magnify it enough you'll find it full of holes. The holes are big enough that most light rays easily pass through and out of the glass greenhouse. That is why we can see through glass. The heat rays, however, are bigger; some of them pass through the glass but others cannot. Of those that do not, some bounce off the glass back to the atmosphere.

Others are smashed on the glass itself, heating it. That is why on a bright spring day the greenhouse glass is hot to the touch even when the surrounding air is quite cool. Then the heat rays which do pass through the glass hit things inside the greenhouse like soil, wood, leaves. Here again some rays are smashed, cease to exist, passing their heat energy to whatever was hit. The remaining rays which bounce off whatever they hit, by virtue of that hit and change in direction, are now bigger and slower. So they bounce out towards the glass roof or walls of the greenhouse they cannot pass out through, because they are now quite a bit larger. So when they hit the glass they become larger still and travel towards the plants and soil within the greenhouse. Where on subsequent hits all these rays cease to exist passing their heat energy onto whatever they hit. The heat is thus captured inside the greenhouse. This is the greenhouse effect. working in an old-fashioned greenhouse.

The Main Actors — Sun and Earth

Now let's go back out into the atmosphere. The main actors, characters or performers of the greenhouse effect, are our sun and our planet earth. Man with all his pollution, destructive behaviour, ego. conceit, and selfishness is in third position. These two performers, the sun emitting the rays of heat and our earth receiving and using them to help create and sustain life here, as we know it. Thus the sun's heat rays warm up the soil, vegetation, buildings, roads and water. As in the greenhouse, when something becomes smashed and that energy is passed on to whatever was hit, heating it. Thus the atmosphere of planet earth achieves the same effect as the glass of the greenhouse. Thus we have the analogous term "Global Greenhouse Effect."

What is a Greenhouse gas? Well, this is a bit of a misnomer. The common dominant gases carbon dioxide and methane, because their molecules are very large especially when compared with the other molecules of the atmosphere, have such a profound increase in heat when reflected back and trapped by the atmosphere. For instance the increase of carbon dioxide from just below $1/3$% of the air to just over $1/3$% has created a notable increase in both earth and atmospheric temperature.

As you have already realized, anything floating in the air can and will be hit by rays travelling down and up in the atmosphere. This includes water in various stages. Clouds are made up of billions and billions of little water drops. As a matter of fact water is by far the dominant greenhouse gas. Also in this category we have other pollutants in our atmosphere, some natural and some man-made like volcanic dust, aerosols, various vaporized chemicals, and smoke-like exhaust from internal combustion engines. In particular, the exhaust from diesel engines powering huge numbers of just-in-time, 18-wheelers. These engines emit both pollutants and a lot more particulate matter than most other sources. And yet these emissions can be greatly reduced by fitting each 18-wheeler tractor with appropriate devices. The technology and materials of construction for building such devices are readily available but the cost would be staggering.

My solution, cheaper and better, is to put those 18-wheeler trailers piggyback on trains. Use the tractors for pick-up and delivery only. Yes the trains are also powered by diesel engines, but we would have one train to several hundred 18-wheelers, each with its own pollution collection and abatement system carrying that same tonnage. This would make the transportation a lot cheaper, and very significantly reduce both greenhouse gases and particulate material. Imagine, if you can, all major highways, with almost no 18-wheelers, all that fuel saved and pollution greatly reduced.

Andrew Dwornik
Welland, Ontario

The Forgotten "Economic Centre"

BOB RAE, former NDP premier of Ontario, resigned recently from the New Democratic Party due to disagreement with the official NDP stand both on the Israeli-Palestinian hostilities and the party's opposition to globalization. In *The Globe and Mail* (23/04, "Beat the Liberals at their Game"), he sets forth his philosophy of government: "There is much current chatter about Canada having become a one-party state. The Liberals, in fact, govern by default. They alone have refused to abandon the centre. They have not seized power. The other parties have ceded it to them by telling the electorate they are all into increasingly obscure niche marketing."

Then, conveniently skipping over his own less than successful attempt to govern from the centre, he reviews the record in various countries and claims to prove his thesis – from Barry Goldwater in the US with his simple slogan "A choice and not an echo," to Margaret Thatcher and the defeat of the Socialists in the recent French elections.

"Most of the wounds in politics are self-inflicted. We live in a time of relative prosperity, of dynamic economic, technological and social change, and above all, in a time when the vast majority of us express confidence in ourselves and our futures." Such is the view from the law firm boardroom to which Bob Rae has retreated for his meditations.

The flaw in Mr. Rae's reasoning is that he concentrates wholly on the *political* center. At most he reaches to hockey for further evidence to support his creed. "Don't give up the centre of the ice, that's where the goals are scored." It would have been more to the point to recognize what eluded him while in office – the importance of holding the *economic* centre. That can be defined as the locus of concerns of most of the population. Had he done that he would not be writing glibly about our time as one "when the vast majority of us express confidence in ourselves and our futures," but more realistically concentrating on the lot of the majority of the population and the changes it has undergone in recent years. That is particularly so in a globalized and deregulated world where the underpaid and underemployed of the Third World have been mobilized to determine the living standards of labour and small business in the advanced countries.

Having done that, he would need go no further for evidence than the very issue of the *G&M* in which his article appears. In it an editorial entitled, "Overpaying Executives": "For many people in Canada's business community 2001 was a tough year. Earnings slumped, share prices fell and jobs were cut. Pain was felt everywhere – except, it turns out, in the executive suite. The *G&M's* survey on executive compensation, found in today's Report on Business, shows that pay packages for the chief executives of Canada's biggest publicly traded companies surged an astounding 54% last year – despite an average 13% drop in profits (not even counting Nortel's $27 billion meltdown) and a 16% decline in the TSE 100 index. Short-term compensation – which excludes gains from exercising stock options, but includes salary, bonuses and other perks – was up 25%.

"The continued bonus bonanza for Canadian CEOs is a betrayal of shareholders, who have seen their investments whittled down severely. After nearly a decade of compensation disclosure this isn't good enough – and it's time shareholders stood up and said so." The editorial page is above all suspicion of rabble-rousing bias.

In the same issue of the *G&M* there are no less than three articles on the plight of our cities. "Martin wants a new deal for cities" by Jennifer Lewington informs us that "Finance Minister Paul Martin says Canada's cities need a 'new financial deal' – including access to new sources of revenue – and called for a national debate on the issue. All options should be considered."

Bleeding Hearts in the Boardrooms?

No less significant is the detail that "Mr. Martin's remarks were made in response to a study by TD Bank Financial Group. The study, released yesterday calls for a 'new way of thinking about Canadian cities,' urging federal and provincial governments to create tax room for them from existing excise and sales taxes." Attention to the problem by the Liberals and the banks is certainly new, but suggesting to solve it out of excise and sales taxes hardly qualifies for that. That does indicate, however, that the Liberal government, that hogs the political centre, is becoming aware of that other crucial centre. With society heading into a morass of world-wide crises, something must be done about it. Even banks are becoming uneasy about the derelict state of the economic center to which they have made so notable a contribution. There is a long stretch of history involving the subject a former leader of a provincial NDP Party should be aware of.

In the early 1930s in the depth of the Great Depression, an ultra-right-winger R.B. Bennett, suddenly realized the need to occupy the economic centre to get reelected. So he brought over socially-minded economists from Britain, and with their help set up the Bank of Canada. It began as a privately owned bank (as was the Bank of England at the time), but like the BoE it was heir to the tradition of the Crown in holding the monopoly for coining and recoining precious metals By virtue of that, it was obliged pass on to the federal government most of the interest charged on the loans that it was authorized to make to the federal, provincial governments, or to any municipality or corporation guaranteed by a federal or provincial government. But the Liberal opposition under MacKenzie King did them one better. They ran and won the campaign of 1935 by outbidding the Conservatives for the economic center. A key plank in their program was the nationalization of the Bank of Canada. And that brought them to power.

Accordingly, in 1938 the Government bought out the 12,000 shareholders of the central bank, paying them a handsome profit. But to continue occupying that crucial economic center the Liberals felt that they had to keep an eye on the CCF – the socialist party that later became the NDP that Bob Rae took to power in Ontario in the early 1990s. While wresting the economic center from the Conservatives, they had to protect their control of it against the CCF. That put the CCF in a position to set the pace for the entire process – especially after the Second World War. Liberal governments looking over their shoulder at their leftist competition, introduced National Health Care, Social Security, and contributed to financing new universities and other post-secondary educational institutions across the country.

The national concern had been expanded to take in those of average and less-than-average incomes. The resultant prosperity allowed huge corporations to develop imperial ambitions. Capitalizing their current growth rate on the stock market, they commited themselves to further growth at the same rate or better. That involved their taking over the economy and government policy. That brought in the age of Deregulation and Globalization.

In 1991 when Canada's banks had lost much more than their total capital in financing mega-gambles in real estate and gas and oil, the Mulroney government stepped in to bail them out. The format of this grandiose act of misplaced charity was the phasing out of the requirement that the banks keep 4% of their deposits from the public as non-interest-earning reserves with the Bank of Canada. This – along with the Bank for International Settlements *Risk-Based Capital Requirements,* which declared the debt of industrialized countries to be risk-free requiring no additional capital for the banks to hold – enabled the banks to take on another $60 billion of federal debt. The same debt held by the Bank of Canada would have saved the federal government some $5 to 7 billion each year. That is the equivalent of a permanent bond of $100 billion. It was to en-

able Ottawa to deliver this annual entitlement to the banks that it slashed its grants to the provinces by an amount of similar magnitude. The provinces passed on the treatment to the municipalities. And that led to the curtailing of educational, social and health programs that federal Finance Minister Paul Martin, so belatedly laments.

The important thing today is for governments and parties aspiring to take over the government to once more recognize the vital importance of the economic centre. Without that holding the political centre will become more hot potato than blessing. As Bob Rae should have learned from his one term in power, and that we are all learning anew from the current plight of the Argentine.

Of course, mere pre-election chatter can in no way qualify as rediscovering the importance of the economic centre. Ever since the Liberals returned to power, Finance Minister Paul Martin has assured us that our "fundamentals are sound" – even as he was extending the policies of the Progressive Conservatives that bailed out the banks. While continuing to honour the $100 billion perpetual bond granted them by the preceding government, he deregulated our banks further. They could thus resume gambling their heads off in every aspect of stock market activities. And all the while he assured us that "fundamentals are sound," presumably because there were enough homeless trying to keep warm on every subway grating in our large cities. Significantly, we haven't heard that winged phrase from his lips for some months now. Instead we have page after page of our press reporting moral rot that has not only overtaken our stock markets, but our accountancy system, and apparently the government itself.

The investigative reporting and the rediscovery of the economic centre will not be seriously begun unless the suppressed facts of the banks' 1991 bailout is opened up for public scrutiny. Only the resources of the central bank as is still provided for in the *Bank of Canada Act,* will make the rehabilitation of our municipalities feasible. Failing that, these resources are likely to be preempted once again for bailing out our high-flying banks from their adventures in Mexico, Venezuela, the Argentine, to say nothing of Nortel, Enron, and Global Crossing, closer home.

William Krehm

The Brussels Consensus?

A S A SYSTEM becomes more complex, unforeseen risks almost inevitably spring up – something that those who rely too wholly on unilateral power positions tend to overlook. With increasing complexity the system they have put together develops vulnerabilities. That is particularly the case when unilateral power has to be presented as a consensus – as in "Washington Consensus" which, strange that it should have been overlooked, is an oxymoron. Occasionally, such unforeseen surprises may even have unscheduled benefits for the surprised party as well. An instance of this has arisen in the economic relationship between the United States and the European Union.

The Wall Street Journal (23/04, "Increasingly, Rules of Global Economy Are Set in Brussels" by Brandos Michener) reports from Hebron, Indiana: "For four years, Michael Aylesworth didn't plant insect-resistant corn on his 21,000-acre farm. The reason: regulations written by bureaucrats 4,000 miles away, in Brussels.

"Since many Europeans doubt the safety of such genetically modified crops, the EU requires that any product that contains even 1% of a genetically altered ingredient to say so on its label. It doesn't matter that many Americans don't care one way or another about eating so-called genetically modified organisms, or GMOs. Multinational food processors don't want to buy any corn that might create marketing problems in Europe."

Tables Turned?

Note the unfamiliar pattern: remote consumers have unexpectedly acquired a veto power over the global corporation that must have a global market to operate economically. There could well be a windfall advantage to the American consumer that he may not care to recognize. What he does recognize in such areas is to a large extent a function of what is allowed to be featured in the media of the corporation's home territory.

"By shunning the high tech seeds, Mr. Aylesworth figures he lost about 7% of last year's crop to a voracious pest called the corn borer. This spring, he took a risk and decided to plant 100 acres with corn that's genetically modified to poison the bug. He hopes to sell the grain as animal feed, which Europeans do not require to be labeled for GMO content – yet.

"'I refuse to suffer anymore,' Mr. Aylesworth says. 'Because of Brussels, I've been using technology that was five to 10 years old.

"Americans may not realize it, but rules governing the food they eat, the software they use and the cars they drive increasingly are set in Brussels, the unofficial capital of the EU and the home of the executive body, the European Commission.

"Because of differing histories and attitudes toward government, the EU, a 15-nation trading bloc with a population of 376 million and the world's second-largest economy, regulates more frequently and more rigorously than the US, especially when it comes to consumer protection. So even though the American market is bigger, the EU, as the jurisdiction with the tougher rules, tends to call the shots for the world's farmers and manufacturers."

This has already resulted in Microsoft Corp. modifying their contracts with software makers and internet-service providers to give consumers a greater choice of technologies. It has induced McDonald's Corp. to eliminate the soft-plastic toys it served with its Happy Meals."

Tweaking Uncle Sam's Nose

To what extent does the phenomenon also include a certain pleasure in tweaking Uncle Sam's nose? That is impossible to quantify, but undoubtedly it is a factor. In the words of the *WSJ*: "Brussels' growing influence is often overshadowed by global concerns about American hegemony. Washington's lead in foreign policy and American culture still dominates the media, but some companies learn the hard way that Brussels rules. It wasn't until EU regulators torpedoed General Electric Co.'s bid to acquire Honeywell Inc. last year – a deal that the US had already approved – that GE began to lavish the sort of attention on Brussels that it devoted to Washington.

"For many of GE's businesses, ranging from light bulbs to plastics, 'almost 99% of new regulations will come from the EU over time,' says Jeffery Immelt, GE's CEO. When Mr. Immelt was head of GE's medical systems unit in the late 1990s, the EU laid down radiation-dose standards for X-ray equipment that were tougher than those in the US. As a result GE worked with European experts to create a dose-management system that it now uses world-wide.

"Regulators on both sides of the Atlantic are trying to figure out how to protect consumers' online privacy. But while the US has mostly promoted industry self-regulation, the EU, in October 1998, laid down the law: Europe's residents have the right to know what data has been collected on them online, and to get that information changed, if it's inaccurate, or force the collector to delete it. Last July, the EU threatened to cut off trans-Atlantic e-mail traffic if US companies failed to guarantee these rights.

"US companies initially fought the regulations, calling them unnecessary and burdensome. But over the past two years, 176 companies ranging from film manufacturer Eastman Kodak Co. to chewing-gum maker Wm. Wrigley Jr. Co. have signed 'voluntary' agreements to abide by the EU rules. Most had little choice. As global businesses they didn't want to go to the expense of creating special Web sites or data-processing procedures just for Europeans. 'There's only one program of privacy protection at Microsoft' and its Europe's.'

"The power to set the regulatory agenda for the US is a relatively new one for the EU which has about 31,500 employees in Brussels. The rules often start as an attempt to reconcile various national standards within the EU, to make cross-border commerce easier. EU critics in Britain, Ireland and regularly bash EU bureaucrats for impinging on national sovereignty.

"When it comes to consumer or environmental protection, EU regulators often invoke what they call the 'precautionary principle.' A sort of better-safe-than-sorry code. The approach evolved partly from a series of food scares in Europe over the past 10 to 15 years, involving such threats as 'mad-cow disease,' the misuse of growth-promoting hormones in livestock feed and, more recently, dioxin contamination. It also reflects the fact that Europeans are more inclined to expect government to protect them.

"Worried about trade with Europe, the Illinois Department of Agriculture last year asked farmers not to plant a Monsanto Co. corn that isn't approved in the EU. Kraft Foods Inc, of Northfield, Ill., says it won't use genetically modified ingredients such as vegetable oil in the Toblerone chocolate and Milka candy bars that it exports from Europe to 150 other countries including the US.

"Greenpeace and other environment activists are pushing the EU to expand its labelling rules to include meat, dairy products and animal feed. That would present a new hurdle for US farmers who would be faced with the choice of eliminating genetically modified seeds or losing buyers who do business in Europe."

There is then such a thing as good globalization, but it is not high on corporate lists.

W.K.

The Widening Gap

THE ALL-PERVADING PUZZLE that has even begun troubling our media is how the greatest boom on record could have turned overnight into the biggest bust. This extends not only to the market valuations of our large corporations but to their morality. The consequent disarray borders on despair because the basic economic theory that we had been educated to regard as a law of nature hinders rather than helps us out of the muddle. Its most recent flowering in the deregulated and globalized market was to have handled all problems: "Fundamentals were sound, because inflation was in check." To the extent that things were not satisfactory, more deregulation was the certified answer. Government had to be kept small, and out of our affairs. Government budgets had to be balanced at all costs, and one of the favoured ways of doing so was to privatize as many public assets as possible. This would not only leave "us" with more money to spend, but with the certitude to spend it wisely since, after all, we had "earned" it.

Government debt, no matter how defined, had to be kept to a minimum, without taking into account the public investments for which it was incurred. This reduced the public sector to impotence. Little did it matter what legislation might be on the books, for there would not be enough staff to enforce the laws.

What Good Are All the Answers
If No Questions Asked?

It was a reassuring doctrine that appeared to hold the answer to all questions, but few questions were asked. That is why when the collapse came, it took the world completely by surprise. All the unquestionables were suddenly brought into question – to the very accountancy. We are faced with the need of figuring out what the economy might be from the bottom up.

We do not have far to go. The trouble certainly has much to do with our supposed knowledge of the future. Though increasingly uncertain, as the world grows more complex and our authorities – academic and governmental – tried understanding it with an idealized model devised 130 years ago to cover up the problems that had already become critical. Through the market and a misplaced spot of calculus, we have been led to believe that we have an unfailing knowledge of the future.

Those of a religious bent can assign the present disarray into a repetition of the primal sin in Eden – encroaching upon the secrets of His Creation, and downgrading Him to a sort of Vice-President with a reduced amount of perks and options.

More prosaic souls will turn to what Greed Unbounded has done to Prometheus, leaving his morality as well as his liver in tatters. The future which by design was to be inscrutable has been reduced to peep-show status, with the financiers ever at the head of the line to see what lies ahead. The rest of society are forever paying admission for questionable reports of what those in power assure them they have seen. That is the set-up that has allowed our financial moguls to coin the unknowable future as a second currency until recently at times more highly prized than the legal tender of the land. The economy itself was reduced to a world of make-believe, until the lights go out, and everybody goes home – those who still have one.

With liabilities, on the other hand, a more modest note is struck. Keeping them off the balance sheet became a specialty of the largest accountancy firms. This is what has happened both with derivatives and with off-balance-sheet partnerships.

But impressing the uncertain future to address the shortcomings of a far from reassuring present turns increasingly difficult as the real facts of the late corporate boom surface. Intercom companies that had yet to earn their first dollar attained stock market capitalizations of billions of dollars. Price-earning ratios lost favour with stock market analysts who accepted in their stead the conquest of market share on the assumption that they could all be translated into earnings. A strange slip-up of many economics PhDs, since market shares – illustrated as cuts of a pie – by definition add up to a single pie. And you don't have to be A. Einstein to grasp that the "market shares" of all but the winning corporations in a given field will fall towards zero in value. But to forestall such mournful thoughts the phrase "Economic Darwinism" was invented. And clearly anybody who had made a killing on the stock market was automatically classified as a superman with elitist genes to go out and conquer.

This was celebrated as the distinctive feature of the "New Economy."

Wherever we look, we find imputed certainties of the future filling holes and cracks not only in the accountancy but in the statistics and the trade relationships. Thus *The Wall Street Journal* (1104, "An Engine of Jobs Sputters as Rates for Insurance Rise" by Christopher Oster): "Tulsa, Okla. – When Bennett Steel Inc., a small construction firm went to renew its insurance coverage shortly after September 11, President Dave Bennett got a shock. There was a 122% increase in umbrella-liability rates, 66% more for liability at job sites, and 51% more for vehicle coverages.

"The higher premiums many small and mid-sized businesses hundreds of miles from New York now face are the legacy of a decade of imprudence among insurers – a period that combined a relentless price war with aggressive risk-taking From 1993 to 2000, underwriters slashed rates, sometimes as much as 40%, and fought for customers by loosening terms on all types of business policies from directors and officers' liability to medical malpractice packages to workers' compensation insurance. Insurers eventually reached the limit." The insurance conglomerates, increasingly dominated by the international banks, and thus occupying seats at the table at the right of the Creator, seemed to think they were privy to His designs. On these, in any case – as a sort of re-insurance – they sincerely believed they held a veto. However, "by 1999, they were paying out, on average, $1.07 in claims and related expenses for every $1 of premium received on business coverage. During the bull market of the '90s, insurers could sustain these losses on underwriting because the shortcomings were more than covered by investment income the insurers earned on premiums."

A booming stock market – which they ordained would go on forever at least in their press releases – automatically confirmed their unfailing wisdom.

"The risky lines of business that appealed to insurers several years ago now haunt them. Cologne Re, a unit of Warren Buffett's Berkshire Hathway Inc., took a $220 million charge in 1999 for losses on workers' compensation business. More recently, Chubb Corp.'s Dean O'hara lamented $143 million in losses the insurer suffered on surety bonds it sold to guarantee delivery of natural gas by Enron Corp."

The wheels on which this grand chariot rides are not only their own knowledge of the future, but the knowledge of the extent to which other companies may be committed to likewise knowing that future. Moreover, the dangers of over-extended bets in space can be as dangerous as those in time. "Shoemaker stick to your last" is a potent argument against too much globalization and deregulation. It should be the motto over the door of every Ivy League business school.

The understatement of insurance and other risks during the late boom exaggerated not only earnings, but collateral, and capitalization in general.

We are witnessing an analogous dependence on futures which heightens the risks of today's transactions in the zero-rate financing of our overexpanded world auto industry.

But another source of explosive surprises is the detail that our link with the future – no matter what form that may take – is interest rates. These in turn are not only used as the "one blunt tool" to keep prices flat by pounding most of society on their heads, but are likely both to reflect and to add to the mounting bankruptcies and capital losses.

If somebody had set out to design a system of inherent and mounting instability, he could hardly have come up with anything more perversely efficient than the one that is collapsing around us.

William Krehm

Dodging the Issue

"'ECONOMIC GROWTH surpassed the Bank of Canada's projections in February, but it's too soon to say whether the surprising strength will persist,' BoC Governor David Dodge said yesterday. 'If the economic data going forward continues to surpass expectations, Canadians should expect interest rates to rise more quickly than expected. We would have to reduce monetary stimulus more quickly,' he told the Senate banking committee. 'It's true that there are going to be pockets of real slack.' He recognized that telecommunications, information technology, machinery and equipment are all lagging far behind the rest of the economy, and the rate hike this month probably won't help them. There is little solace I can offer you, he said, explaining that the bank made its decision to raise rates based on average and aggregate growth figures, and not based on individual regions or sectors.'"

Mr. Dodge is engaged in looking after the health and welfare of favourite aggregate statistics, and nothing will convince him to turn to disaggregated figures to find out what is really happening in the economy. Based on the traumatic lesson of the "Roosevelt depression" that hit the world in 1937, months ago we noted its similarity with the current "recovery." Since inventories had been depleted after years of the deep depression, the Federal Reserve began warning of incipient inflation, and sterilized the gold starting to flow in from Europe in anticipation of the war to tighten money. Result: a resumption of the Depression. The same applies to today's "recovery." The Japanese system of keeping inventories and delivering materials and parts shortly before needed to effect savings on inventory financing has made the economy more vulnerable than in the 1930s to inventory depletion. Moreover, the Deregulation and Globalization that congest our highways and ports, expose us to breakdowns. The Twin Tower Disaster has created tight bottlenecks at all borders. All these factors have pushed up the effects of inventory replenishment.

The rapidly advancing pollution resulting from the population explosion, and the technological advances have widened the gap between the Gross Domestic Production figure, that ignores such "externalities" and the real state of the economy. Clearly if we wish to measure meaningful economic "growth," we must deduct from the raw output statistic the damage to the environment and to society itself (crime, disease. the destruction of subsistence economies) that will have to be remedied at the risk of creating irreparable damage to society. We must in short "internalize" the "externalities."

If we fail to – as clearly Mr. Dodge does – we will be leaving "off-balance-sheet" liabilities in exactly the same way that got Enron, Global Crossing, and a host of other high-tech companies into their present troubles with the courts.

No Routine Matter This

The significant thing about the present crisis seems wholly to escape Mr. Dodge. He deals with it as a routine affair – the turn of the cycle that would inflate prices periodically if our central bank did not forestall that occurrence by raising interest rates. But we are confronted with the spread of corruption within large corporations so recently deregulated and allowed to intermingle incestuously with Wall St.'s ambitions. Leading auditing firms cooperated in the planning of the questionable strategies that left enormous sums off the official books, and played games with the effective due dates of the two sides of a single transaction to show immense fictitious earnings. The supposed moral inspectors were in cahoots with the main players, for rewards of like dimension. Nothing like this has been seen for sheer debauchery of spiritual supervisors since the bubble of simony burst in the Renaissance Catholic Church. That gave rise to the Protestant revolt, and the Counter-Reformation.

And just as the trauma of that sent the doctors of the faith delving into the sacred texts on which the Church was founded, so must our economists – with a determined nudge from the victimized public. They must review what there was about their fundamental doctrines that made this possible, nay invited, such abominations. For without the denaturing of economic theory to hide what was deemed best covered up, such an outcome would have been unthinkable. Towards that end the official economic model assumed an economy of equally tiny traders whose uprightness and candor were guaranteed by the workings of a "pure and perfect" market.

We must not allow Mr. Dodge to trivialize the wrenching problem that has overtaken the world about whether the rate of "growth for the first quarter is likely to be 5% at annualized rates rather than the 3.5% to 4% expected.

But how is this possible, given the tightening of control of the financial interests that profited from and inspired the trend? The answer is simple. The volume of scandal emerging from the late boom has reached such proportions that the veto powers of our financial oligarchs have been shaken sufficiently so that concerned citizens can put some restraint on the shamelessness of their performance.

Evidence of this is coming in on all sides. The militancy has long been there, but it must be informed and organized to fight and win battles as well on more sophisticated planes. The court order blocking Hydro One, the sale of the transmission lines of the former provincial power company is a case in point.

And *The Wall Street Journal* (25/04, "Wall St. has an Unlikely New Cop: Spitzer") reports: "Earlier this year New York Attorney General Eliot Spitzer worried that his probe into possible conflicts of interest involving Wall St. stock-research analysts hit a dead end. Then in January Mr. Spitzer was handed a folder of documents subpoenaed from Merrill Lynch & Co., an early target in the probe. That's when he spotted several e-mails indicating in colorful language that analysts harbored private doubts about many stocks they were strongly recommending investors to buy.

"Get me the damn e-mails! All of them," Mr. Spitzer told Eric Dinallo, the office's bureau chief for investment protection.

"The e-mails – which revealed Merrill's analysts, including former star Henry Blodget, referring to companies as 'crap' and 'dogs' – have vaulted 42-year-old Mr. Spitzer into a lead role in the investigation of research analysts, although the Securities and Exchange Commission traditionally has been Wall St.'s top cop." Across the continent "top cops" haven't been doing an acceptable job. By every means it is necessary to turn up the heat to interest other arms of government and the legislatures to step in where possible.

"The release of the e-mails at a news conference, and the resulting glare of publicity, has brought Merrill to the bargaining table as its stock lost nearly 12% in value following the disclosures."

William Krehm

Showbiz Takes over Government — Happy Days are Here Again!

RECENTLY I saw a movie on the Vietnam War, *Path to War*, produced by HBO. The drama of a nation slipping into carnage, humiliation, and near-bankruptcy was presented as seen in the White House, Congress and the Pentagon. What added to the pathos was the cloven personality of Johnson – a Shakespearean character, if ever there was, embodying vulgarity, cynicism, raw ambition scrawled large over a determination to leave a legacy of greater justice for the downtrodden. The whole Manichean philosophy of the strife between good and evil was bottled up in one man. The very bluster and bullying, meant to clear the decks for his social goals and get him out of the shadow of his predecessor, drew him relentlessly into the cruellest of defeats. Even in martyrdom there are class privileges. Kennedy's assassination made him an icon. LBJ's destiny was to be spat upon by the very classes he had been intent on helping.

The final malignancy of the Greek fates was that his advisers – the Robert McNamaras, the Clark Cliffords – were as clueless as the Pentagon brass of what they were up against in Vietnam – clueless and utterly irresponsible, reversing their original counsel in either direction, and unable to look beyond the next election.

The empty hall was in itself the usual tribute to the excellence of the offering. More astounding was that the admission was marked down – whether in celebration of the Queen's jubilee or a sign of the rotten state of the economy – 2 seniors for $8 and change. Have we beat inflation! Undoubtedly a tribute to Paul Martin's wizardry in the Finance Department before his being sacked by that other wizard who specializes in running upstairs on camera to prove his qualifications for another couple of terms.

Pondering the question, we arrived at another explanation: the statesmen at Ottawa and Queen's Park have driven their respective buffoonery to the point of eliminating the private sector from the comedy business.

Even the columnists have begun cottoning onto what is cooking here. Take Bruce Little's column in *The Globe and Mail* (6/06, "Martin's Finance Legacy secure as ouster fails to move markets"): "Financial markets paid Paul Martin a fine compliment this week after his ouster as finance minister. They wobbled for a moment and then yawned.

"It wasn't that they were happy to see him go; they weren't. It wasn't that they were delighted to see John Manley succeed him, knowing little about John Manley, they were largely agnostic on that point. The market's immediate response was captured in a droll line by economist Douglas Porter of BMO Nesbitt Burns

Inc.: 'We indicated yesterday that the pressure on the Canadian dollar was likely to be short-lived, fully expecting it to last a few days, not minutes.'

"The loonie fell in overnight trading in Asia, but bounced back once the trading floors in North America got busy.

"In a nutshell, that was Mr. Martin's legacy as Finance Minister – an economy strong and Ottawa's finances so sound that they can outlast the man himself.

"All this seems so commonplace now, that many forget how different this is from the years before 1993.

"After nine years in which Mr. Martin exceeded every bottom-line forecast he made, many don't recall that in their deficit forecasts in the 1980s and 1990s the government always fell short of targets, often by a huge margin.

"Does anyone remember the autumn of 1992? Canada was just beginning to escape from a prolonged recession, the deficit was more than $40 billion, Canada was preoccupied with a referendum on the Charlottetown constitutional accord and the currency markets of Europe were in turmoil. The Canadian dollar fell from 84 cents (US) in late August to under 78 cents three months later. Interest rates which had been declining for months, suddenly screamed higher. The bank rate soared to 9% from 5%.

"Or the Mexican peso crisis of late 1994 and early 1995? When the peso collapsed, investors [surely the writer means 'speculators'!] went looking for other high-debt countries to pick on and found Canada. The dollar fell to 70 cents from 74 over three months and the bank rate jumped to 8.5%."

Confounding "speculators" with "investors" is at the root of our troubles and reveals the common game of both Chrétien and Martin.

Hamlet without the Danish Prince

"But look now at 1998, when Asia's financial crisis pulled down a whole region and a Russian bond default sent investors scurrying for safety. World commodity prices – and the currencies of big commodity producers – sank. The Canadian dollar fell from to 63 cents from 68, but this time it took an interest rate increase of only one percentage point – to calm the markets.

"But then, of course, Canada's quarter-century love affair with deficits was over, in no small measure because Mr. Martin had sold the need for change to the Canadian public. He could not do it alone. Without Mr. Chrétien's steady support, we would still be grappling with the stream of deficits that left Canada crippled by rising government debt and vulnerable to sharp interest increases every time global financial markets got nervous."

Surely this version of our financial history is like staging Hamlet and forgetting the Prince of Denmark.

In 1991, after our banks had as a group lost far more than their entire capital, they were bailed out by the Mulroney government. This was achieved by slipping through parliament a bill that did away with the statutory reserves that required them to put up with the Bank of Canada a token proportion of the deposits they received from the public. This enabled the banks to quadruple their holdings of federal debt by taking on another $60 billion without any significant increase in either their capital or the money in their vaults.[1]

The statutory reserves, though not used for the purpose in recent years, had provided an alternative or a complement to raising interest rates in an effort to beat back real inflation. Raising the reserve requirements decreased the leverage of the banks' money creation. Lowering it helped bring the economy out of a recession.

These measures and the high interest rates imposed by the Federal Reserve of the US "to lick inflation" were largely responsible for the explosion of government debt.[2]

The Liberals, on coming to power, made no effort to even question what had been dictated to our government by the Bank for International Settlements (BIS) and the International Monetary Fund. The budget was eventually balanced despite the entitlement assigned to the banks at the expense of the most vulnerable members of our society. The Liberals had been swept into power partly because of their promise to repeal the Goods and Service Tax, a regressive tax that favours the richest sections of society. Mr. Martin did not honour that promise. On assuming office he organized a bogus consultation of economists at a downtown Toronto hotel, where a sifted assortment of economists were given three minutes each to express their agreement. No one who questioned those policies was allowed the floor. The custom of a *papier-mâché* democracy was taken over intact from Mulroney.

Other factors were decisive in reducing the debt and producing a surplus:

1. Most of these originated with the US Fed. The Mexican and East Asian crises and the near bankruptcy had frightened the daylights of the international financial system. A disorderly retreat ensued from the insane high-rate "final solution" of "inflation" that conventional economists had made no effort to understand.

2. Given the deep recession inflicted on the American and world economy by high interest rates at the time, balancing the budget was anything but advisable. *As the private sector suffers massive capital losses and crouches low, the public sector must step in to fill the gap.* The budget was balanced by creating serious deficits in human and physical infrastructures – in health, education, the environment, social security. These deficits were covered up – the exact equivalent of the off-book liabilities that have made a bad joke of the accountancy and morality in the corporate world today. That is the dead rat under the floorboards that befouls the public scene in Canada today. The issues being debated in the pitched battle for the Liberal succession avoid any mention of that most basic problem, but the resulting moral stench is unmistakable.

3. At the very time that the statutory reserves were being phased out, the banks were also being deregulated. This made it possible for them to apply more and more of their enhanced credit-creative powers to build up their own speculative portfolios. The ratio of their aggregate assets to the cash in their possession that had stood at 11 to 1 in 1946 rose to a peak of 405 to 1 in September, 1998. To make matters worse, deregulation had made it possible for the banks to invest more of the credit they created in areas incompatible with banking. Often they were ignorant of the fields they entered. Unlimited greed converted into an ideology was their only radar. Multiple conflicts of interest resulted – for example between market analysis and underwriting, between credit card operations and retail banking. To make matters worse, the assets of the banks appeared on their books at their historic values. Keeping much of their liabilities off balance-sheet became a widespread practice in the corporate world to enhance stock market valuations.

4. The deregulation of our banks shifted the dominant revenue in our society from money-lenders to speculative finance, closely intertwined with the stock market. High interest rates are poison to anything connected with the stock market. This shifted the consensus in financial policy-making away from the dizzy interest rates of the 1980s. Starting with January 1996, the Clinton administration in the US began to depreciate the physical infrastructures of the federal government over their useful life rather than writing them off in a single year. However, this was reported as *"national savings"* in the Bureau of Economic Analysis figures rather than *investment* – something that it most definitely was not since it was not held in cash but spent as investment. Nevertheless, it was a statistic to keep interest rates down that the Clinton administration was after, rather than analysis that could alienate the "political center" that it was determined to hold.[3] The distinction between savings and investment is crucial to Keynes's analysis, the great taboo in reigning circles. That is why Bruce Little talks of "investors" rather than "speculators" going after the currencies of exposed countries in his paean on Martin.

Twisting Auditors' Arms

In Canada the Auditor General refused to give unconditional approval of Martin's two previous budgets until capital budgeting was brought in. After a long standoff it was finally adopted in mid-2000, to be actually brought in during 2002. However, its significance was misrepresented by the Auditor General in his report – he argued that since no new funds would come to the government in this recognition of what had already been spent, it did not warrant new outlays. However, in the early nineties when grants to the provinces had been slashed because of a deficit wildly exaggerated by faulty accountancy, social investment had been reduced on such grounds. Reversing the process and recognizing social investment for what it is, would clearly warrant restoring the cuts in federal spending. Mr. Martin, however, backed the Auditor General into a Faustian deal. He finally agreed to bringing in capital budgeting provided that the Auditor General would in his report include the shameful passage stating that the belated recognition of capital investment did not warrant further capital spending. What does this remind you of? Obviously the current criminal proceedings in the US against Enron's auditors, Arthur Andersen Inc., for their approval of Enron's off-balance-sheet disposal of its liabilities. Mr. Martin's role thus falls short of knight on a white charger.

What separates Chrétien and Martin is little more than an unprincipled contest for power. Statesmanship has been reduced to obtaining the blessings of Wall St. and Bay St. that themselves are beset by massive bankruptcies, financial and moral.

In our last issue we dealt in detail with the antics of the Eves government in Ontario rushing in to privatize the Ontario power system and awarding the former civil servant that heads one of the private successor companies a retirement provision when the privatization is completed of six million dollars with corresponding salary and perks. The public indignation that resulted derailed the initial public offering that Bay St. was depending on to get through a dismal year.

With clowning like that in high political circles, what chance have the best comic-tragic films?

William Krehm

1. Krehm, William (2002). *Towards a Non-Autistic Economy – A Place at the Table for Society* (p. 80). COMER Publications.
2. The Bank for International Settlements *Risk-Based Capital Requirements* introduced shortly before contributed to helping the distressed banking systems throughout the world by declaring the debt of OECD countries "risk-free" requiring no additional capital to hold. The details can be found in Krehm, p. 80.
3. Krehm, p. 125. Due to an uncorrected typo the date of Clinton's introduction of capital budgeting is given as 1966 instead of 1996.

Globalization and Quality of Life

IT IS NOW CLEAR, especially since 9/11, that current globalization brings both good and bad news. Along with increased trade, spreading democracy, intercultural communication, we humans have also globalized crime, terrorism, money laundering, drugs and arms trading, prostitution, child labor and ecological degradation.

To me the issues concern how to optimize the benefits of globalization to reach the 2 billion members of the human family still living in deprivation, ill health, ignorance and despair.

This means globalizing human rights, social justice, opportunities for human development and a new Earth ethics, as symbolized by the 16 principles of the Earth Charter at www.earthcharter.org, which is widely viewed by international lawyers as the companion "people's treaty" to the Universal Declaration of Human Rights.

The traditional scorecards of "progress," Gross National Produce (GNP) and its narrower version, Gross Domestic Product (GDP) no longer adequately measure aspects of society and quality of life. The "Washington Consensus" model of economic development is now under serious question from insiders at the IMF and World Bank no less than by hundreds of scientists from other disciplines, as well as by the suffering citizens of Ar-

gentina and the former "tiger" economies of Southeast Asia.

Broader scorecards of "wealth" and "progress" are needed and now available. Pre-eminent is the Human Development Index (HDI), pioneered by the United Nations Development Program annually since 1990, which was developed by two of my esteemed colleagues, the late Mahub ul Haq and the very much alive Dr. Inge Kaul, editor of the groundbreaking *Global Public Goods* (Oxford University Press, 1999). The World Bank's Wealth Index (1995) added to the debate about "development" by assessing 60% of national wealth as "human capital," 20% as "environmental capital" and only 20% as the "capital" traditionally measure by economists (plant, equipment, infrastructure and financial assets).

This quiet revolution in theories and assumptions about development has yet to hit the mainstream. But the revelation from the Enron and Arthur Andersen scandals have now opened up the entire issue of how we measure not only national wealth and progress, but also assets, revenues, profits and debts of corporations.

The Calvert-Henderson Quality of Life Indicators are Calvert's and my *pro bono* contribution to this re-assessment of national wealth and progress. Calvert and I have developed our Quality of Life Indicators over the past several years as a new tool for assessing national trends.

Why have our Calvert-Henderson Quality of Life Indicators for the US struck such a chord worldwide? The answer lies in the changing debate about how to measure human progress. During the US boom years of the late 1990s, many countries were challenged, even shamed by constantly rising economic indicators in the US. The endured patronizing advice by US economists and officials about following the US model, deregulating their markets, opening up their capital accounts, increasing exports, and generally following the "one size fits all" model of the Washington Consensus.

The dangers of unregulated currency trading were exposed after the Asian crises of 1997 when millions were plunged back into poverty. I predicted in the 1980s that taking down all the "firewalls" between the world's economies would lead to excessive and volatile capital flows.

Our 12 Indicators of Quality of Life in the US: Education, Employment, Energy, Environment, Health, Human Rights, Infrastructure, Income, National Security, Public Safety, Recreation, and Shelter gave them the rest of the story. Many of our multi-disciplinary statistics probed deeper: from the crises in US health care (with over 40 million people without insurance); the misguided military priorities that warned of new vulnerabilities including terrorism; the dis-investment in public infrastructure; the continued lag of energy-efficiency *vis-à-vis* Europe and Japan.

Hazel Henderson

Hazel Henderson's latest books are *Building a Win–Win World* (1996) and *Beyond Globalization* (1999). She can be reached at www.hazelhenderson.com.

Convergence on Catastrophe

IN MY RECENT BOOK, *Towards a Non-Autistic Economics – A Place for Society at the Table*[1] I "drew up a list of every known ransacking of capital accumulation in the real economy…for an unending series of improvisations to fuel the stock market boom" I added: "Our list is necessarily incomplete because it is still ongoing." For these practices do not interact by simple addition.

For the past two years we have experienced a series of explosive lessons on the structures of deception created by the deregulation and globalization of the 1990s. In *The Globe and Mail* (25/04, "A Bright Idea that wasn't: The Emperor had no clothes") Philip Evans, senior vice-president with the Boston Consulting Group in Boston, examines the implications of the head of BCE, Jean Monty, stepping down from his post due to the collapse of the myth of mergers and the synergies of convergence. Without these mirages the recent Mega-Boom and Bust of the stock market could hardly have taken place.

"Like Gerald Levin, whose grandiose visions for AOL Time Warner have similarly succumbed to mundane reality. And perhaps like Jean-Marie Messier, the chairman of Vivendi Universal, who yesterday faced his own angry shareholders.

"The word 'synergy' is almost invariably nonsense. Academic studies show that 80 to 90 per cent of corporate acquisitions fail to return any value to the acquirer. Indeed, acquisitions can be interpreted as conspiracies between the acquiring management and the acquired shareholders – a swap of money for power. 'Synergy' is the fig-leaf.

"In the media and communications industries synergy has a particular and tendentious rhetoric: the rhetoric of 'convergence.' This is the vision of a one-stop provider of information and entertainment, content and distribution, telephone and cable, subscriptions and advertisements. Preferably global. A break from the obsolete past of phone wires and printer's ink.

"When Time Warner merged with America On Line, part of the justification was cross-selling. AOL would promote Time Magazine (for free) and Time would do likewise. There would be tremendous cost savings by not having to purchase such promotions. Except for the obvious point that if the cost is zero anyway, two separate companies could swap promotional space, as they have been doing for years. Another big justification came from the 'creative energy' that would be released by bringing diverse and talented people into a tired, bureaucratic organization, notwithstanding the fact that the diverse and talented people promptly left because – guess what – they don't like working in tired and bureaucratic organizations.

"Another strategy, hinted sotto voce, would be to give AOL privileged or even exclusive access to Time Warner Cable customers. Management was shocked by the suggestion that this synergy might be a euphemism for coercion, but the regulators took no chances: The new convergent conglomerate was explicitly forced to maintain open access, just as if the two firms had never merged.

"So it all came back to the vision thing – a dog's breakfast of properties and technologies from which something unspecified would emerge. A chance for dull businessmen to put themselves on the cover of their publications.

"Convergence really does work if you are a monopoly. Phone companies love monopoly because it is their heritage: In contrast to Microsoft, they are the nice monopoly. Perhaps that explains the appeal of the convergence strategy: It's a way to put the Bell system Humpty-Dumpty back together again."

Elsewhere in the same issue of the *G&M* ("Monty ends twenty years with a clean break" by Gordon Pitts) the bare bones of the tale emerge. "Speaking with little emotion, Mr. Monty announced he had resigned as chairman and CEO of the company. He pointed out that he had brought BCE, the holding company for the country's biggest phone company, into the Internet, satellite TV and a new growth era."

Easy Come, Easy Go

"He also acknowledged what had brought him down – the quagmire of Teleglobe Inc., the long-haul telecom carrier that he had bought for \$7.4 billion in 2000" [for the 77% of it that BCE did not already own].

The figure \$7.4 billion is interesting, because that almost exactly what BCE had come out with by unloading its Nortel subsidiary at the top of the market on an unsuspecting public. It was allegedly the most invulnerable of high tech companies, that not only had a tryst with the future, but in Canada practically owned it. Today it sells for little more than 5% of its peak value. The sales it went on reporting were largely financed under the table by itself creating the illusion of a strong demand for its products. More recently several Teleglobe competitors like 360 networks and Global Crossing have been much in the headlines for the disclosures in their bankruptcy filings. Communication seriously begins in fact when intercommunication companies file for bankruptcy and have to make a clean breast of what is on their books and what is under the table or has already gone bye-bye as rewards to their promoters. BCE has stated that the Teleglobe mess will cost it \$7.5 to \$8.5 billion in the second quarter.

BCE sold a 20% interest in Bell Canada to SBC Communications including a put that allows SBC to sell it back to BCE at a 20% profit. To meet that highly likely deadline Mr. Monty's successor has already arranged to sell 20% in its yellow page directories to pension funds and insurance companies.

And who has been chosen to clean up the BCE mess – one of an interesting group of former federal civil servants who earned their careers in the private sector by setting up the sale for a song of huge public realms, and deregulating the private sector to make possible the miracles of convergence. Then they started new careers at the head of the new corporations. At times the move from the public sector to the private corporations is seamless. No period between his public service and private sector is allowed for the hero to be hung out to dry. The flabbiness of morality even celebrates such "efficiencies."

Michael Sabia, the new CEO of BCE is in the words of Jacquie McNish a man "who has made a career out of turning thankless tasks into triumphs" (*G&M*, 25/04). "As a senior bureaucrat in the Department of Finance a decade ago he helped design and promote the reviled Goods and Service Tax, which now generates more than $25 billion for the federal government." The only thing that remains to add is that this tax comes disproportionately out of the hides of the underprivileged, who spend their entire income rather than accumulate it as capital. That stroke alone would have assured Sabia a glowing career in the private sector. "He joined the Canadian National Railways in 1943 to help transform the bloated, money-losing Crown agency into a profitable company that launched the largest initial public offering of its time in 1995. All this from a 48-year-old former civil servant who was a stranger to the communications sector until he joined BCE in 1999.

"Backing Mr. Sabia's leadership in BCE is Paul Tellier, a BCE director and widely respected CEO of CN. Mr. Tellier, a former civil servant, hired Mr. Sabia at CN and was instrumental to recruiting him to BCE."

Throughout it all there are the giant footprints of the opportunist career man in the sand. He arranges to bring with him into the private sector a portion of the public domain that he was hired to manage in the public interest. What does it remind you of? Of course, of the Russian oligarchs who were high bureaucrats under the Soviet regime, and knew just where the corpses and most valuable assets were buried.

Again in the same issue of the *G&M*, Margaret Wente ("When smart men go so wrong") puts that into perspective: "All across North America people were having stupendous visions of the day when we would all watch movies on our cellphone and trade stocks through our cable companies, E-commerce would be king. The guru of convergence was a revered futurist named George Gilder, who promised that we were on the brink of the great new wireless techno-fibersphere. Risk-taking companies that got there first would get unspeakably rich, and dowdy stodgy companies would be road kill.

"The AOL-Time Warner deal triggered a giddy chain of convergence: Vivendi, Bertelsmann, Canwest, and on and on. No one wanted to be the wallflower at the dance. You would be exposed for not having vision. So Mr. Monty sold off Nortel which he figured was the Old New Thing and set out to find the New Things. BCE did what pretty well everyone was doing in those days. It hired a bunch of big thinkers. The big thinkers would help them identify their core competencies and figure out how to leverage them. That's how they discovered that they were not the boring old phone business after all. They were in the *communications* business.

"Then they bought a bunch of outfits with names such as Teleglobe and Emergis. Most people didn't have a clue what these companies did, but their names were very cool and very modern. Then they bought some content. Which is us [i.e., the *G&M*] I suppose.

"All these acquisitions were supposed to grow like crazy and create synergy. Synergy is the magic twinkle dust. If you have it, you can boost your profits 33% a year forever.

"Instead, the wheels fell off. Teleglobe and Emergis tanked. George Gilder was wrong. Or else he was right, but not yet, which amounts to the same thing.

"At AOL Time Warner, the wheels fell off, too. It just took

a goodwill write-down of $54 billion. Its market value is now one-third of what it was in January of 2000.

"Nortel tanked, too, after Mr. Monty sold it to buy that other stuff. Now he has been replaced by clean-up crews who fire people, sell off things, and count their beans very carefully."

William Krehm

1. Toronto: COMER Publications, 2002, p. 96.

Justice to Whom and by Whom?

DEMOCRACY is a wonderful system, better than any known alternative. But in performing, it frequently kicks up more dust than accomplishment. It can be career- rather than result-oriented, particularly when what is needed is axing the roots of recurrent evils. Easy solutions? We know none. It requires an ever vigilant public, and constantly renewed sources of information and analysis to serve as bees for bureaucratic bottoms. Only that will ensure that good deeds persist beyond the photo opportunities.

A case in point is the meteoric appearance in the sky of New York Attorney General Eliot Spitzer who has grabbed the ball from the federal SEC in the investigation of stock market malfeasance. Chancing upon some e-mail evidence in which big-time analysts of the nation's largest brokerage house expressed their private opinion in barnyard terms of the very stocks they were promoting to unwary investors, he forced a $100 million out-of-court-settlement on the firm. So far so good. But how far does that go and to what good? *The Wall Street Journal* (22/05) trumpets "Merrill Lynch to Pay Big Fine, Make Changes to Settle Inquiry New York Attorney General Wins $100 Million Payment and Oversight of Analysis." Sounds good. But let's take a second look. In this world, if you are confronted with enough money changing hands, you tend to mistake it for a solution.

"Mr. Spitzer's goal is to use the Merrill settlement as a 'template' to wring similar changes and fines from the rest of the industry, especially firms such as the Salomon Smith Barney unit of Citicorp Inc. and Morgan Stanley & Co. that cater to individual investors.

"Many investors who lost money when the technology-stock bubble burst in 2000 say they relied on the bullish calls of Wall St. analysts during the late 1990s boom. They also say they were left holding the bag when analysts remained positive as stocks plunged. *None of the money in the Merrill settlement will go to investors. But the Merrill accord – and any future agreements with Wall St. firms – could benefit investors with civil claims against securities firms alleging they were misled and spawn further litigation.* [Our emphasis.]

"The settlement promises to push the SEC to aggressively pursue its own investigation of analyst practices. SEC Director of Enforcement Stephen M. Cutlur promised yesterday's settlement 'is not the finish line,' though his agency, Wall St.'s top regulator, has been in the unusual position of watching from the sidelines as structural change is forced on a major firm. Competitive pressure on its own may force other firms to match Merrill.

"'This is not just a Merrill Lynch-only settlement,' asserts John Coffee, a security-law professor at Columbia University. 'The rest of the industry will be dragged screaming and kicking into about the same resolution very quickly. [They] can't have Merrill Lynch advertising that the rest of the industry's analysts are shills for their investment banking clients.'"

In the picaresque novels of 17th century Spain a stock character was the old crone whose specialty was repairing impaired maidenheads. Something akin is afoot on Wall St. today. Given the stakes and daring of previous gambles, the $100 million fine handed out to Merrill is just another business expense that will be covered by future business along the lines of the past.

WSJ publishes some of the previous fines that Wall St. firms have paid and gone on to greater heights.

Fines Paid by Wall Street Firms

Year	Company	Amount
1988	Drexel Burnham Lambert	$650m
2001	Republic New York Securities	$569m
1993	Prudential Securities	$371m
1996	Paine Webber	$298m
1992	Salomon Brothers	$290m
2002	Merrill Lynch	$100m
2001–2	Credit Suisse First Boston	$100m
1996	NASDAQ Stock Market	$100m

"At the heart of the Spitzer investigation is the changed role of Wall St. analysts. For years they toiled in relative obscurity, writing reports on the financial conditions of companies or industries, forecasting their earnings and recommending which stocks investors should buy or sell. But with the 1990s boom securities firms competed to underwrite record numbers of 'new' stocks and record fat fees. And the firms' analysts, instead of simply assessing the stocks, increasingly promoted them.

"Analysts have become stars; Merrill's Henry Blodget, Salomon's Jack Grubman and Morgan Stanley's Mary Meeker became symbols of the tech-stock mania and earned millions of dollars for big underwriting deals. In the process they gave investment bankers ammunition to be cheerleaders for companies their firms wanted to do business with."

In Merrill's case, Spitzer got his hands on private e-mails in which their star analysts expressed their contempt for the very stocks they were recommending in glowing prose. "[Their] statement of contrition was less than the admission of wrongdoing Mr. Spitzer had sought.

"Under the terms of the deal reached with Mr. Spitzer Merrill vowed to take a series of steps to separate its investment-banking and research departments. Analysts will no longer be evaluated and paid based on their help in winning investment-banking business. Mr. Spitzer gave up his demand that investment-banking business be spun off entirely.

"Merrill will also appoint a 'compliance monitor' to oversee the firm's research practices. That executive is subject to the approval of Mr. Spitzer. He said he prefers someone not employed by the firm but wouldn't rule out a Merrill executive.

"Under the terms of the agreement, Mr. Spitzer will drop the investigation into individuals examined in the probe. Mr. Spitzer said he expects other security firms to come forward voluntarily to seek settlements with his office. 'I prefer to have the industry take the lead here and get together' to offer him a broad settlement along the lines of Merrill's."

Applied to criminal law, it would save government a lot of money – and presumably increase its efficiency – if it nailed one miscreant with a fine and invited the others to come up and enter the same deal.

There is thus a delicate regard for major financial miscreants who paid many previous fines – much greater – only to go on to bigger accomplishments.

Nonetheless, "Mr. Spitzer has a big weapon in his arsenal: a New York State law known as the *Martin Act* [that] gives the attorney general wide authority in bringing civil and even criminal charges against firms. And unlike the federal securities law, the state law doesn't require Mr. Spitzer to 'show criminal intent.' He merely has to show for example, that a firm failed to disclose a conflict of interest, such as investment-banking relationships, when issuing research that ultimately hurt investors."

Canadians should closely follow the prosecutions of financial conglomerates in their brokerage activities in the US in all their strengths and weaknesses. For the day is drawing nigh when our government will have no choice but address the famous abuses that have flourished in the fields so richly fertilized by the bank bailout of 1991 (the end of statutory reserves) and the deregulation of the banking system that followed in its wake. Just about every major brokerage house has been taken over by a bank, with devastating effects for the small investor. "Compliance" officers do exist in large brokerage houses in Ontario, after which the victim can take his case to the trade association (IDA) where he will be assured of a polite letter. Then he is permitted to direct his complaint to the Ontario Securities Commission, from where he used to receive a similar message in the name of Her Majesty.

Get Yourself a Lawyer and Sue Your Broker — Canada's Version

Today, with stock scandals hogging the headlines, the OSC has barricaded itself against even approach by retail complaints. It is not listed in the telephone directory. If you track it down, you are in effect advised by a recorded message to get yourself a lawyer and sue your broker. Suing a bank is costly sport. The OSC itself is an outstanding scandal. Under cover of such urbanity, the most obvious scams are practised. We will cite a single very obvious one that has gone on for years.

Brokerage houses will sell listed stocks on margin, i.e., if the stock value is over the minimum set by the individual broker, it remains effectively the property of the broker until the debt is discharged. Fair enough. But the broker is allowed to lend the shares used for such collateral to third parties and collect a rental on it. On the client's statement it will then be listed as "segregated" meaning "that it is not available." The only conceivable use that third party would have for "renting" such shares is to sell them – i.e., to "short" the shares to drive down their value in the hope of buying the stock at a considerably lower price to pay the rental fee and, above that, make a profit. Obviously that is against the interest of the person who bought the stock and put it up with the broker as collateral for the unpaid portion of the purchase price.

Neither any part of the rental fee paid by the party shorting the stock to the broker, nor any information – even on request – from the ultimate owner for an explanation of what "segregated" might mean when it appears on his monthly statement is provided.

A case has even come to our attention where a stock below the minimum value to qualify as marginable was parked in the client's account. Repeatedly it was rented out by the broker and marked "segregated" on the client's statements. Then came a day shortly after the collapse of all stock markets in the wake of the Twin Tower attack, and with all sorts of marginable security available in the account for the broker to sell off to put the account into good shape, it went directly to shares that were not marginable and merely parked in the account for convenience, and sold them off days before the shares embarked on an ascent that led to their tripling in value. Abuses of that sort have gone on for years. They have become even more brazen with the increased volatility of the stock market, and the greater need of the brokerage-banks-underwriter conglomerates to make fast bucks to cope with their massive gambling losses.

William Krehm

Do we need Insurance if we can bottle Certainty like Coca-Cola?

THESE DAYS the excessively entrepreneurial are as busy on the dimension of time as Einstein was a century ago. Einstein, however, had a better idea of what he was up to.

Take this front-page story of *The Wall Street Journal* (3/06, "In Echo of Sept. 11, a Bitter Spat Roils Aviation Insurance" by Mark Maremont): "Burlington, NC – Not long after the Sept. 11 attacks, a small army of auditors showed up at a non-descript brick building in this sleepy textile town. Hauling in nine photocopiers, they began sifting the records of Fortress Re Inc., an insurance firm. Though little known in its hometown, Fortress was a bold player in the high-risk world of aviation reinsurance. As an agent for three large Japanese reinsurers, Fortress was a leading seller of policies that covered big chunks of the losses in many aviation catastrophes. For 24 consecutive years, Fortress reported to the Japanese insurers that the business it oversaw was profitable.

"But when 3,000 lives, four jumbo jets and the twin towers of the WTC were lost on 9/11, alarms went off in Tokyo. Concerned about their exposure two of the insurers sent in their own auditors to look at Fortress's books.

"One insurer, Nissan Fire & Marine Insurance Co., contends it has uncovered a massive fraud in which Fortress hid some losses by, in effect, borrowing the money to cover the claims.

While the Japanese insurers were incurring a giant bill, a Nissan Fire lawyer alleged in a hearing in federal court in Greensboro, NC, Fortress's owners were 'skimming off' hundreds of millions of dollars in part via a Bermuda firm they owned.

"Fortress's general counsel, Glenn Drew, denies any fraud or other wrongdoing and says the suit is just an effort by a big insurer to avoid paying losses from risks it knowingly incurred. The insurer profited for years, he says, but 'after 9/11, all of a sudden they didn't like the deal they cut.'

"In Japan Taisei Fire & Marine Insurance Co., one of the three big insurers that worked with Fortress, has become only the second casualty insurer to file for bankruptcy since World War II.

"The events have roiled the global reinsurance market – essentially, insurance for insurance companies, which buy policies from others to lay off part of their own risk. Some who bought policies from Fortress wonder if they'll be able to collect. At the same time, Fortress's sudden absence from the market has exacerbated a post-9/11 surge in the cost of aviation insurance.

"Nissan Fire's suit against Fortress is on hold while the parties pursue arbitration, in which Fortress has filed breach-of-contract and other counterclaims.

"Maurice D. Sabbah, 73, founded Fortress 30 years ago, and was soon joined by Kenneth H. Kornfeld, 55. Despite the 'Re' in its name, it wasn't an insurer. Instead it managed a reinsurance business for the Japanese insurers – committing them to policies that Fortress sold, and taking a share of the profits. Aviation eventually became the main focus.

"Say an airline takes out a policy from a group of primary insurers for up to $1.5 billion per crash. The primary insurers, not wanting to keep so much risk, decide to retain only the first $100 million of it. They unload the rest to reinsurers by buying several policies from them. One might cover the layer of losses from $100 million to $400 million. Another might cover the losses from $400 million to $700 million and so on. These reinsurers, in turn, often seek to minimize their own risks by buying reinsurance themselves, from still other companies.

"If there's a plane crash, every insurer that that has covered a layer of risk has to pay its part. It's a big global industry that includes such prominent companies as Swiss Re Group, General Electric Co., Berkshire Hathway Inc., and the Lloyd's of London syndicates. As an agent, Fortress sold reinsurance policies on behalf of the three Japanese insurers.

"They gave Fortress broad authority to commit them to policies. Some of these entailed hundreds of millions of dollars of exposure, but their deal with Fortress called for it to obtain reinsurance that cut their exposure to just $49,000 per policy.

"The business model: Fortress would collect premiums on the insurance it sold, then attempt to buy reinsurance for a lower premium. The difference – minus fees and claims – was profit, to be shared between the Japanese insurers and Fortress. Such 'managing general agency' setups have been used for decades, but are relatively uncommon in the reinsurance end of the business.

"For years, it seemed to work brilliantly. Fortress in fiscal 1983 reported net profit for its Japanese clients, before deducting its slice of $2 million after taking in $15.4M of premiums. By 1991, premiums taken in had soared to $584 million and profit was $154 million. Of that Fortress earned almost $60 million."

More recently Fortress dominated an estimated 40 to 60% of the aviation insurance niche – that covering losses between $50 or $100 million and $400 million of crash claims. In any major disaster claims are likely to be made within these ranges. It is thus amongst the riskiest portion of the business. And their prices were surprisingly low. Many insurers stepped back from taking advantage of the seeming bargains because they felt that sooner or later Fortress was bound to get into trouble.

Nevertheless, from 1998 to 2000 Fortress reported to its Japanese clients that it had achieved for them – before its commission – $275 million.

"At Nissan Fire, though, executives grew suspicious. There had been a series of hugely costly crashes: TWA 800's explosion off New York's Long Island, the Swissair crash off Nova Scotia, Egyptair and Alaska Airlines planes that dove into the sea, and the Concord disaster on takeoff from Paris. Fortress had exposure to all of these, yet it reported little impact on profits."

From there it was all downhill for Fortress. Nissan Fire requested permission to examine Fortress's records, but the request was fended off. They retained lawyers. September 11 made it clear that huge losses must have been incurred. At that point Nissan Fire was allowed to have PricewaterhouseCoopers examine the books on their behalf.

It is one of the charms of the contemporary business world, that for every big problem there is a seeming solution, that in fact is not really what it appears to be. "In place of traditional reinsurance that transfers risk to others, Nissan's suit says, Fortress made extensive use of a much-less-costly product known as 'financial reinsurance.' Instead of transferring risk, this is like a line of credit from a bank. If there is a claim, financial insurance pays off – but by making what is essentially a loan, which has to be paid back in future years through higher premiums.

"The Japanese insurers knew that Fortress was using financial reinsurance to some extent. But Nissan Fire says it didn't know that most of the protection Fortress bought for them was of this variety. It also says that Fortress improperly treated the proceeds from financial reinsurance – which have to be paid back – like payments from traditional insurance policies. What's more, Nissan Fire says, Fortress improperly used the bogus profit figures to calculate its own commission – one third of the profits. Over the past 20 years Fortress paid itself $528 million as a share of the profits, when the business was 'barely break-even.'" Fortress's lawyer retorts that "it started buying financial insurance for the Japanese companies in 1991 and they were fully aware of it. High prices and scarce availability made traditional insurance 'no longer economically feasible.' Resorting to this was the only way it could 'prudently manage its book and ensure profits to members.'"

And thus the law suits trundle on.

However, this tale raises the question how much risk management and insurance are feasible in our deregulated, globalized world where mobile interest rates are singled out as the one stabilizer and a highly unstable one at that. In such a setting many of our crucial reckonings are based on the fiction that we can foretell future profits sufficiently well to book them as current earnings, and, moreover capitalize them on the assumption that they will continue to expand in the future at the rate at which a questionable accountancy has presented them as having expanded in the past.

To make matters worse, the one remaining financial nexus between the present and the future is interest rates. Beset with all these uncertainties, the further question arises: with so much verging on the make-believe in the economy, why should insurers feel obliged to cling to more rigorous standards? That is the big question that is gnawing at the guts of our society. It must be answered.

William Krehm

Focus on Options

IT COULD BE a game of button, button, for its sweep of territory, and how closely the players approach the button's lair without finding it. But then it had been put out of sight with the closest mating of art and cunning short of fraud. And in our turbulent times that boundary is frail and ever harder to respect.

The creation of money – long a defining trait of sovereignty – had been bestowed on the banks. For its money needs the government itself was made dependent on the bankers who nevertheless come to it at least once a decade when they lose their capital in the gambles allowed them by Deregulation. Not only were they generously afforded the help denied to more deserving needy, but they were freed to do more of what they set their hearts on – lending an increasing multiple of their cash that in many cases they had already lost. For them the very Decalogue had been compressed into a single stricture: if money is kept scarce and dear, except where the banks themselves suffered losses in their adventures, "fundamentals are sound."

But the chosen system has collapsed in a miasma of corruption, and the quest is underway in corporate halls for what brought this on. Commissions of blurred number are enquiring how the laws can be reshuffled to prevent this happening again. But despite all the valiant press releases, the button itself that might keep statesmanly trousers demurely in place has still not turned up.

Inevitably the search has shifted to options, the device by which corporate heads reward themselves by being empowered to buy their corporation's stock years ahead at today's and even yesterday's prices. But let *The Wall Street Journal* (26/3), a sheet noted for seeking out the very indigestible truth in its news columns that it disputes heatedly on its editorial page ("Perk Police – Stock Options Come Under Fire in Wake of Enron's Collapse" by Greg Hitt and Jacob M. Schlesinger): "One day last month lobbyists from 30 of the nation's biggest companies met in a conference room [in Washington] at the offices of software giant Oracle Corp. Another 30 joined in via speaker phone.

"They represented business as diverse as Citigroup Inc., and

Oracle's archival, Microsoft Corp. In the wake of the Enron Corp. scandal, they were united in a common cause: saving stock options – a goodie widely blamed for fuelling many of the corporate excesses of the 1990s. Their common foe: a broad new coalition of lawmakers from both parties, Federal Reserve Chairman Alan Greenspan, big institutional investors and global accountants.

"Their opponents say options have bred a culture of irresponsible greed showering executives with outlandish paydays that sometimes reach into the tens and hundreds of millions of dollars.

"Last month, when he introduced a bill to rein in the benefits of options, Sen. Carl Levin, a Michigan Democrat, described the cycle this way: Most executive pay packages rely heavily on options, encouraging corporate managers to push accounting rules 'to the limit,' to make their financial statements look better so that their stock prices will go up and executives can cash in their options.'

"Options also help companies pump up the earnings they report. Accounting rules don't require companies to treat options as other forms of pay – as an expense that reduces profits. Mr. Levin's bill would deny companies lucrative tax deductions if they don't do that."

Picking Up More than Gum Wrappers in the Aisle

"The last serious clash over stock options was in 1994, and the business lobby won it handily. Odds are that it also will prevail this time around, with a pitch that options make the American economy perform better. As Lisa Wolkst, a lobbyist for the International Mass Retail Association, puts it, 'it makes more likely that employees will pick up the gum wrapper in the aisle.' In the course of the operation, executives, however, pick up a lot more than gum wrappers.

"For years, detractors have complained that options provided executives with obscene returns, but that didn't seem to bother the public so much, as long as other investors prospered too. Then, as the Enron scandal unfolded, the nation learned that top Enron executives had continued to make many millions of dollars by cashing in their options even as they were leading their company toward ruin. Enron Chairman Kenneth Lay realized $123.4 million from exercising stock options in 2000. By contrast, most ordinary shareholders ended losing the bulk of their Enron investments and thousands of Enron workers lost their jobs and much of their retirement savings.

"Testifying before Congress last month, former Enron CEO Jeffrey Skilling conceded that stock options offer an 'egregious way to inflate a company's reported earnings. Essentially what you do is issue your stock options to reduce compensation expense, and therefore increase your profitability,' explained Mr. Skilling, who realized $62.5 million in 2000 by cashing in Enron options.

"Current rules require companies to report the cost of issuing options only as a footnote in their annual reports. Treating stock options as an expense would lower the earnings of nearly every major corporation in the US. Out of the stocks in Standard & Poor's 500, only two companies – Boeing Co. and Winn-Dixie Stores Inc. – have chosen to count stock options as an expense in their financial reports.

"The business lobby is fighting hard to defend options because the stakes are so high. Consider Oracle, which hosted the mid-February strategy session. Oracle CEO Larry Ellison gained $706 million last year from exercising stock options. And according to Bear Stearns, Oracle's operating income was $933M higher for 2001 than if it had given employees cash instead of options.

"Legendary investor Warren Buffet, one of the few business executives who rail against options, makes a simple argument for counting them as a cost: 'If options aren't a form of compensation, what are they? If compensation is not an expense, what is it? And, if expenses shouldn't go into calculations of earnings, where in the world should they go?'

"Accounting-rule writers grappled with the issue as far back as at least 1972. Not only weren't stock options widely used back then, but the challenge of calculating their cost was daunting. So officials decided that options needn't be treated as an expense.

"During the 1980s, however, stock options became increasingly popular, particularly in Silicon Valley. where high-tech startups offered them not only to executives, but to all ranks of employees."

They became in fact a supplement to the official money supply with particular attraction to the payees because of the possibilities of tax evasion or deferment, and even fabulous capital gains. They were like a hybrid of money and a lottery ticket, combining the best of two worlds. In Silicon Valley, not too long ago, suppliers fought to receive them rather than notes bearing the picture of a long-dead politician.

"By the early 1980s, there were sophisticated new methods available for projecting the long-term value of stock-option grants. Companies were beginning to use a mathematical model developed by economists Fischer Black and Myron Scholes to tell employees how much their stock options were worth. Mr. Scholes later won a Nobel Prize in economics for the model. The Federal Accounting Standards Board (FASB) reasoned that if companies could estimate the long-term value of the options to their employees, they could also give shareholders an accounting of the long-term cost of those options.

"And so the FASB voted in April 1993 to require companies to treat options as an expense, based on the estimated future value of those options. In 1994, thousands of high-tech workers gathered in Northern California for a raucous pro-options demonstration called 'Rally in the Valley,' sporting T-shirts and placards with such slogans as 'Stop FASB' 'Federal Accounting Stops Business.' The high-tech sector circulated studies showing corporate profits falling by 50% and that capital would dry up as a result of the new rule.

"The Clinton Administration weighed in against FASB. So did financial investor groups who said the rule change would muddy financial statements."

Today these claims make bitter-sweet reading. Option-happy Enron, Global Crossing, and countless other corporations have applied for bankruptcy protection. The damage has not been confined to any particular group of stakeholders in the companies affected. It undermines the very notion of trust without which there can be no serious economy. For the mathematics underlying the "Nobel" prize for Economics awarded to Scholes and his colleague were based on the premise that all agents in the economy are so insignificant in size that they are helpless to influence prices, or anything that counts. The worth of such "science" is no greater than that of the salesmen on Wall St. who peddled Enron. The "Nobel" jury might as well award its prize directly to the brokerage supersalesmen.

William Krehm

Must we Restructure Economic Theory?

IT IS EITHER naive or excessively cunning to mistake what has happened to the world economy for a cyclical event. What we are confronted with today is the breakdown of the assumptions underlying the "pure and perfect" market and its acrobatic extension into Deregulation and Globalization. These have devastated corporate as well as government accountancy. Not even basic morality has been left untouched.

The time has come to rethink the very structure of economic theory. Despite its immense inconvenience, there is no way of avoiding the task. Like discussions on the trials of old age, what clinches the argument is the alternative.

It wouldn't be the first time economic theory underwent drastic restructuring. Marginal Utility distracted attention from the bloody class warfare that climaxed with the Paris Commune of 1871. The need arose to blinker society's gaze onto the market from the factories whose horrors were portrayed by Dickens and Emile Zola. Wage workers were recast as just traders, each comparing the satisfactions of selling his labour at the wage offered against the joys of leisure in his parlour. Of the three independent creators of marginal utility theory two – Jevons and Menger actually published their great books in the actual year of the Commune, while Leon Walras did so two years later. The theory slackened the bonds with the real world. They provided the genes that eventually, when they put the economy into orbit, gave us Enron.

We must take a hard look at the claims of equilibrium theory to scientific status. Strike one: its profusion of differential and integral signs can't be taken seriously, because of the assumptions to make possible their use – all the actors of the economy are of such insignificant size that nothing they do individually can affect the trend to equilibrium of the "pure and perfect market." Strike two: shoving such non-market areas as the environment, the household economy, the subsistence agriculture of the world, and society itself into the category of "externalities." Clearly this is the distant source of the present off-balance-sheet liabilities that are convulsing the world.

The great classical economists in contrast sought out links with the real world. Their means of achieving this was the labour theory of value, or, alternately, the cost of production theory. These were structured in opposite ways. The labour theory felt that it knew the final value figure in advance. Its approach is breaking up a total rather than adding up the parts to get at the final figure. The amount of "average labour" that enters the production of a good is distributed between capitalist, landlord and worker on the market. It used to be considered a weakness of the labour theory that it was hard arriving at a figure for "average labour." That has turned into a strength: it leaves an "air hole" for new factors previously ignored that force themselves upon our attention. Adam Smith, the real Adam Smith, not the stuffed manikin that economists in uniform have invented – actually switched from one to another of three theories of value, depending on the angle of vision most suitable for the subject at hand. Moreover, value theories are most helpful for what they warn us not to do, rather than for the precision of their answers.

The cost-of-production value theory invites us to add up columns for answers – much as accountants do in their better moments.

The Perils of Number Crunching

This variety of historical value theories suggests the importance of studying interrelationships and structures – rather than just crunching disembedded numbers. That has been the main trend of mathematics used in economics for almost two centuries. Group theory has occupied itself with patterns of symmetry and asymmetry underlying all problems. That is enough to reduce equilibrium theory to dust, for it assumes a symmetry that is not there. The fight against inflation with a single blunt tool rests on the premise that because, other things being equal, an excess of demand over supply will push up prices, the relationship can be turned around: higher prices *in themselves* are deemed to imply an excess of demand over supply.

There is also the detail that in our mixed economy each non-market sector – the environment, the household economy, the government itself – has its own code and purpose. They must indeed communicate with the market, and hence speak its language. But this they do in alien accents. The purpose of the family is to nurture its members from birth to death. For the purpose it must have income. Piling up a fortune, however, is not its prime goal. The purpose of the environmental sector is to preserve a life-friendly setting. If you try to translate that into market logic and sell pollution rights you end up with nonsense results.

Moreover, all non-market sectors of the economy are directly or indirectly funded by the state.

To bring all this together to a first approximation we must follow the procedure of the cost-of-production value theory. We must add the balance sheets of the market and of the non-market sectors to ascertain how the economy and society are doing. If the non-market sectors are being cannibalized by the market, we must estimate what it will take to repair the damage and add that negative item to the bottom line of the market sector to see how the economy is faring.

That rules out a flat price level. As industrialization and

population growth proceed, non-market sectors gain in importance. That deepens the tax layer in price. A factor in raising the price level has developed that has nothing to do with an excess of demand over supply. The same aggregate demand and supply ratio as before, but with a shift of a significant portion of the demand from the private to the public sector must result in a higher price level. This is not a sign of inflation, but of what I call *structural price rise*. Apply high interest rates to flatten price and you will only accelerate its climb by giving more power to the speculative financial community that preys on the non-market sectors.

In my most recent book I use *reduction to absurdity* twice successively to establish the impossibility of enforcing a flat price level by raising interest rates. The proof comes in two stages:

1. Assume that to be possible, but for whatever reason prices do move up. By the assumption to be tested, it would be possible to raise taxes and distribute the proceeds among producers for bringing prices back to where they were. If that is possible, however, there would be no reason for stopping at a single helping of this bonanza. Repeat the procedure until you reach a zero price level. QED. The step method used here is known as "mathematical induction," one of the most frequently used mathematical tools since antiquity.

2. We have proved the absurdity of the proposition when extra taxation for the purpose is distributed among producers. Now comes the second stage. Assume not only that the extra taxation is not distributed to the producers, but interest rates are raised. Instead of reimbursing producers for the taxes they do not recover, they are burdened with higher interest costs. That is an *a fortiori* version of the hypothesis disproved in test #1. QED.

In a pluralistic society price itself must be recognized as pluralistic. Not doing so, is to reject the pluralism of our society.

Instead of disproving the hypothesis with a twig in the sand as the ancient Greeks would, our central banks have acted out *the reduction to absurdity* proof. This has been done at a crushing human toll in mass bankruptcies and crippled social services.

There is a ready way of handling the problems of a pluralist society – systems theory. In science and engineering it has been used for decades: economists, however, have ignored it, for it is incompatible with the notion of a self-balancing market. Its principles are simple enough and directly to the point. If you can identify a sector of the economy, society or the biosphere indispensable to human survival and governed by its own code, it must be treated as a subsystem. Its mutual relations with the other subsystems must be closely monitored to prevent one subsystem from cannibalizing another.

In the case of ecological subsystems the limit of tolerance for their specific vulnerabilities – pollution or whatever – must be respected. For that purpose I have borrowed the notion of *entropy* from physics. But it should be noted that in physics there is a mathematical equivalence amongst the various forms of energy – thermal, gravitational, electro-magnetic, chemical, nuclear. When that important concept is adapted for social

applications, it is essentially reduced to a metaphor, yet a vital one for preventing one subsystem from sapping another. For if that happens the entire system breaks down. What is involved in non-market subsystems is essentially the means and motivations for their survival which can be siphoned off to bolster the negentropy in another subsystem.[1]

Once we set up society as a system, with the economy a single subsystem of the whole, we require other adjustments. We can no longer consider economic data – interest rates, growth, GDP and so forth, as scalars. A scalar is a simple quantity of something that has no sense of direction. A vector, on the other hand, has a sense of direction. The mass of a potato is a scalar, when I drop it, it is drawn by the earth's center of gravitation, a vector. It becomes the product of a scalar and a vector, which is always a vector. When a vector crosses the borders between one subsystem and another it enters another field and interacts with it. A mind pickled in the prejudices of monetarist theory may perceive high interest rates just as a means of "licking inflation." But follow the effects of those rates to the government sector where they lead to a drop in revenues and a rise in the need for more spending for the environment, health, and practically every other subsystem, and disaster is sown.

We must learn to consider economic data vectors rather than scalars and track their influence as they cross subsystem boundaries.

Towards this end, I use a simple tool, known to most economists, but rarely applied to anything that really counts: the so-called Tinbergen Counting Rule. Jan Tinbergen was a Dutch economist who trained originally as a physicist, and thus had a better grasp of what science is about than most economists. His rule merely adapts a principle that everybody learned in her high-school algebra classes: to solve a problem with two independent variables, you need two independent equations. One won't do. Now if you set up a systems-theory mapping of the economy, there must be at least one independent variable per subsystem – there are actually many more. Hence you would have to have as many independent variables in the solution as you can identify in the problem.

Back to High School

Where do we find enough variables for our solutions to match the proliferating variables in our problems? Not only do economic forces change the nature of their impact when they cross subsystem frontiers, but they open recognition of government investment in physical and human capital. That will unfreeze innumerable variables for use in designing solutions.[2] New subsystems can be designed for tactical effect.

We can, for our example, take as target the balance of the public treasury, that depends on two classes of variables – its revenues and its expenditures. Our policy variables in the design of such a new subsystem can be restricted to variables chosen from both of these classes in dosages that will cancel out for a zero-sum effect on the budget balance. Taxes, for example, may be lowered, and interest paid by the Treasury reduced by roughly the same amount. Their *initial* total fiscal effect would thus be nil. Taxes and interest paid by the state are chosen for balanced decrease, because of a broad consensus that exists that, other things being equal, less of these two items are preferable to more. We could call this "the fiscal shrinkage" subsystem. It could be enlarged and varied with *any* pair of measures for overall neutral effect. This would enable us to circumvent pillboxes of prejudice rather than butting our heads against them.

A specific means of achieving this, for example, could be reducing or eliminating the regressive Goods and Services Tax (GST), Canada's version of the VAT, while shifting enough federal debt from the chartered banks to the Bank of Canada to lessen the government's interest burden and achieve a wash. When the Bank of Canada holds government debt, the interest paid on it returns substantially to the Bank's one shareholder, the Government of Canada. These benefits, moreover, are delivered not "in the long run," which in conventional policy usually translates into "never," but immediately. The policy is thus instantly verifiable.

The second step in such policy is passive: monitoring the ensuing bonus as the benign influence of reduced taxation and government interest costs spread through subsystems other than the Treasury. Note that this introduces a "collateral benefit" to the non-targeted subsystems, rather than the "collateral damage" resulting from using interest rates as the BoC's one blunt tool.

Such policy is an application of the modulus congruence calculus of the greatest of 19th century mathematicians, Friedrich Gauss. Don't be alarmed, like Moliere's hero when he learned that he had been speaking prose all his life. You have been using Gauss's modulus congruence whenever you mention a day of the week. Our ancestors could have developed a new name for every day since the birth of Christ, but it would have been cumbersome. So, intuitively, they took seven for their modulus and reverted to Sunday on completing their modulus count.

But for this bird's eye overview of conventional economic theory, I must refer to a congenital flaw of the discipline: it is a hybrid of a stab at being a science and advocacy. In itself that is not a fatal flaw. We are all the offspring of two parents who may not always have gotten along. The problem of economists is one of these parents has done the other in.

The best treatment of the problem I know is that of the late François Perroux, who brought out into the open what no serious economist could have been unaware of. Unless you do so at this late hour, you will get nowhere towards a solution. Compromise is fine, but unless there are benchmarks left to give the deal-makers a sense of what is feasible, it is a futile affair. Only serious economic analysis can provide those benchmarks.

Perroux provides the framework for such analysis.

"The European Occident has passed through successive periods of development, each characterized by a particular morphology of distribution and by a 'dominant revenue.'

"In turn the dominant revenue has been that of the landowners, then industrial profit, then financial and industrial profits in a mixed economy, in which the rate and mass of profit are functions of a complex combination of public and private, of market and extra-market actions.

"During a specific period of development, the dominant revenue is the one to which the others adapt themselves. In an apologetic doctrine it is represented as the revenue that determines whether the given economy functions properly. In the given institutional framework, that in fact is the case; but in another context it would be otherwise."[3] The dominant revenue is first served. If its supporting assumptions are false, there is less or nothing left to trickle down to subordinated revenues.

Since Perroux wrote these lines the role of dominant revenue has passed first to the money-lenders, and then to speculative finance.

Private money played a relatively minor role in financing WWII. The banking system in the US and elsewhere had not only completely discredited itself by its mindless greed in the 1920's, but 38% of US banks had closed their doors by the beginning of 1933. Breadlines snaked around city blocks. In contrast to more recent bailouts by government, in rescuing the banks Roosevelt did not let them dictate their deregulation. They were, on the contrary, put on short leash and restricted to banking. Firewalls were thrown up to keep them out of anything having to do with the stock market.

The war was financed at 2 to 3%. The banks – both the commercial ones and the central bank – indirectly financed the vast bond issues that sopped up civilian buying power. That – along with price controls – kept inflation low. The dominant revenue became the profit of the nation's industries backed by a combination of public and private initiatives, with the trade unions as junior associates. The great absentee were the banks that languished in the dog-house. But health was restored to the banks from this simple regime. and by the early 1950s they experienced a mighty resurgence of their libido. In 1951 the Federal Reserve, behind President Truman's back, asserted its independence in setting interest rates without Treasury interference.[4] Marshall Plan aid had been refused the Latin American countries. In effect they were proclaimed the preserve of the US banks. There was to be no more wonderful way for banks to gamble themselves into trouble again than lending money to corrupt Latin American dictators. The latter were also kept in good supply, courtesy of the US State Department.

Price controls which had been lifted prematurely in the US after WWII, were not reimposed during the Korean War.

Blocking Society's Pluralism

But it was the sixties that provided the banks with their grand opening for scrapping the Roosevelt restrictions. It was a period of massive public investment not only to catch up with 15 years of neglect during depression and war, but to cope with the vast immigration and domestic population explosion. Institutions for a pluralist society and the new technologies were set up. Government accountancy, moreover, treated public investment as current expenditure, thus accentuating the price effect of these outlays. Classifying these as "inflation" offered the financial interests a tool for blocking the growing pluralism of the economy. Interest rates became the blunt tool for stabilization. Thus in Canada, the central bank since 1967 could no longer alter the statutory reserve that banks had to deposit with the BoC as a proportion of the deposits they received from the public, without an act of parliament. By the early 1980s interest rates rose as high as 20% and devastated government finances. Because of these supposedly prudent provisions, the federal debt has risen from $33B in 1973 to around $547B currently.

Today the federal government pays $42 billion annually in interest on its debt. This was due not only to high interest rates, but to the phasing out of the statutory reserves between 1991 and 1993. The bill authorizing the end of reserves was slipped through the House of Commons sans debate or press release.

In 1988 the Bank for International Settlements[5] had issued its *Risk-Based Capital Requirements* guidelines that declared the debt of OECD countries risk-free, requiring no additional capital for banks to hold. Between these two measures Canadian banks acquired some $60 billion of additional federal debt without putting up any significant legal tender of their own.

The purpose was to bail out the banks from their massive speculations during the previous decades (including Dome Petroleum, Reichmann Bros, Campeau's US department-chain-collecting hobby, etc.). Rather than a one-shot affair, it was an entitlement recurring each year. Capitalized, it was the equivalent of a permanent bond of about $100 billion – a third of the federal debt at the time.

Society Becomes a Market for Squeezing Out Interest

But would the increase in base money if the Bank of Canada held so much federal debt not have been inflationary? First of all, the debt would not have risen to such fantastic heights if so much of it had not been shifted to the banks from the BoC. In 1973 the BoC held 20.26%; by 1995 that figure was down to 6.37%. In addition, the tight connection between the Bank's holding of federal debt and the money supply was abolished with the end of the statutory reserves. The effects of that were soon seen when the assets held by the chartered banks which had been 11:1 in 1946 reached a peak of 405 to 1 by 1998. Since, it has hovered around 380. And it should be noted that securities held by the banks are entered at their historic cost. Moreover, the quality of these holdings has deteriorated substantially with ongoing deregulation The multiplier of money creation has quite exploded through the speculative involvements of the banks. The interest charged by their credit cards is as much as three times those of direct bank loans. Society in fact being transformed into a high-powered machine for squeezing out interest. All this just didn't happen. It was elaborately prepared by a virtual censorship in our universities and media to make possible the mutation the financial sector from its role as servant of the economy to its master. What began as the enthronement of the money-lender has given way to the crowning of speculative profit as dominant revenue.

We can see this in the fifth and final edition of an excellent textbook of H.H. Binhammer belonging to an earlier age.[6] Its very qualities were good reason for it having no further edition. And in the final edition we can see not entirely convincing attempts to adapt to the new dogmas that were taking over.

But first let us quote a typical passage where Binhammer explains the process of money creation by the banking system, something never mentioned in official circles today.

"Control of cash reserves is probably the most powerful tool a central bank can possess. Changes in reserve requirements affect not only excess reserves but also the deposit-creation multiplier of the banking system.

"Let us assume that the banking system holds $20 billion in the form of public deposits and $5 billion in reserves. With a 10% legal minimum reserve ratio, and on the basis of the deposits they hold, the banks have to consider $2 billion of their ratio as required reserves. The remaining $3 billion will support a tenfold increase, or $30 billion, in additional deposits. If the reserve requirements are doubled while the total reserves of the bank remain at $5B, required reserves increase to $4 billion, leaving only $1 billion as excess reserves. With the new 20% reserve requirement, the expansion is halved to [multiple] five and the potential expansion of deposits with $1B of reserves is only $5 billion.

"Varying reserve requirements has been considered too powerful and therefore too blunt an instrument for monetary control. Even small increases in reserve requirements can produce undesirable 'shock effects' leading to disturbances and instability in money markets" (p. 300).

Why would Binhammer suggest doubling the reserve requirement to 20% – a level never reached in the BoC's experience? But still more remarkable, when this was written Paul Volcker's "final solution" for what he chose to consider just inflation had brought interest rates to the high teens in the US, and by echo effect in Canada. Surely, increasing the statutory reserves from 10%, if that is where they had been, to 12% would have provided a better basis for comparison between interest rates and raising reserves as anti-inflation tools. Obviously Binhammer was trying hard to make a sixth edition of his book possible. Without success. After all the official party line of the banks by then had become an outright denial that "the multiplier" and "money creation" ever existed.

On page 301 Binhammer informs us: "In some countries the central banks have authority for requiring banks to maintain reserves on assets as well as on deposits. Variable and differential asset reserve requirements may be used to influence the share of bank credit for various users." Binhammer did not specify in which countries the banks have authority to require banks to maintain reserves on their assets as well as on their deposits. But that is precisely what is needed to control the insane leverage of greed that has brought on the present plight of the economy.

By the time the revelations of scams have finished pouring out of the bankruptcy filings of high-tech companies, our banks are likely to require a massive bailout of at least the size of that of 1991. That is why the details of the unholy combination of ending bank reserves and further deregulation of the financial sector in the 1990s must be brought into the open. Canada as we know it will not survive a further ransacking of the public domain in aid of our banks. Their last bailout crippled our social programs. If we fail to prevent it, the next will make us little more than a breakfast for Wall St. A relentless drum-beat has been announcing that for at least a couple of years – in the persistent propaganda for the dollarization of our currency. The wholesale takeover of Canadian firms is already far advanced.

A further bailout of our financial institutions along the lines of the last would put it all in the bag.[7]

Of course, our banks, once the full extent of their massive losses surfaces, will have to be bailed out. But this must not be on their terms as in previous exercises of this sort, but by bringing them back to banking. The acquisition of stock brokerages, credit cards, merchant banking activities, underwriting of stock and bond issues, must be declared incompatible with banking and undone – just as we would consider the merger a hospital with an undertaking establishment.

William Krehm
Paper given at Progressive Economic Forum, at the Calgary meeting of the Canadian Economic Association, May 31 to June 2, 2002.

1. Krehm, William (1977). *Babel's Tower – The Dynamics of Economic Breakdown* (p. 46). Toronto.

2. Krehm, William (2002). *Towards a Non-Autistic Economy – A Place at the Table for Society* (p. 165). Toronto: COMER Publications.

3. *Economie et Societe – contrainte-echange – don* (p. 7). Paris: Presses Universitaires de France, 1960.

4. *FOMC Alert*, 20/03/01, p. 1.

5. Krehm, William (1993). *A Power Unto Itself – The Bank of Canada* (p. 18). Toronto: Stoddard.

6. Binhammer, H.H. (1988). *Money, Banking and the Canadian Financial System.* Nelson Canada, Fifth Edition.

7. Krehm, 2002, p. 183.

We Accuse!

IT IS AS THOUGH Someone above the clouds could no longer stomach the brazenness of our lone superpower replacing the Decalogue with a charter for Mega-Greed. The less fortunate personal traits of George W. simply heighten this travesty on human destiny.

The bare bones of the farce are rattled by Albert R. Hunt in *The Wall Street Journal* (11/07, "Loud Words, Little Action"). "President Bush turned Teddy Roosevelt's famous credo about speaking softly and carrying a big stick on its head in addressing corporate corruption. His unwillingness to match tough talk with tougher regulation and enforcement reflects his view [that] there are a few bad corporate apples but no systemic problems. That is belied by daily headlines about accounting fraud and executive rip-offs causing massive layoffs and pension forfeitures. Tellingly, investors didn't take the president's pronouncements seriously.

"Democratic pollster Peter Hart believes the corporate issue itself may be a winner for his party this November, but more importantly is the cumulative effect of shattered confidence in once-respected institutions: the FBI, the Red Cross, the Catholic Church, the Olympics, and business integrity.

"This may not affect Mr. Bush's long-term political prospects, but it has resurrected his tainted business background. Whether he violated the spirit of the securities in his 1990 Harken Energy transactions obscures a larger point: much of his business career, especially the Harken directorship, was due to cronyism and family connections. He was put on the board of this dubious energy company – this newspaper reported 11 years ago on its link to the sleazy international outlaw bank BCCI – to solicit foreign businesses while his father was president.

"Mr. Bush is incensed that a more than decade old story is being recycled. Remember Whitewater? A major difference is that the Clintons lost money, while Harken director George W. Bush pocketed over $300,000 by selling weeks before the company reported unexpected bad news. If nothing else, this certainly impacts his credibility as a crusader against corporate abuse. But the substance of what he didn't propose is more disturbing, such as:

Conflicts of Interest

Mr. Bush didn't embrace Sen. Paul Sarbanes's legislation, mandating much tougher standards and conflict of interest rules of the accounting profession, currently before the Senate; it has been strongly endorsed by former Fed Chairman Paul Volcker.

"Mr. Bush does nothing about the blatant conflict of an accounting firm auditing and consulting for the same company or a stock touter who provides investment advice to the same company."

Ours has become an extremely conflicted society. The clashes of interest surfacing today merely reflect the still greater incompatibilities buried in the very footings of our financial system in recent decades. More disastrous than even the massive misappropriations of corporate funds, now reported on a daily basis, is the mind-control systematically imposed on economic thinking in government, the media and our universities. That interred what had been learned at a staggering cost during the sixties and World War II.

The purpose of this ruthless censorship was to enthrone the cooking not only of corporate books, but of society's big ledgers as high science brooking no review. The more indefensible its position became, the more absolute the bar to any questioning. That is a formula for maximising inevitable disaster.

An instance: after years of being ignored by the federal government, COMER in recent years had been invited by the Finance Committee to testify before it about once a year. At our last appearance – over a year ago – I cited the leverage run up by money creation by our chartered banks to the legal tender in their tills – from 11 to one in 1946 to a current figure of about 380 to one. I stressed the folly of the bank bailout in 1991 that not only bestowed on the banks an annual *entitlement* of $5 to $7 billion, but at the same time deregulated them to gamble further with fewer restrictions. Capitalized as a permanent bond this entitlement amounted to almost a third of the then federal debt. Our forecast has since been borne out. That is what you are reading about in the screaming headlines of your newspapers today. Significantly COMER was not asked back this year by the Finance Committee.

In the mid-1960s, I had already done considerable work on sorting out upward price movement into its very different components: structural price rise, and market inflation due to an excess of aggregate demand over available supply. In the process I came across the writings of a remarkable group of French economists. François Perroux had formulated the most searching demolition of the equilibrium model and marginal theory known to me. As early as 1962 Pierre Biacabe wrote: "It is necessary either to adopt a new definition of inflation, or to use this term only in its original sense and to find another terminology for the new phenomenon, and that is because we still have no valid model to grasp the contemporary economic system."[1]

However, little remains in France even of the memory of these and other highly relevant economists. I even get the occasional letter from France when somebody has been referred to me as a source of information on Perroux! So thoroughly has thought control been clamped on the world.

The notion that to keep prices and the economy as a whole stable interest rates must be raised high enough to "do the job" was brought in a quarter of a century after World War II. Central banks during the war kept interest rates pegged at 2-3%. If demand outstripped available supply, one of several other measures were used to rein it in. One of these was to restrict the quantity of credit rather than raise interest rates. This was achieved by requiring the banks to leave a higher portion of the deposits they took in from the public as a reserve with the central bank. On such reserves they earned no interest. But beginning seriously in the latter seventies, higher interest rates became the "one blunt tool for fighting inflation." That was pounded into the public's head until today higher interest rates and "fighting inflation" have been accepted as synonyms. Moreover, it was all presented as the law of an impersonal market acting "in the long run" for everyone's good. In fact, it involved the greatest possible conflict of interest. For high interest rates are the revenue of a potentially parasitic class. It is no coincidence that many of the great religions single out usury and even the very institution of interest as a mortal sin. The experience of countless generations must have led to such emphasis. High interest rates assault the revenue of every class but the money-lenders, for they magnify costs in every line of production. Pushed high enough, they drive producers into bankruptcy.

When I first attacked the problem of structural price rise, I leaned heavily on a considerable literature on the automatic shifting of taxes onto price, though they were supposed be absorbed by producers. This suggested that far from a cure for inflation, higher interest rates, as an increased cost both to government and producers, actually contributed to higher prices. Marian Krzyzaniak and Richard A. Musgrave[2] found a shifting of profit tax exceeding 114% for the period 1936-39 to 1955-57. The case of corporation taxes is important: whereas consumption taxes are openly tacked onto price, the fiction of marginalist theory is that corporation taxes cannot affect prices because they are determined by the point at which the least efficient producer just breaks even. There is then at that supposedly decisive point no base for a corporation profit tax. But the researches of Musgrave and others proved that this is not the case. Accountants have always considered taxes a cost that must show up in the price level. Unless, of course, they collapse the economy.

Such matters must be dealt with, rather than ignored. That means the scrapping of all the tendentious views that have taken over our university curricula in recent decades. When that is underway, economics, that has been mugged and kidnapped, will become functional again.

Meanwhile, there are powerful non-technical ways of proving the ghastly conflict of interest in using interest rates, of all things, as the "sole blunt tool against inflation."

No one moving from a small town to New York City will expect his living costs to remain the same. How then can we insist on a flat price level when much of humanity has made a similar move? The number of cities of many millions has risen almost beyond count today and the population on farms has dwindled.

Then there is another major factor readily grasped that has contributed needlessly to an upward trend of our price indexes. Until 1996 the United States treated capital physical expenditures by government exactly as they did the government's purchases of floor-wax – it wrote them off in a single year. In the case of investment in human capital – the most productive investment that can be made – that is still done. In Canada the depreciation of physical capital is supposed to come in this current year. Obviously its absence up to now has distorted the significance of budgetary deficits. Exaggerated deficits, for their part, imposed a conflicted perspective of the economy in favour of the financial sector.

Such grotesque distortions of policy should have warned the world of a mightier conflict of interest lurking at deeper levels. But worse was yet to come. Deregulation and globalization ("D&G") served a double purpose. It allowed the shifting of more of the less skilled manufacturing to countries with the lowest living standards, the least demanding environmental protection, with governments competing to surrender desperately needed tax-base to foreign investors. D&G thus kept commodity price inflation down in the advanced countries. At the same time, deregulation permitted banks to acquire brokerage houses and enter every sort of stock market promotion. That extended dramatically their reach and clutch. The "dominant revenue" whose conflicted interests are confused with the nation's welfare passed from money-lending banking to speculative finance. High interest rates, of course, are anathema to anything connected with the stock market. Applied to less developed lands, they can serve as wreckers' balls to compel admission of foreign interests to areas hitherto reserved for domestic entrepreneurs.

That shift in the "dominant revenue" was very much to the fore in the world-wide bailouts of banks in the early nineties. The spread in interest rates between those charged consumers, small business, and those available to large corporations widened marvellously. The same banks wedded their immensely increased powers of money creation with the buying up of financial and industrial firms for their own account. They invested heavily in credit cards and subpar debt that could fetch them three times the interest from direct bank loans. They were generous investors in the off-balance sheet partnerships of Enron and other energy traders, and covered up their too timely exits with products of their derivative departments. The very name of banking has been dragged through the gory mud.

The Rat under the Floor Boards

The bailout of the banks in the early 1990s laid the foundations of a whole hierarchy of conflicted interests. What is in the headlines today consists wholly of what we might call secondary conflicts. The basic ones – the rat under the floor boards – might as well not exist as far as analysts and the media are concerned. Except, of course, for the unbearable stench it emits, plus the detail that it is likely to prove the most damaging of all scandals.

The whole subject has become immensely timely. It is clear that our banks have once again, as a group, gambled away much, all, or more than their highly leveraged capital in uncharted adventures incompatible with banking. It would be fatal for society as we know it to allow our banks once again to dictate the terms of their bailout. Yet banks are a necessary institution in a mixed economy. But they must be confined to socially useful banking. That will mean insisting that they choose between banking and running highly rigged casinos, with losses to the house practically underwritten by the government.

But wouldn't that be confiscating part or all of the shareholders' capital? That can be handled in a manner eminently fair to both shareholders and society itself. Such an objective rules out a bailout across the industry carried out – as was the last – in stealth. Instead, it must be done in the light of day, and each individual bank bailed out on its own merits as it applies to the government for assistance. Under the circumstances the shareholders' capital of some would appear already to have been gambled away by its management. There would then be little or nothing left to confiscate.

It is not the business of the government to make a gift to such banks to replace their lost capital, so that they can resume their gambles once more. They must be given the choice of closing their doors, trade in their present charters for one confining them strictly to banking.

That done, with the immediate crisis under control, attention can be directed to still solvent banks. Hearings must be held on the consequences of the 1991 bailout – executed under wraps and accompanied with further deregulation. In such cases reasonable compensation for restricting their existing operations would have to be discounted for likely liability connected with suits against them, for excessive past rewards to the high executives. Compensation to them could consist in whole or in part in participations acquired by the government in rescuing insolvent banks.

All this would make possible bringing solvent banks back to banking, with a minimum of discomfort to their shareholders. A further bailout of our banks along the lines of that of 1991-3 is out of the question. It would help bring Canada down to the category of a Third World country.

William Krehm

1. Krehm, William (1975). *Price in a Mixed Economy – Our Record of Disaster* (pp. 35, 51). Toronto.
2. Krzyzaniak, Marian and Musgrave, Richard A. (1963). *The Shifting of the Corporation Income Tax* (p. 13). Baltimore: Johns Hopkins Press.

Missing Model for SEC Sleuths — Russia's Babushka Doll Nests

WHILE the American expeditionary force in Afghanistan is misled by high tech to bomb their Canadian allies and a peaceful village wedding party, bin Laden couldn't have done better if he had his way with Wall St. And evidence is mounting that the key to cleaning up the mess is to be found in Russia's traditional babushka doll.

Take the latest revelation of *The Wall Street Journal* (3/07, page C1, "WorldCom's Disclosure Highlights Estimates that Underlie Reserves" by Henry Sender): "If corporate financial reporting appears built increasingly on sand, it is because in many cases it is. Frequently, the sand in question takes the form of estimates – guesses, really – that go far towards shaping how companies across a wide range of industries report their performance."

Many of the boasted reserves of the financial mega-giants may have been put there not for their posted purpose, but just "for playing around with."

"Reserves, set up to cover adverse developments such as bad debts or anticipated restructuring costs or warranty claims, are found on almost every balance sheet in the US. And many balance sheets have many of them. Here is where the guesswork comes in: 'Companies have huge discretion' in how big or small the reserves are. 'They base their size not on hard, cold fact, but on educated guesses that pass for estimates,' says Douglas Carmichael, professor of accounting at the City University of New York. And that means that management, rewarded heavily by stock options, has an incentive to make the reserves as small as possible.

"Reserves at WorldCom [the world's second largest long-distance telephone provider] were set up in connection with past mergers and acquisitions to cover future payments for such things, say, as layoffs. WorldCom's statement about possible additional accounting woes said only that 'questions have been raised regarding certain material reversals of reserve accounts during 2000 and 1999.' Under such reversals, WorldCom would have released money from its reserves, a tactic that sends funds flowing through the income statement to boost the bottom line.

"Like so many stars of the New Economy, WorldCom was a serial acquirer, taking over dozens of companies. Dennis Saputo, a senior vice-president at Moody's Investors Service Inc., suggests that some reserves may have been overstated so that they could be released later to smooth earnings.' WorldCom reserves may total as much as $10 billion.

"Of course, when companies discover they have overestimated merger-related costs, they are expected to release an appropriate amount of money from the merger reserve. But they are not supposed to deliberately set aside money with the intention of later using it to feed drooping earnings.

"And yet such practices seem widespread, largely because companies everywhere – not just in high tech – are battling slow sales and less pricing power. And the battle may be intensifying despite a recovery of sorts, as companies struggle not only to support their share prices, but to keep from falling afoul of financial performance terms set by their bankers on loans.

"When the SEC sued Xerox Corp. earlier this year for securities fraud, it charged that the copier company had pumped up its earnings nearly $500 million by releasing into income 'cushion' reserves established for some other purpose. The regulators said that 'the intentional or reckless use of reserves for this purpose without disclosure was fraudulent.' Xerox agreed to a $10 million civil penalty to settle the SEC charges without admitting or denying wrongdoing." By such settlements – civil penalties that don't admit "wrongdoing" – everybody's learning curves are kept flat. The culprits are graciously allowed to lose a skirmish, but not the war.

"The SEC cited approximately 20 reputed reserves that had been tapped, including one for vacation pay.

"Reserves are particularly pervasive in the banking and insurance worlds, where they are set up to cover losses for the main products: loans and insurance. But such loan-loss reserves have become more prevalent in the manufacturing world, too, reflecting the huge growth in vendor financing in the telecommunications-equipment makers as telecom stocks soared in the 1990s.

"At Lucent Technologies Inc., for instance, 'one would think, given the failing financial health of many Lucent customers, that these provisions would be increasing, not declining,' says Carol Levenson, an industrial analyst with GimmeCredit, a bond-research boutique. But in the quarter ended March 31, Lucent posted the lowest provision for bad debts since the final quarter of 2000 when it added $370 million to its reserve. The $192 million first-quarter provision was down from $705 million in the year-earlier period."

In an economy based entirely on credit, trust and forecasts are at the very heart of things. Playing hanky-panky with matters so grave – in effect with our money supply – is courting disaster. Nor can you restrict vigilance to the individual firm's reserves. You must go from these to the reserves set up by the government itself to ensure that the cooking of society's accounts is not taking place on a far bigger, more threatening scale.

Thus economic theory that the government guides itself by, and imposes on our universities and media, increasingly leaves such matters as social welfare, the environment, education, health to the "market." It has dismantled and privatized many reserves set up for such crucial purposes on the assumption that "the market" is better equipped than the government for looking after such concerns. But surely the incredible skullduggery that is pouring out of the bankruptcy filings of the leading corporations shows us that "the market" often strikes out in handling its own affairs. The matter of misused reserves is only the very latest revelation of this. How can we then assign to "the market" oversight of the public interest?

Transparency under Water

The government and the public learn about such reserve malfeasance only when corporations file for bankruptcy. And when a mega-corporation has grown too big to be allowed to go bust, the government feels obliged to step in to rescue it. That used to happen with a good sampling of big banks on the average once each decade. But now it emerges that this epidemic of reserve hanky-panky has extended to non-banks as well. Among the assets of WorldCom is vital infrastructure for international communications, both civil and military – a good enough reason for government to intervene in helping it straighten out its affairs.[1]

But moving from one class of reserves to another, as from one babushka doll to the larger one in which it is enclosed, we arrive at the central bank itself. It was set up not only to issue the legal tender backed by the government's credit, but to farm out that faculty to private banks in return for a modest part of the profits from the franchise. To back the credit banks could create beyond the cash they held, they were obliged to put up reserves with the central bank on which they earned no interest. And most of the net earnings of the central bank were remitted to the government – whether it was owned by the government as in Canada or the UK, or by private banks as in the US. In the former case this remittance came to the government as dividends. In the latter case, where private banks held the shares of the central bank, the bulk of the profits of the central bank came to the government by virtue of the monarch's ancestral monopoly in coining of precious metals. Translated into the monetary system in force until about a decade ago, private bank credit rested on a modest base of non-interest bearing government debt – cash – held by the commercial banks at the central bank. That statutory reserve of base-money was the reserve of reserves – the mother babushka doll – in which the whole nest of smaller dolls was enclosed and protected. It was a system that worked reasonably well. By increasing the statutory reserve – the Mother Babushka – the leverage of money creation by the banks was lowered – without having to raise interest rates. Its greatest defect was that it displeased the bankers, because it could be used to force them to stick to banking instead of gambling themselves into bankruptcy.

An Unsolved Murder sans Headlines

Today, despite the chain of scandals revealed in many of our large corporations, the fate of Mother Babushka continues shrouded in mystery like an unsolved murder. In the 1980s the banks of the world, increasingly deregulated and globalized, went on an unprecedented gambling binge in real estate and gas and oil. Many of them lost not only their total capital but much more. Their very deregulation had made it possible for more of them to qualify as "too big to be allowed to fail." So entirely by stealth a world-wide bailout was organized. In Canada the statutory reserves that the chartered banks held with the Bank of Canada were phased out between 1991 and 1993 – with neither parliamentary debate nor press release. Throughout much of the world such reserves had already been reduced from an average 10% of the deposits the commercial banks took in from the public to an average of 4% in Canada and some 3% in the US. By the 1991 revision of Canada's *Bank Act*, they were reduced to zero leaving the banks with no more cash in their tills than was needed to meet their daily net cheque clearance and the requirements of the public. In the US these voluntary cash reserves, essential for routine banking business, are considered part of the statutory reserves. That amounts to almost all of the voluntary reserves. That leaves little or nothing for the former functions of Big Babushka.

On top of that in the latter 1980s the Bank for International Settlements – a bank of technocrats not answerable to any elected government – issued its *Risk-Based Capital Requirements* guidelines that declared the debt of OECD countries to be risk-free requiring no further capital for banks to acquire. This permitted Canada's banks to quadruple their holdings of federal bonds from around $20 billion to $80B without putting up any significant additional funds or even capital.[2] Governments took to borrowing far more money from private banks, rather than creating much of it through the central bank. Indeed, the very system of central banking had been weakened to the point of ineffectiveness. With no substantial statutory reserves left that could be raised or lowered to keep the economy on an even keel, the central bank today can intervene to "cool" the economy only by raising interest rates. That surrendered ultimate control not only of the economy but of the government itself to the money-lenders. It involved a conflict of interest as shrill as a police siren. Moreover, the scam gave rise to a wild turbulence of interest rates in the eighties that accounted for most of the current national debt. It also increased the casualties across society by "friendly fire." Interest rates, in fact, having become a wrecking ball swung across the economy, speculative capital took over from the money-lenders the "dominant revenue" role in our society. We were forced to look at the economy, and indeed the world, through its angle of vision.

When COMER pieced together what had happened in that fateful year 1991 and went public with it, the banks and the government in unison retorted that the statutory tax had been "an unjust tax" – that Canadian trust companies were not subject to it since in theory they had no depositors but just shareholders. Yet not a single major trust company survives today – they have been gobbled up by our banks. When you redefine Mother Babushka, the major reserve of the country, so drastically, distorting its original purpose, what you have done – in the words of the American regulators – is "fraudulent." That is in fact the unhappy position of our government today.

The consequence: the banks were deregulated to operate in just about wherever activity they chose to in Canada or the world. They acquired brokerage houses, financed the partnerships of Enron, occasionally made a billion or so in profits in Global Crossing partnerships, often only to lose their loot and considerably more when the Wall St. bubble burst.[3]

To the SEC, the OSC, and all the innumerable commissions being set up to find out what hit the stock market, we commend Russia's Babuska doll nests for master clues. As a by-product, the deserved popularity of the Babuska Dolls might even revive Russia's privatized economy.

William Krehm

1. "A global network of phone and data lines that stretch from the hot-line between the White House and the Kremlin to much of the Internet, WorldCom could be forced into Chapter 11 bankruptcy protection in the days ahead because 25 lenders, led by Deutsche Bank AG, are seeking a temporary restraining order on a $2.65 billion loan" (*The Globe and Mail*, 16/7, "Congressman cites WorldCom internal memos" by Miro Cernetig).

2. Capital may exist but in highly illiquid forms. Analysts tend to flit over this crucial point.

3. As ultimate call on the entire tax-base of a country, central banks exercise a fatal fascination on private banks on the make. A particularly bizarre case was that of "the Bank of Commerce and Credit International (BCCI), an international bank based in Luxembourg and the Cayman Islands that perpetrated the greatest financial fraud in world history. Founded by a charismatic Pakistani con man named Agha Hasan Abedi, BCCI had been the world's fastest-growing bank for two decades. Its miraculous development was made possible by misrepresenting its largely fictitious capital of $20 billion and serving as a money-laundering conduit for, among others, the Medellin drug cartel, General Manuel Noriega, the CIA, and the terrorist Abu Nidal. BCCI relentlessly sought out new deposits from any source and by any means. One of its most important strategies was to bribe

finance ministry and central bank officials of developing countries to deposit with it national hard currency reserves. Another was to offer high-ranking government officials unrecorded secret accounts to deposit with it national hard currency reserves. Before BCCI's collapse, Bangladesh, Barbados, Belize, Cameroon, Guatemala, Mauritania, Nigeria, Saint Kitts and Nevis, Pakistan, Togo, Trinidad, Tunisia, Venezuela and Zimbabwe had all entrusted some of the hard-earned foreign exchange to the rogue bank, and most of them – along with a million other depositors – lost most of their money. In the small African country of Swaziland, BCCI functioned as the central bank. The World Bank for Latin America used BCCI as its disbursing agent in several African countries." (Rich, Bruce [1994]. *Mortgaging the Earth, The World Bank, Environmental Impoverishment and the Crisis of Development* [p. 21]. Boston: Beacon Press.)

Dead Rat under the Floor Boards

IT IS NOT SUPPOSED to be there. For months financial columnists have been arguing that it's all a matter of boys being boys, and without some by-passing of rules, the economy could never prosper. Just as the race could hardly have survived without the occasional fortifying of bloodlines – a spot of rape rather than churchly sanction. The Sabine maidens and all that contributing to Rome's eventual grandeur. In olden times the objective of military conquest as much as territory included access to genetic banks. All just a matter of "Darwinism." No cause for concern – self-discipline and lectures on sportsmanship will set things aright. Morality will trickle down, just as some of the mega-profits were supposed to. However, the stench persists, deepens and spreads. The independent reporting of a handful of publications hint of a deeper, more elusive truth contrary to the bromides in their editorial columns.

Fourteen years ago COMER and *Economic Reform* began at the opposite end of the matter – spotting the rodent as it chewed its way to build its nest. We predicted pretty well what is now happening.

Our pioneering work provides some benchmarks for assessing the valiant quest of the investigative reporters trying to ferret out the source of the scandals rocking the financial world with little more than their sense of smell to guide them. For the purpose, official economic theory is less than useless. Knowingly or not – it provided the cover-up that brought the world into its present mess.

The Wall Street Journal (20/06, in a series "What's Wrong. Why the Bad Guys of the Boardroom Emerged en Masse" by David Wessel): "Every decade has king-size corporate villains. In the 1970s, Robert Vesco was indicted for looting the Investors Overseas Services mutual funds. In the 1980s, arbitrageur Michael Milken went to jail.

"But the scope and scale of the corporate transgressions of the late 1990s, now coming to light, exceed anything the US has witnessed since the years of the Great Depression."

If even then.

"Enron Corp.'s top executives reaped hundreds of millions as the company collapsed. Arthur Andersen LLP, Enron's auditor, was convicted last week of obstructing justice. Tyco International Ltd.'s lionized chief executive is charged with tax evasion and accused of secret deals with underlings. Cable giant Adelphia Communications Corp. admitted inflating numbers and making undisclosed loans to its major shareholders. Xerox Corp. paid a $10 million fine for overstating revenues. Dynegy and CMS Energy Corp. simultaneously bought and sold electricity in transactions with no point other than pumping up trading volumes." And with them of course, mega-profits or a passing ghostly semblance of the same.

Healer, Heal Thyself

There is no apparent end to the variety of mega-scams among corporations leading to fraudulent bankruptcies. Thus the *WSJ* informs us (8/07, "Merck Booked $12.4B It Never Collected" by Barbara Martinez): "Drug giant Merck & Co. recorded $12.4 billion in revenue from the company's pharmacy-benefits unit over the last three years that the subsidiary never actually collected, according to a filing with the SEC. These co-payments were collected by pharmacies from patients, even though its Medco unit, which manages the pharmacy benefit programs for employers and health insurers, doesn't receive those funds." Between 1999 and 2001, co-payments represented nearly 10% of Merck's reported revenues.

The need emerges for the mighty pharmaceutical industry of the advice from ancient Greece: "Healer, heal thyself."

The latter *WSJ* piece reports a like need in the private educational industry. In its muscular haste to swallow public schools, it seems to have overlooked the basic morality it boasted it would impart to youngsters. "Medco's accounting practice echoes a recent case involving Edison Schools Inc., a commercial operator of public schools which was booking as revenue funds that school districts held directly for teachers' salaries and other costs. Although Edison's accounting practice, which didn't affect net income, conformed to generally accepted accounting principles, the SEC said that 'technical compliance with GAAP 'does not insulate a company from enforcement action if business it makes filings 'that mischaracterize its business or omit significant information.'" That is particularly so since investors are likely to pick the mischaracterization off the page and run with it to their broker, overlooking better-conceived passages which may exist elsewhere in the report.

"Merrill Lynch & Co. paid $100 million to settle New York state charges that analysts misled investors, and other Wall St. firms are under scrutiny."

The extent of the scandal is making the odd member of the Bush cabinet speak like terrorists. The *Journal* article asks, "Is the entire system of corporate governance and regulation flawed? Or was the system abused by a few cleverly diabolical executives who deserve, as Treasury Secretary Paul O'Neill puts it, 'to hang…from the very highest branches?'

"The answer, put simply: a stock-market bubble magnified changes in business mores and brought trends that had been building for years to a climax. The victims: the very shareholders the executives were supposed to be serving.

"One culprit was stock options, which gave executives huge incentives to boost near-term share prices regardless of long-term consequences. No CEO pay package seemed to strike any board of directors as too big. These incentives helped turn the widely practised art of earnings management – making sure profits meet or barely exceed Wall St. expectations – into a gross distortion of reality at some companies. And the institutions created to check such abuses failed. The remnants of a professional ethos in accounting, law, and security analysis gave way to getting the maximum revenue per partner. The auditor's signature on a corporate report didn't testify that the report was an accurate snapshot, says Mr. O'Neill. He says it meant too often that a company had 'cooked the books to generally accepted standards.'

"Measuring the volume of corporate skullduggery precisely is difficult. The SEC opened 570 investigations last year. More than 150 companies restated their earnings in each of the past three years, an acknowledgment that they had misinformed their investors. That's more than triple the levels of the early 1990s, but represents only one of every 100 publicly traded companies. Revelation and outrage always follow the bursting of a bubble. The cycle is immutable. 'At any given time there exists an inventory of undiscovered embezzlement,' wrote John Kenneth Galbraith in *The Great Crash of 1929*. 'This inventory – it should perhaps be called "the bezzle" – amounts at any moment to many millions of dollars. In good times people are relaxed, trusting and money is plentiful. But there are always people who need more. Under these circumstances the rate of embezzlement grows, the rate of discovery falls off, and bezzle increases rapidly.'

"'In depression all this is reversed. Money is watched with a narrow, suspicious eye. The man who handles it is assumed dishonest until he proves himself otherwise. Audits are penetrating and meticulous. Commercial morality is enormously improved. The bezzle shrinks."

The trouble today is that the "bezzle" rather than shrinking is revealed far greater than the past record. Enron, that shocked the business world out of its boots just a few months ago when it declared the largest bankruptcy on record, has now been put in the shadow by the second-largest long distance telephone company [WorldCom]: bad debts are far greater incurred by even more brazen scams. Belatedly the SEC, the regulators of stock markets in the US, announces plans to make the executives at 1,000 big US companies assume "personal accountability" for the accuracy of their reports.

But Harvey Pitt, chairman of the SEC, who not so long ago defended stock market manipulators in court, is simplifying things. As Andrew Willis in *The Globe and Mail* (28/06, "Swearing on a stack of Bibles won't solve this mess") observes: "The truly scary thing about the WorldCom's scandal is that executives believed in the numbers they were producing."

They were carefully brainwashed to do so by the dominant model that proclaims the market the wisest judge of what is best for everybody "in the long run," supposedly its verdicts are determined by the balance between supply and demand. Demand in turn, by the evidence clogging the law courts today, depends on the amount of hype, and misinformation money can buy, on the credit bubbles that can be contrived to produce the growth that society is said to need. Such growth must at least meet the pace already incorporated into stock prices. The slightest short-fall from that severe standard will collapse the whole house of cards.

Worst Variant: The CEOs Actually Trusted their Figures

In the same issue of the *G&M*, John MacNaughton, president and CEO of the Canadian Pension Plan Investment Board, one of Canada's greatest investors, said, "Regulators of financial markets will be strengthened and given more power to police markets so that they can act with more 'force.' Boards of directors will receive more support from shareholders, and the accounting and investment banking business will be 'improved.'" Apart from the detail that the banks – in their new deregulated roles as brokers, underwriters, merchant bankers, derivative peddlers, and what not – have recently been revealed as having shown Enron and other companies how to "structure" their books. Citicorp in particular has shone in that role. Even if that pipedream were realized, even if the CEOs were not allowed to badger and bribe their auditors into producing the necessary pseudo-growth that satisfies the fictitious capitalizations based on stock prices already achieved, that would only widen the gap between hard reality and the perceived "growth" based on accountancy acrobatics.

The problem then centers on the sustainability of a model that drives the CEO to strive towards exponential growth. Exponential growth, the mathematics of the atomic bomb, requires that the rate of growth, the acceleration of that growth, and all higher derivative ("rates" of) growth equal the value attained by the function itself. The success of the first atomic bomb was attested by the destruction of Hiroshima. The current mega-scandals that are devastating Wall St. today are merely evidence that the exponential character of official model has been confirmed. The flattening of morality, the economy, and above of the shareholders of yesterday's outstanding growth corporations merely means that unlimited growth has been achieved. That is what all the official commissions that are being appointed should be investigating.

"Stock options were supposed to solve a problem of the past: entrenched corporate management wasn't serving shareholders – the indictment that corporate raiders made with such ferocity in the 1980s. The solution, widely embraced in American business, was to use stock options to link executives' and shareholders' interests. Executives would benefit if they managed companies in a way that lifted share prices.

"It didn't work as intended. A soaring stock market rewarded executives not for good strategic management, but for riding the roller coaster. And when the stock price dipped below the exercise price – essentially making the options worthless – some companies simply revised the terms or, in Wall St. jargon 'reloaded' them.

"Even worse, the incentives were not to increase profits and share prices over a decade or two, but rather to increase profits – never mind if they have to be restated later – just long enough for executives to cash out. None of the abuses that have been exposed in the past 10 months were committed by chief executives working alone to steal shareholders' money. 'In every one of these cases,' says Mr. Sporkin, the former SEC chief, 'you have professional assistance.'

"The decay of professionalism – and codes of ethics that distinguished a profession from a job – intensified in the 1990s, but it didn't begin then. Reflecting on his 23 years in corporate management, Mr. O'Neill recalls a parade of Wall St. professionals who came to his office with plans for 'new and exotic' financial maneuvers to reduce his company's tax bill or report debt in ways 'not clearly prohibited by the tax code or law.' but not designed to illuminate corporate operations, either. 'They get,' he says, 'into an ethical vacuum.'

"The spectacular crash of 1929 led to modern financial regulation, from bank-deposit insurance to the ban on insider trades, in 1933 and 1934. Despite the obvious parallels, this is a different time. The US is not in an economic depression, nor does George W. Bush see himself as Franklin Delano Roosevelt's heir. The debate over how to repair the system is just beginning to take form.

"The nature and dimensions of the reforms depend on factors that aren't knowable. How many more Enrons and Tycos remain unreported? How swiftly will corporations, boards of directors, the New York Stock Exchange, the National Association of Securities Dealers and other self-regulatory organizations move to reassure investors?"

But all this refers to the mess on the floor. Cleaning it up and polishing the floor boards to a high gloss will do nothing to make the moral stench go away. That comes from the dead rat hidden below the floor: the surrender of the state's sovereign powers of money creation to the commercial banks in their bailout of the early 1990s. This, incredibly paired as it was by the deregulation of the same banks being bailed out, bestowed on the financial sector the power and the glory to embark on unlimited conquest. Who under the circumstances was to tell them 'no,' when they set their hearts on further expansion? Hardly the governments that bailed them out by surrendering to them in stealth its privilege of money creation handed down from monarchies of yore? In other fields those entrusted with administering miracles have historically been put under severe controls – for good enough reason. The Catholic Church, for example, imposes chastity on those entrusted with dispensing the blood and body of Christ. Not so the circumstances under which the governments under the aegis of the international organizations bestowed almost the entire miracle of money creation on the financial community. Deregulating them at the same time was the equivalent of the Vatican not only allowing its priests to marry but to engage in polygamy whenever their hearts really grew fond.

The quickest way of achieving the prescribed growth was by mergers. In this age of fast foods and faster profits, entry and get-away had to be achieved on the run.

That had as one merit: it left the subtleties of accountancy to the next guy. Another buzzword was "synergy" – the parts put together were supposed to be more productive and hence more valuable than they were apart, even after the fees and profits were trucked away. *The Wall Street Journal* (25/06, "Where have the Masters of the Big Mergers Gone?" by Robert Frank) reflects on the big hole they have left behind: "The number of mergers has fallen to its lowest level in a decade. As measured against US GDP, mergers have suffered their sharpest decline since the data were first compiled during the 1970s."

Leaving aside the brainlessness of the statistical ratio – the amount of the mergers to the GDP, what possible economic sense could such a ratio make? – the authenticity of the grief expressed is beyond suspicion.

"Most takeover experts say the slowdown is just another cycle, since merger-and-acquisitions have historically followed the stock market in both good times and bad. Yet a number of deal specialists worry that big mergers may be falling out of fashion and that the merger meltdown marks a pronounced change from the days of $100 billion telecom deals and daily news conferences filled with backslapping and buzzwords such as 'synergies.' Deal activity topped $1.7 trillion in the US in 2000, but it fell below $400 billion during this year's first six months. During their heyday of the 1990s, major firms earned between 10% and 25% of their profits from merger fees, which are some of the fattest on Wall St. Morgan Stanley and Lehman Brothers Holdings Inc. both reported double-digit earnings declines in the latest quarter due largely to the drop in the merger business."

Serious unemployment is turning up amongst merger specialists – something that may receive more attention from governments than joblessness in less exalted strata of society. It will undoubtedly lead to stepping up the pressures to get on with privatizations. "To keep busy, merger bankers are working on smaller deals and taking less traditional assignments, such as bond offerings and capital raising. Some are working on 'reverse M&A,' that is, undoing some of the giant merger-and-acquisitions combinations of the 1990s through divestitures, spinoffs, and breakups.

"'The economy and stock market are partly to blame: Companies prefer to use their stocks as deal currency, but if their stock price is weak, they are less able to make acquisitions. [Moreover], doing deals is all about having confidence in both your own business and the business you're buying,' says Steve Koch, co-chairman of global mergers and acquisitions at Credit Suisse First Boston, a unit of Credit Suisse Group. Right now, we're in unprecedented crisis of confidence.'

"Some of the biggest mergers of the 1990s have also started unraveling. AOL Time Warner Inc., JDS Uniphase Crop. and Vivendi Universal all have taken multibillion-dollar charges to reflect the fall in value of assets they acquired during the bull market. While academic studies have long shown that a majority of acquisitions fail to deliver value for shareholders, the performances of recent mergers offer high-profile proof."

However, a new factor is giving a minor impetus to mergers and acquisitions. The *WSJ* (24/06, "Debt Needs May Drive Telecom Acquisitions" by Robin Sidel) informs us: "Wanted to Buy:

Revenue. At a time when telecommunication companies are grappling with weak sales and continued overcapacity, some investors and analysts are fretting that a few are making revenue-rich acquisitions for the wrong reasons. Instead of buying rivals mostly for their strategic fit, they say, the real motivation is that the deals can help buyers avoid breaking key terms of existing borrowing arrangements. But these critics also acknowledge the flip side: There is also little choice.

"'It's about staying ahead of the debt man. The financial model, not the business model is driving the business – and that frightens investors,' says Scott Cleland, chief executive of Percursor Group, a telecom research company in Washington.

"Last week, for example, Allegiance Telecom Inc., a Dallas-based provider of telephone and internet services to businesses, bought assets from WorldCom Inc., for $30 million. The deals are expected to add $15 million to quarterly revenues towards revenue levels required under a debt covenant, providing Allegiance with a much-needed cushion to prevent it from violating terms of the bank facility." A far cry from triumphant synergy claims that were supposed to lead us into a new golden age.

W.K.

The Ambiguities of Economic Growth

THE ACCEPTED economic wisdom in North America today insists that economic growth in the dollar value of the Gross Domestic Product should have priority over all other economic goals. Any slowdown in the rate of growth of GDP is cause for gloom and even alarm. It is also thought that this type of growth can be maximized by the free movement of capital, surreptitious subsidies in aid of the movement of goods, no restrictions on pollution and resource depletion, and very severe restrictions on the transmission of knowledge other than officially authorized curricula. Therefore all these things are good. In brief: exponential economic growth, in physical terms, is possible and should be pursued with vigour on our finite planet.

This denies rational thought. It is an exercise in immature theology. Scholars like Herman Daly have questioned the concept.

"The economy may continue forever to develop qualitatively, but in cannot grow indefinitely and must eventually settle into a steady state in its physical dimensions."[1]

Daly is saying that we can have economic growth, but we cannot have continues physical economic growth based on the ever expanding use of non-renewable resources. Sustainable growth must be based on quality, not quantity. It cannot be measured by the Gross Domestic Product as calculated by the money value of all transactions.

At the present time the cost of rebuilding after natural disasters such as earthquakes and hurricanes, cleaning up after man-made pollution such as oil spills, acid rain, chemical warfare storage sites and nuclear waste all add to the GDP and economic growth. This type of growth is unsustainable, and any calculation of the social value of economic growth based on GDP figures is nonsense.

Sustainable economic growth depends upon the interaction of knowledge with resources. We know that resources are finite, but knowledge does not seem to be. Each new discovery seems to lead to several more. This means that a very different type of economic growth is possible with a diminishing rate of use of non-renewable resources. The computer industry has proven this point. In this fact lies the hope for a sustainable society.

Let us consider economic growth as the offspring of two parents – an offspring that draws an inheritance from each parent. The one parent, knowledge, is growing in strength while the other, resources, is losing strength. The offspring cannot completely resemble either parent. The offspring, however, can during its growing years, draw strength from where that strength exists and thus grow stronger than if an attempt were made to draw strength from where it does not exist. The offspring (economic growth) can safely maximize benign growth by maximizing dependence on the parent represented by knowledge and minimizing dependence on the parent representing resources. This is the only road to a sustainable economy. It is the opposite of ruling economic policy, which ignores and even subsidizes all kinds of waste of natural resources in the pursuit of instant profit. Present economic policy also restricts the transmission of knowledge, which is essential for benign economic growth.

Robert Good

Bob Good, a founding member of COMER, farms near Guelph.
1. Daly, Herman E. (1993, November). *Scientific American*, p. 57.

Our Mirror-image Economy

IS THE MATTER and anti-matter in Physics being imitated by economists mistaking debt for capital, and the absence of wealth for wealth?

Mathematicians discovered the potential of calculating in imaginary numbers some centuries ago when they began solving quadratic equations – i.e., equations with second powers of variables – like $x^2 + 1 = 0$. The difficulty was that whereas $+1^2$ and $(-1)^2$ both equal $+1$, there is no real number that when squared will give you minus 1. Otherwise stated, -1 has no real square root, only an imaginary one. This caused the great Descartes – founder of analytical geometry – to turn his back on such imaginaries. But some of his contemporaries did not. And their explorations on the subject led to powerful new analytical tools. For by multiplying real numbers – positive or negative by the square root of minus one – designated by the symbol "i" – they were able to weave in and out the realms of imaginary and real numbers with startling results. By segregating the two distinct realms – real and imaginary – before and after arithmetical manipulation – they were able to equate the real and the imaginary parts of the expressions. The result was often like solving two problems simultaneously.

Imaginary Quantities Come to Physics from Mathematics

And in the eighteenth century imaginaries worked black magic in many fields such as infinite series.

It is only decades ago that physicists discovered the realm of anti-matter. In it the world known to us has a mirror image with negatively charged protons and positively charged electrons. However, the negative wealth concept used so extensively by our corporations has no such rigour. It assumes symmetry where it is not present. It is more akin to the art of the counterfeiter where the duplication has a basic non-symmetry with what is real.

This strikes at the heart of policy-making at the highest level.

The Wall Street Journal (2/01/02, "Despite the Recession Americans Continue to be Avid Borrowers" by Jathon Sapsford and Patrick Barta) rolls out an incredible tale: "Ten months into the current recession consumer credit defaults and payment delinquencies are as high as they have been since the last recession a decade ago. This time around, however, lenders, who were quick to reduce the flow of credit during past recessions, have left the tap wide open. That's allowed Americans to continue borrowing to pay for homes, cars and other big-ticket items, bolstering the weakened economy. But the resulting growth in consumer credit – to a record $7.5 trillion at the end of the third quarter of 2001 – also has exposed a potential new economic fault line.

"Rising consumer debt is typically a sign of robust spending. In the short term, consumer spending stimulates the economy. That's clearly what the Federal Reserve had in mind over the past year as it repeatedly lowered interest rates. But the unusual growth in consumer borrowing during the current recession also poses a danger: that at some point the consumers will have to divert more and more of their income from spending on goods and services towards repaying their debt.

"Such a shift would slow the economy, reducing the chances of a speedy recovery. That is, of course, unless the consumers defaulted under the weight of all that debt, packing the bankruptcy courts and spreading financial distress among their creditors. Either way, many economists argue, the current mountain of consumer debt is likely to mean trouble.

"So far, easy credit has helped soften the downturn, and despite months of dire predictions, there has been little sign of a reckoning. Lenders' charge-off rates for bad credit-card debt, for example, were at 5.35% at the end of the third quarter, up from 4.22% at the end of the last recession. But even if that number abruptly shoots higher, most lenders today are far better capitalized than ever before, and thus better positioned to weather their losses."

But are they really? Consequences of such masterly structures of negative wealth as Enron or the fiber-optic giants snake their way throughout our financial institutions. Their total effects are not likely to be fully known for months or years. Corresponding to the negative wealth, a negative accountancy has sprung up to fill a powerful market need, and a negative morality to enable that negative accountancy to operate. We don't really know the financial condition of public companies until they apply for bankruptcy protection. When life savings can disappear overnight, not only our economic, but our social life has been radically restructured in ways that we are just beginning to learn. All this is not irrelevant to the plague of terrorism disguised as religion. George Orwell had a premonition of this less-than-innocent reversal of the plus and minus signs before our most sacred beliefs.

Just as stock market capitalizations confused future "maybes" with clinking coins today, so now consumers are encouraged to go on a buying binge with money that is not there.

The IMF and our central banks have been trying to teach the emerging countries the homely virtues of "transparency" for decades. But it is easier to advise others on the point than to apply it ourselves.

"During the first two quarter of the early 1990s recession, the average American household reacted to those tighter credit conditions by paring its debt by an inflation-adjusted $410, says Mark Zandl, chief economist of Economy.com, a consulting firm in West Chester, PA. That helped leave consumers in shape to borrow anew when the economy ultimately turned the corner. By contrast, Mr. Zandl says that during the first two quarters of the current recession, which began in March, the average US household took on $1,420 of new debt.

"Thus far, low interest rates have helped keep consumers' debt payments relatively manageable. But when rates rise, lots of debt pegged to fluctuating rates – including many credit cards and mortgages – will require higher payments, further stretching household budgets.

"And if the economy takes a turn for the worse, outsized debt levels and rising layoffs could cause far more personal bankruptcies, adding a new layer to the debt debacle already affecting corporations in sectors from telecommunications to energy. The total number of personal bankruptcies for 2001 appears likely to top the record of 1.4 million set in 1998."

But there is another hardly less disturbing intrusion of an imaginary economy today.

I refer to the spread of shorting the market, which has risen mightily, and threatens to duplicate the plundering based on imaginary accountancy that brought market down with its mirror-image. *The Wall Street Journal* (18/07, "Bear Market Encourages Shorts" by Peter A. McKay) reports. "Short-selling, generally considered a speculative way to place bearish bets, used to be practiced almost exclusively by Wall St. pros, especially hedge funds. But fund managers, brokerages houses and on-line trading firms say more and more individuals are getting into the act, particularly as the stock market worsens. In fact, despite yesterday's moderate rise in stocks, some traders say a surge in short-selling has contributed to a selloff in recent weeks."

In short a lot of the gamblers gotten into bad habits during the boom are trying to duplicate their gambling winnings by pushing battered stocks still further down rather than over-priced stocks further up. It is contributing needlessly to the volatility of the market, that is ruining tens of millions.

This whole matter is a can of worms that cries for a can-opener. The extent of the undisclosed practice is indicated on almost any statement of brokerage margin accounts. If you find alongside a security put up as collateral the notation "segregated," it means that it has been loaned out for a rental that goes to somebody who wishes to sell the stock and replace it when it has dropped substantially. Obviously that is against the interests of the owners of the stock who have put it up as security for their loan. In the name of the "transparency" that we hear so much about but is rarely there, the brokerage house should at least be required to translate that notation into what it really means: "loaned out for shorting." The rental, of course, goes not to the owner of the collateral but the brokerage house.

To make matters worse, we are informed of one case of a client of the brokerage of the most aggressive of our banks, and one that is not in the least trouble due to its intercom gambles. This involved not stock put up as security in a margin account, but a substantial amount of shares accumulated over some years that was not marginable. It was simply parked in the account. During the collapsed markets after September 11, the account was technically undermargined, though enough stock had been sold for imminent closings to put it in good shape. Nevertheless, though many times the shortfall was available as security, the firm made a bee-line to a substantial amount of the stock that was merely parked there and was not eligible as security, and sold that. The stock almost tripled in the following weeks.

The Ontario Security Commission has barricaded itself against requests that it look into such matters. Its telephone is no longer listed in the directory. When you find their number, you get a recorded message: "if you have a complaint against your broker, retain a lawyer." That is a wry joke. The cost of suing a bank-broker puts it beyond the reach of their retail clients. Shorting is a menace not only to investors who hold stock on margin, but those whose jobs are threatened by the wild volatility of the market.

There must be a public office to at least sift such complaints of brokers' clients, and advise and assist those that have merit. Otherwise, the traumatic experiences of the recent stock market bubble will be prolonged by the art of fake mirror-imaging.

William Krehm

Gleanings in an Age of Non-Disclosure

PUSHED TO EXTREMES, cunning can become the ultimate simplemindedness. In the thickening murk that is emerging financial columnists are trying to whistle away the lessons of the stock market crash. On wings of globalization and deregulation, these move from corporation to corporation, from one section of the financial markets to another, from continent to continent, from malfeasance in the executive suites to the complicity of auditors, and bankers. What has been undermined is that minimal trust essential for holding together any social system.

During the Cold War it was the contest of superpowers – the US and the Soviet Union – that in a very limited sense occasionally kept greed and rascality of either side within certain bounds. In that perspective what we are going through today may be seen as the revenge of the Soviet ghost. Without a re-thinking of everything, even the basic fundamentals of conventional economic theory, our society will go on tottering on the brink of becoming non-functional

The following postings may help our readers see what leads us to such conclusions.

Traditionally the bond and stock market were seen as balancing each another. As the revenue from one dipped, revenue from the other soared, providing some refuge and consolation for investors in the best of worlds. Hedge Funds were for deep-pocketed gamblers who could turn to the banks and the government itself for succour. This arrangement, to the extent that it really existed, has broken down, adding to the anguish that resounds throughout the financial sector. *The Wall Street Journal* (3/07, "WorldCom Woes Hit Hedge Funds, Stirring Wider Fears" by Gregory Zuckerman) reports: "After rocking the stock market in recent days, WorldCom Inc.'s woes are starting to hit hedge funds and the entire corporate bond market, raising red flags for the rest of the economy.

"Buyers are suddenly in short supply. If things get worse, analysts fear a number of big firms may have to bail out of their positions in WorldCom and other bonds.

"The pain has spread throughout the corporate bond market, hitting both investment-grade and junk bonds, especially companies like Qwest Communications International Inc., Tyco International and AOL Time Warner Inc.'s America On Line, which have been accused of using aggressive accounting or have seen executives under fire.

"The $2.2 billion Obsidian Hedge Fund run by BlackRock Inc., which boasts one of the best long-term records in the bond business, fell 7.5% in June, an unusually steep decline for a bond hedge fund accustomed to grinding out steady returns.

"Firms that specialize in so-called distressed debt have done even worse. Many distressed hedge funds bought WorldCom's bonds when they fell to about 40 cents on the dollar last month, but have seen it tumble further to 15 cents. While those losses pale in comparison with the pain from some stock mutual funds this year, they are startling for investors who have flocked to bond funds to avoid the heavy losses in the stock market. For many bond hedge funds, the past 10 days have been the worst period since Long-Term Capital Management ran into trouble nearly four years ago.

"Many big bond players made hefty bets that WorldCom would be able to make it until at least early next year, thanks to a considerable cash hoard. But when [it appeared that] the company had used accounting maneuvers to boost its earnings in recent years, all its bonds tumbled in price.

"Chris Scibelli, spokesman for Metropolitan West, a big mutual-fund company that recently hired former Vice President Albert Gore as its vice-chairman, is down 4% in a single week after placing 2.1% of its holdings in WorldCom bonds. He comments: 'It is extremely difficult to guard against fraud.'" Fraud, however, runs seamlessly through much of the economy from analysts to auditors and economists. It is as prevalent as mines and legless victims in the former battlefields of Macedonia, Afghanistan and Africa.

Open-endedly the *WSJ* concludes. "Cable and media junk bonds weakened Tuesday on concerns about media companies, sparked in part by a sell-off in AOL Time Warner stock and news involving Vivendi Universal."

The Mexican meltdown at the end of 1994 alarmed Washington enough for it to organize a $51 billion international standby fund. But within a few months what had first appeared as a catastrophe threatening the world financial system turned into bonanza. It opened up key sectors of the Mexican economy that had been off-limit to foreign investors. The Asian crisis of 1997 had like effects, especially in South Korea.

That, however, is notably not the case with the present collapse on Wall St. The *WSJ* (9/07, "Buyout Firms Find Telecom Too Risky" by Kara Scannell and Robert Frank) informs us: "Experts say that with all the assets available for sale and all the money available to buy them, the most surprising aspect on the Leveraged Buyout (LBO) scene is how few deals are getting done. In the case of telecom deals in particular the reason: too much risk, even after asset values have dropped so far. 'Too much uncertainty in the underlying industry and too many accounting questions which makes it hard to have a good sense of the business's trends,' said William Kirsch, a merger-and-acquisition lawyer at Kirkland and Ellis.

"In the early 1990s, LBO firms jumped in when a combination of a recession and falling stock market brought down corporate valuations and the companies remained in business without heading for bankruptcy court. Today some of the biggest companies are heading straight into bankruptcy proceedings, creating a much more complicated process to negotiate deals.

"'The financial misstatements are more or less unprecedented on the scale we're seeing, and that's what created the high level of caution,' said Stephen Schwarzman, co-founder of Blackstone. 'You want to know what you're buying might be true.'"

The substratum of trust that is a synonym for credit has been blown. It is only a decade since Canada's banks were bailed out in stealth and deregulated at the same time – certainly a strange combination of conflicted interests. That suppressed episode itself merits a Royal Commission, to protect Canadians against a replay of that scandalous script, should the banks come back to the government with their begging bowls to get them out of their massive speculative losses. To the banks the 1991 bailout was tantamount to the message: "Go forth and gamble your heads off, courtesy of the Canadian taxpayer." Accordingly, *The Globe and Mail* (6/07, "TD's bond prices under pressure" by Karen Howlett) has a sinister ring: "Bond investors have driven down the price of some of TD Bank's debt securities amid speculations the bank will be forced to take a one-time charge of about $1 billion to deal with further deterioration on loans to the battered telecom and cable sectors.

"Royal Bank of Canada's bonds have also come under pressure once the bank became embroiled in the Enron Corp. scandal through former British employees, debt analysts said. The three have been charged with fraud by US authorities in connection with Enron. They are also at the centre of a lawsuit launched by Rabobank of the Netherlands against RBC over a separate Enron issue. Spreads have widened significantly on

TD's trust securities and are wider than similar securities issued by other banks, debt analysts at CIBC World Markets Inc. said yesterday in a report. TD has the biggest exposure to the telecom sector among the big banks, with $4.9 billion in loans at the end of the second quarter.

"Kevin Choquette of Scotia Capital Inc. said the bank might take a special writedown of between $500 million and $1 billion this year."

William Krehm

TINA Banner Hoisted High

GIVEN THE SWARM of bankruptcies that have taken over, including that of public morality itself, it is becoming ever more difficult to defend the status quo. For such occasions, the TINA argument ("There Is No Alternative") gets spread out like a magic carpet to bridge over a few missing syllogisms to the desired conclusion. When NAFTA was brought in, Sylvia Ostry and other ambitious folk were arguing for the North American Free Trade Agreement. However, today Ms. Ostry is one of the few repentants on this circuit. On a recent television show I was astounded to hear her plead that she had not examined carefully enough what NAFTA would impose on us, and how little it would give us. Of course, she should have. However, amongst her colleagues, she stands out for her rare courage in going public about her error and should be applauded.

Yet the allure of TINA continues, particularly since a more exigent cast has taken over in Washington. In a shrinking academic universe, it is hard for academics to go quietly into the night of retirement. The fate of the generation of mandarins who so brilliantly introduced Keynes to Ottawa before and during the war could not present a more uplifting warning, if their heads had been impaled on Parliament's Bell Tower.

When you get to continental defence, the issues not only tend to be more strenuously argued though with even more gossamer logic. But then aggressiveness is a not uncommon trait among military scholars, veterans of so many wars with pen and computer.

In *The Globe and Mail* (20/06, "Strong and Free? Then Act that Way"), Stephen Clarkson reviews the text published by the C.D. Howe Institute urging military integration with the US. "Today, retired historian, J.L. Granatstein will stand up at a lunch meeting in downtown Toronto to say that, in the interests of preserving its independence and sovereignty, Canada must make a dramatic move into further military integration with the US.

"If he sticks to the text the Howe published over his name last week – *A Friendly Agreement in Advance*, he will go on to state that Canada has no choice but to support the US administration's other priorities: weaponizing space and attacking Iraq. If Ottawa doesn't endorse these initiatives, it risks economic retaliation from an angry Washington. Because Sept. 11 created 'a new situation and new threats,' Canada's policies cannot risk being perceived as anti-American or based on morality." Perish the thought!

And yet we do owe it to our friendship with the US to speak out when we feel that its government of the day is ignoring not only its own higher interests, but the survival needs of humanity. By warning Washington in good time of the bloody mess they were getting into on behalf of the "domino theory" (remember?), we honoured our obligations. We are proud to have provided a haven to thousands of young Americans who refused to participate in that senseless butchery. The one-eyed chap owes it to his blind neighbour, no matter what his bulk, to warn him when he is headed towards a precipice. Of course, the chances of a US government on a roll taking our advice is slight enough. Yet it should be clear today that it would have benefited immensely in the case of Vietnam if it had. In all its history no such military defeat was suffered by the US, one particularly humiliating because it was in an unjust cause. It almost tore the land of Lincoln apart once more. On our side, it was one of the most courageous stands in the annals of our foreign policy. That should encourage Ottawa to refuse to become involved in US policies that we disagree with on higher grounds. It should also suggest to Washington the wisdom of listening patiently to the dissenting views of friends.

William Krehm

Sorting Out Cart, Donkey and Driver

THE HEAVENS, officially taken as the source of the free-market gospel have suddenly opened and emptied upon us the plagues of Egypt. It is not enough to denounce the results as "evil," punishable by prison sentences. Greed is a human frailty, and that is why in all reasonably run societies it is subject to some serious controls. What is unique in our present meltdown, is that not only were such restrictions removed, but the frailty was promoted to the basic economic virtue. No ceiling on its appetites was recognized. Its rate of growth and expansion of that rate were projected into the future, and capitalized as present assets. Once embodied into the market price of the asset, that rate of growth, real or simulated, had to be maintained if the stock market – the ultimate pontiff of the system – was not to crater. Survival needs present an awesome temptation. But the chief villains in the drama are not those who succumbed to it, but those that stood the norms of human decency on their head. Unless we sort out the basic responsibilities – those who set up the system – punishing individual actors conforming to its non-rules will hardly solve the immense problem that has overtaken the world.

The need of the hour, in short, is to sort out cart, donkey and driver.

That is why clues towards that end emerging from the countless investigations are of key importance.

The Wall Street Journal (24/07, "Energy Deals Made $200 Million In Fees for Citigroup, J.P. Morgan" by Paul Beckett and Jathon Sapsford) offers some helpful clues: "Citigroup Inc. and

J.P. Morgan & Co. made more than $200 million in fees from transactions that helped Enron Corp. and other energy companies boost their cash flow and hide debt, according to congressional investigators and others.

"Investigators also laid out evidence from company documents that suggested the bankers knew of Enron's aim to avoid scrutiny through the deals. Along with the banks' acknowledgement that they marketed such schemes to other energy companies, some legal specialists said that raised the specter of possible criminal or civil liability for the nation's two largest financial institutions. The hearing yesterday, before the Senate Permanent Subcommittee on Investigations, aimed to determine how much Wall St. enabled the complex arrangements that helped fuel the spectacular rise and swoon of the energy industry. As it went on, shares in both banks plunged. In 4 p.m. New York Stock Exchange composite trading, Citigroup share sank 15.7%, J.P. Morgan stock was down 18.1%.

"'If it looks like the banks gave companies intricate instructions on how to do all this, the banks are going to face a significant chance of being indicted,' asserted Christopher J. Bebel, a former consultant for the Department of Justice and a former Securities and Exchange Commission investigator."

Pitch Books Presented Alleged Facts in Pitch-black Darkness

"The structures the banks were promoting to Enron and [other] energy companies involve prepaid oil and gas forward contracts, in which money is paid up from for future delivery of the commodity. Those are common in the industry. But by involving a special-purpose vehicle established by the banks in an offshore location, energy companies could book that cash as part of their trading operations – instead of as debt – and also keep investors in the dark.

"To help sell these financing deals, Citigroup and J.P. Morgan developed pitch books about how companies could use their services in a way that, critics allege, deceive investors by masking a company's true financial health.

"In submissions to the subcommittee Citigroup said it engaged in prepaid trades involving special-purpose vehicles with Arka Exploration Co. in 1992 and Amerada Hess Corp. in 1993, as well as with Enron in 10 transactions most recently in 2001. The biggest of the Enron transactions was a series of deals dubbed 'Yosemite.'

"Citigroup also said it had made presentations on financing arrangements similar to Yosemite to many of the best-known players in the energy business, including Williams Cos., El Paso Corp., Reliant Dynegy, and Duke Energy. But none of those companies took the bank up on its offer."

The present Pontiff of Rome, the saintly Paul II, was not more dedicated to his missionary work than America's two leading financial institutions were to theirs. The "special purposes" of this new technology they were spreading *urbi et orbi* were how to cook the books and bilk investors.

Nor was J.P. Morgan a slouch in its mission. "[It] said that besides Enron seven other companies used the same offshore vehicle it established, called Mahonia Ltd. The bank named

Columbia Natural Resources Inc., now part of NiSource Inc.; Occidental Petroleum Co.; Ocean Energy Inc.; Santa Fe Snyder Corp., now part of Devon Energy Corp; and Tom Brown Inc. Spokesmen for those companies said the transactions with J.P. Morgan were all accounted for properly."

Were J.P. Morgan still alive, his bulbous nose would light up in pride over the spectacle of his old corporation scoring so smashing a revenge for the rough ride he was subjected to by an earlier Republican president.

"In a statement J.P. Morgan said, 'Prepaid forwards, widely used by a large number of companies, demonstrate that several outside firms found that they were legal and appropriate.'" This would seem a newly burgeoning point of law that might hold: if bank hold-ups became frequent enough, they might pass under common law as an accepted practice.

"Citigroup and J.P. Morgan already are being investigated by criminal prosecutors at both the Justice Department and the Office of Manhattan District Attorney Robert Morgenthau, as well as the SEC, which handles civil cases.

"Documents uncovered in the congressional investigation provided new details about the extent to which the banks knew Enron was seeking to use the transactions to mask debt as trades. 'Enron loves these deals as they are able to hide funded debt from their equity analysts because they (at the very least) book it as deferred revenue or (better yet) bury it in their trading liabilities,' one J.P. Morgan executive said in a 1998 email to colleagues."

The conclusion of all this: the largest banks, that have been coddled by the government with regular bailouts and deregulation are not left with a desire to reciprocate all this largesse. Size and power carry their own immunities and privileges. The Bush government must not be allowed off the hook by putting on TV the handcuffing of three members of the Rigas family for their crimes against their shareholders and the public at large. The only meaningful response to the present meltdown of the scandal-ridden market is to make banks stick to legitimate banking rather than run training courses for major financial crimes.

William Krehm

Facing the Mother of Financial Scams

THERE ARE FEW THINGS to rejoice about when elementary business morality lies in the ditch. Yet for the first time in three decades there is a healthy regurgitation of the supposedly eternal truths that have been force-fed the public: "Leave it all to the market," "fundamentals are sound."

We are in the early stages of this liberating process: the scams of leading financial conglomerates are still coming to light as yesterday's star firms file for bankruptcy. And the disappearance of so much capital is bound to scar every area of the economy.

Like our own government in Canada, the Bush administration is trying to wriggle out of such reckonings. More than accountancy and corporate cash boxes have been tampered with. The language itself has been twisted to eliminate all alternatives to the policies that led to this crisis. Many of the most dearly bought lessons of our history have been buried.

The initiative for all this came from outside Congress and Parliament and behind their backs. The Bank for International Settlements (BIS), originally a purely technical body for handling transfer problems connected with World War I reparations, served world bankerdom as the Afghan caves did bin Laden – a den for plotting the take-over by private banking of the central banks. The main steps for this:

• Spreading the conviction that governments are not to be trusted with creating the nation's money supply. Instead it is to be entrusted to the private banks. This flies in the face of the record: more frequently than once a decade the governments of most countries have bailed out the private banks. Yet, incongruously, the image drilled into the public mind is that the creation of our money supply must be farmed out to the private banks, who then lend much of the money to the governments at a rate of interest fancy enough "to lick inflation." When the central government creates credit, it is denounced for "printing money." When private banks do the same thing, it is prudent business practice.

• It was established as a law beyond discussion that any upward inching of price was a warning which if ignored would bring on hyperinflation such as wiped out the German currency in 1923. However, Germany in 1923 had lost a war. Its hyperinflation was set off by the occupation of its industrial heartland by the French and Belgian armies to collect war reparations. In response, the whole country – left and right – went on strike. But the BIS, through myriad channels, spread the version that even the tiniest bit of "inflation" tolerated would end up reduplicating the German hyperinflation of 1923. The implication of this gospel was that if interest rates had been pushed up high enough, there would, retroactively, have been no World War, no occupation of the Ruhr by the French army, and no general strike. To the drumbeat of such illiterate propaganda, most of Canada's federal debt was run up in the early 1990s.

Not only was that frivolous, but it involved glaring conflicts of interest – higher interest rates, i.e., the revenue of loan sharks, was declared the one blunt tool for stabilizing the economy. The very word "Deflation" was banned from polite discourse even when prices dropped below production costs. Involvement in this arrangement, active or through silence, hangs over the head of every politician in the land. We must recognize this leverage in discussions with our elected representatives to fix their attention on society's plight and its root causes.

• Prices in fact can go up because of too much demand over available supply. That is real market inflation. But an inching up of price was the inevitable consequence of the rapid urbanization in all countries, and of the higher technology that required more services that the state alone could provide. *Nobody moving from a small town to London or New York can expect his living costs not to rise. How then can you expect flat prices when the exploding population of the world makes a similar move?*

• But the greatest encroachment of the banking system was achieved by identifying "fighting inflation" with raising interest rates. The two have become virtual synonyms. Higher interest rates, however, shift wealth from every other group in society to money lenders and banks. They drive firms into bankruptcy and create mass unemployment. Such policy is the economic equivalent of the collateral damage that in Afghanistan rained down from the US air force onto their Canadian allies, and on a civilian wedding.

Maximizing Collateral Damage

On the other hand, before the revision of the Bank of Canada Act in Canada in 1991, an alternative way of dealing with real inflation had existed in Canada as in all leading countries of the world. The chartered banks were required to deposit with the Bank of Canada (BoC) a token part of the deposits they held from the public. On this "statutory reserve" they got no interest. When the economy was really "overheated" – i.e., when the demand for goods and services exceeded their possible supply – it could be "cooled" by raising the required statutory reserve without raising interest rates. When that occurred, it reduced the leverage of credit creation by the banks: they had to put up more cash with the BoC for existing loans, and it increased the amount of cash needed to support new loans.

But in the 1980s the banks in Canada – as in the United States – had lost much or more than their capital financing gambles in real estate, gas and oil, and US department store chains. To bail them out, a bill was slipped through parliament without debate, phasing out these statutory reserves. At the same time BIS, to rescue overextended banks throughout the world, had already issued its *Risk-Based Capital Requirements* for banks that declared the debt of advanced (OECD) countries risk-free, requiring no additional capital for banks to acquire. Between the two measures it became possible for Canadian banks to quadruple their holdings of federal debt – to some $80 billion – without putting up any significant amount of money. Rather than a one-shot bailout this is an entitlement that comes to the banks each year. Translated into a permanent bond it amounted to some $100 billion – about one third of the outstanding federal debt at the time.

It was to support this largesse to the financial community that Ottawa slashed its grants to the provinces in the early nineties and introduced the harshly regressive Goods and Services Tax. This led to the cancelling of social services across the land.

In other countries – like the US – where the statutory reserves were not wholly abolished, they were reduced to the point of becoming almost meaningless.

At the same time as they were awarded this entitlement, the banks were further deregulated. They were allowed to take over brokerage houses, do merchant banking, underwriting of public stock issues, engage in just about every sort of stock-market activity as principals or financing their clients. The fire-walls established in the thirties between these incompatibles were weakened or abolished. Without this, the mega-bubble that has blown up in the faces of our governments could never have occurred. And unless the lessons from it are learned and applied, no matter how many CEOs are paraded before cameras in handcuffs, the ground will be left ploughed and fertilized for another crop of financial malfeasance. And this was the handiwork of international non-elected bodies that consider public money spent on schools and hospitals inflationary!

The Dead Rat under the Floor Boards

We have called the entitlement-cum-deregulation of our banks in the early nineties the "dead rat under the floorboards." It is the source of the moral stench that fills the air and prevents the financial system from being made whole again. That is what must be addressed.

That is why a spot of analysis is essential to compare the alternatives – the use of the central bank to finance federal public investment on a near-zero interest basis, as opposed to the interest-free bailout of the banks in 1991 that made possible the late financial bubble.

Let us begin by noting that the control of money creation by our central bank and the surrender of that control to our private banks both end up restricting the amount of credit available to its ultimate users – whether private consumers, corporations, or all levels of government themselves. However, if the control remains with the central bank the government has access to almost cost-free credit by the fact that the profits of the central bank almost entirely revert to it. That is so in the case of Canada because the federal government is the sole shareholder of the central bank. In the case of the US Federal Reserve, which is owned by private banks, it is a continuation of the ancestral monopoly of the crown to coin precious metals. When the private banks provide the bulk of the credit – even to the government – that is not so. During a recession when the debt of the private sector becomes of doubtful quality and there are few

lenders and even fewer reliable borrowers, this raises serious problems. Then it becomes important that governments step in to make essential investments to revive the economy. When the government is reduced to paying interest to the financial sector for the credit-creation it has surrendered to banks – that is not possible. Then the most obvious public capital expenditures – even the maintenance of watermains, and disease control are vetoed with question" "Where is the money coming from?" That must be answered with another question: "Where did the money go?"

Having privatized the bulk of our money-creation,[1] concerned primarily in improving its own balance sheet, the private financial sector now intervenes as a highly conflicted intermediary. That is the background for the present plague of CEO crime. The main concern of financial corporations during the stock market bubble was to improve their balance sheets amidst violent deflationary pressures. That required that they incorporate their dreams of future profits into their market valuation which must be kept high enough to peddle their stock.

Of all of this, conflicted interest is the driving engine. It not only makes possible collateral damage, but runs on it.

We must make use of the provisions in the *Bank of Canada Act* to enable us to cope with the oncoming tidal wave of deflation as was done after the Bank of Canada had been founded for the purpose in 1935. Anything short of that, will merely guarantee a replay of the 1991 surrender of money creation to our sporting banks. Society surely cannot survive a replay of that disgraceful episode.[2]

William Krehm

1. Actually "near-money" creation since the banks' loans to the government bear interest. Legal tender (or cash) when it was gold or silver, or now when it is government borrowing from the central bank does not. When you reduce government borrowing from the central bank to make room for more borrowing by the government from the banks, you are imposing a an additional burden of interest on everything throughout the economy.

2. The story of the bank 1991 bailout was first fully documented in *The Bank of Canada – A Power Unto Itself* (Krehm, William [1993]. Stoddard: Toronto). This book is still available at a special rate of $5 plus $3 for postage and handling, or as a free gift with an annual subscription to *Economic Reform*. (Price: $30).

[Sidebar]

"Ecuador's Central Bank director, Leopoldo Baez, said it will propose to President Gustavo Noboa raising the statutory reserve requirement of the country's bank by two percentage points each month until it reaches 10%, up from 4% now" (*The Wall Street Journal*, 19/08).

Poor little Ecuador that has tried just about everything – not excluding dollarization – is finally attempting to rejig its central bank for its original purpose. However, it would be more fitting for the powerful countries to take the lead in dealing with the results of their failed policies. The same *Wall Street Journal* issue in an article by Jon. E. Hilsenrath quotes Donald Ratajcazk "a widely followed inflation watcher": "the biggest risk for Fed policy makers is that prolonged economic weakness push the sharply slowing inflation rate into a bout of deflation." In fact such a bout is already well under way, and for it the central banks of the leading powers and the international institutions are completely unequipped. Even the mention of "deflation" in central bank circles there leads to mouth-washing with soap suds and a blighted career. Years ago central bankers forgot how to spell the word and now they are suddenly confronted with the reality.

Banks in the Spotlight

AS STOCK MARKETS cave in, dragging corporate bonds with them, investors in search of a haven are coming to remind us of the boatloads of refugees who sail the seas looking in vain for a country to offer them a chance of survival.

That has brought bank shares into the spotlight as candidates to fill this role. But they are not passing the scrutiny of better analysts.

Consider the article of Gretchen Morgenson (*The New York Times*, 28/07, "Banks are Havens (and Other Myths)"): "Since the bear market began in March 2000, investors have been told that even if the economy suffered, the risks of investing in bank stocks were far lower than in the recession of 1990. New and sophisticated risk management practices had enabled them to unload much of their lending risks to other market players, the argument went, while the institutions' ability to generate fees continued apace."

We have emphasized that the so-called risk management models are based on derivatives that in turn posit a market of players so minute that nothing they do or don't do can affect prices. That explains why a few years ago Long Term Capital hedge managed by two economists who had been awarded the so-called Nobel Prize in Economics had to be rescued by a $51 billion standby fund hastily put together by Washington. This was to prevent a crash of the international financial system.

Ms. Morgenson does not dig that deep, but she has done some significant spadework: "But a risk that the banks cannot expunge is the fear taking hold among investors that the country's largest financial institutions were central to the financing of the stock market bubble.

"That perception is not only punishing banks stocks, which not so long ago were seen as a haven for investors, but it is also casting a pall over the entire market, fund managers say. If banks are found to have facilitated corporate misdeeds – such as hiding losses in Enron, as has been alleged in Congress – severe damage will be done to already battered investor confidence in the entire financial system.

"The banks have been both the least visible and the most important components of the financing of the new economy over the last 10 years,' says Jonathan H. Cohen, of JHC Capital in Greenwich, Conn., and former head of Internet research at Merrill Lynch. 'Investors know that most Internet and telecom companies were part of a bubble, and that many brokerage houses were involved in sustaining it. Now people are getting around to focus on the role of the commercial banks.'

"Bank stocks, as measured by the Philadelphia Stock Exchange/KBW Banks Index, have lost 10.4% in the last two weeks alone. 'Until recently, the feeling among investors was that banks have regulators and that will keep them out of trouble,' said David A. Hendler, an analyst at CreditSights, a research firm in New York. 'But no one was thinking that banks enabled the rest of the world's business problems, and that will eventually get reflected in the operating performance of the financial companies.'

"As bank stocks outperformed the market, their weighting in the Standard & Poor's 500-stock index grew. Their recent downturn has hurt the big, popular mutual funds that mirror the performance of the S&P.

Our Banks Headed for World-class Insolvency?

"Some of the nation's biggest and most trusted banks are in this fix at least partly because of their increased reach in all areas of financial services in recent years. The Financial Modernization Act in 1999 eliminated most of the barriers to certain business set up for banks under Glass-Steagall, the legislation that came out of the Great Depression. This allowed commercial banks to compete with investment banks for the right to sell securities to investors. And the larger banks approached the business aggressively.

"For example, in May 2001, WorldCom raised almost $12 billion in a bond offering managed by Citigroup. The offering came when WorldCom's was still a high-grade name in the credit markets, and was presented to investors as a benchmark issue against which other investment bonds would be judged. Because the WorldCom deal was a benchmark, any portfolio manager running a bond mutual fund had to own the security. So when WorldCom began its free fall earlier this year, a throng of bondholders were holding the bag. The bond sale allowed WorldCom to clear out a lot of the bank lines of credit and push back the maturity dates on loans.

"Now, with WorldCom filing bankruptcy a little more than a year after the bonds were sold, investors are questioning how much due diligence was done by the banks that sold the securities. There are considerable risks associated with the growth of financial services conglomerates. One is that top management and the board cannot possibly know what lower- and middle-level employees are doing inside the bank. 'Senior management and the board of directors must have comprehensive orientation, knowledge and understanding of what's going on, and in many instances that is not the case,' said Henry Kaufman of Henry Kaufman & Co. in New York.

"'And the nation's financial system,' he said, 'is put at risk when these companies become huge conglomerates.' The banks' pitch,' he said, 'is essentially this: We want to be your banker, which means we want to make you the loan, syndicate the loan, underwrite your bonds and distribute them, we want to do your stock issues, we want to place your commercial paper and we want to manage some of the assets in your pension funds. This not only diminishes competition, but creates institutions that are too big to fail. If they did they would create a systemic risk.'

"Some analysts say that in the interest of grabbing more of the lucrative securities underwriting deals that had been the province of investment banks, commercial banks may have been eager to advise companies on how to get around tax rules and accounting regulations or leverage their balance sheets excessively. Such strategies are now drawing the attention of Congress and regulators and the ire of investors."

William Krehm

Standing on our Heads — Thinking with our Feet

THE GOSPEL from on high was that economics had shrivelled to a single strand of wisdom: "inflation was always a monetary phenomenon." Money, then, was the major problem. If zero inflation was in sight fundamentals were sound. Most of Canada's federal debt was run up during the watch of John Crow. As Governor of the Bank of Canada, Crow, a Brit with a previous career as a proconsul of the IMF in Latin America, was a fanatical believer in "zero inflation." And of course, there was no institution in recent years that created as much credit-money as our deregulated banks did on the stock market. From 11:1 in 1946, the ratio of their assets to the cash in our banks' possession rose to about 400:1 today. But somehow that wasn't deemed inflation, because the hilt of that mighty weapon was in the proper hands. Since there is no money but credit, this powerful surge of stock market winnings changed the face of the world economy. It gave rise to a new class of billionaires; rewards to CEOs came to equal the wages of a regiment of factory workers.

But suddenly all this turned out to have been based on illusion. Increase in the money supply had elbowed out minor concerns such as accountancy and even morality. The implications of this were bottomless. And that leaves our governments – already in sorry repute for their role as shills of the stock market bubble – in further trouble.

From a mere by-product of the money supply ("always monetary phenomenon"), the economy was suddenly presented as being independent of the stock market, i.e., of the money supply. Thus *The Globe and Mail* (25/07, "Central bank plays down financial market volatility") reports the Governor of the Bank of Canada, Mr. David Dodge, emphasizing "the possibility of booming domestic demand, spurred by low interest rates" being as strong as "market volatility spilling over into the broader economy."

Strange that the Governor should be referring to the supportive effects of low interest rates as he slapped on his third interest rate increase in weeks bringing the Canadian rate a full per cent above the discount rate in the US.

The chief economist of the Royal Bank, Craig Wright, is quoted in the same GM piece as "agreeing with Mr. Dodge that the economy is strong and somewhat immune to the volatility on the market. Raising rates is the right thing to do."

On the other hand this is too much to swallow for other bank economists "'I was surprised that Mr. Dodge was so sanguine about the financial market debacle that we're going through,' said Sherry Cooper chief economist at BMO Nesbitt Burns Inc. She said her phone is ringing off the hook with tearful pensioners who are seeing their life savings go up in flames on the stock market, and she disagrees with Mr. Dodge that regular Canadians are detached from the stock market. The central bank should be very cautious before it raises rates again, she added."

The present crisis and the reactions to it gives you an x-ray of the clique that have taken over the central bank. David Dodge won his spurs as Deputy Finance Minister in charge of pushing through the Goods and Service Tax, a regressive bit of legislation that help cover the cost of the 1991 bank bailout at the expense of the most vulnerable members of our society. It mattered little that the Liberals came into power partly on the strength of their promise to repeal the GST, Dodge showed Messers Chrétien and Paul Martin, by making it possible for them to break their word on the GST, that he was "independent" enough to run the Bank of Canada. His present stance only highlights what the alleged "independence of the Bank of Canada" really means.

It requires a good deal of brass to pretend that the BoC is "independent of the government" when that government is its sole shareholder (article 17(2)). The *Bank of Canada Act* (article 14(2)) sets forth the power of the Finance Minster to impose his view of Bank policy if a major disagreement should arise.

The position of the federal government as sole shareholder of the Bank of Canada is no small point. For it means that all net profits of the Bank belong to the shareholders. Part of the stock market mess can be traced to the trend of large corporations to reduce their dividends towards zero. Exactly the same thing has been done with the dividends of the Bank of Canada. The bailout of the banks in 1991 took the form of having the Bank of Canada reduce its holdings of federal debt from well over 20% of the total outstanding in 1975 to a mere 5%. The difference came to be held by the chartered banks without putting up any significant money of their own.

But that misrepresentation – the independence of the Bank of Canada – shows why financial scandals on the scale that we are experiencing are possible. The art of government has become to a large extent the thwarting of key laws on the books. The control of the media and the educational system on these key matters makes this possible. The present deepening crisis provides an opportunity to challenge this system and bring democracy into flower once again. It must not be fumbled.

Of course, we, as in 1933, will to a considerable extent be influenced by what happens in the United States. *The Wall Street Journal* (24/07, "What Could Bring 1930s-Style Reform of US Businesses?" by Gerland F. Seib and John Harwood) offers its perspective: "In the early 1930s a shattered economy, a devastated stock market and revulsion towards the business class produced sweeping changes in the way business and finance were conducted. Now Americans face the possibility of a similar wave of reform. Today's economic woes hardly rival those of the 1930s, and Congress's rush to clamp down on corporate misconduct is mild compared with the legislative earthquake that shook the business world then. But the country is beginning to appraise the celebration of the free-market forces that marked the 1990s. And early political tremors of public opinion hint at greater fallout to come.

"Political momentum to restrain government regulation is waning. As they await the government's response to a wave of business scandals, six in ten Americans say they are worried regulators won't go far enough.

"AFL-CIO President John Sweeney call this the best chance in years to 'fundamentally change the way corporate America works.' And free-market apostles, ascendant since Ronald Reagan, fear that even a Republican White House may join a popular stampede. The 2002 market meltdown could turn into a historic turning point in American politics and regulation if two significant changes occur.

"First, the present crisis of confidence in business and markets would have to turn into a broader economic decline. When Franklin Roosevelt embarked on the New Deal, one in four Americans was out of work, four times today's unemployment rate. The spread of stock ownership means Main St. is feeling Wall St.'s pain, but so far that pain has produced public anger not desperation."

However, it took well over three years for the 1929 stock market crash to play out throughout the economy. Since at the time a substantial portion of Americans were still living on farms, these were – until their farm was foreclosed – assured of a miserable something to eat and a roof over their heads.

Deregulation and Globalization (D&R) in our day has, moreover, created a tight mesh of economic vulnerability throughout the world. Subsistence agriculture has been shattered in many areas. This must have two distinct effects. The response to the Wall St. debacle is already registering in the flight of foreign capital from American shores. It had been drawn there in large part as a refuge, and it did much to fuel Wall St.'s orgy. Weaker domestic currencies will to an extent improve American and Canadian export industries. But since the purchasing powers of other continents will be adversely affected by the US meltdown, that will have limited scope.

On the other hand the deteriorating international situation will encourage US rearmament, and military interventions throughout the world – at least until the body bags start coming home in serious number. Neither of these perspectives is encouraging. But they could converge to strengthen the demand for basic economic changes.

There is another potential advantage that we have over our grandparents. We have the example of the New Deal and its fire walls to show us the way. We have, too, the very use of the central banks of the advanced countries in creating a substantial part of the financing of War II at nominal rates. There was, too, the lesson of the first two decades of peace when 16 years of neglect during the Depression and the War were repaired. No such models existed in the thirties. The need is to catch up with those who have suppressed the memory of these dearly-bought experiences. Rubbing out those key chapters of our history is as grave a crime as the purloining of billions of shareholders' wealth.

I recently watched a Donahue TV show out of Houston on which Ralph Nader addressed an audience of Enron former employees who lost much of their retirement funds as well as their jobs. Not only was I impressed by Nader's command of the situation, but by the high educational standards of many of the victims of the bankrupt high-tech corporations. There is no comparison between the average capacity of today's victims to mount an effective political response and their corresponding numbers in 1930.

Having been burned by fraudulent claims in high places, they should have no difficulty in grasping what COMER has come to call the "Dead Rat Under the Floorboards." That refers to the Central Bank's master hanky-panky in bailing out the banks from their past gambling disasters by surrendering to them the financing of the government – i.e., bulk of money-creation. Without these master central bank scams there could have been no Enron.

William Krehm

The Hierarchy of Fraud

ONE THING should be made clear. As great as the financial scandals have been, they are not the trunk story line of the skullduggery that has brought down the American model. They are mere symptoms of a deeper swindle. That by-product – palpable body counts – of course, is easier to quantify than the cause. But suppressing key information, including crucial cuts of our history, and substituting a twisted version of the setting, is what made possible the financial malfeasance. Send to prison all the miscreants who cooked the books and made off with the boodle, but leave in place the underlying web of fiction, and it will all start over again in no time flat.

That achievements of all the venturesome attorneys and reporters are significant only because they alert us where we must do further digging. And with persistence – for each disclosure leads to the next more astounding one.

That is why *The New York Times* (28/02, "Once Upon a Time, a Restless CEO" by David Leonhardt) deserves our applause.

"Welcome to story time in corporate America. The old story went like this: the chief executives were in such demand that they were apt to jump ship at any moment. The next story is already emerging. It says executives will begin quitting in droves if boards force them to hold on to their company stock in an effort to tie the executives' pay to their company's long-term health.

"The storytellers have most often been the executives and the recruiters and consultants they hire. By suggesting that the job market for chief executives is fluid, the tales of executive wanderlust have conveniently offered an economic rationale for enormous executive pay. The evidence, however, is about as impressive as the wardrobe of the emperor in that other fairy tale.

"The job of CEO is fabulously attractive, allowing somebody to lead thousands of people, often in an organization where they have spent years. Few people leave voluntarily before they are ready to retire. Surprisingly few have even been willing to leave one corner office for another elsewhere.

"Since 2000, a year in which executive turnover spiked, 77 of the 200 biggest companies have hired a new boss, according to Pearl Meyer & Partners, a compensation consulting firm in New York. How many of those companies had to do so because their CEO took another job? Two. Most departing chiefs retired and remained on their company's board, according to news accounts. A good number were forced out.

"Yet many companies, including USX and Verizon, lavished their executives with so-called retention bonuses. Dozens of others cited retention to justify big pay packages, even – as was the case at Enron recently – when the executives could hardly expect to be sought-after candidates for other jobs."

Senator John McCain, Republican of Arizona, has proposed requiring top executives to hold all their company stock as long as they are in their jobs. Congress is unlikely to adopt the plan, but some analysts think that boards of directors might enact milder versions of the policy on their own. Executives have begun to fight the effort, saying that talented leaders would quit after the stock price had risen, sell the stock and find new work.

"If boards are wise, though, they will realize that finding a new company to run is not easy. Bank One and Citigroup already have stock-holding rules for top executives, and neither has suffered an exodus. Boards and investors simply have to decide that they will not bend to executives' wishes as often as they did in the slap-happy 1990s." ⌘

History of Mathematics for Future Economists?

THERE IS ENOUGH RELIGION of a tattered sort about our economy to warrant reaching to the Old Testament for guidance. There we note that rather from the Temple, the greatest prophets came out of the desert. No surprise then that Chairman Greenspan's much awaited utterance on the economy should be found wanting (*The Wall Street Journal*, 17/07, "Greenspan Issues Hopeful Outlook as Stocks Sink" by Greg Ip). Despite his unhappiness with the situation, his analysis was essentially an inside job.

"Saying an 'infectious greed' had gripped business in the late 1990s, he warned that breakdowns in corporate governance could undermine the trust necessary for an efficient market. That prospect threatened to 'significantly erode the economy's impressive gains in productivity.' He praised the Senate's sweeping legislation aimed at shoring up accounting standards and corporate governance, and noted that even without congressional intervention companies such as Coca-Cola have voluntarily begun to record their stock-option grants as expenses. With inflation now low, he said Fed officials are sticking to their current stance until they see evidence that obstacles to growth 'are dissipating enough to allow the strong fundamentals to show through more fully."

In those few remarks there are enough windows left open for the miscreants to be back at their games in no time flat.

What, for example, is "inflation"? This he sees as low enough for the Fed not to raise interest rates – unlike his headlong Canadian counterpart. If prices were flat despite the increased government measures against terrorists, with so much run-down infrastructure in our cities, the neglect of our educational, health and social services, that would surely indicate not a victory over "inflation" but actual deflation. Prices would have fallen far short of what is necessary to replace the public investment being used up. The monumental hanky-panky disclosed in our greatest corporations' books must have left holes in society's balance sheets as well. And what really lurks behind the term "productivity" that serves as ground base for the Chairman's optimism? Statistically that is the total amount of all goods and services divided by hours worked, or wages and salaries paid. Though a causal relationship between numerator and denominator is implied, it isn't necessarily there. For example, the spoliation of the environment and the degrading of our social services will not be recognized in the numerator of the productivity ratio. Whatever economists don't want to recognize, they declare an "externality." Wasn't that what Enron and Global Crossing did with much of their debt and deficits? How much of Mr. Greenspan's celebrated "productivity" is actually just bad bookkeeping?

The ongoing collapse of our economies will not be set aright by the automatic workings of the economic cycle. Economics began as a stab at a science, but it was also an instrument of advocacy and power. Over the past century the power element has completely taken over. Behind a forbidding screen of misapplied mathematics, the governance of the world has been surrendered to speculative capital. Packaging the future of which they have little knowledge and incorporating it into stock market valuations, the desired end-result is obtained. A clear case of garbage in and billions of fictitious dollars out.

The law of the deregulated stock market is that stocks must perform to substantiate the rate of increase of stock market valuation monetized in advance. The result tends to the pattern of the exponential curve: the rate of increase of the rate of increase must equal the rate of increase already attained. If it fails to, the price takes a dive. It was due to this striving to exponential increase that earnings per share were replaced by revenue per share, and revenue redefined to include expenses, and capital often to include debt. The atomic bomb was proved successful when it flattened Hiroshima. In a similar sense their exponential compulsion proved successful when it flattened the world's stock markets. All that was implicit in the model. That is where research on the causes and cures of our disaster must begin.

In my book *Towards a Post-Autistic Economy* I have dealt with the necessary switch to pluralistic price theory. This would bring onto society's balance sheets the cost of unpriced services, the amortization of public investment, the cost of repairing the damage inflicted on the environment and on human capital. The price effects of government spending for such purposes – or the debit run up by not attending to such matters – must not be confused with real inflation, i.e., an excess of market demand over available supply. It must instead be considered as "structural price rise." Today all such vital matters are ignored as "externalities." In effect then we have been trying to steer our complex world by a rogue discipline. Here I wish to suggest a valuable resource for dealing with this nightmare: the introduction of courses in the history of mathematics in university economics curricula.

A few of the benefits that would accrue.

• It would breed a reverence for the human mind in its quest of knowledge. That would help protect society against the degrading of mathematics by economists to a pitch for peddling stocks and bonds.

• One of the greatest of all challenges faced by mathematicians was handling the black magic of infinity. That is the precisely the altar at which conventional economists worship. Whenever a zero appears as the denominator of the ratio of two rational numbers, mathematicians found themselves in difficulties. If the numerator were a real number other than zero – the value of the ratio becomes infinity. Using the infinity concept often yielded remarkable results, but it could also lead to wrong answers. It was only towards the end of the 19th century that mathematicians developed a rigorous way of dealing with the infinitely large and the infinitesimally small. Georg Cantor and others achieved this in a way as remote as possible from the "number-crunching" that constitutes economists' entire bag of tricks today.

Learning from Mathematicians the Limitations of Growth

Numbers can be viewed either as absolute values (cardinal) having no particular sequence; or in a distinct order (ordinals). Studying the infinity concept in their cardinal aspect leads nowhere – there is no way of encompassing infinity by simply adding up or subtracting – i.e., by number-crunching. However, if you line up the odd numbers as ordinals – 1, 3, 5 and the even ones 2, 4, 6, etc., directly below, and tick off a number in the upper series against one in the lower, you have proved the equivalence of the sums of the even and the odd numbers. But the numbers in the odd series (if you leave out zero) are individually less than the corresponding ordinal number in the even. That doesn't matter: you can go on adding numbers to both series at the far end of the process – that is the essence of infinity. What is of key importance is the one-to-one correspondence of the individual terms – the essence of "set theory" that became crucial in dealing with this and many other problems in mathematics. Cantor singled out a cross relationship between the even and odd ordinal numbers. Instead of trying to walk the problem step by step to infinity, he allowed the relationship to cover the endless mileage to a sound proof. Thus the infinity of the even numbers equals that of the odd numbers or for that matter of all numbers, odd and even. Cantor, indeed, went on to prove that there was more than a single order or "power" of infinity. (He designated them by the first letter of the Hebrew alphabet "Aleph" with a numerical subscript.) Thus for each irrational number there is a rational number to the left of its deci-

mal point and an infinity of other numbers to its right – that is what makes it an irrational number. It cannot be expressed as a simple ratio of two rational numbers. So the irrational or "transcendental" numbers, are infinitely more numerous than the infinite sum of the rationals. The most familiar of these transcendental numbers is "ϖ," the ratio of the circumference of a circle to its diameter.

That eliminated errors in the handling of infinity by some of the very greatest mathematicians. Obviously what economists stand in need of is a method that would protect them against their mistaken ways of handling endless economic growth. That is the ultimate source of the current crisis We could learn from mathematics how to put the voracious beast of infinite growth on a leash.

There are other powerful tools that economics could borrow from mathematics.

Making a Valuable Tool of Absurdity

An important one is the method of "reduction to absurdity." The model to be tested is assumed true, and then the implications of that assumption are studied. If this leads to the conclusion that the assumption is not true, we have disproved it in the most rigorous way. Its refutation is found within it. This was the method that of the Greek geometers developed almost two thousand years ago. Euclid's book on geometry was widely used as a standard textbook right into the last century.

This method of *reductio ad absurdum* cries out to be applied in economics. For example, it would be easy to prove with a pencil and paper that you cannot stabilize prices and the economy by continuing to increase interest rates until they flatten out our price indexes. For interest rates add to the cost of everything produced: they extract wealth from the economy for the benefit of a class that directly produces nothing. Eventually that must lead to the breakdown of the economy and society itself. Instead of arriving at this proof with a pencil and paper, right-thinking economists chose to have society act it out at a devastating cost. And now that the *reductio ad absurdum* disproof of that model has come crashing on our heads, they still persist in not recognizing it.

Mathematicians have been ever less concerned with specific numbers than with the internal structure of a mathematical model. At the beginning of the 19th century, "group theory" revealed the essence of any mathematical model in terms of its inner patterns of symmetry and asymmetry – whether it was valid if read backward or not. Identical patterns of this sort were found to extend to the most different fields of mathematics, so that it became possible to solve problems in the most seemingly dissimilar areas at one crack.

Our economists do just the opposite. They assume that an asymmetric model can be flipped over and read backward. Thus, because, other things being equal, market prices will rise if demand exceeds supply, they take for granted that if the price level has climbed it means that there is too much demand, i.e., "inflation." But in the mixed economy that has developed since World War II, the price level can go up for quite other reasons. When anybody moves from a town of 10,000 to New York City, he doesn't expect his living costs to stay the same. How, then can we expect the price levels to stay flat when humanity is making a similar move? Many other such things create a growing layer of taxation in price. Economists handle this by putting it under the table – just as Enron did many of its liabilities. Even a limited knowledge of the history of mathematics would expose such evasions.

Above all, nobody should allow herself to be intimidated by a few mathematical symbols. What is needed to refute the abuse of mathematics by economists is a "defensive" grasp of mathematical principles to penetrate the aggressive false mathematics upon which most conventional economics is based. Much of that can be gotten from an understanding of what mathematics can and cannot do. It is a discipline that contributes nothing factual to our understanding of anything but of mathematics itself. What it does do, gloriously, is reveal the implications of the premises fed into a model. If those premises clash with the reality studied, we know that the claims of that model are counterfeit. Thus the whole notion of a self-balancing market is based on the assumption that all actors in our economy are of such tiny size that nothing they do or leave undone individually can influence the result. That in the age of Enron, Microsoft, and General Electric, is clearly nonsense. You can therefore dismiss such models out of hand.

There are few mathematical principles that cannot be explained in perfectly accessible language for the reader with little mathematical background. A course in the history of mathematics for economics students would be of immense use in training economists to examine critically whatever is put before them.[1]

Today governments and central banks are clearly at their wits' end to explain the grotesque results that have ensued from their "solid fundamentals."

William Krehm

1. A highly readable work on the subject is James R. Newman's four-volume *The World of Mathematics* (New York: Simon and Schuster, 1956). In my recent *Towards a Post-Autistic Economy – A Place for Society at the Table* (COMER Publications, 2002, p. 165), I outline a simple way of designing policy in gradualist steps, by pairing dosages of generally desired effects for a joint zero-influence on the public treasury – i.e., cutting interest rate costs to the Treasury by shifting a limited amount of federal debt from the chartered banks to the central bank, and at the same time curtailing the government's revenue to an equal amount by reducing the regressive Goods and Service Tax. The immediate total effect on the Treasury will be a wash, but the bonus will appear when the consequences of these measures work their way throughout the economy. After the effects of the first dosage of such paired policies has been assessed, it can be repeated – with the same two countervailing factors, or quite different ones. This is an application of Gaussian modular congruence, but it is not necessary to know that to appreciate its enormous potential in getting society out of its present dilemma. Keynes grazed the idea when in his *General Theory* he remarked – "We send Denmark cookies and they send us cookies. Wouldn't it make more sense if we exchanged recipes?" It would certainly decongest all channels of communication, cut down pollution, and needless bustle.

Mail Box

A SYSTEMS VIEW

Security and Denial

AMONG THE FORCES that act on stock markets, in addition to fear and greed, are hopes for security, as well as more or less denial of risk. Some denial of danger may certainly be normal, indeed may be an aspect of courage. Adaptive mechanisms of more extreme denial are brought into play when we are confronted with facts and situations which are more than a little disturbing, which threaten our well being and about which we do not know what to do.

Much current evidence seems to indicate that world society, and particularly the Western world, is involved in one or more existential dilemmas which are shaking the foundations of civilized life. It this is the case, it will have consequences for us, whether we understand and admit the facts intellectually or not. Laws of nature are inexorable, and wishful thinking or ignorance alone cannot alter circumstances.

In coping with change, much depends upon the reliability of our mental maps.[1] In particular, our notions of freedom, security and power deserve special care and attention.

A confused understanding of freedom and security, one based largely on denial and self-interest, threatens both freedom and security. The problems of our time in relation to terrorist assaults, corporate fraud, stock market decline, economic travail – and perhaps the future of the capitalist system – all impact upon real and imagined security and the urge to drastic action. Yet actual security also involves issues of equality, fairness and trust, so essential for personal and social well-being.

And security implies power. Whose freedom is to be traded for what kind of security? Threats to the integrity of the moral and financial foundations of our society have greatly shaken complacency and have decreased public confidence in governments.

If we would reestablish and validate the bonds of societal trust so essential for civilized existence we must supplement our traditional values with new tools for understanding. If we fail to appreciate the context and relations of core values, we risk misunderstanding the values of both freedom and security.

Freedom, of course, is more that just the absence of constraints, and often depends upon special conditions, e.g., education, information, specific skills, and resources. Freedom entails available alternatives, and effective means. Choice also involves the evaluation of consequences, and hence responsibility.

Many will seek ideological answers to questions they do not understand in order to support beliefs involving denial. But in the quest for freedom or security no answers can be absolute, and in an open society both will be depend greatly upon facts as well as sound methods.

While security involves provision for essential needs as well as avoidance of undue risks, taken to an extreme the quest for security may lead to impoverishment and death. All living systems must at times deal with unexpected contingencies and a secure civilization depends upon freedom to entertain new ideas and possibilities, perhaps stabilized by institutionalized systems of checks and balances. And while security against terrorism must include counter-terrorist thinking, the attainment of true "homeland security" will depend upon positive objectives and inclusive strategies, and will only be threatened by denial or fixed defensiveness.

System dynamics

Living structures depend upon a balancing of opposing forces, stabilized by feedback or knowledge of results. And in general, forces in balance provide platforms of stability at various levels which make possible emergent functions and growth, and in effect, new levels of adaptive freedom. But such freedom depends upon adequate structure.

While the specifics of successful arrangements cannot be predicted in detail, certain principles are clear. Productive accommodations over the long term must provide for benefits to an organization as a whole, including its essential components and relevant environment. Nor can reliability be assumed without quality control via feedback, which for a healthy society will require an informed electorate.

Analyses of the road ahead fill the business pages as well as the general press, and there is great preoccupation with the opinions of the market professionals who have lived through and observed past economic cycles.

But there are perhaps two other major kinds of factors or influences, outside the financial markets, that hang darkly over our common future. Both are attributable to human actions, impossible at this time to quantify, but are clearly growing. Both are influencing events and slowly penetrating popular consciousness and adding greatly to uncertainties. And both affect financial markets profoundly.

The first is the apparent lack of reliability of much public information concerning not only corporate but also governmental accounting, not least at state levels, where the juggling of finances has been used for political rather than public benefits. The meaning of this in terms of declining infrastructure and/or indebtedness to future generations is only gradually dawning, but is simply too important to be ignored for long.

Secondly, similar considerations also apply to scientific and popular concerns over the environment, climate change and attending problems. Such concerns include increasing population pressures and demands, dwindling resources of water and energy, increasing pollution and many other factors and trends.

A leader who encourages or relies on denial of realities stores up many potential problems for the inevitable days of reckoning. These days are upon us. We see growing popular consciousness of incompetence, even betrayal of public interests, by too many among those in the elite levels of governance, public and private. To the extent that this is the perception, and grounded in facts that are becoming ever more obvious, questions of responsibility lead on clearly to issues of legal liability. The challenges are real, the problems stressful, and behind the comparative composure of leaders much active denial still continues – clinging to past illusions, not knowing what to do.

Freedom requires self-awareness and effort. Societal well being depends upon information that is relevant and accurate, but facts require interpretation, and telling truth to either the public or those in power is seldom a simple business.

Those who wish to remain ignorant find many ways to do so. The security of structures of informed decision-making and governance must be cultivated with care if we are to find our way in all this. More attention is needed to the "hermaneutic round" – the cyclic or systemic process which seeks to interpret a growing body of facts ever more precisely within a continually revised and upgraded perspective on the whole. Our institutions of science provide for this kind of intelligence in ways that those of our political culture and news media appear to actively discourage and deny.

Long term security depend upon freedom not only to ask questions but to engage in serious dialogue. As a condition of human survival, the days of propaganda must come to an end. The required prescriptions will be seen by many as radical. but serious public questions such as the following must be addressed without prejudice, and the level of discourse raised above partisan bickering:

• What is the real evidence for the presumed benefits of corporate globalization?

• How are we to interpret the evident disconnect between the alleged purposes and actual results of interventions by the World Bank, the International Monetary Fund and the World Trade Organization?

• How can we assess and improve public debate so that money and vested interests do not overwhelm serious discussion of issues?

Such questions are usually dismissed as naive by cynics in denial, who have given up on any attempt to improve the common understanding or the human condition. Nevertheless, if humanity is to surmount the difficulties ahead, governments will be obliged to earn the trust of citizens, and this cannot be done without pursuing the whole truth. To the extent that trust continues to be lost, the future of mankind will also be lost.

Bruce Buchanan

1. Schumacher, E.F. (1978). *A Guide for the Perplexed.* HarperCollins.

Canada's Image Badly Dented?

AS A SECONDARY POWER, Canada is particularly sensitive to its image abroad. It took particular pride in its success of remaking its social structure while groping its way out of the Great Depression. The influx of a penniless refugee immigration brought its own reward in helping replace our stuffy colonial pieties with a new pluralism. And in all this no mean factor was a talented group of scholars who returned from studies under Keynes at Cambridge to become Ottawa's celebrated "Mandarins." Unfortunately they disappeared into retirement, heirless and forgotten, a generation ago.

The record of this heritage gathers dust in underfunded libraries. Even mentioning the uniqueness of the Bank of Canada and its achievements in funding the war and postwar is enough to cost an academic his tenure and keep him off the national broadcasting system. This new regime blew in under the remote guidance of the Bank for International Settlements (BIS) that at the Bretton Woods Conference in 1944 – under its Resolution Five – was slated to disappear because of it had been too serviceable to Nazi Germany. BIS, that allows no member of a government to attend its sessions, declared inflation the primary problem of the world economy, and high interest rates the one "blunt tool" for dealing with it. "Zero inflation" was proclaimed mandatory under its general manager, Alexandre Lamfalussy, in 1991. The slightest rise of price indexes, if unrepressed, was seen bound to expand into hyperinflation of the sort that gobbled up the German currency in 1923. In "Facing the Mother of Financial Scams" in this issue, we debunk this myth. By sheer force of disinformation that BIS version was imposed on Canada by Governor John Crow, imported from Great Britain in 1988 to head the Bank of Canada. His previous career had been as an International Monetary Fund official in Latin America, an assignment he carried out in the style of a viceroy of a long disappeared empire presiding over a durbar from elephant back.

This policy resulted in running up interest rates in Canada five percentage points beyond those in the US. That plunged the country into deep recession, and multiplied the federal debt during his incumbency. The odd thing is that Canada at no time had sought aid from the IMF, and there was no reason for such a policy being imposed on it. Under the Government of Brian Mulroney it slipped into colonial status once again, substituting Washington for Westminster.

In 1991 without debate in Parliament or explanatory release in the press our banks that had lost much or more than their capital in manic financing of energy and real estate bubbles made possible by their previous deregulation. The tale is also told in "Facing the Mother of Financial Scams."

But even more incredible, at the same time that the banks were bailed out, they were deregulated and allowed to use the vast powers of money creation surrendered to them by the Government in taking over stock brokerages, underwriting stock issues, acting as merchant banks, acquiring and selling almost any type of companies. In the process the leverage of the credit created by the banks to the money in their tills had risen from 11:1 in 1946 to over 400:1 today.

To make room for all this money creation, the Bank of Canada reduced its holding of the federal debt from well over 20% to 6%. The consequence: when the central bank holds federal debt the interest paid on it almost entirely finds its way back to the government as dividends. For since 1938 the central bank had only a single shareholder – the federal government. When banks acquire such bonds, they keep the interest the government pays.

To help cover the growing federal deficit arising from those interest payments to the banks on the additional federal debt they held, Ottawa slashed its grants to the provinces. They passed on the courtesy to the municipalities. And that brings us the subject of this piece, the deteriorating image of Canada as a caring, well-run country.

A Young Land of Archaeological Infrastructures?

In *The Wall Street Journal* (07/8, "Canada's Cities Grapple with Age" by Joel Bagole) we read: "Canada's famously well-ordered cities are looking the worse for wear. Its infrastructure is sagging, services are slumping and mayors are seething. Despite the country's recent economic rebound and hefty federal budget surpluses, a funding crunch has left cities from Halifax to Vancouver struggling to upgrade dilapidated municipal works. While the cities continue to attract an ever-increasing percentage of Canada's population, decrepit roads, sewers and buildings threaten to undercut the nation's reputation for having some of the world's most livable urban centers.

"Vancouver, for example, is so cash-strapped that the city of 2.2 million is replacing its rusted sewer pipes at a rate of 1% a year. We should be finished sometime after the year 2030, says Mayor Philip Owen. Halifax, an Atlantic-coast city of 375,000 has no sewage treatment plant and dumps raw sewage into its harbour."

Possibly the public imagery department of government could be enlisted to do something about these things, where the ministries directly concerned with the environment and public health have struck out.

"The problem, Canadian mayors say, is that Canada's municipalities have much less authority than U.S cities to raise funds. Canadian cities derive half their revenues from property taxes and rely on transfer payments from provincial and federal governments for the other 50% of revenue.

"While balancing their own budgets, the federal and provincial governments have cut their combined transfer payments to municipalities by 22.6% since 1995, according to Statistics Canada, a government agency. Although 80% of Canada's 30 million citizens live in urban centers, only 10 cents of every dollar goes to cities.

"Making matters worse, provinces have downloaded greater financial responsibilities to cities for services ranging from ambulances to highway repair.

"The Federation of Canadian Municipalities, an Ottawa-based lobby group representing 1,000 municipalities, estimates that Canada's cities need C$44 billion in infrastructure upgrades, and that cost is growing by C$2 annually.

"While Canada's cities remain clean and safe by US standards, urban congestion and housing shortages are rising. In Toronto, homeless people crowd downtown parks. In Montreal, pothole-riddled streets have become the stuff of local legend.

"Canada's mayors are demanding more independence and greater taxation powers. Pointing to US cities, mayors here say they, too, want the power to levy income, sales and highway taxes, and to share in the national fuel tax.

"The issue is drawing attention. A federal task force on urban issues is now finalizing a report that supports the mayors' position. Some provinces are starting to help. Alberta and British Columbia for instance are giving their cities a small cut out of the national fuel tax.

"Judy Sgro, chairwoman of the federal government task force on urban issues, is urging the federal government to develop and fund a national transportation program for roads and transit, a long-term infrastructure fund and an affordable-housing program for cities. Though the ideas are supported by some parliamentarians, the government has made no commitments so far."

How the Bank Bailout Trickled Down

There is a key missing link in this presentation of the problem, the key one that we summarized at the beginning of this article: the slash in federal grants, which has now visibly trickled down to the municipality level, was the direct result of the shift of funding to bailout our chartered banks. Worse still, it was brought in as an entitlement rather than a one-shot affair. Along with deregulation it provides a capital platform for the banks' stock market and other gambles. Now that process must be reversed. Not only to clean up the accumulated neglect of municipalities in the past but to forestall the next bailout of our banks that is in the offing.

The Globe and Mail (08/8, "Ottawa's surplus vanishes" by Heather Scoffield) informs us: "Turmoil on financial markets and expectations for a weaker US economy mean Ottawa is going to have to constrain its spending this year, Finance Minister John Manley warned yesterday. The surplus for the fiscal year 2002-3 is $6 billion less than last year, and reduced expectations for federal coffers could seriously dampen Prime Minister Jean Chrétien's hopes for immediate action on an activist fall agenda that would fund social causes."

Repeatedly individual municipalities, often making use of COMER research, have proposed to the Federation of Canadian municipalities that they propose that the Federal government make use of article 18(c) in the *Bank of Canada Act* – "The Bank may buy and sell securities issued or guaranteed by Canada or any province" – to finance the capital disrepairs in our physical and human municipal infrastructures. If this were done the interest paid on such loans would return end up substantially with the federal government as BoC dividends. Part or all of this could be passed on by Ottawa to the municipalities involved to reduce the effective interest rate to the municipalities. That would only be minimal justice, since the municipal crisis is basically the result of the 1991 bailout of our chartered banks, the details of which neither the government nor the banks dared make public. This suggestion should be made in the politest possible language but in a way that would emphasize where the "savings" from the cuts in the grants to the provinces went. With a federal election in the offing, the timing could not be better. The time has come for taking off gloves.

William Krehm

REVIEW OF A BOOK BY BRUCE RICH, BOSTON: BEACON PRESS, 1994

Mortgaging the Earth — The World Bank, Environmental Impoverishment, and the Crisis of Development

ONE OF THE THINGS that make this 8-year old book so invaluable is that it is written by an ethnologist rather than an economist. He brings to his subjects the insights of such alien thinkers as Max Weber on the role of bureaucracies of whatever political stripes. There is no more powerful way of reducing humanity to a becoming modesty when it is overtaken by the itch to rearrange the biosphere to its convenience.

"In a famous essay published over two decades ago, 'The Original Affluent Society,' anthropologist Marshall Sahlins pointed out the ultimate paradox of modern development: 'the most 'primitive' hunting and gathering societies on earth, Australian aborigines and African bushmen, enjoy material and social plenty, working at most an average of three to five hours per day at a leisurely pace to satisfy all of their material needs. They 'keep bankers' hours, notably less than modern industrial workers (unionized) who would surely settle for a 21-35 hour week.'[1] The considerable leisure time at their disposal – enough to make the average two-job household jealous – is spent socializing, sleeping, and in surprisingly sophisticated cultural activities.

"Claude Levi-Strauss's description of the cultural life of Australian aborigines, spent in endless elaboration and discussion of fine totemistic classifications and distinctions, focuses on aboriginal culture's extraordinary social complexity and – there is no other word – development, the product of long isolation.

"Moreover, this development was not undergone passively. It was desired and conceptualized, for few civilizations seem to equal the Australians in their taste for erudition and speculation and what sometimes looks like intellectual dandyism. But lest there be any mistake about it: these shaggy and corpulent savages whose physical resemblance to adipose bureaucrats…makes their nudity yet more incongruous…were in various respects… real snobs. Theorizing and discussion was all the rage in this closed world and the influence of fashion often paramount.

"For Sahlins, not only hunger but especially poverty is socially produced, ironically, through the process of economic development itself. Poverty, he observes, is above all a relation of relative status amongst people. Although 'the world's most primitive people have few possessions, they are not poor.'

"How did this conception of social organization, which most of the humans who ever existed did not know and lived well enough without, become in less than four centuries, not only universally desirable but something perceived as unstoppable.

Nature as Booty

"The ultimate answer of how we got to here takes us back to 1619, a 23-year-old French mercenary in the pay of the Prince of Nassau, Réné Descartes, later recalled in his *Discourse on Method*. 'It was in the Bavarian town of Ulm.[2] I spent the whole day shut up in a room heated by an enclosed stove, with the aim to seek the true method of arriving of knowledge of everything – a practical philosophy through the invention of an infinity of devices by which we might enjoy, without effort, the fruits of the earth and all its commodities.' Descartes is promising us not only an infinity of new inventions to master nature, but the entire earth, without effort. The goal, Descartes wrote, was not just knowledge, but power and welfare. 'I shall not perhaps appear to you as too vain if you consider that as there is only one truth of each thing, whoever finds it knows as much about the thing as there is to be known.'"

As the inventor of analytical geometry that allows geometric problems to be formulated and solved by the routine procedures of algebra, Descartes as much as any human could be forgiven such hubris. But it turned out a pitfall.

"The Cartesian approach was an almost totally novel, alien vision of the world in 1637. Its promise of unimagined power entailed a Faustian bargain – the 'progressive devalorization of being,' a world reduced to an extension occupied by objects for a rationing, calculating subject."

"But if Descartes was the metaphysician of modernity, Francis Bacon was the prophet of technocracy. A year after Descartes had his vision in Ulm, Bacon published his *The Great Instauration*. It was nothing less than a program to lay the foundation of human utility and power. 'His project bore much in common with Descartes' – a grand vision of the domination of nature, as well as of human affairs, through the application of the "new philosophy." One finds embedded in Bacon's writings many of the sociological implications of modernity that would become manifest centuries later. He envisages the critical role of instrumental reason in a world rationally directed to the conquest and utilization of nature….' The goal is not to win arguments with academicians but 'to command nature in action.' As money will fetch all other commodities, so this knowledge is what should purchase all the rest." In his *Novum Organum* he exhorts the reader to consider what a difference there is between the life of

men in the most civilized provinces of Europe and the wildest and barbarous districts of the New India – enough to justify the saying that "man is a god to man."

In his own life Bacon acted out some of the less lovely implications of the new faith, "In 1618 he was appointed to the highest legal office in England, Lord Chancellor, from which he personally supervised the torture of prisoners when the practice was illegal, issued monopolies to curry favor with the court, accepted bribes and favors from prospective litigants and tampered with trials and judges. In 1621 he was indicted by the House of Lords for corruption, pleaded guilty, and was banished from London, as well as permanently disbarred from public office and fined 40,000 pounds, a huge sum for the times."

Rich quotes Martin Heidegger, "Chronologically, modern physical science begins in the 17th century. In contrast, machine-power technology develops only in the second half of the 18th century. But modern technology, which for chronological reckoning is the later, is, from the point of view of the essence holding sway within it, the historically earlier." Rich enlarges on this: "C.S. Lewis in a marvelous essay called 'The Abolition of Man' advances the thesis that the birth of science and the modern age are often misinterpreted, especially by those who claim that magic and the occult were medieval remnants to be swept away by the Enlightenment: 'There was very little magic in the Middle Ages: the 16th and 17th centuries are the high noon of magic. The serious magical endeavour and the serious scientific endeavor are twins: one was sickly and died, the other strong and throve. But both were born of the same impulse For both alike the problem is how to subdue reality to the wishes of men: the solution is technique.'

Meet the Other Mr. Newton

"The most striking proof of this lies in the life of Sir Isaac Newton. On July 14, 1936, several thousand pages of manuscript just rediscovered was auctioned off at Sotheby's and John Maynard Keynes was the successful of three bidders for almost half the offering. To his surprise, on studying his purchase, Keynes was astounded to have to conclude that Newton was not a 'rationalist,' but rather an alchemist and magician. 'Newton was seeking the philosopher's stone, the Elixir of Life, and the transmutation of base metals into gold. He corresponded extensively on the subject with Robert Boyle, formulator of the celebrated law on the behavior of gases, who himself published many alchemical and occult tracts, and even a treatise in which he claimed to have found the philosopher's stone which enables the transmutation of lead into gold. Newton was so concerned with the apparent discovery that he argued that the knowledge was 'not to be communicated without immense damage to the world.' John Locke's correspondence shows that he shared Newton's obsession with the subject, and on his death they exchanged the different incantations the old alchemist had had left them."

Richard S. Westfall, Newton's biographer, notes that Newton "started with sober chemistry, and gave it up rather quickly for he took to be the greater profundity of alchemy."[3]

What was common to both of Newton's interests that are

considered incompatible was a common will to power over nature. Eventually that led Newton to abandon physics and mathematics to become Warden of the Mint. In this post his experience with alchemy was of assistance in assaying the proper proportions of gold and silver in the coinage of the realm. 'A fascinating aspect of Newton's tenure at the Mint was the energy with which he hunted down counterfeiters, setting up networks of informers and spies all over England, visiting, incognito, taverns and quarters infested with thieves to ferret out information. In a single nineteen-month period (June 1698 to Christmas 1699, he appeared in 123 separate days at the Mint to interrogate some 200 informers and suspects, many of whom were subsequently executed' (Manuel, Frank (1979). *Portrait of Isaac Newton* (p. 230). Washington, DC: New Republic Books). On that the solvency of the realm could depend.

Rich traces the portentous vision of applying spur and whip to nature. He finds in the system-building mania of Claude-Henri Saint-Simon a common ancestry of both international development banking and socialism. Oddly enough, he fails to mention Karl Marx, who certainly belongs in the grand vision of a liberating future based on the subjugation of nature.

The Common Ancestor of Socialists and Bankers

"In a life filled with surrealistic escapades, the French count Claude-Henri Saint Simon fought as a 19-year-old adventurer in the American War of Independence and years later was interned in the same insane asylum as the Marquis de Sade. Saint-Simon's early experience in America inspired his life's mission – to work for the improvement of humankind. Material production and technology would be the means to accomplish this improvement, the total reorganization of society.

"Saint-Simon was arguably the first international planner. Following the American Revolutionary War the young count traveled to Mexico where he tried unsuccessfully to convince the Spanish viceroy to invest in a canal across the isthmus of Panama. In 1787 he surfaced in Spain, attracted by rumours that the government was committed to building a gigantic canal to link Madrid to the sea. He landed a job consulting with the king's financial advisor and chief architect of the project. But the French Revolution broke out and the plan was abandoned.

"He suggested that the Papacy be replaced with a 'Supreme Council of Newton' in which 21 eminent men of science would govern the world. Society would be 'one workshop' directed by the council.' He promoted an Anglo-French union. As a consequence of his thesis on the prevalence of the will to power in human nature, social equilibrium would be guaranteed through gigantic internal and international economic development programs.

"Saint-Simon died in 1825, but by the early 1830s his writings had attracted a large following and spawned a journal, *Le Globe*. The editors extolled huge development schemes such as canals across Panama and Suez; and a political and economic union of Europe and the Near East, linked by a system of railroads and canals to be financed by new industrial development banks.

"Though Saint-Simon was a proponent of liberal econo-mists like Adam Smith and J.B. Say, an important number of his followers concluded that the principal obstacle to the technocratic utopia was private property. In February 1832, *Le Globe* invented one of the most fatal neologisms of the modern age – 'socialisme.' That, considered seditious, brought the editor, Barthelemy Prosper Enfantin, a year in prison.

"Enfantin's approach was more like that of an idealistic Peace Corps worker than that of a World Bank consultant. Enfantin and his associates worked on the Nile dam through 1836, refusing to accept money and insisting on living and eating with the native workers. Fever and disease caused the project to be abandoned. But several of the Saint Simonien engineers stayed on in Egypt to build highways, founded the Polytechnique School in Cairo, head the Artillery School and direct the School of Medicine.

"The Saint-Simoniens Isaac and Emile Pereire founded the first railway in France, and with other Saint-Simonien bankers and engineers promoted railways during the Second Empire in Switzerland, Italy, Spain, Hungary, Austria and Hungary. The Pereire brothers set up the first industrial development bank, the Credit Mobilier, in 1852. It became the model for modern continental banking.

"The movement also produced a political right wing, headed by Auguste Comte, who had been Saint-Simon's secretary. It was particularly strong in Latin America. Comte elaborated a systematic (and authoritarian) philosophy of history, society and politics, in which humanity evolved in three stages, the final, modern phase being the 'positivist' approach. Its motto would be "Order and Progress" which is still to be found on the Brazilian flag."

In the mid-twentieth century the Saint-Simonian technocratic faith flared high during the first generation of the new nations. Nassar proclaimed that after the construction of the Aswan dam Egypt would be paradise. Nehru called India's gigantic new dams its "modern temples."

Why we Need Double Vision when Looking at Descartes or Newton

An important caveat is called for. Throughout the excellent work the terms "Cartesian" and "Newtonian" are used as though these men contributed nothing but their philosophical view of human affairs – their Weltanschauung. Without their seminal work in mathematics and science, the ecological critique that Rich handles so ably would be unthinkable. Crucial for the warnings of the hothouse gas effect, for example, was the ability of astrophysicists to devise and deliver exploratory machines to the surface of Venus that opened the likelihood that there may have been rudimental life on that planet until it lost its atmosphere. And the alternate models that Rich calls for could not be formulated without Decartes' great mathematical innovation that made it possible to translate relationships in any sphere into the tongue of algebra, accessible to its routine processing. Both Descartes and Newton, for all their genius, were children of their age, subject to its worldly outlook. Surely it would be helpful to distinguish their time-bound world "philosophy" from their timeless scientific heritage. Failing to do this would repeat the gaffe of many well-intentioned environmental activists who from the abuse of mathematics by free market theory, disapprove altogether of applying mathematics to economic problems. Mathematics has no independent factual input. It merely reveals the implications of assumptions made.

The positive contributions of Descartes and Newton for stopping the rapine of the biosphere outweigh beyond measure their negative contributions as social philosophers. Newton destroyed the dogma of man as the pre-ordained belly-button of the universe. Descartes freed mathematics from its origins in the need to resurvey the fields after the Nile's annual floods. Referring to their social musings as the Newtonian and the Cartesian systems is not only grotesquely unjust. It helps confuse what should be clarified. It ought to be expunged from an otherwise excellent book.

William Krehm

1. Sahlins, Marshall (1972). *Stone Age Economics* (pp. 34-5). Chicago: Aldine-Atherton.
2. Einstein's birthplace. A case of lightning striking twice in the same place!
3. Isaac Newton had heaped scorn on the chronologies drawn up by Egyptian scribes vain enough to claim that their ancient monarchy was "some thousands of years older than the world." "Before Civilization. The Radio-Carbon Revolution and Prehistoric Europe" in Braudel, Fernand (1990). *The Identity of France* (vol. 2, p. 22, Sian Reynolds, Trans.). Harper Collins Publishers.

The Many Dimensions of Deflation

WHILE the Bank of Canada and other central banks are manning the ramparts against inflation as the one peril that they see threatening the world, it is actually deflation that is taking over. In central bank orthodoxy imposed several decades ago, the main threat is always inflation, while the very word "deflation" is unspeakable. In 1997 when the predecessor of the present BoC Governor, Gordon Thiessen, uttered his concern about deflation before a Senate Committee, he was back in a week to apologize, expressing his likely regret for the rest of his life for having mentioned the word. Nobody seated at the political table above the salt even asked the obvious question: why would the head of a central bank founded in 1935 to try to pull the country out of a disastrous decade of deflation have to apologize for mentioning the subject? And at whose behest?[1]

Deflation is a distemper that has since come at us from just about every point of the compass. To begin with, the terms of the Deregulation and Globalization have been more effective in importing into the First World the lowest labour costs and environmental and health standards from wherever these are to be found. And the market bubble, compounding hot air and corruption at the highest executive levels, once punctured, becomes a powerful engine of deflation. The amount of fictitious capital that has disappeared in the US alone is reported in the $7

trillion range. That is within hailing distance of a whole year's GDP – and the process of sorting out fact from fiction in stock valuation has hardly spent itself. Though the ban was on the mention of deflation in the world of commodities and services, the contrary was the case when it came to stock market valuations. There even an expression of concern by Chairman Alan Greenspan himself about the "irrational exuberance" of the stock market was slapped down. That mighty walking-ikon was told to stick to commodity inflation and leave the stock market alone. The Chairman complied and spoke no more about the overheated state of Wall St. until the roof had collapsed, and it was too late.

The post mortems on the raunchy tales of immorality and corruption that fuelled Wall St.'s finest decade have shaken not only the accountancy of the financial sector but the basic morality necessary for any business transaction. That means that capital is harder to raise for launching firms. Fewer people trust their counterparties in deals. With less lending and financing to replace the massive holes ripped in the near-money supply, powerful deflationary gusts are sweeping the economy. Nor is there any lack of whistling in the dark. From high government sources on either side of our undefended border we have been fed endless nonsense: though the stock market has had both legs and reputation shattered, the fundamentals in the rest of the economy are declared sound. So Wall St. is a basket-case, but consumer demand is healthily brisk. Boasted government surpluses have disappeared as earnings of corporations are being restated for years back, and unemployment mounts.

As corporation after corporation files for bankruptcy protection, hundreds of thousands of workers are being laid off throughout the world each week. New unsuspected channels by which the plague of deflation spreads are coming into view. Thus *The Wall Street Journal* (14/08, "Telecom Glut Could Linger as Failed Networks are Rescued" by Dennis K. Berman, H. Asher Bolande and Almar Latour), reports the latest of these: "Buyers have begun rescuing financially troubled fiber-optic telecommunications networks for cents on the dollar, but by giving these companies new life they risk perpetuating the world-wide capacity glut that sent the industry into a tailspin.

"Just last week investors took over Global Crossing Ltd., a bankrupt Bermuda company that was once a darling of US investors. In its heyday, Global Crossing built undersea fiber-optic cables capable of handling unprecedented volumes of voice and data traffic. But it and other companies flooded the market with capacity at a time when demand started to falter. When a number of these companies filed for bankruptcy, including Metromedia Fiber Networks Inc., 360 Networks Corps., and Williams Communications Group Inc. of North America and KPNQwest NV and Energis in Europe, it appeared that the industry was undergoing a sensible correction that would flush out unneeded communications systems.

Bankruptcy Restructurings Fuel Deflation

"Now with rescue efforts underway for a number of these telecom providers, including the latest bankruptcy filer, World-Com Inc., that [excess] capacity may be here to stay. 'If you want to solve the problems with the telecom industry in North America, you better liquidate, period.' says Stephane Teral, research director at RHK of South San Francisco.

"As struggling companies are bailed out, and the massive debt they incurred to build their lines is wiped away, they 'are in a much stronger position to compete on pricing,' says To Chee Eng, a Singapore-based analyst with the US market research firm Gartner Inc.

"A revived WorldCom could be an especially nettlesome competitor of the likes of AT&T Corp. and Sprint Corp. Upstart companies such as Global Crossing or Williams still have to fight inch-by-inch to win the largest corporate customers. But WorldCom already has those relationships, and if it eventually slashed prices, it will put the most direct pressure on big competitors such as Ma Bell." That could mean more massive layoffs, and more bankruptcies.

No contagious disease spreads faster than deflation. Yet the mere mention of it was *verboten* by the deep thinkers who run the world's central banks. Such inevitable results can be traced back to the drive towards exponential growth incorporated into stock market valuations.

"'If a carrier erases its debt costs, it can start offering 'bandwidth' as telecom capacity is called, at a price close to its barest operating expenses. For example, between London and New York, a basic fiber-optic connection cost $22,000 annually at the start of 2001. The glut has forced the price down to $5000 today. For a carrier without any debt payments the price may drop to $2000, Dr. Jean-Pascal Crametz, a former Stanford University professor who studies telecom pricing, says. 'I don't know how the Sprints of the world can compete.'

"The Global Crossing bailout, meanwhile has set a benchmark for what creditors will accept for financially distressed networks. Hutchison Whampoa Ltd. and Singapore Technology Telemedia Pte. have offered just $250 million for a 61.5% stake. That bid values the company, which had $12 billion in debt when it filed for reorganization in January, at just one cent on the dollar."

Nor is this killer aspect of deflation confined to the telecoms. *The Wall Street Journal* (16/08, "Europe Airlines Fear Impact of US Carriers' Woes" by Daniel Michaels and Scott McCartney) report the identical phenomenon amongst the tottering international airlines: "'We've long been concerned by the American airlines' ability to go into Chapter 11, rid themselves of debt and come out and compete again,' said Paul Moore, a spokesman for Virgin Atlantic. 'Bankruptcy protection – on top of the US government bailout – is a safety net their competitors simply don't have.'"

William Krehm

1. See Krehm, William (Ed.) (1999). *Meltdown: Money, Debt and the Wealth of Nations* (p. 312). COMER Publications.

Our Dysfunctional Central Bank

THE *Bank of Canada Act* is the logical point of departure for assessing our central bank's performance. The preamble (Chapter B-2) states the purpose of its founding: *"to regulate credit and currency in the best interest of the economic life of the nation, to control and protect the external value of the national monetary unit and to mitigate by its influence fluctuations in the general level of production, trade, prices and employment, so far as it may be possible within the scope of monetary action."*

Its mission then is to minimize either "deflation" or "inflation" when either occurs. That, however, is quite the opposite of what the BoC has been up to for the past quarter of a century.

Thus in the June 1996 issue of *Economic Reform* we read: "On May 8, Gordon Thiessen, Governor of the Bank of Canada, acted out the scenario of man biting dog, and thereby earned himself a front-page spread in *The Globe and Mail* (8/5/96). He had announced his worry about 'deflation developing within the next two years.'"

He was in fact dead on. Two years later – almost to the month – the collapse of stock markets and economies began in Thailand and ripped throughout East Asia, Latin America, Russia and North America itself. This ushered in a period of deep deflation.

Proud Governor with a Face Full of Humble Pie

Forecasts of such accuracy rarely if ever occur in official circles. You might have imagined that it would have been celebrated with brass bands and Roman candles. Not so. "Eight days later Mr. Thiessen, appeared before the Parliamentary Finance Committee with a face full of humble pie: 'I probably will regret forever that I mentioned the word "deflation"' (*G&M*, 16/5).

Uttering the unutterable may indeed have cost Mr. Thiessen a second term as Governor of the central bank. Thiessen is about as far as you can get from your rebel, martyr type. His rising to the commanding post in the Bank of Canada these days is proof enough of that. If the word "deflation" burst from his mouth when protocol required his babbling on about the perils of inflation, that indicated his stress under the party line.

So contrite an apology to an anonymous address is a symptom of the dysfunction of the Bank of Canada. No less significant: no member of the parliamentary committee even asked him to explain his contrition.

It is not by oversight, that the passage quoted above from the preamble, along with others of like sort are still be found in the *Bank of Canada Act*. In the May 1992 issue of *Economic Reform*, under the caption "All the News Fit to Print" we reported one of several unsuccessful attempts to replace these with the goal of "zero inflation."

"For months the government and the BoC had prepared their coup. With the economy already badly dented to the beat of the "zero inflation" drum, the plan was to elevate that policy to a state religion not subject to worldly testing. First came the scholarly papers churned out by friendly think-tanks proving the scientific necessity of putting 'zero inflation' into the *Bank of Canada Act*, and to establish the sovereignty, pardon, the 'independence' of the central bank from the elected government. Like Strasbourg geese, the media were force-fed with disinformation describing the present mandate as a 'mishmash' of goals.

"All the more remarkable then that the three-party caucuses of the parliamentary committee joined in recommending that the proposed amendments be turned down. Not a word of this appeared in the two leading business papers of the land, *The Globe and Mail* and *The Financial Post*."[1]

Running Up the Jolly Roger on the Mast

But the government and the Bank of Canada were not ready to be denied.

On 26/10/92 a *Globe and Mail* editorial in a heroic non-sequitur ran up the Jolly Roger on its mast: "Whether it knows it or not, the federal government has been given a mandate in this referendum. The Conservative government is obliged in the time it has left, to fulfill the electorate's preferred prescription of its duties. The Government should make good on its earlier promise, and entrench in law the BoC's one true mandate: to maintain a stable monetary standard." The government had actually received a thorough bashing in the constitutional referendum. Although it had originally proposed putting "zero inflation" in the constitution, the matter was dropped for good cause.

And then on 11/12 there appeared a remarkable article by the *G&M's* editor-in-chief, William Thorsell: "Why have we paid so little attention to deflation, its risks and consequences? Because the intellectual priesthood of price stability has a hammerlock on public discourse. Indeed, the most powerful of the current crop of politically correct nostrums insists on the virtue of absolute price stability." An ordinary reader of the *G&M* in recent years would have difficulty in getting a statement like that accepted in the *G&M's* "Letters to the Editor."

Who Edits our Editors-in-Chief?

Economic Reform (1/93) went on to observe: "The *G&M* owes its readers an immense catch-up on information it has withheld from them over the years. Uttered by the editor-in-chief of Canada's National Newspaper, 'the hammerlock on public discourse' is a ticklish phrase. Can it mean that the *G&M* and other papers are not edited by their editors-in-chief? And if so, by whom?"

The answer to that, too, is not difficult to document from

official sources.

Subsection 4 of Section 457 of Chapter 46 of the Statutes of Canada 1991 in its decennial revision of the *Bank Act*, phased out the requirement for our chartered banks to maintain reserves with the Bank of Canada [as a percentage of the deposits the banks held from the public]. "On the first day of the first month following the month this section comes into force, the primary reserve referred to in subsection 2 shall be reduced to 3%, and thereafter on the first day of the first month of each of the next three succeeding three-month periods, the primary reserve as modified by this subsection shall be reduced by 3%, and on the first day of the twenty-fifth month following the month in which this section comes into force, the primary reserve referred to in subsection 1 shall be nil."

The Tell-tale Thumbprints in our Law Books

The statutory reserves put up with the BoC had earned the banks no interest. Even before this bill was carried, they had been whittled down from 10% in legal tender, plus 8% in government debt to less than 4% in legal tender. The purpose of this was to bail out the banks from their headlong gambling losses.

The insertion of the "zero inflation" goal into the Bank of Canada Act, the Constitution – why not into the national anthem? – had clearly been part of the original plan for bringing in the new dispensation. An embracing campaign was organized as well to assert the independence of the BoC. However, the Bank of Canada Act clearly establishes the federal government as sole shareholder of the Bank (section 17(1)); empowers the minister of finance, in the event of a disagreement with the Bank Governor on basic policy, to give him 30 days to comply (section 14(2)); and authorizes the BoC to hold federal debt, funded or unfunded, or even guaranteed by the federal government (sections 18(c) and (j)). You are left wondering what the "independence of the Bank of Canada from the government" might possibly mean. The highly public campaign to legitimize this led nowhere. The technical legislation for the end of reserves was put in place – in the separate Bank Act that deals with the private banks – without so much as a mention in the press or debate in Parliament. But this clashes with the key purposes of the central bank still in the *Bank of Canada Act*.

This incongruence points to the exotic origins of the whole "zero inflation" campaign. To appreciate the consequences for government finances of all this, we must bring in a further actor, The Bank for International Settlements. It opened its doors in 1930 as a purely technical facility with the task of converting the German World War I reparations into hard currencies. The BIS shareholders were originally to consist entirely of central banks, but on isolationist grounds the US Fed was unwilling to take up its allotted shares. A syndicate of American commercial banks acquired the shares reserved for it. Characteristically, the BIS voting rights are still retained by the original members in proportion to their original subscriptions even though they may have sold some of their shares since then. This is but another instance of BIS's allergy to anything that smacks of democratic procedure. No government official – other than a central banker – is allowed at their sessions.

At the Bretton Woods Conference in 1994, Resolution Five presented by several governments-in-exile was carried requiring that BIS be liquidated at the earliest possible moment. The reason: BIS's too cozy relationship with the Nazi German government before, and some said, during the war.[2]

For the first few years after the peace BIS kept a low profile in the shadow of the noose. But by 1951 the bankers in the United States managed to do away with the fixed low interest rates that had financed the war, and were in need of a bunker from which to direct their further comeback. The low-profile culture of BIS, insulated from all elected governments, fitted them like a glove. Though you can buy and sell its shares on European stock-markets, BIS has more say on the destinies of Canadians in some key respects, than their elected Parliament. That is known in official parlance as the "independence" of the Bank of Canada. In fact the "independence" is entirely from Canada's elected government. Its dependence on BIS is absolute.

Thus in his annual report, delivered in Basel on May 23, 1991, BIS General Manager Alexandre Lamfalussy laid down the "zero inflation" party line in more severe terms than even Bank of Canada Governor John Crow, a monetarist fanatic of IMF background, dared impose:

"It has been argued that a quality bias in price level calculations implies that inflation in the range of 1-2% may be considered price stability for all practical purposes. Nonetheless, the move from an environment of low or moderate inflation to one of no inflation implies a psychological shift. It has proved very difficult in recent decades to do better than achieve merely low inflation than to move toward actual price stability, even in those countries with the best price performance.

The Forked Tongue of the BIS

"From all this it must be clear why central banks – even if they enjoy full independence from governments – find it difficult to pursue the objective of absolute price stability. An obvious condition is a sufficient degree of social consensus, since in a world in which unavoidable price increases need to be offset by price declines, the consequences will be felt differently by different social groups.

"But would such a pessimistic conclusion be justified? Perhaps not: several developments, with converging lessons, provide a ray of hope. As the environmental debate illustrates, it is by no means impossible to convince large segments of the population that the systematic undervaluation of future interests needs to be corrected. Something similar has also happened with the public perception of the need to combat inflation."

In actual fact, environmental clean-up and "zero inflation" rather than converge are irreconcilable. The costs of protecting the environment must inevitably show up in the price level, and in the eyes of BIS that is "inflationary."

Mr. Lamfalussy concluded: "Even more important is the behaviour of bond market operators who have worldwide acquired a much longer time-horizon with a strong, well-founded interest in the future course of inflation. They are able to deliver a more convincing message to all policy-makers on the appropriateness of monetary policy than any academic speculation regarding the tolerable level of inflation."

This heavy reliance on decibels to cover dubious content in many of the BoC's official declarations is a sure symptom of dysfunction. Let me quote from *Economic Reform* (2/93): "The Governor of the Bank of Canada is spending more of his time in foreign capitals taking bows for having 'licked inflation' back home. Is he attempting the ultimate in salesmanship – peddling to unsuspecting foreigners the culls that can no longer he sold at home? Or is he merely repaying an old debt to the land that gave us the Baron von Muenchhausen, the delightful teller of tales taller than our bankrupt skyscrapers?

"The good Baron realized that the gullibility of his audience grew as the square of the distance from the settings of his stories. In keeping with this, Governor Crow decided to work the Germans.

"'The German newspaper *Handelsblatt* reported last week that John Crow, governor of the Bank of Canada, had told it that the growing economic recovery in Canada means that there is no further need for interest-rate cuts. That sent bankers and economists in Canada scrambling for dictionaries for a retranslation of these comments (*The Globe and Mail*, 13/1/91).'

"Along with New Zealand, Canada is being presented abroad as having put 'zero inflation' and the 'independence of our central bank' into the law of the land. The facts are different: last February the government's proposal to amend the *Bank of Canada Act* in this sense was turned down by a parliamentary subcommittee.

"We have long known that Governor Crow sees the credibility of the central bank as the polar star around which the heavens turn. The trouble is that in his mind credibility is wholly a matter of what you can get away with."

The Long Shadow of BIS

What we have here is the long shadow of the BIS. The strategy of the bailouts, just as the regime that had got the banks into trouble, was conceived and promoted throughout the world through the BIS and the Bretton Woods institutions. For years the BIS refused to control derivatives – the wildly leveraged gambling tools without which the recent Wall St. bubble could not have happened. Since bank capital had been swallowed up in the speculative new ventures to which deregulation had given the banks entry, it was liquid capital that had to be improvised to fill the vacuum left by their losses. As always the next best thing to cash was leverage. At the national level this had been provided by the phasing out of the statutory reserves mentioned above. In countries like Canada and New Zealand these reserves were abolished altogether. In the UK they were reduced to a fraction of one percent. In the US they remained at a nominal three percent average, but since this included the non-statutory voluntary reserves of the banks to meet their operational obligations, the effective statutory reserves were reduced to about a single percent, Yet having the reserve system left in place, even if diminished, makes it easier to increase them to a significant level again in a major crisis.

In the latter 1980s when few banks in the world were in good shape, BIS put together its *Risk-Based Capital Requirements*. These declared the debt of OECD countries – the most industrialized ones – to be risk-free. Between the phasing out of reserves in Canada and these new BIS capital requirements it became possible for Canada's banks to increase their holdings of federal debt from about $20 billion to some $80B without putting up any significant amount of cash or capital. A detail that has escaped economists of just about every stripe is that the requirement of reserves in legal tender was shifted to "capital" which in a deregulated world is an ever more different affair. Banks' capital comes to them through the sale of their shares and through their undistributed earnings. But it is not left in the form of cash – even overnight – because cash does not breed interest unless it is lent out or otherwise invested. But in that case it is no longer cash. The cash held is kept strictly to the needs of the public's withdrawing their deposits or the individual bank's needs to meet its net cheque clearances with other banks. Moreover, provided they hold less than 20% of an issue of a given security, banks enter their assets on their books at their historical cost, not their market value. The criterion of bank solvency was shifted from "cash reserves" to "capital requirements." Moreover, deregulation allows banks to take over every aspect of stock market activity from brokerage firms, merchant banking, underwriting, insurance, derivative boutiques. The result: the leverage of bank assets to cash holdings has moved – the aggregate for all banks – from 11 to 1 in 1946 to over 400 to 1 today. That is a terrifying backdrop for the questionable deals our banks have become involved in. Enron, Global Crossing, WorldCom that are occupying criminal prosecutors in the US today are just the more prominent samples of this.

This would have been impossible if the firewalls between banking and speculative activities had not been removed. The involvement of our banks in such activities is further evidence of the dysfunction of the Bank of Canada.

The Cost of the Bank Bailout to Canadians

This has been at a staggering and ever mounting cost to the citizens of Canada. The cost to the government of the $60B increase in the chartered banks' holdings of federal debt is some $2.4B annually – but that varies with the rate of interest. Even more important is the fact that the banks are relieved of the need to put up reserves for the amount of deposits they already held prior to the end of reserves. In July 1990 this amounted to $472 billion of assets in domestic and foreign currencies, and the discontinued reserves on it would have been almost $19 billion.[3] Such discontinued statutory reserves put up with the BoC, served the government as cash since they enabled it to draw on credit from the central bank without exceeding the limits in force.

This, moreover is no one-shot bailout. It recurs annually like the solstices. It is in fact an entitlement.

Dysfunction comes in degrees. Assigning vastly increased powers of money-creation[4] as the means of bailing the banks out from their previous indiscretions was in itself dysfunction of a higher order on the part of the BoC.

But that is not the end of the climb.

The Degrees of Dysfunction

If you have whittled down your mission to "licking inflation" with a "single blunt tool," you would have to recognize the villain before you do him in. President Bush did not send his Special Operations elite soldiers into the Afghan caves without providing them with photos of bin Laden. But the Bank of Canada seems to have only the vaguest notion of what inflation is or looks like.

"Until a couple of years ago, the orthodox view was that higher taxes kept inflation down. We might have hoped that the Goods and Service Tax, showing up on the consumer's invoice, would make it clear that some of our price rise may merely reflect the cost of more public services. Vain hope. To get around that embarrassment the term 'tax inflation' has been introduced."[5]

COMER and others prevailed on the government to make some sort of distinction between price increases that merely reflected an increase in taxation on a given product, and those that could not be identified in this way. That still left such items as income taxes and corporation taxes unaccounted for, but clearly the revenues they bring in go to pay for a good many necessary public services. But the Bank of Canada – long before the 43rd US president – has a unilateral way of disposing of problems. It doesn't let go easily.

During the first week of September 2002 it seemed that the BoC was about to up interest rates the fourth time in recent months, when the US economy to which the NAFTA has welded us was in steep descent. The reason: consumer prices posted their largest increase in nearly a year in July, fuelled by rising energy prices and higher cigarette taxes. However, the *G&M*, with skepticism, commented, "The surge in cigarette prices was one of the key ingredients in the upward move in inflation last month and reflects the rise in excise taxes in mid-June. Without the increase, the overall inflation rate would fall to an annual rate of 1.8% from 2.1%."

Just reflect on this. The excise tax on tobacco was raised to cut down the rate of cancer which apart from destroying humans drives up health and other expenditures. Respond by raising interest rates at a time when there is distress throughout the economy, and you will add further to costs across the board which means that prices will rise further as will bankruptcies.

The response of the stock market was violent enough to cause the Bank of Canada to draw back from the rate increase it had already all but announced. So blunt a lone tool applied so indiscriminately is doubly dysfunctional.

William Krehm

1. Reproduced in Krehm, William (Ed.) (1999). *Meltdown: Money, Debt and the Wealth of Nations* (p. 79). Toronto: COMER Publications.

2. Krehm, William (1993). *The Bank of Canada: A Power Unto Itself* (p. 18 et seq). Stoddard.

3. In previous estimates of the cost of the 1991 bailout of Canadian banks I confined myself to the interest paid by the Government on debt that the BoC had held and now had been shifted to the chartered banks. Here I have for the first time added the discontinued cash reserves the banks had put up on their deposits from the public. This conforms entirely to the model in the fifth edition

of H.H. Binhammer's *Money, Banking and the Canadian Financial System*, Nelson Canada, 1988. In the July 2002 issue of *ER* ("Must We Restructure Economic Theory?") I discussed the Binhammer treatment of statutory reserves – in its strengths and weaknesses.

I cannot miss the occasion for a tribute to our underfunded librarians in preserving the valuable heritage of an economic literature that is rarely acknowledged to exist in the lecture halls of our universities. The time is ripe not only for a course on the history of mathematics for economics students, but for a course on "the disappeared texts of yesteryears."

4. Actually "near-money" creation, since cash earns no interest unless it is lent out.

5. *Economic Reform*, 1990, May.

Letter to the Editor

IN HIS RECENT COLUMN, "A Systems View: Trust and Confidence" (*Economic Reform*, Aug/02), Bruce Buchanan described a set of related symptom complexes in financial establishments which seem to accumulate and interact to produce what we all can agree is destructive social behaviors.

This account recalled to my mind the system of human development known as Spiral Dynamics (SD), based upon the research of Dr. Clare Graves. That research found that the psychology of the individual emerges in response to changing life conditions. The psychology affects individual feelings, motivations, ethics, values and belief systems. As a developmental application SD has been employed in post-apartheid South Africa as well as the revitalization of communities and organizations in a variety of countries (www.swin.edu.au/afi/Spiral_Dynamics.htm).

It is evident that the feedback loops involved in such spirals can be positive or negative in their societal consequences, and that system properties may at times produce consequences which go far beyond the specific intentions of individuals.

Don Chisholm

The Public Sector is Not Left Behind

WE HADN'T PLANNED this as a morality issue. It was just that when we were reading proof we noticed that almost all the issues dealt with basic morality as much as with economics. Nor is it consoling that the public sector, so badly neglected in other connections, is as much involved in accountancy and other scams as the private buccaneers.

Thus *The Economist* (10/11) and the *G&M* inform us of Italy's circumnavigation of the entry requirements of the Maastricht Treaty, i.e., a maximum 3% budgetary deficit to get into the European Union. Not to worry, a report of the International Market Association (ISMA) informs us that the government is as adept in cooking the books with derivatives as any corporation with a bond issue to peddle. Swaps like other derivatives convert the uncertainties of future arithmetic into the supposed certainties of current figures. This is usually done by trading one cashflow for another in the opposite direction – whether in different currencies or interest rates. The derivative operation is kept off the books. Usually the two streams, however, do refer to the same time span. But that was not so in the case of the manipulation that allowed Italy to meet the Euro Union entry requirement. "The deal, unusually made use of a negative rate of interest, to defer payments on 200 billion yen of government debt from 1997 to 1998. This cut the deficit heroically from 6.7% in 1996 to 2.7% in 1997. What was unique – even amongst the plentiful scams based on derivatives – was the two income streams referred to different time periods.

The author of the report, Gustavo Pega, a former adviser to the Italian Treasury, did not mention Italy by name, but the media had no difficulty identifying the culprit. "Sophisticated investors and even the Bank of Italy (which lost a lot of money in Long-Term Capital Management) know this only too well. Mysteriously Pega's report vanished from ISMA's website the day it was posted.

∾   ∾   ∾

Another borrowing of private sector "efficiency" by government surfaced in *The Globe and Mail* (17/11, "The Story of Nortel's Fall" by Fabrice Taylor): Discussing the long list of Nortel customers who couldn't pay their bills, Taylor notes "Nortel's cash flow situation might have been worse if not for the Export Development Corp., a Crown corporation. The EDC doesn't report details of its deals, but it does provide financing for some Nortel customers. That's good news for Nortel's shareholders, even if it might not be for taxpayers." Just add it to the list of mega-bailouts, beginning with the granddaddy of them all, the bailout of the banks in 1991.∾

Have We Already Begun Blowing the Next Bubble?

THE SOAP SUDS are stirred, the clay pipe is at hand. The clay gods who preside over the ritual are intact on their altars. The world has not begun coping with the trauma of the last bubble-burst, and Wall St. is already preparing the next.

To understand its compulsion, a word of introduction. No one has to be told that the world has become terrifyingly complex except orthodox economists. A key way in which they manage to avoid recognizing that unpleasant fact is by the liberties they allow themselves with the dimension of time. Time is what links our past and future with the present. This means that we must distinguish between what took place in the past and note its significance for the present. And of the future we have only imperfect knowledge. And yet it is the happy hunting ground for security salesmen, bagmen and promoters. The least we can do is get a firm grasp on how the past feeds into the present. And

on what might occur in the future that can conscientiously be presented as a present asset. Graphically this could be shown by arrows: one direct from the past to the present. The other from the present to the future. This is the simplest (one-dimensional) instance of dimensional analysis. And it is one that, scandalously disregarded, has contributed richly to the world's current crisis. If you distort the way in which the past affects our present, or how something that may even not happen in the future affects our present, you are blowing soap bubbles. And hardly with the innocence of a child.

Instead of arrows leading from the past to the present and from the present to the future, we end up with a dot that has no dimensions. Otherwise expressed, instead of analysis we end up with number-crunching, that essentially ignores that great spoiler – the time dimension. Let me give you a couple of examples of misleading dimensionless number crunching.

The treatment of capital investment in the public sector. Rather than writing off over its physical period of usefulness (depreciation) and noting the repayment of its monetary cost (amortization), the investment's value is written off as a current cost in the year it is made. If this were done in the private sector most companies would be bankrupt. As for households, it would be equivalent to calculating your net worth by recording the mortgage on your house as a debt, but omitting the asset value of the house to offset it.

Contrast this with the practice of corporations capitalizing not only their anticipated flow of earnings in the future, but their anticipated market share. Especially in the case of high-tech corporations, it didn't seem to matter whether that market share has been achieved by selling the company's product at a profit or as a loss. The assumption is that after achieving a dominant share – say 100% – the competition will be stone-dead and then your firm's prices can be raised to bring in handsome profits. This obviously is a grotesque new instance of Keynes's "Fallacy of Composition." That story-line if realized might work for the victorious corporation, but it involves all the competitive companies going broke. Passing from the individual to society at large, the result would be disastrous. We are witnessing today the hopelessly deflated market for fibre optical inventories which has left no victors.

But let's get on to the subject of our article. *The Wall Street Journal* (9/9, "While Auto Makers Sputter, Their Dealers Go Full Throttle" by Karen Lundegaard): "At a time when Detroit's big auto makers are scrambling to slash costs to rebuild razor-thin margins and are watching their stocks get hammered, many car dealers are prospering.

"With auto makers pumping money into the costly promotions that have consumers thronging to dealerships, retailers are enjoying some of their best years ever. Stocks of the big publicly traded dealer groups such as AutoNation Inc., based in Fort Lauderdale, Fla. and Dallas-based Group 1 Automotive Inc. have more than doubled during the past two years, while auto makers' share are down as much as 50%.

"The divergent fortunes of car dealers and car makers add up to a striking anomaly of today's shaky economy. In past downturns, when car-makers saw demand sliding, they cut production, and even, in some cases, scaled back discount deals to ride out the storm. Car dealers suffered along with the factories.

"Now auto makers face a fundamentally different landscape. Even with strong sales, the North American auto industry, including the overseas plants that feed it, still can make about 20% more vehicles than the 17 million or so that they sell each year. Any producer that pulls back risks a long-term loss of market share, if rivals choose to fill the gap."

In short with their present profitless production automakers are just keeping their chairs warm for future profit-making. And, more or less, they are all doing the same thing and the new instance of Keynes's "Fallacy of Composition" takes a firmer hold.

"For Detroit's Big Three, scaling back production doesn't save much on labor anyway, because union contracts in the US, make labor in effect a fixed cost. And cutting production means less cash coming in the door to finance growing pension obligations."

In the Greek legend, Sisyphus in Hades rolling his rock uphill each day only to have it roll back each night for all eternity. But at least he didn't have to worry about meeting a payroll, and keeping his bank at bay.

"So the car makers have been pouring on the discounts to keep production moving, and consumers have been snapping up the output in a surprisingly robust level of spending. Rising take-home pay, declining mortgage rates, low inflation and relatively low unemployment have all helped keep wallets open.

"But as the Big Three have used ever-deeper discounts to protect market share, they have seen their profit margins shrivel. Last year, the second-best sales year in US history, brought a $5.45 billion loss for Ford and $2.12 of red ink for Daimler-Chrysler AG's Chrysler group. General Motors eked out a profit of $1.5 billion, a mere $8/10$ of a cent per dollar of revenue.

"GM says its deals this summer cost the company at least as much as the sweeping 0%-financing offer it rolled out as an emergency measure to resuscitate sales after September 11. In the second quarter, the prices paid for comparable vehicles were down 1.9% from the year before.

"'We have learned to live with this.' says GM vice chairman John Devine. That has meant a stepped-up focus on cutting costs. Despite the sales boom, the Big Three have announced plans to cut more than 50,000 jobs and suppliers are facing new demands to lower prices.

"And Toyota and Honda are expanding their North American productive capacity to celebrate a brilliant year. Even though auto makers have cut dealers' margins over the years – charging them more for the cars – dealers have been able to make that up since big rebates and cut-rate financing have fewer customers haggling over the price of the car or the value of a trade-in."

"Also manufacturers foot the bulk of the marketing bill needed to sell cars. AutoNation's Mike Jackson estimates that the manufacturers spend about $2,500 a vehicle on incentives and $500 on advertising and other marketing, while AutoNation is spending just $300 a vehicle. At the same time – low interest rates keep down inventory expenses – one of dealers' biggest costs."

More Gloomy Epitaphs Rarely Found on Tombstones

The day after carrying this report, *WSJ* carried a story (10/9, "Ford Expects to Post 'Small Profit' for Third Period, Beating Forecasts" by Joseph B. White and Norihiko Shirouza) with the following incredible tidings: "Ford's market capitalization of $19.7 billion is less than the $24.9 billion in gross cash the company has on its books, which means investors are effectively assigning a negative value to Ford's $131,5 billion a year automotive and finance business!" More gloomy epitaphs are rarely found on tombstones. And this particular tombstone is over an economic system rather than any single exponent of it.

And into this china shop, Governor Dodge of the Bank of Canada has barged with higher interest rates – yesterday's rule of big-toe for fighting inflation.

Meanwhile, "the public dealerships are using their sudden favor on Wall St. to expand, betting that the combination of demographics and industry dynamics that has kept sales strong can continue. Last Thursday, four of the groups boasted of their latest expansions. AutoNation announced it was buying five franchises in Corpus Christi, Texas. Charlotte-based Sonic Automotive, Inc. said it would buy four dealerships around the country. Group 1 announced plans to open a new Nissan store in Los Angeles, and Detroit-based United Auto Group said it has opened two Hummer stores in Arkansas and one in California.

"The publicly traded dealerships have spent the past couple of years trying to distance themselves in the eyes of Wall St. from the ailing car makers. They present themselves to analysts as specialty retailers, along the lines of home improvement chain Lowe's Companies, Inc., rather than auto companies."

What it amounts to is another derivative bubble. The dealerships are a derivative of an already bursting bubble – the auto companies. They are packaging a future that cannot survive for long the disappearance of the supporting bubble that they have mistaken for terra firma. Obviously when the bankers of the manufacturers force the auto companies to throw in the towel and write off their bad loans, there will be no one to make up the deficits the are currently fuelling the dealership boom. The losses of the manufacturers are being regarded as an endlessly profitable trail into the sunset for the dealers. Once again – as in the case of the fiber optics conglomerates there is no serious communication between the two. The stage is being set for a new round of victimization of the innocents.

William Krehm

P.S. There is an important corollary to this simple exercise in one-dimensional economic analysis. The collapse of the international financial system leaves society with a numerous tribe of highly overpaid people with no other skills or training than bucaneering on a highly manipulated world securities market. No economic revival worthy of the name can be fashioned around the priority of finding gainful employment for jobless high executives at the lofty remuneration they have become accustomed to. They will simply have to be retrained for more useful posts at far more modest salaries.

Deregulation and Globalization was conceived with little concern for the tens of millions that were deprived of their livelihood and even of their savings. In reshaping the world to more sustainable activities, there should be more humanity shown in helping these unhappy unemployed high executives to more useful careers. But ways of achieving this must be undertaken at once. Returning infrastructural assets to the state where the privatized companies are in trouble can be helpful in this respect. Significantly the British government has bailed out British Energy PLC to the tune of $998 million to help it meet its immediate financial obligations which include the 82.4% of Bruce Power. The share price of the mother company fell 65% in a single day. And it seems that there is desperate need for deprivatizing the eight nuclear reactors in Ontario rather than having the financial markets take over further public assets.

But first and foremost it involves rethinking what has passed for economic theory for the past quarter of a century. In fact that is now being exposed to have been little more than the battle hymn of the world's stock markets elevated to the dominant economic group.

SECOND INSTALLMENT OF A REVIEW OF A BOOK BY BRUCE RICH, BOSTON: BEACON PRESS, 1994

Mortgaging the Earth — The World Bank, Environmental Impoverishment, and the Crisis of Development

ON THE IFFY ORIGINS of the World Bank, Rich writes: "Harry White, top adviser to the Secretary of the Treasury Henry Morgenthau, delivered to him his 138-page "Proposal for a United and Associated Nations Stabilization Fund and a Bank for Reconstruction and Development" in April, 1942. Morgenthau shunted aside Roosevelt's initial suggestion that Treasury first share White's plan with Cordell Hull, State Secretary, and the following day Roosevelt endorsed Morgenthau's recommendations. The Treasury had won the turf war of the century, and the State Department has been trying so regain influence in international economic affairs ever since.

"According to one commentator (Richard N. Gardner) Hull actually believed that the fundamental causes of the world wars lay in economic discrimination and trade warfare. Some of his aides went so far as to propose a trade agreement with Nazi Germany in 1939 as a means of avoiding the Second World War. Had Hull been Roosevelt's Duchess County neighbor instead of Morgenthau, we might have ended up with an International Trade Organization and not an International Monetary Fund."

The unprecedented predominance of the US on the world stage at the time inevitably asserted itself – it accounted for one half of the world trade and had the only international viable currency But this took place in an unlimited surge of New Deal rhetoric – environmental or economic for an "unlimited prosperity" for all mankind. No people will again tolerate prolonged and widespread unemployment. In his broadcast remarks at the close of the Bretton Woods Conference Morgenthau envisaged "1. The creation of a world economy in which the peoples of every nation will enjoy, increasingly, the fruits of material progress on an earth infinitely blessed with natural riches All else must be built on this. For freedom of opportunity is the foundation for all other freedoms.

"The original capital of the Bank was set at $10 billion, the equivalent of at least $70 or $80 billion in 1993. Twenty percent of the capital subscriptions would be paid in by member countries, and the remaining 80% was would be 'callable' as a guarantee. The guarantee by major industrialized nations (the Bank's callable capital" allows the Bank to raise money for lending by borrowing in international capital markets; the Bank charges borrowers a rate of interest typically .5 percent above its own borrowing cost, pocketing the difference to pay its operating expenses and to add to reserves. Membership in the IMF is a prerequisite for joining the Bank."

The mighty opponent of the Bretton Woods Agreement was the Republican senator Robert Alfonso Taft. He warned that Wall St., as opposed to Main St. would welcome the Bank. It is almost a subsidy to the business of investment bankers and will increase the business done by the larger banks. Though dismissed as a prejudiced rightist at the time, by the 1960s Taft came to be praised by the New Left for his prescience.

The Perils of Bureaucratic Rationality

"The Bank was very much a product of the New Deal and of a pioneering optimism about the ability of government and centralized planning to manage economic forces. Little thought was given to the political and moral risks associated with such an enterprise, though the literature of modernity from Max Weber onward is replete with warnings of the human consequences of bureaucratic rationality divorced from political and social accountability.

"No one embodied this technocratic faith more than [J.M.]Keynes, who envisaged the Bretton Woods institution as virtual technocratic priesthoods, beyond the vulgar machinations of national politics that had led to so much grief in the past. But to vest institutions with unprecedented financial and political power without corresponding accountability to those affected by their decisions is a dangerous path indeed, and technical reason cannot legitimize power – it only rationalizes and magnifies the consequences of its exercise."

Our readers will be aware of COMER's indebtedness to much of Keynes's writings. However, he was very much the product of his time, his country, and his social group And, indeed, he fell victim to his very talent. It was an age when economic reasoning had broken down to where the society was denied the use of much already discovered technology. In the Soviet Union, Lenin literally equated electrification with socialism. In a similar heart-throb, Keynes and many others in the thirties saw in technology the missing bridge to resolving society's problems. They had no eyes for the new problems that it might create. He was British, accustomed to government answerability. As an academic, and son of an academic, he spent his entire life in the atmosphere of one of the great universities of the world, used to differences being solved in a setting of cordiality and gentlemanly give-and-take. He had little experience of the muddy trenches of class warfare that divided the world, not excluding Britain herself. His immense self-assurance drew greatly on this comity, indeed, took it for granted. Finally his own gifts seduced him into the belief that hack politicians were the victims of stupidity or a faulty education.

In contrast, Max Weber, the German historian-sociologist, whose spirit hovers over the Rich book, had a background diametrically opposed to that of Keynes. Son of a wealthy industrialist who had abandoned his early liberalism to move closer to Bismark, he was much under the influence of a mother burdened with a Calvinist conscience. That not only filled the parental house with tension but led Weber to tireless questing through history and exotic faiths for release from it. He suffered a severe nervous breakdown.

When he emerged from it years later, he reversed his earlier position in favour of German expansion which would help produce a sense of responsibility. Instead he developed the concept of "official secret" as the specific invention of bureaucracy. Bureaucracy naturally welcomes a poorly informed and hence powerless parliament.

His opposition to Germany's annexionist war aims caused General Erich Ludendorff to brand him as a traitor. He died in 1920.

Keynes's sad awakening from some of the illusions bred of intellectual privilege came during his negotiations with the US before and during Bretton Woods. There he was turned down in his advocacy of a postwar world in which dealing with imbalances of payments would be a responsibility of creditor as well as debtor nations. In it creditors would have to help reduce their mounting credit balance – by raising the exchange value of their currency, lowering interest rates, purchasing more goods from debtor nations. If their positive balances continued growing, they would eventually become forfeit to the international organization to be used for humanitarian projects of the international organization.

Keynes towards the end of his life arrived at a wormwood conclusion: since bankrupt Britain would not be seen as a candidate for an international dole, her only hope was to espouse the cause of all needy lands.

The misgivings about the future of the World Bank were soon fleshed out. After a six month tenure of Eugene Meyers, publisher of the Washington Post, he was replaced by John J. McCloy, a "prominent Wall St. lawyer who was to earn the sobriquet of Mr. Eastern Establishment" and was to move on to posts and non-posts that shaped US Policy: Allied High Commission for Germany, director of the CIA, conduct negotiations with the Saudi government on behalf of both his oil company clients and the US, while the US ambassador waited in the adjoining room for the outcome.

In his powerful unofficial capacity he held back or released the lightning bolts that could overthrow elected Latin American governments. He arranged the merger of the Chase and Manhattan banks, and much, much else. John Kenneth Galbraith saw him as the most influential person at the cutting edge of US policy. McCloy left a deep footprint on the Bank's future career.

Blanket Paternalism Combined with Breath-taking Naïveté

"The Bank declared that [its] technical assistance and intellectual leadership would 'define the shape of a sound over-all development program.' Development theory in the 1950s and 1960s emphasized the capital-intensive approach. Walt Rostow spoke of the economic 'take-off' once the catalytic effect of capital investments had spurred increased productivity and growth. Early Bank lending was biased not toward the need of borrowing countries, but toward what was easiest for the Bank to lend for. Power and transportation projects were easily appraised, involved technology transfer and planning that appeared the same all over the world.' [The approach] combined blanket paternalism with breathtaking naivete, rooted in *a priori* macro- and micro-economic assumptions, rather than in empirical understanding of local social political and economic realities."

"Since the demand for development projects the Bank could finance was less than expected, the Bank's strategy from the 1950s onward was to create it. A primary focus was institution building, most often taking the form of promoting the creation of autonomous agencies within governments – EGAT in Thailand and NTPC in India are typical examples. Such agencies were intentionally established to be relatively independent financially from their host governments, as well as less accountable politically – except, of course, to the Bank. The Bank exerted increasing influence over the evolution of critical economic sectors such as agriculture by linking loans for specific projects to the acceptance of technical packages of fertilizers, pesticides, and technical trading, provided mainly from the outside. A serious pressure began to appear at the end of the 1950s – net negative transfers from its borrowers: some countries began to pay more money back to the Bank than the Bank disbursed to them in new loans. For most banks this is a simple fact of life: disbursements from a lender to a borrower will be heavily in the borrower's favor in the early years of a loan; in later years the flow reverses as the borrower pays the loan back. To keep increasing the volume of loans so that the net transfer over the short term from bank to borrower remains positive is obviously building a house of cards. But a well-run commercial bank does not face this prospect if it can recruit a constant stream of new customers to lend to, corporate or individual.

Maximizing the World Bank

"In 1963, 1964, and 1969, India transferred more money to the Bank than the Bank disbursed to it. In 1968, India was obliged to reschedule its long-term debt, followed by Indonesia in 1970. In 1970 debt service payments for developing countries already equaled 40% of the total transfer of funds to them from the industrialized north. Enter Robert McNamara.

"In physical terms, McNamara drove the Bank to expand at a pace unprecedented for a large institution. From 1968 to

1981, lending increased from $953 million to $12.4 billion, and the Bank staff from 1,574 to 5,201. It was McNamara, too, who created in 1970 an environmental office. In the 1972 Stockholm UN Conference on the human environment he declared: 'The question is not whether there should be continued economic growth. There must be. Nor is the question whether the impact on the environment must be respected. It has to be. The two considerations are interlocked.'"

We will quote summary samples of the practical results of this grand vision.

"In Malaysia, the Bank supported with numerous loans the massive forest-clearing and agricultural settlement activities of the Federal Land Development Authority (FELDA) – an autonomous development agency of the kind fostered by Bank 'institution building.' The Bank viewed its FELDA projects as unusually successful: 'They met or overfulfilled goals of land clearing, crop production, and settlement: with more than 1.3 million acres developed and 72,600 families settled since 1960, FELDA is undoubtedly one of the most important and efficient settlement agencies in the world.' These 1.3 million acres covered 4% of the entire land of peninsular Malaysia and accounted for the destruction of about 6.5% of the remaining forest cover in the 1970s. But the cost per family of these forest clearing and settlement schemes was astronomical – nearly $40,000 in 1993 dollars. In contrast, the much more criticized Indonesia Transmigration and Brazil projects of the 1980s averaged $6,000 to $8,000 per family settled.

Elephants Smarter than World Bank?

"The most severe environmental consequence of these Malaysian settlement schemes was intentional" the clearing of huge areas of intact tropical rainforest. But there were others. Massive pollution from Bank-financed palm oil factories was one. The rapid decimation of forests also created difficulties with rampaging wild elephants, boars, and porcupines. Deprived of their forest home, the elephants stampeded onto the newly established oil palm and rubber estates in the Jahore project. 46% of the oil palm stands were destroyed by rampaging pachyderms, who in the opinion of some observers, bore signs of uncanny purpose and intelligence. Nearly a hundred miles of electrified barbed wire fences had to be constructed to keep the elephants at bay so that the palms could be replanted with a 96% cost overrun.

"The Colombia Caqueta Land Colonization Project attempted to promote spontaneous migration of settlers to the Colombian Amazon rainforest through the construction of 200 kilometers of roads and subsidized credit for cattle ranching. The Cameroon Niete Rubber Estate Project was the first of two loans to clear and develop 37,000 acres of tropical forest for rubber plantations. The deforestation proceeded so crudely that logs were not even salvaged for commercial use.

"By the late 1980s it became clear that the performance of Bank agricultural projects was abysmal in the Bank's own terms of meeting appraised rates of return, and reaching the poor. Nearly 45% were judged unsatisfactory. In 9 of a total of 21 irrigation projects, agricultural production after investment phase was completed. Of the 17 of these irrigation projects in Asia, 10 were considered overall to be failures.

The World Bank professes to carry out adequate feasibility studies before embarking on projects. However, many have been rushed through without adequate analysis because the decisive factor was the urgent need of the host country for the resulting foreign exchange to meet its obligations to the IMF.

"One of the most important regions for McNamara style poverty projects was Brazil's northeast. The World Bank approved more than a half dozen projects in the late 1970s to support the Northeast Integrated Area Development Program (POLONORDESTE), an ambitious agricultural and livestock development scheme that purported to target the landless and poor, small-scale farmers. Let the Bank's Operations Evaluation Department speak for itself: 'By 1980 only 37% of the projected number of farmers had actually been assisted, 18% had received credit, fewer than 6% of the anticipated land titles had been distributed and less than a third of the planned health posts and water supply systems had been built. Benefits, moreover, had for the most part been monopolized by 100,000 owner occupiers, with the bulk of the program's three million low-income rural families being largely excluded from credit and agricultural services.' The list could go on for ten times the space at our disposal.

"There was a more sinister side to the McNamara years, one that went beyond wasted money and environmental devastation. On July 18, 1977, Senator James Abourezk of South Dakota, a Democrat, rose on the US Senate floor to denounce the World Bank's predilection for supporting military regimes that tortured and murdered their subjects, sometimes immediately after the violent overthrow of democratic governments that the Bank had previously refused to lend to. The habit continued in subsequent years as well – an incomplete list of this shameful record includes Chile, Uruguay, Argentina, Brazil and the Philippines. and Indonesia.

Even Ceaucescu of Romania was a recipient of the Bank's largesse. According to former Bank staff member Aart Van de Laar, at one meeting McNamara responded to questions on Romania with a statement that he had "great faith in the financial morality of socialist countries in repaying debts." At which point a Bank vice-president acerbically observed that "Allende's Chile had perhaps not yet become socialist enough."

Rich heads the chapter where this is revealed "The Faustian Paradox of Robert McNamara."

W.K.

The Next Generation of Irridescent Bubbles

IN OUR PIECE on the automobile dealership boom coinciding with the near record auto manufacturing slump (page 7 in this issue), we introduced the concept of derivative speculative bubbles: moon bubbles spinning around aspects of the earth speculative bubble that has in fact already burst. A high school student will tell you that if the mother planet has gone up in smoke, there will be no gravitational force to keep the moon in orbit, but economists shun raising such obvious problems. They would needlessly complicate the sale of stocks and bonds. The pattern can be detected across the world economy. Thus *The Wall Street Journal* (10/09, "Foreclosures Hit Record Levels" by Queena Sook Kim) deals with the soft underbelly of the housing boom that has been hailed as one of the few guarantees against a "double-dip recession": "In recent years, the housing industry has bent over backwards to allow people to buy houses they couldn't previously afford. Lenders require smaller down payments and allow buyers to devote more of their income to mortgage payments. And many borrowers are being lured by adjustable rate mortgages with low teaser rates that quickly climb, pushing up house payments.

"Now the bill is coming due. In the second quarter, a record 1.23% of all home loans were in the foreclosure process, above the first quarter's tally of 1.10%, and surpassing the previous record of 1.14% in the first quarter of 1999, according to a report of the Mortgage Bankers Association of America. The same report found 4.77% of all home loans outstanding were at least 30 days delinquent. That's one of the highest rates of the last decades, though it's well below the record delinquency of 6.07% in 1985 [at the height of the Savings and Loans super-mess].

"If the delinquency rate worsens, lenders could tighten lending standards, making it harder for many potential home buyers to get financing and resulting in a weaker overall housing market. That would be bad news for the economy since surging house prices are a big reason that consumers have kept spending even as the stock market slumped.

"The derivative aspect of the housing boom, is that it was fueled by a growing problem of the house builders – their inability to move their housing without luring buyers into taking on financial commitments that many simply can't afford in a crumpling economy. The cheerful house-buying boom has been based largely on the already deeply insecure housing market. That confirms our new category of a 'derivative boom' that sets its foundations in an already collapsed bubble.

"Part of the reason the housing market got so hot is that lenders rushed out loans designed to cut monthly payments so that buyers could get bigger homes. It is some of these very loans that are now experiencing problems. One indication: Conventional adjustable-rate mortgages, popular with budget-stretched customers, currently have a 5.29% delinquency rate vs. a 2.75% rate for conventional fixed-rate mortgages.

"In the San Diego county town of Vista, the Mullins think their brokers steered them into a home they couldn't afford. The couple, who are in their 30s, had racked up $20,000 in credit-card debt after buying their first home in 1999. Mr. Mullins figured that monthly mortgage payments on the Vista home would eat up about 60% of their take-home salary and exceed the 36% of gross income that once was the banking industry's usual limit.

"The couple say that their broker, Patty Villanueva, steered them towards a 'stated income program; which allows borrowers to simply write their income on an application without submitting tax returns. The interest rate on a state-income program is between an eighth of a percentage point and one percentage point above the conventional rate.'"

The real motivation of such plans is to use the customers' credit card elbow room (another bubble in the process of coming apart) to stave off the house builders' bankruptcy, with too many of the buyers merely patsies victimized as fodder to keep the derivative boom going.

William Krehm

When the Circus Came to Town

A MEMORY from my remote childhood was when my school class was taken to watch the circus come to town. Arriving by train they were marched through the streets towards the exhibition grounds, a sort of Noah's ark in reverse gear. A literal-minded believer could take it as the ultimate proof of the Scriptures; an evolutionist as a broad proof of Darwin. But what stuck in my little mind was the way the trunk of one elephant clutched the tail of the one ahead, the whole resulting in a tidy chain. It gave you a sense of a world properly organized according to whatever script you chose.

Somehow that came to mind when I read *The Globe and Mail* story (27/08, "US solidifies its ranking as the world's biggest jailer" by Miro Cernetig): "The US has cemented its status as the world's No.1 jailer, with a record 6.6 million behind bars, on probation, or paroled last year.

"These latest statistics published yesterday by the Department of Justice, mean one of every 32 adult Americans is in the penal system – six times the incarceration rate in Canada.

"The growth of that figure slowed last year to 2.6% from an average annual increase of 3.6% over the previous five years." But the US is far from losing the championship. "Civil liberties groups believe US prisons have become a weapon against the poor, especially against blacks.

"Blacks represent more than 45% of the prison population, even though they comprise only 12% of it.... On any given day, 'one in nine black men between the age of 25 and 34 are locked up,' said Marc Mauer, assistant director of the Sentencing Project, a Washington-based advocacy group. 'In 2001, the US had 1.3 million people in prisons, and 631,240 in jails, 3.9 million people on probation and another 731,147 under parole supervision. The US incarceration rate is five to eight times higher than in other democratic nations.'"

Here the first interlacing of the elephant's trunk with his

colleague's tail makes its appearance: "One consequence for the world's most powerful democracy: about 4 million US citizens can no longer vote, because a felony conviction means a lifetime ban on casting a ballot.

"Mr. Mauer said 'enough prisoners have been stripped of their voting rights to sway several key states, most notably Florida which President George W. Bush won by a few hundred votes in 2000.'

"It wasn't always so. In the 1950s, the US put people in prison at a rate more in line with other Western countries. But in the sixties, the violent anti-Vietnam War protests and President Richard Nixon's first salvo in the war on drugs in 1968 started a trend towards tougher sentencing." Of course, like the interpretation of the elephant chain of the arriving circus, there are always a couple of juries out on such issues. One has the connections that count, the other doesn't.

"It soon became good politics to implement harsher sentencing for drug crimes, a trail blazed [of all people!] by New York Governor Nelson Rockefeller. In 1973 he imposed 15-year mandatory sentences for possession of small quantities of drugs. Policies further hardened in the 1980s and 1990s, culminating in the so-called three-strikes law that put people away for a minimum of 25 years if convicted three times on relatively minor felonies." Second interlacing of trunk and tail.

Some might find these massive statistics on the jailed a striking contrast with the couple of photos of manacled Wall Street high-flyers taken into custody that have recently received such prominent play in the media. However, it does keep down the number of officially unemployed in the land.

"In 1980 there were about 40,000 people in prison for drug offences; today it's about 450,000.

"Experts believe the incarceration rate shows no sign of reversing soon, even though there has been no major upward trend in crime rates."

William Krehm

October Mail Box

I thought you might be interested in a speech excerpt (06/06/02) by Gurmont Grewal, Alliance MP representing Surrey Central. I send it to you even though I am Green.

Thankful fan and student,
David Walters, Surrey, BC

We are indebted to David Walters for bringing to our attention Mr. Grewal's remarkable statements. Like green shoots breaking forth from a well-manured field, it is a sign of the times than an Alliance MP should be publicizing what parties further center and left are carefully tip-toeing around. We quote from the excerpt:

"The government has been cooking the books. This draws an exact parallel to dubious accounting practices at WorldCom, Xerox and Enron.

"As a former member of the public accounts committee, I remember that Auditor General Desautels was very critical of the government for not following generally accepted accounting principles and blamed this weak federal government for unilaterally changing its accounting rules to balance the books in 1998.

"When the government was running a deficit before the election, it deferred payments to the next year so that the amount of the deficit is minimized – front-end loading. When the government has more surpluses and it will be quite some time until the next election, then it hides away the money so that it can dole some out just prior to the election to buy votes from Canadians with their own money – back-end loading.

"The government had also hidden money in entities that did not even exist at the time the payments were made. The Auditor General was very critical and questioned the credibility of the federal government's books. To avoid political pressure to reduce taxes and pay debt, the Liberals avoided reporting a surplus during that time.

"The Auditor General qualified his audit of federal government books in 1996-7 because the Liberals overstated the deficit by $800 million. This arrogant Liberal government inappropriately recorded the $800 million transfer payments to the Canada Foundation Innovation before March 31, 1997, a foundation not legally created until April 1997. The government books closed on March 31, 1997. The money for the foundation was not supposed to be spent until the year 2000. If a businessman or manager had done that he or she would be in jail.

"Let us look at the further arrogance of the Deputy Minister of Finance and the Secretary of the Treasury Board who wrote a letter bullying the Auditor General, registering their profound astonishment that the Auditor General would publicly state his objections.

"The practice has not stopped yet. According to a newspaper report, the Auditor General has identified at least another $30 billion that has been secreted away in separate slush fund accounts that she cannot access or question. Only the Prime Minister and the cabinet have access to these funds, and by legislation, they are accountable to nobody. (Notwithstanding the fact that the Finance Minister took $25 billion from the excessive $40 billion Employment Insurance surplus to balance the governments' books.) This shell game must end and we need honesty in the government's accounting practices." [Gurmont Grewal]

Coordinating Investigation of Scams in the Government

As impressive as these unventilated matters are, coming from an Alliance member of Parliament, they merely scratch the surface of what lies buried. Conscientious parliamentarians for inspiration must look to the prosecutors who are examining the irregularities of many high-tech and other corporations. Every time a major scam is identified, and a further insider turns state evidence, greater fraud implicating ever more powerful corporations comes to light. Why then should parallel irregularities in government not be pursued to their very roots?

Grewal has revealed Auditor General Desautels' confrontations with the Finance Ministry, but stops short of the entire story. There are tales too important to be cut off half-way. This is one of them. It is the record of the perversion of our society that could well cost us its survival.

Before he would provide unconditional approval of the federal books, Auditor General Desautels prevailed on the Government to bring in Accrual Accountancy, also known as "capital budgeting." Up to now the government has been writing off its physical investments in a single year – unless they are set up as crown corporations, in which case they follow accountancy rules prevailing in the private sector. When the government itself constructs a building or a bridge it treats it exactly as it does money spent on floor-wax or paper-clips. Though its useful life may extend over decades and the land it sits on actually increases in value, it is carried on the government books at a token dollar. Four royal commissions over the past 40 years recommended that the treatment of capital investment obligatory in the private sector be extended to the public sector. A bill passed in 2000 by Parliament provides that this change in government accountancy be brought in by mid-2002. Mr. Grewal should be asking why we have heard nothing further on this matter. It was not reassuring when the measure became law the Auditor General in his report made a most surprising statement: since no new money is brought into government coffers by the accountancy change, it cannot warrant increased public spending. But if that were so, why was the bogus deficit created by these arbitrary write-offs used as the pretext for slashing social services in the early 1990s? Why then would the recognition of the government investments – those made in the past and those to be made in the future – not warrant resuming needed public investments?

Obviously Finance Minister Paul Martin, and the top bureaucrats in the Ministry of Finance had used precisely the sort of arm-twisting on their auditor, for which Enron and Global Crossing *e tutti quanti* are being indicted on criminal charges in the US.

Nor does the story close there. The legislation bringing in capital budgeting referred only to physical capital. But from the rapid reconstruction of devastated Japan and Germany after World War II economists came to recognize that the most productive of all investments is in human capital – education, skills, and hence also in health and social welfare. (This recognition came in only in rare footnotes and a Nobel Prize for Economics for Theodore Schultz, rather than in economists' operative models.) When all government investment – physical and human – comes to be treated as such in the state's books there is little doubt that the net worth of the governments of the developed lands will be greatly positive. That will warrant a drop in interest rates just as the present bogus deficit led to their being held disastrously high for over two decades.

Nor is even that the end of the story. Somebody long since pointed out that in human affairs there are few really independent story-lines. And the one apt in this connection is the oldest of them all – primal sin. It comes with a grim warning attached – Eden did not survive its attempted cover-up. Our bureaucratic Adams must come out of the bushes.

In fact in the best American tradition the tale has a "three strikes and out" wrinkle. In the 1980s the North American banks – as many elsewhere – had as a group lost their entire capital and more in wild gambles financing gas and oil, real estate, and other mega-ventures. The bailout was staged as a necessity since governments are not supposed to be trustworthy to exercise the powers of money creation, while the private banks are. And to celebrate the principle, the bailout took the form not of a one-shot rescue, but as an entitlement, recurring each year. The deregulated banks were literally piped into the national treasury, and the funding of their gambles received priority over any other government obligation. In essence it applied very much the logic of the International Monetary Fund in dealing with Third World countries – suffocate them in debt, and from the vantage point of creditors, dictate the distribution of their national income.

All this should be of interest to our democratically elected representatives, whether they are left or right of center. Our applause to Mr. Grewal has a single condition – that he continue his researches until he gets to the dead rat under the floorboards.

The Editor

Has the Master Performer Forgotten his Scales?

IN THIS AGE of uncertainty the conductor himself seemed to have forgotten the score. The expression of confidence offered on the point by *The Wall Street Journal* is far from reassuring (9/08, "Fed Faces a Delicate Balancing Act" by Greg Ip): "The Federal Reserve is concerned about the economy's recovery, but not as worried as Wall St. So while the central bank isn't likely to cut rates next week, it still has to figure out how to acknowledge the risks without sounding either panicked or complaisant." That's like reassuring you that you have more reason for optimism than the man in a death row cell.

"Just five months ago, expectations were high that the banks would be steadily raising rates to stem a resurgence of inflationary pressure. The stock market's plunge during the past month along with a run of weak economic reports turned those expectations."

That's no detail for the Fed. It has convinced itself that its main (if not sole) business was to "fight inflation," and its one-time arsenal for achieving this has been reduced to a single hatchet – raising interest rates. That equips it shoddily for dealing with deflation. So it ends up pretending that it is never there. The sheer technical reason for this is daunting: how much can you raise interest rates? Mr. Greenspan's predecessor Paul Volcker explored the inflationary seas and ended up driving interest rates well towards wrecking the economy and sending up the national debt like a rocket. But if you recognize deflation – falling price levels – to be closing in on you, you run into a problem. The current discount rate is 1.75? How much lower can you go? The Japanese central bank battling deflation for most of the decade has pretty well – like our desperate car manufacturers – reached zero interest rates – or a bit better. Go below that and you would subsidize borrowers. Our governments are more experienced in subsiding banks than borrowers.

On the other hand when central banks still made use of increasing the statutory reserves – that is the modest proportion of the deposits they took in from the public – to bring down the banks' leverage in creating credit – they could reverse that tool for handling the opposite problem – lowering the reserves to deal with deflation. Since for decades those statutory reserves were in the 10% region, that gave central banks a long bow for fighting deflation. If the statutory reserve were at 10% during a boom period you could bring it down quite a way to dig the economy out of a recession. In combatting a speculative boom you simply removed some of the banks' leverage in creating credit without pushing the economy over the cliff with lofty interest rates. You would have both less deflation to wrestle and adequate means for doing so.

"Yesterday (8/08) futures markets were forecasting that the Fed would lower its target for the federal funds rate from to 1.5% by November, from its current 40-year low of 1.75%. No matter how badly the spell of deflation ahead of us may turn out, our central banks are with little ammunition for handling it. Possibly that is a contributing factor in refusing to recognize the serious potentials of such a prospect."

More powerful influences, however, have been at work. With the deregulation of banks – which strangely enough took place when they had just been bailed out from their gambling losses – they were allowed to engage in just about every type of business connected with the stock market. They took over brokerages, underwriting stock issues, and acquiring chunks of the businesses that they financed ("merchant banking"), they sat on multiple chairs. Their main loyalty was to pushing up the price of their stock. And for that high interest rates were poison. And in 1996, when Chairman Greenspan warned against "irrational exuberance," he was told by Wall St. to mind his own business – and that was looking after inflation of commodities not of stock market prices. And, like a docile lamb, the great man obeyed. The message went forth that Wall St. ran the land and the world. That is what gave us the Enrons and the WorldComs. It has left little room for the basic morality that makes possible meaningful transactions.

An important point should be clarified. When you hear that the Fed has lowered its discount rate to 1.75% and might possibly reduce it further, do not for a moment conclude that happy days are here once more. That is the rate for banks to borrow from the Fed for overnight purposes. Most borrowers – including large corporations – are being stiffed by historically high rates, because of the mistrust that pervades the economy, and to help cover the banks' huge losses on the stock market and associated endeavors. Consumers – except for mortgages and financing purchases of autos – are increasingly dependent on their credit cards and pay credit card rates. The spread between these and the Fed discount rate is at historic highs. Bank fees are another rich chapter.

The *WSJ* piece ends on what can only be described as a dead

note: "Some economists have said the Fed officials wouldn't cut rates for fear of repudiating their previous upbeat statements and sparking panic. Such fears aren't likely to be a factor if officials are really convinced that the economy is in trouble. 'We need to do what we need to do' is a popular refrain among Fed policymakers." Then why didn't they do it to rein in the "irrational exuberance" when Chairman Greenspan first went public on the matter?

William Krehm

Chain Questions Raised by Europe's Floods

EUROPE'S FLOODS are wreaking great physical damage, but no greater than their toll on institutionalized dogma.

Before we embark on our tale, we would advise our readers to check their calendars to confirm that the year is indeed 2002, a half-century after the governments of Germany and Japan were already well advanced in rebuilding countries that had been flattened in the war. And in the process they helped make possible one of the greatest mass migrations that gave both the defeated lands and the victorious allies the most prosperous years of their history.

What then is the trouble today? Let's first gauge the extent of the confusion. *The Wall Street Journal* (20/1, "Flood Damage Forces Germany to Delay Tax Cut" by Philip Shishkin and G. Thomas Sims) informs us: "Germany and other nearby governments are taking drastic steps in an attempt to finance billions of euros in damage from the worst flooding to hit Central Europe in more than a century.

"German Chancellor Gerhard Schroeder unexpectedly announced plans to postpone 6.9 billion euros (US$6.8 billion) in tax cuts scheduled for next year to free up funds for an estimated 15 billion euros in damages. The Czech Republic, meanwhile, canceled a $1.2 billion plan to modernize its air force, hoping to redirect the money to cover flood damage estimated at nearly $2.8 billion.

"The effort in Germany to pay for damage without incurring new debt underscores the limited resources of the cash-strapped country, which was already brushing up against European Union spending limits before the floods hit Bavaria and eastern Germany." The European Union requires that its members produce a government surplus of 3% of the GDP.

But, "meanwhile, the Czech Republic's decision not to replace its old fleet of Soviet-built MIG fighter jets with 24 Western planes follows a similar move in Austria, which said it would reduce the size of a planned order of new Eurofighter jets to help free up money for flood aid."

Is God a Frustrated Keynesian?

A propos of which, some years ago, the late Lynn Turgeon coined the phrase "God is a Keynesian, perhaps the last one around." Nor is it hard to understand the reasons for the Almighty's occasional anger. Like so many others, Turgeon had noted that when natural disasters occur – especially in God's own country – tornadoes, forest fires, earthquakes – jobs increase, cash registers tinkle more quickly, and the GDP goes up. And with a vibrant economy, government revenues surge, and a frowning system smiles once more. But why must we await a disaster to use our economy sensibly, and not only as a private hunting ground for the greedy privileged?

What is the difficulty in financing the clean-up of the present floods?

Let's give the word to the *WSJ* once more" "Some economists hope the flood repairs could revive Germany's stagnant economy later this year, even though a loss in output is likely during the current quarter. Elga Bartsch, an economist with Morgan Stanley in London, estimates that Germany could gain as much as a point in economic growth over the next year as reconstruction takes place."

Doesn't that mean that if reconstruction does not take place,

Germany would be missing this "growth." (To simplify things, we are assuming it's all going to be good and not just add to the pollution and to the cementing over of Mother Earth that contributed to the floods.) And if the damage were not duly repaired, would we not have to deduct the unrepaired damage from the economy's balance sheet? Doesn't that suggest that the very concept of the GDP is under water?

And why would the Chancellor not mention that with East Germany's unemployment in the upper double-digit region there would be considerable savings not only in unemployment insurance, but in the moral waste of the unemployed?

But these are seditious chain questions. Ask one, and inevitably an even more disturbing one springs up as an answer. Why would a government, especially one headed by a Socialist politician, have to wait for a national disaster to put willing unemployed to work?

William Krehm

Lessons from the Pampas

IT WOULD BE WRONG to mistake Argentina for just another disaster-prone "emerging" land unable to cross that magic line into developed, democratic status. Its levels of education and cultural attainment are up to those of Western and Central Europe. In the first quarter of the 20th century it was referred to as Britain's unofficial "sixth dominion." Buenos Aires, indeed, was a world cultural centre to a degree that no city in Britain's actual dominions could match.

With its overtones of European fascism, the dictatorship of Peron initiated the downward drift. A murderous military regime, similar those imposed by Washington in neighbouring Brazil and Chile, hastened the decline. It involved the country in a senseless war with Britain over the Falkland Islands that the Iron Lady also needed when she ran out of options. Then the International Monetary Fund and the World Bank stepped in to truss the wounded land like a fowl for the oven. All restrictions on the free movement of trade and hot money were done away in return for IMF loans. That denied Argentina the self-defence without which the US and European countries could never have become leading industrial powers. It could issue further domestic currency only if fully backed by US dollars. That deprived its economy of even a wind-break for shelter when the going got rough. Argentine exports were priced out of the world market. A paved escape route was provided speculative money to safety abroad. IMF loans boosted the hard-currency value of securities that had been bought for devalued pesos. Nothing was left for the Argentinians but the interest and eventual redemption payments in US dollars.

The pension fund had been privatized, which meant that the government – unlike the governments of the leading countries – could no longer have the use of monies that would not be called upon until years ahead.

When International Finance Sinks its Fangs into a Country's Vitals

Argentine thus offers us an opportunity for understanding how a country privileged with physical and human resources can be reduced to helplessness once international finance sinks its fangs into its vitals. It must serve as a laboratory not only for understanding how that can be remedied, but prevented from happening elsewhere. For not even the world's lone superpower is secure against privileged debt. A recurrence of the worst features of the Dirty Thirties hangs over the heads of all of us.

The 1930s became a period for the founding of new central banks and a groping towards focussing of their powers of money-creation to lift the world out of its depression-trap. The process did not really get under way seriously until the war and the postwar. Then it financed a move towards a more just, pluralistic society.

These very achievements of the western world brought on a brilliantly organized reaction of international finance to reverse the trend. The turning point was the so-called US Treasury-Fed Accord of 1951 that unpegged interests rates behind President Truman's back – at the very beginning of the Korean War![1] A key part of that strategy was presenting the subject of money creation as infinitely complex beyond the understanding of average citizens. In reality the subject is far less complicated than the reigning model of the self-balancing market. It calls for nothing more than the sort of arithmetic that you use whenever you go to the supermarket.

All you need is to grasp that you cannot automatically turn around a relationship just as you flip a pancake. When somebody holds a loaded revolver to his head and pulls the trigger, he falls dead. But that doesn't mean that when somebody falls dead, he has shot himself in the head. That, however, is the sort of logic underlying the monetary policy of the past three decades. If there is an excess of demand over available supply on an idealized market, prices will go up. From that, however, you can't conclude that if prices go up, market demand has outstripped supply. It could mean that the public sector is providing more essential unmarketed, unpriced serves paid for by taxation. If so, that extra taxation makes up a deeper layer in the price level.

That must not be confused with "inflation" caused by excess demand bidding up the prices of insufficient supply.

There is no need for complex mathematics to prove the point. In 1929 an estimated 90% of the world's population lived in the countryside, and only 10% lived in large cities. Now those figures have been reversed. Before World War II you could count the cities with populations of several millions on the fingers of your hands. Today the number of cities of several millions run into three digits. Nobody moving from a town of 5,000 to New York City or London, expects his living costs to stay the same. How then could prices remain flat when humanity as a whole has made such a move? A huge urban population requires physical and human infrastructures undreamt of in the countryside. Cities are the brains of modern societies where most of the world's creative thinking is done. That means universities, libraries, art galleries, costly transport and sanitation systems, and so forth.[2] If these aren't supplied, then the cost of the missing public services must be deducted from what is being provided for the taxes and prices charged, to ascertain what the real price level is. When the price level is not adjusted to reflect this explosion of urbanization, it is not a true indicator of the real degree of price stability. And urbanization is not the only such factor contributing to such "structural price rise." This has nothing to do with market inflation (the excess of available over available supply). Unrepaired damage to the environment, neglected education and social services must be entered as a shortfall, with a resulting increase in the price per unit of what has actually been delivered. Central banks today have been seeking "inflation" under the wrong beds.

A Glaring Conflict of Interest

At the very time that this increased pluralization of our society was producing an upward ramp of the price level, the financial interests shifted the very purpose of the central banks. In all this, I take the Bank of Canada as our example, not only because we know it best, but because it is one of the extreme examples of the take-over of the central banks for the sole purpose of "licking inflation." And to make matters worse, the policy kit that the central bank has at its disposal to stabilize "inflation," was by the late 1970s reduced to a "single blunt tool" – raising interest rates until prices lay flat. But interest is the revenue of money-lenders, a group that needs no encouragement to become predatory. Higher interest rates transfer revenue from the rest of society to the money-lenders. There is thus a glaring conflict of interest in declaring their revenue the one blunt tool of central bank policy.

The central banks in the 1930s had as their main goal the creation of the base money – the legal tender or "cash" that must by law be accepted by creditors for extinguishing a debt. Our "cash" since 1971, is entirely central government debt (as in our two-dollar bill). In this our governments are the historical successors to the monarchs of Europe who had a monopoly for the coining precious metals – their "right of seigniorage." It is called base-money because it served as the basis for the far more voluminous "near-money," the interest-bearing loans made by banks. Base-money earns no interest by its mere existence. The same was the case of gold when it was used as money…. In the case of money borrowed by the central government from the Bank of Canada, such interest-free base money is created because about 95% of the earnings of the Bank of Canada find their way back to the Government as dividends, for the government of Canada is the sole shareholder of the Bank of Canada. But that holds even in the case of the US Federal Reserve system which is owned by private banks. There the formal reason is that the federal government has assigned its rights of "seigniorage" inherited from the British monarchy. Interest-free money is an important attribute of base-money, because its value must be kept as stable as possible – and that means it must not vary with any change in the prevailing interest rate.

The credit created by the banks in granting credit as a multiple of the cash they hold does earn interest by its mere existence. That is why it is called "near-money."

Until 1993, the link between base-money and "near-money" was assured by the "statutory reserves." This was a modest portion of the deposits the banks took in from the public that they had to deposit with the BoC. On such "statutory reserves" they earned no interest. This served an important purpose apart from allowing the central government to borrow more interest-free money from the BoC without infringing the limits on such borrowing in force. Assume the economy was suffering perceived "inflation," that is prices were moving up…. Instead of being restricted to using what is its present "one blunt tool" – raising interest rates – it could leave interest rates alone, or raise

them to a lesser degree, and raise the statutory reserve requirement instead. This would reduce the amount of credit banks could offer their customers as a multiple of the deposits from the public it held. The leverage of the banks' money creation would be reduced. Not only would the banks be unable to create as many new loans, but they would have to put up more statutory reserves to underpin the loans they had already made.

When interest rates are raised, that not only hits those who have been doing too much trading, but quite innocent parties who may just have to renew their mortgage, or the government during a recession that wishes to finance vital public works that will provide employment for jobless workers. Using higher interest rates to stabilize prices thus guarantees a maximum of "collateral damage." The term is familiar from the US air force error in Afghanistan bombarding their Canadian allies and native wedding parties celebrating the occasion by firing into the air. It should be a sobering thought that our central bank – along with those of most other countries – have for three decades been using such "friendly fire" to stabilize the world economy.

The trend of deregulation of the banking systems of the world initiated in the US in 1951 was continued on an ascending scale. The severe rules that confined banks to banking introduced in the mid-thirties, were stripped away one by one. Banks became deeply involved in financing huge speculative real estate, gas and oil, and other adventures. The statutory reserves in Canada which had stood at 10% for years, by 1991 had already been whittled down to an average of 4%. That increased the leverage of their money creation at the same time they were able to stray farther and farther into activities incompatible with banking. When they had lost all or more than their capital, a bold bailout was arranged behind the scenes.

Counter-revolution without Press Release

In 1991 a bill was slipped through the Canadian parliament without debate, or press release, phasing out the statutory reserves altogether by 1993. This immediately released 4% of some $473 billions total deposits held by the banks in Canadian and foreign currencies, or amounting to around $19 billions. Since the bank rate at the time hovered around 10%, this represented a savings of over $2 billion a year to the banks, and more than that as an added cost to government in having to find financing outside the central bank. Moreover, we are talking of base-money – cash – that enabled the banks to lend out many times that amount on that monetary base.

Moreover, the Bank for International Settlements[3] had already issued its *Risk-Based Capital Requirements* guidelines for banks to help bail them out of difficulties not unlike those in which Canada's banks had gotten themselves. These guidelines declared the debt of OECD (the most developed countries) to be "risk-free" requiring no additional capital for the banks to acquire. This enabled the Canadian banks to quadruple their holdings of Canadian federal debt without putting up a significant amount of money. The interest on the additional $60 billion of federal debt at the rates in force at the time were around $6 billion. However, with the end of statutory reserves, the banks were no longer confined to the 10:1 base multiplier (which with the redeposits of the additional money into the system amounted to a net increase of far more than that). With the end of reserves theory there were no limits on money creation by the banks, except for the ceiling on the multiple of the capital they employed. But banks do not leave their capital in the form of cash – except for the bare minimum needed to meet their customers withdrawals and their net cheque clearance balances with other banks. Left as cash, money earns no interest. And their assets are recorded on their books at their historic costs rather than at their market value – except where they hold 20% or more of an issue. It is hard to say what the actual worth of a bank's capital might be when stock market values and the credibility of many businesses are far from their highs.

At the same time as the leverage allowed the banks was vastly increased in the above way, they were further deregulated. Since 1991 they have acquired brokerage houses, underwriting and merchant banking firms, derivative boutiques. As a result the indications are that many of them – perhaps most – have lost their entire capital – and are ready for a new bailout.

We can sum up the lessons of the Argentine experience as follows:

1. Statutory reserves are the key element for the functioning of central banks. In countries where they have been abolished they must be brought back to lessen the dependence of central banks on changing interest rates as a policy tool. Where they continue to exist but have been reduced to vestigial importance as in the United Kingdom their scope must be broadened. Exchange controls must be brought in where the availability of foreign currency is a key problem. Tariffs and import quotas where necessary must be brought back. Restrictions must be placed on the entry of short-term speculative money. A country with critical monetary and economic problems must be able to make use of the classical tools of central banks to overcome acute social and monetary crises.

In doing that an important distinction must be drawn between projects that require foreign currency for their execution, and those that do so only to a minor degree.

The Argentine is an extreme case, in having almost everything for attacking basic problems of housing, food, clothing, both the raw materials and labour force. A firewall must be established between the foreign exchange credits and the purely domestic credits for purposes of new investment.

Even the smallest, most backward African nation produces what is needed for their primitive housing, and, except where natural disasters occur, for the production of their food supply. In many such countries, for example, housing is built of local wattle and mud. What imported items are necessary should be financed through foreign aid programs or by husbanding what net foreign exchange the country receives.

The domestic money needs of government, and of government programs, must be arranged through the central bank, so that in effect it is an interest-free loan. New economic projects must not be wholly directed to maximize the volume of exports. Providing critical domestic needs must be the prime objective of projects financed in the domestic currency.

The corruption endemic to many of the Third World countries should be addressed by careful oversight, whether purely domestic, where no foreign assistance is involved, or a combination of domestic and foreign where foreign governments or NGOs have provided the economic assistance. Already contracted foreign debt must be restructured in a way that will allow such projects to proceed.

As in domestic social projects, the proper use of the central bank is a key ingredient in such programs.

William Krehm

1. The story is told in closely documented form, in *FOMC Alert* (20/3/01) of the Financial Market Center, a non-profit organization that monitors the US Federal Reserve.

2. Fernand Braudel (1990). *The Identity of France* (vol. 2, p. 415 et seq, Sian Reynolds, Trans.). Harper Collins Publishers.

3. The Bank for International Settlements was originally set up as a strictly technical facility to handle transfer of the German WW1 to the former Allied countries. The Bretton Woods Conference in 1944 passed Resolution Five providing for the liquidation of the BIS at the earliest possible opportunity. The reason? It had too cozy with the Hitler regime certainly before the war when it handed over the Czechoslovak gold left with it by the Prague Government the moment the Nazis took over the country. During the subsequent decades it cultivated a low profile under the shadow of the noose. That low profile commended it to the bankers of the world as an ideal bunker to formulate and carry out the strategy for the banks' comebacks. To this day, no one occupying a government post (central bankers excepted) are allowed at its sessions. Much of the world's monetary policy is formulated and propagated by BIS (Krehm, William (1993). *The Bank of Canada – A Power Unto Itself.* Toronto: Stoddard).

Mail Box

TO THE EDITOR:

I have been interested in monetary reform since encountering members of the now defunct Social Credit Party of Great Britain and North Ireland in 1948. I was, for a period, a member of the Social Credit League of Ontario and had a national program published in the Canadian Social Crediter. I was a delegate to the Provincial Convention in Ottawa that year and witnessed an attempt by the vicious fascist and anti-Semite Ron Gostick to take over! (He was given short shrift). Although you would never have known it from the media, the main program of the party was still monetary reform (à la Douglas), including the distribution of the National Dividend, and the Just Price. The power to control credit was to be taken away from the chartered banks and given to the people through their elected representatives, to which the Bank of Canada would be responsible.

I still have the profoundest admiration and respect for Douglas's three foundations for social credit, viz. the increment of Association, the Cultural Inheritance, and the Wages of the Machine. I also loved some of the slogans of the British Social Credit Party: "Not less for some but more for all," and "Not full employment but full enjoyment" – which reminds me of Oscar Wilde's quip, "Work is the curse of the drinking classes." The fundamental view was that the right to live a decent life (hence the necessary money) should not be dependent on employment, but should be a birth right for all. Anything earned would be gravy and you didn't have to work if you didn't want to! I now believe, as a libertarian socialist, that in the ideal society there will be no money or property, that all labour will be volunteered, and all the product will belong to the common.

My last political involvement was as candidate of the Green Party of Canada in Kingston-and-on-the Islands in 1984. We had an election collective, of which I was the "spokesperson," which really worked. Every speech I made (which got fantastic response) contained material from all members of the collective who approved the speeches before they were given. That original Green Party – an anti-political political party – was thoroughly anarchist in its principles, like the original German Green Party, although both have now morphed into a "regular" political party!

We had no leader but had to pretend we did to be registered as a party! Our slogans were "Think globally, act locally," "We do not inherit the earth; we borrow it from our children" (stolen from the German Greens). And "There is no way to peace, peace is the way" – the last particularly relevant in the present-day world. I know what peace is, but what the hell is a "peace process"? Peace simply consists of laying down your arms, and that is the only process there is. Political solutions come afterwards.

Looking at the current show put on by all those idiots competing to replace Harris, their eyes (the very low-key lady excepted) positively bugging out with the lust for power and status, my belief that no one who seeks power should have power is reinforced. (One thing Plato was right about.)

E. J. (Ted) Bond,
Professor Emeritus of Philosophy
Queen's University at Kingston
Tamworth, Ontario

O Canada! What are we doing to thee?

THE GLOBE AND MAIL (25/09, "Ontario Power prices rival rates set in US" by Martin Mittelstaedt and Luma Muhtadie) delivers some doleful if perfectly foreseeable tidings: "Ontario, which had an electricity cost of 4.3 cents a kilowatt-hour before opening the market to competition on May 1, had lower prices in May and June, but has been near or above prices in most of the US since July.

"So far in September, the Ontario price has averaged 8.2 cents a KWH according to Navigant Consulting Ltd., a Toronto energy consulting firm, well above the rating in western New York state, New England and Pennsylvania, New Jersey and Maryland high-priced areas of the US.

"Today's price forecast by the independent Electricity Mar-

ket Operator, the provincial agency that operates Ontario's wholesale power market, was expected to exceed even levels in California. Toronto residents have not faced the higher prices because Toronto Hydro has kept charges at 4.3 cents per KWH. It will make periodic adjustments if prices stay high. "In many other Ontario municipalities, [however,] residents have opened bills this month that are higher than ever before.

"In Wawa, the deregulation of electricity prices charged by Great Lakes Power Limited has put the city 'on the border of crashing,' Chris Wray, the city's chief administrative officer, said. We've got 3,600 people in this town, and a lot them are on old-age pension or a fixed income. The provincial Ministry of Energy even issued a study just before the market was opened predicting that competition would save consumers $3 billion to $6 billion over the next eight years.

"He said rates have been high this summer because of hot-weather demand for air conditioning when supplies have been curtailed because of drought, cutting cheap hydro-electric power. I just got a call from a woman whose pension comes to $1,000 a month and her hydro bill for 50 days was $500.

"Wawa resident Roger Guindon got a power bill of $537 that nearly matched his $575-a-month rent.

"Before deregulation, Ontario had prices that were high by Canadian standards, but generally lower.

"He says delays in restarting idled nuclear reactors have also cut the power available."

To which must be added the detail that the British company that acquired the privatized eight Bruce Peninsula nuclear generators is in financial difficulties and has had trouble providing the bond for insuring the rehabilitation of those reactors, until it arranges a bailout by the British government. A stunning footnote to the over-advertised merits of privatizing government assets.

Before privatization, weather spikes and other such temporary misadventures were averaged out to keep consumers bills smooth. But that was before Ontario's power needs were attached to the big crap game invented by Enron south of the border. The "savings" were capitalized in advance and the executives who executed the privatization were rewarded with salaries, bonuses, and retirement benefits that pretty well foretold the orbiting of consumers rates.

How can you average out price oscillations, if you rush to capitalize every price increase in the most generous way, and take home that capitalization as a reward for your ongoing financial brilliance? That would take out the fun of the game as played from the high executive chairs.

"New Democratic Party leader Howard Hampton says high electricity rates are a lightning rod for public concern . At a farm fair in South Western Ontario last week many farmers told him the rates threatened their livelihoods."

What we are witnessing is a mix of shameless ideology and Tammany Hall politics stood on its head to line the pockets of the best-connected adventurers who are supposed "to get things right." Next step? Perhaps we will be redoing our national flag by adding a WC for "Washington Consensus."

W.K.

What has Happened to the Joys of One-stop Financial Services?

A DECADE AGO we were overwhelmed with the campaign for one-stop financial services. Just think of all the shoe leather we would save, if we could go to our friendly bank and do all our financial business without having to so much as cross the road!

If you were not sold by the pitch, friendly commentators were quick to point out that there was in any case no use opposing the trend – it was inevitable. It was a deal you couldn't turn down. Not only because it was good for you, but you had no choice. Hadn't we heard this before?

In Nazi Germany and Stalin's Russia?

Besides, to serve you better, our banks had to merge so that they could compete on the world markets against those ultra-powerful Japanese banks who were umpteen times the size of our modest counterparts? What was omitted was the detail that these Japanese role models of our banks had already gambled away their capital and were undischarged bankrupts. They had withdrawn from issuing further euro and other foreign financing. It is not only the light from distant stars that reaches us with considerable delay.

What was kept from the public was that the government had recently bailed our banks from their massive gaming losses of the 1980s…. That took the form of doing away with the statutory reserves – a portion of their deposits from the public that they had to hold with the Bank of Canada that earned them no interest. Between the amount of additional federal debt that the banks were allowed to acquire without putting up further funds of their own (some $60B) and the release of the statutory reserves that were supporting the $470 billion of deposits they already held, the resulting entitlement bestowed on the banks amounted to about $20 billion a year.

But adopted as it was in the deepest stealth, it did even more. It convinced the banks that the realm of money-creation had been surrendered to them. Only in this way can we understand why the further deregulation of the banks was sped up at this point to allow them to take over brokerage firms, the underwriting of shares, acquiring pieces of industries in return for financing (merchant banking), derivative boutiques, and much else. Most of these activities are incompatible with banking. Enacted immediately after the massive bailout of the banks, this further deregulation is nothing less than scandalous.

Piping into the Public Treasury

Having been allowed to pipe into the public treasury, the banks were in command of money creation, and through it of the economy as a whole. NAFTA and all that merely formalized the fact that the deregulated banks needed the planet for its playing field. Henceforth Wall St. would call the shots.

There is one hitch to all this: allowing the banks to take over practically the entire world economic space, less and less remains to provide them with the their next bailout. Our own banks – hardly the modest violets that they pretend to be – ap-pear ever more deeply in the soup as the investigation of the American bankrupt high-tech corporations proceeds.

Thus *The Globe and Mail* (23/09, "Banks may face Enron setback" by Karen Howlett) informs us: "Royal Bank of Canada and Dutch financial group Rabobank Group already embroiled in a nasty law-suit tied to a complex Enron Corp. transaction, could face a setback in efforts to seize $400 million (US) of stock in an Enron-spinoff.

"In a report released this weekend, the court-appointed examiner says transactions Enron characterized as asset sales could in fact be reclassified as loans. If so, assets valued at about $500 million would be added to Enron's estate.

"Lenders may have a claim on the underlying asset for their recovery. The interim report looks at six transactions involving Enron special-purpose entities. In all, these provided Enron with cash totalling $1.38 billion. In most of the transactions, an Enron entity 'purported' to sell an asset to a special-purpose entity in exchange for cash and other considerations. Enron or an affiliate agreed to repay the debt incurred by that entity. The single largest transaction involved the RBC and Rabobank. RBC lent an Enron affiliate $517 million in November, 2000, and then swapped the loan to Rabobank.

"Rabobank has refused to pay the $517 million owing RBC as a result of the swap transaction because it alleges that RBC ought to have known Enron was a house of cards about to collapse. RBC lent the $517 million to Enron to allow it to have one affiliate buy 11.5 million shares of Houston oil and gas producer EOG Resources Inc. with a market value of $400 million from another affiliate.

"RBC and Rabobank have been embroiled for several months in a legal dispute with a group of hedge funds led by Silvercreek Management Inc. of Toronto over shares held by Enron in EOG.

"Earlier this year, the banks asked a US Court to order the immediate sale of the EOG shares and distribute the proceeds to them. RBC, acting as agent for Rabobank, is also being sued by the Dutch bank over the same transaction.

"In its financial statements for the nine months ended Sept. 2001, Enron reported that its debts totalled $12.98 billion. But in a presentation with its bankers in New York on Nov. 29, 2001, the same day the third-quarter results were released, Enron told its bankers that its debt in fact totalled $38.1B, the report says.

"More than half of the additional $25B in debt was incurred through structured finance transactions involving the special-purpose entities. Enron met with its bankers in an effort to restore confidence among creditors and discuss its proposed merger with Dynergy Inc."

And it was to empower Canada's banks to play in this league that the our government not only bailed out our banks from the equally scatter-brained financing of Dome Petroleum, the Reichmann Brothers' Canary Wharf venture, and Robert Campeau's buying spree for US shopping-store chains and much else in the eighties. It actually deregulated them further to pursue their games on a far larger scale. For them too it was to be a land of the Rising Sun. And it was to cover the interest payments on its debt that the chartered banks held, that now Ottawa slashed its grants to the provinces. And provinces in the fullness of time passed on the compliment to the municipalities. And that is why thousands of Canadians are sleeping in the streets, as we ride over ever deeper potholes, and our hospitals are gasping with financial asthma. Textbooks on economics have been rewritten, and our universities are upping their fees and increasingly displaying the brand of our mega-corporations.

Not one of the scams of Wall St. surfacing in the sundry investigations south of the border quite matches the effrontery of further deregulating our banks after their two massive bailouts within a decade. It should be the subject of an open investigation. And well before the next federal election.

William Krehm

Varied Perspectives

WHEN CONFRONTING a maze of possibilities with many uncertainties, including the future, we need useful maps. Love, money and power may provide motivation and resources but they are no substitutes for reliable guiding perspectives.

Of course a map is a kind of representation, not the thing itself, and will be selective of entities and relationships. There are many different kinds of maps; in genetics, mapping locates a gene or DNA sequence in a specific region of a chromosome and also in relation to other genes. Maps are designed to serve specific purposes.

What might be an adequate map of ways in which to envision the worlds of today and tomorrow? We need to identify avenues which may maintain and increase possibilities of freedom, as well as dead ends to be avoided and traps which may be lethal. As emphasized by E.F. Schumacher[1] such a map must deal primarily with the ideas, concepts and values in terms of which we apprehend truth and realities; it must also be adequate to the complexities we are likely to encounter.

The map will also allow for relevant measures of progress and feedback of guiding information. The map must relate to everything of concern; anything less runs risk of introducing perhaps fatal diversions of energies, materials and attention.

A persuasive effort to provide perspectives of this kind is set out in *Spiral Dynamics: Mastering Values, Leadership, and Change*, by Beck and Cowan,[2] which builds upon findings in psychology to take account of the characteristics of the human observer as he or she seeks to relate to the complexities and challenges of the world.

The core concept is that we all are tied to our individual stages of development, in part the results of personal experience. We all attach primary values to our own particular views, and indeed can hardly know anything else. If we would communicate reliably, we first need to take account of those values and perspectives which orient our understandings.

Recent studies suggest that such perspectives may be usefully mapped, i.e., framed and related, in terms of Memes – considered as controlling views or concepts somewhat analogous to genes, but at higher levels of organization. Memes include individual and cultural values which govern attitudes, ideas and behaviours. They are also subject to learning and development.

Recognition that the observer is involved as part of any observation is not a new idea. It is part of ancient wisdom that human perception reflects both the world and the values we bring to bear; if we judge others harshly we are likely to feel harshly judged. "To see ourselves as others see us," admittedly difficult, appears important.

To improve accuracy of perception in such ways we require a map which takes personal prejudices out of the equation as far as possible. The ideas set out in *Spiral Dynamics* make a significant contribution towards this end.

It is obvious that the world views of a small child, a young student, or a seasoned veteran, such as they may be, will be markedly different. However it has been found that, given supportive external conditions, human development progresses in spiral stages that can be described with some precision. An average population, of course, includes persons at many different stages; unfortunately not all have equally full potential, nor the conditions required for optimal development of their capacities. So people will see the world in very different lights.

In an overview perspective, Beck and Cowan describe eight stages of developmental equilibrium, each of which builds upon the preceding stages. The eight stages may be summarized, beginning with requirements for life, and in the order of increasing consciousness and complexity, as Memes or patterns of dominant Values which may apply both to individuals and groups, roughly as follows:

1. Physiological needs, goals of survival based on instinctive behaviours.

2. Safety and security originating in kinship and tribe; individuals feel they owe their lives and souls to their parent-like group (cf. aboriginal peoples).

3. Values of power and action which are egocentric and absolute; might is right; strong leaders provide security and rewards (cf. mafia, etc.).

4. Stability and purpose in life depend upon accepted truths; work is a duty, to be done "the best way," failure is punished (cf. traditional conservatisms).

5. Material success and independence are the goals, motivated by competition and material rewards (cf. individualism and "free enterprise").

6. Harmony and equality are goals which depend upon co-operation; satisfaction and acceptance emphasize community (cf. social democratic ideals?).

7. Responsibilities and qualities of life are evolving, systemic, and integrative; freedom leads to more enjoyable and productive work (cf. "cultural creatives"?).

8. Renewal and synthesis based upon a broad experience lead to holistic views; meaningful work, health and life take on a unifying spiritual dimension.

The above account is much too condensed to give anything more than a very general idea of the kinds of developmental progressions in evidence, and there may be variations with respect to details of the above. However, the transitions or passages from one level to another involve very definite adaptive challenges and stress. Attainment of any level involves individual capacities and particular relations with the external world. The levels and stages are not absolutely distinct, and different levels may be attained in relation to various spheres of life – such as marriage, work, civic attitudes, etc. But these categories and relationships may be seen as useful orienting ideas within their limitations.

Crossed Wires

A little study of possible crossed wires and complications leads to the wonder that useful communications across such different perspectives are ever possible at all.

It takes little imagination to realize, for example, that when governments (mostly level 5) ask the police (level 4) to deal with protesters (levels 6 and 7), serious misunderstandings are inevitable. Those whose views are grounded in ideologies of various kinds (levels 4 and 5) are likely to see those who appeal to the evidence of their own experience (e.g., levels 6 and 7) as lacking absolute moral foundations, an interpretation which falsely belittles those whose opinions differ. And rather than simply reject as "evil" the values of those at levels 2 or 3, an attitude which is itself destructive, it may be more useful, once security is ensured, to identify areas where communication may be possible.

From the point of view of the reformer in economics it may be important to take account of the misunderstandings which may be expected between levels. An individual who has already met with conspicuous success (e.g., at levels 2-5) may have every reason to cling to what he or she knows. It will take a very real threat to the status quo to motivate interest in alternatives. Moreover those whose perspectives are fixed at the earlier stages are most likely to believe they have found "the truth" and be impatient with logic and arguments.

Transitions between levels are not without pain and even risks to sanity. "True believers" are likely to ascribe to others motives which reflect their own prejudices. As we know, personal and social development require openness and tolerance for ambiguities and complexity, and also carries risk of failure.

But the hazards of transition from one stage to another are only part of this story. On the positive side, an awareness of such differences enhance leadership resources. Leadership in a complex world requires not only the recognition that people live at different levels but also an understanding of the relationships among the levels. Such understandings require insights only arrived at in the overview stages (7 and 8). Without an understanding able to accommodate a range of values and perspectives it will obviously be more difficult to engage the interests and integrate the activities of any organization. While some may think that such flexibility indicates a lack of values, what is actually at issue is the search for the most productive values.

Since so much lies in the eye of the beholder, thinking which makes a purely logical case for economic reforms may be necessary but cannot be a sufficient condition for change. Economics includes a variety of theories associated with values which often go unrecognized, sometimes in disguise. The focus of neo-classical economics is perhaps on the assumption of rational motivation by material rewards and promises of independence (level 5), which indeed may promote certain kinds of personal, societal and economic growth. Yet such growth may be impossible to reconcile with sustainable equilibria and other values without expanding the frame of reference (e.g., by moving to levels 6 and 7).

The lesson for managers as well as political leaders appears to be the need to recognise and work with those who perceive and act upon realities at various levels, and to involve the full range of talents and resources which may be available.

Bruce Buchanan

1. Schumacher, E.F. (1978). *A Guide for the Perplexed*. HarperCollins.
2. Beck, D.E. & Cowan, C.C. (1996). *Spiral Dynamics: Mastering Values, Leadership, and Change*. Blackwell Publishers.

A Sermon for our Finance Ministers?

EVEN AFTER THE COLLAPSE of the stock market was under way, Wall St.'s professional cheer leaders were pushing for entrusting it with more retirement monies. They proclaimed that the solid fundamentals of the economy ruled out a "double-dip recession," a euphemism that evoked the ice-cream cones of our innocent childhood. With the economy in the gutter, you might expect those who had peddled such advice would be apologizing to those who to their sorrow had taken it. Instead, a thundering silence blankets the subject. However, an unexpected phenomenon is filling the void. Many established charitable foundations, shocked by their losses on the stock market, are giving their capital away and closing shop. They feel that it would be far better investing in human capital, something not even acknowledged to exist on the government's balance sheet. In their opinion, that has proved a far better use of their capital than flinging it into the bottomless canyon of Wall St.

For the details, let us turn to a source beyond suspicion of leftist bias. *The Wall Street Journal* (10/09, "Socked by Stocks Some Foundations Spend What's Left" by David Bank) reports: "With the stock market slump taking a bite out of charitable endowments, many foundations are cutting back spending to preserve assets. But to a growing number of philanthropists, a different approach makes more sense: spend it all and close up shop.

"Applying business practices to their giving, they are analyzing the 'time value' of their money and concluding that a dollar spent now can be worth more than one, or even two spent later. They argue there is plenty of money on hand to accelerate spending on today's critical problems. They also say that despite the recent downturn in the stock market, long term economic growth will generate more [gifts] to deal with tomorrow's issues.

"One such donor is Charles F. Feeney, the reclusive millionaire who co-founded the Duty Free Shoppers Groups Ltd. chain of airport stores. Earlier this year, Mr. Feeney pushed his foundation, the Atlantic Philanthropies, to adopt a plan to exhaust its $4 billion endowment over 15 years or so. Now 70 years old, Mr. Feeney told his board that the prospect of going out of business would focus the foundation on bold problem-solving rather than self-perpetuation.

"The foundation, which approved about $100 million in grants in 1995, will now give away $400 million each year. That puts the Atlantic Philanthropy, which until last year made nearly all its grants anonymously, in the top ranks of private givers. As part of its recent deliberations, the board decided to concentrate on the aging population, disadvantaged youth, and global public health.

"A federal tax-code change in 1981 relieved foundations of the obligation to distribute at least as much as they earned on their assets each year. Since then, overall foundation 'pay-out' rates have drifted down to near the legal minimum of 5% of assets. Most long-established foundations such as the Rockefeller Foundation, the John D. and Catherine T. MacArthur Foundation and the Pew Charitable Trusts – continue to manage their endowments for perpetuity.

"Some of them, such as the Ford Foundation and the David and Lucille Packard Foundation, have increased their payout rates to cushion the impact of their stock-market losses on their grant-making. But foundation executives and their trade organization, the Council on Foundations, have resisted any permanent increase in the payout rate. They argue that instructions from donors obligate some foundations to maintain their foundations in perpetuity."

The Paradox of Accelerating the Disbursement of Endowments

"The stock market's slump only strengthens the case for accelerated spending, says Paul Jansen, director of consultant McKinsey & Co.'s Institute on the Non-Profit Sector, in San Francisco. By almost any estimate, he argues, the long-run financial returns on foundation investments are lower than the expected returns on the 'social' investments they might make in the form of grants. Such social returns include families lifted from poverty and children spared disease through vaccination.

"In making his calculations, Mr. Jansen used a standard business analysis of the time value of money. Just as financial returns need to be more heavily discounted the further in the future they are likely to occur, so must social returns delayed by conservative spending policies.

"Factoring in a typical discount rate, Mr. Jansen found that a $100 million endowment of a foundation that paid out only 5% or $5 million a year in grants really had a 'net present value' of just $50 million or so.

"'There's a tremendous cost to society of this behavior. The tax deduction has been received. The money is there. The commitment is there. The question is, when do we convert the dollars into social goods? Our answer is, just do it – sooner.' [Our italics.]

"With nearly $500 billion in US foundation endowments,

an increase in the payout rate of two percent would make an additional $10B or so available each year. To understand what such a figure might mean, consider that the United Nations Secretary-General Kofi Annan has suggested that $10 billion a year is the amount needed to reverse the global AIDS epidemic. US foundations contributed about $312 million to domestic and international AIDS effort in 2000, according to Funders Concerned about AIDS, in New York.

"To philanthropists such as Richard Goldman, 82, the way to provide more is to dispense with the goal of maintaining perpetual endowments altogether. 'I don't think anything should be in perpetuity, certainly not foundations,' says Mr. Goldman, a retired insurance executive and president of the $430 million Richard and Rhonda Goldman Fund in San Francisco. 'I think there's too much money accumulating in foundations that should be put to use. The needs are out there, so give it away.'

"The Goldman Fund focuses on environment, population, social services and Jewish affairs. Mr. Goldman says some opportunities can't wait, such as parcels of land that can be saved from development. Other investments, such as education for young girls in the developing world, offer such 'high returns' that they are hard to pass up. In addition, he says economic downturns create greater social needs and put organizations trying to meet them under greater pressure, making increased spending more important.

"The Goldman foundation's assets increased dramatically after the 1996 death of Rhoda Goldman, a Levi Strauss & Co. heiress. Two years ago, the fund raised its annual grant-making budget to about 10% of assets, and adopted a plan to cease operations within 10 years of Mr. Goldman's death.

"The spend-it-all approach has some precedent. In 1913 Julius Rosenwald, chairman of Sears, Roebuck & Co., declared, 'Permanent endowment tends to lessen the amount available for immediate needs.'

"In the first half of the century, Mr. Rosenwald's fund gave away the equivalent of more than $700 million in today's dollars, placing Mr. Rosenwald alongside Andrew Carnegie and John D. Rockefeller as one of the great early philanthropists, says Waldemar A. Nielson, a historian of philanthropy. Yet Mr. Rosenwald is scarcely remembered, in part because he ordered the fund to spend itself out of existence within 25 years of his death, which came in 1932. (The trustees beat the deadline by a decade.)" Wisely so, since the 15 years of spending beyond the norms already set by him covered the worst years of the Depression and the War.

"Mr. Rosenwald contributed to the construction of nearly 5,400 schools for black children in the South. In the years following World War I, an estimated 60% of American blacks who completed primary school had been educated in Rosenwald schools."

Obviously, Mr. Rosenwald had managed to get his ego under control, possibly the supreme reward in the human experience. Humanity would be greatly benefited if more politicians followed his example.

William Krehm

Weird Tale

THE WEIRD TALE I am embarking on requires some preliminaries to the telling.

In the 1960s the "just society" promised during the war was actually being realized. To accommodate the baby-boomers new schools, universities, hospitals, and housing were built. The institutions of social pluralism were set up. Under such circumstances, I was puzzled that economists should be characterizing the upward inching of prices taking place as simple "inflation." Still worse, higher interest rates had begun being touted the one method for repressing it.

These institutions couldn't possibly be delivered while prices lay flat. However, whatever is not done for profit was banished from the operational core of the official model as an "externality." It simply does not enter into its reckoning.

Nevertheless, these new or extended public services do have their costs. And they must be covered by taxation that turns up as a deeper layer in the price of marketed goods. It is as simple as that. The official price theory, however, holds that if prices climb it means that there is an excess of demand over supply. Yet the higher interest rates that were being applied as the one blunt tool" against "inflation" can bring down prices temporarily only by pushing up bankruptcies and unemployment. In doing so they shrink the tax-base and the revenues of government, and thus inexorably lead to still higher prices. Interest rates are played like an accordion to find the magic level at which prices would lie dead. That invited financial speculation at the expense of the productive economy.

Perceptive French Economists

During the 1960s there was still considerable freedom of discussion. In the course of my work fleshing out these thoughts, I came across the work of not one but two French economists, who had clearly posed the problem. J.P. Mockers wrote: "In most cases observed, the years of economic slack correspond to periods when price increases have been most marked.... We have here quite the opposite phenomenon to that postulated by the traditional price theories of the cycle. We must begin by devising a terminology that will distinguish between a price rise that can be traced to an overheated economy, with more demand than can be supplied and a price increase that coincides with a slack economy. That must be caused by other factors."[1]

As early as 1962, Pierre Biacabe discussed these new "structural aspects of price rise. It is necessary to adopt a new definition of inflation, or to use this term only in its original sense and find another terminology for the new phenomenon that we are trying to track down. But no one has yet detected the new phenomenon, and that is because we have no valid model to grasp the contemporary economic system. Thus we go on calling inflation a phenomenon that no longer has the same form, the same object, or the same function as formerly. We continue viewing it as a sinister thing, harmful and destructive, because of the effects that it might have had in a previous economic system."[2]

The champions of the reigning economic doctrine were just beginning to feel threatened. A considerable space still existed for heterodox views. The forty-plus-page paper that I wrote on the subject was actually purchased by the leading French economic journal at the time, *La Revue Économique*, and carried in its May 1970 number. That was no accident: much later I learned that both Mockers and Biacabe were on its editorial board. More remarkable still, Calmann-Levy, a leading French publisher, wrote suggesting that I expand my article into a book which they were interested in publishing. I spent the next year writing that book, and sent it to them. But the Ice Age by then had closed in. I still have received no acknowledgement from Calmann-Levy.

I published the book intended for France in English – *Price in a Mixed Economy*. It has stood up very well over the subsequent quarter of a century plus, and received flattering reviews in a half dozen European countries including the *Economic Journal* of Cambridge. But on the whole the following paradox emerged.

A Pall of Silence

Not in a single instance has an economist taken issue with the thesis – that price in a pluralistic society must reflect the increase in taxation that pays for unpriced public services.

Yet not a single economist has espoused this notion of pluralistic price publicly. And yet an elementary sense of responsibility would have required them to do one and/or the other. That was especially so in view of the official remedy for "licking inflation" that was being wheeled into place.

To understand the roots of this failure of the profession throughout the world we must refer to another signal achievement of the French school – the theory of "the dominant revenue" of François Perroux. He held that in every historical period the revenue of a particular group in society is held to be the index of the well-being of society as a whole. For that group the official price model is a citadel of power, and is defended by every conceivable means. In Britain after the Napoleonic Wars it was the income of the landowners, who fought for the maintenance of the Corn Laws. With their repeal, the privileged revenue became that of the industrialists. During the Great Depression the role by practical default passed to an alliance of industrialists, and the public sector, with the trade unions as a junior partner, while the financial sector sat in the doghouse.

With the crowning of interest rates as the "one blunt tool" for preserving a balanced economy, however, the dominant revenue was recaptured by the banking interest. And when interest rates were pushed high enough to bankrupt many lenders along with their borrowers, the sceptre passed to speculative finance. Economic modelling became a closely guarded privilege as the keys to the national cash box, which in a sense it was. And the more dubious the understanding of what those who ran the show were up to, the greater their determination to suppress any challenge to their assumptions.

In an attempt to clear these barricades and reach the mind of the reasonably literate citizen, I have attempted to illustrate technical arguments by a single example that would show that a flat price level is ruled out today. For the purpose I have chosen the notable urbanization of just about every country in the world. Cities with multi-million populations were few indeed fifty years ago. Today they are to be found on every inhabited continent in growing numbers. Obviously they require far costlier infrastructures, and far more educated citizens than did small towns or country townships where the bulk of the world's population resided fifty years ago. Nobody who moves from a town of 10,000 to New York expects his living costs to rise steeply. How then can society as such do so when it makes a similar move?

But more than merely higher costs, a new intensity of life and spirit developed as the large cities came into being. The French historian Fernand Braudel[3] has explored the development of French town life in the late Middle Ages.

Town and Country

"For between towns and villages there lies an ineradicable frontier, that has always existed, a line as clear as the Pyrenees, of which it used to be said that what is true on one side was false on the other.

"In France, as in Europe, there were for a very long time indeed far fewer people living in the towns than in the countryside. Between 1450 and 1500 the peasant population represented at least nine-tenths of the population. This figure – 10% of the population in the towns – 90% in the countryside, is an approximation, of course, only probable at best. During the Hundred Years War, French towns gradually freed themselves from their seigneurs, a significant liberation despite the many long-last remnants of feudalism which would persist until the very end of the *ancien régime*.

"After 1450, and the return of peace, the towns came back to life with renewed vivacity. Everything was in their favour: not only the leap in the birth-rate, the rapid rise in productivity in the countryside, but also the flowering of urban activities and the commercial economy. The prices of town-produced commodities, began to rise, while farm prices slumped. The price 'scissors' effect operated in favour of the towns. With the lively growth and recovery of the 16th century, accompanied by the price revolution which boosted everything, urban activity in particular. The towns would soon be able to do as they pleased with the surrounding countryside, now virtually defenceless against them."

In all this – especially the "scissors" price effect with the urban price blade rising in tandem with the agrarian prices falling – you will not fail to note a presage of the contrast today between prices of the high-tech First World products and services and the prices of agrarian and other raw materials of the Third World. Then as now that has as much to do with disparities of power and financial might as with mere technology. In the earlier period cited by Braudel there was even a stark split between the currencies used by the town and country, one gold, and the other silver and copper rapidly losing their intrinsic value and becoming in effect a fiat currency – like paper money.

Today we have the hard currencies of the developed countries and the fragile currencies of the Emerging and Third Worlds, with the International Monetary Fund dictating what the debtor countries dare spend for social survival and what they must export at desperately low prices. No army that over-ran a conquered land exerted more raw power.

Behind their walls, towns generally were the nurseries if not always of democracy, at least of resistance to the arbitrariness of the Church and the Crown. For good or evil they became head and brains of the realm. If population density outstripped the infrastructures to accommodate them, large cities or their poorer sections could become living infernos. Properly equipped, they could open new vistas of human achievement.

The economic backwardness of France until after World War II could in fact be traced in part to the stunted development of its towns outside Paris. They replenished their population and manned their industries from the countryside. With the slow but systematic advances of agricultural techniques, the countryside was constantly shedding its population. 91% of the French nation lived in the countryside in 1800.

In England between those dates the countryside dwellers had fallen from 77% to 21%, and in Europe as a whole from 88% to 13%.[4] Clearly if living costs were far higher in rapidly growing cities and towns than on farmland, the component of "structural price rise" in the price climb as contrasted with market inflation had risen portentously. Yet economists still seek ways of bludgeoning the supposedly self-balancing market into the perverse Utopia of "zero inflation." Some day, by the grace of God, economists will discover history.

William Krehm

1. Mockers, J.P. (1969). *Croissances économiques comparées, Allemagne, France, Royaume Uni* (pp. 1050-67).

2. Biacabe, Pierre (1962). *Analyses contemporaines de l'inflation* (p. 222). Paris: Sirey.

3. Braudel, Fernand (1990). *The Identity of France* (vol. 2, p. 415, Sian Reynolds, Trans.). Harper Collins Publishers.

4. Braudel, p. 447.

The Strange Discourse between Japan and America

VIEWED through history's lens, Japan and the US are a study in ultimate contrasts. Japan is set on tight volcanic islands; the United States sprawls luxuriantly across a continent. America has been an open society thriving on immigration. Japan is turned inward, emphasizing social solidarity, focussed purpose, education, and a high symbolic sense of destiny. From its earliest days, with the better half of a continent behind it, the US has been an importunate knocker on other folks' doors. That found early expression in the Monroe Doctrine, refurbished by Teddy Roosevelt at the turn of the century, and now sent into orbit as the Dubya Doctrine. Inevitably this has led to epic interactions, negative or positive between the world's two largest economies – from Commodore Perry to Hiroshima. At a great disadvantage in physical and military arsenals, the Japanese have been noted for the subtlety of their strategies.

On the subject, we wrote, "Over the decades the Japanese have developed special skills for keeping their overseas rival-

mentor, the United States, appeased, while holding their own and occasionally better" (*ER*, 7/99).

Even today, in spite of the sickly state of its economy, the Japanese automobile industry is painting circles around Detroit on its native turf. Toyota sales in Canada also doubled to 127,754 last year from 67,956 in 1995.

That Other Dodge Circumvented

A classic factor in this achievement is how Japan reorganized her goals after WWII.

"In 1945, Joseph Dodge, an old-line Detroit banker, arrived in Tokyo to implement the US reconstruction policies. In a country devastated by war, mass unemployment, and industries bankrupted by unpaid wartime government bills, Dodge insisted on absolute budget-balancing with only short-term debt to be issued. All new subsidies and further loans from the Reconstruction banks were ruled out. The policy was to be severely deflationary on the assumption that the problem was too much demand, not the grievous lack of production." No, just in case the thought may have crossed your minds, that Dodge was not a relative of the current governor of The Bank of Canada.

"The Japanese were in no position to argue with their conqueror, but they did tactfully contact the US General Headquarter Economic Scientific Section and persuaded it to issue a "Tight Money Neutralizing Measure." Under it the Bank of Japan provided credit to buy the government bonds held by financial institutions, so that they might serve as money base for the creation of further bank credit. And then the Korean War providentially increased both Japanese exports and spending in Japan by the American military personnel." That allowed the Japanese to lay the footings for their economic miracle.[1]

The Rising Sun of the Low Yen

In a broad way their approach can be useful to the world today.

"Its essence was to focus its scant financial resources on export industries that would show the greatest value added and the least import component." This would have been ruled out today by Globalization and Deregulation. By shifting to heavy and chemical exports from the pre-war emphasis on cheap textiles, they concentrated on improved output of steel, coal, large generators, hydro-electric dams, to prepare for the next stage of export-oriented development – earth-moving machinery, automobiles, domestic appliances, synthetic fibres. To such strategic industries the government made available inexpensive financing, tax advantages, but avoided taking up ownership positions. Cartels were tolerated, and when an economic downturn seemed ahead, a single corporation each year was allowed to carry out the only expansion in the industry. This made it possible for firms to pursue aggressive policies at less risk. Labour relations were nurtured with an informal policy of lifetime employment.

Note the immense difference between this and recurrent proposals originating in the US to have lesser countries adopt various forms of a "common" currency with the US. Thus the Argentine's strict dollar-backing of their currency contributed

in a major way to the collapse of its economy.

Eventually exports boomed in highly profitable areas and the vast influx of foreign currency actually become something of an embarrassment. A yen low *vis-à-vis* the dollar was kingpin of the plan. The Ministry of Finance (MOF) directed financial institutions to load up with long-term US securities. David Stockman, a pillar of the early Reagan regime, has written that the US government was surprised to find Japan providing Washington with the means of coping with the craters the Laffer Curve policy left in its budget. Soon up to 30% of American Treasury issues were being sold in Japan, and the influx of Japanese money was driving up the value of the dollar. Heavy US equipment makers like Caterpillar anguished.

The US parried by proposing that the yen become an international reserve currency. But losing control of their low yen was the last thing in Japanese minds. "They smiled across the table at Donald Regan, the Secretary of the Treasury, described as 'the greatest bond salesman in history,' gratified at his cluelessness, and offered to help in the super-marketing effort." But they went their own way.

Because the MOF discouraged the development of a domestic debt market, Japanese issues had to be floated overseas. This was to prevent the development of a powerful constituency of domestic bond traders that would strip its central bank of control of the commercial banks.

This was the opposite of the Bank of Canada's course in the 1950s when it bribed Bay St. firms to morph into short-term money traders. Before these legendary young men in red suspenders," its very own creation, the government has ever since cringed in terror whenever the slightest problems arose.[2]

"It was through the use of its banks to shovel out to second-tier Japanese firms credit created by the BoJ, that the MOF frustrated the Plaza Accord to bring down the dollar-yen ratio."

Fiat — Let There Be Darkness

But how did MOF ensure that such credit would not end up just stoking inflation? "The answer is in the collateral principle underlying Japanese banking. Japanese bankers are not trained to analyze business projects; they depend largely on the collateral in stock market shares and land put up to back their loans. The valuation of either of these items is highly rigged by the MOF. This ultimate security for bank loans becomes something not dissimilar to the fiat money of the West, where a dollar or a mark is worth largely what the government says it is – so long as the system goes on working. A whole school of Japanese economists have summed it up as a 'land standard.'" The shortage of space on their islands reinforces the effort. And the shift of so much North American money-creation to Wall St. via the deregulated banks makes the comparison less fantastic. Our stock market valuations are now exposed to have been largely fiat.

"Ultimately, the brazen confidence of Japan's banks rested on their cushion of hidden assets. On the surface Japanese banks might look thinly capitalized. But financial reporting there did not require the banks or companies to adjust their assets to their market values. In a pinch the banks or companies could dispose for $50 million of a small parcel of land kept on its books since the last century at $300." This was in notable contrast to the recent Wall St. boom when land and all other assets tended to be booked at tipsy levels.

"The moment of truth arrived in installments. First there was the collapse of the American real estate market in which the triumphant Japanese banks had been bemused to plunge. Their domestic pattern may have disposed them to picking up major interests in American icons like Rockefeller Center. And then came the hammer-blow of the 1997 East Asian meltdown."

Two Fiat Systems Collide

"Under American pressure, the Japanese had agreed to many things that finally destroyed their insular financial system. A major instance is the Bank for International Settlement's *Risk-Based Capital Requirements.* 'Japan's negotiators at Basel could not say, "Look, it makes little difference what the reported capital bases of our banks are. They are going to price loans to get the business, and we will support them in that. Moreover, MOF controls the value of their assets and the extent of their capital cushions." So they ended up agreeing to the BIS capital adequacy guidelines, even if with a lot of exceptions for Japan. That gave the banks incentives to do things the authorities wish they hadn't done."[3]

The Japanese financial system was caught in the crossfire of two incompatible fiat systems – that of their own MOF valuation practices on land, and the collapse of the US model in Eastern Asia in 1987.

That explains the daunting news out of Tokyo. Reuter's News Agency recent report: "Japan's central bank, moving to allay fears of a financial crisis, has announced unprecedented plans to buy corporation shares directly from banks. Sailing into uncharted waters for a central bank, the Bank of Japan said the plan was aimed at preventing market volatility and banking system instability from feeding on each other." More bluntly put, the Japanese central bank proposes relieving the commercial banks of the highly dubious corporate debt that prevents them from making the further financing that its industries need. "The Economics minister was taken by surprise."

"The move – described by ratings agency Standard & Poor's Corp. as 'shocking' – follows a fall in the Nikkei share average to 19-year lows this month. That raised concerns about a financial crisis ahead of the half-year book-closing on September 30.

"The announcement came just an hour after the bank decided to leave its monetary policy unchanged. The bank has kept short-term money market rates at virtually zero under its 17-month-old 'quantitative-easing' policy."

A Dress Rehearsal for the Next US Bank Bailout?

The Wall Street Journal (19/09, "Japan's Central Bank Will Buy Stock Held by Troubled Lenders" by Phred Dvorak): "The unexpected announcement from the central bank came just a week after Prime Minister Junichiro Koizumi promised President Bush faster action on banking problems." Here again the addiction of the lone superpower to barking out orders from the bridge hasn't been helpful.

For clearly when the BoC buys corporation shares of ques-

tionable value to restore the banks to liquidity, it gooses the value of the shares on the stock market. And that can inject not only the shares involved but eventually the stock market itself with fiat value. "The stock-buying plan also marks a significant departure for Japan's conservative central bank: not only is it highly unorthodox for central banks to purchase stocks from private companies, but it could be dangerous. Indeed, Bank of Japan Gov. Masaru Hayami has long resisted calls for the bank to combat price deflation by buying unconventional assets such as stock or bad loans, arguing that such tactics could destroy the credibility of the nation's lender of the last resort."

Is this just another instance of Washington's irrepressible need to pressure the rest of the world to do its bidding, or might there be another factor involved? The US Federal Reserve has abdicated much of its control over the monetary system at home to the short-term money-traders. By virtually doing away with the statutory reserves (without doing so formally as in Canada) it will be impossible to design another bank bailout – should that become necessary – by reducing the reserves further. There is simply nowhere further to go along that road. Hence the immediate effect of this proposed Japanese "solution," if carried out, would certainly be closely followed by other central banks. For they all have their faces to a wall, as the consequences become apparent of their deregulation of their banks shortly after their massive bailout in the early 1990s.

The words of BoJ Governor Masam Hayami have suggestive overtones: "There is no central bank in the advanced world that buys shares. But I think the BoJ should take steps to eliminate worries. Call it crisis prevention or stabilization." That novel device has in fact been brought in as a sort of monetary Prozac rather than on other merits. On 12/10, *The Globe and Mail* carried a Bloomberg News dispatch reporting that the BoJ will buy US$16B of Japanese corporation shares from 10 banks to help them cut their losses.

We have often emphasized the advantages of using statutory reserves rather than short-term interest-rate as the main lever for stabilizing the economy. The main disadvantage of the latter course is the screeching conflict of interest it involves. Interest does happen to be the revenue of money-lenders and can devour the producing classes in society. That policy adopted by central banks in the 1970s is in fact the Mother Conflict of Interest that became the model of the countless others that have made our financial sector a bordello. Moreover, high interest rates as the one tool against "inflation" hits everything that moves or stands still in the economy. In military terms it maximizes "collateral damage."

So destructive are its effects that eventually it may inflict damage beyond the power of central banks to remedy by reducing interest rates. If the economy is still on its back when the rate of interest reaches zero, there is nothing left for the central bank to do with its proudly proclaimed "one blunt tool." Moving to a negative interest rate is tantamount to subsidizing insolvent banks in open public view – not behind screens of silence, as in the epic bailout of the Canadian banks in 1991. And all the while the ever impatient US Treasury is pressing the Japanese to "address the nonperforming bank loans and deflation so that it [can] play the role that it should in the world economy" (R. Glenn Hubbard, chairman of the president's Council of Economic Advisers, *The Wall Street Journal*, 27/09). Presumably, this includes resuming purchases of US government debt to help finance Washington's overseas adventures.

Another factor entered the picture in the 1990s. With ongoing Deregulation and Globalization banks acquired brokerage, underwriting and merchant banking firms that live by their stock-market gambles. To almost anything connected with the stock market high interest rates are poison. This has caused the banks to see their survival interests pass from high interest rates spreads to low interest rates. That means that the spread between boom market rates and zero have remained lower than any other time in our history.

Hence the BoJ, distraught with the pressures on it to do something about the collapse of the stock market, has decided to continue descending the interest scale by single steps into negative territory. Given the risk factor in the shares of insolvent companies, what might result is not a careful one-step descent, but a headlong tumble into the abyss.

William Krehm

1. *The Postwar Japanese Economy, Its Development and Structure* (Takafus Nakamura, University of Tokyo Press, 1995) and *The Real Price of Japanese Money* (J. Taggart Murphy, Weidenfelt & Nicolson, London, p. 164) provided much of the material for an article, Rearmament for Japan, in *Economic Reform* (7/99) from which I quote.

2. Krehm, William (1999). Fashioning the God of Clay. In Krehm, William (Ed.). *Meltdown: Money, Debt and the Wealth of Nations* (p. 226). COMER Publications.

3. Murphy, R. Taggart. *The Real Price of Japanese Money* (p. 164). London: Weidenfeld & Nicolson.

Social Self-help at Grass-Root Level?

WHO HAS NOT been saddened at the patent evidence of society's disintegration even when our political leaders were crowing about their alleged victories on the GDP front? That is why a front-page *Wall Street Journal* story (12/06, "Southern Pastor Has A Mission to Deliver His Flock From Debt" by Ellen Graham) sounds resonances of promise. Is Western society developing early signs of a rudimentary immunity system at the grass root level?

"Norfolk, VA – Carl and Janice Beaver went to church one night recently owing $10,500 on a slew of credit cards. When they walked out two hours later they were debt free.

"Now all they owe is gratitude to their brethren at Mount Carmel Baptist Church. About once a month the church holds a 'debt liquidating revival' a foot-stomping, hand-clapping outpouring of music and financial generosity aimed at lifting members out of credit-card debt. How generous? The Beavers are the 56th family to have been 'delivered' from debt since the revivals began about a year ago.

"In a single night in May, church members not only raised the Beavers' $10,500, but an additional $5,400 to liquidate the debt of another couple, and there was $500 left over for the next time. To date the congregation has wiped out a total of $318,000 of debt.

"Their feat is all the more striking because Mount Carmel isn't some suburban mega-church catering to the country-club set. It is in a vaguely seedy section of downtown Norfolk, and volunteer security guards watch parked cars during services. The church's predominantly African-American members are mostly under 50 and are drawn from across the economic spectrum. Many are from military families posted at the huge naval base here, home of the Atlantic Fleet.

"'The credit-card companies don't like me too well,' says Mt. Carmel's pastor, 48-year-old Bishop C. Verne Russell Jr., an imposing figure with a graying, Santa Claus beard who accounts for all repaid debts in a pocket-sized, green note-book. But he insists, 'you can't serve your Master and MasterCard at the same time.'

"To an overextended generation accustomed to instant plastic gratification, Bishop Russell preaches the evil of 20% interest rates and the virtues of saving and paying cash. At his urging, 1,000 church members have cut up their credit cards, and the shreds are kept in a glass urn on the pulpit. People whose debt has been liquidated are asked to donate at least $300 at subsequent revival meetings to help others.

"The amount tithed is up 25% in the past year, according to the bishop. In addition to money collected at debt revivals, Mt. Carmel takes in more than $2 million annually to fund operations and community outreach missions, such as feeding and clothing the homeless. The goal is to have the 3,000-member congregation debt-free, except for mortgages and car loans. 'When you do something collectively, it's better,' Bishop Russell says."

Others' Good Fortune

"Excitement pulsed through the congregation as members streamed into Mount Carmel's sanctuary on a recent Friday night. The floorboards throbbed with the beat of a brass, drum and keyboard combo. Plump grandmothers in flowered dresses waved fans and handkerchiefs. Dressed-for-success working couples cuddled infants snoozing through the din.

"Janice Beaver arrived figuring she'd 'have a good time getting someone out of debt.' For a year the 40-year-old retired Navy cook has regularly attended debt revivals, reveling in others' good fortune. But, she conceded, 'You definitely hope the Lord will bless you too.'

"Still, she had no reason to believe that she and her 43-year-old husband, Carl, also recently retired from the Navy would be blessed that night. The bishop never chooses beneficiaries before arriving at church and says he has no special criteria for picking candidates. 'The Lord gives me insight as to show who should be called,' he explains."

Yet the Lord must distinguish between those with an income to keep out of debt, once they have been redeemed by the congregation, and those who get into debt for lack of employment and an income. To be successful, the project would have to make the distinction, whether it comes from up high or from the Bishop's judgment. A common source of employment, the navy, in the case of many of the congregation could strengthen a sense of community and discipline. And of course the religious ties would carry that farther.

What we seem to be witnessing is a tighter communal restructuring familiar in many fundamentalist religions – above all in the Islamic world. It resists and undoes the damage of preying usury, with faith, and enlightenment on the dangers of uncontrolled debt. Precisely the information that tends to be kept out of official school systems that may be openly sponsored by financial corporations, or by politicians who depend on those same corporations for their political funding.

"When the Beavers married two years ago, their credit-card debt totalled $40,000. Since then they have cut up their credit cards, increased their monthly payments and applied a bequest from Mrs. Beaver's grandfather to the balance. In the past year, they've paid off nearly $30,000, while starting second careers. They've also managed to give $200 and sometimes even $300 at each monthly revival meeting.

"'The devil is defeated, he is defeated,' the congregation chanted. A troupe of young dancers in black T-shirts fanned out into the aisles, and soon everyone was on their feet, elbows akimbo, stamping and strutting.

"Whoops of delights greeted the announcement that Earl and Lanitha Hudson had been chosen to get out of debt. The Bishop's wife summoned debt-free parishioners to come forward with offerings. 'Those who can plant a seed of $1,000 get into line.' Behind them came those offering $500, then $300, then $100. Small children clutched dollar bills. The deacons collected and counted the contributions while the pastor snipped credit cards with large shears.

"Finally the good news resounded: 'The Hudsons are out of debt,' the pastor shouted. 'We have $7,000 left. It's time for somebody else – Brother and Sister Beaver,' announced. Janice Beaver gasped and sank down in her seat, as friends rushed to embrace her.

"During Bishop Russell's 19 years at its helm, Mount Carmel has grown from 35 to 3,000 members. Three Sunday-morning services are needed to accommodate the crush. It was overcrowding that indirectly inspired him to begin the revivals. How could he ask his congregation to support a new building fund, he wondered, when so many struggled to pay their own bills?"

The Example of the Early Christians

"Turning to the Scriptures, he read in Acts about the early Christians who shared what they had with each other. 'The notion of following their example was something the Lord placed on my heart,' he says. 'The first revival was the hardest, because there were no previous beneficiaries pledged to help others. Still, that day $5,600 was raised.'

"Church members whose debts are erased bring their bills to Bishop Russell after the meeting. He goes over the figures, initials the statements and gives them to a church trustee who writes checks to the creditors.

"Those newly freed from debt must attend a seminar on staying solvent. Then the pastor meets with them periodically to see where they stand. So far, he says, there have been no backsliders.

"He concedes that some members probably are growing impatient waiting their turn. But he points out that if a family is $5,000 in debt at 19% interest and is paying off only the minimum each month, it will take 55 years to retire that debt. 'If it takes the church two years to get around to them, they are still 53 years ahead of the game.'

"If current trends continue, everyone at Mount Carmel should be out of debt in another year's time, the Bishop estimates. He has told his flock he will be the last to be called for debt liquidation because, he jokes, 'You guys will have so much more money then.'

"'In fact,' he says, 'he pays off the full balance on his single American Express card each month.'"

Apart from the benefits of such solidarity it is an antitoxin against the vicious marketing of the credit card interests.∾

Falling Off the Flat World of Zero Inflation

FOR AT LEAST a quarter of a century, the Bank for International Settlements[1] directed an international campaign to enforce "zero inflation" with the "one blunt tool" of higher interest rates. In its 1991 report Alexandre Lamfalussy, its then general manager, minced no words: "It has been argued that a quality bias in price level calculations implies that inflation rates in the range of one to two per cent may be considered price stability for all practical purposes. Nonetheless, the move from an environment of low or moderate inflation to one of no inflation implies an important psychological shift. It has proven very difficult in recent decades to do better than merely low inflation and to move on to actual price stability, even in those countries with the best price performance."

Nonetheless, on 8/05/97, the then governor of the Bank of Canada, Gordon Thiessen, was reported by *The Globe and Mail* worrying about deflation. Clearly, by that time the BIS "zero inflation" campaign could claim a victory of overkill. But eight days later Mr. Thiessen was back assuring the House of Commons Finance Committee "that he will probably regret forever having mentioned deflation." The unanswered question: on whose orders did the Governor of a supposedly independent central bank make so remarkable a statement when industrial commodity prices were down nearly 10% after sliding for more than two years – the largest decline in a half-century?

And today the "important psychological shift" is hardly the one that Mr. Lamfalussy foresaw. What we are in effect witnessing in high policy-making circles is a state of disorientation and sheer blue funk. Suppressing even the word "deflation" – the plague that just missed doing in society in the 1930s and brought on the Second World War – has left our central banks clueless about how to deal with that problem. *The Wall Street Journal* (6/11) reported a 1999 discussion of US Fed high officials in which they anguished over how the Fed can reactivate the economy when it has already lowered short term interest rates to zero. Using the "sole blunt tool" to which it has limited itself – high interest rates – there is simply nowhere left to go. In the ensuing brainstorming the suggestion was made that the Fed could start buying used cars to pump credit into the inert economy. The most obvious solution to the problem was not even mentioned: the use of the central bank to fund the government to deal with the vast backlog of neglected public investment that has piled up since the bailout of the banks by the federal treasury in the early 1990s.

While dumbing down the general public, the central banks of the world have themselves ended up paralyzed with the fear of falling off the edge of the flat economic world of their creation.

Like the navigators of the remote past, our economists must awaken to the fact that the world isn't flat, but has more dimensions than conventional theory chooses to recognize. The drop of the price index is not entirely due to price deflation, i.e., a shortfall of demand over supply. Likewise the increase of the price index in earlier decades was not wholly due to "inflation," i.e., an excess of demand over supply. Both have had other contributing causes. And it is in those other dimensions, that the solution to either of these problems is to be found, i.e., when they really exist. That was learned in the 1930s at a staggering cost. And that price is being needlessly paid once again today.

Let us list some of these other dimensions, those that caused the Great Depression of the thirties, and others that have arisen since then with the development of our pluralistic society.

Some of these other factors in deflation and inflation had been brought to light by a brilliant generation of economists, of which John Maynard Keynes was only the most eminent member. The essence of their great discovery – had in fact been identified by great "outsiders" like Karl Marx and Major C.H. Douglas – and elaborately ignored by those in power. It was that the "market" of capitalism is not self-balancing. Inevitably it leads to a short-fall of demand which only massive investment by the government can remedy. This it must do by creating essential infrastructures without which capitalism itself cannot function.

It was this so-called "Keynesian revolution" that made possible the relatively prosperous quarter of a century after the war. What had not emerged before Keynes's death was the inevitable price effects of this necessary increase in unmarketed public services. Unmarketed services have no price, and hence their increase cannot be picked up by a simple two-dimensional price index. Just as the two-dimensional charts of early 15th-century explorers lacked the notion of the third dimension that allowed them to return home from the east from their daring far-western journey.

Rising prices can reflect not only an imbalance of demand and supply, but changing proportions of the public and the market components of the economy. And when the private sector has had the stuffings knocked out of it as it has by recent the stock market collapse, the private sector shrivels. Consequently the public share of the economy must increase in relative and even in absolute terms to restore the necessary ratio of supply to demand. Like the economy and society itself, price too has become pluralistic. The costs of more public services in the output mix can only be covered by a deepening layer of taxation in market prices.[2] The flat-earth price theory reduces to the assumption that essential public services come cost-free.

The Ignored Dimensions of our Problems

One of these ignored dimensions of economic policy can be found in the *Bank of Canada Act*. Elsewhere in this issue we quote the passages of the *Bank of Canada Act* that make it possible for our central bank to create the credit to lend to the

Government of Canada on a virtual interest-free basis – practically all the interest paid by the Government to its central bank on such debt comes back to it as dividends since it is the sole shareholder of the central bank.

But would the use of the central bank to provide such credit to the government not be wasteful? To judge that we have need of still further dimensions of enquiry. It makes little sense to have further deregulated our banks immediately after having bailed them out at a crushing cost from their gambling losses made possible by their previous deregulation. Obviously, the elaborately peddled notion that the free market is always efficient and government always wasteful can hardly stand up in a context of the endless scandals that made possible our recent stock market boom. But to pass judgment on such matters in a calmer and more rational way, we would have to introduce capital accounting to the public sector. Up to now, both the US, the UK and the Canadian governments treated government capital investments – the acquisition of buildings, the building of bridges, universities as a current expense. Until recently they all wrote it off in the year in which it was made so that the debt incurred for the investment appeared on its balance sheet, but the value of the capital asset created did not. Obviously no serious assessment of what investment is wasteful and what is worthwhile is possible with such skittish bookkeeping. Both the US government and Ottawa have moved to change this in recent years – the Clinton administration in its Business Economic Analysis figures since the beginning of 1996, and the Canadian government in 2002 by finally yielding to pressure from a series of Royal Commissions and Auditor Generals over a period of almost 40 years. But this has been done or committed to in stealth. In the US government investment in physical infrastructures was classified as "savings" which it most definitely is not since it is not held as cash. And in Canada the change that was to have come in by mid-2002 has never been mentioned again, though it is crucial to just above everything in the headlines: the reform of our health, education and social services, the proposed merger of our banks, the choice of a new prime minister, the morality of our stock markets.[3]

Not only the long-denied problem of deflation, but just about everything in the economy, domestic and international, requires the free flow of information that has been withheld for at least four decades. Without it we are being sucked into a period of high-tech military solutions that can only lead to disaster beyond all our nightmares.

Instead of seeking out these neglected dimensions of our mixed economy, our politicians of just about all political stripes insist on inciting fears that we must balance federal budget and reduce the federal government's debt – even pay it off entirely. But federal debt has been the only legal tender since the early 1970s. What does our Finance Minister propose to pay it off with? Government debt of a different colour? These and other such questions must be asked.[4]

William Krehm

1. The Bank of International Settlements (BIS) is a private club of the world's central bankers that allows no official of a government to attend its sessions. This status was the model of the supposed "independence" of the central banks throughout the world from their elected governments. It was founded in 1929 as a purely technical body to handle the transfer problem of Germany's WW1 reparations. At the Bretton Woods Conference of 1944 Resolution Five was passed calling for the liquidation of BIS at the earliest possible moment. That was because of its too ready surrender of the Czechoslovak gold entrusted to it the moment Hitler's troops marched into Prague. (Krehm, William (1993). *The Bank of Canada – A Power Unto Itself* (p. 18 et seq). Toronto: Stoddard.)

2. Krehm, William (May, 1970). *Revue Economique.* "La stabilité des prix et le secteur publique," Paris. This paper was expanded in the book *Price in a Mixed Economy – Our Record of Disaster*, Toronto, 1975. In it the notions of capital budgeting, public investment and human capital were developed and related to the concept of a non-inflationary component in the price ramp of the 1960s.

3. The only mention in the media of the legislation introducing capital budgetting was in *The National Post* (20/7/99) in an article by Kathyrin May based on the Auditor General's report. *The National Post* was a rightist publication that was desperate for readers.

4. Krehm, William (1999), *Meltdown: Money, Debt and the Wealth of Nations* (p. 312). Toronto: COMER Publications.

Practice Confirms Theory

THERE ARE MOMENTS when our readers must have wondered why we go to the trouble of developing what may seem an entirely new way of approaching economic problems – systems theory. The answer is that it obliges us to examine problems and solutions according to their impacts on all subsystems of our economy – e.g., the environment, our household economies, the public sector. Why don't we instead stick to those comfortable "eternal truths" of the market, that we hear about whenever our Finance Minister assures us that "our fundamentals are sound"? The answer is simple: when we are examining the effect of that measure in the market subsystem, the market is host and its house rules are the only ones that count. When we track the effects of that same measure into an environmental subsystem, say the carbon dioxide subsystem, that subsystem becomes the host, and its needs become paramount. They become the criteria for judging whether or not the given measure is house-broken according the rules of that particular house. Systems theory helps us foresee at the planning stage crises that might result from a proposed measure.

Take for example, the matter of using the market in the form of trading polluting rights, as the way to go for handling environmental concerns "most efficiently." Hadn't conventional "equilibrium theory" taught us that the market is the most efficient of all institutions, even though the advocates rarely specify which of the many conflicting markets they are talking about?

It elevated "the market" and its "logic" into the one dominant code by which the effects of a measure not only could, but had to be judged. That necessarily reduced the other subsystems of the economy – and society itself – to subordinate subsystems. It is another aspect of systems theory that one subsystem must never be allowed to cannibalize another, since they all have to be in good working order, each by its own rules, for the entire system to function. And the only way in which that could be ensured would be to judge their effects by the local rules as we tracked them across subsystem boundaries. Otherwise put, the variables of a given measure had to be considered not as absolute unchanging truths, i.e., *scalars,* but as *vectors* with a sense of direction. It was like an electron entering a different electromagnetic field, or an asteroid entering the gravitational field of a planet. As soon as it does, its behaviour undergoes a change.

To be treated as a scalar, the given quantity of any substance must be "fungible" – a term related to "function." It means that every sample of it is exchangeable with any other sample. A grain of a given variety may fulfill this, or coal of given specifications. They are known – in a special sense as "commodities" suitable for the trading in bulk with no further reference to the parameters within which this can happen. High-style tailoring is not a commodity in this sense. Nor is it fungible. On the contrary, those in charge devote their energies to establishing it as a distinct "brand" which is the opposite of being fungible. Within a given market, pollution rights – say of CO_2 – is perfectly "fungible" – one sample of carbon dioxide is perfectly interchangeable with another. The ultimate example of this is the term "chemically pure." But when you cross from the market subsystem into the CO_2 subsystem of the environment, all that changes since your pollution sample has become a vector that has found its way into a different field with its own house rules. What will be decisive on this side of the subsystem frontier will be the amount of CO_2 pollution already reached and how close and on what side of the "limit of tolerance" for CO_2? A given sample of CO_2 in the area entered is no longer fungible, because fungibility now depends in part on the local parameters of the given pollution already reached. It no longer resides entirely in the characteristics of what is being traded, but on where it ends up.

Is Pollution Fungible?

The Wall Street Journal (20/11, "Report Faults Emissions Trades for Dirty Air in Some US Areas" by John J. Fialka) provides confirmation of the effectiveness of our "fungibility" criterion; and of its vector rather than scalar status.

"Washington – A federal emissions-trading program that has helped power plants cut their sulfur-dioxide output by 32% since 1990 has left some areas of the US with dirtier air than they had before, according to a report from an environmental group.

"The study produced by the former enforcement chief of the Environmental Protection Agency says one result of emissions trading is that residents of 16 states face an increased health hazard from small particles of soot.

"We've got some places that have been left behind," said Eric V. Schaeffer, noting that antipollution efforts have been uneven. He blamed emissions-trading laws that allow owners of coal-fired plants that don't meet tighter air-quality controls to keep operating by buying credits from plants that exceed their emissions-reduction target." In short they violate a basic principle of systems theory: one subsystem must not cannibalize another.

"Congress might expand the so-called cap-and-trade system next year, as the Bush administration proposes to make deeper cuts in emissions of sulfur dioxide, nitrogen oxides and mercury during the next 20 years. The plan calls for expanded emissions trading."

That means that the flaws of the "solution" will be further stepped up to wreak still greater damage in some of the most vulnerable areas of our environment. Obviously, we are confronted here with a serious flunking of the Tinbergen Counting Rule – we are applying a simplistic solution with fewer independent variables than can be identified in the problem – for example the distance remaining between the degree of a specific type of pollution already attained and the local limit of tolerance to that pollution.

"Mr. Schaeffer left the EPA in February and heads the Environmental Integrity Project, a nonprofit research center in Washington backed by the Rockefeller Family Fund. 'Two troublesome clusters of increasingly polluted air occur over the Carolinas and Virginia and over western Pennsylvania,' according to the study. The clusters could worsen, Mr. Schaeffer said, if the EPA relaxes a separate set of rules covering maintenance of older coal-fired power plants. The rule change could be announced later this week."

Foresight (which is really an aspect of hindsight) is one of the supreme gifts bestowed on mankind by the Creator. Before we allow our political leaders to number-crunch us into a coma on the subject, we must reclaim the use of our minds.

William Krehm

The Rotten Core of our Most Spectacular Privatization — the CNR

CANADA'S picture poster of successful privatizations has suddenly made the front pages. *The Globe and Mail* (27/11, "CN slashes 5% of work force – Asbestos claims bring $175 million charge" by Paul Waldie) reports: "Canadian National Railway Co. announced 1,146 job cuts yesterday and a $175 million provision to settle a growing number of personal injury and asbestos claims in the US." The shares of the company fell by a full 6% on the Toronto Stock Exchange. The job losses are the result in part of the drought in Western Canada which has reduced the CN's grain revenue by 13%. It also needs fewer workers because it has been cutting the number of locomotives and rail cars in recent years by 32% and 12.5% respectively.

"Asbestos lawsuits have become a huge issue in the US where the number of cases has quadrupled in the past decade. Railways currently face nearly 10,000 claims from employees who say they were exposed to asbestos and repair shops."

The bad weather of the past year would hardly in itself justify massive layoffs. The CNR's shopping spree buying up American railways has transformed it into the largest North American railway. It has turned its axis from east-west – the purpose for which it was created at considerable cost to the Canadian taxpayer – to north-south – once again at the cost to the Canadian taxpayers in money and services. One might imagine that such decisions were best left to our government, rather than to a corporation adept at seeking private advantage at public expense.

The Iron Lady Put in the Shade

In certain respects, the details of the CNR privatization leave even Maggie Thatcher's classic disposals of public assets in the shade.

As the world's industrial pioneer, Britain almost inevitably ended up with many obsolescent industries, that became ideal candidates for either nationalization or privatization as the political winds might blow. Moreover, corporations having to do with communications like railroads or telephones may hold hidden crown jewels beneath pools of red ink. These could become tempting to civil servants themselves poised on the brink of privatization.

In *The National Wealth – Who Gets What in Britain*[1] Dominic Hobson summarizes the complex record of privatization in Britain: "By 1997, privatization had become the stock-in-trade of satirical comedians. Their efforts, and those of tabloid journalists, gradually reduced the public appreciation of privatization to massive pay rises for bosses, higher prices for customers, and a pay cut or sack for employees. Caricature has erased memories of what went before. At the time it was privatized BT had 250,000 customers waiting for a telephone line to be installed. The public telephone boxes doubled as public lavatories. Electricity and gas prices went down before elections, and up after them. In the water industry, the sewers were crumbling, the beaches a disgrace, the rivers filthy, and water shortages commonplace. The public images of British Rail, its timetables regularly undone by 'the wrong sort of snow' and leaves on the line, was of grubby trains and surly staff." Clearly the author of this book is no doctrinal opponent of privatizations.

Hobson continues, "Few remember these things now. After twenty years of privatization, *how* public assets were sold matters more than *why*. The main criticism is that they were sold for less than they were worth. From 150 sales between 1979 and 1997, the government raised £90 billion in real terms, or about half the net value of the nationalized industries. The size of this gap is the reason why the shares in privatized companies almost always soared in value in the first few days after the sale. Shares in Amersham International, British Airways, British Telecom and Rolls-Royce were all worth a third more than the offer price within a week. A reluctance to sell shares in stages, or organize competitive auctions, usually denied the taxpayer any stake in the appreciation of the stock.

"The chief architects of privatization, Margaret Thatcher and Nigel Lawson, have both admitted that they were prepared to sell nationalized industries cheaply to speed their exit from the public sector and to widen share ownership. In February 1982, Lawson was responsible for the privatization of Amersham International, the radio-chemical company. Its shares soared to a premium of 35% in early trading after being oversubscribed 25 times at the offer price. But the former chancellor is unapologetic: 'The serious underpricing of Amersham, though in no sense deliberate, may have been no bad thing. The enormous publicity given to the profits enjoyed by subscribers conveyed the clear message that investing in privatization was a good thing.' There lies the crux of much of the world's trouble – "the good thing" consisted largely of the illusion that such outrageous speculative profits could be actually earned by the efficiency of the private companies, rather than in a give-away of public assets, a waning condition for such state of bliss.

"To attract ordinary people, privatization shares also had to be sold at a fixed price rather than by auction, because they could not guess the right price to pay. The two sales priced by auction, Britoil and Enterprise, both flopped, But the subsequent performance of fixed price issues often made the initial valuation embarrassing. BT shares, which City advisers had insisted would flood the market, went to an immediate premium of 91%. Under pressure from the National Audit Office (NAO) and the Public Accounts Committee, the government slowly got better at pricing privatization issues It appointed an independent adviser on pricing, and began to take a more sceptical view of City advice.

"At privatization, nobody even thought to charge a premium for the public land under which BT cables were laid. The NAO later believed the government had sold the English and Welsh water industry for £2.3 billion less than it was worth. The Medway Ports, bought by the management for £29.7 million in March 1992, were sold eighteen months later to Mersey Docks and Harbour Company for £103.7 million. Ownership of the National Grid was transferred to the regional electricity companies at a valuation of £1 billion in 1991. Just four years later the companies themselves valued it for sale at four times this amount. Even the Conservatives were sufficiently embarrassed by this cheeky plan to threaten its owners with a windfall tax. Royal Ordnance, sold to British Aerospace in April 1987 for £190 million, turned out a bargain. Within a year, unwanted factories sold by the taxpayers for £5 million were sold to property developers for £450 million."

Unheeded Lessons for the CNR Privatization

All this is highly relevant to the privatization of Canadian National Railways. Even Margaret Thatcher eventually learned that privatizations could take place in several instalments, so that by the time the market had come to appreciate the give-away feature of the first offering, the government could at least participate in the share prices that reflected these in the later installments.

That was not done in the case of the CNR. To prepare it for privatization in May 1995, the government as seller reduced its long-term debt by $1.4 billion, and threw in a $900 million equity contribution. It transferred to itself all non-rail assets for future sales, where the Thatcher government relied on a clawback clause that gave the right of the state to half of the proceeds of future sales of such assets when the privatized company sold them. In this way instead of exposing itself to the greed of the stock market and its own record of incompetence in the very deal it was negotiating with the privatized railway, it would piggy-back on the resale deals that company might strike with other private companies.

"'Clawbacks,' in which the government reserved the right to reclaim the proceeds of post-privatization asset disposals, became a regular feature of sales as the British programme matured. When electricity was privatized, the government reserved the right to clawback half the profits made by the regional companies on the sale of surplus property, and withdrew the Central Electricity Generating Board headquarters (near St. Paul's) and Bankside Station (in Southwark) from the sale rather than see them sold or redeveloped after privatization. When the bus companies were privatized, many of their most attractive city centre properties were withheld and sold separately.

"The sale of British coal which put one of the greatest landed estates on the market, was shaped by this growing [very British] awareness of the value of real estate. Though its land holdings were much reduced since the 1940s, British Coal still owned around 250,000 acres and in its last years of public ownership, earned £35 million a year from sales of unwanted property. R.J. Budge, which bought virtually the whole of the English coal industry, acquired a mere 14,000 acres of freehold land, and other buyers acquired negligible leaseholds. Any profits from property disposal by the new owners were clawed back fiercely, and the bulk of the estate was retained for future sale.

"The privatization of British Rail, sometime owner of an estate of over 200,000 acres, was accompanied by a similar division of the spoils. The operational assets of the railways – tracks, stations, signalling equipment and engineering works – now belong to Railtrack PLC. But non-operational land was retained by the British Railways Board. Its property subsidiary is now landlord to outmoded buildings, disused yards, vacant plots and disused viaducts and bridges. (British Rail did not know how much property it owned.)

"In its anxiety to privatize the railways, the government allowed some gems to escape. One reason Railtrack shares rose from £3.90 on flotation in May 1996 to over £10 less than two years later was the over-endowment of the company with property. Railtrack owns a portfolio crammed with rent-producing assets and commercial sites ripe for redevelopment or disposal.

"Most of the 2,500 stations are leased to the train operating companies, but Railtrack has retained the right to redevelop the most promising. Railtrack will make of £1 billion from property rents and developments during its first years in private ownership.

"The first train franchises to be sold had to be fattened with high subsidies." At least the Brits have had the educational advantage of their National Auditing Office conducting a post-mortem that helped them recognize that they had been had. Nothing of the sort has happened in Canada. Hence the botched privatizations of Ontario Hydro. A post-mortem on the CNR scam could have saved the Ontario public much wealth and sorrow. According to the NAO, the seven British Rail train maintenance depots were sold for only £32 million when they had £17 million of cash on their balance sheets. The track

maintenance units went cheaply too. A construction company called Jarvis bought the Northern Infrastructure Maintenance Unit for £11 million in 1995. A year later it was worth £50 million. These losses escaped public censure. But the underpricing of the rolling stock leasing companies (Roscos) was too large to lose in the financial pages. Assets valued at £3 billion were sold for £1.3 billion. Within two years, all three Roscos were sold to new buyers for an additional £790 million. A Japanese bank made £330 million when one of them was sold. The management buyout team at another turned a joint investment of £300,000 into £83.7 million, a three hundred-fold increase in a matter of months.

For an idea of the extent to which the Canadian public was taken to the cleaners appears from the course of CNR stock. The high in its first year 1996 was $28.50 which was roughly double its low for that year. By 1999 it had touched a high of $54.58. Options were issued to insiders exercisable for as little as $13.50 a share. In March 2001 the CNR completed the sale of its 50% interest in the Detroit River Terminal Company, showing a post-tax profit of $82 million over the book value at the time of the sale.

The Missing Sage Provisions for Privatizing in Other Lands

We also miss the sage provisions in some lands that prevent an ex-civil servant from dealing in public assets for some years after his retirement. But Paul Tellier, the CEO of the privatized CNR had been Clerk of the Privy Council, who knew where all the dead bodies and the family jewels were buried.[2] All in all it was done in a style that could have made a central Asian ex-Soviet republic proud. By slipping up on the nationalization of the CNR, the government and its watchdogs were emitting encouragement to the privatizers of Ontario Hydro. However, this did help instill some signs of life in an already moribund stock market. That in fact was the prime purpose of the operation.

The ultimate theme of the Hobson book is the relative merit of nationalization and privatization. But to see that more clearly we must satisfy ourselves on at least two matters:

(1) Does the accountancy of the public sector distinguish between a capital investment by amortizing it over its useful life, or not? Obviously if it does not, there is no basis for comparing real as opposed to reported costs of nationalized and privatized services.

(2) Were near-interest-free credit of the central bank available to the government for essential public services, the scandalous giveaways that passed for sales would have been unnecessary. Inexpensive capital could have been raised for rationalizing essential public companies via the central bank against government guarantee. Since the interest paid on such loans would revert to the sole shareholder of the Bank of Canada – the Government of Canada – it would have been a virtual interest-free loan. That might have made privatization unnecessary.

The Hobson book is thus useful on a variety of planes. It discloses some of the safeguards against the corrupt exploitation of privatization that even Mrs. Thatcher eventually learned, but have still to reach our shores.[3]

The nationalization of the Canadian National Railways by market criteria – and not many others have been in vogue in recent years – was the most successful of our privatizations. In three or four years its market value rose by a multiple of approximately four. That paper bonanza was interpreted as a sign of the wisdom of nationalization – but it might also have raised doubts about whether the privatization was a sale, or a case of a high civil servant using his inside knowledge and his connections to make a killing.

Historically the CNR was the government's collection of walking wounded. It had gathered into the public bosom the bankrupt and near-bankrupt railways that had provided the heavy stitching necessary to create the country called Canada. That could hardly have been left to the wisdom of the market. Naturally, unprofitable lines have been abandoned or sold off by the CNR to smaller operators. Even the first Canadian transcontinental that had joined the country together further south required generous financial lubrication by the government that left an epic scandal in its wake. However, the CPR incident besmirched our early history as a nation will in time be downgraded to kids cheating at marbles by the dubious CNR privatization in our adulthood.

William Krehm

1. Hammersmith, London: Harper Collins Publishers, 1999.
2. Since this was written, Tellier has resigned his post as CEO of CNR to become CEO of Bombardier, an already privatized concern that stands in need of major government assistance. The Globe and Mail (14/12) quotes a close friend: Mr. Tellier's knowledge of how government works would be an advantage in any business."
3. The near-encyclopedic range of Hobson's review was bound to leave some poorly covered areas. It is unfortunate, too, that the outstanding of these should be the Bank of England, the independence of which from government is treated as just another manifestation of the systole and diastole that keeps the economy pumping. "In theory, there is no reason why competition should not confer the same benefits in the markets for money as it does in the markets for other goods and services. Competition between many different private and state 'brands' of money would not necessarily lead to chaos. Counterparties would conduct their business in the most reliable and stable currencies, and competing currencies might or might not be convertible into a basic form, such as gold or a basket of goods and services."

This ignores that the use of non-interest-bearing reserves that before the 1990s had been put up by the commercial banks as a ratio of the deposits they have accepted from the public. This had been a modest remnant of the *seigniorage* of ancestral monarch's monopoly for coining precious metals. Equally important, those statutory reserves provided the central bank an alternative to higher interest rates for controlling "inflation." Interest rates are after all the revenue of a an economic group that should not be encouraged to become predatory. Moreover, the very concept of "inflation" – that identifies all increase in the price level with an increase of demand – is in need of re-examination. A modern economy is unthinkable without higher educational, social, and health standards. And these do require an ever more massive investment of public capital that must show up as a deepening layer of taxation in price. It is very well talking about having private and public currencies compete for government acceptance, but that sidesteps the crucial question of the deregulation of our banks that forced national corporations to seek their capital on the stock market and in wildly leveraged derivative gambles covered in the Hobson book.

Risk Management or Risk Creation?

THERE WAS A TIME, not so long ago, when stock market analysts and promoters had a sure-fire thing by the tail. In making the leap from fact to fiction, they needed only to utter the words "risk management," mention the name of a couple of academics who had won the so-called Nobel Prize for Economics for a paper in which a few rows of differential and integration signs were supposed to prove "scientifically" that the market would take care of things. That left the CEOs free to plot ever more complex deals, and cash in their options.

And of course, if you have high science at your bidding you don't harness the beast to a creaky cart. You fuel it with the greatest power and prevarication and let her rip to "maximize growth." The only risk left in so well-ordered a universe is standing still.

There is little mood for wasting time with just compound interest, you "conserve your capital" by betting on the growth of the market value of shares that you don't necessarily even own into the remotest future. Hundreds of millions in profits may be raked in that way, but somehow rather than bleeding the economy, it is seen as improving its "sound fundamentals."

And that makes our job editing a contrarian monthly review on a minimal budget so easy, virtually a sinecure. Today we can quote from the better financial journals the evidence of the inevitable swindle of such overhyped markets. That, indeed, is the moral of this tale.

On the front page of its Money & Investing section (5/12, "A Market Backfires, and Investors Pay – Though Greenspan Praised Them Credit-Derivative Trading Mutates; Instead of Stability – Instability" by Henry Sender) *The Wall Street Journal* spills the beans: "At the beginning of October, the cost for investors to buy credit protection against a default by several large German banks, most notably Commerzbank AG, suddenly began to rise. And while there was a lot of bad news at the time, the dramatic move in prices in the market where such protection is bought and sold seemed disproportionate.

"Then, concerns about Commerzbank's health suddenly eased. Today, it costs $140,000 for each $10 million of default protection on Commerzbank's bonds, down from $200,000 not long ago – even though there has been no significant change in the bank's financial condition. To some analysts, the incident came as a warning that the young market for what are known as 'credit-derivative swaps' doesn't always reflect the underlying economic reality. Indeed, some market players have magnified potential credit problems far beyond the level they deserve, critics contend, creating an ever-bigger sense of doom about an underlying company's prospects.

"This poses a conundrum: a market originally designed to provide stability by letting investors hedge their credit risk has instead in some instances become a source of the very instability it was meant to reduce.

"The potential for disruption is particularly vexing, observers say, because in the five years since credit-default swaps have become widely used, the market has won praise from such regulators as Federal Reserve Chairman Alan Greenspan, who has applauded the way in which it has helped banks reduce their exposure to risky borrowers.

"The buying of the insurance protection pushes up the price of the insurance, much like the buying of many financial products pushes up their price. Then, because the young market has something of a reputation as an early warning signal for spotting corporate debt problems, the higher insurance prices themselves can cause other investors to worry – and thus push a company's bond prices even lower. This then prompts other investors to worry about a possible default and to buy insurance protection, in turn driving prices in the credit-derivatives market even higher.

"While much of the trading of credit protection is still done by banks and other investors that are owed money or own bonds, an increasing amount of trading in the unregulated market appears to be driven by hedge funds that often don't own the bonds. Instead, they aim to make a profit by buying the insurance protection and reselling it when the price goes up. Because the credit-derivatives market is private and limited to professionals, there are no market-manipulation rules in the way there are in the stock market."

In short, the increase in the price of the derivative on its own distinct market becomes a derivative of a higher order, with a life and purpose of its own, that ends up blocking the alleged purpose of the derivative of the lower order on which it is based. The phenomenon is of crucial importance, since it reveals the flight from reality to exploitative fiction that has taken over. It needs only be mentioned that even in the "regulated" stock market the rules haven't set the world on fire in protecting investors from crooked manipulations.

"Among those sounding the alarm that savvy players are whipsawing the market to their advantage is William Gross, managing director of Pacific Investment Management Co., or Pimco, the largest bond investor in the US with more than $300 billion under management.

"In a recent newsletter, Mr. Gross warned that hedge funds, which have used the stock market to place bearish bets, have turned their sights to the bond market. Mr. Gross and other critics say that the new credit-derivatives market allows these hedge funds, along with in-house trading desks of banks and investment banks, to place leveraged bets with huge potential upside returns and little downside risk.

"There are fresh negatives to haunt traditional corporate bondholders that emanate from the growing power of hedge funds and their willingness to play fast and loose with the solvency of struggling companies,' Mr. Gross noted.

Apparently this sort of pressure was applied even on Ford Motor Co. "well before the bond market became uneasy about the ability of Ford to boost its market share and profitability in an increasingly competitive car market and became nervous about the company's near $150 billion in unsecured debt."

Right-thinking analysts and even academics used to dismiss this sort of thing as a mere case of the "healthy Darwinism" of "the market." However, when a predator eliminated a weaker species it had proved its ability to run, claw and bite better. It did not stay in its lair and manipulate some phony figures of its own creation. But that is what our hierarchy of increasingly rigged markets has become.

William Krehm

On the Perils of Insuring an Economy Navigating by the Wrong Charts

THE MOST BASIC SOURCE of our economic troubles is this: we treat the relationship between past and the present in the opposite way that we do that between the present and the future. But since time, like the geologic plates beneath the oceans, moves on, the past-present link transmutes into the present-future one. When that happens, the clashing treatment of these two transitions throws up mountain ranges of contradiction.

In the past-present pairing, we ignore the vast investment of the various levels of government: highways, canals, ports, sewage and water systems, health, social security and educational institutions. These have risen in Canada from about 15% of the total annual output of the economy 70 years ago to some 40% today. In the Scandinavian countries the figure is closer to 60%. Near the bottom of the list is the United States in the lower thirties. In all these countries such investments were handled as current expenses and written off in a single year – like floor-wax or paper clips. The only aspect of the great enduring investment left is the debt incurred to finance them. And that debt, without the offsetting assets that it was incurred for, is the most overworked tool in the ideological kit of politicians. Yet it is like calculating a private person's net worth by including the mortgage on his home among his liabilities, but omitting the house it financed from his assets.

All this is converging into a new tangle of problems even though we have not succeeded in clearing our courts from the old ones described above. Insurance was one of the three pillars of finance that it had been the ground rule to keep separate. The other two were banks, and the stock market. The reason for that was obvious. Insurance was the ultimate security against the gambles that are the bane of financial markets. Banks, however, have been driven to become the masters of all they see. And the last bailout of the banks from their loss of their capital in the eighties, was, incredibly, accompanied by their further deregulation. Because of that, insurance companies today find themselves close to the epicentre of the skullduggery that you have been reading about in the stock market and our banking system. *The Wall Street Journal* (30/10, "Some Bets May Come Back to Haunt Insurers" by Christopher Oster and Henry Sender) reports: "Insurers face possibly substantial losses from an array of business activities tied to the ability of corporations to pay off their bond debts.

"In a relatively new line of business, some property-casualty insurers have sold a brand of protection under which they're stuck for the payment of corporation bonds if an issuer defaults. Ace Ltd., American International Group Inc., the American Re unit of Munich Re, Chubb Corp., Swiss Reassurance Co., XL Capital Ltd., and Zurich Financial Services Group are notable players in this young but rapidly growing market, according to the report.

"As investors wonder which industries are most at risk if the economy worsens, insurers seem increasingly to be in the bull's eye. Moody's new update on the property-casualty insurance sector follows one in August that found life insurance companies held $23.4 billion of securities of problem issuers, nearly 10% of the industry's total capital. Life insurers have other stock-market worries as well, including declining fee revenues from market-linked products and minimum-return guarantees they made on variable annuities.

"Some analysts contend that AIG, Chubb and other property-casualty insurers stand to profit now that premium rates are rising 30% to 100% in many lines. But Moody's believes exposure to problem credits threatens to postpone yet again the promise of improved results of many companies.

"For the property-casualty insurance sector, the pile-up of economy-related exposures is partly the outgrowth of a decade-long price war that lowered premium rates and expanded coverage. The Sept. 11 terrorist attacks, with their steep insurance losses, effectively ended the price battle, and since then insurers have tightened terms and reduced coverage limits of many types of policies, including directors' and officers' liability insurance. But many customers purchased multi-year CDO policies [that] remain in effect.

"In another expansion of their business to fight falling revenue during the price war, insurers sold more and different types of surety contracts. Before the price war such contracts were written only to guarantee the completion of construction contracts, but ones currently in place have been used to back up complex business transactions, such as the delivery of oil and gas by now-collapsed Enron Corp. Chubb and AIG booked $220 million and $57 million respectively in charges related to such transactions earlier this year.

"Increasingly the insurers have gotten into the business of credit derivatives, giving themselves yet another way to lose money when companies default on debt. Some participate in the oddly named credit-default swap market, where investors with large exposures to an individual corporation can buy insurance that will pay them if an individual company fails to make payments on its debts. In addition, some insurers both guarantee and invest in complicated pools of sliced-and-diced corporate debt, as well as pools of individual credit-default swaps, known as collateralized debt obligations (CDOs).

"Insuring credit derivatives accounted for more than 30% of Aace's Ace Guaranty Re unit's total revenue of $125 million last year."

Re in the name of an insurance company stands for "Reinsurance" – the part of the risk that insurance companies incur in the business they write that they choose to rewrite with such Re companies – to keep their exposure within manageable limits. Usually such reinsurance covers an upper chunk of that risk that the prime writer could itself not safely handle.

There is thus a connection between the present clouds over the world insurance industry and the stubborn resistance of the US and international regulatory authorities to the very suggestion that Over-the-Counter derivatives be regulated that we reported in our last issue.

The Crisis among Reinsurers

In The Wall Street Journal (29/11, "Munich Re Posts 3rd Quarter Loss as Outlook Clouds" by Charles Fleming) we are confronted with the end fruits of all this:

"Munich Re AG has some bad new for almost everyone.

"The world's largest reinsurer disappointed stockholders with news that it had sunk deeper in the red in the third quarter from the second quarter under the combined woes of its exposure to Germany's weak banks, the worlds' troubled stock markets and this summer's Central European flooding.

"It also had grim news for insurance buyers everywhere, warning that increase in natural catastrophes would mean further sharp increases in the cost of insurance coverage for at least the next two years.

"And it offered a barely veiled threat to the stumbling German banks in which it holds large stakes – namely Commerzbank AG and HBV Group AG – that they should get their acts together but couldn't rely on Munich Re. Munich Re reported a $850.7 million net loss for the third quarter yesterday. That greater-than-expected loss and the grim outlook for the fourth quarter caused Munich Re share to fall against the market's broader trend.

"Munich Re, like all of Europe's insurers, has been especially hurt by the precipitous decline in stock market values over the last two years. European insurers have suffered much more than their US rivals on this score because US insurance reserve requirements act as a disincentive to US insurers holding too much of their assets in equities.

"Under German accounting rules, insurers have to take such 'impairment charges' when shares held on its own account have traded below book value for a certain time.

"Another element that will hurt Munich Re's earnings at the end of the year will be the delayed impact of heavy third-quarter losses at Allianz AG and HVB Group, both of which are consolidated in Munich Re's accounts because it holds more than 20% in each."

Negative factors ricochet in all directions between the reinsurance market and stock markets, the state of the financial system at home and abroad. The virtues of firewalls and enough isolation to reconsider our most sacred dogmas is becoming evident. In addition to the above-quoted article, the menace of this overhang in the European Re industry appears grave enough for the *WSJ* to devote an editorial to in the same issue: "Global stocks have been creeping up since October is good news. Each little ratchet-up makes it less likely that the world financial system will suffer a major meltdown. But what if...?"

"European companies hold a greater proportion of reserves in stock than do US firms (30% vs. 4%). Moreover, the values of their own stock are down by almost two-thirds since the beginning of the year, making it difficult for them to write new business. Bad enough, but it gets worse. Both American and European insurers are exposed to a variety of risks in the credit market at exactly the same moment that the corporate credit market is experiencing a severe and intense downturn."

"They are also exposed to the credit markets through the writing of commercial surety bonds – instruments that directly insure companies, or specific financing for projects, against credit risk and/or default."

"Many insurers have taken on additional risk in the credit-derivatives market. Credit derivatives allow credit risk on an underlying asset to be transferred from one party to another."

"Although the market itself is only about five years old, insurance companies, especially those writing property and casualty lines, have become aggressive players through credit-default swaps and instruments known as collateralized debt obligations or CDOs.

"Companies have been selling credit-default swaps (guaranteeing the debt of other entities) for investors with large exposures to an individual corporation; the swaps allow investors to buy insurance that will pay them if that corporation defaults. Insurers have also been involved, as guarantors and investors, in CDO's, complicated pools of sliced-and-diced corporate debt as well as pools of individual credit-default swaps."

Reinsurers, in short have played God concerned with every sparrow that falls but needing no insurance Himself. This is the ultimate spire of the cathedral of market faith.

"Accounting rules for insurance companies are – to put it politely – lax. Balance-sheet disclosure is inadequate and transparency is best described as exceedingly opaque. Government oversight is also haphazard. In the home markets of the two largest reinsurers, Munich Re and Swiss Re are mostly unregulated. A few weeks ago, worries over the impact of hidden insurance problems propelled the Organization for Economic Cooperation and Development to agree to create an information exchange on reinsurance companies within their jurisdiction."

We can gauge the extent of the trouble by referring to the statistician's use of the concept of "bias" as something to be avoided. Much of his art has to do with just that in calculating probabilities. "This is illustrated by the results of large experiments conducted on several thousands of school children in Lanarkshire in 1930 to measure the effects of feeding them with milk on their growth during the experiment – about six months. At each school the children were divided into two comparable groups; one group received the milk and the other did not, and the effect of the milk was to be measured by comparing the growth rates of the two groups. In an experiment of this kind, the accuracy depends very much on the two groups of children being similar on the average before the feeding begins, i.e., on one being unbiased with respect to the other. To secure this, the children were selected for the two groups either by ballot or by a system based on the alphabetical order of the names.... But the whole thing was spoiled by giving the teachers discretionary powers.

"Presumably the substitutions were not done on the basis of the actual weights of the children, but were left to the personal judgement of the teachers. It has been suggested that teachers tended, perhaps subconsciously, to allow their natural sympathies to put into the 'milk' group more of the children who look as though they needed nourishment. The substitutions of the children could have been done without introducing bias, had the actual weights been made the basis."[1]

When we turn to the insurance companies who are supposed to protect the economy against unpleasant surprises, rather than with an innocent bias we are confronted with a militant ideology. That ideology is a brood-hen that not only has laid all the eggs, but sits on them protectively until they hatch. Rather than the future being foretold from a random sampling of the past and present, present valuations are made by projecting their alleged present rate of growth into the remotest future. And this spurious knowledge of the future underpins the wild leverages that derivatives make possible. Accordingly accountancy and data banks are contaminated and Globalization and Deregulation guarantee the spread of the contagion.

William Krehm

1. "Sampling and Standard Error" by L.C. Tippett in Newman, James R. (1956). *The World of Mathematics, Vol. 3* (p. 1466). New York: Simon and Schuster.

The Derivative Economy

SO STRONG is the compulsion to growth in our current economic culture that the distinction between healthy and malignant tissue is lost. More often than not, healthy flesh is hacked away to make room for morbid mass. For unlike pathological cells, the normal ones on maturity stop growing – and that is rated an "inefficiency" by conventional economists. On occasion, however, our lips can be more perceptive than our minds, and the parallel between diseased expansion and healthy growth turns up in our speech. That is why the most destructive of all financial growth-pills devised are called derivatives, which is the term for the growth of a mathematical function with respect to its variables. The first derivative – the rate of growth – itself has a rate of growth, the acceleration of the underlying function. That second in turn has a rate of growth – the third-degree derivative of the function itself, a fourth and so forth to infinity.

To crown all this, the stock market has arrogated to itself a godly foreknowledge of the future, and loses no time in translating this into the coin of the realm. A company's stock price tends to incorporate the rate of growth, and the acceleration of that growth already attained, extended into the remotest future, and all discounted for presumed present value. That means that the rate of growth is under a compulsion to match the rate already attained that is already tucked into the current share price. That tends to reproduce at various levels the process already embodied in price; for each is the first derivative of a lower derivative. Add a healthy ingredient of hype and promotion, and the result strains towards the pattern of the exponential function, the mathematics of the atomic bomb. So long as the economy is driven by this model, similar outcomes are unavoidable.

There is then an urgent need to gear down this growth mania. That is no easy task: we must not underestimate the political clout of numerous groups of disproportionately rewarded people suddenly threatened with unemployment. To ease the transition to a more sustainable pattern we must arrive at an understanding of the underlying structures of the problem. Without that we are unable to design the policy tools to make possible as smooth and compassionate a transition to sustainability as possible.

Elsewhere[1] I have introduced Gaussian modular congruence as a simple instrument for this purpose. Long before it was developed by the greatest of 19th century mathematicians,[2] various cultures had made intuitive use of it: instead of bestowing a distinct name on each day since Adam bit the apple, they used three different cycles for naming the days of the week, the month, and the year. These three distinct *moduli* conveniently identify any particular day.

Once we encounter a needless or even harmful factor swelling our economic activity, we must express it in modular terms. Let x be the symbol of that factor quantified as a modulus, occurring in y in a multiple n leaving a remainder of say z less than x. In terms of modulus congruence the value of x then is z. If we can ignore or eliminate the multiple of the modulus and deal only with the remainder, our purpose is advanced. If we can lower the multiple of the modulus in stages we are making progress in the right direction. To slim down the economy to sustainability, this is an essential tool. It has not been explored by economists.

COMER has combined Gaussian modular congruence with systems theory which identifies the essential subsystems that must be kept in working order for the system as a whole to function. The other ingredient in our analysis is what economists call the Tinbergen Counting Rule. That matches the number of independent variables in proposed solutions to those that can be identified in the problem. Essentially, it is what you learned in your first-year high school algebra lessons – to solve a problem with two independent variables, you need two linear (i.e., first-degree) equations. One will only give you the value of one variable in terms of the other.

Once we grasp the basic principle of Gaussian modular congruence we have an untapped trove of unsuspected resources for policy-making. To solve linear equations we eliminate some of the variables one at a time and, after having solved for the value of the remaining ones, we complete the solution by dealing with the variables first eliminated. In a similar way we must deal with the complex problems of our crisis-ridden economy. We can plan the temporary elimination of suitable variables to set up tactical sub-systems to work our way around the pillboxes of prejudice set up to defend vested interests.

The 1980s and particularly the 1990s were a period when the world banking system was both globalized and deregulated, and to bail it out from its repeated losses ever further powers of money creation were shifted from the government to private financial institutions. In this way the public treasury took on hundreds of billions of debt to private institutions. This in turn left governments without the funds to look after essential capital investment in physical and human infrastructures. As more and more of such infrastructure programs fell into neglect, they were shifted to lower levels of government without the funding to deal with them. Essentially our sporting financial institutions had elbowed out the most needy social groups from the relief lines. The uniform answer to Non-Government Organizations who demanded attention to human and environmental needs was" Where will the Money Come From?" "The Government incurring more debt for social programs would be inflationary."

Circumventing the Pillboxes of Prejudice

To work our away around such objections, I designed what might be called a tactical subsystem. I quote from *Towards a Post-Autistic Economy – A Place for Society at the Table*, p. 165: "We take as our [initial] target the public treasury, the state of which depends on two variables – its income and expenditure. Our policy variables accordingly are also two, chosen because the broad public will agree that, *other things being equal*, these are better directed downward than upward. These two variables could be, for example, doing away or reducing the Goods and Services Tax, an unjust regressive tax that hits the most vulnerable groups in society. Before coming to power the Liberal party had agreed to do that, but has not gotten around to it. That would reduce the revenue of the fisc. To balance that a carefully calculated part of the federal debt could be brought back from the commercial banks to the central bank. Held by the Bank of Canada, the interest paid on the debt shifted would revert to the federal government as dividends since it is the sole shareholder of the BoC. The result would be a zero joint effect on the fisc. Such is Step One of our plan.

"Step Two is entirely passive. We monitor the bonus that ensues as the resulting lower interest rates and the lower taxation work their way through the economy. Obviously the tonic effect of all this on the essential infrastructural, environmental conservation, and investments in human capital by the government, will broaden the tax-base and head off the deflation that is taking over.

"Step Three. Instead of relying on an 'eventual trickling down of benefits' (when have you heard that promise last uttered?), evidence will be available for planning the next step before a year is out. It could be a further dosage of the same two countervailing policies employed in Step One, or a quite different combination." A complete commitment to the Kyoto Plan could be covered by the shift of a further amount of federal debt to the Bank of Canada from the chartered banks. Or enough grants to the provinces to finance the reduction of university fees, and adequate funding of home-care, and public schools. Or the $15 billion needed for health care according to the Romanow Report could be made available. In return for such federal funding, the provinces and municipalities would be required to observe federal standards in the projects funded in this way. This would open up a new chapter of cooperation amongst the various levels of government.

But the potential of Gaussian modular congruence for policy making does not end there.

We hear a great deal from our financial institutions about risk management. In actual practice it has not worked out too well. In part this was because too often it was based on the assumptions of the self-balancing market. Also with such cuckooland certainties, it was inevitable that the leverages and off-balance sheet temptations of Over-the-Counter Derivatives should prove irresistible. What purported to be hedges guaranteeing risk management have brought in famously huge losses and conflict-of-interest suits.

Hedging of a far safer sort against some fundamental risks is possible through a considered used of Gaussian modulus convergence.

Risk Management that Cuts Rather than Increases Risk

But first let us go back to the Gaussian formula and suggest an important extension. Note, to begin with. that whereas the modulus is expressed as an arithmetical or algebraic quantity, it has important qualitative effects as well. It deals with the mutual interaction of vectors moving from one field to another. The intensity of these interactions is quantitative; the nature of the effect, however, is qualitative. A vector coming from the market sector into the public sector and leaving a big hole in the fisc, lessens the likelihood that the government will undertake vital conservation measures. That certainly is negative qualitative content.

Keynes made no explicit use of modular congruence, but he came close to it in a celebrated epigram: "We send the Danes our cookies, and they send us theirs. Wouldn't it make more sense if we exchanged recipes." That clearly had to do with the quality of life, less traffic, less pollution – the elimination of *moduli*. Were we to analyze the order of the derivatives that increasingly drive the economy to less and less useful purpose, that would give us a sense of the needless human costs of our financial bustle.

Next point. The modulus congruence hedge we are about to propose is *not* a win-lose proposition. One or the other variables might come to perform as hoped in different degrees, but no matter what happens, but these variables can still be chosen to bring in social advantages rather than liabilities. That is an important aspect of the quantitative-qualitative mix in our chosen modulus. For what we are doing is combining analysis to different modules. That can add to its qualitative dimension.

To illustrate the point, I need only quote some passages from my *Babel's Tower – The Dynamics of Economic Breakdown*, 1977. "Subsystems Three Four and Five – the Social Lien [the layer of taxation in the price level, Social Revalorization, and the Personal Services System] especially those that call for a high portion of unrecognized human capital into their production – e.g., health, education, social services] – contribute to a price gradient [a secular price ramp]. If we were to set ourselves price stability as a priority we should be depriving society of all choice concerning the quality of life. After a certain point of economic development, it is personal services rather than commodity production that determine the quality of our existence The only way in which price could be kept stable would be through so powerfully exponential a rate of expansion of our mass production commodity sector, that its effects on price would balance the upward pressures on price generated by subsystems such as those mentioned above (p. 40). That, however, is most definitely unsustainable.

"Detaxing – thinning the layers of taxation in price – is bound to leave serious holes in the state's finances. To fill that gap a companion technique is called for – tax-bonding.

"Certain classes of entrepreneurs [and private citizens] would be given the option of subscribing a portion of their taxable income in tax-bonds, long-term government paper bearing interest substantially below that of the market. Before their maturity the price gradient would shrink the real value of such securities. Businessmen are accustomed to operating within different time horizons; nor is it always the most distant horizon that they can afford to steer by. Such tax-bonds [which would make available to them the taxes they were spared] would offer the entrepreneur important defences in his present menaced setting: in a pinch the bonds could be sold or borrowed against.

"If sold, they would, of course, be subject to a discount reflecting the difference between their interest coupons and the market rate. If borrowed against, their value as security would likewise depend on this factor. If a government found that the economy was really 'overheated' – i.e., that demand was pressing against the limits of productive capacity – it could 'cool' it by *lowering* the interest rates on tax-bonds. The idea of fighting real inflation by lowering interest rates is important rather than just picturesque. It would help break the vicious cost spiral [for interest is a cost to producers] that has shaken the private sector."

Lowering the Secular Price Gradient

Why bother with tax-bonds when the government could satisfy most or all of its needs simply by having the central bank hold its debt. There are several reasons – one of the most important is that government debt is our only legal tender with the resources of the nation behind it, and there are many purposes for which it is essential in the hands of the private sector – retirement funds, reserves of financial institutions. Moreover, the financial interplay between public and private sector is vital for the health of both. The tax-bonds making available to corporations the use of taxes that would otherwise have to be paid is a line of defence for them for which they will pay a relatively painless price in the erosion of the real-value of the bond through the price gradient. The crowning virtue of the scheme is that it would tend to attenuate that price gradient rather than contribute to it.

Finally it is a hedge in a very different sense that those constructed with financial derivatives. To the extent that it moderates the price gradient, it will have reduced "inflation" (whether it is real market inflation or structural price rise) by lowering rather than raising interest rates. To the extent that it has not performed up to expectations in that regard – i.e., the price gradient will have continued substantially as it was – it will give the government a capital gain in the shrunken real value of the bond. Interest rates could be included in the tax-immunity or not, depending upon the rest of the arrangement.

The final advantage is that by increasing the kit of policy instruments, it will contribute to the number of variables in the solutions to match those in our problem-ridden world. By managing the list of industries and private tax-payers having access to tax-bonds the government will be able to focus its policies to minimize collateral damage. At present, the use of high interest rates as our central bank's "one blunt tool" maximizes such slaughter of the innocents. The mere fact that central banks could have described their policies in those terms gives you the measure of economic theory's dark age.

Note that tax-bonding was formulated a quarter of a century ago – long before I had concerned myself with Gaussian modulus convergence. My concerns about the price gradient were ignored by the profession and the government. Logically enough, since the grand push to undo the pluralism of society and elevate the speculative sector was just beginning. Now all that high-powered control of minds and media is in a state of unlovely collapse. Surely the present need is to make up for lost time. Interest must be harnessed as a two-way affair to give policy makers some essential alternatives for policy design.

William Krehm

1. Krehm, William (2002). *Towards a Post-Autistic Economy – A Place for Society at the Table* (p. 163). COMER Publications.
2. Carl Friedrich Gauss, 1777-1855.

Reply to Two Questions from a Candidate for the Leadership of a Federal Party

QUESTION 1. The proportion of debt that COMER believes should be repatriated from the public sector.

There is no such magic number. Moreover, the very statistics are so addled by the absence of any serious distinction between government investment and current spending that any attempt to run the economy by "balancing the budget" or "reducing the national debt" can only be misleading.

Let me mention the two main sources of this confusion:

(A) Despite the recommendations of four royal commissions over four decades, it was only in 1999 that a bill introducing "accrual accountancy (also known as "capital budgeting") passed through parliament. This occurred because the Auditor General refused to give unconditional approval of the government's two

last balance sheets without it. However, nothing further has been heard of the matter. The accountancy for the change was to have been completed by mid-2002, and here we are celebrating Xmas with no further word of "capital budgeting." It should be added that the "accrual accountancy" contemplated did not include human capital – health, education, social security – in government investment.

A probable reason that "accrual accountancy" has not been heard of since, is that it explodes the notion that public investments must be privatized to get the government out of debt. And Bay St. has urgent need of juicy privatizations to help it out of its present difficulties.

(B) Identifying any rise in the price index with "inflation" – i.e., an excess of demand over supply – seriously distorts what is happening in the economy. Whereas it is true – other things being equal – that an increase of aggregate demand over supply will push up prices, you cannot flip that proposition around: a rise in price does not necessarily mean that demand has exceeded available supply. It might signal that more of society's total output has taken the form of unmarketed and unpriced public services and less of the whole is being produced in the private sector, i.e., is marketed and priced. The cost of the increased public sector's unpriced output is covered by taxation that must show up as a deeper layer in the prices of what is marketed. This I have called *structural price rise*. Confusing this with an excess of demand and attempting to suppress it with "a single blunt tool" – higher interest rates – is the source of endless mischief. It not only unhinges the finances of government, and condemns a great part of the population to marginal if any employment, but shifts power to the financial sector. That holds society to ransom through the speculative movement of prices and interest rates.

A pretty obvious example should make the point. Nobody who makes the move from a farm or a town of 5,000 to New York City can expect his cost of living to remain the same. How then can economists expect a flat price level when human kind makes just such a move. Even fifty years ago you could count on your fingers the number of cities with a population of say 5 million and more throughout the world. Today there are several such on every inhabited continent and urban concentrations of 30 million are not unusual. How could the price level not move higher – whether the necessary infrastructures to make such cities people-friendly have been put in or not?

Whether the broad electorate can grasp such matters is a moot point. But political leaders must do so, if they are to be effective. It is true that politics is to a large extent the art of compromise and consensus. But unless the leaders understand these deeper flaws in official statistics, they will lack the benchmarks for judging at what point compromise becomes surrender. The statistics on deficit, debt, and inflation must never be used without emphasizing how unreliable they are.

Hanky-panky with the Ownership of the Bank of Canada

Having said that, let us return to Leadership Candidate's Question One, "The proportion of the debt that COMER believes should be 'repatriated' from the private sector."

The Bank of Canada was founded in the depth of the Depression of the thirties (1935) for very different purposes than the use it is put to today. Moreover, its original purposes are still set out in the *Bank of Canada Act*. A logical point of departure for a return to its original purpose could be regaining the 22% of the federal debt that was held by the central bank at its highest point in the mid-seventies. The shift of a corresponding amount of federal debt held by the chartered banks today must take place to finance essential public investment – both human and physical. Some of this can take the form of transferring federal debt as it matures to the Bank of Canada which would effect at least a 95% decrease in the interest the Government would pay on such debt because of the increased dividends the government would receive as sole shareholder of the BoC. Special care would have to be taken to ensure that the government investments financed in this virtual interest-free way were really of the highest importance for the nation's welfare. Since the provision of many of these vital services have been downloaded from the federal government to the provinces, who in turn have done the same vis-a-vis the municipalities, some of the new federal financing arranged under such a shift would take the form not of new federal direct debt, but a federal guarantee of provincial and municipal borrowing from the BoC (under section 18(c) of the *Bank of Canada Act*). Such a policy would open a new dimension for constructive compromise amongst the three levels of government.

By negotiation, the federal government could agree to return to the province or municipality part of the interest paid on this debt to the BoC from the corresponding dividend to the federal government. This would be a *quid pro quo* for the said province or the municipality agreeing to observe federal standards in the project financed. The total effect would be borrowing by the junior levels of government at a fraction of market rates.

We refer you to item (A) of this memo on the bill that passed Parliament in 1999 to introduce capital budgeting in 1999 that has never been heard of since. We noted that this did not include human investment which even conservative economists in the 1960s came to recognize as the most productive of all investments – based on the rapid reconstruction of war-smashed Germany and Japan. Ted Schultz of the University of Chicago even won a Nobel prize for his work that proved that. COMER will provide you on request with complete documentation on that including our presentation to the Romanow Commission. We would suggest that in presenting your views to your party on using the Bank of Canada to finance public investment, you suggest treating the $15 billion over several years mentioned by Romanow as a possible cost of his proposals as a public investment. It is not really a debt in the conventional sense: it will cost the Fed practically no interest and the investment in health will continue being productive. It is in fact a public investment. But you may say that human capital was not included in the bill that passed. So what? Physical capital was definitely included and has apparently been relegated to the ash-can. Respectfully we would suggest that your party should stop being neutered lambs and revert to a bit of the spirit of Tommy Douglas.

Having achieved the 22% plus of the federal debt that was held by the BoC in the mid 1970s over a period of two or three years – depending on how deeply the incipient deflation bites – there would be every reason for moving cautiously to a higher degree of "repatriation."

Since political leaders are understandably concerned about the possible reaction of the broad electorate, COMER has devised a strategy for circumventing rather than colliding head on with the wall of prejudice against anything that would increase the government debt or require a hike in taxation. This can be done by choosing two measures that most people would prefer turned downward rather than upward – all else being equal – and having opposite effects on the treasury. For example, one would decrease its tax revenues; the other would lessen the interest payments it makes. *These could be applied in calculated dosages for joint zero effect on the treasury.* One such pair could be the reduction of the Goods & Services Tax – an unjust regressive tax that the Liberals had promised to do away with when in opposition – and on the other side a shift of federal debt from the chartered banks to the Bank of Canada. That would be Step One of this plan.

Step Two is purely a passive one. The effects of the lower GST and the lower interest payments in bringing down interest rates generally would be monitored as they moved throughout the economy. Both of these would spur a revival of business activity through the private sector and reduce the cost of all non-government programs to conserve the environment, to maintain and improve social services. Rather than the promises of "trickle down" that were rarely realized but simply forgotten, we would have an immediate "collateral benefit" throughout the economy instead of the present "collateral damage." That would justify a second application of such a paired dosage of tax reduction and interest rate reduction achieved by shifting a further amount of federal debt from the private banks to the BoC.

The details of this plan are to found both in my *Towards a Post-Autistic Economy – A Place for Society at the Table*, 2002, p.165. A complimentary copy of the book will be sent on request to you or to any other candidate for the leadership, or leader of any democratic party, no matter whether right or left of centre. I understand that Herbert Wiseman has made available to you a copy of the video put out by COMER Publications on Money Creation. That too is available on a complimentary basis to any candidate for the leadership of a democratic party as above.

Our Ghostly Money Supply

Question 2. With respect to money supply expansion, what is the size of the money supply expansion that COMER has recommended and what are the results of any analysis of the various effects that this would have on various processes and indicators.

Our ideas of what constitutes the "money supply" must be revised. The amazing thing about the bailout of the banks in 1991 is that not only were they freed from the need to deposit with the BoC an average 4% of the deposits they took in from the public (for decades it had been 10%) but they were even allowed virtually to dictate the terms of their further deregulation. This made it possible for the banks to acquire brokerages, engage in merchant banking, i.e., acquire interests in almost any concern, underwrite stock issues, issue credit cards, derivatives. All these activities, some of which were incompatible with banking, added to the effective money supply when they prospered, and destroyed money supply when they folded.

When the banks were bailed out under Roosevelt, they were not allowed to dictate the terms of that bailout. On the contrary they were severely confined to banking and not allowed to engage in any aspect of stock market activity. Caps were placed on what interest they could charge or pay. The opposite course was followed in 1991. From Bank of Canada statistics, COMER has compiled what this meant in the leverage that the banks could employ in their new speculative activities. In 1946 the ratio of Canadian bank assets to the cash in their possession was 11 to one. Currently it is 400 to one. But that understates the real situation. The equities owned by the banks are listed at their historic cost, not their current value – unless they own 20% or more of an issue. Many of their involvements – for example Over-the-Counter Derivatives do not even appear on their balance sheets.

The implosion of the US stock markets in the recent two years has destroyed a reported 8 trillion dollars of value – a figure within hailing distance of a full year's GDP. And the damage is just beginning to come to light as more and more corporations apply for bankruptcy protection, and deflation collapses one emerging economy after another in which Canada's banks were allowed to become involved.

Given the official leverage of our banks (assets to cash in their possession) of 400 to 1, any sizable retreat of the stock market could wipe out the entire liquidity and even the entire capital of our banks. After the 1929 Wall Street crash it took over three years before the consequences for the banking system to fully appear. Ours have still not done so. There is little doubt that as a group our banks will have already lost most of their capital. In 1991 the banks were bailed out in complete stealth. It took over a year even for COMER to track down the bill that did the job, and blow the whistle. We related it to the Bank for International Settlements *Risk-Based Capital Requirements* that declared the debt of OECD countries risk free requiring no additional capital for the banks to acquire. That and the end of the statutory reserves made it possible for the Canadian banks to take on another $60 billion of federal debt without putting up any significant money of their own and released the statutory reserves that they had to put up to support the $470-odd billion of deposits they had taken in from the public. Depending upon what the interest rates happened to be shoved up to, that represented an annual entitlement of anywhere between $5 and 8 billion dollars. That entitlement and the further deregulation of our banks – supposedly to be able to compete with the Japanese banks who in fact had already lost their capital and had stopped lending – allowed them to gamble their heads off in areas of which they had little knowledge. The contempt of our banks for the public and our political leaders was without bound. They were allowed to represent the Canadian banks as though they were just a another sports team upon whose victory amongst the international biggies our national pride depended. The importance of our banks to the economy is their ability to help provide consumers and producers with their legitimate capital needs. It is precisely those functions that our banks have turned their backs on.

Will We be Surprised by the Next Bank Bailout?

There is every indication that our banks will be back for their next bailout before long – and certainly very long before the public learns about it. When it does, as in the 1991 case, the danger is that it will be too late. Our government will have committed itself to the next bailout. The $15 billion dollars that the Romanow Commission calculates will be necessary to put our health care system in shape over several years is supposedly not there. But we may well learn that that much and more has been committed to rescue the our sporting banks once again from their gambling losses.

The only way in which that can be forestalled is for the candidates for the leadership of any democratic party to commit themselves to a Royal Commission to investigate how the banks in 1991 were both bailed out and further deregulated in hasty sequence. This is not to exact retribution for the scams of the past. It is to protect what is left to us of a future.

Certainly the banks who need it and have not lost their entire capital should be helped into liquidity when the need for that arises. But not by equipping them for international gambles as in the Enron partnerships, and Argentinian and Venezuelan banking. As in the US in 1935, the banks will have to be brought back to banking. If they prefer running casinos, they need only surrender their bank charter and apply for a casino charter, or a brokerage licence.

Where banks have lost their entire capital, it is not the business of the government to make them whole again. Of their own doing, those banks have put themselves out of business. It will be enough for the government to make sure that depositors will be able to count on their deposit insurance being effective.

When the Bank of Canada in 1938 was nationalized 12,000 shareholders were paid a handsome profit on their BoC shares that they had held only during three depression-ridden years. Now for some years we have been told that the Bank of Canada is independent of the government of Canada. But that disregards the ownership rights of Canadians as a nation. The purpose of our central bank is clearly established in the *Bank of Canada Act*, that declares (in the Preamble) its purpose is: "to mitigate by its influence fluctuations in the general level of production, trade, prices and employment, so far as may be possible within the scope of monetary action." Why then did a previous Governor of the BoC apologize to the House of Commons Finance Committee for having allowed the word "deflation" to slip out of his mouth in predicting that a wave of deflation would overwhelm the world within two years – a dead-on prediction? Governor Gordon Thiessen declared that he would probably regret using the word "deflation" for the rest of his life. Does that not contradict the above-quoted statement of purpose in the *Bank of Canada Act* preamble?

In Article 14 the *Bank of Canada Act* sets forth that in the event of a difference of opinion between the Minister of Finance and the Bank concerning the monetary policy to be followed, the Minister may give the Governor a written directive concerning monetary policy in specific terms and applicable for a specific period, and the Bank shall comply with that directive.

Article 17 provides that the capital of the Bank shall be divided into one hundred thousand shares of the par value of fifty dollars each which shall be issued to the Minister of Finance to be held by the Minister on behalf of Her Majesty in right of Canada.

Article 18(c) states that the Bank may buy and sell securities issued or guaranteed by Canada or any province:

"That then establishes fully the ownership and the control of the BoC by the Government of Canada, its ability to determine the policy to be followed, it purposes to mitigate not only inflation but any fluctuation in the general level of production, trade, prices and employment."

There is on record the terms of the generous buy-out of the private shareholders of the BoC by the Government, i.e., by the taxpayers of Canada when money was as scarce as hens' teeth.

By whose authority then was the Act contravened to declare the "independence" of the BoC from its shareholder?

William Krehm

The Elusive Openness of Governor Dodge

THERE IS A SENSE of unreality on the earth and in the heavens. Our central bankers are weighing whether we are suffering from too much deflation or inflation. President Bush is deciding whether to bomb the daylights out of which evil empire first and why not at the same time, since it would make them virtuous all the faster? But meanwhile there is disturbing evidence that at least one of the brain lobes of those in command might be coming down with mad cow disease, genetically modified by the Americans to make the deregulated market work.

Are we exaggerating? Just listen to this item from *Bloomberg News* reproduced by *The Globe and Mail* (27/12, "Morgan defends Enron trades"): J.P. Morgan & Co. regarded the financial mechanics of its secret energy trades with Enron Cop. and offshore company Mahonia as 'innovative' and 'proprietary,' a bank official testified yesterday.

"The deals are at the heart of a suit by the second-largest US bank against 11 insurers that have refused to pay it $1 billion in surety bonds that guaranteed the trades against default by now bankrupt Enron. The insurers, including Chubb Corp. and CNA Financial Corp, have argued that they don't have to pay because the bank deceived them about the deals, which they regard as disguised loans.

"'We considered them innovative transactions,' Richard Walker, a J.P. Morgan executive, said of the deals. He served as the bank's primary account manager for Enron, which filed the second-largest US bankruptcy a year ago. 'We felt they were a proprietary structure meeting the client's needs. It was an alternative to other forms of financing.'

"The bank was so proud of its proprietary financial product that Mr. Walker ordered commemorative pens to celebrate passing the $1 billion mark in the prepaid energy trades. He sent the pens to at least seven Enron officials, including a former chief financial officer, who was indicted on fraud charges in October."

Remember when banks in their fake Greek temples stood watch over business morality, scrutinizing their mom-and-pop clients for "character, character, character?"

From that brief media item let us carry away the genome of the new morality: "innovative and proprietary."

And in its light we will peruse the lead article of the same *Globe and Mail's* "Report on Business" (January 2003, "Who is David Dodge?" by Konrad Yakabushi), on the Governor of the Bank of Canada. The article loses no time in accepting on faith the badge that the Governor has chosen to pin on himself: "That Dodge is by far the most public of the seven governors who have headed the BoC since its creation in 1934 maybe

because he is also the only one since the first governor Graham Towers to come from outside the bank." In fact John Crow, the most unpopular of all those governors was hired from the IMF where he had developed an imperial style pushing around Latin American governments. This is an indication of the ignorance of our economic history that has become almost a requirement for a journalist aspiring to a career in the financial media.

Yakabushi goes on in this vein, "[Dodge] is transforming the institution – secretive, stuffy and doctrinaire, the financial-sector equivalent to Freemasonry – into a dynamic and increasingly open one. He is the first governor to grant an in-depth one-to-one interview – to Report on Business – scrubbing an unwritten central-bank rule."

That may settle the measure of the Governor's "openness" in terms of Yakabushi's professional needs. As far as openness to the public, you would have to ask 'open about what'? For example, where is there in all the near incoherent ramble of Yakabushi the slightest suggestion that policy alternatives to the use of interest rates even exist, let alone played a very significant role in our history? "Openness" as used by Dodge, with the help of analysts like Yakabushi, amounts to little more than an artless peddling of the dogma of the financial group that has put him in a position of power.

Here there is a genuinely "proprietary" and "innovative" use of the term "openness." But as for awarding him the palm for "openness" on the available options open to the Bank of Canada, just consider the following answers of the first Governor of the Bank to questions from the Commons Subcommittee on Banking and Commerce in 1939:

Q. "But there is no question that banks create the medium of exchange?"

A. "That is right – that is banking business just as a steel plant makes steel" (p. 287).

Q. "95% of all business is being done with what we call the exchange of bank deposits – that is simply bookkeeping entries of banks deposits – that is simply bookkeeping entries in banks against which people write cheques?"

A. "That is a fair statement" (p. 223).

On the availability of money to pull a country out of depression: Mr. Towers: "The real cost of government expenditure to the country as a whole is the amount of labour and equipment required to carry out the various projects. When the question is asked is whether we can finance a certain government expenditure, the fundamental problem is whether we can afford to devote a certain amount of our productive resources to the projects in question. How the government can obtain the money that will give it title to the use of the labour and equipment may present considerable technical difficulties, but it is not the fundamental problem."

What we have here, is not the sort of "openness" that Governor Dodge shares about his mind-set in one-to-one interviews with writers who take dictation from the BoC. Instead Governor Towers set forth the basic facts of the problems of the economy and the option that are available to deal with them. Between the two uses of the word there is a world of difference.

And Dodge's background is of a single piece with his brand of "openness."

"Well before he took over the helm at the BoC, Dodge's thinking was coveted in Ottawa. He piloted the Mulroney government's controversial introduction of the GST (Goods and Services Tax). By the time he became Paul Martin's deputy and architect of Ottawa's deficit reduction strategy, Dodge was easily the most powerful and respected bureaucrat in the capital. Which is why, as central bank governor, he can wade into policy debates – subtly touting Canada-US integration, admonishing politicians to keep the faith of fiscal restraint – that go well beyond the realm of monetary policy. No previous governor dared so much."

Besides, controverting the charter of the Bank (see Preamble, and articles 14, 17 and 18) in asserting the "independence" of the central bank from the government, he imposes the dependence of the government on the Bank of Canada and through it on the unelected Bank for International Settlements. It was in this way that the ending of the statutory reserves was imposed in utter stealth under the governorship of John Crow in 1991. To the tune of an entitlement of anywhere from $5 to $8 billion a year, the February 1992 budget presented the bill for that reverse bank heist. It was Dodge's main legacy as Deputy Minister. For starters, it announced spending cuts of $25 billion over three years, a reduction in transfers to the provinces of $7 billion and the elimination of 45,000 civil service jobs.

Notably, the figures of the federal spending reductions tally broadly with COMER's independent estimate of the average annual entitlement resulting from the end of reserves – both the interest on our extra $60 billion of federal debt the chartered banks took on without putting up either their own cash or capital, plus the interest on the reserves of some 4% on $470 billion of pre-existent deposits that were released.

Dodge provided the seamless bridging from the Trudeau regime to Mulroney, responding to US pressures en route. As chief bureaucrat in the Department of Employment and Immigration in 1982 "he warned that 250,000 jobs lost in the 1980-81 recession – [the peak of the high-interest rate insanity of the BoC] – were gone forever and criticized the government's job-creation schemes." It was a practical way of endorsing "the natural rate of employment" then coming into vogue. "Privately no one questioned Dodge's analysis." For Dodge and his interviewer there was simply no room for doubt on such matters. Such is the background of the "new openness."

And in 1984 Trudeau [had] promoted him to assistant deputy minister of fiscal policy in the Finance Department. The Liberals' defeat that year meant Dodge's money-saving ideas, including to stop indexing baby-bonuses and old-age pensions to inflation, were left to Brian Mulroney's Tories to implement. Seniors protested on Parliament Hill over the partial deindexation of their benefits, forcing Finance Minister Wilson to retreat.

"Dodge, though, was unscathed. He was a man with a mission." Wilson promoted him in 1986 to head the department's tax policy branch, putting him in charge of a massive overhaul of the federal income- and sales-tax systems. That reform poisoned public sentiment towards the Tories. Frustrated by opposition attempts to stall the GST, Dodge strode into the political fray telling MPs the government intended to push through the tax 'in military fashion.' He was roundly criticized for this glaring breach of civil-service etiquette.

Turning Out the Light at the Tunnel's End

"When Dodge moved into the deputy minister's office, he hung a plaque on his door. It read: 'Due to current financial constraints, the light at the end of the tunnel will remain off until further notice.' It set the tone for his five years in the post – a period of deep, deep budget cuts."

Our banks had been bailed out with an entitlement equivalent to a permanent bond of around one third of the outstanding federal debt at the time. Yet incredibly, when it came to the needs of widows and orphans, the banks were soon being deregulated further to play at every conceivable speculative game. The banks evidently were neither widowed nor orphaned. Soon their massive losses in these adventures at home and abroad began to come to light. Not all of them brought their reputations out of that trial unsullied.

"One of Dodge's earliest policy moves was to extend a formal agreement between the bank and the Finance Department on inflation targets. Inflation had been the bank's preoccupation since John Crow persuaded the government to formalize the targets in 1991. Crow had been squeezed out of the job in 1993 when he pushed for lower targets" – i.e., closer to the "zero inflation" goal that the Bank for International Settlements had advanced. Of course, a flat price index at a time when rapid urbanization was underway would have really represented deep deflation. Nobody moves from the farm to New York City, expecting his living costs to stay the same. How then could the Dodges of the world expect a flat price level when humanity is making just such a move? And many other changes in our society increase the proportion of unmarketed public services with the same effect.

Indeed, when the GST was first imposed on a protesting population, the Bank of Canada actually proceeded to raise interest rates, because the GST had added to the bottom price figure on invoices. Only wide protest forced it to retreat – at least part time – from that gaffe. But the inevitable conclusion of that retreat by the BoC escaped economists – all taxes because they are payments for public services that are *not* sold must show up in the price level because they are all payments for public services that otherwise would be judged cost-free.

When Statistics Canada showed that higher price level had been due not to more government spending on projects as a proportion of the GDP, but to higher interest rates, the response of the government was to slash StatCan's budget. No weak open-mindedness in the official stand on such matters! At the time Dodge was already a power to reckon with behind the scenes.

Finance Minister Paul Martin appointed Gordon Thiessen as

Crow's successor as central bank governor with a stated goal of keeping inflation between 1% and 3%. More important, Dodge explicitly stated that he would aim for the midpoint of the target range, 2%. Says Dodge, 'at the last renewal in 2001, we actually had a lot more evidence to operate on than we had when we went into the game in 1991. Our research guys beat their heads against the wall and we couldn't find any compelling argument that 2.5% or 1.5% was any better than 2%.' But that is not what the BIS had said – it had argued that the slightest increase of inflation would end up reproducing the hyperinflation of Germany in 1923, when a war had been lost, and the French army had moved into its industrial heartland to collect reparations, precipitating a general strike from right to left, and practical civil war. But never ever does the BoC or the BIS from which it takes its instructions recognize a major error. It merely soldiers on to the next disaster. What the media mistakes for Governor Dodge's open-mindedness is in fact just open-mouthedness.

After September 11, 2001, Dodge did slash interest rates repeatedly, the lowest level in 40 years. But they were still higher than those of the US. The Twin Towers catastrophe created a drastic requirement for getting the BoC to abandon its 'one blunt tool' of high interest rates.

The interest cuts achieved their main objective: keeping Canada's economy above water. But investors dropped the Canadian dollar in droves, saddling the Chrétien government with a full-blown currency crisis. Martin and Dodge scrambled to New York in January to assure Wall St. about the strength of the Canadian economy. Some bank watchers see Dodge's subsequent increase of the key rate to 2.75% and recent talk of further tightening as an attempt to put a floor under the dollar, but subsequent reductions by the US Federal Reserve Board and tightening by Dodge have increased the differential in favour of Canada to 150 basic points. The real reason for the increase is to support the currency. However, it is deflation that most humbler Canadians are worrying about.

William Krehm

Rowbotham on Money Creation

E LSEWHERE in this issue we reproduce a letter from a reader questioning whether the near-money created by a loan is destroyed when the loan is repaid or somehow lives on. I use the expression "near-money" because legal tender earns no interest by its sheer existence. That is what makes it fungible – one sample exactly like the other – and not subject to change with every quiver of interest rates, our central bank's "sole blunt tool." The view asserting its survival on the repayment of a loan has somehow been cropping up with increasing frequency. One of our correspondents has reminded us that it was actually advanced by Michael Rowbotham in his eloquent and in many respects excellent *Grip of Death* (1998). I remembered having expressed some fundamental differences with Michael's views

on money at the Bromsgrove Conference that we both attended in 2000, but the subject of our disagreement had escaped my mind. I owe it to a reading of David Boyle's charming and wide-roaming anthology *The Money Changers, Currency Reform from Aristotle to e-Cash* (2002) to have had my memory refreshed on the matter. Rowbotham is important enough to merit a careful consideration of any view of his.

Let us begin by his statement disputing that a debt paid off to a bank destroys the money created to make it, though, of course, not the interest collected on it (pages 28-29 of his *The Grip of Death*, 1998):

"It was argued that when someone paid money into their overdrawn account, the debt and that amount of money were set against each other and cancelled each other out. This idea grew up in the early part of this century, and was enshrined in the infamous admission by the Rt. Hon. Reginald McKenna, one time Chancellor of the Exchequer and former chairman of the Midland Bank, who stated: "'I am afraid that the ordinary citizen would not like to be told that the banks, or the Bank of England, can create or destroy money. The amount of money in existence varies only with the action of the banks in increasing and decreasing deposits and bank purchases. Every loan, overdraft or bank purchase creates a deposit and every repayment of a loan, overdraft or bank sale destroys a deposit.'

"According to this argument, banks were able to claim that, yes they did create money, but not for themselves. This bank credit was, in principle, temporary. Bank credit only lasted for the duration of the loan, and upon repayment was cancelled out of existence."

Here Rowbotham shifts the subject under discussion. It was not for whom the money was created, but whether the money created by a specific loan perdures or disappears when that loan is repaid. That shift of subject is as relevant as asking whether a baking conglomerate bakes its bread for its customers or for itself.

"But this is not what actually happens at all! As any bank manager will confirm, when money is repaid in an overdrawn account, the bank cancels the debt, but the money is not cancelled or destroyed. The money is regarded as being every bit as real as a deposit: it is regarded by the bank as the repayment of money they have lent. And that money is held and accounted as an asset of the bank.

"The fact that upon repayment, money that they have created is not destroyed, but is accounted an asset of the bank, proves beyond dispute that when banks create money and issue it as a debt they ultimately account that money their own."

The good Lord knows that our deregulated banks have employed every accounting trick that their accountants could invent, but have still not dared to count discharged debts as assets.

"The only factor which disguises their indisputable ownership of the money they create is that this returning money is usually rapidly reloaned."

Should he not rather be talking about their charter that allows them to create money by rapidly lending again rather than powers of "recreating" money already lent? Banks can and do create and lend money for their own and their preferred clients' needs, but not by grace of having previously lent out the same money. The fact that lending during a boom is on a wildly expanding scale implies that a lot of it was *not* previously lent and repaid. And once that is conceded, what remains of the argument that money is not destroyed when a debt to a bank is repaid?

Rowbotham's difficulty arises from the tempting assumption that if something is true, more of it must be better and more truthful. His missing tool is double entry-bookkeeping that would show an asset-and-liability pair created on the books of both lender and borrow when the loan is made, and reversed when it is repaid. You might even say that double-entry bookkeeping was essentially an anticipation of the Tinbergen Test – with each recording of the accountancy showing a double-pronged grasp of the double-pronged transaction.

The Importance of the Vestigial Reserves Retained by the UK and US

In the course of this minor self-indulgence, Michael has not only disparaged the memory of a remarkably open-minded banker (McKenna was a close ally of Keynes); he loses sight of the importance of some very residual surviving institutional details in his readiness to emphasize the sheer explosion of unstructured debt. To his merit he does distinguish between the10% legal tender reserve requirement that used to exist (the statutory reserves) and the capital reserve (BIS *Risk-Based Capital Requirements*) that have replaced it. Capital is raised or earned as cash but is not allowed to stay in that form for long since cash earns no interest. Capital, indeed, can be in the form of securities booked at their historic rather than market values. Few economists or analysts make that distinction. COMER in Canada tracks it – from 1946 when the ratio was 11:1 it has grown to 400:1, because the statutory reserves have been wholly abolished and a little more than 2% of the banks deposits are held in cash for strictly operational needs – end-of-day net cheque clearances and to meet the public's demand for cash. Deregulation of the banks has allowed them to use their powers of money creation for speculative plays of their own or their clients. That is what gave our table its unprecedented leverage. The reserve/asset requirement in the United States has been preserved at 3% average, with it would seem about one third of that not required for such operational purposes. In Britain the proportion of deposits is reported to be about 0.5% which if anything is barely enough to meet such operational needs. Yet Britain and the US are still in a better position than Canada and New Zealand, where in an emergency special Acts of Parliament would be necessary to bring back the statutory reserves.

The symbolic value that the UK's circa 0.5% reserves that still appear to exist could be enhanced by explaining what they are a sorry vestige of. The time has come to seriously begin working out the strategy for meeting the next banking crisis. Otherwise we shall most certainly once more be surprised to learn that the banks have been rescued again at the expense of our neediest citizens.

William Krehm

Mail Box

TO THE EDITOR:

One of my current interests is to understand money creation, i.e., private bank created debt-money and government created non-debt money. I am having trouble understanding a very crucial point in money creation by banks. To quote from your book page 175: "John Smithin argues convincingly for the Post-Keynesian position that money is borrowed by the entrepreneur when he starts production and is created by the bank that lends it. Upon the completion and sale of the good produced, if all goes well, "the loan is repaid and the money created by it is destroyed, with the exception of the profit." My logic indicates to me that when the bank loan is repaid, the bank, through the 'magic of money creation,' receives the full principal plus interest in real "non-debt money. The paper credit entry in the loanee's bank account becomes real non-debt money when repaid to the bank. More significantly however, when the bank spends this principal and interest of non-debt money, the money supply is permanently increased by this amount! My logic indicates that the debt-money created by the bank is not destroyed.

Gerry Masuma

Dear Gerry Masuma,

You write: "When the bank loan is repaid, the bank…receives the full principal plus interest in real non-debt money. The paper credit entry in the loanee's bank account becomes real non-debt money, the money supply is permanently increased by this amount!" Double-entry bookkeeping will help you over this bump. All debt in any country – unless specified to be in a foreign currency – is in the legal tender of the land. and hence a claim on real money, which happens to be central government debt. When the bank makes a loan to a client it puts a double entry into its books: (1) an asset in the form of the debt to it of the client; (2) a liability in the form of the deposit created in the client's account. The latter is very real since when the client writes a cheque on that deposit created the bank, the recipient of the cheque can deposit it in another bank, which will clear it. When that happens the lending bank will have to come up with legal tender to the amount of the cheque. When the loan is paid back to the bank it extinguishes both the loan asset on its books and its deposit liability in the client's account. However, the interest it has received from the borrower stays with it and stays created. The borrower will have to borrow it elsewhere or earn the wherewithall to extinguish it. Once you bring double-entry bookkeeping into the picture, there is no ambiguity.

Bill Krehm, Editor

A Memorable Critique of the Ailing Banking System

W E ALL OF US these days find more to criticize in what comes out of the United States than we would wish. But let us never lose sight that historically the United States has itself often generated the antitoxins to its own particular venoms. It should never be forgotten that some of the most fundamental criticism of the monetary policy at the core of the so-called Washington Consensus is of American origin. And no mean part of it, moreover, has been bred within the elite federal bureaucracy itself.

Jane D'Arista is director of programs at the Financial Markets Center, where she conducts education seminars and authors *Capital Flows Monitor*, a quarterly analysis of international financial developments, a quarterly commentary on the Federal Reserve's main compilation of domestic financial statistics. Previously, she served as an international economist at the Congressional Budget Office, and as a staff member of the House Banking Subcommittee on Telecommunications and Finance of the House Energy and Commerce Committee."

The Financial Market Center leaves one with the impression that it keeps far closer track of what goes on within the Fed than the Fed's own high brass. Her latest study: "Rebuilding the Transmission System for Monetary Policy, November 2002," could hardly be more timely. It traces the crumbling of the Fed's mighty apparatus of power, undermined by its own eagerness to serve the ideology in the saddle – to the point where, quite literally, no one is left minding the store.

"Open market operations – first used in the 1920s and formally acknowledged as a policy tool by the *Banking Act* of 1933 – have for many years remained the primary means for changing the price and supply of money and credit…But while the tools themselves remain in place, the institutional context in which they are employed has changed dramatically. These changes include a relative decline in the banking sector's role in credit creation, reductions in the level of required reserves and the ascendancy of market forces – particularly unrestricted international capital flows – in determining the pace of credit expansion in a world of increased financial integration.

"This paper assesses the impacts of these far-reaching changes on the process of monetary implementation. It argues that the failure to modernize aging policy tools has deeply damaged the Fed's ability to influence credit expansion…. Unrestricted credit expansion, in turn, fueled unsupportable debt levels for households, businesses and financial institutions. And unchecked credit growth helped inflate asset-market bubbles. Moreover, weakened policy tools now hamper the Fed's ability to implement effective countercyclical policies in the event of a significant downturn.

"The paper also contends that this underlying problem can be remedied by introducing a new system of reserve management that assesses reserves against assets rather than deposits. This new approach would enhance monetary control by applying reserve requirements to all segments of the financial sector."

Canada's case, where the statutory reserves against bank deposits were not just slashed and neutered by "switch accounts" and other such devices used in the US, but abolished altogether, is in this respect more drastic. *ER* readers may remember that with the abolition of denominator in the old multiplier banking statistic (the ratio of deposits held by the banks to their cash holdings), we started publishing the "Indicator," the total assets of our deregulated banks to the legal tender they held for purely operational purposes. The alternative would be a zero denominator for the multiplier that would have given the ratio a meaningless infinity figure – i.e., the statistical system would have broken down in theory as it has largely done in practice.

"Over the past quarter-century, the US financial system has undergone a transformation, as household savings shifted from banks to pension funds and other institutional investment pools. Between 1981 and year end 2001, the assets of all depository institutions plummeted from nearly half of total financial-sector assets to 24%. Meanwhile, spurred in part by the funding requirements of the *Employee Retirement Income Security Act* (ERISA) of 1974, the assets of pension funds and mutual funds soared from 23% to 38% of financial sector assets. The shift in individual savings from banks to pension and mutual funds also produced a symmetrical increase in borrowing through capital markets, since securities constitute the primary assets held by institutional investors. As investors increased their demand for credit market instruments, corporations borrowed less from banks and issued substantially more bonds and commercial paper."

"Slicing and Dicing" — A Dubious Efficiency

"Credit flows to individuals also moved into the capital markets as government-sponsored enterprises (GSEs) such as Fannie Mae and Freddie Mac and federally related mortgage pools securitized more mortgages and asset-backed securities. (ABS) issuers used securitization techniques to fund car loans and other consumer receivables. Between 1991 and 2001, the liabilities of GSEs and mortgage pools – used mostly to finance single-family housing – rose by \$3.6 trillion to \$5.1 trillion. During the same period, assets of ABS issuers jumped 530%, soaring to \$2.1 trillion." ["Securitization" is the process of "slicing and dicing" huge blocks of individual loans and selling them to other institutions. The organizing bank takes an up-front profit but often leaves the debt unmonitored – no one is left "minding the store." On the surface it seems more efficient.]

"Asset management has become the dominant function in US financial markets and trading has become the principal activity. Bank lending remains important, particularly to small business borrowers that lack access to capital markets. But banks, too, manage mutual funds and offer asset-management services through their trust departments. And since passage of the 1999 *Gramm-Leach-Bliley Act*, larger banks have expanded their securities, asset-management and insurance operations through financial holdings companies. Since the 1970s [too] these institutions have been the dominant foreign-exchange market-makers. And more recently, they have developed a highly profitable niche – supported by their special relationship with the lender-of-the-last-resort – providing financial insurance as dealers in derivatives and sellers of committed lines of credit to back issues of commercial paper and other securities.

"The size and importance of over-the-counter foreign exchange and derivatives markets and the dominant role of large US banks in these markets ensure that the Federal Reserve will intervene to support the banks' derivative positions and financial guarantees. When the bond and derivative markets seized up and the dollar fell 17% against the yen during the last quarter of 1998, the Fed fulfilled its own [off-balance-sheet] guarantee of the guarantors' role.

"Policymakers have long recognized the influence of these institutional changes on the conduct of monetary policy. In 1993, for example, Fed Chairman Alan Greenspan told the Kansas's City Fed's Jackson Hole Conference, 'the fairly direct effect that open market operations once had on the credit flows provided for businesses and home construction is largely dissipated' due to the diminished role of banks, the increase in savings channeled through institutional investors and the growth of securitization…. The Fed can still affect short-term interest rates, and thus have an impact on the cost of borrowing from banks, from other intermediaries, and directly, in the capital markets. [But] this effect may be more indirect, take longer, and require larger movements in rates for a given effect on output.' [Indeed], during the 1990s, the Fed kept real interest rates higher in a non-inflationary environment but its policy failed to moderate the rapid rise in stock prices, credit or GDP in the final years of the decade. In 2001, the central bank reversed course and undertook an aggressive easing campaign. Yet more than a year later, this effort had still not produced the intended impact on output.

Dismantling Quantity Controls

"At the same time…lawmakers and regulators were dismantling the quantity controls that once constituted a key feature of financial systems in the US and other countries. These [included] interest rates ceilings on deposits, international capital controls, liquidity and reserve requirements and direct limits on credit expansion. Historically, these 'macro-prudential' policy tools have contributed to financial stability by systematically restraining credit expansion and promoting the soundness of individual institutions. However, limiting the credit they can extend to customers also restricts the opportunities of financial firms for profit. During the 1970s and 1980s, offshore banking activity grew explosively as US depository institutions sought the higher returns available in external markets lacking reserve requirements and other restraints on lending. The rise of the unregulated Eurodollar market gave the Fed and other central banks a powerful incentive to relax or remove quantity controls to moderate the shift in deposits and loans from domestic to external markets.

"After experimenting with direct limits on bank lending in an effort to manage capital outflows in the 1960s, the US abolished capital controls in 1974. Six years later, the *Monetary Control Act* ended Regulation Q interest rate ceilings on depository institution accounts.

"Despite moving decisively in the direction of deregulation, the US has not eliminated reserve requirements – the primary quantity control used by the Federal Reserve and the tool most critical to implementing monetary policy. However, reserve requirements have been seriously weakened. In response to international competitive pressures on US banks during the late 1980s, the Fed supported a zeroing-out of reserve requirements on time deposits to make the cost of domestic CDs comparable to Eurodollar sources of funds. The central bank also lowered reserve requirements on demand deposits from 12% to 10%, as of 1992."

The foregoing paragraph is of special interest to Canadians. The American banking system may have had no direct interest in strengthening Canada's large banks to compete with them at home and abroad. However, the end of the restraint on their credit creation helped qualify them as ideal fall-guys on whom the largest US banks could unload some of their more questionable securitized paper. Above all, there was a strong, ideological interest in imposing unrestricted capital movements throughout the world. Through the Bank for International Settlements and the IMF the Fed leaned heavily on the Bank of Canada and New Zealand, whose monetary and social security arrangement were a living refutation of the new gospel of financial deregulation. New Zealand had run into serious foreign exchange problems and was at the mercy of the IMF. Canada was not. Here it was essentially the servility of the Mulroney government that brought us the free trade arrangement with the US. Canadians today are thus at a disadvantage with respect to the US, when it comes to designing a monetary system that could best serve our interests. The D'Arista document should accordingly be obligatory reading not only for our federal, provincial and municipal authorities, but for those of our Non-Government-Organizations that resist even recognizing the way in which our banks' statutory reserves were done away with in stealth. That, however, more than any other factor, led to the wholesale slashing of our social programs.

"Simultaneously, the Fed played a key role in negotiating the Basle Accord, which set capital adequacy standards for all multinational banks in the G-10 countries. By establishing these standards at levels previously applied to US banks, the Basle agreement eliminated a key advantage enjoyed by non-US depository institutions. Moreover, the Basle standards represented the kind of prudential requirement acceptable to liberalization proponents, since they ensure that market forces – i.e., the providers (or withholders) of capital – determine the amount of loans banks can extend."

Ensuring that Depressions will be Deeper

"Over time, the Basle capital standards tended to displace rather than complement the role of reserve requirements. And this displacement created problems for monetary control." COMER for almost a decade has emphasized this displacement of statutory reserves, plus the detail that in Canada and the US the capital monitored is not always really there – securities are recorded at their historic rather than their market value.

"And this displacement created problems of monetary control. Since markets inevitably supply more capital during a boom and less during a downturn, capital requirements tend to impose a pro-cyclical bias on bank lending.... Direct limits on lending remained a primary monetary tool for the UK and other European economies into the 1970s. European countries and Japan also extensively used regulations that required banks to match the maturity of assets and liabilities. Only by the end of the 1980s did all the EU nations undertake capital account liberalization to fulfill conditions of monetary union."

This in fact is no small detail in the inability of the EU to climb out of its deepening economic rut.

"As reserve requirements continued to weaken, reserve balances with the Fed fell from peak levels of $35-40 billion in 1986-1989 to $7 billion by 8/02 In large measure this steady decline mirrors the fact that the Fed has been applying its lowered reserve requirements to a proportionately dwindling universe of liabilities.

"During the past half-century, depository institutions' share of financial sector liabilities declined in tandem with their share of assets. While financial sector liabilities expanded by more than 150% between 1991 and 1001, checkable deposits increased by a comparatively paltry 37% – with virtually all the growth occurring at savings institutions and credit unions (commercial banks' checkable deposits grew by less than one percent over this period).

"Among other things, these trends reflect banks' growing proclivity to sweep customers' deposits from transaction accounts into time and money market accounts that are not subject to reserve requirements. [This is a daily process of moving such balances from checking accounts that require reserves to non-checking accounts that don't. It takes place at the end of business hours each working day, and back again the next morning at opening hour.] From 01/1994 to 7/02, sweep accounts rose from $5 billion to $501 billion. Like the movement to capital requirements, these techniques increase the financial system's procyclical bias, providing greater access to funds at lower cost in a boom and less access at higher cost in a downturn. They undermine the Fed's capacity to implement anticyclical initiatives." And that had been a prominent goal when the system was founded in 1913 and reformed almost beyond recognition in the mid-1930s.

"As banks' reserve balances shrink, the Fed has tried to compensate by altering some of its operating procedures. Since it began announcing its target federal funds rate in 1994, the Fed has increasingly relied on the announcement – as opposed to actual open market operations – to implement policy decisions. In operating 'open mouth operations,' the central bank essentially waits for market participants to adjust to the new rate level, based on their belief that the Fed can enforce the rate.

"Sweep accounts, repurchase agreements and securitization have expanded the role of non-reservable liabilities in credit creation and thus weakened the ability of reserve requirements to restrain bank credit growth. At the same time, non-bank financial firms have become much more prominent sources of domestic credit. [As a result] debt levels and debt burdens have grown explosively and crimped the central bank's influence over output."

The US Debt Bubble

"At year end 1971, outstanding US credit market debt totaled $1.8 trillion, equaling 155% of GDP. By 2001, outstanding domestic debt had climbed 16-fold to $29.5 trillion and reached 289% of GDP. The dangers inherent in those developments may be heightened by changes in their composition. During the 1980s, the debt of all US nonfinancial sectors surged from 139% of GDP to 191%. Over the next decade, these sectors' aggregate borrowing remained at virtually the same level relative to GDP, but the burden of debt dramatically shifted from the federal government to household and non-financial corporations. During the past 30 years, household debt soared from 45% to 76% of GDP while nonfinancial corporate debt d from 35% to 49%.

"As debt loads increased, their constraints became more apparent. At year end 2001, outstanding household debt ($7.7 trillion) equaled 104% of disposable income, up from 87% in 1990. And debt as a share of nonfinancial corporations' net worth stood at 59%, up from 40% in 1990.

"Meanwhile, the financial sector itself experienced extraordinary increases in borrowing that reflected the dramatic shifts in its products, practices, and structure. From 1990 through to year-end 2001, financial institutions' debt rose by $6.8 trillion to $9.4 trillion. Overall, the financial sector's share of total annual borrowing jumped from about 20% in 980 to about 50% at the end of the 1990s. In other words, at the height of the 1990 expansion and during the following downturn, financial firms routinely borrowed more than their domestic customers.

"It seems clear that this unrestrained credit boom played a crucial part in financing the US stock market bubble of the late 1990s. Growing volumes of margin debt and home equity credit enabled households to bid up equity prices to unprecedented levels. In addition, executives and other employees borrowed heavily (often from their companies) to exercise stock options – a practice that also put upward pressure on share prices. At the same time, debt-financed stock buybacks by corporations substantially reduced the supply – and thereby propped up the price – of their shares.

"In addition, the unprecedented scale of financial-sector leverage carries troubling implications. Widespread borrowing among financial institutions exacerbates the possibility of problems in a few of those firms spreading to many others through their web of debt and derivative obligations.

"For the economy merely to move forward, household and business borrowers must set aside large portions of their income just to service debt. And the financial sector must continue to raise the mountain of funding needed solely to refinance its own and its customers' existing borrowing.

"During the past decade, the foreign sector became a large net supplier of credit to US borrowers. As net US obligations to foreigners swelled during the course of the decade, the gap between US ownership of foreign assets and foreign ownership of US assets rose from -$165 billion, or -3% of GDP in 1990 to -$2.3 trillion, or -23% of GDP at year end 2001.

"Foreign lenders offered particularly strong support for the corporate bond market, becoming its dominant buyers during the second half of the 1990s. By year end 2001 they owned 24% of outstanding corporate bonds, up from 13% in 1990.

"Foreign investors also own $1 trillion (about one third) of outstanding Treasury securities and, as the supply of new Treasury debt dwindled in the late 1990s, they ramped up their purchases of [government] agency securities.

Borrowing Daisy-chains

"Foreign purchases of US credit market instruments played a prominent, albeit indirect, role in pumping up the equity bubble of the late 1990s. More than any other class of investors, foreign buyers purchased corporate bond issues supporting the stock buybacks that helped prop up unsustainable equity prices. To a substantial degree, these huge inflows of foreign funds reflected monetary policy decisions by the Fed – though not always in ways the central bank had intended. In February 1994, for example, the central bank began a series of interest rate hikes to preempt inflation and prevent the economy from overheating. Rising rates [however] helped attract inflows from foreign investors, encouraged US investors to shift back into domestic assets, fueled domestic credit growth and interrupted what had been a consistent outflow of funds to Mexico (thereby precipitating the December 1994 peso crisis).

"Over the rest of the decade, the Fed maintained interest-rate differentials between US and other G7 countries that favored dollar investments. As the US current account deficit widened and inflows of foreign savings soared, domestic credit expansion blossomed into a full-fledged boom. While the strong dollar restrained inflation (aided by recurring financial crises), it did so at the expense of manufacturing and other export sectors while shifting a larger share of credit flows to household and to corporations financing equity buybacks. And at the peak of the 1990s expansion, the strong dollar-soaring inflows-expanding credit-strong consumption daisy-chain exerted an increasingly powerful pull on asset prices.

"However, should US demand falter and import growth decline, new foreign investment in US financial assets will diminish as the investors' export income recedes. And a reduction in inflows will strain the ability of households and businesses to refinance extremely high levels of debt, thereby disrupting economic activity. In addition, a shock to the US economy or a substantial loss of confidence could precipitate a dollar crisis. Should that occur, the Fed might feel forced to push up interest rates to halt capital outflows – a lingering prospect that underscores the degree to which monetary policy has become captive to high levels of foreign investment."

Though it has been likened to a high-power computer capable of keeping track of an ever increasing number of balls in the air, it could end up more like a case of lobectomy, unmindful even of its own history.

William Krehm

The second instalment of this review of the D'Arista paper will deal with her suggestions for the restructuring of our monetary system.

Grass-root Powers of Recuperation in the Argentine?

TOO GREAT a preponderance of power and certainty leaves no elbow-room for doubt. Consultations become a time-consuming formality; disagreements an impertinence. The case of the Argentine illustrates the point. Once the most promising of the Latin American countries, its recent troubles began in 1991, when it pegged its currency to the US dollar, renouncing its power to issue its own currency without 100% backing in US dollars. Though not openly imposed on it by Washington, the persistent propaganda for such moves has turned up throughout the Americas, Canada not excepted. It was presented as a short-cut to solving just about any country's foreign exchange and other problems. It also fitted neatly into the management of the US's ever more problematic foreign debt.

Like Canada, the Argentine in the postwar period sorely missed the historic UK market for its farm exports. That had disappeared with the United Kingdom's exchange reserves in WWII. And once again through Britain's entry into the European market. Canada's response – like that of Australia – was to let its currency decline. But it was precisely against Canada, Australia, and indeed the United States itself that the Argentine had to compete in selling its wheat and beef. In addition the over-muscular peso invited the flight of capital abroad. Inevitably, the Argentine depended more and more on financing by the IMF. Its economic policies became determined by that body.

Let *The Wall Street Journal* (20/12, "Self-Reliance Helps Argentines Endure Economic Chaos" by Matt Moffett) pick up the thread: "During much of the 1990s the [Argentine] was hailed in Washington as a model for free-market reform. US banks and companies loaned or invested tens of billions of dollars there, and now find themselves trying to salvage their losses. Moreover, with globalization, the contagion of ailments has grown in several Latin American economies.

"Argentina's resilience hasn't resulted from any grand strategy. Neither the government nor the Bush administration has offered significant ideas to revive Latin America's third-largest economy."

On the contrary the IMF, to which Washington is the largest contributor in money and advice, pretty well washed its hands of the Argentine. The then Secretary of the Treasury met its devastating crises in which depositors suddenly found themselves cut off from their savings, with the observation that Washington had nothing further to contribute: "the Argentine had made its choice."

Unwittingly, a double message was conveyed in that remark: (1) Deregulation and Globalization had struck out; (2) The Washington Consensus, always more Washington than Consensus, had nowhere to go.

Rescue from the Grass Roots

The very finality of that response, imposed the need to seek alternative solutions.

"Argentina has been saved for now, by the resourcefulness

of hundreds of grass-roots leaders in schools, factories and neighborhood associations. Educators have improvised a safety net so effective at providing food, social services and jobs that classrooms in much of the country are being kept open as summer comes to the Southern hemisphere. Operating on their own initiative, scores of [local] leaders have launched emergency relief efforts.

"With both foreign and national investors skittish about maintaining operations here, workers have often had to take the initiative for keeping plants open. In more than 100 factories undergoing bankruptcy liquidation, workers seized control and kept them operating, saving 13,000 jobs, according to the National Movement of Recovered Businesses, an umbrella group of the employee-led firms.

"It's like someone kicked up an ant-hill,' says Jose Abelli, a leader of the Cooperativa Travi poultry plant that was revived out of bankruptcy by workers. 'It looked like there was disorder, but all the ants were building something new.'

"When the liquidation agent from bankruptcy court arrived at the gates of Cristaleria San Justo glass factory in July, 200 workers and family members blocked his way. To make sure that the factory assets weren't removed and sold, workers maintained a round-the-clock vigil in a pup tent in front of the factory for 10 weeks. Finally the workers won a court battle for control of the plant. Using the same expropriation statute that allows the seizure of houses blocking highway construction, they argued that their action served the public interest. The worker-run plants have to make up the most fundamental rules as they go along. After plant workers and administrators of Tractores Zanello, a big tractor maker in Cordoba, took control of the insolvent firm, they faced a dilemma: How would customers pay for tractors, when cash was so tight? The answer: along with pesos, the plant also accepts three different varieties of the bonds or script that a number of provinces issue as legal tender, and even soya beans. The plant will sell 240 tractors this year, ten times the number sold last year."

There you have, under duress, those endless discussions about what money might be about, translated into life-saving reality.

"The jury-rigged recovery is still extremely precarious. This year's crisis has exacerbated long-standing poverty problems in the provinces, where numerous children have died of malnutrition. Moreover, political infighting ahead of presidential elections in April may trigger renewed economic instability.

"But for now, there is stoic resolve. 'The crisis has brought out two qualities in Argentines overlooked during better times: solidarity and creativity,' says Jorge Selser, a surgeon at the Argerich Hospital. When he isn't helping run a soup kitchen that feeds 60 people, Dr. Selser designs medical equipment that can replace imports that are now too expensive. He has come up with a $1,000 locally made bone screw that works just as well as the $4,000 imported model."

Other Argentines are turning back to the land for sustenance. 'We're rediscovering the survival tactics that our grandparents learned after the great wars in Europe,' says Angela Bianculli, an organic food expert. This year, she estimates that tens of thou-

sands of hard-pressed Argentines have seen her presentations of growing your own food and cooking meals that are both inexpensive and nourishing.

"Perhaps no group better represents the Argentine knack for improvisation than the cartoneros, the trash recyclers. Pushing their two-wheeled carts, they have become as commonplace on boulevards as yuppies in Italian suits were during past boom times. The number of those who earn their living scavenging trash has doubled in the past two years, to an estimated 40,000 of the 13,000,000 of greater Buenos Aires. Before the devaluation Argentine imported $100 million of paper a year from Brazil. Now it exports recycled cardboard.

"Other initiatives have faltered, partly because the Peronistas are preoccupied with internal power struggles ahead of next year's presidential election. The government has counted on swiftly reaching an agreement with the International Monetary Fund to bring cash and credibility. But the IMF and Buenos Aires have been publicly sparring over details all year. Argentina has failed to comply with several earlier agreements, and the IMF says it's reluctant to be burned again.

"Argentines assert that the IMF is withholding assistance to make an example of the Argentine and discourage other debtor nations from defaulting. Argentines also complain that the US is too preoccupied with the war against terrorism to press for aid for Argentina.

"'You could die waiting for the IMF and the government to solve Argentina's problems,' says Walter Blas, an activities coordinator at School 502 in the Buenos Aires suburb of Ezeiza.

"Typical of how educators have served as a line of defence against the crisis, Mr. Blas developed his own assistance program at School 502. The school radio, which can be heard for miles around, airs aid requests from residents in urgent needs. When one family couldn't afford medicine for an epileptic daughter, the station got the medicine the same day. It has sponsored rock concerts to build up the school's food bank.

A Forgotten Heritage of Self-help

"Every bit makes a difference. Several students have fainted in class this year because they were not eating well. With cash and jobs scarce, the teachers and parents set up a market that allowed neighborhood families to barter goods and services and use tickets issued by the school to make purchases. Participants could come to the school and buy a loaf of bread for two tickets or get a car tuned for 20 tickets.

"With the barter market running out of steam in May because of counterfeit ticket and other problems, the neighborhood launched a recycling cooperative. A local businessman donated bricks to build an oven that will produce enough bread for the school's needs and for a surplus to sell for cash.

"The principal says any earnings will supplement the budget for the school cafeteria which will stay open during the summer."

The crisis on the Plata has in fact brought to light a forgotten heritage of self-help and communal solidarity that had been buried under the avalanche of free-market hype. The countless schemes of alternate currencies and barter throughout the world, the recycling concerns of environmentalists, the study-groups on alternate life styles, volunteerism rather than maximizing one's personal take as a goal in life, study groups on heterodox economic theories, and much else more than just "off the wall" oddities have now been disclosed in the Argentine as exercises that preserve survival habits menaced by greed at the throttle. The United States in Afghanistan and elsewhere has proved far more competent at smashing societies than at putting them together again. The world may still be beholden to the Argentine for ways to cope with menacing disaster.

William Krehm

The Best Laid Plans of Mice and the White House

WHO COULD BEGIN estimating the cost in blood and treasure of Washington's double-decade effort to impose free movement of speculative monies? Politicians and analysts were corrupted so that hot speculative money might pass quickly in first-class comfort across boundaries wherever there was a currency still to be unhinged, a government to be overthrown, and Wall St.'s booms nurtured to last a bit longer. But now all that doctrinaire wisdom is being regurgitated – and precisely in two countries that were long cited as proof that the Washington Consensus was doing fine.

The Wall Street Journal (9/10, "US Trade Talks with Singapore. Chile Hit Impasse" by Neil King Jr.): "Trade talks with Singapore and Chile are hung over a vexing question about the rules that govern the global economy: Should countries seek free-trade deals with the US be forced to lift all controls over the flow of foreign money across their borders? The US treasury says they should. But Singapore and Chile, both generally regarded as market-economy success stories, object. The impasse imperils two agreements at the top of President Bush's trade agenda and is causing a rift between the Treasury and US Trade Representative Robert Zoellick, who was unable to close a deal with Singapore because of these differences.

"'This is puzzling, given that the US has been severely criticized for being too doctrinaire on the question of capital controls,' says Edwin Truman, a former top international-economics official of the Federal Reserve and the Clinton Treasury."

With the cold fingers of deflation tightening on the throats of both the East Asian and Latin American economies, the question is asked why their countries should be denied the means that in its day were used by the United States itself to become master of its own destiny. Under Roosevelt – to combat deflation – Washington not only dropped the exchange value of its dollar to defend its exports and discourage imports, but made it compulsory for its citizens to surrender any monetized gold to the Treasury.

Given the deepening gloom pervading the US economy, and Wall St.'s desperate need for "big deals," the growing trouble of US trade negotiators merely reflects a deepening cleft between speculative finance and the industrial sector at home.

A Rift in the Councils of the Superpower

"In the US, the tussle pits the interests of big banks and investment houses, which oppose all controls, against US manufacturers and other exporters, [and] are keen to see the trade deals signed and approved by Congress. To try to allay mounting concerns, Treasury's undersecretary for international affairs, John Taylor, met with nearly 20 business leaders last week to explain why the US was holding fast to its position. 'Reaction ran from strong support to consternation,' said one industry participant.

"The difficulties come as US trade negotiators huddle in Washington for the final week of trade talks with Chile after years of sporadic negotiations. Top Chilean officials say that capital controls have emerged as the biggest hurdle.

"Both Chile and Singapore have used limited capital controls to protect their economies from instability that comes from big inflows of foreign money, particularly short-term loans or deposits, that can flee rapidly in a panic. For years, Singapore required foreign financial institutions to seek government permission before borrowing Singapore dollars. The rule prevented investors from borrowing money to speculate in currency markets as happened elsewhere in Asia."

And Over It All Looms China

But that is what helped fuel the Wall St. boom. Once the noose of foreign-currency-denominated debt was fastened on a country, it was at the mercy of the American financial conglomerates. It enabled them to dictate the slashing of social programs, the selling of domestic real estate and corporations for a song, and to enforce compulsory exports at whatever what prices. That been a key factor in both the relative drop in perceived "inflation" within the US, and the disastrous deflation in both Latin America and East Asia.

These countries are already under pressure from the massive export drives of China where wages are one tenth of those in Japan and one-fifth those of Singapore and other East Asian countries. However, the vulnerability of East Asia and Latin America translates into the possibility of massive bargain-basement buyouts, and mergers that Wall St. is missing today. Washington's aggressive stance on the removal of currency movements arises from its concern to solve Wall St.'s unemployment problem at the CEO level. It aims to do so at the expense of living standards in the emerging world.

"In Chile, the *encaje* system required companies bringing money into the country to deposit a portion of it in a non-interest-bearing account for a year, to discourage short-term borrowing from abroad. The levy topped 30% in 1998, but is now at zero. Economists say the system protected Chile during the financial turmoil of the late 1990s."

Our readers will note that the mechanism resembles strikingly a beefed-up version of the statutory reserves with which central banks were able to discourage inflationary booms until the early 1970s, without depending exclusively on raising short-term interest rates. Exchange volatility fueled by uncontrolled movements of speculative money across frontiers is the equivalent of shaking the dice in a casino.

"[Controls are] important for our own stability,' says Ricardo Lagos, the son of Chile's president and one of the country's top trade negotiators. 'We think we should keep various prudential measures in place, just in case, and the US doesn't like it.'

"Treasury officials concede that the debate goes well beyond Singapore or Chile. 'What's important is that these are precedent-setting agreements for many agreements to come,' said one Treasury official."

Chile Agreement: Washington's Template of the Future

"Treasury's Mr. Taylor insisted to the industry representatives he met last week that none of this is new. Demands that countries forgo capital controls, he noted, are already part of 45 US investment treaties with other countries as well as the 2001 free-trade deal with Jordan and the 1994 North American Free Trade Agreement with Mexico and Canada. But his critics point out that NAFTA permits at least some controls if a country faces a serious balance-of-payments crisis. With Chile and Singapore, Treasury wants to scrap that provision as well."

Quite understandably: since these earlier treaties were signed Wall St.'s unemployment problem at the CEO level has dramatically worsened, and by the nature of things, it is likely to receive more attention than that of ordinary jobless stiffs.

"Columbia University's Jagdish Bhagwati says, 'It is absurd after the Asian financial crisis and the 1994 [Mexican] crisis that the pressure is still relentless to open up and knock down every conceivable barrier on capital flows. These countries have good reasons to be cautionary.'"

US trade officials and many US companies say they have been surprised by how the capital-control issue has blown up out of nowhere. The Bush administration figured that both the Singapore and the Chile deals were in the bag weeks ago.

"The Chile agreement is about so much more than just Chile, a small economy whose trade with the US amounts to about $6.5 billion a year, counting both imports and exports. But a deal with Chile is seen widely as a step toward the US goal of having a free-trade bloc with every country in the Americas except Cuba by 2005."

On the other hand, securing the foreign exchange portal, would empower countries to use their central banks in an emergency for domestic money creation to look after such needs as housing programs, food supply while another department would control what foreign exchange was available to finance the acquisition items not available at home. What the Bush administration is doing is trying to prevent the world from drawing the necessary conclusions from the Argentine disaster. Having such a system in place would make it available for emergency use as the need arose. So long as foreign exchange was no great problem there would be few restrictions except in the case of short-term money. But since the world seems headed for deflation, the sudden stiffening of the US position is just a

foretaste of the eye-gouging to protect Wall St.'s control of the world economy.

Since the above *Wall Street Journal* articles appeared, Washington has won its point with Chile and Singapore (*WSJ*, 16/01, p. 10). But such victories are doomed to be Pyrrhic. They merely store up a binful of crises throughout the world, to nurture Washington's hope of reviving the Wall St. bubble. Nothing is more disastrous for society as a whole, than the efforts of those who profited from a failed system to tighten their hold.

William Krehm

A SYSTEMS VIEW

Phony Idealism

EARLY IN THE 2003 New Year, the host of a Sunday morning TV news show asked a political aspirant: "George Bush says his favourite philosopher is Jesus Christ. Who is your favourite philosopher?" The interviewee sidestepped the question, probably an indication of his political skill. But the contradictions implicit in the President's statement, which there seems no reason to disbelieve, verge on the surreal – an oddly dream-like quality to the values of the American chief executive.

First, and most obviously, Jesus was not so much a philosopher as a thinker and activist. He was at the least a gifted religious mystic, but also was seen as a political threat, although he said that his kingdom was not of this world, and went to his death because he rejected worldly power. His teachings were refined by others who came after, some of whom were philosophers (e.g., Augustine and Aquinas). Yet it must be clear that earthly survival and political power were not among the primary values taught by Jesus. So what is going on here?

God and the Devil

There is, of course, the obvious attempt by Bush to associate himself with religious values in the interests of political power – a kind of identity-theft – which in fact does violence to those values. This is so brazen that one assumes it must be automatic and unconscious on Bush's part; he is beyond his depth and does not understand the contradictions involved. The mistake, however, is far from innocent; it is deliberately exploitative, even malignant.

Malignant is not too strong a word. In effect, Bush takes on a mantle of loving kindness in order to operate through a screen of misleading rhetoric, thereby to subvert the values, which he pretends to support. The example is important because it is so unconscious and revealing, and so typical of the systemic difficulties produced by political and economic ideas applied out of context.

Among the tools of civilized mankind, few are as important as language. And crucial to language is the capacity it entails of giving stable forms to abstract thought, of enabling speakers to articulate and communicate ideas clearly. This is largely what a formal education, particularly in science, is about. Exposure to experience and methods must be adequate and systematic.

Language and Learning

However the processes involved are beset by hazards. Many people simply do not think in abstract terms; they limit themselves to concrete personal considerations, and translate what for others are abstract ideas into either vague generalities or specific examples, which reflect personal experience. Such people tend not to engage themselves with science or politics except as tools for personal advantage.

Of course there are many areas of human experience where different and contrasting styles of thought are appropriate. However there are also many areas of politics and economics where sudden shifts of meaning and changes of subject lead to great confusion.

Learning requires some structure, and the correction of mistakes requires feedback. In the absence of a commonly understood framework there may be no possibility of feedback and learning; there are simply no standards of comparison, and therefore nothing, which requires correction. No learning is required or possible. Under such circumstances confusions reign supreme.

For example, there are those who argue that indefinite growth is possible on a finite planet, and that resources are available without any foreseeable limits – when the facts are in obvious contradiction. People frequently believe in things simply because they want to. Public opinion, as well as government and much elite opinion, reflects many such confusions.

Those who cannot agree on decisive values i.e., on the direction we want to take as a society, cannot know what constitutes progress. Under such circumstances they find themselves confused and going in circles; discussions of policy and the public interest are then easily sidetracked by special interests. The approach taken by Bush almost guarantees such confusion.

Before the days of Newton and other pioneers of modern science, the concepts of energy and work were folk ideas – as they still are for many people. The Romans and other peoples of course had much useful understanding of materials and mechanics, but nothing so subtle as to enable them to build really powerful engines, nor could they replace the need for slave labour, required to support the societies of the time. We in our time retain a confused mixture of values, including the views of political power and the exploitation of peoples as practised in earlier ages.

Advances by the 17th century made possible new inventions, previously inconceivable. Along with precise concepts of force, mass, energy and heat, related consistently in terms of exact formulae, modern physical sciences and benefits became possible. All the advances of modern science are built upon refinements of concepts and language, including the accurate observation of relationships.

By the 19th century it was clear that modern technology had overcome the need for a society to require slave labour. Yet the values of an elite that takes for granted the use of human beings as replaceable parts are still operative today in the use of sweat shop operations. Such practices have not caught up with modern thought and the enlightened social order new insights make possible.

In relation to the concepts we have of societal organization and responsibilities, we still live in a benighted time. Much relevant knowledge is available, but those who make decisions, which affect societies, tended to be guided unapologetically by the most primitive instincts for manipulating power. And the complexities of life may lend apparent support to many such illusions in the short term.

Neither politicians nor business people have a privileged vantage point on which to pronounce the truth about affairs. The integrity of the whole depends on clearly distinguishing the roles and the sources of knowledge and power of all sectors, including the civic sector, and achieving a creatively balanced view. In particular, the civic sector involves the clearest awareness of human needs and concerns and of the real world in which people live and die.

Over recent decades we have experienced increasing distortions in the balance of ideas and interests necessary to sustain a healthy world. The pronouncements of leaders in government and major corporations have become increasingly unbelievable in their attempts to appeal to diverse interests. Claims to understanding and responsibility regularly outrun performance in both government and business.

Meanwhile, the proposals advanced and policies adopted to attract various constituencies with opposing interests are rife with contradictions. Opportunists attack big government, demanding tax cuts and individual responsibility, but also increased expenditures on defence and crime. Aided by polling, they learn what to say in order to garner votes, but at the price of perpetrating contradictions, illusions and eventual disappointment.

The American "War on Terrorism," with its guiding principle of "Whoever is not for us is against us," is a challenge that promises to be extremely costly to many sectors in many ways. Tragically, it does not address the real issues in a serious way. In a very primitive and prescientific way it identifies destructive behaviour with "evil-doers," agents of the devil. This is pre-Christian primitivism, a kind of scapegoat morality, which is the cause of societal problems, not part of any useful solution.

The compartmentalization involved in this primitive thinking leads logically to calls for programs of detection and prevention, which grow whole industries of surveillance and control. This reflects a kind of obsessional neurosis, admittedly a response to damage, but a response, which is not directed realistically and must fall short.

Our society certainly needs better protection. But too many of our leaders now operate on the basis of delusions (i.e., beliefs which cannot be corrected by evidence). In the service of an absolute ideology they are ready to redirect public attention to any convenient scapegoats, and to use such scapegoating to help them achieve expanded powers and other objectives.

What is to be done? The Christian teaching is that truth shall make man free. George W. Bush has a long way to go if he would absorb and provide an example of this teaching. In the meantime we would do well to cultivate a political climate, which does not allow absurd claims to pass unchallenged.

Bruce Buchanan

An Angry Boil to be Cleansed

AS THE INVESTIGATIONS and bankruptcy filings roll on, there seems no end of scandal that fuelled the New Economy. By strict journalistic criteria the subject should long since have yielded the front page to the latest rumpus in the private lives of the British royals or of some Hollywood star. Yet, like an angry boil, it holds our attention crying out for lancing.

Thus the Fifth of a series "What's Wrong?" in *The Wall Street Journal* (23/12, "Tricks of the trade – As Market Bubble Neared End, Bogus Swaps Provided a Lift" by Dennis K. Berman, Julia Anwin and Chip Cummins) reenacts the scene with the high drama of crumbling empires:

"It was 10 p.m. on a Friday, 50 hours before Qwest Communications International Inc. was due to close the books on its third quarter of 2001. CEO Afshin Mohebbi sat down in his 52nd floor office at the telephone giant's Denver HQ and tapped out a desperate e-mail to his top salesmen. The subject line: 'Help!!!!!!!'

"Mr. Mohebbi was alarmed because a series of sweet deals he urgently needed weren't working. The plan was for Qwest to swap connections to its phone network for connections to other companies' networks. Phone companies had been making trades like that for years, but lately there was a twist: Both companies would book revenue from these transactions – inflating their financial results even though they were swapping assets of equal value.

"But Qwest couldn't make these latest swaps work. It had agreed to buy $231 million in access to telecom networks. But the companies on the other side of the table had committed to spend less than $108 million with Qwest. The company was going to have to squeeze more money out of the deals if it was to meet the projections given Wall St.

"What's happened to the creativity of this company and its employees?' Mr. Mohebbi wrote in his e-mail. 'Let's not have a disaster now.'

"In the end, disaster did strike. Ten months later, Qwest's new CEO, Richard Notebaert, soberly read a script during a conference call with press and analysts. He announced that the company's swaps had violated accounting rules. The company later said it would restate $950 million in revenue, erasing the deals from the company's prior results.

"When the business history of the past decade is written, perhaps nothing will sum up the outrageous financial scheming of the era as well as the frenzied swapping that marked its final years. Internet companies such as Homeshare Inc. milked revenue from complex advertising exchanges with other dotcoms in ultimately worthless deals. In Houston, equal amounts of energy were pushed back and forth between companies. The beauty of the deals, from the perspective of the participants, was that everyone walked away with roughly the same amount of revenue to put on their books."

And this was at a time when a demand for 5% wage increases would draw the wrath of the Federal Reserve because of its inflationary effect!

However, "the swaps rage turned out no bargain for investors. The bad deals contributed to an epidemic of artificially inflated revenue. In many cases, swaps slipped through legal loopholes left in place by regulators who had failed to keep pace with the ever-changing deal-making of ever-changing industries. The unravelling of those back-scratching arrangements helped usher in the market collapse. It led to the realization that the highest-flying industries of the boom – telecom, energy, the Internet – were built in part on a combustible mix of wishful thinking and deceit. The amount of restated revenue from swaps totals more than $15 billion since 1999, according to an analysis of the *WSJ*. The number is especially significant since investors focused on revenue in new industries that had little earnings to show."

Gross revenue came to replace earnings, whether the sales took place at a loss or a profit. The next step, to meet the pressures for capital gains on company stock, was to replace real gross revenue with a fictitious version of the same.

"Swaps were used by at least 20 public companies, including AOL Time Warner Inc., CMS Energy Corp., and Global Crossing Ltd., which are all under federal investigation.

"It is no accident that the swaps frenzy sprang up in industries with newfangled, intangible products. Putting a price tag on online ads, energy or telecom-transmission contracts and moving them back and forth, is a lot trickier than dealing with a fleet of trucks or a cement plant. Swaps essentially involved 'manipulating an abstraction,' says Andrew Lipman, a telecom attorney in Washington. 'These swaps morphed into devices to satisfy the God of quarterly performance.'

"Along the way, the reciprocal deals became an accepted part of a business culture obsessed with revenue growth.

"Swaps have been around since Old Testament days, when Joseph traded food for horses and donkeys of hungry Egyptians. In the 1980s, corrupt savings and loans traded real estate back and forth at increasingly overblown prices. This was known as trading 'a dead horse for a dead cow.'

"The telecom industry for decades got around the expense of building fiber-optic lines by exchanging access to each other's networks. Everything changed when the industry was deregulated in the mid-1990s. Telecom companies bloomed, laying miles of new fiber. By late 2000 it became obvious that there was nowhere near enough customer demand to use up all the capacity.

Mutual Back-scratching Takes Over

When not scratching each other's back, "'…everyone was scratching their heads about how to make the numbers,' recalls Darek Gill, a former vice president of 360networks that filed for bankruptcy in June 2001. A Canadian telecom builder, 360networks held what salespeople dubbed 'stoke the fire' meetings. They stood before top executives and listed the closed deals and sales prospects. People who didn't deliver their quotas were considered failures.' Adds Mr. Gill, 'I talked to my friends across the industry and no one was selling.'

"That's when swaps began to take on an entirely new motive: adding revenue onto quarterly financial results. They turned each other into their best customers. 'The buzz was that when we saw an announcement for $300 million or $500 million we thought it was b-s-,' says John Shaban, an executive director at Energia USA, a subsidiary of Spain's Telefonica S.A. 'The first question was, "is it a swap? If it was, who cares?"'"

The little liberties with accountancy had evolved into a major breakdown of basic morality. That is why the photo-shots of an occasional hero of these episodes in manacles evade rather than address the real problem. The roots of that reach back to the early 1870s when the focus of economic theory was wholly shifted from production and the work place to the interplay of supply and demand on the market. Until then the various schools of economic theory had concurred in the primacy of the production of goods over their sale. That was reflected in the importance they assigned to some *value* theory rather than to just *price* theories. Adam Smith, far from the mannikin that he is presented as today, used no less than three different value theories depending on which problems he was wrestling with. Each of these emphasized the relevant link between the problem and real production – whether it was the amount of "average labour" needed for the production of a given commodity, or the amount of labour that could be hired with the proceeds from the sale of given goods, or adding up the costs of producing such goods.

But between 1848 and 1871 the workplace had become crisscrossed with barricades. A need arose to shift attention away from factory floor to the marketplace. No longer was there a welcome for a deeper notion of the "value" other than the last sale price. All economic actors were presented as just traders, comparing the satisfactions of accepting what the market offered for their labour with the joys of leisure in their parlours. If there was mass unemployment it was just that those who had only their labour power to trade had opted for the latter. Like the bankers they were seen as diligently maximising their rewards and with it the efficiency of the economy. What is more, the market assumed that all the agents on it were tiny enough to allow the application of infinitesimal calculus. That was presented as "scientifically" guaranteeing that the prices and terms set by it were both just and inevitable. What more could you ask? Of course, it was all nonsense, since this "marginal utility" theory was brought in at the very time of sped-up concentration of finance and industry into behemoth corporations rather than of inconsequentially tiny operators. Anyone with a serious grasp of what mathematics is about, would have trashed such a model without going beyond its assumptions. It was cutting the customer to the cloth.

Acquiring Title to Eden

Profits were attributed less to production than to the excess of market demand over supply. From there it was but a short step to manipulating that market and scarcity itself as the prime source of wealth. As in any brothel or B movie, the black arts of advertising and promotion could whip desire into a lather. Nothing was left unrevised. The very Decalogue, in a lone undoing of the digital revolution, was replaced with a single stricture – the free movement of capital. "In the sweat of thy face shalt thou eat bread" applied only to the drones. The serpents, morphed into CEOs, lawyers and accountants, acquired key and title to Eden itself and lost no time in listing it as a REIT on the stock exchange.

The *WSJ* (31/12, "How Energy Trades Turned Bonanza Into an Epic Bust" by Paul Beckett and Jathon Sapsford and Alexei Barrionuevo) wrote: "Trading became a means for fudging financial results. And a cozy group of traders in Houston and elsewhere colluded on sham transactions aimed at fooling investors about the volume of activity in the new market. In the midst of an energy crisis in 2000, California officials accused avaricious traders of ripping off the state. Questions arose about concealed liabilities at Enron Corp. and dubious gas deals at Dynegy Inc. Not everyone took this route. But enough companies did for that energy trading to be in shambles. Investors in the trading companies have lost billions of dollars. The entire affair raises serious questions about whether such a complex market can operate safely without regulation."

In fact, some of the physical constraints of energy trading were deliberately disregarded.

This brings the *WSJ* onto the very door-mat of revelation: "Not so long ago, supplying electricity and natural gas wasn't so complicated. Heavily regulated utilities that enjoyed local monopolies sold power and gas to consumers large and small. Beginning in the early 1990s, however, federal and state regulators were scaled back, and utilities were forced to open their transmission lines to rivals. The idea was that suppliers and traders would compete for business by cutting prices and moving energy around the country more efficiently. Buyers would obtain more stable supplies by entering long-term contracts." A central challenge is to figure out how to value such contracts, given the unpredictability of such variables as the cost of power years in the future and weather shifts that affect demand for heat and air-conditioning.

"Companies scrambling for position in the trading market went after the brain power to crunch the numbers representing these factors. Williams, in Tulsa, Okla., for example, hired Anjelina Belakovskaia, a Ukranian chess grand-master, to help quantify the weather effects. Trading companies also lobbied in Washington for flexible new accounting rules that would allow them to account for anticipated revenue and income from long-term contracts as if the cash were coming in immediately. In 1992, the Financial Accounting Standards Board, an accounting industry group, signed off on the switch, as did the SEC. The adjustment helped the companies impress Wall St. with what looked like quickly bulging bottom lines.

"Enron quickly signed up some big customers. In 1998 it struck a $246 million long-term deal with the Archdiocese of Chicago to provide electricity and natural gas for churches and schools. Later, it signed a $610 million deal with IBM Machines Corp. and a $600 million deal with J.C. Penney Co.

"However, it soon became clear to industry insiders that electricity was much more difficult to trade than natural gas. Electricity can't be stored and is hard to transport over long distances. Even brainy number-crunchers found it difficult to value over long periods. [Yet] the online exchanges Dynegy-Direct and EnronOnline exploded. EnronOnline racked up more than $180 billion in transactions in the first year after its October 1999 launch.

"Energy-trading stocks soared. Enron's shares rose 78% in the three years after 1996, as investors bought the story that the company and its top rivals were powered more by intellect than electricity and gas. For about three years, beginning in 1998, Enron traders selling power to California utilities artificially increased congestion of the state's transmission lines, knowing that they would be paid later to ease the situation, according to a federal plea agreement in October by a former Enron trader, Timothy Belden. The scheme worked, even though the traders didn't relieve the clogs. In fact, the electricity was generated in California, shipped out and then brought back in.

Gouging and being Gouged

"By reporting false price information to the price index keepers, traders could inflate the value of contracts they held. In November 2001, Todd Geiger, an El Paso Corp. trader, allegedly fabricated 48 natural gas trades and sent fake volume and price information by e-mail to "Inside FERC's Gas Market Report," a trade publication. Earlier this month, federal prosecutors charged him with wire fraud and reporting false market information. Dynegy has agreed, without admitting wrongdoing, to pay $5 million to settle charges by the Commodity Futures Trading Commission that it tried to manipulate price indexes.

"Until such practices came to light, senior executives of Enron, Dynegy, El Paso and Williams saw their pay packages balloon, fueling an impressive degree of excess in some quarters of Houston. At one dinner in 1998, nine El Paso traders and brokers racked up a $13,000 bill at Pappa's Bros. Steakhouse, thanks in part to a $150-a-glass Remy Martin Louis XIII cognac, according to participants.

"On another night, a group of more than 15 traders ranging in age from mid-20s to late 30s gathered in a private room at Sullivan's Steakhouse. Over drinks and cigars, several of them, including Mr. Geiger of El Paso, challenged each other to jab steak knives between outstretched fingers in a show of machismo. Finally, one of them, according to participants gouged himself, bloodying the white tablecloth. He left, cursing, and later got stitches. Mr. Geiger and a few others began throwing knives into the restaurant's wood paneled wall. 'It was like an adult fraternity,' says Stephen Fronterhouse, the restaurant's manager at the time. 'They were making a ton of money and having a great time." Tight professional and social relationships created a milieu in which traders covered each other's backs in deals that seemed aimed more at increasing the volume of their business – and thereby creating the impression of an expanding market.'

"CMS Energy Corp. in Dearborn, Mich., played the willing foil in 'round trip' trading in which two companies exchanged the same amount of power or gas, at the same time, at the same price. Ultimately, the CMS's round-tripping with Dynegy and Houston's Reliant Resources Inc. accounted for 80% of CMS's energy trading in 2000 and 70% in 2001, the company later said in a statement.

"The accounting rules gave company managers huge leeway in valuing long-term gas and power contracts, leading to more dubious behavior. In December, 1999, Lawrence Whalley, then president of Enron's trading unit, asked a group of subordinates to 'find' $9 million in additional profit to help the company meet end-of-year goals, according to a trader and another employee.

"The energy-trading companies also turned to investment banks such as J.P. Morgan Chase & Co. and Citigroup Inc. to help engineer some questionable deals. In some cases, the banks extended financing for the future delivery of gas and oil. The energy companies booked the financing as if it were cash flow from operations, even though under ordinary analysis it looked more like debt."

Hiding Smokin' Guns à la Saddam

"Some bankers involved in these deals were shocked to discover the degree of Enron's dependence on the tactic. In October 2001, Richard S. Walker, a J.P. Morgan banker in Houston, sent an email about Enron to a colleague, George Serice: '$5 billion in prepays!!!!!!'

"'Shut up and delete this e-mail,' Mr. Serice responded.

"As inquiries into the California's energy mess gathered steam, revelations began to pour out about round-trip trades and other abuses. With every bit of bad news, the stock market punished the traders' shares. Since last year, power-trading volume has shrunk by as much as 70%, according to industry estimates. Firms such as El Paso, Dynegy, and CMS are ditching all or most of their energy trading to return to their roots as pipeline and utility companies. El Paso peaked in March /01 at $74, but is now traded at about $7. Dynegy's shares, after hitting a high of $57.50 in September, 2000, is now trading at about $1.

"Energy trading could have been a profitable business without all of the chicanery,' says Mr. Fusano, the industry consultant. 'They could have made a lot of money because there was so much volatility in natural gas and power. But a lot wasn't enough."

Doesn't that sum it up for the entire Deregulated and Globalized economy?

The model – out to maximize growth, not troubling of what – simply settled on the growth of remote generations of its financial derivatives instantly incorporated into share prices that had to be maintained at unsustainable levels. The Bible Belt can read the current overflowing of the courts with disquieting exposures as the coming to pass of the divine prophecy that woman's seed "shall bruise the serpent's head, and thou shalt bruise his heel."

The trouble is that we have lost all sense of what is head and what is heel.

William Krehm

Will the Chrétien Legacy Match that of Mackenzie King?

SURPRISINGLY, from the scratchy leadership race in the Liberal Party is finally emerging a sign that democracy is still alive in the land. *The Globe and Mail* (11/2, "Infrastructure packet will be in the budget" by Simon Tuck and Shawn McCarthy) informs us that "The coming federal budget will include a 10-year infrastructure package with an initial value of more than $2.5 billion, much of which will be aimed at projects that are good for the environment and Canadian cities. But sources say the $2.5 billion, which will fund only the first five years of the program will also be used to leverage considerably more money through private-sector involvement in many of these projects. That way you end up with a bigger pot,' one government source said. 'It's not all public money.'"

The unasked question, however, is "whose pot?" The answer to that question will largely depend on what information is available in our media, in parliament, and our universities concerning our economy. For many years now, that has been suppressed.

The above item, for example, could set the stage for future privatizations of public assets developed with public money that could and should be financed on a near-interest-free basis through the Bank of Canada. The arrangement for that is to be found in the *Bank of Canada Act*. The one shareholder of the central bank is the Government of Canada. Accordingly, when the federal government borrows money from the Bank of Canada, the interest paid reverts substantially as dividends to the Government of Canada. As simple as that.

But isn't it a recognized fact that governments aren't to be trusted in handling money, while private financial corporations are? To ask that question today takes a bit of gall. The media are brimming with scandals in which the world's banks and other large corporations have presented liabilities as assets, and on top of that, kept other massive liabilities off their books.

But aren't our governments at all levels running deficits and shouldering deficits? How could we possibly know? The books of the federal government and most of the provinces register the debt incurred in making investments, but carry the resulting assets on their books at a token one dollar. The government's infrastructure scheme could be seen in part as a plan to back that big milch-cow into Bay St.'s stall for future privatizations.

Messy ambiguity? Definitely. But the extent to which it is depends on how adequate the permitted flow of key information. That predetermines what politicians will be tempted to get away with to stay in office.

We had already drafted this article when the press carried word that at long last – 3.5 years after the bill introducing

capital budgeting (a.k.a. accrual accountancy) had been slipped through parliament without mention in any of the national newspapers with the exception of the *National Post* and forty years after it had been recommended by the first of four Royal Commissions. That happened as a deal between the former Finance Minister Paul Martin and the then Auditor General Denis Desautels. Unless accrual accountancy were brought in, the AG had refused to give unconditional approval of the 1998-9 balance sheet of the government. Partly to break the deadlock the Auditor General had understated the government assets as $50 billion.

Elsewhere in this issue, we indicate that based on the US figures for a not dissimilar move in 1996, the Canadian figure should be not $50 billion but closer to $100 billion. Extended to include the federal investment in human capital – education, health, and social security – the total unrecognized capital assets of the government would at least equal that in physical capital. That would bring the total unrecognized capital assets of the Ottawa to at least $200 billion. That collateral is far, far more than enough to finance the total infrastructure program planned without help of private financing. Of course, most of the work for such infrastructures will be contracted out to private firms, but the financing can be done wholly on a virtual interest-free basis through the Bank of Canada.

Our Forgotten Ownership of the Bank of Canada

The Bank of Canada was founded in 1934 to help the country grope its way out of deflation. Today, deflation is overtaking this country and the world once again, though the Don Quixote at the head of the Bank of Canada is still breaking lances against "inflation." In 1938, 12,000 private shareholders of the central bank were bought out at a fat profit after four lean depression years of ownership. But by the early 1990s the BoC and the government itself were conducting a campaign claiming that the central bank was independent of the government. That is not what the Bank of Canada Act says. But if it were so, why was the Treasury not reimbursed for the money it paid to buy the Bank? What is ownership without the advantages of ownership?

And then for the next three and a half years we heard nothing further about "accrual accountancy." Meanwhile the federal surplus is slipping towards a deficit again. And then as a bolt out of the blue *The Globe and Mail* (along with the other newspapers) informed us (13/02, in an article by Simon Tuck) that Finance Minister had declared that "Full accrual was recommended frequently by the Auditor General and by everybody who wants full, transparent accountancy in our books. I expect to announce in the budget that for 2003-4, we'll have the first year in which the government's books will be on a full accrual basis."

But it goes on to spread the old misinformation: "The government's decision will not directly alter Ottawa's financial health or the amount Canadians owe in debt." That is tantamount to saying that if your personal net worth statement included the mortgage on your house as a liability, but omitted to include the house that it helped pay for as an asset, it would not alter your "financial health." You would be refused credit by your bank, or if you got a loan it would be at a far higher rate of interest. So, too, those cooked government books helped the central bank shove up interest rates into the 20 percent range. There is then no stopping at half-deeds and half-truths. From bitter experience we should know that they lead to full lies and total disasters. It is essential that the government explain to the public the full significance of accrual accountancy in establishing our credit. Since the early 1970s, money has been nothing but government credit and credibility. It thus determines the interest rates we pay. A relevant figure for government assets must be arrived at by extending recognition to the government's investments in human capital: education, health and social security. In prudent steps federal debt must be returned from the chartered banks to the Bank of Canada – to attain the 22% of the total debt figure that the bank held in the mid-1970s. En route, the needs of the provinces and the municipalities can be met.

If Prime Minister Chrétien initiates such a program, he will go down in history alongside William Lyon Mackenzie King who in 1938 nationalized the Bank of Canada. What a legacy that would be!

William Krehm

Restructuring the Fed

This is the second of two installments. The first part appeared in our February issue.

THE REMEDIAL SECTION of the D'Arista document starts with a flare of trumpets: "The developments already covered have placed the Federal Reserve in a situation reminiscent of the early years of the Great Depression, when the central bank's passive reserve system proved inadequate to deal with bank failures. With the 1929 Crash, gold outflows limited the Fed's ability to conduct the open market operations pioneered by the New York Fed chief Benjamin Strong. Slowing economic activity reduced the amount of paper eligible for rediscount and as collateral for note issues, compounding a dramatic contraction in the supply of money and credit.

"More significantly, the Fed's maneuvering room was severely limited by its statutory inability to use the banking system's large holdings of US government securities as collateral for discounts and backing for note issues. In 1932, emergency legislation authorized the use of Treasury securities for Federal Reserve Notes. This authorization, reaffirmed in the *Banking Acts* of 1933 and 1935 and made permanent in the 1940s, provided the framework for system operations still in use today.

"As financial-sector changes render this framework increasingly ineffective, the US central bankers now find capital inflows limiting their actions in somewhat the same way gold outflows handcuffed their predecessors 70 years ago. In addition, the Fed's contemporary balance sheet – now composed almost exclusively of Treasuries on the asset side – offers the central bank far too little operational flexibility, much as the balance sheet of 1930 stymied policymakers of that era. US central bankers [then] are confronted with four basic choices. They can rationalize the erosion of their primary policy mechanism by changing objectives. They can attempt to muddle through. They can simply surrender to the powerfully procyclical market forces. Or they can acknowledge the need for new policy mechanisms as decisively as their predecessors did in the 1930s.

"As the Fed's policy transmission system has worn down, the central bank's policy objectives have narrowed. Many central bankers [declare] price stability the most important prerequisite for sustainable output and employment growth.

"Even though widely shared – and it offers a seemingly neat rationalization for weakened policy tools – this view has several major flaws. Focusing on a single goal would require a change in the *Federal Reserve Act*, which directs the central bank to pursue full employment and maximum output as well as stable prices.

"Equally important, the sustained pattern of divergence between credit and output growth over the last two decades points to a form of inflation that has not been curbed by the Fed's interest rate policies. The persistence of credit inflation adds an important dimension to the longstanding debate over the relative influence of money and credit on macroeconomic outcomes.

"As long as depository institutions hold less than one-quarter of total financial assets, discount-window reform and other bank-focused initiatives can exert a limited influence at best on general credit conditions. Such initiatives may very well allow the Fed to defer a day of reckoning. But they will not cancel the event."

An Unpretty Outcome

"While most Fed officials acknowledge the importance of monetary policy in managing the economy, proponents of an unregulated economic system might argue that the difficulty of maintaining effective monetary tools makes the case for simply throwing in the towel and allowing market forces free rein. But the growing financial disruption over the past two decades suggests the outcome wouldn't be pretty.

"If shorn of all restraining influences, the procyclical bias of market forces would ensure boom-bust cycles of increasing frequency. And since markets, unlike central banks, do not have the power to create liquidity in a crisis, these violent swings would further destabilize both economic and human development.

"Finally, the Fed could try to regain meaningful control over money and credit by modernizing – rather than fiddling with – its policy transmission system. Given the gravity of the situation, a thorough overhaul appears to be the most practical long-term remedy."

"No plausible scenario suggests banks regaining their once-hegemonic role in credit creation. As a result, [we] must establish new channels for exercising monetary control over all financial institutions. And nonbank financial firms cannot participate in the transmission-belt function unless they too meet reserve requirements.

New Transmission Belts

"1. One sensible approach would be to use the *Gramm-Leach-Bliley Act's* definition of activities deemed financial in nature and apply reserve requirements to such activities. Requirements should be imposed only on those portions of a company engaged in financial activities (for example, on GMAC but not on those portions conducting nonfinancial operations (e.g., GM's auto-making divisions).

"2. Despite their growing dominance, non-bank financial intermediaries are not designed for money creation [i.e., the loan to buy a new car when spent does not echo back as a deposit with General Motors as does a line of credit – minus statutory reserve – into the banking system]. Moreover, the liabilities of institutional investors such as pension funds and insurance companies are in longer-term contracts, rendering reserve requirements on those liabilities impracticable. In short, a liability-based system doesn't permit central banks to create and extinguish reserves for nonbank financial firms.

"Efficiency and equity therefore require that reserves be held against assets. Though this notion may appear exotic, it actually embodies a range of real-world experiences, including the current model for US insurance regulation. For years, states have required insurers to hold reserves against their assets and in 1992, insurance commissioners instituted an asset valuation reserve (AVR) that assigns risk weightings to various asset types. Although these reserves were imposed for soundness purposes (as opposed to conducting monetary policy) and are held by firms themselves, they nonetheless illustrate the feasibility of systematically reserving institutional investors' assets.

"The experience of European countries during the Bretton Woods era provides additional examples of asset-based reserve systems – some designed to control overall credit expansion and others to shield key sectors from cyclical excesses and droughts. [such measures [were used] in Sweden for housing-related assets, 1972 for Netherlands credit ceilings 1967, and the Bank of England before 1971. France, 1967, targeted both deposits and assets. Italy [made use of them] to restrain inflation periodically, and Switzerland imposed credit limitations 1972-75]. Only by targeting financial firms' assets can a reserve system hope to influence total credit extended to non-financial and financial borrowers and to ensure greater balance in the distribution of resources across the business cycle.

"By shifting reserve requirements in this fashion, the Fed would be able to extend monetary control to an assortment of assets that, as of year end 2001, was 36 times larger than the universe of reservable deposits ($35.8 trillion versus $998 billion).

"With the move to an asset-based system, reserve requirements would become far less onerous to depository institutions, represent a small burden (at most) to nonbank financial firms and remove a longstanding competitive inequality by leveling the field for the entire financial sector."

To the Canadian reader, this discussion of debt-based re-serves in the present tense coming out of the United States, might seem like a message from outer space. When COMER revealed the phasing out in stealth of the statutory reserves from our *Bank Act* in 1991, we were told it had been an "unjust tax." In fact it had provided an alternative to the ruinously high interest-rates imposed by the Bank of Canada as "the one blunt tool to lick inflation." It also offered the government the use of considerable interest-free deposits as a *quid pro quo* for the transfer to the banks of most of the government's historic franchise for the creation of money. Depending on the rate of interest at the time, this represented an entitlement to our bank system of from $5 to $8 billion annually.

Repurchase Agreements as Central Bank's Primary Operating Tool

"Repurchase transactions are ideally structured to interact with all financial firms on the asset side of their balance sheets. For example, the Fed can use a repo to buy government securities (or agencies, corporate bonds, loans, mortgages, commercial paper, etc.) from any institution holding these assets – commercial and investment banks, mutual and pension funds, insurance and finance companies, or GSE (Government-Sponsored-Enterprises).

"Broadening the holdings on its balance sheet would bring the Fed closer to the practices of other central banks.[1] More importantly, authorizing the Fed to conduct repos with any sound financial assets would strengthen the central bank's ability to halt runs, moderate crises and curb excessive investment across the entire financial system, from over-the-counter derivative markets to the mutual fund industry.

"Extending the Fed's range of eligible holdings would eliminate the central bank's need to own a vast amount of Treasury securities – and its reliance on the federal government maintaining relatively high levels of indebtedness. The requirement that one government liability (government securities) be used to back another (outstanding currency) was redundant at the time of its adoption in 1932. While outstanding currency should of course remain a Federal Reserve liability, the central bank does not need to hold Treasury obligations to make good on that claim because it already wields a more powerful guarantee – the ability to create and extinguish Federal Reserve notes.

"In an asset-based system, the Fed could still acquire government securities as backing for repos. But most of its vast current holdings of Treasuries would be released for purchase by investors and financial institutions seeking the ultimate safe-haven asset.

"In a system of universally applied reserve requirements, financial institutions would book reserves on the liability side of their balance sheets rather than on the asset side. It would more accurately reflect the role of both reserves and the central bank in America's current financial system. Defining reserves as liabilities to the Fed would make explicit that reserves represent the financial sector's obligation to serve as a transmission belt for policy initiatives to affect economic activity. Recognizing reserves as liabilities to the Fed [i.e., as Fed assets] would meet the contentious issue of paying interest on reserves – removing a longstanding sore point for depository institutions and a potential expense for taxpayers… The Fed has maintained a set of bookkeeping arrangements that continue to treat its assets and liabilities like those of a mere bankers' bank. Defining financial sector reserves as assets of the central bank would modernize these outdated arrangements by confirming that: (a) the Fed's major function is to create and extinguish liquidity; and (b) it enjoys the unique ability to create the reserves that accomplish this function.

"Reserves would be recorded on the asset side of the Fed's balance sheet, mirroring their entry as liabilities to the Fed on the balance sheets of banks, insurance companies, pension funds, mutual funds, GSEs and all other financial institutions.

"Meanwhile, repurchase agreements and discounts would move from the asset to the liability side of the Fed's balance sheet to reflect the Fed's liability for the private sector assets it acquires when it creates reserves. Foreign exchange assets (international reserves) also would become liabilities rather than assets since they too would be acquired through repurchase agreements. Outstanding currency would remain a liability, manifesting the Fed's congressionally mandated authority to create money and manage its value.

"Since the Fed would no longer earn interest on holdings of government securities – and since it would back repurchase agreements and discounts with non-interest-bearing reserves – the central bank would no longer have income to pay interest on its repos. *But because financial institutions receive invaluable interest-free liabilities when they 'loan' the central bank assets through repos, it seems eminently reasonable to compensate the central bank to receive earnings on the collateral backing these repos.*"[2]

Defence Amnesia of Financial Institutions

Time was when economists referred back to ancestral monarchies and their right of seigniorage – the coining of precious metals – to put the non-interest-bearing reserves into historical perspective. History, however, is hardly the strong suit of the profession: bankers and economists make a point of not remembering even what happened a decade ago. Asset-based central banking as proposed by D'Arista would help combat this tendency of the guild to amnesia. The creation of reserves by the central bank is a highly valuable service. Not only do the services of the central bank allow depository institutions to create credit many times their net worth, but they provide assurance of liquidity when a crisis threatens. It is helpful to bring that to the fore, rather than treat it as a sterile "tax." What is involved is by no means the sort of accountancy fraud that recently almost flattened the world's stock markets, where debts became assets and assets debt for monumental fleecing of the unwary. Here double-entry bookkeeping is observed, and broadening the reserve base to include all financial organizations should keep the charge for this modest. "With all financial institutions participating in the federal funds market, volatility would decline as a result of those institutions making portfolio adjustments by purchasing and selling reserves rather than assets."

Up to now our central banks exerted themselves to create an ever more complicated universe through deregulation while narrowing their policy kit to a "single blunt tool" – interest rates. But interest does happen to be the revenue of a potentially parasitic economic group, and using it as the central bank's one big stick entails a screeching conflict of interest. Broadening of the reserve system and shifting the accountancy from liabilities to assets will permit focusing on specific problem areas. Planned economy? No more than our fire departments are planned to cover emergencies only when and where they arise. They are not programmed to actually light fires.

Of course, even with the important D'Arista's central banking reforms, system would be left with some serious distortions. Let me mention two of these.

The treatment of government investments as liabilities has gone on for decades. They have been handled as current expenses, and written off in a single year. But as of January 1996 the Bureau of Economic Analysis under the Secretary of Commerce began treating such assets as an investment to be depreciated over its useful life. But it didn't call them "investment," but "savings" which is hardly apt, since they are not held in cash. Why? We can only surmise: The Clinton government was interested in just a statistic that bond-rating agencies would smile on; Clinton was determined to avoid arousing the lightly sleeping dogs of the right. Carried forward several years, the adjustment produced an improved balance sheet for the government of over one trillion dollars and helped achieve the lower interest rates that the government sought. Government investment – a term that reeked of the influence of Keynes – was not even mentioned.

In Canada in July 1999 a bill introducing accrual accountancy (a.k.a. capital budgeting) was passed on the insistence of the Auditor General before he would issue an unconditional approval of the previous two years' accounts. But nothing further was heard about it until mid-February 2003, when the government, beset with budgetary surpluses melting into deficits, crumbling infrastructures, commitments to restore slashings of grants to the provinces for health education and social services, pressure for increased military spending to meet the Iraq crisis, widening divisions in all parties, the disasters of privatization and of Deregulation and Globalization, with the Bank of Canada blowing the whistle about the danger of inflation when the world economy was clearly sinking into deflation. And then, out of the blue, the new Finance Minister, John Manley announced that capital budgeting would be introduced in the budget due in a matter of days.

The other similar reform that has been denied so much as a mention is the ever deepening stratum of taxation in the price level. This pays for the ever greater unpriced public services needed to keep our economy and our society functioning.

Were a flat price level retained as the main goal of the central bank, it would frustrate the proposed new transmission mechanisms for monetary policy that D'Arista proposes. These additional challenges lie beyond D'Arista's mission. We can therefore hope that others will be inspired by her achievements to carry forward the analysis into these closely related fields.

William Krehm

1. "Expanding the Fed's eligible holdings would also confirm the wisdom of former Chairman [Marriner] Eccles, who argued that the *Banking Act* of 1935 should be amended to free the Fed to buy or discount 'any sound asset.' At that time, the *Federal Reserve Act* permitted only trade bills to serve as backing for currency and bank reserves. The reluctance of a few powerful members of Congress to change this provision almost defeated the effort to extend emergency legislation that added government securities as eligible paper. Since then, government securities have attained the status trade bills once had as the enshrined central bank asset."

2. "If the Fed kept the earnings on financial assets held under repurchase agreements, the income – along with fees for check clearance and other services – should prove sufficient for it to continue operating at or near current levels."

A SYSTEMS VIEW

Problems of World Security

IN HIS RECENT BOOK, *The Hidden Connections*,[1] Fritjof Capra deals with issues of political power and creativity from a systems science perspective. Beginning with current understandings of the nature of life and social reality he goes on to consider the networks of global capitalism. He pulls together many of the themes advanced by critics of capitalism, and relates them to fundamental science. Capra also draws upon the work of Manuel Castells[2] and others.[3]

This leads to a very useful perspective on current economic and political problems of American foreign policy. Castells advances the hypothesis "that all major trends of change constituting our new, confusing world are related, and that we can make sense of their interrelationships."

Information and Money Flows

Central to this thesis is the common observation that we have moved into an "informational society," which makes possible financial networking on a global scale. It is noted that the rise of globalization has proceeded through processes that are characteristics of all human organizations. While many effects are intended, some are emergent, not clearly observed or delineated, and are very poorly understood.

Among these, as is well known, have been the rise of global capitalism and the dominance of money flows which ignore the social and environmental costs of economic activities. This uncontrolled process has involved the gradual dismantling of the social contract between capital and labour, deregulation of financial trading and privatization of many services. This new capitalism is global, requires continuing innovation, and is structured largely around networks of finance. Profits are channelled back into the meta-network of financial flows to move rapidly from one option to another in the search for investment opportunities. Information technology, and the cultural capacity to use it, are essential for both productivity and competitiveness. To promote this process, transnational corporations are supported by the World Bank, the International Monetary Fund and the World Trade Organization, which were created for that purpose.

However the multiple systems – social, economic, governmental, industrial – are in practice so complex, turbulent and unpredictable as to defy analysis in conventional economic terms. Financial flows do not follow market logic alone; they are also the consequence of computer-governed investment strategies, subjective decisions, political events and the complex turbulences involved in the many interactions, which escape the possibility of timely analysis. Severe financial crises have been among the results. In the wake of the Asian financial crisis (1997), Paul Volker, the former Chair of the US Federal Reserve, stated that "something has been lacking in our analyses...and there is every indication that [the problem] is systemic."[4] We have unresolved problems of instability, and we know from the study of complex living systems that stability is a requirement for life.

Moreover, the new economy may be seen as shaped in its fundamentals by networks of machines programmed according to a single value – money-making for the sake of making money – and to the exclusion of all other values. In the words of Castells, "We have created an Automaton at the core of our economics [that is] taking control of our world...."[5]

Values Shape the Future

Yet this is not an inevitable process. The critical issue is not technology per se, but politics and human values. And in view of the social and cultural impacts this question of alternative values and strategies looms very large indeed.

Central to the argument being pursued here is that in the competition for livelihood in the world are two major kinds of labour – unskilled and educated. Unskilled workers are not required to access information and need only understand and follow orders. Such workers may be replaced at any moment by fluctuations in global financial markets. Thus increased poverty and hopelessness have made life a nightmare for ever larger numbers of people, expendable under the present rules.

Whole countries and regions are now thus afflicted. The systemic effects of the new economy is having disastrous social consequences all over the world, contributing to marginality, criminality and to attitudes and cultures of anger and hatred which are on the increase. These tend to be attributed to America, somewhat of a scapegoat but partially responsible.

Nor does "free trade" based upon the premise of continuing economic growth on a finite planet hold long-run hope for all the well educated. The promise of benefits from "free trade" have not met their short term goals, and the long-run trends seem ominous to many informed observers.

Because the stakes are so high – the future of the world is at issue – it is worth considering the hypothesis that some of the internal and external difficulties facing the United States, as addressed by President Bush in his State of the Union speech on January 28, 2003, involve some of these unanalyzed connections. The primary political concerns are the domestic economy and jobs as well as international affairs. These are clearly closely related and involve a matrix of problems not primarily attributable to terrorists or individual bad actors such as Saddam Hussein. As we know, mischief and worse are attributed to Saddam, certainly partially responsible but also somewhat of a scapegoat for more general fears.

Diagnoses: Systemic Disorders

It is characteristic of human nature to look for concrete and practical solutions for even the most complex problems. Yet accurate diagnosis and sound management strategies are all important. Where the problems are systemic in nature this should be understood before tackling individual symptoms.

Certainly there are underlying problems in many developing countries where people young and old feel dispossessed, for reasons they do not understand or cannot accept, who therefore support what may appear to others as irrational policies, including terrorist acts. But to the extent that this is the case, terrorism cannot be simply suppressed. To eliminate terrorism requires its replacement with strategies that take account of economic needs and realities. Such an appraisal may not be the whole truth, or the only truth. Even if it is partly true, it points to a useful approach to problems both on the domestic and foreign affairs fronts. There are also many in the relatively prosperous West who are also much concerned for the future and for their children, who show their concern by demonstrating, often without a clear idea of what the real problems are or who to blame.

To rely on a theory which is mistaken adds to problems and makes a solution more difficult. And unfortunately, much political and economic thinking is built upon supposedly practical and "hard-headed" analogies with physical combat. Capra cites the clear distinction between reliance on the leverage of physical force, and recognition of the role of values, creativity and autonomy in coordination of civilized human behaviour.

Seductive Simplifications of Power

The contention offered here is that an important part of the problem facing the civilized world is the disorder and inequality being served up by the Automaton of uncontrolled financial networks. To the extent that this is the case, then to misidentify and locate some specific agent or devil is not likely to lead to good results. While one cancer may be removed, if conditions are not changed, others will take their place. If the diagnosis is faulty or inadequate, and the remedy tangential to the real problem, the outcome will not be successful. The underlying problems will continue unabated – the rage of those dispossessed under current arrangements will continue to fester – and the attempted remedies lead to problems more grave than those they were intended to resolve.

In the field of foreign relations the resort to analogies of mechanism and threats of physical force may seem the only guarantee of security. And often this may be so – even with its risk of lost opportunities. Each nation will insist upon its own autonomy; As Bush said in his State of the Union speech, to much applause: "This nation does not depend upon others." Of course, the same logic applies to other sovereign nations. Yet the fact is that every nation is stronger when it benefits from the support and cooperation of others, and weaker when it does not.

No matter how sincere leaders may be in their beliefs, if they view politics as the manipulation of citizens they pose a threat to the integrity of their own societies. Leaders whose assumptions revolve around power and its rewards are not those whose creative energies shape the future. Power has its advantages in the short run, but these fade away as time horizons and challenges broaden. To destroy what is seen as evil is not enough; it is also necessary to cultivate values and relationships, which actively promote the good.

Leadership cannot be justified by power alone, but depends fundamentally on a creative vision, which can be shared. Intelligent attention to financial and market systems is required. Only then will a just peace become possible.

Bruce Buchanan

1. Capra, F. (2002). *The Hidden Connections: Integrating the Biological, Cognitive and Social Dimensions of Life into a Science of Sustainability.* Doubleday.
2. Castells, Manuel (1996). *The Rise of the Network Society.* Blackwell.
3. Mander, J. and Goldsmith, E. (1996). *The Case Against the Global Economy.* Sierra Club Books.
4. Quoted by Capra, p. 140.
5. Quoted by Capra, p. 141.

The Tricky Perks of a Lone Superpower

A WHOLE NEW AREA of vulnerability has opened with the unique status of the United States today. There are certainly vast perks that come with its position as sole superpower both in a military and a financial sense. Money and people flock to it for security. Since the early 1970s money has been even in theory nothing but debt. But all that depends on the trust inspired by the debtor. Clearly the debt of the superpower, other things being equal, wins here on several counts. Once its credit is accepted as reserve currency by central and commercial banks, and, not least of all, by speculators, the superpower needs only touch its computer keys to produce further reserves. Third world and emerging countries must export to the superpower at any price to earn the dollars to service their dollar debt. That deflates wages and other costs in the debtor country. It gives the superpower, however, more absolute power over the subject land than could be obtained with an army of occupation. By setting the terms of debt restructuring, former colonized lands can be deprived of the possibility of ever acquiring a degree of economic and hence political independence. Globalization and Deregulation prevents the subjected country from resorting to the tariffs and exchange controls that allowed the United States to develop its economic and financial might. The US in fact has sacrificed a good deal of its low-tech production to take advantage of this financial monopoly. More and more in lower-tech industries the actual production is being transferred to branch plants in East Asia, Mexico, and now to China itself.

But as this process has enabled the speculative financial sector within the US to take over, it has begun undermining the dollar's preeminence on the international arena. That is possible because of the unique position the dollar holds as reserve currency. It required the influx of foreign loans and investments into the United States along with the privileged position of its fiat money as reserve currency. For only that allowed the US to absorb the cheap exports of most of the world, and to entrust the relatively unskilled processes of manufacturing to the emerging lands. The Euro was introduced in Europe to challenge the US in this lucrative field that assigned much of the hard dirty work to lesser nations. 45.7% of cross-border loans were denominated in US dollars compared with 28.7% in euros at the end of March 2002. 70% of the world's foreign exchange reserves were denominated in US dollars and 17% in Euros.

Today these perks of super-power status are rapidly eroding – to some extent by the very folly of the US government. Historically, the most serious weakness of the US has been to ascribe its vast advantages to Manifest Destiny rather than to a constellation of circumstances. These had to be carefully nurtured not only with gunboats, but with a sensitivity to the feelings of lesser nations on which its supremacy rests. Philosophers like Hegel would say that supreme status of any single state is to an extent a reciprocal relationship. It calls for a degree of acceptance by the lesser partners.

The collapse of the US stock market bubble – the largest on record – has made its contribution to the threatening debacle. The loss to date amounts to over 70% of a full year's US GDP.

Until the beginning of 1999, there was no serious alternative to the dollar as reserve currency. The euro launched at the beginning of that year provided that alternative. The US stock market boom and the American voracity for imports caused the new currency to fall by 30% during the first two years of its existence. In the most recent year it has come to exceed its original parity with the dollar by 10%. The corruption revealed in the accountancy of some of the largest failed corporations, the high technologies of deception designed by its very auditing firms, did nothing to buttress the credibility of the US. A crisis of morality of such proportions knows few boundaries. Countries with bones to pick with Washington have lost no time in exploiting this vulnerability. Iraq has asked that the $10 billion in its frozen bank account in New York be converted into euros. Iran, proclaimed part of the axis of evil, has been threatening a switch to the euro for both its oil and non-oil trade. "The euro could become our currency of choice" should it make further gains against the dollar (*Agence France Presse*, 31/12/01). There are rumblings in Saudi Arabia on the same theme. As oil prices climb, and the expenditure for American military adventures abroad mount, it is not unlikely that US hedge funds, starved for profits, may shelve their patriotism long enough to join in shorting the dollar.

After all the supreme law of self-interest and the all-wise market has been instilled into heads by government, universities, and the media.

"In a report commissioned by Russia's Central Bank in July 1999, the Russian Academy of Science said: 'The introduction

of the euro alters the conditions for Russian integration into the world economy. In the final analysis, the consequences are to the benefit of our country" (*Asia Times*, 19/5/01).

"Another likely candidate for switching to the euro is Venezuela, whose leader Hugo Chavez the US has been attempting to oust over the last year. The more countries that switch to the euro, the more attractive the euro becomes"(*Aspects of India's Economy*, December, 2002).

A multilateral agreement with friendly and not-too-hostile powers could at least retard the drop of the dollar in euro terms. But surely the rejection of multilateralism in more instances than we have fingers to count on, weakens the case for Washington playing the multilateral card to defend the right-of-first-night of its currency. Indeed, the diplomats of other nations who have been jolted by Washington's arrogance in dismissing its obligations under the Kyoto Protocol, the International Criminal Court, its rejection of the anti-personnel mines ban treaty, its withdrawal from the Anti-ballistic Missile Treaty; its threat that the UN would become irrelevant if it did not follow the instructions of the US on the invasion of Iraq, its increasingly aggressive conduct in trade matters, and much else are likely to return to haunt it.

As the world sinks into deflation, and the protectionism of the 1930s is reappearing, the stage is set for some rude awakenings.

The tens of millions who demonstrated against the deadline for the invasion of Iraq across the globe had an important message for the US government. It should not miss the point. History has similar warnings. But they are not heeded.

Pretzelizing History

Let us take the evidence *The Wall Street Journal* (29/01, "Capital Journal – Ambitious Agenda Poses Risks for Bush as 2004 Approaches" by John Harwood): "In the evening quiet of the White House, the commander-in-chief worried about the collision between foreign and domestic priorities. He sought authority for military attack just as Congress was considering his economic agenda.

"'Will it kill, or help us?' the president asked a top aide. The aide couldn't offer him any certainty.

"George W. Bush can't be any surer today than Lyndon Johnson was about mixing his war on poverty with a war in Vietnam in that tape-recorded exchange 39 years ago, recounted in Michael Beschloss's book *Taking Charge*."

But surely what brought Johnson to grief was a war that never should have been. It was based on the folly of the "domino theory" that held that if Communism were allowed to come to power no matter where – in Nicaragua or Vietnam, every neighbouring country would keel over into Communism until the US would be left to confront the Communist hordes in Virginia and the Dakotas. In its day "the domino theory" was presented as absolute a truth as the need for a preemptive strike against Iraq is today. In the process of heading off that imaginary peril, they dragged the prestige and fair name of the United States through the bloody mud, alienated many of the brightest and unselfish of its own younger generation. It finally emerged that the Soviet Empire would have crumbled under the burden of its own iniquities. The bashing that the Americans took in Vietnam if anything retarded the Soviet collapse. That, however, has been one of the great Unlearned Lessons.

"Harry Truman saw the Korean War sap attention from his Fair Deal and limped from office without achieving national health assurance." However, rather than a budget overstretched by the Korean War, what did in Truman and his plans was the virtual *coup d'état* of the Federal Reserve in cahoots with the banking establishment undoing the essence of the Rooseveltian banking reforms. That ruled out financing that war and the scheduled social programs substantially through the central bank, as was done in WWII.

In its March 20, 1991, issue, on its 50th anniversary of the event, *FOMC Alert*, the publication of the Financial Markets Center, recounted the episode that led the world directly into its present mess.

"Under the leadership of Marriner Eccles, the central bank had worked intimately with the Roosevelt Administration to combat deflation during the great depression and finance America's effort in World War II. Throughout the second half of the 1940s, though, the Fed chafed at Treasury 'pattern of rates' dictates."

Fed Elevating Interest Rate as Sole Stabilizer Destabilized Muslim World

"As it moved to overturn this arrangement, the central bank displayed uncanny bravado. Despite its subordinate status – economic historian Daniel Vencill labels the Fed of the late 1940s 'a sorry, dowdy operation' – the central bank marshaled support from key members of Congress and the financial press. And it precipitated a showdown with the executive branch under astonishing circumstances.

"As US ground troops poured into South Korea in the summer of 1950, the FOMC [the Federal Open Market Commission] coolly approved a request from the Federal Reserve Bank of New York to hike its discount rate, citing concerns over rising inflation. With this act, the central bank signaled its refusal to take marching orders from Treasury. [And this was] at the onset of a military action widely expected to trigger broader conflict and in a culture accustomed to mobilizing all institutions for global war.

"Months later, the confrontation came to a head. In January 1951, President Truman invited FOMC members to the White House to... 'reestablish a working formula for debt management and credit policy.' After the meeting, Truman announced that the central bank had agreed to resume its peg.

"The Fed officials came away with a different impression. Two days after the president's statement, Marriner Eccles – bypassed by Truman for another term as chairman but still a powerful presence as governor – personally released an internal Fed memo that flatly contradicted the White House version of events.

"'I was given assurance at this meeting that the Federal Reserve would support the Treasury's plans for financing the action in Korea,' Truman wrote in his memoirs, 'and when they

left I firmly believed that I had their agreement to cooperate. I was taken by surprise when subsequently they failed to support the program." Thirty-two days after the meeting, Truman's Treasury okayed an accord on the Fed's terms.

This initiated the process that eventually elevated interest rates to the status of ' lone blunt tool' for stabilizing the world economy. In doing so it contributed to the suicidal terrorism that concerns us so deeply today. For on the subject of interest, let alone usury, the Muslim religion minces no words. And by that very token, the most powerful tool in the war against Bin Laden, would be to return to the use of the Federal Reserve and central banks throughout the world to provide a major part of the credit needs of governments for essential investments on a virtual interest-free basis. How would foreign exchange problems fit into such a scheme? With exchange controls, two-tiered central banking could be brought in. To mobilize the domestic resources available for many public capital projects, credit in domestic currency could be created by the national central bank. What imported items for the purpose were needed could be provided through a system of exchange controls. And such capital projects – inexpensive housing, schools, hospitals, water systems would be entered in the government books for what they in fact are – investments that should be written off gradually over their useful life rather during the year of construction. In Canada, for example, though a bill was passed by parliament in mid-1999 on the insistence of the Auditor General, nothing has been heard about it ever since. Such public investments are carried on the official books at a nominal dollar while the debt incurred to create them is carried on the liability side of the ledger. Obvious this does two things: it exaggerates the public debt, and it sets up government capital assets for bargain-basement privatization that it is hoped will revive the stock market boom.

In the United States capital accountancy (also known as accrual accountancy) was introduced at the beginning of 1996 in great stealth, but misrepresented as an increase in government "savings." All the Administration wanted was an improved statistic to get a higher rating from the bond rating agencies, without alienating Wall St.

If we are serious about defending our world against terrorism, we must go beyond having corps of writers revise the President's speeches. We must in fact review our economic theory, our accountancy, and our statistics. We must restore the possibility of free discussion to identify what in our suppressed history might be useful to help us out of the economic troubles closing in on the world. However, when Canada finally was compelled to introduce some capital budgetting by its Auditor General, it made some fleeting reference to what it was all about on budget day. And then the subject was buried in the media in silence and misrepresentation.

Until the 1970s, the statutory reserves that banks had to leave with the Fed as a proportion of the deposits made it unnecessary to depend wholly on higher interest rates to rein in inflation. This arrangement limited the amount of lending banks could do during a boom, as well as the rates they could charge.

Hand in hand with the move away from the reserve system,

went the deregulation of the banks to allow them to enter financial activities in conflict with their banking function.

Globalization and Deregulation are rapidly bringing the world to conditions disturbingly like those of the 1930s. Defending the world against Hitler would have been impossible without putting the economy of the democracies in order. That is why our history and its lessons must be made available once more.

We have developed a technology for digging up our land mines. But not those we bury in our economic policies.

William Krehm

As Fly in Spider-Web, Entangled in Past Lies

ELSEWHERE IN THIS ISSUE we hail the government for at long last switching to accrual accounting (a.k.a. "capital budgeting"). This permits our Finance Minister in his new budget to use the credit that was always there to attend to some of our most urgent needs in childcare, welfare, health, infrastructural disrepair, housing, underequipped defence forces, a crumbling educational system. The bill that made this possible was passed in mid-1999 and reported in only a single national paper, apparently desperate enough for readers to be reduced to honest reporting.

For the government it was a shot-gun marriage, the blushing bride ten-months pregnant. The Auditor General of the day, Denis Desautels, had simply withheld his unconditional approval of the government's books unless the Finance Minister brought in such elementary accountancy. But then Finance Minister Paul Martin spent months working out a Faustian deal – in which the Auditor General would get the desired accountancy, but was obliged to misinform the public about its significance.

Up to now when the federal government buys or builds a bridge, a building, a naval vessel, it writes off the entire cost in the first year as a current expense – hence requiring more taxation. After that, though an asset may last ten or forty years, it is carried on the books at one dollar.

If Mr. Martin Kept his Shipping Line with One-year Capital Write-offs

If Mr. Martin kept his shipping company's books that way, it would have gone bankrupt and/or been prosecuted by the government. Were a private person to do so, he would calculate his net worth by entering the mortgage that helped pay for his home as a liability, but omit entering the house as an asset. End result: he would end up paying through the nose for what credit he could get. That is precisely what happened with the government and its finances. Except that on top of that, the central bank, mistaking accounting irresponsibility for "fiscal irresponsibility," shoved interest rates up over 20% to impose prudence. The country ended up in the pawn-shop. The absence of serious

bookkeeping created most of our national debt in the 1990s.

The Auditor General – his arm twisted by Mr. Martin – finally consented to declare that since no new money was brought into the treasury by the change in accountancy, it should not be taken as a sign that more money was there to spend. That is mischievous nonsense, and Mr. Desautels knew it when agreed to such a declaration.

Mr. Martin put himself in the position of Enron, Global Crossing, and umpteen other American mega-corporations convicted of auditing their auditors.

Since the spurious deficit and debt had been the pretext for slashing social programs and driving up interest rates, the present recognition of our capital assets can and should reverse that process. The budget that is being brought in is living proof of that.

On the point Finance Minister John Manley himself was frank enough: " Full accrual was recommended frequently by the Auditor General and by everybody who wants full, transparent accounting on our books." Apart from the accounting profession – behind closed doors – over the past three decades I and later COMER have carried on that campaign with practically no company. Transparent accounting on the government books was termed "loony." Once you have *gleichgeschaltet* against you the press, the CBC, the central bank, and professordom (when speaking on record), it is true you must have a streak of madness to persist in taking a contrary position, just because it is leading the world to hunger, break-down, and wars. That streak of madness is also known as principle.

One of the many difficulties about cooking books, is it is hard stopping to do so without an implicit confession of what you've been up to.

Are the Homeless in Better Shape than the Royal Bank?

The same holds for switching to honest newspaper reporting on subjects previously verboten.

Thus *The Globe and Mail's* report announcing the accountancy changes continues immediately after the above quotation from Mr. Manley. "The government's decision will not directly alter Ottawa's financial health or the amount Canadians owe in debt." The last comparison is meaningless. The Royal Bank of Canada owes more money than any homeless person sleeping on the sidewalks. That does not, however, mean that the latter is in better condition than the RBC. It is its net debt, i.e., debt less assets, and net revenue that count. Besides, the fact that the Government is now doing all these fine new things gives the lie to its claim that it does not "directly alter Ottawa's financial health."

The Globe and Mail is stumbling and bumbling to cover its tracks. On 17/02, in addition to an editorial of the same quality, it ran a column by Brian Milner, "Our politicians are fiscally more frugal than Americans," "Chrétien doesn't want to go down in history as a loony who was only held in check by Paul Martin."

Then Milner gets the accounting subject mixed up with Fed Governor Alan Greenspan's "strange notion that budget deficits would not drive up long-term interest rates. He also repeated his advice that the government switch to the accrual method of accounting, which would provide a truer, more transparent picture of the fiscal situation by taking into account such long-term obligations as Social Security and Medicare payments, as well as future revenue obligations such as Social Security and Medicare payments." Corrections:

1. Milner might have added education, and much else. These are all government *investments in human capital*, which economists have long since recognized in foot notes as the most productive of all investments. Theodore Schultz of the University of Chicago was awarded a Nobel prize in Economics for having reached that conclusion from the rapid reconstruction after the war of devastated Japan and Germany. It was due to their rich human capital, which emerged from the war almost intact. Human capital has not been included in Canada's 1999 recognition of accrual accountancy. Had it been, it would have more than doubled the neglected public investment to be recognized.

2. "US politicians are loath to approve such a change, because the liabilities are so huge the government would be awash in red ink." Adding the neglected investments in human capital to what has been recognized would have further improved its ability to take on more debt for productive purposes. Only then would the term "full accrual accountancy" that Mr. Manley uses be justified. Our government as sole shareholder of the central bank, can borrow from it at a near-zero-interest basis, since the bulk of the interest paid on government debt held by the BoC reverts to the government as dividends. With a balance sheet improved by the recognition of public investment in human capital, financing productive public capital projects would be prudent and desirable. Of course, there would have to be less borrowing from the private financial system by the government. Fiscal responsibility in this new context of total "full accrual accountancy" would require that the aggregate investment of the private and public sectors be kept within limits of real resources in labour and materials available in the economy.

A New Campaign of Misinformation?

3. "US politicians are loath to approve such a change." Wake up Mr. Milner! Wake up *G&M!* Accrual accountancy was snuck in by President Clinton beginning with 1996. The story is told in *Meltdown*, edited by W. Krehm, 1999, pp. 224-226. I will quote a section of the coverage to convey what effort goes into finding the real facts about legislation that may affect the lives of the entire world population. A.W. Caughey of Valencia, Pennsylvania puts out a modest xeroxed review of economic statistics, and is a subscriber to *Economic Reform*. "We are indebted to him for bringing to our attention a quiet revolution in the official US statistics that literally reduces to nonsense the central issue around which the presidential campaign is being run: the deficit. He writes: 'Overnight the nation's savings data jumped by $132.2 billion for 1994 and even more for some prior years. This is due to the fact that the Bureau of Economic Analysis [under] the Secretary of Commerce now incorporates the government investment in arriving at the total. Prior to January of this year, when the government purchased assets with

long lives, such as buildings or computer systems, the Bureau of Economic Analysis (BEA) treated the purchase as an investment to be written off 100 percent in the year of purchase. The effect was to understate the nation's total saving and to overstate the government deficit. All of which reveals the budget-balancing charade for what it is – an assault on public service expenditures. Budget balancing is valued not as a goal but as a process to undo the progressive legislation of the past sixty years. The foregoing data can be verified in the *Survey of Current Business* for Jan.-Feb., p. 13, *Economic Indicators*, p. 34, and the *Federal Reserve Bulletin*, table A-4.'"

The only change we made in Caughey's excellent analysis was to point out that listing such investment as "savings" distorted the picture – as the government undoubtedly intended: since Keynes's mature contribution to economics a deep distinction must be made between "savings" and "investment." Investment spurs the economy and when necessary lifts it out of a recession. Cash saving by the government or the reduction of its debt has the contrary effect.

The very term "government investment" causes free market ideologues to see red. Governments are proclaimed incapable of investing, only capable of wasting tax-money. Which of course, is true when they bail commercial banks out on so wholesale a scale from their gambling losses as happened in the early 1990s, and then proceed to deregulate them further. But the immediate purpose of this note is to record the beginnings of a campaign to distort and sabotage the real nature and purpose of accrual accountancy. You can expect it to crescendo by all means fair or foul. Join us in countering it!

William Krehm

P.S. In bringing down the budget on February 18, the Finance Minister referred repeatedly to accrual accountancy, but in doing so encountered neither applause nor understanding among his own caucus. Noting this, he started explaining what the term might mean. Since Parliament had passed the bill introducing accrual accountancy over three and a half years ago, you might ask what the House – with substantially the same Liberal caucus – might have thought it was voting for.

By the next day *The Globe and Mail* reported the new budget only in terms of who got what, what tax went up or down, but not so much as a mention of accrual accountancy. Meanwhile three of its columnists lashed into the Chrétien and Manley for their "People's budget" and their return to the deficits of Trudeau and Brian Mulroney! The new art of running democracies would seem to exclude sharing with the voters or Parliament what the government is up to.

A Scorched Field in the Battle for Capital Budgeting

THE INTRODUCTION of capital budgeting (a.k.a. accrual accountancy) had been, in the words of our Finance Minister, John Manley, "recommended frequently by the Auditor General and by everybody else who wants full, transparent accountancy in our books."

Let us pause to give credit where it is due – to the great number of hard-working accountants who, irrespective of where their monetary interest lay, defended meaningful accountancy against the crunching of rigged numbers.

Obviously the Auditor General who stood up to the then Finance Minister Paul Martin is high on that list, though a shameful compromise was imposed on him by Mr. Martin. to hide rather than disclose what accrual accountancy can reveal. The staff of *The Bottom Line*, an accountants' trade publication that leaked the information about that hard bargaining merits our thanks.

Accountants as a profession in the past couple of years have been victims of a bum rap. Some of the largest accountancy organizations in the US have been convicted for devising the scams that enabled corporations like Enron, Border Crossings and many more to cheat their shareholders, the public and the government. All the greater reason for acknowledging with gratitude the struggle over decades of other accountants to prevent governments from cheating the more vulnerable members of society on behalf of the most privileged.

Meanwhile, in a matter of a day or two, the subject has been twisted to create more confusion than the promised transparency. It is in fact hardly if ever mentioned any more in the media discussions of the Manley budget. It is vitally important to understand how this has been achieved. The method in fact is the same by which accrual accountancy was kept out of the government books against the advice of accountants and royal commissions for some four decades.

Essentially it has been to trivialize the issue to the production a couple of statistics that lend themselves to the desired number-crunching as of yore. Notably these are the balance of the *cash* budget, and the growth rate (GDP). But these figures are a can of worms. A public investment that really qualifies as such is not to be judged by the amount of public debt it involves but only by its effects on the economy and whether the real resources are available to undertake it. If not, and if it is vital enough for society and the functioning of all its subsystems, it may be pared down to what is barely essential, but not ignored.

In short, capital budgeting is not to be judged by its usefulness for the crunching of a couple of misleading statistics assigned crucial importance by a totally failed economic model. That would in fact prolong the stranglehold of that failed theory to the bitter end. Reduce capital accountancy to that and you are continuing the cooking of the books, but simply shifting the process to a microwave oven.

W.K.

War as Viagra for the US Economy?

FROM THE EXPERIENCE of War II it was widely assumed that a war against Iraq would help the world economy cope with the bind that Globalization and Deregulation has gotten it into. But *The Wall Street Journal* informs us that this is not so (4/02, "Spending on War Won't Outweigh its Negative Impact on Economy" by Bob Davis and Greg Jaffe). "Military spending is one of few recent bright spots in a weak US economy, but an Iraq war won't provide the stimulative jolt that military conflicts once did.

"A surge in orders for military goods was the only reason orders for big-ticket factory goods rose in December. Outside the military sector, oil suppliers from giant Exxon Mobil Corp. to tiny Apache Corp. reported steep rises in fourth-quarter earnings, as crude oil prices soared on fears of war.

"But the $100 billion or so the US is likely to spend fighting and then rebuilding Iraq won't make much difference to the $10 trillion-a-year US economy. The harmful effects of war – sharply reduced consumer confidence, a sagging stock market and reluctance by businesses to invest – now overshadow any gains from military spending."

And then comes the punch-line: "Military research-and-development profits don't have the powerful commercial spin-offs they once did. World War II projects to develop nuclear power, jet engines, and radar spawned new industries that helped power a post-war boom. Nowadays, the Pentagon struggles to keep up with advances in computing and communications pioneered by commercial firms."

Indeed, the indications are multiplying that our economy is less and less able to maintain the military and quasi-military technology. Thus *The Globe and Mail* (3/02, "NASA faces big questions" by Paul Koring) informs us: "Nearly a year ago, Richard Blomberg, then chairman of the Aerospace Safety Advisory Panel, warned 'the safety margin has eroded too far.' After the damning report NASA removed five of the panel's nine members and two of its consultants.

"Former NASA technician Don Nelson told a British newspaper he had asked the White House last summer to intervene to 'prevent another catastrophic space-shuttle accident' because of safety fears."

In short, while the White House has been prattling about Star Wars ever since Reagan, they were nickel-and-diming the astronauts. These ended up risking their lives so that Wall St. might have the right-of-way for its own space flights.

The final insult heaped on injury to their Cold Warrior lineage: the disasters in America's space program have left it dependent on Russia for some of the most rudimentary life-saving needs of the space program.

Thus *The Wall Street Journal* (5/02, "The Hard Questions for NASA: Can the Space Station Survive? – Forced to Rely on the Russians"): "The greatest engineering challenge ever attempted, the International Space Station is over budget, behind schedule and so dumbed-down that it will be hard-pressed to perform its primary task, space-based science. Another of its original purposes, as a launch pad for a mission to Mars, was scrubbed because of outsized costs. Still incomplete, the station has undergone a decade of funding cutbacks and design modifications in pursuit of another lofty goal – as an orbiting platform for international scientific collaboration.

That, too, hasn't worked out as planned for the 16 countries in the project. The Canadians, for instance, are miffed that cutbacks have limited their research allotment to 30 minutes a week. The US has gotten angry with the Russians because they have required more than $1 billion in direct funding support from the National Aeronautics and Space Administration to keep up with their commitments.

"Meanwhile, NASA and its partners confront more-immediate issues: how to get the current crew back to Earth, whether to launch a replacement crew and whether to mothball the station. Subject to atmospheric drag, the station received periodical nudges from visiting shuttles to help maintain its orbital position. On its own, the facility can maintain a safe orbit only as long as it has adequate fuel for its boosters before it starts falling back to Earth.

"In the short run, as the Columbia investigation unfolds and America's remaining shuttle fleet is grounded, the station will have to depend on the Russian space program. Yesterday, an unmanned Russian Progress craft arrived at the station with fuel and food. But Russia lacks the money to fly more missions to the station or contribute more for construction. The Russians are already suggesting that the USD will have to foot the bill for their expanded interim role.

"'For us, it's big money. For the US it's kopeks,' says Valery Ryumin, deputy head of the RSC Energia Corp., which builds the Progress ships and the manned Soyuz spacecraft. Soyuz, like the shuttle, serves as a ferry to the station."

An Uneven Power Rivalry Carried from Planet Earth to Cooperation in Space

And that brings us to the uneven partnership carried over from the economic power-game to the space program. "The space-program has always been an uneasy marriage of science, politics, business and diplomacy." It was a perfect problem for system analysis. For it to fly, no subsystem can be allowed to cannibalize another. Instead, however, it largely mirrored the power relationships in the economic sphere.

First proposed by President Reagan as "Space Station Freedom" in 1984 as a permanently crewed lab, space factory and staging station for missions to Mars. The price tag was then $8 billion and the target completion date was 1994. But industry showed little interest in space manufacturing. President George W.H. Bush's 1989 proposal for a manned Mars mission within 30 years failed to gain traction after NASA, despite far lower private-sector estimates pegged the cost at $500 billion.

But the decisive point was the break-up of the Soviet Union. As in many areas, the optimum behaviour of the US depended on the presence of a rival superpower. For military programs money seems ever available. Science per se, and non-marketed programs cannot stand up to the imperatives of balancing a budget that still sees public investment as nothing more than simple "spending."

"That left science the only survivor of the station's original justifications. Then a new one quickly emerged: international cooperation with space-faring nations such as Canada, Japan, members of the European Space Agency, and especially Russia." After the Soviet collapse, keeping Russian engineers busy building one-third of the station rather than peddling their services to North Korea or Iran suddenly "seemed a good idea. In1993, Russia was invited to help build the station.

"A Russian Proton rocket ferried up the first piece of the station in 1998, depositing it in a 250-mile-high orbit. The facility is currently the size of a three-bedroom house.

"Russia's contributions were supposed to save NASA $2 billion, since Russian salaries and maintenance costs are much lower than their American counterparts. But when Russia pleaded penury in the mid-1990s, NASA had to pay to avoid massive delays. Russia received $1.4 billion for its station services, including $660 million to make sure it completed the 20-ton Zvezda service module, which was finally sent aloft in 2000, three years behind schedule. In addition to providing temporary living quarters for the crew, Zvezda controls the station's orientation in space and periodically fires small boosters to help keep it in orbit. Overall, the original estimated price tag of $8 billion had soared to $19.4 billion by 1993 to $23.3 billion in 2000, and to $35 billion last month.

"Another problem can be seen in the project's contract changes for 1998 and 1999. NASA ordered 593 alterations to the station's prime contract at a cost of $897.7 million. About half of these changes and about 98% of the additional cost came from contracts authorizing work without a negotiated agreement with the contractor."

This highlights the unmanageable complexities when private contracting introduces the usual mouse-and-cat game between the government and contractors – when time pressures and the irrelevance of costs in life-saving emergency measures often prevents formally negotiated contracts. "To compensate for wildly spiraling costs, NASA has scaled back the scope of the station on several occasions. To save $3 billion it eliminated the habitation module, with crew living quarters, and a crew re-entry vehicle. When NASA attempted to identify the specifics of the projected savings, instead of $1 billion NASA analysts identified new areas of cost growth. That resulted in a net increase in total space-station spending."

How could it be otherwise when you are planning missions to Mars?

But to make ends meet, NASA cut its science budget for the project. "By 1996 it had halved funding for gravitational biology to $250 million. Cutting the habitation module meant room for three rather than seven astronauts at any one time. That gives the Canadians half an hour a week for research – based mainly on its funding contributions – while the European Space Agency gets about two hours. The agency is phasing out experiments in evolutionary biology, environmental health, and reflects a lack of industry interest in materials processing. The unending cutbacks have infuriated scientists.

"The one country that has made the best of it so far is Russia, for whom space-station funding is a critical underpinning of its underfunded space program. Besides the US Shuttle, Russia's Soyuz and Progress vehicles have been the primary ferries to the station. That's expected to intensify during the period that the US fleet is grounded. A 2000 US law allows NASA to provide funding if the Russians are conducting work to prevent 'imminent loss of life' or 'grievous injury' to astronauts."

The illusion is that peace comes both cheap and must yield a profit to a Wall-St.-listed corporation.

W.K.

Ottawa Uncooks Its Books — Somewhat

WE GULPED on our breakfast coffee as we glanced at the front page of *The Globe and Mail* (13/02, Ottawa gives itself $3 billion windfall" by Simon Tuck) and read: "In an interview yesterday, Finance Minister Manley confirmed that the government will move to full accrual accounting, which will free up additional room for spending on priorities outlined in last fall's Speech from the Throne."

Mr. Manley remarked: "Full accrual was recommended frequently by the Auditor General and by everybody who wants full, transparent accounting in our books."

That would certainly not include the present government and its predecessors.[1] In the second issue of *Economic Reform*, Fall 1988, I wrote: " Today the federal government writes off purchase of land, buildings, and equipment in a single year. No inventory of our government's non-financial assets exists to set off against its debt. Such assets should be compiled – not only for physical investments that remain within the jurisdiction of the federal government, but for a reasonable portion of such assets created through grants to other levels of government and to the private sector. The sole criterion for regarding an expenditure by the government as an investment is whether it expands its tax-base" [as contrasted to increasing the taxation on the existing tax-base].

Ignoring the investments of the federal government distorted the significance of its deficits and debt. It would be like calculating your net worth by noting the mortgage on your house in the debt column but leaving out the value of the house from the assets. Obviously, if a loan were granted, it would be at a much higher interest rate. Why did the government resist bringing in the sort of accountancy used in the private sector? Because the banks and other financial institutions adhered to the doctrine that governments can only waste money, not invest it. Only private corporations could invest seriously, even though our governments have bailed out our banks more frequently than once a decade.

Having government assets on the government books at a nominal $1 has made privatizations possible at a small fraction of their market value. Once acquired, they are revalued at mar-

ket and launched as public companies.

These certainly have been important factors in successive governments fighting capital budgeting – with increasing ferocity in recent years.

Three or four royal commissions in the past 40 years recommended it to no avail. It is to the credit of the then Auditor General, Denis Desautels that he refused to give unconditional approval to the government's 1998-9 books unless Finance Minister Paul Martin agreed to the step. For weeks the two were at loggerheads. That was reported only by an accountancy trade publication *The Bottom Line* (14/05): "A more conciliatory Auditor General has hinted that he has buried the hatchet with the Finance Department and will likely approve the books for the 1997-98 fiscal year."

The compromise reached required Desautels to fudge the significance of the Capital Budgeting that was to be brought in. The momentous event was reported in only one of the national papers, the *National Post*, which was avidly in need of readers. In her article in it, Kathryn May quoted Desautels, warning that the sudden appearance of $50 billion of assets won't bring in new money.

However, that much value missing from the government's balance sheet caused the rate of interest on government bonds to move upwards. It served to whip up panic for cutting grants to the provinces, which resulted in the slashing of vital services. Reclaimed, these assets must have the reverse effect. That is in fact finally confirmed by the current Finance Minister crediting them with giving the government 'additional flexibility' to increase its spending by $3 billion. Then why would these simple facts have been disputed in the compromise that Finance Minister Martin imposed on the AG in 1999?

A Gross Understatement

That gives you the moral profile of Paul Martin. Traced back further to the Mulroney regime, that disregard for the facts enabled the Bank of Canada to push up interest rates to well over 20%.

The $50 billion dollars of additional assets that the AG recognized to have been wiped off the books is a gross understatement. In general, Canada's aggregate economic statistics pretty well amount to some 10% of the corresponding ones in the US. At the beginning of 1996 Washington had included the asset value of federal physical investments on its balance sheet to improve the government's bond rating and help revive the economy, without disturbing Wall St. To achieve this the Commerce Department revised the government's "savings" figure – carried backwards several years – increasing it by well over $1 trillion dollars. Nonetheless, the rediscovered assets were certainly not "savings" but investments, for they were not cash. But listing them as government investments would have disturbed the philosophers of the right; for according to their hymn book governments are as incapable of investing as eunuchs of paternity.[2]

By this criterion, where the government estimates another $5 billion available annually, and of this is prepared to spend $3B, the figures should be about $10 billion, if we followed the

US figures.

But that is not the whole understatement. Theodore Schultz had been a member of the corps of economists sent by Washington to Japan and Germany at the end of the war to assess how long it would take them rebuild their economies from the rubble. Later he pondered how wide of the mark their conclusions were. The reason, he concluded, was that far more important than the physical destruction those two countries had suffered was that their highly educated populations had come out of the war substantially intact.

Conclusion: investment in human education, and hence in health and social services, is the most productive investment a nation can make. That netted Schultz a Nobel Prize. Consequently the investment of our government must be revised to include its direct investment in human capital. Nor does it matter whether it leads to assets registered in the Government's name or in that of provinces and municipalities, or is housed in human heads and bodies. So long as it broadens the central government's tax base, its outlay in human capital is at least as important as the physical investments that it has finally recognized in part. The additional $10 billion a year, can thus be expanded to something more like $20 billion.

How will we find the money to pay for that? By financing both investments of the federal government in physical and human capital through the central bank of which it is the sole shareholder. Accordingly, the interest Ottawa pays on the federal debt the BoC holds finds it way substantially back to the treasury as dividends. But only by returning the Bank of Canada to the goals that are still in the *Bank of Canada Act*, will Canada reap the full advantages of the serious accountancy that it has now embarked on.

The Government's first step in the matter of capital budgeting deserves our applause. If the Chrétien government persists along this path in careful but resolute steps what a legacy P.M. Chrétien will leave on his retirement! It will stand out alongside that of William Lyon Mackenzie King who nationalized the Bank of Canada in 1938. That made possible the financing of WWII at 2 to 3% rates, and laid the basis for our social security system.

William Krehm

1. Keynes, on the other hand, based his policy proposals to get the world out of the Depression precisely on the distinction between investment and savings. But Keynes had been declared a non-person, an "inflation-monger. " Interestingly, he had briefly fought for accrual accountancy, but gave up the fight as a politically lost cause. Long before COMER was founded in the late 1980s, the undersigned had raised the point, and stayed with it because he recognized that little could be done to preserve our socially oriented mixed economy without it.

2. It has been a lonely battle, and we sincerely congratulate the federal government in rallying to the cause. My *Price in a Mixed Economy*, 1975, devotes an entire chapter "Society's Forgotten Capital Assets" (it's an elaboration of a paper that appeared in the economics publication *La Revue Économique* of Paris, May, 1970). But the federal government had no ears for the subject, and soon it became impossible to get a mention of it inserted in the media with a shoe-horn.

Do the Issues Determine our Elections or Vice Versa?

THE MATTER may seem a fine point but it has a bearing on whether our world gets to run or is run over. The point is: do the issues involved decide the elections, or do the elections determine the issues? A striking example is the imminence of Washington's war against Saddam Hussein.

Margaret MacMillan, author of *Paris 1919: Six Months that Changed the World,* updates the half-forgotten tale of the origins of Iraq when it was being stuck together after WWI from highly incompatible parts. That was certain to preserve British influence as umpire over their squabbles. The story, highly relevant for the present day crisis, is told in *The Globe and Mail* (23/01, "Iraq's twisted British roots"): "Britain, the world power at the end of the First World War also tried to create the Iraq it wanted, to ensure access to oil and safeguard crucial routes to India.

"'Regime change' Sounds mild. So did the League of Nations mandate that Britain should take of Iraq until it was ready to stand on its own feet.

"Iraq is a very new country – in spite of the ludicrous attempts by Saddam Hussein to position himself as the heir to Nebuchadnezzar (Babylon's ruler around 600 BC and conqueror of Judea). Present-day Iraq was thrown together by the British out of disparate bits of the defunct Ottoman Empire. To serve as the new country's ruler, then British colonial secretary Winston Churchill put in Faisal, son of the Sharif of Mecca who had helped lead the Arab revolt against the Ottoman Empire.

"After the British authorities had thoughtfully arrested (or bought off) opponents to Faisal's candidacy, a Council of State unanimously asked him to be their king. The subsequent referendum – Faisal was the only candidate – saw him elected with what was claimed to be 96% of the votes." Sound familiar?

"The stage manager of the charade was an extraordinary Englishwoman, Gertrude Bell, who knew the Arab world well and was convinced she knew what was best for Iraq. Will Condolezza Rice be the kingmaker in a post-Saddam Iraq? Faisal and his successors faced a series of revolts; the final one toppled the regime for good in 1958. His grandson, Faisal II, was strung up from a lamppost, something the king's relatives among the ruling family of Jordan no doubt still remember. The prime minister, Nuri al-Said, was murdered. Baghdad's buses ran over Nuri's corpse until little was left.

"It is dangerous to have states that don't work. The British called their creation Iraq, Arabic for 'the well-rooted country.' It was anything but.

"A majority of the Arabs thought in terms of a pan-Arab nationalism that excluded the quarter or so of the population who were Kurds, Assyrians, Jews or Persians. The Kurds in the north were mostly Sunni Muslims, the Persians in the south were Shia Muslims.

"The British expected that the nation's very divisions would make it easy to manage. They also assumed they had a huge technological edge. When the country erupted in revolt in 1920, the British used airplanes to bomb civilian targets. Iraq came to heel. But the resentments against Britain remained. They have now been inherited by the US. Administrations tend to think from election to election. But what the Bush administration does today will cast its long shadow down the future just as the actions of the British in the interwar did in their time."

The State of the Nation

IT WAS IN SOME RESPECTS the most impressive of rituals to be seen on earth. Under the Capitol Dome were gathered several hundred of the most powerful people of the planet, whose collective whims tend eventually to become law on all continents. With hand on heart they swore their dedication to freedom at home and throughout the world. Most attention was given to the achievement of a near-dyslectic president, brought to power with less than a majority vote and trained to deliver fateful lines written by others. This most political of all audiences was perfectly aware that many of the President's promises were not wholly his to fulfill; that his assurances re a sinking economy were slippery evasions rather than a meaningful undertaking. The enthusiastic applause reinforced by most of the audience, Republican or Democrat, rising to their feet, was less than voluntary with the TV cameras keeping its unforgiving record. It was obvious, too, that the cost of the imminent military crusade against Iraq was fudged, as would certainly be exposed by TV commentators licensed to talk freely at least on the perils of budgetary deficits, as they called for the reduction of the national debt.

Yet there is a not a serious economist in the land not aware that the federal debt cannot be paid off except with other federal debt, possibly in bills of a different colour. For federal debt is the nation's only legal tender. The only officially acceptable alternative is to continue running up the debt of the US to the rest of the planet, which exposes it to rude surprises. So the lone superpower goes on piling up two-tiered debt, at home and abroad. That of the underdeveloped world is managed to keep living standards there ever lower. That makes disease starvation and terror and warfare inevitable and provides the cheap imports to keep the US commodity markets "inflation-free." That in turn allows the relatively low interest rates that hopefully will revive the morbidly swollen US financial sector that lives on the debt of the producing economy at home and abroad.

The world's superpower had been packaging its growing vulnerability as strength and uprightness. It is as though a curse has been laid on great empires: their arrogance, begotten at the zenith of their economic might, continues to swell even as they run out of easy prey. And as though on special antennae their victims and bested rivals pick up the message that their overweening pride has a lining of fear. Significantly, several of the leading American newspapers have been publishing series of articles probing the misgivings they have come to feel in the marrow of their bones.

The *Chicago Tribune's* effort in this respect was entitled "The Economics of Glut. Bloated industries put the economy in a

bind. Glut is making it hard to shake off the recession (William Neikirk, 15-18/12/02). In it we read, "The world's auto industry can now produce 20 million more cars than consumers can buy. When supply outstrips demand, equipment sits idle, costs go up, workers are laid off, and investments are postponed." The *Tribune* sees a swamp of excess capacity in airline, auto, machine tool, steel, textile, and high-tech industries, even commercial space and hotel rooms. "According to the Federal Reserve, manufacturers are using only 73.5% of capacity, far below the 80.9% average of 1967-2001, and 3.5% percentage points below the level during the 1990-1 recession."

No CEO in his right mind would deliberately choose such an outcome. However, Deregulation and Globalization incorporated the growth rate attained into share prices, extrapolated into the indefinite future and then discounted for present value. And that malediction leaves them no choice. The merest stumble will cause the collapse of the entire house of cards. What is at work here is not just compound interest but exponential rate of growth that is the mathematics of the atomic bomb. It is as though some malignant ancient god had granted them their wish to fully realize their greed for one year, but to this is attached the curse that they must match that rate of increase year after year. Increasingly the US economy has had to live an eternity on borrowed time. Think that over: how suitable a punishment for the enslavement by debt that made them mighty!

So while the American President prepares to declare war on Saddam Hussein on suspicion of his preparing an atomic weapon, Americans themselves have incorporated the mathematics of that weapon into their economics and life style.

The telecommunications industry incurred $2.1 trillion in debt between 1996 and 2000 from fibre optic lines and telecom networks that are being employed at 3% of their potential. That was the meaning of stock market valuations and financing based on market share achieved 1996 to 2000 and increased its investment by 15% annually in real terms. Since the financial sector is merger-and-stock-market driven – it has in fact become a derivative of the real producing economy and is judged by the increases of the projected rates of increase of its earnings. Or where no such earnings exist, of its revenue as the next best thing. And if the growth of revenues fail them, their accountants may instruct them how to put liabilities in the asset column, or keep them off the balance sheet, or in offshore tax-shelters. The legendary ingenuity of the American people has come to be most handsomely rewarded when it is devising scams to escape the curse of accelerating growth for another year. The same pattern takes over in every conceivable dimension: first in the stock market valuations, then in the accountancy of firms, then in the field of options that allows high executives to decamp in good time with their profits, leaving the store in smoldering ruins, as creditors, staff and pensioners fight over the slim remnants in bankruptcy courts. Bankrupt steel companies can no longer hope to be acquired by buyers, domestic or foreign, as going concerns, because that would mean taking over the obligations to their pension funds that have been ransacked. So bankrupt steel companies – some with legendary names in American industrial history – must sell their dismembered assets, not the going firms, so that their workers and retirees may be left shivering in the cold.

The regulatory authorities, embarked on career-making campaigns to try, convict, and imprison the falling idols of the recent boom, are having second thoughts. The economic system itself depends on the revival of the stock market, and that beast feeds on "irrational exuberance." That requires promoters who stop at little to whip up demand. The free market system holds to no other value than that indicated by market demand. And the more abstract the market equities become, the greater the rewards. Debt is disguised as assets. And tax evasion is mistaken for increased value, in the inverted pyramid of make-believe called equilibrium economics.

William Krehm

Brief Course on Capital Budgeting for Parliamentarians

AFTER FORTY YEARS of evasion our government took a great step in bringing serious accountancy onto its books. Kudos for that to Auditor General Denis Desautels who in July 1999 refused his unconditional approval of the government books unless accrual accountancy (a.k.a., "capital budgeting") was adopted. Desautels was one of a long line AGs who, along with four Royal Commissions, had raised the point. He, however, dug his toes into the effort. Against crushing odds, some of the founders of this humble newsletter, long before it appeared, had fought for such a move. Without it, bottom lines can become a mousetrap. Misleading statistics for debt and deficit block programs essential for society.

Dumbing-down Parliament

Most non-government organizations avoided the matter like the plague, arguing that it was too complicated for the public to understand. You could have used the same logic against exposing the scams of Enron and other stock-market pin-ups, who also kept what counted off their balance sheets.

Letting those in power dictate what the public is too stupid to understand is the ultimate surrender. Today governments, beating the war drums and their shill economies in tatters, have begun acknowledging some off-book assets to be able to borrow more. But that has caught our non-government organizations unprepared. In the peculiar society that has evolved, legislatures will make it their business to understand only what concerned citizens won't allow them to ignore. The educational process in public affairs is from the bottom up, not from the top down. For it is at society's bottom that the victims are buried. Our NGOs themselves have moral accountancy to rethink. For lack of it, they have flubbed a rare opportunity.

After a couple of days of vague references to the novelty of accrual accountancy that justified a modest amount of overdue program spending, the editorials and the parliamentary discussions reverted to the old number-crunching – the spending binge, can we afford it? Accrual accountancy had been trivialized to meaninglessness.

In calculating your personal worth you include the value of the house in your assets and not just the mortgage on it in your liabilities. If you didn't, you would pay through the nose for further credit. Besides, the government might crack down on you for tax evasion, and other misrepresentations. Had other NGOs joined us in educating more people to the anti-accountancy on which key official statistics are based, the government could not have misrepresented the purpose of capital budgeting even while adopting a limited version of it.

What you must do to prevent this happening again is go through the list of NGOs to which you write a cheque each year, and ask why they had not forewarned the public about this mother of all government scams. Our problems will never be resolved without an informed public backing up the AG on the matter. Yet a beginning has been made. On bringing down his budget, Finance Minister John Manley even tried explaining accrual accountancy to his uncomprehending caucus. Yet it was essentially the same caucus that had passed the bill bringing in accrual accountancy in 1999.

Exactly the same thing happened in 1991 when the *Bank Act* was amended to do away with the statutory reserves that banks had to leave with the Bank of Canada as collateral for the lucrative money creation assigned to them by the Government. No explanation was given to parliament. No debate took place. Nary a press release was issued. I have met former cabinet ministers who were not aware of the bill two or three years after it became law. Continue along these lines and all our males will be wearing obligatory moustaches like that of the Governor of the Bank of Canada – some future one since Mr. David Dodge is bare-faced.

One of the most vicious forms of usury is known in the trade as "subprime debt." That is plied by "money shops" in lending to those who have no bank account, or "no documents." They are uneducated people, some with little English. They are not told, nor does it occur to them to ask, what the rate of interest will be. Their only concern is how much their total monthly or weekly payment will be. Not how long it will go on. In short, like our government in its own books until recently, neither they nor the shark that exploits them, make the distinction between capital and interest. Our financial institutions, having lost boodles of their shareholders' money on mega-gambles incompatible with banking, are today expanding their involvement in subprime debt. The government invites them to do so by having no ceiling in civil law on interest rates – in criminal law it is 60%. But what does it matter if their victims are too "dumb" to understand? Perhaps night-school courses could be opened to explain to such people how to defend themselves against such abuses. Members of parliament, too, must become conversant with the distinction between capital and current spending. For basically our government for the convenience of our banks has been running its affairs as "non-prime debt."

Microwaving the Government Books

The government, and most of the provinces, had made no distinction in their books between the government's treatment of the wax they use in polishing their floors and of the floors themselves. Their buildings, bridges, roads, and all the other physical investments that last for decades, and the land beneath the buildings that is likely to appreciate in value over the years – to say nothing of the human investment by government in education, health and social insurance – are depreciated in a single year. By year two of their acquisition, such assets are carried on their books at zero value. But the debt incurred to acquire these vanished assets, more than anything else, occupies our editorials and political debates.

Yet it is impossible to balance such books, without subjecting the country to severe deflation. Even the attempt to do so must leave a deeper layer of taxation in price than is necessary. On top of that, for its one blunt tool "to lick inflation" the central bank has chosen a high enough rate of interest. And yet it is no secret that moneylenders with the slightest encouragement tend to become predatory. Not for nothing have several great religions committed usurers to eternal hell-fire.

To establish a monopolist role as an anti-inflation tool for interest rates, the *Bank Act* was amended in 1991 to do away with the statutory reserves. These had provided a complementary method of combating inflation, real or perceived. The statutory reserves required a modest portion of the money deposited by the public in chequing accounts to be redeposited with the central bank by the bank. That earned them no interest. The availability of these funds to the government was a modest consideration for the monarch's assigning to the banks most of its ancestral monopoly in coining precious metals known as *seigniorage*. Since government credit has been the only backing for legal tender since the early 1970s, that seigniorage had grown wondrously – the cost of producing a dollar bill or a computer entry is far less than the former costs of creating gold and silver coins. The statutory reserves had enabled the central bank to cool an overheated economy without raising interest rates or raising them less than would otherwise be necessary. All it would have to do is increase the reserve that would lessen the money base on which the banking system can create its multiple of near-money (i.e., interest-bearing credit). Using interest rates instead of this hits anything that moves or stands still in the economy, not only those who may be investing or consuming too much.

Software of Debt Slavery

The resulting bogus deficit and debt figures are the software that imposes debt slavery.

Amongst the military, such unfocussed destruction of the innocent is known as "collateral damage." And great effort is made to avoid it. The Bank of Canada, however, glories in the extent to which it inflicts such destruction. It is testimony to its omnipotence. I have searched the *Bank of Canada Act* and have found nothing that might authorize our central bank to be more indifferent to innocent victims than the armed forces we train to kill. I invite our government to bring to our attention anything that I may have overlooked.

I found in the preamble, Chapter B-2, that the central bank was established "to control and protect the external value of the national monetary unit and to mitigate by its influence fluctuations in the general level of production, trade, prices and employment, so far as may be possible within the scope of monetary action, and generally to promote the economic welfare of Canada." Note that it is directed to mitigate…fluctuations in production, trade, employment as well as prices. That means

deflation as well as inflation, unemployment as well as an overheated economy in which not enough workers can be found. It is not then just "collateral damage" that is at issue, but the very chosen target that defines what collateral damage might be.

Nor can our government wash their hands of responsibility for what the BoC does. Section 14(2) sets forth unequivocally: "If there should emerge a difference of opinion between the Minister and the Bank concerning the monetary policy to be followed, the Minister may give the Governor a written directive concerning monetary policy, and the Bank shall comply with that directive."

That makes the government the accomplice of the Governor for the illegal target he has set the Bank. With the world sinking into deflation, BOC Governor Dodge has raised the bank rate a second time, with a third boost promised because the unusually cold winter, the impeding Iraq war and the Venezuelan strike have pushed up oil prices. Does he really believe that will improve the weather or bring peace to Iraq and Venezuela?

And to come away with clean conscience for the dreadful damage inflicted on our society by its "one blunt tool," the Bank and the government would have to examine the underlying economic theory that made such massive misfire possible. Not only has this not been done, but also anything that might resemble meaningful examination of alternative economic models has been eliminated from our universities and the media.

Elsewhere in this issue ("Economics and the Test of Falsifiability" by a new contributor, Dix Sanbeck), you will read about the work of Karl R. Popper: "There can be two reasons why a hypothesis must be discarded as false. The foremost one is failing when tested against observations. For instance, a hypothesis about a flock of swans, claiming they are all red, will be labeled false if an observation returns the report that they are, in fact, all white. But according to Popper, a hypothesis must also be discarded as non-scientific if it is not falsifiable, that is capable of being tested conclusively against observations. This is the case if a hypothesis is couched in an open-ended language so that no matter how many false observation reports one gets, the hypothesis cannot be gotten rid of. 'Some swans are red' is unscientific because even if all known observations come back with the result 'false,' it is not possible to get rid of the hypothesis by confronting it with these observation reports. The person questioning the hypothesis can never be sure that there might be some red swans somewhere that just have not been seen yet."

That is precisely the pattern of our central bank policy over the past three decades. The damage inflicted by interest rates high enough to win the battle against "inflation" led to widespread bankruptcies. The banks, once bailed out by the government, were deregulated further to allow them to seek the Holy Grail of a self-balancing "pure and perfect market." They got deeper into ever more speculative ventures incompatible with banking. The pattern was that of the gambler with a doting uncle who simply cannot leave the casino until he wins back his losses and takes home the pot. That purpose flowed over into the bailout of the early 1990s. Without the micro-cooked books of non-accrual accountancy, the surrender of our banking institutions to the stock market could not have taken place.

At the same time the very suggestion that a flat price level (identified with zero "inflation") might be an impossibility in a rapidly urbanizing high-tech economy, was denied even a hearing. What should have been met in the open and refuted – were that possible under light and logic – was ignored.

The growing need for costly physical and human infrastructures to run such a society requires a rapid growth of essential public services that only the government can provide. These are paid for by taxation, not by sales. Since they are not marketed, they have no price and therefore are ignored by a theory that identifies value with the price of the last transaction on the market. This is the deepest root of the classification of all non-marketed services as "externalities." Equally obvious, since all unmarketed government services are financed through the growing layer of taxation in price, flattening out price caters to those who oppose as an extravagance government spending for anything other than police, defence, jails, and hangmen. This fits handily with the resistance to accrual accountancy that declares capital expenditures of government an "externality." For by writing off the cost of public investments in a single year, while noting the liabilities incurred to acquire them, the deficit and the debt can be puffed up to intimidate.

That also set the stage for the fire sale of government investments carried on the books at a token dollar. You could sell a public asset at one tenth of its value and use the proceeds "prudently" to reduce the deficit and the debt.

Putting Together the Jigsaw Puzzle of Deceit

But what could the government do about such things? For aren't we told that the Bank of Canada is "independent" of the government? Yet article 17(2) of the *Bank of Canada Act* reads: "The capital [of the Bank] shall be divided into one hundred thousand shares of the par value of fifty dollars each, which shall be issued to the Minister to be held by the Minister on behalf of Her Majesty in right of Canada."

There is in addition a highly relevant detail. The Bank was founded in 1934 by the ultra-conservative government of R.B. Bennett. The shares were sold to some 12,000 private stockholders. In 1935 the Liberals under Mackenzie King scored a sweeping victory on a program that included the privatization of the Bank. And in 1938 the shareholders were bought out by the government at a handsome profit – especially for those depression years.

It turned out an excellent investment for the government, essentially because article 18(c) that authorized the bank "to buy and sell securities issued or guaranteed by Canada or any province." These are immense powers, essentially the rights that go with ownership under capitalism. They could be made use of in two ways.

1. Securities of the federal government held by the BoC. Almost the entire interest paid on such debt (over 95%) would find its way back to the federal government as dividends.

2. Guaranteed by the Federal government and/or the province, loans could be made to municipalities. That, however, would not result in the return of the interest paid to the munici-

palities, since they are not shareholders of the Bank of Canada. Nor are the provinces. But such arrangements would open a new dimension of cooperation rather than confrontation between the different government levels. In return for the municipalities agreeing to observe federal standards in the investments financed by such loans, part of the dividends corresponding to the interest paid to the Bank of Canada could be refunded to the provinces or the municipalities. In this way the lower levels of government could be helped out of their present straits. The brutal downloading onto first the provinces and then onto the municipalities of social obligations without adequate funding would be repaired. That would do more to improve the relations of the different levels of government than a baker's dozen of constitutional conferences.

But for all this, accountancy that distinguishes between public investment and current spending is an essential link. But that will require a proactive democracy that seeks out rather than buries essential information.

William Krehm

Kingdoms of Cover-Up

OURS IS SAID TO BE a globalized culture that unites the world in a sameness of advantage.

Even the bubbling broth of dialects that provided delights of English letters from Shakespeare to Dickens was reported vanishing under the smooth vocal cords of the BBC. Reality, however, has a bad habit of cutting off expectations at the knee. Clefts are widening between the different meanings of key words no matter how they're pronounced.

Alan Murray, Washington Bureau Chief of CNBC, considers one unpublicized instance in his *Wall Street Journal* column (8/10, "Narrowing Tax Gap Should be Priority of Next Congress"): "Congress will leave town in a few days having addressed only half of the credibility crisis that afflicts corporate America. The Sarbanes-Oxley bill passed in August will make it harder for companies to mislead shareholders about how much they are earning. But nothing has been done to deter them from misleading the Internal Revenue Service about how little they are earning.

"On July 2, I wrote a column pointing out that between 1996 and 2000, WorldCom reported $16 billion in earnings to its shareholders, but less than $1 billion in earnings to Uncle Sam. I suggested a modest solution: Public companies should be required to make their tax returns public.

"Several US senators took up that cause, including Democrat Charles Schumer of New York, and Republican Charles Grassley of Iowa."

Senator Grassley notes that between 1996 and 1998 the gap separating book income reported to shareholders and tax income prepared for the Internal Revenue Service widened by 97%, from $92.5B to $159B. Most of this came from large corporations.

A good bit of this is probably the result of puffery to boost the market for its shares. On that mirage of achievement, the tax rates have been trimmed "to encourage productivity," but much of it, from evidence in the courts, has hidden actual earnings. In that it has preempted the resources that are famously absent whenever it comes to urgent social programs, education, infrastructures upon which everybody depends in a functioning society.

"On July 8, Sen. Grassley wrote Treasury Secretary O'Neill and Securities and Exchange Commission Chairman Harvey Pitt asking for their comments. Their replies in letters to Grassley are a study in contrasts. O'Neill, who has a political tin ear but doesn't shy from challenging established practice, was open to the spirit of the suggestion. Chairman Pitt dismissed it, saying companies already disclose enough." As always the important words are unspoken: "For whom"?

"In his letter, Secretary O'Neill rejects the notion of releasing complete corporate tax returns to the public, arguing these contain much 'proprietary information' of little use to the SEC or the public but of considerable interest to competitors. And he gamely suggests rewriting the tax laws and accounting rules to reduce the differences.

"Cut through the jargon, and his point is simple: income is income. Allowing one definition for the taxman and another for the shareholder invites deception. [Doing away with it] won't be easy. The tax code, after all, is a creature of Congress, full of provisions designed to curry favor with powerful interests. Public accounting standards, on the other hand, are controlled largely by the Financial Accounting Standards Board, a private-sector organization set up by the accounting industry. (In Iowa we call this 'letting the fox into the henhouse,' Sen. Grassley writes.)"

Steaks in the Future

Taxation is not the only henhouse with a foxy presence. There is, for example the domain of derivatives by which present values are derived from future maybes. The narrow literal meaning on financial markets is something "derived" from a real security – the rate of interest earned in a particular currency, or the increase in the price of a company share, or a debt instrument, or the change in the value of one currency in terms of another. Underlying all these constructs is the current credit system, which is itself a derivative of the real economy. All these abstractions add up to highly stacked bridges of hope built into the future.

Unless you have footings of absolute credibility to support the structure, you are asking for big trouble. But where do you find all the credibility in an economy, which depends on a steep upward ramp of winnings resulting from its basic price theory to its latest off-balance sheet scam designed by some of the world's greatest auditing companies?

The derivative market appeals both to extreme conservative investors and extreme risk-takers. In theory pairing an extreme sporting soul with the conservatism of another may seem a match made in heaven. The conservative may wish to invest in a mining stock but has a mortal fear of two things – neither of which really has to do with the physical mine. One is the future price of the metal, which will in part depend on the state of the economy and a host of other things, like the relative value of currencies, interest rates. So what is the problem? Didn't the Lord put big gamblers on earth to take over such gambles? Trouble is that gamblers can read the future no better than other self-appointed prophets. The future of anything is a demurely veiled lady, who while never exposing herself, is ever coyly alluring. Your conservative investor, or banker, may sell puts – an option to sell his mine shares to the big gambler, who had gambled so big that when the time comes for him to purchase the worthless mining shares he may already have evaporated, i.e., gone bankrupt. That caveat applies not only to individual gamblers who sell puts, but to gambling banks. And the world is always, by a benevolence of providence, amply stocked with gamblers to provide at least the semblance of security in the form of eager counterparties (a.k.a., "risk management").

But let us get back to the broader subject of this column – which is the forked tongues of prophets. *The Wall Street Journal* (8/10, "Derivative Growth Has Helped Banks, Greenspan says" by Greg Ip and Rebecca Christie): "Proliferating financial derivatives have helped banks withstand rising corporate defaults, but they also can fuel speculative excess, Federal Reserve Chairman Alan Greenspan said: "Financial derivatives have grown at a phenomenal pace over the past fifteen years, Mr. Greenspan said in prepared remarks to the American Bankers' Association convention in Phoenix. Banks appear to have effectively used such instruments to shift a significant part of their corporate loan portfolios to other institutions. For example, significant exposures to telecommunications firms were laid off through credit-default swaps and collateralized debt obligations."

In these seemingly harmless sentences Mr. Greenspan put the face of innocence on one of the most vicious recent practices of banks unloading through syndication – and through the anonymity of derivatives – securities of Enron and other dubious corporations. That has not only resulted in enough legal suits to keep a generation of litigation lawyers prosperous, but has had disastrous results on the public image of our banks. Mr. Greenspan, however, seems convinced that "transferring part of the risk to other institutions" and "laying off through credit-default swaps and collateralized debt obligations" solves anything of importance for the economy and for the bank system. To believe that means to believe the "taking in one another's laundry" is the essence of a sound economy. It is impossible for the economy as a whole to hedge against systemic risk or the asset-inflationary effects of deregulating banks that have been entrusted with most of the economy's money creation *as the form of bailout from their previous speculative excesses.* For surely the counterparties to the derivatives hedging all-embracing risks must come from the economy. They cannot just be declared "externalities," as the good Chairman is doing.

"These transactions represent a new paradigm of active credit management and are a major part of the explanation of the banking system's strength during a period of stress," the Fed Chairman said.

But hedging the boldness of the statement as a keen energy trader is supposed to his plunges, the Chairman went on to add: "But more sophisticated risk-management techniques and especially the various forms of derivatives are, by construction, highly leveraged. They are thus prone to induce speculative excesses, not only in the US but throughout the world. This potential for systemic risk can be contained through a combination of risk, supervision and private sector action, including better public disclosure. But ultimately, some of the systemic risk must also be absorbed by the central banks," he said. That means since the net income of the central bank goes to the federal government, parts of those losses are downloaded on the most vulnerable by the slashing of government services.

It is one of Mr. Greenspan's distinctions to burnish devastating realities into euphemism. Thus "systemic risk" is a housebroken term for a chain-reaction of bank insolvencies due to bad debt or failed speculations. And the reference to the "ultimate absorption of some of the systemic risk by the central bank," means that through tighter credit and higher interest rates the taxpayers will once again be bailing out our sporting banks. The high "leverage of derivatives" covers the notorious fact that made possible the gambling by our banks in ever-greater volume and leverage. And this at a time when Globalization and Deregulation have enabled our banks to move into geographical and financial areas of which they are not only badly informed, but are incompatible with their banking function. By no stretch of the imagination can that be described as risk management. Rather it is risk creation on a scale never seen before. Mr. Greenspan would seem to stand in need of some risk management of his own when he declares. "Our banks have been able to retain their strength in this business cycle in contrast to the early 1990s when so many either failed or had near-death experiences." It is a bit early in the day to make such positive statements about the banks' health in any part of the world, let alone the US. There is scarcely a week in which a new mega-scandal of a transnational corporation doesn't make the headlines with compromising disclosures revealed for the first time as it files for bankruptcy. There is not one of these that does not involve one or more of our mega-banks or their brokerage and other financial arms.

The reporters observe, "Mr. Greenspan has long been a fan of derivatives, as well as a leading opponent of moves to impose new regulations on them. He recently spoke out against a proposal by Sens. Tom Harkin (D., Iowa) and Richard Lugar (R., Indi.) to regulate some energy derivatives, a move sparked by alleged abuses by Enron Corp." This, of course, happens to be the position as well of the Bank for International Settlements, and the Bank of Canada.

Meanwhile the trade in derivatives outside exchanges, and hence unregulated, reached an estimated record $128 trillion US during the first six months of 2002. That was 15% higher than the year before.

In his annual letter to his shareholders, Warren Buffet, the legendarily successful head of Berkshire Hathaway, warned that derivatives are the "silent weapons of mass destruction."

The choice of these words at this particular time could not be more alarming.

When the inspectors finish with Iraq, possibly they should be sent into this murky kingdom of cover-up.

William Krehm

Shaping America's Future

AT THIS TIME OF WRITING (late Feb/03) there is much discussion of possible justification and likelihood of a war in Iraq. The facts are subject to debate and arguments are complex but deal almost entirely with geopolitical considerations. While economic factors are mentioned, these tend to be ignored or dealt with rather superficially, as though a discussion of oil supplies and the need for post-war aid and support exhausts the important economic concerns.

Meanwhile, financial markets are not happy, and even if some resolution short of war is found, for example if Saddam were to accept peaceful exile, this would not solve all the important problems.

From a systems perspective it is a truism that complex system problems are functions of the perceptions of all the participants. In this sense it may be said that failure of the Americans to understand how they may be part of the problem means that they will be unable to understand the nature of an optimal solution. If the American way of life is seen quite simply as *the* solution to world problems, it becomes impossible to think outside this box, perhaps to consider environmental, resource or equity issues involving the world problematique or other potential contingencies. This may add to problems, because surprises are inevitable.

Views of terrorism, or the use of violence against civilians for political means, also depend somewhat on observers, even if destructive purposes and effects justify condemnation. As often said, one man's terrorist may be another's freedom fighter. Once again it may help to recognize that the observer may be bringing something to the observations. This makes thought and analysis more complex but may be a source of new opportunities.

Transnational Corporations

Among the realities at work, and strongly identified with America and its influences, are the operations of transnational corporations throughout the world. While based in many countries, and beyond the direct control of most nations, they are notably associated with capitalism, American power and its global reach. There is an awareness that policies in many Western governments are heavily beholden to the business interests on which they rely for financial contributions and electoral support. The interests of transnational corporations overlap the geopolitical interests of all major states.

Of course it is not in the interests of the wealthy supporters of political parties to direct public attention to the ways in which those parties serve the interests of money rather than the general public, but most educated citizens have become aware of how such games are played. This helps account for low voter turnouts at home as well as restive resentments abroad.

It is easy to misunderstand such resentment as based on envy. Underlying problems are pervasive, difficult to articulate, and depend more upon attitudes than specific facts and logic. Such attitudes are based upon hopes and fears, which are part of life's realities. For too many people, free trade and globalization spell exploitation and inequality rather than personal freedom and opportunity.

Of course, increased economic activity and trade are essential for any country that would improve the standard of living of its citizens. Yet capitalist enterprises do tend to exploit such vulnerabilities as human greed and ignorance. The best of intentions and results in one area may be offset by carelessness or worse in others. We need only think of death-dealing sales of tobacco to the young, the pollution following from the use of depleted uranium shells, or the willful ignorance associated with lack of policy follow-through and accountability.

Such considerations may seem far removed from the questions of risk posed by Iraq. However they are relevant to the specific role of the United States as the exemplar of the values needed for the world's rescue. And much depends upon the economic and social, as well as the military, behaviour of the United States.

Political and Corporate Interests

It adds to the problems that the interests of American politicians may be identified or confused with those of powerful transnational corporations. Such perceptions of interested powers are part of the problem.

While capital markets may be important engines of prosperity, they are not without problems. Among such problems is the neglect of supposed externalities (e.g., pollution, environmental degradation, exploitation of labour, growing social inequities, neglect of safety) and the ignorance or denial of needs for regulation in the public interest. There is widespread recognition of such problems, and some corporations (e.g., Pepsico, Motorola, Heineken) have withdrawn from some repressive regimes, e.g., Burma. But corporations less in the media spotlight still find it in their interests to exploit situations where governments and regulations are inadequate to protect the interests of the vast majority of people.

Some of the relevant factors have been explored in the recent book, *The Silent Takeover*[1] by Noreena Hertz, which argues that over the past twenty years governments across the globe have withdrawn from the public sphere and surrendered to global capitalism. It is precisely because these developments are so widespread, and now beyond the influence of any individual, group, party or nation, that they are so difficult to specify and subject to societal control. Yet the effects of these realities cannot be ignored for long (problems that are merely repressed are bound to return in some form), and will inevitably appear in forms otherwise difficult to fathom.

Hertz suggests that there is a need for supranational bodies or powers able to tackle such problems. The United Nations carries the hopes of many. Others look to the World Trade Organization, although, along with the International Monetary Fund and the World Bank, these are seen by many as servants of shadowy special interests.

Yet adequate remedies for complex systemic problems are not to be found in particular policy proposals offered in isolation – e.g., redistributive taxation, or special programs of social support. Larger systems will always try to reject specific changes incompatible with entrenched values.

The problems which need attention lie at a deeper level. An essential part of the debate concerns whose voices are to count in the matter of running the world. Yet questions of representation and globalization – dealing with the economics of trade, wealth and fairness – have been crowded out by violence, e.g., threats of terrorism and Iraq. Once the immediacy of these threats is contained, we need a way to cope with rampant power and confront the more fundamental issues of economic development and its dependence on justice and equity.

There is not space here to explore these issues adequately. For example, difficulties are compounded by the fact that corporate needs and governmental policies are almost dictated by factors of technology over which decision makers have little real control. Alan Hedley[2] points to the role of technology as the driver and principle problem confronting developed countries and indirectly affecting all humankind. The imperatives of new technologies, as carried by scientists and entrepreneurs as they appeal to capital markets, are ever-expanding, irreversible, and cumulative. Technology exists to fulfill its own promise without plan except for conditions of profit on which it feeds. The United States' war machine is a modest example, but there are many others, including genetically engineered crops and foods and the hazards of environmental contaminants, which also contribute to a climate of protest.

To translate our consideration from terms of Western facts and logic to those, which may resonate more deeply in relation to cultural attitudes, it may be said that the image of the United States as a careless cowboy has penetrated deep into the psyche of vast numbers in the Islamic world, and even beyond. It is far more important to transform this image than simply to kick Saddam Hussein out of Baghdad.

It is at the level of public opinion that opposition to United States' policies is most strongly expressed. It adds to the problems that the simpler logic of power politics is a reflection of perspectives narrowed by corporate interests and technological might.

These are some of the grounds for the distrust of America, which is abroad in the world. It should be the first object of American statecraft to understand and cope with basic problems of communication on which so much else depends. A systems perspective suggests that a more adequate overview of all such factors at work must be the centrepiece of any war on terrorism.

Bruce Buchanan

1. Hertz, Noreena (2002). *The Silent Takeover: Global Capitalism and the Death of Democracy*. Free Press.
2. Hedley, R. Alan (2002). *Running Out of Control – Dilemmas of Globalization*. Kumarian Press, Inc.

REVIEW OF A BOOK BY RODNEY SHAKESPEARE
AND PETER CHALLEN, NEW EUROPEAN
PUBLICATIONS, LONDON, 2002

"Seven Steps to Justice"

THIS LITTLE BOOK opens minds to the erosion of yesterday's topographies. "All people are invited to forget, for just a moment, their own view of things to try and see if there is something which helps them think about broadening their ideas, and so, join up a little more with others. Some people like to have views on books without bothering to read them."

A charming aid towards this is the book's format – a chairperson, objections in the audience to the last speaker's views, audience members sent out to check moot points at sources. There are even coffee breaks until the answer comes in. It is a lesson in courtesy to others' opinions. For all this credit goes to Plato's *Symposium*.

"In the world as a whole, 20% of the population have only $1 per day to pay for everything, 20% have only $2, and a further 15% have $3. 25,000 die each day have been estimated as a result of dirty water."

That raises the question of money creation, and why some 97% of our money supply should be interest-bearing credit created by private institutions in a system that has eliminated all traditional quantity controls. This has left interest rates the one means of reining in perceived inflation.

"A member now arose saying that there was some unpleasant historical information to impart. Two US presidents had understood that governments could create their own interest-free money and – would you believe it? – had been assassinated. The chairperson thanked the member. In respect of Kennedy, she had heard that Executive Order 11,110 [supposedly providing the motive for his killing] was a technical amendment, which has been misunderstood. It did not create authority to issue new money. However, she wished to add that assassination was only one of a range of powerful weapons by powerful interests – blackmail, bribery, and besmirching of characters are often used." The gently imparted message was that reformers must not overstate their evidence. Their privilege is to be in a position to avoid this. At times you almost feel like pitying those in power who don't dare utter what they are up to.

Example: "Why can't a state, instead of borrowing for its capital spending, create its own money and pay no interest?" To find an answer, the chair suggested they return to the letter from the Governor of the Bank of England, which read in part, 'It is perfectly true that governments may borrow money from banks – or indeed from the central bank – and in that sense they can perhaps be seen as "creating money." But to the extent this does happen, it reduces the funds available for borrowing by the private sector given the overall constraint.

"Very clearly, the Governor allows that a government may borrow from the banking system (and so have to pay interest). Equally clearly, he allows that it could borrow from the central bank, which would *not* be allowed to charge interest. Odd that the Governor fails to mention that point.

"'Now wait a minute,' protested a man who worked in the City, 'the Governor isn't saying that. He says that when governments borrow from private banks, or even from the central bank, it reduces the amount available for borrowing by the private sector. As everybody knows, the private sector runs things efficiently – and the state wastes money. That's what it's all about.'

"'Rubbish!' snapped a voice. 'The Governor knows that in any society there is always a large amount of public capital spending. It should be done at the lowest possible cost, i.e., without interest. That in no way crowds out the private sector. It only means that when public capital spending is done, it should be done cheaply, instead of expensively.'

"In the discussion that followed it became clear that the crowd-out-the-private-sector argument is very weak. There is always going to be a large amount of public capital spending. That spending can go to private companies who put up the buildings, construct the waterworks or lay the roads, but those companies don't have to be paid with money that has interest attached to it. We must stop the rip-off."

Interest-free Money Created for the State

That brings the discourse to the creation of interest-free money by the state. It is extended from public investments to private ones. It could become possible for all individuals "over time, to have a substantial independent income from their ownership of some capital, *if* all really did mean *all* – including those providing care, the retired, the sick, the unemployed, women, children and men. Then poverty would be banished."

To achieve this S&C (Social Credit) favour Binary Economics, developed by Louis and Patricia Kelso in their *Democracy and Economic Power* (1991). "Most important is the view of *who or what actually creates wealth*. People will always be in poverty because they own little or no capital.

"So where does the idea that labour does all the work come from? It comes from Adam Smith who did his thinking *before* the industrial revolution. As a result, Smith got something wrong. Quite simply, Smith said that labour creates all wealth."

Now the time has come for us to catch the chairperson's eye and express our dissent. First, the labour theory of value is one thing about the real Adam Smith that the "free market" supporters rarely mention. Over a century ago their intellectual ancestors abandoned that theory, because it helped socialists draw attention to the inequities of the "free market" just as S&C are doing today. They flocked instead to the marginal utility theory that was devised to recognize no value other than the price of the latest market transaction, not only of useful goods, but of wagers on the future price of corporation shares. However, demand for such gambles can be manipulated more easily than Saddam Hussein stuffs his ballot boxes.

We must then appeal to the Chairperson to ask why S&C who so deplore our casino economy would endorse Binary Economics? From their description of it, it utilizes the quantity theory of the "self-balancing market" with an implant of capital made available (under the name of "Capital Homesteading") by the government to all citizens to be paid for by interest-free loans. Such loans are to be held until redeemed by future installments of such government grants.

The idea of such grants is fine. But they should not be tied down to their being invested to make capitalists of their beneficiaries. Not all people have the knowledge or talent for investing. They would become dependent on brokers and consultants. And that would contribute to another bubble to match the one that so recently burst to shake the world. To keep their unsustainable system going Wall St. and Lombard St. ransacked every pool of capital in sight. They would do it again with those juicy escrowed "Capital Homesteading" accounts.

Wouldn't it be better, Ms. Chairperson, to offer everybody a freely disposable "second income." Should they feel entrepreneurial urge stirring within them, they could buy shares and bonds. But should they prefer, they could use it as an aid to dropping out of the rat race and adopting an alternate life style. That would diversify society, enrich it, and make it less vulnerable.

A Freely Disposable Second Income for Everybody to Spend on Whatever Lifestyle They Choose

The notion that everybody must become a capitalist is a morbid one. It stems, I believe, from the bizarre notion of the Binary Economics people that machinery itself produces wealth. It doesn't.

The machinery that Binary Economy contrast for its superior productivity over labour is itself entirely the product of human labour. What distinguishes it from current spending is that its usefulness will go on for many years, unless human effort and talent conceives still more productive machinery to render it obsolescent. And not only was it built by human effort, but the capital accumulations and the social framework that made it possible can be traced to the contributions of generations of slaves, serfs, thinkers, martyrs, burned, mangled or hanged, navigators, philosophers, scientists. We must, accordingly not dehumanize, indeed deify technology as something that has replaced human effort.

C.H. Douglas, the founder of Social Credit, summed up the situation in his concept of "social heritage." He, too, proposed a sort of "social dividend," but one that would encourage citizens to cultivate alternate ways of living. The Argentine disaster is proof of the wisdom of that. There the improvisations of such gropings such as barter and community currencies in a great crisis are adding up to an impressive promise to save society's future.

There are several misunderstandings that have led S&C into the facile vision of everybody becoming investors. Believe that machines have replaced humans as the ultimate source of value, and there is no need for concern about these things.

Let me, add in justice, that S&C do a magnificent in exploring "these things," but then without realizing if they have left a gaping hope for the "free market" fanatics to come back and take over.

A key factor in this weakness of the fine S&C book is that they have underestimated the deadly compulsion that the existing system is under due to its built-in agenda of insane expansion. Like so many monetary reformers they have mistaken compound interest with exponential growth that puts our financial elite under the need to shred everything – morality itself – in its desperate urge to survive (page 108).

In reality exponential is *infinitely* more high-powered than compound interest. Let me resort to a parable beloved of monetary reformers. Had the Virgin on the birth of Christ deposited single shekel in a bank that paid 6% and didn't go broke, its value today would exceed all the silver mined and unmined in the world. The point, however, is that the Infant would have had to wait 2000 years for such a result. Hiroshima, visited by a bomb of exponential power, reached an infinity of destruction in seconds. Unlike compound interest, which works at a fixed rate of interest, the exponential function is artfully designed as an infinite series with a rate of growth that always moves up to equate the value already attained by the function itself. Say that, and you are saying that the rate of acceleration (second derivative of the function) keeps step and all the higher derivatives of the growth rate do likewise.

What has this to do with our Stock Market Unbound model? Simply this: the rate of growth – real or faked – already attained by a stock is extrapolated on an ever exploding base into the indefinite future, and then discounted at a fixed rate for present value and incorporated into the share price. That done, the stock must continue to move up at the same increasing rate and at the same rate of growth that determined the share price already reached. Failing that, the whole game collapses.

It is not that the numerous CEOs who were role models in the recent planned boom planned becoming criminals. It was just that, without quite realizing what they were letting themselves in for, they made a deal with the Devil. "I will grant you your greatest success on the stock and option markets," said the Great Persuader, "but on one condition, you must match that success on your own year after year. Sign here." Under such a compulsion, the Decalogue is a lost cause.

And into this jungle the Binary people will send the downtrodden masses with their Second Income to do their investing.[1]

A further word on the perils of misused mathematics. The Binary people inject a new item "Capital Homesteading Plan" into the standard Quantity Theory equation relating the quantity of money, its velocity of circulation, price and the quantity of product. But the Quantity theory is posited on the notion of a self-balancing market. Money creation today is not confined to the demure promises of the Quantity Equation. With statutory reserves that banks had to hold with the central bank as a modest collateral quota to back their money creation abolished or almost so depending on the country, banks can create unlimited money. That power is regulated with little but the Bank for International Settlements *Risk-Based Capital Requirements*. Instead of creating credit to lend out, they used it to buy brokerage houses, derivative boutiques insurance companies. That is why so many huge banks became holding companies. But the statutory reserves were in legal tender; the BIS constraints that have almost wholly displaced them throughout the world are in capital not cash. And the US and other law courts are jammed investigations concerning the fictions of capital devised by accountants and others to put capital on the books that never existed, and keep liabilities off the books. What could result for the "Capital Homesteaders" is likely to be a replay of that immortal classic "The Slaughter of the Innocents."

Paying for the "Capital Homesteading" will inevitably give rise to a deeper layer of taxation in price. I have called such price increases that reflect not an excess of demand over supply which is real inflation, but the redistribution of income to "internalize" essential public services, a "structural price increase." Such public services have been declared "externalities" by the quantity theory and other models incorporating the dogma of a self-balancing market.

Likewise, the surprising S&C's adoption of Say's Law, that holds that every commodity creates a market for itself by the very act of its production. Obviously, this blows up just about everything that S&C deal with in the excellent portion of the book out of the water – forced unemployment, the maldistribution of wealth and so forth.

An apology, Madam Chairperson, because I have already taken more than my allotted time. The moral of all this is important. Never was a more persuasive book written on the need to reform this crumbling, unjust and unworkable social system. But to walk the seven steps to justice that the authors identify, we need a radical mind-cleaning of the dogmas of the system in power. Otherwise what well-intentioned reformers throw out through the door, will come back to mock their efforts via all windows and the chimney. The limitations of space have led me to list some serious misconceptions of this partly excellent little work, instead of celebrating its many virtues. The *Seven Steps to Justice* is good enough to merit at least seven editions. But for the second of these they must address the weaknesses I have listed. We trust that can be done at future sessions of your excellent Symposium. Count me in for its sessions.

William Krehm

1. For a simple examination of the Exponential Function, with the high-school or freshman maths needed, see my *Towards a Post-Autistic Economy – A Place for Society at the Table*, COMER Publications, 2002, p. 99.

The Portent of the Kiwi

AS WE ENTER ever more deeply into the brave new world of Globalization and Deregulation, we are becoming aware that what was presented to us by its promoters was an advertising logo rather than an honest picture of what lay ahead. Hence the multiple surprises that call to mind the scratchy scramble of the 1930s for larger pieces of a shrinking world market rather than the brave New World promised by politicians.

Much of the disturbing news comes out of China. Its population, cultural background and worldwide outreach may eventually reduce even the US to a middle-power – as the US did Britain. The combination of Confucius and its brush with Marxism may turn out a formidable blend. Just a few years after President Clinton proclaimed that democracy would come to China on the wings of free trade, there are signs that China is opening up to Western trade with a surfeit of aggressive cau-

tion. In a recent issue we reported how China has demanded a maximum of technological transfer as the price for granting market access to US corporations. With wage levels one tenth those of Japan and one fifth those of Taiwan and Singapore, and somewhere between 100 and 200 million unemployed and displaced persons, China is a far better manufacturing base for American firms for their exports to the West than a consumer market. 40% of microwave ovens and 25% refrigerators sold in Europe are at present produced in China.

The same is turning out to be the case in the field of agriculture and biotechnology. There, too, China is learning to defend itself against the trade offensives of the US, and even to turn them around.

On that the humble kiwi – identified by the world as a New Zealand fruit – has a tale.

"When Xue Dayuan talks about the future of biotechnology in China, he starts with the kiwi. About a century ago, the Chinese scientist says, visiting New Zealanders found a fuzzy grape-size object on a sacred Buddhist mountain and took it back to their country. Researchers discovered how to make the fruit plumper, sweeten its green insides and ultimately export the kiwi to its ancestral home, China, where it sells for five times its domestic counterpart.

"If China had developed the same species, maybe its fruit would occupy the world market," writes *The Wall Street Journal* (20/01/03, "China Tries to Stake its Biotech Claims" by Peter Wonacott).

"Many Chinese scientists and bureaucrats are worried that China lags behind the US and other countries by such a margin that it can't hope to compete in determining what Chinese plants, trees, herbs and fruits may someday yield scientific breakthroughs and commercial riches. Fears that foreign companies may start to patent genetic material obtained from native Chinese products are now behind stepped-up efforts to police biotechnology. Recent efforts to restrict access to China's biotech market have prompted complaints from foreign industries, who says government protectionism is stifling investment and export opportunities.

"'A country should protect its genetic resources. It's just like territory,' declares Mr. Xue, an adviser to China's State Environmental Protection Administration, or SEPA. The 47-year-old, who has done academic stints in the US and Australia, is involved in drafting a secret list that will try to keep the genetic makeup of certain goods out of foreign hands. Culled from thousands of medicinal herbs, plants and vegetables, the list will seek to isolate agricultural species deemed quintessentially Chinese, and safeguard their genetic material in a government-run repository. The list will be broken into three categories: gene matter that can be freely exchanged between Chinese and foreign scientists; material that can be exchanged under certain conditions; and material off-limits to the outside world.

"Other countries maintain such gene banks, but China appears more reluctant to share what it has, according to biotech experts.

"The effort is an offshoot of a global trademark movement that has swept countries touting their own special foods, like

French winemakers in Bordeaux, or Italian cheese-makers in Parma. China's growing unease over how a globalized economy is blurring lines between what belongs to countries and companies is shared by developing nations. Pakistan and India, for example, have fought a US patent on a variety of South Asian rice.

"When US biotech company Monsanto Co. tried to patent a gene of a soy-bean grown in China for thousands of years, Chinese media kicked up a fuss. And in recent months, Chinese newspapers have focused on the fact that 70% of Peking ducks in China's restaurants now are products of a UK company, Cherry Valley Farms. British geneticists have used computers to develop a hybrid fowl that grows faster, lays more eggs and eats less than its Chinese cousin.

"Over a 5-year period that ends in 2005, the Chinese government has pledged $600 million to boost biotech research. But China is slow to commercialize the science That caution is in line with the other side of the global biotech debate represented by the European Union, where consumers have resisted the lab-altered foods. In contrast to almost every other area of the Chinese economy, Beijing has battened down the hatches to foreign investment in agricultural biotech. Last March it barred foreign investment in precious agricultural breeds, including genes in plants. These areas were lumped together with weapon manufacture, the smelting of radioactive mineral products and tiger-bone processing."〜

An X-Ray of our Economic Process

THE WALL STREET JOURNAL (24/05, "How a Nursing-Home Empire Built on Medicare Collapsed" by Lucette Lagnado) provides us with a colorful vignette of the US health system that is so often held up as a model to Canadians. The facts, considerably condensed, are taken entirely from the WSJ. The interpretations are ours.

"On January 28, 2000, Robert Elkins, founder and chief executive of Integrated Health Services Inc., put the finishing touches on a project that had drawn his passionate devotion for nearly a year. IHS, one of the nation's largest nursing-home chains, was fighting for its life. The federal government had slashed Medicare reimbursements to nursing homes, resulting in billion-dollar losses for the Sparks, MD, company. Creditors were circling, having lent IHS $4.1 billion when it was the great hope of for-profit health care for the elderly. The company's stock, as high as $39 a share 18 months earlier, was trading at less than a dime.

"But the deal that Dr. Elkins's company closed that day had little to do with the health of IHS or its patients. Using company money, contributed to a retirement fund set up for him, Dr. Elkins directed the purchase of 'The Holy Family with St. John the Baptist and an Angel' by Guido Reni, an early Italian baroque painter, for $1 million.

"It was the last of more than a dozen purchases at auctions in London and New York through which the retirement plan amassed a collection valued at $8.2 million – booked as company assets. Among the paintings were a Canaletto, a Lucian Freud, and Dr. Elkins's favorite, 'Madonna and Child with Adoring Angels,' by Rodolfo Ghirlandaio.

"'Beautiful, innocent,' Dr. Elkins, 58 years old, says of the Ghirlandaio. Many paintings hang on the walls of his seaside villa in Naples, Fla." The high-flyers of the late stock market boom seem to have developed a taste for expensive art, especially that paid for by shareholders.

A week later, IHS had filed for bankruptcy protection from its creditors. The company that Dr. Elkins had founded in the late 1980s and developed into a giant concern with 86,000 employees and 45,000 beds in 47 states, chalking up $3 billion of revenue annually.

Before long Elkin's handiwork was being investigated for Medicare-fraud. It is only at such moments that the investors and the public at large learn the fate of their investment and tax dollars. That makes for drama. Newspapers have never had it so good. Little energy is wasted scratching heads for sensational headlines.

"Shareholders were outraged to learn that IHS executives had received nearly $60 million – most of it going to Elkins himself – under a 'loan program' that turned into a giveaway when the loans were forgiven.

"Despite the ill-timed art collecting and the cash handouts to top brass, this isn't simply a tale of executive self-indulgence at others' expense." It sheds light on the clash of codes of public and financial sectors, that makes communication between the two as dicey as that between sheep and wolves.

"Within the industry Dr. Elkins was lauded as a visionary and spawned many imitators. Even his most vocal critics credit him with having found a way to provide exemplary care of the elderly and disabled – and to do so profitably so long as Medicare, the federal health-insurance program for the aged, kept paying.

"IHS ran a 'pretty good operation, qualitatively,' says Bruce Vladeck, who oversaw Medicare when Congress began the rate cuts that helped bring down IHS. '[Dr. Elkins] found a hole in Medicare policy through which one could drive a truck.'

"'There is a major disconnect between the government giving of public funds and its oversight' of those funds,' says Cynthia Rudder, a director of the Nursing Home Community Coalition of New York State. She says the issue is looming larger as Medicare again ratchets up reimbursements for a revival of the for-profit nursing-home industry.

"Dr. Elkins's innovation rested on what is called subacute care – turning nursing homes, accustomed to doing little more than warehousing seniors, into minihospitals for stroke victims and other sick elderly people who otherwise would be placed in hospitals. That way, IHS could coax larger reimbursements out of Medicare and other insurers for types of care hospitals provide, while leaving IHS more profit because its overhead was not nearly as great as that of hospitals.

"Wall St. loved it because it seemed a sure-fire bet for profits.

"For a while at least. Looking to rein in growing costs and abuses, Medicare cut reimbursements for subacute care by as much as 50% in the late 1990s. IHS wasn't the only one hurt. Around the same time, four other nursing-home companies that emulated IHS's methods found themselves unable to meet payments on debt of more than $10 billion and filed for bankruptcy protection. About 12% of the US nursing-home population now lives in institutions whose owners have sought bankruptcy in the past five years.

"[As a student] Elkins, unable to get into an American medical school, had attended one in Rome, Italy. During breaks in his studies, he visited the art galleries of Florence, and became a 'self-taught' connoisseur of art. Later, during a psychiatric residency at the Massachusetts Mental Health Center, he took a job at a failing psychiatric hospital. There, he says, he got involved in running the facility, and enjoyed the work. 'Once I had a taste of that, it was very hard to practice medicine,' he says.

"He discovered his entrepreneurial flair. In 1988 he turned his attention to nursing homes, which he says were a very inexpensive business. 'They were horribly unpopular. I thought I could change that.' Nursing homes had been the orphan of the health-care industry. Most were small, family-run operations where little actual nursing went on. Much of the care was delivered by nurse's aids.

"Hospitals, however, were often charging fees of $1,000 to $2,000 a day – and because of rising costs were still not making money. It wouldn't take much money to build a subacute care wing and add monitoring equipment, piped-in oxygen or critical-care nurses. He and his associates developed a road show to demonstrate to investors how extremely sick elderly patients – those recovering from a stroke, for example, or depending on respirators – could recover at an IHS facility as well as in a hospital. Insurers and HMOs, saw a means of holding costs.

"Under Medicare rules at the time, IHS could ask for reimbursement of 'reasonable costs' as defined in Medicare manuals thousands of pages long. In addition, companies like IHS could apply for 'exceptions' to cover the cost of caring for the severely ill. Thus nursing homes that received $300 or $400 a day per patient from Medicare could ratchet up the payments to $600 or $700 a day.

"'Until money got tight later in the 1990s, IHS tried to keep an intensive-care nurse in every subacute unit. Executives kept a close watch on care, parachuting in at any hint of trouble,' says Gary Singleton, who oversaw clinical issues for IHS, 'While reimbursements were high, so was quality.'

"Dr. Elkins adds: 'You had to apply for exceptions, but Medicare paid for all of them 100%…. We had sicker and sicker patients. I should have sold the company then. We were darlings of everybody.' The more desirable IHS seemed as a growing company, the more eager banks were to lend. The company's debt ballooned to $3.2 billion in 1997 from about $142 million five years earlier, and then to $4.1 billion by the end of the decade.

"'Soon the success spawned imitators. There was this euphoria that Wall St. would be there and the banks would be there,' said Mr. Singleton. In 1998 Dr. Elkins signed off on an executive loan program, drawing on suggestions by a consultant on how to retain talent. It grew to include more than two dozen executives, receiving millions of dollars with which they were advised to buy IHS stock. According to a creditors' lawsuit a large portion of the proceeds were not used for the stated purpose.

"But as the 1990s waned, trouble was brewing. In January 1998, a year before the big Medicare cutback, IHS spent more than $1 billion to buy a slew of long-term-care facilities from HealthSouth Corp. In January 1999, after Medicare had slashed reimbursement for home health care, IHS had to sell for just $26 million a home-health-care company it had bought in 1986 for about $300 million.

"Medicare's cost-based reimbursement system, enriched by aggressive use of exceptions, helped fuel health-care inflation through the decade. The number of patients in nursing homes increased to 1.8 million in 1998 from 600,000 in 1990."

Medicare Pulled the Plug on Nursing Homes — When Banks were Bailed Out from S&L Losses

"When Medicare pulled the plug in late 1998, it put in a regime that paid nursing homes a set rate per patient, depending on how sick they are. Average reimbursements plummeted 25%, from around $370 a day to $275. But the decline was much steeper for companies like IHS that had thrived on exceptions.

"'It was like moving patients out of a Marriott into a Motel 6,' says Laurence Lane, a vice president at Genesis Health Ventures Inc., a nursing-home chain outside Philadelphia.

"It was the beginning of the reckoning for IHS and its ilk." Filings for bankruptcy began multiplying. IHS itself laid off hundreds, including many physical therapists. Its stock price started 1999 at $14 a share, less than half of where it was for much of the previous year.

"But the company still continued to pay into a special executive retirement plan it had set up a couple of years earlier for Dr. Elkins and a few other top executives. By 1999, the plan held $26.5 million, and began to invest in art.

"'I had no doubt the paintings would be worth more than the stupid mutual funds' he had been investing in. 'You could at least look at the paintings.' Dr. Elkins flew to New York to attend pre-auction showings at Christie's and Sotheby's."

What he didn't mention is that it later appeared that those art auctions were later shown to be as rigged as some of IHS's billings for "reasonable health-care costs."

"More recently, the nursing-home industry has shown signs of revival as government has loosened the purse-strings. In response to loud complaints from the companies hurt by the 1998 Medicare cuts – as well as damning federal reports on conditions in nursing homes, Congress approved an additional $2.7 billion in 2000 in Medicare funding for sicker nursing-home patients over five years and the next year another $2.2 billion over two years.

Some of IHS competitors have managed to come out of bankruptcy, but not IHS. The federal Medicare fraud investigation goes on. Dr. Elkins, no longer in prominent view, has remarked. "'The system is so screwed that the motivation is to give the least care.'"

In this lengthy tale we are offered an X-ray of the motivations driving the financial speculative system that our economy has become. Two high-powered groups fed upon one another each completely unconcerned with the constraints the other was subjected to. Neither the nursing-care entrepreneurs, nor Medicare made any serious effort to understand the full implications of the social problem it was supposedly addressing. Such distractions were blotted out by their own compulsive agenda.

Right-thinking economists could be of little help. For they tend to concentrate on the extent that growth can be recorded or foreseen. Dr. Elkins was able to spot unmistakable growth in the demand of our aging population and in their need for nursing care, and in the consequent shortage of hospital beds to accommodate them. And he lost no time translating all that into a listed corporation dedicated to maximizing its growth.

The population explosion and the increase in life expectancy were sure things. There was no attempt to analyze the growth of each social factor involved, to determine what might be growth of healthy tissue, and what was plain cancer. Growth was growth, and only a fool looks a gift horse in the mouth. Obviously, we must dig deeper to get to the roots of the world's problems. Economic thinking is itself in a bankrupt state.

The factual material on Dr. Elkin's adventures in the private health system was taken from *The Wall Street Journal* (24/05/02). The same publication, notable for the excellence of much of its factual reporting even when it thumbs its nose at its editorial columns, reports on the fictions of the accountancy of HealthSouth Corp. As mentioned above Dr. Elkin "bought a slew of long-term care facilities for more than $1 billion." In the *WSJ* (20/03/03, "Health South Faked $1.4 Billion Profits, The SEC Alleges," it gives us an intimate glimpse of how, under our speculative, growth-maximising economy, the great deceivers in turn get greatly deceived, and the skyscrapers of deception shoot into the sky until no one can say whether those GDP growth figures are fact or fiction.

"Eight days ago, the former chief financial officer of Health-South Corp., approached federal prosecutors in Alabama and told them: Senior executives at the health-care giant had been falsifying results for more than five years. Weston L. Smith's statements to the US Attorney in Birmingham said that the company's founder and chief executive, Richard Scrushy, had met regularly with him and another chief executive to inflate earnings to meet Wall St.'s estimates. The get-togethers were known as 'family' meetings, and bogus accounting entries were known as 'dirt' to fill a 'gap' or a 'hole' in the earnings numbers. The SEC accused HealthSouth and Mr. Scrushy of 'massive accounting fraud' alleging in a civil case that they had overstated earnings by a total of $1.4 billion since 1999. Mr. Scrushy had returned to the HealthSouth CEO post only two months ago, after a six-month period during which a law firm's inquiry found the insider-trading questions groundless. The one-time gas-station attendant had made a fortune by targeting a health care niche and riding trends in demographics and Medicare's reimbursement. His outpatient rehabilitation and surgery-services business, founded in 1984, had made HealthSouth into a kind of McDonald's of outpatient care.

"In the fall of 1997, according to the SEC, some accounting

personnel of HealthSouth appealed to Mr. Scrushy to abandon the earnings manipulation. Mr. Scrushy refused. The agency said that he said, 'Not until I sell my stock.' In 1998 its all-time high was $30.56. Currently it is trading at $3.91."

In a separate article in its same issue (*WSJ*, 20/03/03, "Unscrambling the Accounting"), Jonathan Weil sums up the system used to baffle auditors: "If they plowed all the illicit revenue into one type of assets, they might detect it. So they spread the improper entries far and wide in tiny pieces across HealthSouth's balance sheet, according to prosecutors."

A question arises: if you assess the cost of these many-storeyed structures of deceit, the losses to shareholders, the broken families, the suicides, the resulting loss of jobs, the disarray, the legal costs to track down the fraud, the alienation caused at home and abroad, and occasionally perhaps even a little war to wipe the slate clean and begin all over again, do we really know whether our society is progressing or falling apart? Even those with a passing knowledge of Russian history will be aware of Grigory Aleksandrovitch Potemkin, the long-time lover of Empress Catherine II, who set out to colonize the Ukrainian steppes, built a Black Fleet Navy, with the hope of eventually winning Constantinople. In 1787 he arranged a trip for his Empress to Crimea so that she could see his achievements for herself. The only problem was that much of what was there was an unholy mess. Undaunted, he had special display villages built, with well-scrubbed peasants in fine houses, well-dressed and trained to dance their native dances. The Empress was enchanted. The technique has gone down in history as "Potemkin villages," and is by no means restricted to Russia. Must we not ask ourselves whether our economy with its lasagna of deception may not in fact be largely imposture – a Potemkin economy?

William Krehm

Economics and the Test of Falsifiability

"Only hypotheses capable of clashing with observation reports are allowed to count as scientific." – Karl R. Popper

AN IMPORTANT FEATURE of modern epistemology is the demand that scientific theories be falsifiable. By this is meant that it should be possible to submit theories to falsification tests by comparing the predicted outcomes with the ones observed. Only hypotheses capable of clashing with observation can count as scientific. Thus, there can be two reasons why a hypothesis must be discarded as false. One is its failure when tested against observations. For instance, a hypothesis about a flock of swans claiming they are all red, will be false if an observation shows that they are, in fact, all white. This, of course, is a long-standing methodology of science.

But, according to Popper, a hypothesis must also be discarded as non-scientific if it is not falsifiable, that is, capable of being tested conclusively against observations. This is the case if a hypothesis is couched in an open-ended language that, no matter how many false observation reports one gets, the hypothesis cannot be gotten rid of. "Some swans are red" is unscientific because even if all known observations came back with the result "false," the person questioning the hypothesis can never be sure to have seen all swans. And that will give its defender room to claim that there might be some red swans somewhere that were missed.

In a more general sense, we can say that all hypotheses based on absolute claims will, by the very nature of absolute statements, always be open-ended. Because of this, they are not falsifiable and they must therefore be relegated to the realm of non-science. Many of the totalitarian ideologies that were sweeping Europe in the 1930s and 1940s, when Popper wrote his major works, were based on absolute or open-ended claims.

A similar case arises with religions. Typically, religions are based on sets of absolute claims. Such systems can play an important role in the spiritual and ethical understanding of life, where the demand for scientific form is irrelevant. However, when absolute religious claims are used to justify wider social and political purposes, they move into a realm where their accessibility to falsification tests must be considered.

Turning to modern neo-classical economics, we can say it consists of a set of claims and hypotheses about the relations within modern industrial societies. However, seen in a Popperian light, a major part of the hypotheses underpinning the neoclassical framework either fail falsification tests, or are not falsifiable.

One such is the theory of consumer choice that assumes that rational economic agents possessing complete and perfect information will make choices that best serve their self-interest. It is not hard to find a multitude of data that contradicts this: examples of people knowingly rejecting choices in their self-interest to reach or serve a more important personal or social goal. Such examples are reinforced by behavioural psychology that tells us that people in general have varying degrees of irrational elements in their behaviour. In management sciences, as taught in all business schools, this is shown in simplified form in the Johari window:

	Known to self	Unknown to self
Known to others	Open motives	Suppressed motives
Unknown to others	Secret motives	Deep hidden motives

The Johari Window

The fact is that entrepreneurial activity is to a high degree driven precisely by the circumstance that much information related to economic activity is exclusive and not available either to the general public or to their main competitors.

Finally, from the Popperian angle, the assumption of complete and perfect information is an open-ended claim since we can never pin down what complete and perfect information is.

A similar situation exists with the other central claim of neo-classic economics about the *existence* of perfect competition. The widespread existence of monopolistic and oligopolistic competition has forced the neo-classical theorists to modify

this pretension. Instead it has been altered to the assumption that all markets are constantly trending towards perfect competition. This credo is clearly not falsifiable and is therefore, non-science.

This puts the claim into the open-ended, non-falsifiable category, parallel to the claim about the red swans. The neo-classical defenders can always postulate: Well, just wait long enough, it will eventually materialize, somewhere, some day.

Dix Sandbeck

A Time for Indicting Even Higher Fraud?

SINCE WE ARE REGALED with photos of Wall St. operators in handcuffs being marched off to jail, we marvel that basic scams exposed years ago should go right on.

Thus *The Globe and Mail* Report on Business (22/08, "Consumer prices in July, boosting inflation to 2.1% by Marian Stinson) recounts: "Consumer prices posted their largest increase in nearly a year in July, fuelled by rising energy prices and higher cigarette taxes. The 0.5% rise from June in the consumer price index – higher than analysts had forecast – has bolstered expectations that the Bank of Canada will push up interest rates again in September.

"The core rate, which is closely watched by the central bank, was steady at an annual rate of 2.1% in July."

To appreciate the extent of the misinformation, we must go back 12 years ago when under pressure from COMER and others, the Government was forced to recognize that when it increases consumer price taxation, the resulting jump in end-prices has nothing to do with inflation. It is palpably something for which the government itself must answer. And when the Bank of Canada responds to that by raising interest rates "to lick inflation" – it becomes double-tiered fraud. How clearly we set this forth at that time appears from the following:

"Belatedly the hoax of salvation through usury is being uncovered. That task seems already underway at Statistics Canada. Thus it reports that the Consumer Price Index posted a 4.5% increase in the 12 months ending in May, down from 5.0% in April. That was the biggest monthly drop in nearly six years. The most important factor in the drop was the removal of the federal excise increase on tobacco and gasoline.

"Douglas Peters, chief economist of the Toronto-Dominion Bank and later member of the Chrétien government, summed up the disclosure: 'The inflation numbers tell us what we've known for a long time – inflation has stayed at 4% for the last six years except for the idiot taxes that keep getting added in.' The 'core rate of inflation' that excludes volatile factors of food and energy, fell to 4.4% in April from 4.9% a year earlier. The concept of a 'a core inflation' was introduced by the late Otto Eckstein in 1981.

"Far more important than the volatility of certain market factors is the part played in price movement by factors not originating in the market at all. It is essential that the price indexes be unbundled according to their component causes."[1]

However, it is notable how those in the saddle make use of or eliminate the non-core items according to their advantage at the moment. For example in the 1990 quotation when the tax on tobacco had been decreased, that was noted in accounting for inflation. Today when it has been increased, it is not mentioned in sounding the tocsin on inflation. The common purpose would seem to be exaggerating the extent of inflation. If you add to that, the detail that the previous BoC governor, Gordon Thiessen, apologized for even uttering the word "deflation" you have a case of cooking society's books that can match anything on Wall St.

The recent *G&M* article continues in a mood of guarded skepticism. The caution has good cause. However, academia and journalism are littered with the blanched skulls of those too insistent of speaking the whole truth.

"The surge in cigarette prices was one of the key ingredients in the upward move in inflation last month and reflects the rise in excise taxes in mid-June. Without the increase, the overall inflation rate would fall to an annual rate of 1.8% from 2.1%.

"Electricity rose 3.2% in July, almost entirely because of a 9.2% increase in Ontario after it moved to a free-market pricing system. Rising demand because of heat waves caused prices to move higher during the month, Statscan said."

Two months earlier, *Economic Reform* quoted Greg Ip (*Financial Post*, 30/03/90): "Interest rates resumed their upward march yesterday raising concerns among some economists that the price of the BoC's battle against inflation may be too great." The real point is not that the product is over-priced, but that it is fraudulent, contributing to the very problem it is advertised to solve.

"Until a couple of years ago, the orthodox view was that higher taxes kept inflation down. One could have hoped that the Goods and Service Tax, appearing as it does on the consumer's invoice, would make it clear that some of our price rise may merely reflects the cost of more public services. Vain hope. To get around that little embarrassment the term 'tax inflation' has been introduced."[2]

But the distortions mentioned are the mere beginning of the tale. There are many other taxes – those on producers and property, for example, that consumers never set eyes on and hence are not aware exist. That helps identify any price increase with an excess of demand over supply that requires higher interest rates to repress. For interest rates a quarter of a century ago were proclaimed the only blunt tool against inflation. The many other successful methods used during WWII and the early postwar years have been done away with. Notably the fixing of interest rates at a low level in times of crisis, and the increase in the statutory reserves that private banks had to leave with the central bank as token collateral for their deposits from the public. While these reserves existed, instead of shoving up interest rates as a 'one blunt tool' to calm a speculative boom, the central bank could leave interest rates alone and merely raise these reserves. That would cut the credit the private banks could create. This made it unnecessary to push interest rates up

to levels that clobbered the entire economy.

Most disturbing is the dogged resistance to recognizing that not all price rise can be identified with an excess of demand over supply. In fact a good part of it stems from the development of a high-tech, pluralistic society. That requires many more public services; and these for the most part are neither marketed or priced. However, they are not without cost. The obvious conclusion is that their cost – through a broadening layer of taxation – turns up in the price of what goods and services are marketed. Once that is recognized the whole economic model changes beyond recognition.

Though these lines of thought may seem novel, they are not that difficult to grasp. Far less so than the discredited official model of a self-balancing market to which all concerns must be left.

A Glaring Conflict of Interest

And beyond the respective technical merits of the two models, weighty moral issues are involved. The "one blunt tool" chosen – paradoxically – to enforce the model of a self-balancing market, happens to be the revenue of a distinct economic set – money-lenders. And these have been known, when opportunity beckons, to become voracious. That is attested by the stand of several great religions against usury and even against interest as such. The traumatic experience of millennia must have led to such a position. High interest rates take a toll on all producers. There is thus a glaring conflict of interest in the "zero inflation" model, and the elevation of interest rates as "the one blunt tool" to impose it. Worse yet, with the abandonment of even the notional gold standard in 1971 and the reduction of money to pure credit, the scope of that conflict of interest grew awesomely.

How then it could it have been overlooked by the very authorities who are playing sheriff to enforce morality on the high-flyers of Wall Street? That is the key question of our troubled times. There is not a doubt that proclaiming interest rates the one stabilizer has led to the transfer of more trillions of dollars from frayed pockets to the very wealthy than all the skullduggery on Wall St. that is now rocking the world. Moreover it helped set the stage for the latter. All this has still to be addressed in official circles.

As is the case with many of the key puzzles of our economy, at least the framework for an answer was worked out decades ago. Our problem is that such answers have simply been suppressed.

The best of these for our present purpose was provided by a leading French economist of the 1950s and 1960s, François Perroux. In his concept of "dominant revenue," he held that in every historic period the welfare of society is officially measured by the volume and rate of revenue of a particular class. In the early 19th century Britain it was the landlords with their ultra-protective Corn Laws. Then in sequence came the industrial capitalists, the speculative financiers who struck out with the collapse of the system in the great Depression of the 1930s. The creaking world economy was started up again by a coalition of industrial capitalists and government, with the trade unions as junior partner. In the 1970s this was replaced by the private banking system, and with the deregulation of the world economy by highly speculative financial capital. That system has crumbled resoundingly, and that is where we are.

Behind the elevation of a privileged revenue as the barometer of the system as a whole lies a bold assertion of power. The dominant revenue and its supporting theory are not advanced as a hypothesis to be defended against rival doctrines. They are proclaimed as a revealed faith. Alternative theories are simply eliminated from the media, the educational system and public discourse. Indeed the very language has been restructured to exclude competing models. In this way the reassessment of basic policies is ruled out.

Today the absolute power of deregulated and globalized finance is without precedent. To fashion their regime, bankers have studied and applied all the hard lessons they learned during their long years in the doghouse – 1933 to 1951. That experience was reviewed, analyzed, and strategies and tactics elaborated. Not the least of these was the complete occupation of the intellectual space so that critics do not have to be answered.

By silencing all warnings, such an arrangement guarantees not only major crises, but guarantees that they will swell to disastrous proportions before they are recognized for what they are. If Her Majesty's government has no opposition in Parliament on the policy that led to our economic meltdown, little remains of democracy and its built-in defences. That situation in the economy today has seeped into our very political process.

William Krehm

1. *Economic Reform*, July 1990, reproduced in Krehm, William (1999). *Meltdown: Money, Debt and the Wealth of Nations*. COMER Publications, p. 39.
2. Krehm, p. 33.

History's Surprises Are Like an Alligator's Tail — Watch Out

Let *The Wall Street Journal* tell the story (11/3/03, "Fast Wallet, Free Agent: Russia Goes its Own Way" by Alan Cullison). As ever, we treasure sources above suspicion of left-wing prejudice. "Moscow – Russia's resistance to a US-led invasion of Iraq is a sign that the diplomacy of dependency may have run its course. After recovering from the post-Soviet economic deterioration of the 1990s, Moscow is awash in cash and not so easily plied by the West's handouts."

Private sources report that Muscovite tune-smiths are working on a blend of the International and the Czarist anthem to lyrics thanking the American insatiable appetite for SUVs for making possible their regaining economic independence. What is at stake is more than just the physical oil that the US can't consume enough of, but the denomination of the oil trade in US currency. That has permitted the US to pay for its oil imports in currency of its own making. The drop of the dollar *vis-à-vis* the Euro shortchanges the oil exporters. That has not been lost on the oil exporters.

The reserve status of its currency enabled the US to print bills or computer entries at practically zero cost to import goods and securities from the entire world, even while its balance of payments worsened. That has led to a climb of the Euro in dollar terms since 1999 from about 83 US cents to a current $1.10 plus. That is an increase of about 45%. That earned Saddam Hussein a fat currency gain when he instructed the UN to shift the approximately $10 billion in his blocked currency account from dollars to Euros. This hasn't been lost on Iran, another of Bush's evil axes, a ferocious rival of Iraq, and a far greater oil exporter.

The Saudis, who have their own internal problems about Washington's Iraqi war, ditto. How long will it be before US hedge funds will put a wet finger to the wind, and place their patriotism in their safety-boxes long enough to make a killing shorting the dollar? Meanwhile Russia is doing fine since oil prices have risen from $11 crude to just under $40. At the same time, China is proving a hard-knuckled negotiator not only for branch plants and the jobs it sorely needs, but access to technology as the price of American entry to the Chinese market. They threaten to compete the pants off the Detroit Big Three and General Electric. They are taking over huge market share in Europe and America and Asia in everything from micro-wave ovens, to refrigerators, knock-offs of stringed musical instruments of at least orchestral caliber. Stradivarius is reported twisting in his grave, since the Chinese went to his native Cremona to learn the violin-making craft at the local violin-making school. They even send their violins to Cremona at times for the coats of varnish that authenticates them a bit more.

But back to the *WSJ*. "With an imminent UN vote that could lead to war, the opposing camps led by the US and France have focused their lobbying on a handful of Security Council members – Angola, Guinea and Chile. US National Security Adviser Condolezza Rice has openly suggested that the Bush administration offer aid to nations in exchange for support, saying: 'We're talking to people about their interests.'" It used to be known as "bribery" and involves thousands of innocent lives.

"Western purse strings were a factor Russia had to consider when formulating its foreign and even domestic agendas through the 1990s. With its economy in a shambles, Moscow feared punitive rulings from the Paris Club and London Club groups of creditors, which held billions of dollars in Soviet-era debt. It also relied on the World Bank and IMF to plug budget gaps.

"When NATO bombed Yugoslavia in 1999 in response to 'ethnic cleansing' of Muslims and others, IMF aid was seen as an important incentive that kept Russia's often-symbolic support of the Yugoslav government from turning into active defence.

"The alchemy of Russia's financial relations has since changed. Vladimir Putin, chagrined by the contemptuous 1990s characterization of Russia as 'Upper Volta with rockets,' focused on the nation's sickly economy after he became president in early 2000. He put a stop to IMF borrowing when a recovery in world oil prices gave Moscow some financial relief. Unrest in the Middle East and Venezuela has helped prompt a sharp rise in oil prices since then. Russia is now cash rich, and the government has been using its huge surpluses to pay down the national debt.

"Last week, the day after Russia joined France and Germany in declaring its firm opposition to a new UN resolution clearing the way for force against Iraq, the Russian government announced that it intended to repay IMF loans next year ahead of schedule. Nobody could miss the connection. In December, it announced it was ending the work of the Peace Corps in Russia. The mission of groups like the Peace Corps is to assist developing nations.

"'They haven't been on their knees for some time,' said a senior US diplomat based in Moscow. The US has steered clear of any outright offers of economic incentives in exchange for Russian support of an invasion of Iraq, adding that the Russian government has made it plain it isn't interested in such offers.

"To the extent that economic enticements enter into Mr. Putin's thinking on Iraq, it isn't clear that Washington can offer more than France or Germany. Germany is one of Russia's greatest trading partners, and most of its gas exports go to Europe.

"President Saddam Hussein has promised Russian companies the chance to develop more than 25 billion barrels of oil in Iraqi fields. The Russian government, meanwhile, would like to be repaid Soviet-era debts that totaled $8 billion when Iraq stopped paying in the early 1990s.

"Russia [however], has indicated it is more worried about world oil prices than any oil contracts or the Soviet-era debt, the US diplomat said." But those prices depend upon whether oil internationally continues to be quoted and paid for in terms of a sinking US dollar or in Euros.

"The Kremlin already has amassed a lofty financial cushion against any decline in oil prices in the aftermath of the war. Its 2003 budget is based on any average oil price of $21.50 a barrel.

"'In the past, Russia tried to convince the world of its greatness by building rockets,' said Roland Nash, head of research at Renaissance Capital investment bank in Moscow. 'Putin has concentrated on the economy with essentially the same end in mind.'"

If the American administration would consider the costs in wealth, lives, morality, and sympathy among nations of its present autistic policies as a sole economic superpower, it would accept the erosion of its highly vulnerable position with grace. As did Britain and France in their day. That would not only provide an answer to the question that is bothering more and more Americans, "Why does the world hate us?", but a solution to the problem.

William Krehm

Crocuses in the Snow

THE PLANET is seeded with land mines of policy. The technological preponderance of the lone superpower has been translated into a disregard for the sensitivities of other lands. The mind of economists is held hostage at the altar of a self-balancing market in a world that was rarely ever so out of kilter. But in this daunting mess, cropping up in the most unlikely places, the reaction of the forces of survival are beginning to push up like crocuses in the snow. There are the improvisations in the Argentine, reduced to poverty by its previous adhesion to the dogma of the Washington Consensus. There are the magnificent anti-war demonstrations across the world, matured into the dignity of non-violence. Humble church communities in the US south that bail out their debt-ridden members in sequence set by benign lotteries. And now out of religious circles in darkest Alabama a tax-lawyer has started a campaign for a measure of social justice.

The Wall Street Journal (12/2, "Seminary Article Sparks Alabama Tax-Code Revolt" by Shailagh Murray) informs us out of Tuscaloosa: "An unlikely force is setting off a tax revolt in Alabama: religious fervor. The catalyst is Susan Pace Hamill, a tax-law professor who used a sabbatical at a divinity school to write *An Argument for Tax Reform Based on Judaeo-Christian Ethics.*

"'How could we, a bunch of Christians, have the most unjust tax structure you could have dreamed up?' she asked in the *Alabama Law Review*. Leading churches of the state are citing the paper in a pamphlet borrowing from Jesus for its title 'The Least of These.' It is being distributed by Samford University where Ms. Hamill attended divinity school. Alabama is at the bottom of the list of states in which income-tax liability kicks in. In 2001 the level there was $4,600 for two-parent families of four, with Kentucky next at $5,500 and Illinois at $14,300.

"By contrast, wealthy agricultural and timber interests are well protected against a revision of their state-tax bonanza. To change their tax code individual counties need permission from voters and even from the state legislature. Counties on their own, however, can raise the sales tax, some of which goes to the state, on their own. Result: more than half the state's revenue come from sales tax which has reached as high as 11%. That hits African-Americans with a wallop. They account for a quarter of the state population but one half of its poor.

"The new Republican Governor, Bob Riley, is on board of the campaign. He has appointed a commission to clear the constitutional table for 'comprehensive tax reform.' The United Methodist Church, the Presbyterian Church (USA), the Alabama Southern Baptist Convention, the Episcopalian Church, as well as local Roman Catholic and Jewish officials have joined the crusade. State business leaders have set up a coalition to promote a new tax structure that would support schools and other public services even if it means that companies would have to pay more.

"Yet there are battles ahead. The Governor has to push constitutional reform through the legislature where powerful farming and timber interest are strongly represented. Some conservative Christian groups and Alfa, the Alabama Farmers

Federation, that also represents timber growers, are resisting the changes in the tax code.

"In her stump speech, which she gives at least twice a week, Ms. Hamill reminds her audiences that both the Old and New Testaments condemn oppression of the poor. She quotes Micah 2:1: Woe to those who plan iniquity, who plot evil in their beds!

"Ms. Hamill, 42, is a Florida native, who, after graduating from Emory University and Tulane Law School, worked at the Sullivan & Cromwell law firm in New York and with the Internal Revenue Service in Washington. Eight years ago, she moved to Tuscaloosa to teach at the University of Alabama Law School. Feeling like an outsider among Alabama's large evangelical population, she spent her sabbatical at Samford University's Beeson Divinity School. There she read a local newspaper explaining how Alabama taxes families of four with very low incomes. 'I assumed the $4,600 figure was a misprint.'" Not so.

Before the Civil War Alabama depended for most of its income on a slave tax. After slavery disappeared, the state raised property taxes to fill the resulting gap. That brought on a backlash from the whites who owned most of the land. State constitutions adopted in 1875 and 1901 put and tightened the cap on property taxes. The goal was openly stated "to establish white supremacy in this state."

"That Jim-Crow effort sharply restricts Alabama's tax base today. Forests stretch across 71% of the state, but timber land is taxed at 95 cents average, compared with and average of $4 to $6 per acre in Georgia.

"Ms. Hamill has little first-hand knowledge of those she seeks to help. She hasn't visited many of the poverty-stricken parts of the state she has written about. She described Alabama as 'the modern version of ancient Israel. The land's being gobbled up. There's no minimum opportunity. And we're staying afloat on the backs of the poor.'

"'Until recently, most of my field trips out of the ivory tower were speaking engagements to the business and tax crowds,' says Ms. Hamill.

"She was a guest one recent Sunday at Vestavia Hills Baptist Church in Birmingham. She was invited back for another session.

"Other groups are more stubborn. Once area of resistance: the state's Black Belt, a cluster of former cotton-growing counties mostly in the state's western mid-section, nicknamed for its dark soil. Though rich in timber, the region has a paltry tax base and some of Alabama's least-equipped schools. Yet in the antebellum town of Marion, Zion United Methodist Church Pastor Fairest Cureton predicts many of his black parishioners will resist.

"He says he will preach in favor of reform. But he says poor people tend to like the sales tax, because they pay it in small increments."

Obviously information about the basics of public finance is kept at a premium. It rather reminds you of the bulk of more sophisticated taxpayers being brainwashed to concentrate their concern about the government's debt and deficit, without suspecting what may lie behind those siren words.

Thomas Jefferson summed it up: "If a nation expects to be ignorant and free, it expects what never was and never will be." Those that run the show these days are applying that wisdom in the negative at both ends of information process: Little gets through on the media that sheds any basic light on the economic process in our country. And with the schools fallen into decay and the universities and media muzzled, we are approaching the point where most folk will have just enough learning to read the ads. That is why these multiplying initiatives of concerned citizens, whether right or left of center, must be coordinated into one great revival.

William Krehm

ON PROPOSED BANK MERGERS AND FREEDOM OF INFORMATION

A Public Letter to the Commons Standing Committee on Finance

T*HE GLOBE AND MAIL* (20/12) informed us that "The central bank released the first issue of its new semi-annual publication, the *Financial Systems Review*, as part of the bank's strategy to increase openness about its operations." We are therefore suggesting some vital areas to which this excellent new policy should be applied.

"'In the face of elevated levels of financial stress, the Canadian financial system as a whole has shown itself capable of effectively meeting the current challenges,' the central bank said.

"'The environment of uncertainty and changing views of risk associated with financial assets and declining willingness of among investors to take on risk led to sharp movements in equity and bond prices,' the bank said, 'which affected the revenues and profitability of financial institutions.'

"To cope with the pressures of the past two years, Canadian banks and insurance companies increased their loan-loss provisions, the bank said. As well, chartered banks managed their exposure to credit risk, and some of them plan to reduce the proportion of their capital targeted to corporate lending."

There is no hint that these changing views of risk may have arisen from the disastrous failure of Bank of Canada policies in the 1990s. The chartered banks had been bailed out from their huge losses in gas and oil and real estate. This rescue took the form of discontinuing the statutory reserves they had put up as collateral for the public's deposits they held. Such primary cash reserves earning no interest had been as high as 12% in the case of chequing accounts, but had already been whittled down to an average of 4% across the whole range of accounts by 1991. On top of that there had also been the secondary reserve requirement of interest-bearing securities done away with in 1980.

In the late 1980s, the Bank for International Settlements *Risk-Based Capital Requirements* declared the debt of OECD countries risk-free requiring no further cash or capital for the banks to hold. Between these two measures our banks were able to quadruple their inventories of federal debt to some $80 billion without putting up significant money of their own. When the Bank of Canada holds such debt the interest paid on it comes back to the federal government almost entirely as dividends. For the one shareholder of the Bank of Canada since 1938 has been the Government of Canada. In contrast, when the banks hold such debt, that interest stays with them. The phasing out of the statutory reserves by 1993 made it unnecessary for the banks to put up reserves to support the $470-odd billion of deposits it already held from the public in 1991. That figure is some 50% higher today. The banks were rehabilitated at the expense of our society.

Even in 1993, the bailout amounted to anywhere between $5 and $8 billion a year, depending on how high the Bank of Canada had pushed up interest rates. Nor was it a one-shot affair. It was an entitlement, paid once again each year.

That left a crater in the finances of the central government. To fill it, grants to the provinces were slashed. The provinces in turn downloaded onto the municipalities responsibility for social programs, without adequate funding.

The statutory reserves had also been a virtual interest-free loan to the federal government within the constraints in force. Historically this harks back to the Crown's monopoly in coining precious metals, long a major source of its revenue. Gold and silver have long since been replaced by credit.

The Great Unspoken Secret (GUS): Deregulation after a Bailout

But most incredible of all, shortly after the banks were bailed out in so grand a way, they were deregulated further to enable them to acquire brokerage houses, engage in stock underwriting, merchant banking, operate derivative boutiques. It was a case of the drunk the morning after the night before being prescribed the hair of the dog that bit him. This equipped our banks for ever more highly leveraged gambling, on their own account as well as for clients. Many of these operations resulted in conflicts of interest. That is what the mega-scandals that are rocking the United States are about. The very largest US banks' $1.4 billion-plus settlements with the regulatory authorities still left them their most profitable year on record. Our Canadian banks have not been subjected to similar scrutiny at home.

Though reduced to dwindling significance, the statutory reserve system continues in the US and in Great Britain. Canada and New Zealand were singled out by the Bank for International Settlements to serve as examples, precisely because they had been outstanding for their social institutions.

We have not always been judicious in our choice of what we copy from our southern neighbour. I would recommend to you the publications of the Financial Markets Center, whose mission is to monitor the Federal Reserve. Last November its highly competent head – Jane D'Arista – who formerly served at a high level in the Congressional Budget Office and other congressional committees – issued a special study on the statutory reserve system of the Fed, of its surrender of many of its powers and the need to restructure and extent the entire system of banking reserves that has been abolished in Canada. Do give it your attention.

It is rare enough that banks will bail out their own clients in serious trouble, but never ever do they allow them to go on to more daring speculations with the funds that had been tossed to them as a life-belt. This, however, is what happened in Canadian banking in the 1990s.

Today two of the largest of our banks are subject to class actions in the US for their involvement in the off-balance-sheet partnerships, and "round-trip" trading that created fictitious market activity in California and drove up energy prices to fantastic levels.

It is surprising that our central bank should refer to this unedifying panorama as "an unusual series of adverse shocks." Unusual it most certainly is, since there was no precedent in the history of central banking of so massive a hushed-up bank-bailout followed, moreover, with an unprecedented degree of further bank deregulation. If in the Bank's words, there is a "declining willingness among investors to take on risk," it is largely because our banks and financial institutions abused those investors in countless ways.

"To cope with the pressures of the past two years, Canadian banks and insurance companies increased their loan-loss provisions, the bank said. As well, chartered banks managed their exposure to credit risk, and some of them plan to reduce the proportion of their capital targeted for corporate lending."

The real point is not how much more loan-loss provision they have already taken, but how much more they are likely to take. And who is going to insure the staggering risks created by our multi-storied casino economy? For that is the essence of risk management.

The Wall Street Journal (29/11/02, "Munich Re[1] AG has some bad news for almost everyone") reported: "The world's largest reinsurer…had sunk deeper in the red under the combined woes of its exposure to Germany's weak banks, the world's troubled stock markets and this summer's Central European flooding. And it offered a barely veiled threat to the stumbling German banks in which it holds large stakes – Commerzbank AG and HBV Group AG – that they couldn't rely on Munich Re that reported a $850.7 million net loss for the third quarter yesterday" to inject more capital into them."

In addition to the above-quoted article, the menacing over-hang in the European Re industry appeared grave enough for the *WSJ* to devote an editorial to it in the same issue: "European [insurance] companies hold a greater portion of reserves in stock than US firms (30% vs. 4%). Moreover, the values of their own stock are down by almost two-thirds since the beginning of the year, making it difficult for them to write new business. Bad enough, but it gets worse. Both American and European insurers are exposed to a variety of risks in the credit market at exactly the same moment that the corporate credit market is experiencing a severe downturn.

"They are also exposed to…the writing of commercial surety bonds – instruments that directly insure companies, or specific financing for projects, against credit risk and/or default.

"Many insurers have taken on additional risk in credit-derivatives markets. Credit derivatives allow credit risk on an underlying asset to be transferred from one party to another.

"Companies have been selling credit-default swaps (guaranteeing the debt of other entities) for investors with large exposures to an individual corporation. Insurers have also been involved, as guarantors and investors, in CDOs, complicated pools of sliced-and-diced corporate debt as well as pools of individual credit-default swaps."

Today the international insurance companies are themselves undermined by the risks taken on by world banking since it has become one flesh with the stock markets. It is therefore difficult to understand Bank of Canada's assurance that, "heightened levels of volatility relative to historical norms, financial markets continue to function relatively well." Relative to what? Surely not to the time when the Re companies were still able to under-write risks on land, water and in the air.

For years, since Globalization and Deregulation were foisted on the world as something inevitable, alarm bells have been drowned out by the thundering placebos of the central bank's releases. On 8/05/97, *The Globe and Mail* reported the Governor of the BoC, Gordon Thiessen worrying about "deflation." But a week later in the *G&M* (16/5) he was back assuring the Commons Finance Committee "that he will probably regret forever having mentioned 'it.'" Yet Mr. Thiessen's warning could not have been more timely. The following year, the economies of the so-called East Asian Tigers – Thailand, Malaysia, Singapore, Taiwan, and South Korea – had collapsed and carried that of Latin America and the Soviet bloc with them. Why did Mr. Thiessen feel he had to recant in public? And on whose behest?

The Illegal "Independence" of our Central Bank

If we consult the Bank of Canada's Charter, we find in its very preamble that the Bank was established "to mitigate by its influence fluctuations in the general level of production, trade, prices and employment, so far as may be possible within the scope of monetary action." That enjoins the bank to concern itself as much with "deflation" as with "inflation." Indeed, the Bank was founded to help lift the Canadian economy out of a disastrous world depression that eventually led to the Second World War. However, Mr. Thiessen's sound prognosis probably cost him a second term as governor of the Bank of Canada.

But has Parliament the right to look into such matters? Have we not had it drummed into our heads that our central bank is independent of the government? Let us then see what its charter says about that.

Article 17(2) reads, "The capital shall be divided into one hundred thousand shares of the par value of fifty dollars each, which shall be issued to the Minister to be held by the Minister on behalf of Her Majesty in right of Canada."

Article 14(2) provides that "should there emerge a difference between the Minister and the Bank concerning the monetary policy to be followed, the Minister may…give to the Governor a written directive concerning the monetary policy, in specific terms and applicable for a specified period, and the Bank shall comply with that directive."

Article 18(c) provides that the Bank may "buy and sell securities issued or guaranteed by Canada or any province." That implies the right to hold such securities. We have already noted that when the Bank holds such securities, practically all the interest paid on it ends up with the federal government as dividends on its shares. When private banks hold the same debt, the interest stays with them. By far the greater portion of our present federal debt originated in that way, plus, of course, sky-high interest rates as "the one blunt tool" of monetary policy.

The three articles cited – the ownership of all the shares of the Bank; its ability if need be to instruct the Bank on its policy, and the right to the bulk of the earnings of the central bank as dividends – add up not only to the ownership but to the ultimate responsibility for the Bank's policies. All this is clearly stated in the Queen's English and French. The taxpayers of Canada acquired that ownership in 1938 when they bought out 12,000 private shareholders at a fat profit when cash was as scarce as hen's molars. What then does the "independence of the Bank of Canada" consist of? Under whose seal was it given? Because of that fiction, our banks have been allowed to pipe into the public treasury.

That suppressed period of our history must be brought into the open, for along the road that we have been speeding on for the past quarter of a century, all bridges are down. We have already done away with the statutory reserves that had allowed us to brake speculative expansion in a relatively gentle way: it equipped the Central Bank only to reduce the leverage of credit creation without hitting with high interest rates everything in the economy. No reserves are left to repeat that sort of bailout of our banks from their most recent losses. And where will we find a reinsurer to reinsure Canada's insurers of the last resort?

The Suppressed Alternatives

However, if we really open up our minds, we will discover a wealth of unsuspected options. Remember your first year algebra class in high school when you learned to solve first-degree equations? We had it drummed into our heads that if the equation has two variables we need two equations for a solution. A single one won't do. Unfortunately the governors of our central bank and our finance ministers must have skipped that class. Otherwise, they would have realized that their "one blunt tool" to "lick inflation" could not possibly work. Even in the movement of prices alone there are too many independent variables loose to be handled by a single tool. Ever more services are needed to run modern urbanized societies. Many of these can only be provided by government on an unpriced basis. They are paid for by taxation that accordingly makes up an ever-deeper layer of price. Raise interest rates and the need for those services doesn't go away. Eventually society itself starts unraveling.

Nor does it help to label all the non-marketed needs "externalities." In those elementary algebra classes we were taught how to solve a pair of equations with two such variables. We eliminated one of these variables temporarily by multiplying one of the equations by a factor that would make the coordinates of one of the variables variable in either equation identical. And then we subtracted one equation from the other. That gave us the solution of one of the variables. Then we substituted that solution in either of the original equations and we solved for the second variable.

In our economy we have many subsystems all of which must be kept in working order, if the whole system is not to break down. That means that no single subsystem, say the market, can be allowed to cannibalize any other – for example, the environment, the household economy, or the public sector.

However, you may say that sort of reasoning will lead to the government spending beyond its means and bring on inflation. COMER has developed a simple safeguard against that. It is based on an elementary but immensely powerful method of the greatest of all 19th century mathematicians. His name is Karl Friedrich Gauss and the tool he fashioned is "modular congruence."

Don't be alarmed; our ancestors used it instinctively. Instead of giving every day since Adam bit the apple a distinct name, they used only seven names, and started all over again on each eighth day. The modulus was seven and the remainder is what was vital for many purposes. They did the same with the monthly modulus of thirty, important for biological, navigational and other purposes. And finally with 365 relating to the seasons. For sheer computational purposes it does away with the useless burden of having to deal with multiples of the modulus. You can add, subtract and multiply the remainder with identical results as with the original huge numbers. Keynes, who didn't make use of Gaussian modular congruence, came close to it when he asked: "Denmark sends us cookies, and we send them our cookies. Wouldn't it make more sense if we exchanged recipes?" Of course, it would bring down the GDP. But that just shows how misleading that and so many of our key statistics are.

Modular congruence highlights the fatal vulnerabilities of Globalization and Deregulation. If we had exchanged fewer goods with China and more recipes, Toronto and Vancouver would not have acquired notoriety as world foci of SARS.

And don't let anybody dumb you down by convincing you that all this is too complicated for the ordinary mortal to grasp. Remember Moliere's hero, who was astounded to learn that he had been talking prose all his life?

Obliging our Finance Minister to Listen to Gauss

Let us make use of this Gaussian device to design a model that will achieve goals that at present are dismissed as beyond our means, while allaying all possible fears that it will increase the federal debt, or contribute to inflation.

STEP ONE. Let us single out a single target, say the public treasury, focusing on not adding to its deficit. Let us choose two measures with contrary effect on it that most people would agree, other things being equal, are better pointed downward than upward. Our first step is to calculate dosages of these two so that their joint effect on the fisc will cancel out. One of these measures will decrease its revenue, the other will decrease its spending. Together they constitute a wash. We could for example reduce or abolish entirely the Goods and Services Tax (GST), which was an electoral commitment of the Liberal Party that still awaits fulfilment.

To compensate for the loss of revenue from that we would move just enough federal debt from the private banks to the central bank, so that the interest paid on it would return to the federal treasury as increased dividends from the BoC.

STEP TWO is entirely passive. The direct effect of our paired measures on the fisc will be zero. But those measures will echo through every other subsystem of the economy – the business world, the cost of environmental repair, the household economy, and come back with secondary benign effect to the fisc. The reduction of the GST will show up on most invoices in lower costs to the producer and consumer. And lower government interest payments will also reduce taxes and tend to lower interest rates across the board. Each of these indirect factors will tend to stimulate the private sector. The paired reductions will reduce the costs of environmental conservation. They will both decrease the stress that households are under to make ends meet.

The evidence of such bonuses would appear within a year. That would be a helpful contrast to the usual trickle-down promises of benefits bestowed directly on the banking and large corporations that trickle into oblivion and are heard of no more.

STEP THREE is a second application of the same technique. For this, the same two variables could be chosen, or another pair. For example the federal government could make available the $15 billion dollars over several years that the Romanow Commission has recommended – which would reduce the net revenues of the fisc. That could be balanced with a further shift of federal debt from the private banks to the Bank of Canada, which would reduce the interest burden on the Treasury.

However, to judge seriously what the condition of the fisc might be, we must remember in that in mid-1999 a bill was passed by Parliament introducing accrual accountancy, also known as capital budgeting. That was nearly forty years after the first of several Royal Commissions recommended it.

This was done because the Auditor General of the day withheld unconditional approval of the government balance sheet without it. There was no discussion of the bill in Parliament, and to the best of my knowledge it was reported only in the *National Post*. Meanwhile Bay St., to help it out of its mounting troubles, is pressing for more privatizations. Privatizing without accrual accountancy is an invitation to giveaways. In good part, the current difficulties of our economy can be traced to a strange incongruence: whereas leading corporations in their accountancy have been known to capitalize fictitious earnings, our government persisted in treating its vast and crucial investments, in physical and human capital, as current expenses.

Modular congruence, which we explained in our submission, has important qualitative aspects. It deals with the mutual interaction of vectors moving from one subsystem of the economy to others, most of which are categorized by conventional economists as "externalities," i.e., as matters that really don't count. The intensity of these interactions are quantitative; their mix, however, introduces a qualitative dimension. A vector coming from the market sector into the public sector, say higher interest rates, leaves a big hole in the fisc, and lessens the likelihood that the government will undertake vital conservation or public health measures.

This and much else along similar lines was submitted to the Committee on Finances on innumerable occasions. Our experience over at least some 15 years indicates a lack of access to those in power that resembles the Chinese bureaucracy's handling of SARS. Twenty years ago there was considerably easier approach to parliamentary committees – if not to the government itself – for proposing alternative policies for the problems crowding in on us. Some of these had in fact proved their positive value right into the sixties when they were suppressed by the financial group that had taken over political power and revamped our monetary system in ways that contradict the *Bank of Canada Act.*

Our recent submission to the Commons Standing Committee on Finance dealt with these matters, as had innumerable submissions of COMER over previous years. The disturbing fact, however, is that the more the validity of our positions has been recognized, the less the readiness of the group in power to consider any real alternative to the failed policies of Globalization and Deregulation. The most recent report of the Standing Committee "Large Bank Mergers in Canada: Safeguarding the Public Interest for Canadians and Canadian Businesses" is evidence of that. There is no way of forming an intelligent position on large bank mergers, without studying the cost to Canada of the bailout of 1991 and the subsequent further deregulation. Without the information that we have resumed in this article, Parliament and the voters are flying blind.

Must We Learn Openness from Beijing?

Our first temptation was to compare that suppression of crucial information affecting the basic flow of resources of the nation to the censoring by the Beijing government of all information of the SARS outbreak in Guangzhou last November. That suppression gave the mutated virus the opportunity of spreading to other continents and has been widely condemned as "criminal." On second thought, as reprehensible as its conduct in the matter was, we became convinced that would be unfair to Beijing. At least by April, Beijing had come clean and allowed world health authorities access to the origins and spread of the plague in China.

With the monetary policy forced upon the country in 1991, the contrary has been the case. The greater and more pervasive the damage resulting from Globalization and Deregulation, with interest rates proclaimed the sole stabilizer of the world's economies, the greater the clamp-down on any proposals for alternative policies. The urgency of free public dialogue on such matters should be clear when a crisis of deflation is closing in on the world economy, and the growing indebtedness of the lone superpower is leading to dangerous military solutions for problems that could at least be contained by economic information, dialogue and compromise. But no alternative to the presence disastrous course is possible without a free flow of relevant information. Without that democracy itself risks becoming a farce. The latest report of the Standing Committee on Finance warns us of that.

William Krehm

1. "Re" in the name of an insurance company stands for "re-insurance" – the part of their policies that they rewrite elsewhere to keep their exposure within manageable limits. Usually such reinsurance covers an upper chunk of its contracted risks.

Resurrection on Wall St.

A MIRACLE is under way on Wall St. Not the hoped-for revival of the stock market boom, but the resurrection of some of the villains who devised the scams that made it possible. A new generation of aspiring politicians have been laying the footings of a future political career as prosecutors pursue recent Wall St. stars. But their zeal seems to have been reined in by the administration as the need for a replay of the last boom becomes apparent. It was after all what produced budgetary surpluses and drew the world's investors to the United States like flies to honey. For the US is the most indebted of nations and cannot live with a stock market in the gutter. Hence, the sudden recognition that delving too deep into the shenanigans of Wall St. may not be in the national interest. If a boom is what you want, don't put those who know best how to beat the big drums in the hoosegow.

It is some weeks now since we saw front-page photos of famous Wall St. Tycoons being marched handcuffed off to their lawyers' offices to arrange for bail.

The picture gallery of the rehabilitated villains is headed "The Second Act on the Street" (*The Wall Street Journal*, 2/04). It includes Michael Milken, the former Drexel junk bond king who pleaded guilty in 1990, served two years in jail, and was barred for life from the securities business. In 1998, he settled SEC charges that he violated the ban, disgorging $42 million plus interest. He has returned as an investor in Leapfrog and Nextera.

John Gutfriend: Forced to resign as CEO of Salomon in Treasury bond bidding scandal; barred from serving as CEO. In 2001, he joined C.E. Unterberg, Towbin as senior managing director.

John Meriwether: Served 3-month suspension in 1993 after the Salomon scandal; led Long-Term Capital Management hedge fund to its near collapse in 1998, forcing government aided bailout. Now back for Act 3 with new hedge fund.

The Spotlights from Christ to the Thieves

And for the final case of "Life after Death on Wall St.," Jack Grubman: "A symbol of Wall St. stock-analyst conflicts is bullish on the ultimate turnaround story – his own" ("Grubman Still rates himself a 'Buy'"). He may be inspired by the approach of Easter, but the lead role seems shifting from Christ to the two characters who framed His passion.

"The former star communications-stock analyst at Citigroup Inc.'s Salomon Smith Barney has told people he hopes to return to provide consulting services about the telecom industry, despite facing a lifetime ban from the securities business. He believes he could function in such a job as long as he remains unaffiliated with a brokerage firm.

"This is the same analyst who has been vilified by regulators and investors for remaining bullish on dozens of stocks that generated hundreds of millions in fees for Salomon – and as much as $20 million a year for himself. And his flaunting of the dual role he played as an investment banker and a research analyst helped spark regulatory probes that culminated in a $1.4 billion industry-wide global settlement, together with a host of regulatory changes. As part of that civil pact, Mr. Grubman, 49 years old, is expected to pay $15 million and be barred from the securities industry for life."

Mr. Meriwether rebuilt his career in the mid-1990s. But he suffered an even higher profile setback in 1998 when LTCM's near collapse required a $3.6 billion government-aided bailout, threatening the global financial system. ["Too big to be allowed to fail" – the ultimate tribute to "growth" and "maximization."] He now runs another hedge trust, JWM Partners.

On the same front page of the Money and Investing section of the same *WSJ* ("Meeker Won't Face Securities-Law Charges" by Charles Gasparino and Susanne Craig) is a lengthy piece on another falling star that has been saved to dimly light up the firmament: "Morgan Stanley tech-stock analyst Mary Meeker – once dubbed 'Queen of the Internet' for her bullish calls on highflying tech stocks – won't be charged with securities-law violations as regulators this week make final their broad settlement over allegations that the nation's top securities firms misled small investors with biased stock research during the 1990s market bubbler, according to people familiar with the matter.

"In a draft settlement, regulators led by the New York attorney general's office and the Securities and Exchange Commission have informed Morgan Stanley that neither the firm nor Ms. Meeker will be cited for securities-fraud violations, and that the firm will face less-severe record-keeping violations and pay $125 million to settle the matter, the people said.

"The development comes as Ms. Meeker continues to work at Morgan Stanley and publish research. Regulators are putting the finishing touches on a $1.4 billion global settlement with Wall St.'s largest securities firms over allegedly misleading stock research, an accord that if worded harshly could be used in private claims filed by aggrieved investors." The purpose then is to keep investors past and future aggrieved, and the sinners in business.

William Krehm

ER Mail Bag

B ANK MANAGERS can have a heart, too. On one of the coldest days in February I met one of Kingston's finest as we marched in unity with other marchers all over the world to protest the looming war against Iraq. Later I asked him if he had heard of COMER. He acknowledged he had and agreed to have lunch with me to learn more about it. I told him I would like to invite him to speak at our next meeting, but suggested he wait until our lunch before he decided.

Our manager is very affable, and during our lunch, for which he paid, we talked about many things (including the mortgages I would have to renew in the not too distant future). On COMER, one of the concepts he questioned was where the BoC would get the money to lend to the government without borrowing it first from someone else. I replied that the BoC would create the money the same way that private banks did. As I recall, he replied that the BoC would need a base of deposits, which would have to be borrowed from others, which led to a discussion of reserves. According to our manager the reserves were not abolished in 1991 by the Mulroney government, but merely changed and increased from 5% to about 8% and later to 9% based on a bank's total capital rather than just on deposits. On this point I had to acknowledge that I did not know enough to comment, but suggested we could talk about how the BoC could be used to finance public capital expenditures at the Kingston COMER meeting where I expected others would have more information. I gave him a copy of the February issue of *ER*, which is mainly about banks. Our banker agreed to come, but to our disappointment he did not get there. We hope he will come another time because we could learn from each other.

Richard Priestman
Kingston Chapter, COMER

PS: "Reserves" are discussed on many pages throughout *Meltdown* and particularly in Appendix B of *Towards a Post-Autistic Economy*.

"Why Do They Hate Us?"

THE ANSWERS to that question, which is troubling Americans, is suggested in S.N. Eisenstadt's *The Decline of Empires*.[1] To that compilation, I am indebted.

Particularly pertinent is the message of cultural universality that accompanied the previous rearing of vast empires. "Christendom and Islam may be regarded as universal nomocratic states, while Judaism was a parochial divine nomocratic state." Theocracy exists only where God is regarded as the immediate ruler – as in the case of the Tibetan Lama or under Shintoism in Japan. In the Mosaic religions, God's representatives on earth were charged with enforcing God's laws. One of the significant lessons of history is that a recognition of cultural diversity arose as a protest against parochial conditions.

"The universal ideals current in the Hellenistic world arose as a result of the conquests of Alexander the Great. For Alexander, steeped in Greek philosophy by his teacher Aristotle[2], nevertheless abandoned his notion that all non-Greeks should be treated as slaves, and turned from parochial to universal values. The Stoics carried Alexander's ideals further and expressed their philosophy in terms of universal concepts and values. The Romans translated Alexander's ideas and Stoic philosophy into a system. Both Christianity and Islam developed under the impact of these ideas. After the great Arab conquest, the Muslims became Hellenized." Judaism, which developed before such concepts were accepted, was naturally parochial: the Jews were regarded as God's chosen people. Their state, therefore, was national and not a universal state.

Cultural Universalism vs. Coca-Cola

However, in the Hellenistic setting, Judaism did develop ecumenical offshoots, as Christianity itself and the Essenes bear witness. "The universality of Islam, as preached by the Prophet Muhammad did not necessarily carry with it the conception of a universal or world-state. But the legal prerequisites were already there, such the equality of races before *Allah* and law and common allegiance to one head of state."

What cultures choose to see above the clouds will have a great influence in shaping their behaviour amongst themselves and towards other cultures. It is a serious weakness of the Washington Consensus that unlike Alexander it has embarked on its world conquest with little more intellectual baggage than the brand logos of Coca-Cola and P&G. Worse still, it has elevated interest rates to the "one blunt tool" for keeping the price level flat. But the price level can approach flatness only by eliminating all public services paid for out of taxation.

Freeing entire nations and their governments from debt-bondage provides the resources to allow other options in the relationship of gods and men.

Since gold was replaced in the early 1970s throughout the world with central government credit, government debt is today the only legal tender. It makes no sense for the government to borrow its debt from the private banks, when it could do so from the central bank on a virtual interest-free basis. But wouldn't that be inflationary? Not if the government limited such borrowing to essential government investment programs for which resources are available.

In the 1980s the deregulated banks as a group lost much and even more than their capital in hotshot gambles in real estate and gas and oil. The debt of Canada and other developed countries was declared risk-free that banks could hold much more of without putting up more of their own capital. And the private banks were deregulated so that they could take in more deposits from the public and use them to create higher multiples of credit to lend out – actually 375 times as much as the cash in their tills to meet the public demand for the return of their deposits. In the mid-1970s over 22% of the total federal debt was held by the Bank of Canada. It is now down to less than 6%.

This has involved a massive shift of revenue from the most vulnerable classes in our society to the banking system. Internationally, the same management by debt manipulation has imposed a similar form of debt slavery. Loans are made through the International Monetary Fund and the World Bank, essentially controlled by the US government. Interest rates have been repeatedly raised by the Bank of Canada because bad weather and the preparations for war against Iraq have allowed speculators to drive up oil prices. Yet higher interest rates cannot possibly change the weather. If you want lower oil prices while fighting a war, you must control those prices and cut down the number of SUVs produced. If Washington must have its little war against Iraq, then do something about war profiteering.

High interest rates force the Third and Emergent Countries to cut their export prices and export more even at losses to earn the dollars to keep up their payments on their dollar debt. The US, however, need only print more of its bills that costs it nothing – so long as the rest of the world is ready to accept its money as reserve currency. The end result is debt-slavery. That does not make for warm ecumenical feelings – in religion or politics.

A Needless Provocation to Islam

To declare interest rates the one sole blunt tool against inflation is an incredible provocation to the Muslim world. For the Koran bans any sort of interest – high or low – as a mortal sin. There are many domestic reasons for abandoning the use of interest rates as a cure for inflation. Prices will rise even if there is no excess of total demand over total supply, but because more essential public services are delivered as unmarketed public services and hence a deeper layer of taxes in price. You would also have to recognize public spending for infrastructures that will last many years – even generations – as investments. They will continue producing value for many years – in the case of investments in education and health even for generations. Until very recently they were treated like soap or floor wax used in the daily clean-up and written off in the year of their acquisition. Their significance is still lost in routine number-crunching as plain "spending."

Is there a common cause in the decline of empires? From Eisenstadt's review it somehow involves the redistribution of power and a similar re-allotment of revenue.

"A.H.M. Jones finds that among the major reasons for the decline of the Roman Empire were the deterioration of the civic spirit, the growing spiritual emphasis which deflected energies from the political scenes, the continuous expansion of the bureaucracy, the shrinkage of the cultivation area, the shortage of manpower, and the development of a *landed-rentier class*.

"Similarly B. Lewis, in his discussion of the Ottoman Empire, stresses the detrimental effects of the large and inefficient bureaucracy, the heavy burden of a *growing rentier class*, the decline of commerce, and the alienation of the non-Muslim merchant classes.

"George Ostrogorsky's analysis of Byzantine economic and social history focuses on the struggle between the forces of centralized polity and those of the aristocracy, with the rulers attempting to promote an *independent peasantry* which could provide a source both of military manpower and revenue, while the aristocracy continuously attempting to thwart this effort (and ultimately succeeding)." [Italics ours.]

Obviously the redistribution of power and wealth occupy central roles in these analyses.

But nowhere has the scale been pushed to exponential patterns as in the current economy. The multipliers of money creation (once a carefully chaperoned banking prerogative) has shacked up with every aspect of a deregulated stock market. That converts the steady bleed of ordinary usury into the hammer blows of an abattoir. Companies become available as inert basement bargains, and the government balance sheets are thrown out of kilter with unrecognized assets. Driving the whole frantic exercise is the extrapolation of the attained profit and its rate of growth into the indefinite future. Note the frantic insistence of Finance Ministers on "growth" – at times it does not seem to matter too much of what as long as the pattern of growth can be monetized. That becomes a drive to the mathematics of the atomic bomb. That unprecedented technology of destruction the Washington Consensus has turned on its own economy.

That brings not ecumenism but tattoos that accompany the fall of empires.

Surely Washington can squeeze in one more think-tank to study the evidence of history on the point.

William Krehm

1. Eisenstadt, S.N. (ed.) (1967). *The Decline of Empires*. Englewood Cliffs, NJ: Prentice-Hall, Inc.
2. Khadduri, Majid (Eisenstadt ed.). *The Nature of the Islamic State*, p. 33. The equivalent would be the elder Bush hiring John Dewey to tutor the infant George W.!

How the Oil Cartel Leads the Superpower by the Nose

THE WORLD OIL SITUATION and its relation to the SUV and to the Iraq Crisis, are a snake-pit where not one but a cluster of reptiles are intertwined. The slogan of many protesters "Iraq is about Oil" is not incorrect, but it doesn't begin to cover the sinuous interlacing of distinct plots about oil and other crucial matters. It is not that the US hasn't alternate sources of petroleum to the Arabian lands, if much more costly ones. It has. But the Saudis have long since perfected a means of keeping the superpower helplessly addicted to imported oil in ever swelling quantities. Equally important: with the American dollar, the reserve currency for most of the world in which oil is quoted, the US is able to produce dollars to pay for all their oil imports at a nominal cost – that of printing currency, and running their bank computers. In our last issue we noted that the euro – the currency of a potential bloc of 500 million – has strengthened because of the collapse of the US stock market in a miasma of investigation. This has put question marks over the morality of the US economy and its very auditors. The euro in dollar terms has surged by some 35% in the last couple of years. The recrimination between the US and most of its hoped-for allies over the Iraq war, and the open bribery and threats that Washington is using to dragoon nations to the warring camp are not helping. A further deterioration of the record trade balance can result in a flight from the dollar, which would mean the collapse of the entire Globalization and Deregulation program.

The Wall Street Journal (18/03/03, "How OPEC Keeps America Hooked on Oil Imports") lays out some incredible details.

"All six presidents of the past 30 years have tried to wean the US off imported oil. All have failed. In 1973 when Nixon made the commitment to prevent oil imports from rising they amounted to 40% of the oil it consumed. Today it is 60%, and going higher. President Bush says hydrogen power will lead to hydrogen independence. Mr. Bush is certain to be wrong at least in the next couple of decades."

At the root of the trouble is that Saudi and its neighbours are managing their oil sales with the skill of great performers for one purpose: maintaining America's dependence on their oil. The Persian Gulf states not only hold two-thirds of world reserves, but their average cost is as low as $2 a barrel. Around those stunning statistics they have perfected an act that keeps oil prices higher than they would be on a really free market, but low enough to make alternate fuels and technologies uncompetitive.

North Sea oil costs about $15 a barrel to produce, so there is a broad playing field for the Saudis. Only once have American oil imports shrunk substantially – between 1979 and 1983. These were years of the deepest depression since the 1930s. Others factors were the Iranian revolution of 1979, and the jump in fuel-efficiency of US automobiles as new fuel efficiency standards were brought in. The American public turned to smaller cars. President Reagan put an end to oil price controls and triggered a boom in domestic drilling increasing home production.

During that trying period oil prices hit $40 a barrel – $100 present equivalent allowing for the increase in the general price index. Prices were expected to double from there. President Carter advanced a plan for synthetic oil developed from coal and shale. The Saudis put on their thinking caps to head off such doomsday.

Virtues are Accidents; Vices are Planned

They dropped their prices to several dollars below the $34 figure of OPEC. Then as Alaskan and North Sea output shot up; Saudi and Kuwait decided that the time had come to pursue market share rather than higher prices. Sheik Yamani, the Saudi oil minister, minced no words. "Let's see how the North Sea can produce at $5 a barrel." Prices fell to $12 a barrel, and Vice-President George H.W. Bush toured the Persian Gulf countries urging them to drop production and raise prices. The US had surrendered on the oil front. Eventually Mr. Bush convinced the Saudis to rein in production to attain $18 a barrel price. OPEC. OPEC has since set its sights on $22 to $28. What has since delivered the US to their mercies is the US gluttony for oil.

Today the US needs only half the oil that it did in 1973 to produce the same economic output. That was the most important lesson of the Saudi attempt to push their dearer production off the economic map. Electric utilities and other large consumers switched to natural gas, which, of course, is also cleaner. For which the Saudis earned some unintended brownie points. Natural gas was not only cheaper but more abundant in North America. The proportion of electricity produced from oil dropped from 13.5% in 1973 to around 3% today.

Such is the complicated world of today. Virtues happen by accident. Unwise policies are usually planned.

Accordingly, when oil prices declined after 1985, the pursuit of fuel efficiency relaxed. In the 1990s gasoline prices fell lower than they had been at any time since the oil embargo of 1973, after inflation had been taken into account. Its lesson learned, OPEC kept prices low enough to hold onto market share and chase those extra rigs to the scrap yard. And with the economy, courtesy of the stock market, booming again, consumers went mad buying SUVs, minivans and other big burners.

"To lessen dependence on oil, the US would have to raise the price of gasoline by an additional $1 a gallon tax on top of the average present tax of 41 cents to reduce consumption a quarter."

Britain has a $3.15 per gallon tax on gasoline, Japan $1.75, and that makes people choose smaller, fuel-efficient cars. Germany, France and Japan consume only one half the oil for the same amount of economic growth as the US. That is another of the vulnerabilities of the superpower. But Satan and his minions have a way of showing up wherever some virtue still holds out. On the troubled oil set, he takes the form of a strengthening euro, which not only cheapens the US-denominated oil price, but seems about to snatch away some of that privileged status for the euro. That would not only keep oil prices low in euro terms, but move part of the privilege of producing cost-free euros for oil purchases to the member countries. That may prove the crimson path to oil-enslavement that is helping to undermine US supremacy. The transition will be easier because of the established presence of Daimler, GM and Ford in Europe.

This is one of several factors that must be subsumed in the answer to the question, "Is the Iraq war about oil?"

William Krehm

Returning to Tobacco for Currency?

THE PROOF OF THE PUDDING is in the eating. But what is the corresponding test for the GDP, compounded as it is with useful goods and disasters? No surprise then that the plight of the states in the world's richest and loneliest superpower should be making the front pages of the financial press. Thus *The Wall Street Journal* (2/04, "Once Tobacco's Foe, States Are Hooked On Settlement Cash" by Gordon Fairclough and Vanessa O'Cannell): "They are poised to try to rescue the country's biggest cigarette companies in one of their darkest hours. State governments, once the tobacco industry's fiercest foe, now find themselves in an unusual position. In 1996, Washington state Attorney General Christine Gregoire sued: 'The tobacco industry has targeted our kids, withheld safer products and deliberately misled the public about the safety of smoking,' Ms. Gregoire said at the time. Opening the door for a slew of additional litigation, the state suits shattered the aura of invincibility that had surrounded the tobacco companies.

"Now, however, Ms. Gregoire and other state attorneys general may go to court to protect Philip Morris USA, the maker of Marlboro. At issue: an Illinois state judge's order that Philip Morris, owned by Atria Group Inc., post a $12 billion bond to appeal a massive defeat in a class-action lawsuit. Altria said the bond requirement could force it into bankruptcy court.

"Ms. Gregoire, more importantly, said 'it could deal a significant, unnecessary financial blow to the states.'

"The very states that won huge tobacco settlements in 1997 and 1998 became hooked on the money which for many states is staving off budgetary catastrophe. The Illinois court order threatens the tobacco cash flow and has sent the states scurrying to switch sides.

"Under the tobacco settlements of the late 1990s, major

manufacturers agreed to pay over 25 years to settle lawsuits. The companies also agreed to a series of restrictions on the way they sell cigarettes. The settlements have given state governments a huge additional interest in the continued financial health of the tobacco industry in these days of widening state budget deficits. Many states have also relied increasingly on cigarette-excise taxes.

"Philip Morris, for its part, is aggressively playing on the states' dependence. The company is warning the states that it may not be able to pay $2.5 billion due them by April 15.

"Several states had planned to issue bonds backed by expected tobacco-settlement payments. Virginia's treasurer, Jody M. Wagner, yesterday put on hold the sale of $767 million in such bonds scheduled to close on Thursday. 'We spoke with the underwriters, and they told us they couldn't proceed with closing this deal. The state had planned to use the bond money to revitalize its slumping tobacco-growing regions. With the possibility of the Philip Morris money not arriving, several state attorneys general were preparing to enter the fray. Illinois ordinarily requires a bond equal to the entire trial judgment.'

The Wall Street Journal (15/04) reports that Judge Nicholas Byron of the Madison County Circuit Court has relieved Philip Morris of the need to increase its previous bond.

"The bond requirement stems from a $10.1 billion verdict late last month in a suit over Philip Morris's low-tar cigarettes. In the first class-action alleging such labels mislead smokers into thinking that such cigarettes are less harmful, the same Judge Nicholas Byron had ordered the company to pay $7.1 billion in compensatory damages and an additional $3 billion in punitive damages. The judge tacked on $1.8 billion in fees for the plaintiffs' lawyers.

"Various states have recently taken legal action to enforce marketing action that the settlements imposed on cigarette makers. New York, which is hoping to sell bonds based on tobacco-settlement payments to deal with its budget woes, last week enacted one of the nation's toughest laws restricting smoking in public places. But there is a broad alignment of economic interests between cigarette makers and the states. Considering both cigarette taxes and the settlements, 'the states make more money from each pack of cigarettes sold than anyone else,' said Tommy J. Payne, executive vice president of Reynolds, the nation's No. 2 cigarette maker.

"Between November 1998, when the tobacco industry signed its main settlement with 46 states, and 2002, cigarette-makers paid those states more than $21.6 billion. An additional $5 billion is scheduled this year. States have increasingly come to rely on this money as they struggle to cope with their worst crisis in 20 years.

"In the 1990s, states became accustomed to plentiful tax revenues, in part because of the rising stock market."

Elsewhere in this issue we examine the quandary of those who were determined to reform the stock market, on which the present casino economy is so utterly dependent. To lift this economy out of the gutter, it feels that it must revive Wall St. Now the view is prevailing that straight morality must be watered down with a little opportunism, since it is impossible to bring back the prosperity of the latter nineties without the questionable craft of those who blew its iridescent bubbles. The only alternative is to rethink how we got into this mess, and go back to where we were learning how to organize a more humane and workable society.

Could it be that the next step along the path that we are embarked on would be for the states to accept payment for their settlement with the cigarette companies in cigarettes and retail them to the public at a discount? Or flog dubious stock market shares by special arrangement with Wall St.? If you dig deep enough in history you will find antecedents for almost anything you are looking for. For lack of gold and silver in the early Middle ages taxes in certain Balkan provinces were paid by selling children to the state as slaves. That would certainly have helped them avoid costly family allowances. In the early colonies tobacco leaf served as currency. If the state abandons its age-long monopoly of money-creation to Wall St. so that it can gamble bigger and better, just about anything can follow.

William Krehm

The Decay of Empires

WHEN THE ROMANS ruled much of the known world, they not only built fine roads, but stone walls that set a prudent boundary to their ambitions. The Manchus in China also understood the wisdom of the wall. That has been replaced with Globalization and Deregulation that unshackles inordinate dreams of power.

At the very pinnacle of their might, the Romans showed a great sensitivity for other cultures, especially that of the Greeks. The Greeks in turn had not been above sitting at the knees of the Phoenicians, just a bit down the coast, to learn their technological breakthrough of a phonetic alphabet. That reverence for our common culture helped them preserve a minimum of cordiality with their subject peoples. Indeed their leaders made a point of mastering the Greek language as well as their own. The United States is already paying dearly for its failure to follow their example.

The Washington Consensus – better described as an imposition than a consensus – is based on a price level flattened by raising interest rates. But higher interest rates not only add to costs in the public and private sectors, but encourage usury to which the Third World is particularly vulnerable. IMF loans denominated in dollars forces overproduction and exports of commodities such as coffee that have replaced subsistence food crops to earn the dollars to service their foreign debt.

Ours has become a culture that in every area lavishes all its wiles in expanding superstructures, to the neglect of infrastructures. That has been lodged in the very cut of our economic theory where price, a superficial happening monopolizes the attention of economists to the neglect of infrastructures. In the time dimension longer-term considerations have given away to perfecting getaways at lightning speeds. Obviously these are not favourable features for building realms of duration.

From the time of Polybius (208-123 BC) through Edward Gibbons on the fall of the Roman Empire of the West, to Oswald Spengler, the decay of great empires has obsessed historians. It is not reassuring that the brashest and most powerful of political leaders today give it no second thought.

That warning was delivered in unmistakable form in the failure of Secretary Rumsfeld to spare a tank or two to protect the Baghdad archeological museum to shelter the oldest treasures of our common culture from looters.

William Krehm

The Birth of the Immortal Free Lunch

I F THE RECENT STOCK MARKET bubble taught us anything it was that the key to success was to have your auditors in your vest pocket. The excellence of that recipe is proved by the ability of the same tight group to live down their failed predictions in the most varied fields. Some details are given in a "Political Capital" column by Alan Murray (*The Wall Street Journal*, 01/04, "'Dynamic' Scoring Ends Great Debate With a Whimper").

From it appears that away back in 1974 it was the Rumsfeld-Cheney team that sold the Reagan regime famous Laffer's Curve that promised balanced budgets with abundant trickle-down by cutting income taxes. The outcome was a disaster. Instead of lying down and committing well-behaved euthanasia, the federal deficit and debt rose to unprecedented heights. But that misadventure rolled off the well-oiled Rumsfeld-Cheney hides. They survived as both behind-the-scene lobbyists under Clinton and as cabinet potentates in Republican governments. That princely immunity to reassessment has continued right up to the goose-egg they laid in predicting Shiite uprisings to welcome the American coalition forces. And just to prove that the world is round and never ceases spinning, the purpose of "doing Iraq" on the cheap was, guess what? – To apply the Laffer Curve – slashing income taxes to bring back prosperity and a balanced budget.

Murray's column dips into the 30-year record of the Laffer Curve in academia and government. "The problem with Mr. Laffer's graph [on that cocktail napkin and in its subsequent reincarnations] was that it had no numbers on the axes. How much would growth be boosted? At what taxation would tax cuts become self-financing? These remained the big unknowns as the issue became a central question of American politics.

"In Washington, the debate became a bureaucratic battle focusing on the Congressional Budget Office and Joint Committee on Taxation, the two agencies responsible for advising Congress on the costs of budgets and tax changes. By convention, both use 'static' scorekeeping that assumes budget and tax changes have no effect on overall economic growth. Supply-side proponents have criticized both agencies relentlessly for this, but to no avail – until last week.

"Enter Douglas Holtz-Eakin, an economist on leave from Syracuse University and an avowed advocate of supply-side 'dynamic' scoring. A few months ago, Republican congressional leaders picked him out of a job at the White House and made him director of the CBO. Last week, in his analysis of President Bush's tax and budget plan, he provided his new bosses with their first taste of dynamic scoring. The results: some provisions of the president's plan would speed up the economy; others would slow it down. Using some models, the plan would reduce the budget deficit from what it otherwise would have been: using others, it would widen the deficit.

"But in every case, the effects are relatively small. And in no case does Mr. Bush's tax cut come close to paying for itself over the next 10 years. Only two of the nine different models used to analyze the president's plan, only two showed a large improvement in the deficit over the next decade as a result of 'supply side' effects. Both these models get their results by assuming that after 2013, taxes would be *raised* to eliminate the remaining deficit. Advocates of dynamic scoring have tried to make the most of these tepid results, calling the report a good first step. 'You've got to crawl before you can walk, and you've got to walk before you can run.' But it should make both sides wonder what the hubbub of the past 30 years has been all about."

It just happens that in my book *Towards a Post-Autistic Economy – A Place for Society at the Table* (COMER Publications, 2002, p. 165), I have developed a model that answers the "dynamic scoring" criterion of the neo-supply-siders through a vastly different approach and with indisputable results.

The details can be found in the lead article of this issue. The purpose of this note is to bring to our readers' attention how timely it has become in the light of the revealed charlatanry of the Laffer Curve.

William Krehm

Not to be Taken Internally by the Doctor!

W ASHINGTON'S CONFIDENCE that the Iraqis would rebel in gratitude for the bombs dropped on them, was the basis for budgeting its invasion "on the cheap." That wouldn't interfere with the central plank in the President's re-election platform: cutting income-tax rates. The lesson to draw is that the White House's future prescriptions should carry a warning: "Not to be taken internally by the Doctor!"

Good cartoons help focus our thinking. The news out of Iraq brought to mind a cartoon I saw in the Mexican press more years ago than I care to remember. A baby was shown nursing at an enormous motherly breast while a passer-by, a hand over his incredulous eyes, gasps: "Caramba! chupa ó sopla?" – "Is the little bastard sucking or blowing?" Centuries under Spanish rule and corrupt governments of their own have bred a wry, ribald cynicism south of the Rio Grande. That cartoon fits the present US quandary in Iraq like a glove. The very channels supposed to bring in reliable information to guide the war chieftains ends up confusing them.

For the moment their staggering superiority in armament might make such nuances of no importance. But by imposing Globalization and Deregulation on the world, Washington has multiplied enormously the balls it is juggling. To cope with this, it has need of the sort of system theory in its policy-making that it employs in the design of its smart bombs. Trouble is that in the long run, bombs can be no smarter than the policy they serve.

The automobile is a familiar enough example of a system. It consists of several subsystems, each of which must be in working order for the system as a whole to perform. These subsystems include the mechanical, the fuel system, the engine, the electrical, the electronic. It won't do to average out their efficiencies. *Each* must be in a good state or the car won't be safe. No subsystem must be allowed to cannibalize another. The channels between subsystems must deliver information and resources as needed from one subsystem to another in either direction. No subsystem can be declared an "externality" and put out of mind – as economists do with the environment, education, health, the investment of the public sector, in fact with every subsystem except a highly idealized market.

Let us examine some of the alarming reports out of Iraq that bear witness to incredible violations of these system rules.

Cooking the Ledgers of Conquest

Can the US – even with the support of Micronesia, Iceland, and other tiny powers that Washington has bullied or bribed into "joining" its "coalition" – afford such a war, especially if non-monetary costs such as the loss of the respect and friendship of other nations are included in the bill? If you confine the costs to those of immediate conquest, and disregard your failure to provide policing to protect one of the greatest museum that guard all humanity's heritage, then Washington lucked out. But no figure can be placed on the ultimate costs of such false economies. For a culture that has driven marketeering to virtuoso levels, it is astounding how insensitive the superpower can be to world opinion. Unless a juicy contract can be put out to a friendly advertising agency to handle, a problem does not exist. No contract, no cost. As simple as that.

It is somewhat in this vein that *The Wall Street Journal* (21/03, "President's Dream Changing Not Just regime But Region" by Robert S. Greenberger and Karby Leggett) tells an amazing story of how a tiny professional lobby induced an indifferently prepared President to rewrite the law of nations and possibly open a chasm between Western cultures and Islam for decades." The vision is appealing: a region that has pro-American governments in the Arab world's three more important countries: Egypt, Iraq and Saudi Arabia. Reducing the influence of radicals helps make Palestinians more amenable to agreement with Israel.

"[But] in the short run, it's entirely possible that the influence of radicals may grow, fertilized by America's intrusion onto Arab soil.

"One of the places the idea was born was the Project for the New American Century, a fledgling neo-conservative think-

tank in 1998. That's when it told President Clinton that the time had come to depose Saddam Hussein.

"In a letter to President Clinton put together by the group's director, former intelligence official Garry Schmitt, the group declared: 'The only acceptable strategy is the one that eliminates the possibility that Iraq will be able to use or threaten to use weapons of mass destruction. In the near term this means a willingness to undertake military action. In the long term, it means removing Saddam from power.

"It was an audacious declaration. The group had only one full-time staffer and an intern. But it managed to get its message signed by 18 national security hawks. Such messages are usually lost in the din of countless think tanks in Washington. But in this case the message grew because over the next few years more and more of the signers moved into the foreign-policy camp of George W. Bush.

"Even before the 1998 letter the seeds of a regime change in Baghdad to foster Middle East stability were being sown. In a 1996 letter to the then newly elected Israeli Prime Minister Benjamin Netanyahu, Richard Perle, a hard-liner from the Reagan administration, proposed replacing Mr. Hussein with Jordan's King Hussein." A close relative of King Hussein imposed by the British as King of Iraq after World War I had been lynched by the Iraqis. Mr. Perle's ideas of democracy have always tilted to the quaint. Under Reagan he was an extreme hawk in initiating a quarter-of-a-century of murderous civil war in Central America.

The genome of declaring inconvenient costs "externalities" is to be found in the marginal utility theory taught in our colleges for the past century. It recognizes no value other than the price of the latest market transaction. That disposes of environment, health, education, and much else. Whatever is not marketed and hence not priced becomes an "externality," i.e., an inconsequential footnote in key reckonings.

But Mr. Perle has made the headlines recently in quite another connection. *The New York Times* (28/03, "After Disclosures, Pentagon Adviser is Stepping Down" by Stephen Labaton and Thom Shanker) informs us: "Richard N. Perle resigned today as chairman of an influential Pentagon advisory board in the wake of disclosures that his business dealings included a recent meeting with a Saudi arms dealer and a contract to advise a communications company seeking permission from the Defense Department to be sold to Chinese investors. The departure came after growing criticism of Mr. Perle's business ties while serving as chairman of the Defense Policy Board, a collection of experts and former government officials who have access to classified information and are unpaid advisers to the defense secretary on military issues. The Pentagon said Mr. Perle, who has many friends in the senior ranks of the administration and was appointed to the chairman's post in 2001 by Defense Secretary Donald H. Rumsfeld, would remain on the board.

"The communications company, Global Crossing, also announced that Mr. Perle had decided to sever his ties with it.

"Senator Carl Levin of Michigan, the senior Democrat on the Armed Services Committee, wrote a letter to Mr. Rumsfeld urging him to force Mr. Perle to choose between his job on the Defense Policy Board and his business.

"For months some senior Defense Department officials have expressed discomfort with Mr. Perle's public statements on foreign policy and military affairs. Mr. Perle's statements were often far more hawkish than the Bush administration's public line. "His recent troubles began with an article in *The New Yorker* by Seymour M. Hersh that disclosed that Mr. Perle had lunch earlier this year with the arms dealer Adnan Khashoggi. Mr. Perle responded by calling Mr. Hersh a terrorist and threatening to sue him in a British court for libel.

The Two Externalities of Washington

"Last week, Mr. Perle and lawyers involved in Global Crossing's bankruptcy disclosed that he had been retained to advise the company on how to overcome the Defense Department objections to its sale to an Asian venture led by Hutchison Whampoa, controlled by Li-Ka-Shing, the Hong Kong billionaire. Global Crossing is rewriting its proposal for the sale. The Defense Department and the FBI had objected, raising national security and law enforcement concerns. Mr. Perle said he was retained by Global Crossing to gain the approval of the transaction by the committee because of his former job as an assistant defense secretary in the Reagan administration and his current position on the Defense Policy Board."

All this compels us to conclude that there are two very distinct categories of "externalities." In one, the household economy, the environment, education, health, social insurance, is pushed out of economic theory's back door into the cold darkness. On the other hand, whatever and whoever caters to the power of those in control are deemed "externalities" in the sense of being above rather than beneath the protection of official science and laws. So long as the individuals are dedicated to these goals, they will be looked after and assured personal fortunes. What would be deemed conflicts of interests in another context are easily straddled with the help of "old boys" clubs.

William Krehm

Nonsense Machine

FEED ABSURDITY into the premises of your policy-making and you will guarantee spectacular nonsense in the results. High interest rates are as destructive of empires as moths are of wardrobes. The indications are that the European Union is setting itself up for just such a fate.

Conventional theorists reached a local pinnacle of the ridiculous some twenty years ago when they elevated interest rates as the chosen vehicle to flatten prices. The higher these were, the better, since flat prices were ruled a law of nature. It was seen as a mere coincidence, not worthy of mentioning, that interest happens to be the revenue of moneylenders.

The Wall Street Journal (21/03, "France and Germany Could Benefit – Budget deficit restriction relaxed" by G. Thomas Sims) reports: "France and Germany already may be benefiting from a war in Iraq that both nations so fiercely opposed.

"Until yesterday, the euro Zone's two largest countries appeared on course to pay hefty fines for breaking strict rules that cap budget deficits. But just hours after US bombs began falling on Baghdad, the EU's budget policeman, European Monetary Affairs Commissioner Pedro Solbes, declared the war an 'exceptional circumstance' – a ruling that could partly unleash countries from a pact that prohibits deficits from exceeding 3% of gross domestic product."

This law is all the more absurd since the EU makes no distinction between investment for infrastructures and current spending. If an EU member spends more than their current income for investments such as water purification plants, building new schools and hospitals, that is treated just as their spending for military parades, even though such investments will produce value for many years to come.

"Last year, France and Germany were the only two of 12-euro zone nations to break the 3-percent limit and both are likely to do it again this year as the economy sags and tax revenues dwindle. Fines can total 0.5 of a nation's annual GDP – about 7.6 billion euros ($8.03 billion US) in France's case and 10.5 billion euros in Germany's.

"The development marks a set-back for Europe's smaller countries. Belgium, Austria and Spain have recently balanced their budgets [on such fines] and have been calling for strict interpretation of the rules enshrined in the Stability and Growth Pact.

"The ruling is also annoying for the European Central Bank, which sets interest rates for the euro area. The bank relies on the budget standards in Europe to make a common monetary policy for a basket of sovereign nations. 'Countries should not now use Iraq as an excuse to renege on their commitments to put their public finances in order,' the bank said in a monthly report last week.

"Pressure is mounting on the ECB to cut interest rates, just two weeks after its most recent cut.

"The commission wouldn't say how much leeway the Iraq war would give countries. A month ago the commission signaled that a country must send troops to get more lax tax treatment under the pact's 'exceptional circumstances' clause, but that distinction was hazier today.

"The pact has repeatedly come under attack, especially during the past two years as the economy slowed. Critics said it hurts the economy by limiting spending during slowdowns, exactly when stimulus is needed.

"Last fall, European Commission President Romano Prodi even called the pact 'stupid', leading to a review. Two weeks ago, after months of wrangling, finance ministers agreed to make the pact slightly more flexible by taking the state of the economy and the countries' debt levels into consideration when judging governments' fiscal performance."

But on the whole the message appears to be that a little war is the best way of bringing down interest rates a bit for a little while.

William Krehm

The Golden Heresy of Venice

OVER THE THOUSAND YEARS of its independent existence, the Venetian republic was a uniquely successful state. Founded on swamp-girt islands by refugees from the barbaric invasions of the Roman Empire, it developed into a very special maritime community, dominating the sea routes through the Adriatic and the Eastern Mediterranean right through to the Black Sea towards India and Eastern Asia. It fell heir to the maritime outposts of the Byzantine Empire, and founded a trading Empire that stretched from Egypt through Asia Minor, Cyprus, Crete, the Peloponnesos to the Alpine passes into central and Northern Europe. Brilliantly administered as an aristocratic republic, it was long immune to dictatorships that plagued mainland Italy.

In just about everything it did, Venice contradicted the current model that ascribes to unregulated private markets unique efficiencies.

"Where trade was concerned, the state left nothing to chance; and by 1470 it was taking over more and more of Venetian economic life. The days of private enterprise on the grand scale were almost gone. All the merchant galleys were built in the Arsenal and were state-owned; the Republic kept the monopoly on many of the most profitable routes and cargoes. Even the ships that remained in private hands were obliged to conform to the strict specifications laid down by the Senate. The advantages were obvious. Given such conformity, all the vessels in a given convoy could be trusted to behave similarly in bad weather and so, with luck, to stay together; the convoy's speed, and consequently its arrival dates, could be more accurately estimated; standardized spares could be kept available in agencies and outposts overseas and quick convertibility to warships was guaranteed in an emergency. By the end of the fourteenth century there were normally six of these trading convoys a year, each consisting of up to 500 ships – and each bound for a different destination, but each sailing on appointed dates, and following specified routes, fixed months ahead. Most would be state-owned, their command – which was open to the nobility only – leased by auction to the highest bidder for the duration of the voyage; but every merchant and captain involved, whether owner or lessor, was bound by oath to obey the instructions issued by the Senate and to uphold 'the honour of St. Mark.'

"As always, increased public ownership led to increased taxation. A hundred years before, Venetian taxes had been among the lowest in Europe. No Longer. Not only were there the soaring costs of the Arsenal and its 16,000 workers to be met, but the spread of state control had spawned an army of eagle-eyed tax collectors famous for their niggling accuracy – all of whom had to be paid by the Republic. Small traders continued to be encouraged; if they could not afford, or spare, ships of their own for their ventures they always enjoyed the right – so long as they were Venetians – to demand cargo space on the state-owned convoys at fixed and reasonable rates.

"The most important branches of industry were rigidly protected, with bans on the export of certain raw materials; skilled artificers were forbidden to leave the city, while to reveal the secrets of key manufacturing processes was an offence punishable by death. (Foreign craftsmen, on the other hand, such as German makers of looking glasses and the silk workers from Lucca were encouraged to settle in Venice and even, as a special inducement, exempted from taxation for the first two years of residence.)"

Pioneers in Public Health

"Public health was early accepted as a state responsibility, and to the Venetian Republic must go the honour of having founded the first national health service in Europe, if not in the world. After the establishment of the state-run School of Medicine in 1368, licensed medical practitioners were required to attend monthly meetings to exchange notes on new cases and treatments.

"Alone of all the states of Catholic Europe, [Venice] never burned a heretic. Alone she maintained that moderate, humanist outlook which had sprung from the Renaissance and which must have seemed oddly out of place in the world of the Counter-Reformation. She allowed the Greek Orthodox community a church of their own, the Jews their synagogues in the Ghetto, the Muslims their mosque in the Fondaco dei Turchi, the Armenians their monastery on the island of San Lazaro. That made her a centre both for enlightened liberal thought and – through her printing houses – for its dissemination. That gave her university at Padua (there was none within the lagoon) a prestige unrivalled in Europe."[1]

The end to her period of glory came when her very successes involved her in the politics of mainland Italy. Her paramount strength lay in the sea, but to fight wars on the mainland she became dependent on hiring mercenaries and their paymasters – the condottieri who were the curse of Renaissance Italy. Even more serious, the Portuguese discovering the sea route to Indian and Eastern Asia around the Cape of Good Hope, shattered Venice's monopolist access to the land caravans from India and China. Central and Northern Europe were no long dependent of getting their imports from Asia by the land routes across the Alps through Venetian-controlled territory.

However, the echo of its glory perdured. Though plundered by Napoleon (who put an end to its 1,000-year independence), and generations of British collectors, it remains in the opinion of many the most beautiful city in existence. It taught Europe manners and the art of living. "Like most intelligent young men of the age (circa 1730), Horace Walpole learned more from his Grand Tour than at university (Cambridge)."[2] And the climax of the obligatory Grand Tour was, of course, Venice "where every rich British visitor longed for at least one picture of the city to remind him of one of the most remarkable experiences of his lifetime. Virtually all Antonio Canaletto's best work is in England – Venice possesses scarcely a single canvas." Giovanni Gabrieli and Claudio Monteverdi had been organists at St. Mark's, and it is only since World War II that the world came to appreciate that Antonio Vivaldi, dismissed as a rather minor composer by British musicologists, was in fact considered by Bach and other pinnacles of German music as their peer. Titian, Tintoretto and Veronese adorned the city with their genius. Its wedding of sea and land, of the Byzantine and the Renaissance have no equal elsewhere.

And to economists of the West intent on constantly ever-sputtering growth, it is a reminder that much of society's survival-craft has to do with nurturing the legacy of the past.

William Krehm

1. Norwich, John Julius (1983). *A History of Venice*, pp. 282, 283, 284. Harmondsworth, England: Penguin Books.

2. Hobson, Dominic (1999). *The National Wealth*, p. 179. London: Harper Collins Publishers.

Question Mark Over Our Newly Discovered Deflation?

THE WALL STREET JOURNAL (8/05, "What Deflation? Why Your Bills Are Rising?" by Jeff D. Opdyke and Michelle Higgins) poses a minus $40,000 question. For decades central bankers were too busy looking for inflation under every bed to utter the word "deflation." One of the colourful episodes in Canada's monetary history was when our central bank governor Gordon Thiessen in 1996 warned a parliamentary Committee of impending deflation. Within a week he was back before the same committee to apologize for having mentioned the unmentionable.[1] And it turns out he was dead on. Within a couple of years the East Asian meltdown took place with disastrous repercussions in Russia and Latin America. Thiessen's perspicacity probably cost him a second term as Governor. At whose bidding did he apologize for the one precise prediction in his career? Today the evidence is growing that the statistics of wages and prices – across the board – are in persistent sag. The main exceptions are unemployment and bankruptcies.

Why then is the WSJ asking, "If the Federal Reserve is so concerned about deflation, why are so many of the everyday costs of life on the rise? The price of postage stamps, sporting events, auto insurance, real-estate taxes, and even haircuts has been increasing in recent years at a faster pace than the official inflation rate. The establishment's Consumer Price Index has averaged just 2.5% annually over the past three years. In the same period, by some measures, cable-TV costs are up 9.1% annually, auto insurance is up 7.6% a year, and even movie popcorn is up more than 3%.

"Health-care costs, college tuition and the price of heating your home have been rising at far faster rates – in the case of natural gas, around 21.4% a year. These increases stand out all the more given that the Fed announced Tuesday that it may cut interest rates later this year to stave off even a hint of falling prices. That marks the first time in decades that the Fed has publicly worried about deflation."

What underlies all this confusion is the state of economic theory.

Elsewhere in this issue is my paper read at the ICAPE Conference at the University of Missouri at Kansas City. In it I discuss the process by which the group in power in any economy restructures economic theory to serve as a bristling pillbox in defence of its privileges. Towards this end it simply cuts down the number of recognized variables without which alternate policies cannot be drafted. "Information" becomes brass-knuckled disinformation. High on the list of these has been the Globalization and Deregulation (G&D) of trade and finance that removes all defences that could help less advantaged groups defend their positions against the slew of variables unleashed by the privileged group. I would suggest that you read that article in this ER issue, and then come back to this note.

Grim Surprises from Overextended Supply Lines

Much of the deflationary pressures in the real economy comes from the use of mounting debt to impose the slashing of vital social services. This has systematically curtailed the purchasing power of the Third World. It has put a question mark over the quality of much of the debt in the portfolios of the large First World Banks. It has wiped out the production of many consumer products in the United States and other First World lands. It has undermined the health and educational systems in the advanced countries and exposed the whole world to grim surprises from hopelessly congested supply lines. And, by increasing the burden of existing debt, deflation transfers massive wealth from the debtor to the creditor. Eventually debtors go bankrupt to produce liquidation bargains for those with deep pockets.

What results is the equivalent of a high-powered machine of a nightmarish complexity with circuits all mixed up. Transmission-line voltage is delivered to where it is bound to kill, but it fails to supply electricity stepped down for light-bulbs and kitchen ranges. Cutting down central bank policy to one blunt tool lets loose a wild number of variables in the G-Ded world and creates a hopeless mismatch between proliferating problems and available solutions. The latest instance of this is the SARS epidemic when the public health resources across the world have been mowed down to keep our deregulated banks in high boom.

A double-tier economy has resulted. At one level – the Third World and the unemployed and underemployed in the First – there is deflation. At the others – financial adventurers profit from the disarray for daring coups and quick getaways. Incredibly, such high-jinx are mistaken for the economy. The governments themselves depend for their revenue on these excesses. Increasingly, the Third and Emerging Worlds are doing more and more of the globe's real manufacturing. Wages in China are one tenth those in Japan and the United States. But that ten-to-one difference in labour costs is peanuts alongside the gap between winnings of CEOs of large public corporations and the earnings of semi-skilled workers. $20 million a year with handsome protection against taxes compared to $15,000 a year for rank and file workers is not uncommon. The firewalls put up to separate conflicting areas of finance and get the world out of the depression of the 1930s have long since been done away with – for example between banking and stock brokerage As a result we have had a stock market collapse that dwarfs that of 1929.

Morality a Hormonal Deficiency

The speculative economy that has emerged depends for its booty on the spread between the rewards of financial speculation and Third World wages. It extrapolated the rate of growth and the acceleration of that rate of growth – real or imagined – into the remote future, and then incorporated that, discounted for its supposed present value, into current stock market prices. This imposes a sort of servitude on the very rulers of this unbalanced world; for they have to make good commitments already embodied in the price of their company shares. If they don't, the very price of their stock becomes a noose around their necks and a trapdoor beneath their Gucci shoes. In so unhinged a "New Economy" old-fashioned morality rates as a hormonal deficiency.

Hence the difficulty of our authorities in deciding whether inflation or deflation is parked on our door-mat.

No distinction has been made between capital investment of governments and current spending. Until recently – 1996 in the US and 2003 in Canada they were written off in the year of the investment, so that there was no asset value carried on the government books to offset the debt incurred to make the investment. The above-mentioned corrections are only partially effective because they still do not include government investment in human capital – in other contexts recognized as the most productive of all investments. Besides the partial shift to accrual accountancy (capital budgeting) was made in stealth. As a result its real significance has been suppressed. To obtain better grades from bond-rating agencies and hence lower interest rates for its bonds, the government needed only an improved single statistic – a lower net deficit after public assets had finally been recognized. What they avoided doing was bringing in the notion of government investment – banned from the textbooks as a Keynesian sedition. So instead of double-entry bookkeeping throughout the economy – public as well as private – we got more number-crunching within the framework of a closed ideology. In the US that is what the endless political argument over the size of President Bush's tax-cut is about today.

In our Kansas City paper we note the public sector output – measured at cost, i.e., the payments by government salaries, supplies and sub-contractors – are counted twice, once as an expenditure of government, and again as the taxes paid by private individuals and corporations. That exaggerates the output of the economy and hence of growth. And growth is considered a key factor in containing inflation.

Net debt – i.e., after including public investment – is replaced with the absolute debt of the government. By that criterion the street people who sleep on the sidewalks are in sounder financial condition than the leading banks. For they have little if any debt, while the banks are loaded with it for their investments. The purpose of such accountancy is to forestall even a recognition of government investment. But little infrastructure would have been possible without public investment – in whatever form. Tax concessions to corporations, for example, are in every sense a government investment. They should be recognized as that on the government books, or not be made.

The *WSJ* article cited provides some key instances of price rises that cannot be attributed to "inflation," i.e., to an excess of demand over supply on a free market:

"Even Pat Jackman, economist at the Bureau of Labor Statis-

tics, which calculates the official inflation rate, says the widely reported numbers understate the rising cost of life from one year to the next. In compiling the consumer price index, the BLS relies on roughly 80,000 price quotes that flow into its offices each month. The bureau smooths and adjusts those numbers to account for improvements in quality, among other things.

"For example, the bureau looks at the price of a car today and the price of a similar version of that car in the past. If the car now costs more but comes with a lot of extra features, the bureau may consider just a minor price increase or even a price reduction. That's because the consumer got a higher-quality product for roughly the same cost. But the reality is that you're still paying more money for a car than you used to. 'You had to pay.'" The simpler car you replaced no longer has an equivalent on the market.

The High Cost of Cooking the Books

"The government's Consumer Price Index has averaged increases of just 2.5% annually over the past three years. In the same period, by some measures, cable-TV costs are up 9.1% annually, and insurance is up 7.6% a year." But most branches of TV are coming out of questionable promotions in which books were cooked with the complicity of accountants, earnings replaced with market shares, and sales faked. Obviously the transition under the gun of investigators leads to considerably higher prices in many fields.

This is achieved by incorporating a special high-technology of mergers, patenting genes, making use of the in-house brokerage and financial services to promote and unload stocks, corrupting auditors, to introduce an exponential pattern in manipulated stock pricing.

Wherever a pool of savings was to be found, it was appropriated to keep the boom in ascent. The pension funds of large corporations in particular have been devastated, for Wall St. carried out successful campaigns to put pension money into corporation equities rather than leave them in "stick-in-the-mud" government securities. The tragic consequences of that for retirees has just begun coming to light. In both the US and Canada the retirees of many large corporations are learning that their contracted pensions have lost much or all of their value with the collapse of the stock boom. Thus *The Globe and Mail* (12/5, "Pension shortfalls threaten to explode" by Elizabeth Church) reports, "Canada's largest corporations face mounting demands on cash and higher expenses because of dramatically deepening losses in their employee pension plans. A Report on Business study of the 104 companies on the S&P/TSX index with defined-benefit pension plans showed…all the companies saw a pension funding shortfall of more than $18.7 billion in 2002. And there is more bad news on the way."

And south of the border, on the same day, *The Wall Street Journal* ("A Retired Steelworker Struggles With a Health-Insurance Crisis. The Ailing Industry Breaks Promises of the Past to Stay Afloat today" by Robert Guy Mathews) informs us, "More than 200,000 retirees and dependents, at roughly a dozen steel companies, likely will be stripped of their health-care benefits, as their former employers reorganize or liquidate in bankruptcy.

If a company goes out of business and sells its assets to another, neither is obligated to pick up the tab for former workers. That leaves retirees in a no-man's land.

"What makes the predicament of retired LTV workers so striking is that their old bankrupt company is now operating profitably under a new name. International Steel Group paid $1.5 billion for LTV and assumed nearly all its liabilities, not including the cost of paying health insurance for retirees. The jobs of younger workers were preserved by taking away the benefits of retirees. A similar situation awaits the retirees of Bethlehem Steel Corp., National Steel Corp. and others that are now becoming parts of leaner, stronger competitors. These buy their assets but abandon promises made to former employees in better times.

"The same fate may befall retirees in other struggling industries, which have managed so far to pay retiree benefits but are increasingly looking for ways to relieve themselves of such obligations.

"Decades ago, steel makers agreed to generous benefits for their retirees, in large part because of pressure from the White House. Steel makers didn't want to spend their profits on higher wages when steel was in demand. So instead they promised generous retirement benefits, postponing the day of financial reckoning in the hope that when it dawned they could afford the payouts. But they can't."

Another instance of what is laying our economy low: a proprietorial claim on the unknown future, converted into an immediate clinking profit on the stock.

All these are gruesome symptoms of deflation.

William Krehm

1. The incident is documented in *Meltdown: Money, Debt and the Wealth of Nations*, edited by William Krehm, COMER Publications, 1999, p. 211.

Time to Restructure our Economic Theory?

The following paper was delivered by William Krehm at the first World Conference on the Future of Heterodox Economics at the University of Missouri at Kansas City, US, June 5-7, 2003.

MUST WE free our thinking from an excessively entrenched economic model? That's a dreadfully big subject, but it answers a dreadfully big need. Globalization and Deregulation (G&D) was advanced to maximize shareholder equity and spread the blessings of the free market. In the past three years, however, it has stripped tens of millions of stakeholders of their jobs, pensions, and savings. What was presented as a scientific model has mutated into a lethal syndrome.

If a single structural flaw is to be singled out as point of departure for our enquiry, it is this: is the model really self-balancing as represented? In other words, is it symmetrical? Can it be read as validly backward as forward? That is no small detail: it involves basic structure – the main concern of mathematicians

in the 19th century.

Let's go back to a main watershed. Until the latter 1980s there had been two major tools for central banks to deal with perceived "inflation." The first was increasing the statutory reserves. These were cash deposits banks put up with the central bank as a percentage of their deposits from the public in accounts requiring little or no notice for withdrawals. Such reserves earned no interest. By raising the reserve quota, the central bank could reduce the leverage of the banks' money creation. It could thus rein in "inflation" without pushing up interest rates.

The other major tool was increasing the rate charged by the central bank for overnight loans to the banks for their operating needs – their daily net cheque clearance and the cash to meet the requirements of the public. That rate serves as benchmark for interest rates throughout the economy. In Canada and New Zealand the statutory reserves were completely terminated. In the United States they survive only in enfeebled form.

Much ingenuity has been applied by the Fed towards curtailing its own powers. Thus, sweep accounts shift deposits from reservable to non-reservable accounts at the close of the each business day, and back again at the opening of the next one. Moreover, in calculating the statutory reserves the funds kept in the banks' own tills or voluntarily deposited with the central bank for operational purposes are included. In Canada where the statutory reserves were abolished outright in the 1991 revision of the *Bank Act*, such operational reserves had not been reckoned part of the statutory reserves. In the UK statutory reserves have been reduced to .35 of one percent.

That left interest rates the sole blunt tool for "fighting inflation." This move was highly questionable on several grounds. At the very time that G&D was multiplying the number of variables of perceived inflation, the central banks reduced the variables for designing solutions to the resulting problems from two to one. That solitary variable, moreover, is suspect: it is the revenue of moneylenders, who need no encouragement to become predators.

The stand of the three great Mosaic religions against usury must have summed up millennia of bruising experience. The Koran extended its ban to interest as such, and its penalty for a relapse into interest-taking ("riba") is eternal hell-fire. The elevation of interest to the one tool for keeping the price-level flat could do nothing to improve the relations between Islam and the Western World.

A Counting Rule for What Really Counts

In our first-year algebra classes we learned that to solve problems with two independent variables, we need two linear equations. One simply won't do. That was brought to the attention of economists by Jan Tinbergen. But economists rarely apply his "counting rule" to problems that really count.

A self-balancing market implies a power symmetry between transactors. Yet at the same time as the banks were bailed out from their speculative losses at the beginning of the 1990s, they were further deregulated. They were allowed to engage on their own account and for their clients in most aspects of the stock market – brokerage, merchant banking, underwriting, insurance, and derivatives. That multiplied the conflicts of interest, the uncertainties, the unfamiliar counterparties, and off-balance-sheet deals, and hence the number of loose variables in their mounting number of problems.

Above all, it made possible a breath-taking increase in the leverage with which bank holding companies can create credit through the stock market, credit cards, and other non-banking channels.[1]

To make matters worse, a flat price level ("zero inflation") was declared the prime goal of central banks.[2]

G&D has hopelessly entangled the underdeveloped world in dollar-denominated debt. And the dictates of the International Monetary Fund and the World Bank severely cut down the variables with which the debtor countries can defend themselves. To service their dollar-denominated debt, they have little choice but to increase the export of their staple crops no matter how demoralized the markets; and to slash their sketchy social programs. That dollar-debt, moreover, becomes ever more burdensome as the local currency falls. The resulting bargains help keep prices and interest rates lower in the First World. Tariffs and exchange controls that enabled our industrialized countries during their development stage to work their way out of dependence are not available to the underdeveloped world today.

The conflicts of interest created by G&D have deepened and spread. We are told that we must put up with joblessness and fewer public services because the world economy is being "restructured" – an expression that bristles with engineering know-how. However, if we summed up our global restructuring, it would be that markets, especially financial ones, are to be freed from all restraints. When the prices of stocks and even derivatives go up, it is said that value is being "created." But any upward blip in the prices of real goods must at once be repressed with higher interest rates. Those higher rates stimulate the appetites of those who juggle securities to add further storeys to the financial superstructure. But the same high rates eat away at the footings of the top-heavy economy. Such a construct is increasingly exposed to collapse.

"That has begun to happen. The Bank for International Settlements, habitually as silent as the grave on such matters, has taken to issuing alarmed releases.

"In a report by BIS, central bankers from the world's 11 major industrial countries said many banks don't appreciate the size or complexity of settlement risk and they lack the formal mechanisms to measure and cope with their exposures. The amount at risk even to a single counterparty could easily exceed that bank's capital. Some 80 of the major international banks studied acknowledge that their senior executives have never been fully briefed on the foreign exchange settlement process and associated risks" (*The Wall Street Journal*, 28/03/1996).

"Yet BIS and the central banks have consistently pressed for ever more deregulation of finance. Even when banks, mutual funds, local governments, and industrial corporations were losing astronomical amounts of money on complex derivative gambles, central banks recoiled in horror from any suggestion for imposing a modest tax on financial transactions."[3]

To such a degree that rather than just deviant behaviour, such irregularities in theory and practice must be recognized as a root phenomenon. For their study, the "dominant revenue" concept of the late French economist François Perroux provides an indispensable framework: "The European Occident has passed through successive periods of development, each characterized by a *dominant revenue*. In turn, the dominant revenue has been that of landowners, then industrial profit, and then financial and industrial profits in a mixed economy. During a specific period, the dominant revenue is the one to which the others adapt themselves. It is presented as the revenue, which, by its rate and mass, determines whether the given economy functions properly. In the institutional setting corresponding to the given dominant revenue, that in fact is the case. In another context it would be otherwise."[4]

A major institutional change of this sort took place with the virtual ending of statutory bank reserves already mentioned. Shortly before, the Bank for International Settlements' *Risk-Based Capital Requirements* addressed the bank crises across the world. These Guidelines made two questionable contributions: They shifted the crucial statistic for monitoring banks from *cash* reserves to their *capital*. Capital, of course, does originate as cash from the sale of bank shares, or as undistributed earnings. But rarely does it stay in that form. For cash breeds no interest.

A Launch Pad for World-wide Gambles

The second important change: the BIS Guidelines declared the debt of OECD governments risk-free, needing no additional capital for banks to acquire. As a result the banks loaded up with government debt. In Canada they quadrupled their holdings of it to C$80 billion without putting up any significant money. In the United States, corresponding to the retention of the statutory reserves on a diminished scale the jump in the commercial banks' holdings during a roughly equivalent period, increased by half the Canadian figure – from $372 billion in May, 1989, to $781 billion in November, 1993 (*US Federal Reserve Bulletin*, 01/1994).

This was not a one-shot bailout, but an annual entitlement. And in addition to the new government debt the banks took on, they no longer had to maintain reserves with the BoC for the $470 million of deposits they already held. Depending of how high the central bank has pushed up interest rates "to lick inflation," this bailout amounted to anywhere from $5 billion to $8 billion annually. That stood the power relationship between banks and government on its ear. The banks, so generously bailed out, were free to denounce the growth of the government's debt and deficit, and demand that the fisc show fiscal responsibility by cutting social programs. To make this charade possible, the massive bailout of the banks had to be kept secret. That emphasized another privilege of the dominant revenue – systematic disinformation.

This bailout of the banks provided them with a launch pad for worldwide gambles conflicting with their banking function. In the perspective of the dominant revenue, however, it was perfectly logical that further deregulation should follow the bailout. Power demands constant exercise of muscle.

New problems arose from the downloading of programs to the junior levels of government without adequate funding. And that process ricocheted from the provinces to the municipalities. Junior levels of government across the world have been added to the list of "externalities."

This is reflected in the US states' growing dependence for solvency on the ability of the tobacco corporations to pay the damages awarded them by the courts (see *The Wall Street Journal*, 2/04/03, "Once Tobacco's Foe, States Are Hooked on their Settlement Payments"). Certain states have stepped in to secure the reduction of the bond that had been required by the court to guarantee a loan that would enable Philip Morris to make its payments to the states.

There is no more overweening expression of power than a government ignoring its own laws. The preamble of the *Bank of Canada Act* still sets forth its goals as "mitigating by its influence fluctuations in the general level of production, trade, prices and employment, so far as may be possible within the scope of monetary action." That would include "deflation" as much as "inflation." Article 17(2) of the Act reads: "The capital shall be…issued to the Minister to be held…on behalf of Her Majesty in right of Canada." Article 14(2) provides that 'should there emerge a difference between the Minister and the Bank concerning the monetary policy to be followed, the Minister may give the Governor a written directive concerning the monetary policy, and the Bank shall comply with that directive." Article 18(c) provides that the Bank may 'buy and sell securities or guaranteed by Canada or any province." That implies that it may hold such securities.

Municipalities Left Holding the Bag

By these articles, it was possible in the early 1990s, instead of slashing social programs to fill the fiscal hole left by the bank bailout, to finance such programs through the Bank of Canada against federal and provincial guarantee. The federal government could have returned to the junior level of government all or part of the dividends from these loans reaching it as sole shareholder of the Bank. In return, the junior governments could have been required to observe federal standards in the programs financed.

In Canada and the UK the government is the sole shareholder of the central bank, and by virtue of that, almost the entire interest paid on the debt held by the central bank (some 95%) comes back to it as dividends. In the US the shareholders of the Fed are private banks, but because of the ancestral monarch's monopoly in coining precious metals, the percentage of the profits of the Fed that goes to the government is of the same magnitude as in Canada and the UK.

This would have opened a new dimension of cooperation between the various government levels. Conflicts between the provinces and the federal government today are taking over front-page headlines again. That, however, would have undermined the prerogatives of the dominant revenue. As a result there was no mention of that option in Parliament or in the mainstream media.

Instead, the supposed independence of the central bank from its government was trumpeted forth. Yet the provisions from the *Bank of Canada Act* assert the nation's ownership of it in every sense of the word. The Bank was founded in 1934 by a staunchly conservative government as a privately owned institution. In 1938, the Liberals, honouring an electoral promise, bought out its 12,000 shareholders at a handsome profit. For the Bank and the government to join in violating the hallowed rights of ownership is bizarre. A far from reassuring further detail is that this was done on the initiative of the Bank for International Settlements, a purely technical body that makes a point of allowing no elected representative of a government at its sessions.

By the light of the Tinbergen Test, a more useful policy would have been to internalize the various non-market subsections of the economy now treated as "externalities."

Systems theory must be designed for rectifying asymmetries such as those that have sprung up between our market and non-market sectors. There is no other way of ensuring a sustainable economy. However since the early 1970s economists have not even acknowledged systems theory to exist. The very tag "externalities" is like the slam of a door. System theory maps the interactions of the subsystems and leaves the effort open-ended. That not only prevents one subsystem of our economy from preying on another, but makes it possible to incorporate new subsystems as they may arise.

In the natural sciences, such a relationship is covered by the entropy concept – without a difference in energy levels (negentropy), energy, though always present in matter itself, cannot be harnessed. Not only will the victimized subsystem be undermined, but in consequence so will the entire system. Were this not so, the victim would simply not qualify as a subsystem.[5]

In the natural sciences a mathematical equivalence exists among the different forms of energy – chemical, gravitational, thermal, electro-magnetic, nuclear. That is not the case in the social disciplines. Applied to their problems, "entropy" is a metaphor – but a very useful one. What is involved are the "means and motivations" to keep a given subsystem working. Such means and motivations vary from subsystem to subsystem but include some common factors – for example, funding; an overarching theory that recognizes the needs of all subsystems and assures them the necessary physical resources, political support, and enough variables for its solutions to match those of its survival-problems.

A high-tech, pluralistic economy has multiplied the non-market subsystems of the economy. There is ever-greater need to protect the environment, for more public investment in education, health and social security, and to provide infrastructure for the various new technologies. Most of these, directly or indirectly, are funded by the public sector. They cannot be left dependent on someone making a big buck.

The aggressive use of debt as a stabilizer has drastically reduced living standards in the Third and Emerging worlds. The result has been a massive suction of scarce human capital from these lands to the developed countries. In the long run, however, these too facile victories of the dominant world revenues will prove anything but cost-free. SARS could not have happened if

G&D had not replaced the subsistence agriculture of China with frantic stock raising for overseas markets, to the point where humans almost shacked up with the livestock. This permitted the crossbreeding of viral strains in man, swine, chickens, and ducks to create deadly mutations. And these were immediately transported to other continents on our bankrupt airlines.

Disproving a Flat Price World

The very notion of a flat price level in a pluralistic society undergoing rapid technological development can't withstand scrutiny. This can readily be proved by *reductio ad absurdum*. This assumes the proposition to be tested to be true, and then traces the implications of that assumption. If that leads to a conclusion contradicting your assumption, you have disproved the proposition in the most rigorous way.

I will apply this test twice to the proposition that as the public sector grows within the economy, while the total supply and demand of the public and private sectors remain unchanged, it is possible for the price level to remain constant, other factors remaining the same. Assume this, but for some reason the price index has risen. Increase the taxation on the private sector and apply the added taxation to subsidize producers to lower their prices to where they were the previous year. By the assumption, this is feasible. Having done this, there is no good reason for not repeating the performance, again and again. Eventually the price level would reach zero. Q.E.D.

Let us now assume that the added taxation goes not to producers to reimburse them for the higher interest rates, but stays with the government. Obviously the previous proof is an a fortiori version of this. The latter therefore has already been proved.

The December 1988 *Journal of Economic Literature*, carried a review of Robert Eisner listing weaknesses of the national product estimates that include the following:

"The total national product obviously includes both that portion that is produced and marketed commercially, and that portion that is produced and consumed within each family unit. The long-term trend has been away from non-commercial and towards an increasing proportion of commercial output. Therefore, the real per-capita commercial output overstates the increase in real per-capita total output. In recent years the increasing proportion of women in the workforce, many with young children, has increased the demand for commercial services in education, childcare, food preparation, etc., services previously supplied in the non-commercial home economy. That increased the reported real commercial output, but may well have reduced the quantity and quality of those services.

"If environmental considerations are to be fully recognized both the consumption of natural resources and the degradation of the environment must be considered. The introduction of a rigorous concept of value added in the estimates of total national product would achieve that goal. That would have to be net of natural resources consumed, of previously produced physical capital consumed, and of the environmental degradation.

"Eliminating the Double Accounting of Output in Joint Purchase Situations."

In *Economic Reform*, of 12/1989, Harvey Wilmeth, one of the founders of COMER, used the following parable to explain the point: "Merchants frequently offer some additional products 'free of charge' as a bonus to stimulate sales. For example, a free $100 bicycle might be offered as a bonus with each purchase of a $400 television. How should such a transaction be measured for national output purposes? Did a $400 joint purchase take place, or did the buyer receive a free bicycle worth $100 plus a $400 TV? Most observers would agree that a joint purchase took place at a total price of $400, and that the amount should be allocated appropriately to each item.

"Now, instead of a free bicycle, think of free government services. Using a joint purchase example again, assume that the government levies taxes that can only be recovered from increased prices of goods sold over what the prices the prices otherwise could be. Funds from the taxes then permit the government to pay for goods and services that are given way, yet their costs are also included in the GNP. This illustrates how the cost of government services are included once in GNP through the higher prices necessary to recover tax costs, and a second time by including a cost-based value of 'free' government output. That double counting overstates the nominal value added and distorts measures of inflation. Inflation should measure increases in factor costs not increases in joint purchase costs."

In the same issue of *Economic Reform* I added the following note: "The growing layer of taxation in our price structure I have termed the 'social lien.' The value of the output of the public sector must be seen as transferred to the output of the private sector through the social lien. Aggregate price would thus include the value produced by both sectors, though it is attached to the output of the private sector alone. 'The "external diseconomies" of the private sector would come into better focus.'

"Let us subject the phenomenon to further analysis: If the output of the public Sector (P) is subtracted from the GDP to correct this duplication, the quantity of the GDP will be adjusted by the factor $G/(G+P)$. Dividing the numerator by the denominator we get the infinite series $1 - (P/G) + (P/G)^2 - (P/G)^3 \ldots$.

"This is a remarkable result achieved with some tuppenny mathematics. It shows that the effect on the price level of unpriced government services is more complex than simple addition. That is because the cost of public services must be borne by a real GDP that is in fact smaller than would first appear – in its pricing the cost of the public services turns up twice. But a smaller private product as a proportion of GDP means that the output of the public sector is relatively greater. And since it is counted twice this means a further shrunken real GDP to support this correction, and so forth. The correction of the double counting echoes back and forth between the P and G and gives rise to a converging infinite series to show the ultimate effect on price of unpriced public services."

Here I will note a single of the many "externalities" that even alone rules out a flat price level. At the beginning of the 20th century the population of the world lived largely in the countryside; the balance, generally estimated at 10-15%, inhabited very large cities.[6] Now those proportions are approximately reversed. Greater Tokyo and the eastern seaboard of the US from Washington to Massachusetts house populations of 35 millions each. Nobody moving from the countryside to New York City expects her cost of living to stay the same. How could we then expect the price level to stay flat when humanity as a whole makes such a move?

I will mention a few more random disparities between the variables in our problems and those available for their solutions.

In most countries no distinction was made until recently between capital investment by governments and current spending. If a government built a bridge, road or bought a building, its cost was written off in the year of acquisition. After that it appeared on the books at a token dollar. Nothing was on the asset side of the balance sheet to offset the debt incurred. This breached the laws of double-entry bookkeeping practised in the private sector since the 14th century. It provided a pretext for raising interest rates to protect the economy against "inflation." To cope with the exaggerated net deficit, assets of the government recorded at a token value on the books could be sold to private interests for a high multiple of their book value ($1) which would still be a tiny fraction of what they could fetch on the market And that tiny fraction, with due patriotic flourish, could be applied to "reduce the debt." Many of these assets, reorganized as public companies, were then resold on the stock market at rich multiples of their cost. That was a major factor in fuelling the stock markets of the late 1990s.

Before the Cure Contaminated the Evidence

In the 1960s when the price level began its climb and the evidence had still not been hopelessly contaminated with the high interest-rate cure, I concluded that prices can rise for either of two very different reasons. It could indeed be "market inflation" (too much demand for available supply). But part or all of the price rise might merely reflect the deepening layer of taxation to cover the cost of increased public services. But wouldn't that be inflation? You can call it whatever you wish, but it is confusing labelling two different phenomena with the same name. Recognizing two sets of independent variables where only a single one was deemed to exist multiplies the available options for designing a solution. I therefore coined the term "social lien" for the layer of taxation in the price level.[7]

Disregarding various structural factors responsible for a significant price climb reduces the variables available for handling the problem. It is important to treat public capital outlays as investments, and to finance them through the central bank at near zero-interest cost. The focus must be not on the absolute amount of government debt but on net debt after entering the properly depreciated value of its past investments in both physical and human capital. Who in these days of SARS can question that government spending to train doctors, nurses and scientists is a critically important investment?

The sixties were a period of much public investment throughout the world. The baby boomers had reached university age and new post-secondary campuses were springing up across every developed land to accommodate them. One of history's greatest migrations had been housed, a huge backlog of infrastructures neglected over a decade of depression and six years of war was retrieved. The social lien effect was exaggerated by the absence of the very concept of investment in the public sector. To the extent this accountancy shortfall was covered by taxes it exaggerated the perceived inflation: for the additional taxes inevitably showed up in prices. To the extent it was not, it exaggerated the real deficit and net debt. In Canada over a period of forty years no less than three royal commissions and a series of Auditors General had recommended capital budgeting to no avail.

A measure of accrual accountancy was introduced into the figures for US government savings as of January 1996, but was incorrectly listed not as government investments but as savings. This it was not, since it wasn't held in cash.

The purpose was to introduce just enough capital budgeting in stealth to improve government balance sheet without arousing the sleeping dogs of the right. Robert Rubin, Clinton's Secretary of the Treasury and former Wall St. ace, was the man for the job. He needed only a single statistic of lower government net debt to show the bonding agencies and get a lower interest rate to keep the market boom going. Carrying the revision back several years, it brought to light $1.3 trillion of "overlooked" government assets. Calling it what it was – "investments" – would have brought to mind J.M. Keynes and his emphasis on the distinction between savings and investment. So "savings" is was. It showed up for the first time in the January 1996 Bureau of Economic Analysis figures of the Department of Commerce. In essence it put an end to the one-year write-off of the physical investments of government. Government investment in human capital – education, health, social security – still remain unrecognized And by listing government physical investment under the wrong heading, capital budgeting was reduced to number-crunching that provides a single statistic rather than all the relevant variables that must be monitored for managing the economy in a sustainable way.

It took the Canadian government three and a half years and an ultimatum of its Auditor General to catch up with Washington in this respect. The AG simply refused an unconditional approval of the government's balance sheet unless this was done. But the Minister of Finance, Paul Martin, imposed a Faustian bargain on him: in his report, the AG argued that since the accountancy change had brought no new money into the treasury it must not be taken to warrant increased spending. However, the misleading figures for the debt and deficit in the absence of accrual accountancy had been good enough reason for slashing grants to the provinces and thus indirectly for cutting social programs. But when it was finally brought in February 2003, it was made the occasion for a grab bag of increased spending which did include some health and social services. Again, instead of putting it in a form where it could increase the variables for policy-making, it was degraded to another exercise in number crunching. After an attempt by Finance Minister John Manley to explain what "accrual accountancy" might be to his own caucus, who obviously didn't know what they had voted for in 1999, it was reduced to another exercise in the futile debate between spending vs. fiscal responsibility. By that logic Canada's street people who sleep on our sidewalks are in sounder financial condition than our big banks because they have no debt at all. That is the goal that all the parties set in principle, though it is not clear what they would use to pay off the existing debt. Since gold is no longer legal tender, it would have to be notes of a different colour.

Resistance to Capital Budgeting

Why the resistance to recognizing capital budgeting in its full implications? One factor was that, misrepresented as fiscal irresponsibility, it spelled windfall opportunities for speculative finance. The subject of the pioneer nationalizations in Britain under Margaret Thatcher is dealt with in detail in Dominic Hobson, *The National Wealth – Who Gets What in Britain,* Harper Collins, London, 1999. After the National Audit Office had revealed the grossly low prices of the initial privatizations (BT, the English and Welsh water industries, Mersey Docks and Harbour company), all of which lost no time in reselling assets at several times what they had paid, the Thatcher government came to rely on a clawback clause. This gave the state the right to half of the net proceeds of future sales when the privatized company resold them. In this way, instead of exposing itself entirely to the greed of the stock market and its own record of incompetence in negotiating deals, the government piggy-backed up on possible resales that the private companies might do. Significantly, such clawbacks were not imitated in the sale of the Canadian National Railways to a company headed by a high former civil servant, and in the sale of Ontario Hydro. The stock market badly needed such windfall listings to lift itself out of the gutter.

The essence of banking is money creation on a base that is mostly borrowed or held in trust. The more the banks are deregulated to engage in conflicting non-banking activities, the more the government is exposed to costly bank bailouts. While the bias of deregulation advocates is for "small government," the larger banks, grown "too large to be allowed to fail," are bailed out quite regularly to prevent the entire financial system from collapsing. But the increasing extent and frequency of the bailouts carried out in semi-stealth, entrenches the dominant revenue further. In addition, over the past three decades the dominant revue has shifted from industrial corporations and conservative banking to speculative finance. That explains in part why the bailouts have invariably been followed by further deregulation. The seemingly endless revelations coming out of investigations by the SEC and other government departments in the US have disclosed auditors of bank holding-companies advising their clients how to keep liabilities off their books and assets beyond the reach of the tax-collector. In Canada equivalent disclosures have not even begun.

Unholy Mix of Bailout and Deregulation

But for this unholy mix of bail-out and deregulation, recent stock markets could not have soared so high or fallen so low. The weakening of Wall St.'s moral constraints have sapped the credibility of the United States. Washington is in a sorry state to preach morality to the world.

The classical banking model provided for the creation of interest-earning credit. When the bank made a loan such "near-money" was created; when the loan was repaid money was destroyed. Double-entry bookkeeping took care of that. But all that changed with the removal of the firewalls between banking and other financial businesses. Bank holding companies were supposedly set up to "maximize their shareholders equity" by incorporating into current prices the growth rates of shares and options extrapolated into the remote future and then discounted for presumed present value. Note well: such evaluations were derivatives in a multiple sense – they were functions of the rate of growth as extrapolated into a remote future made all the less predictable by the incorporation of the uncertainties of Globalization and Deregulation into capital values. But there have been overlooked by-products of that process: the ghost of loans supposedly expunged when the original loan was repaid to the bank, often lives on because the artificial asset values achieved served as collateral for new investments or loans. It thus goes on reproducing itself, and spreads a fatal infection around the world. The "asset," of course, at times is shorn of the balancing liability – no great problem with the new boneless accountancy. When you violate double-entry bookkeeping at any stage of the complex financial structures that have arisen, double-entry accountancy is doomed at higher levels.

A new fatal model for the valuation of shares had been developed: the extrapolation of ill-defined growth into the remote future and then discounted for present value. The resulting market price increase projected into the indefinite future was incorporated into the current share price of such privatized enterprises. That imposed the obligation of management never to allow the corporation returns to fall short of last year's returns. That put corporations under a compulsion towards exponential growth, where reckonings are strictly in rates of higher order. This is a formula for disaster for exponential growth does happen to be the mathematics of the atomic bomb.

The ingenuity with which the books were cooked was thus preordained in the "maximization of shareholder value." Since many of the star high-tech stocks had never shown a bean of profit, "earnings" were replaced with "market share" as the guiding statistic. That, however, left open whether the "market share" resulted from a real sale, or was a dodge financed by the seller. It was as though the Great Tempter had done a deal with Wall St. promising to grant all it could desire but only for a single year, and on condition that it continue to maximize shareholder value at the same rate for ever and ever. Failure to meet the schedule a single year would bring down the house of marked cards. Perfectly sober and honest CEOs ended up paying their accountants to dream up the scams to stave off the inevitable reckoning.

Economic theory has becomes a manual of black magic by which the group with political and economic power defends its claim to a privileged share of the national product. Management's own disbelief in its number-crunching is betrayed by the short-term horizon of many outstanding operators. They cash in their options when they can and move to the nearest exit.

Should anyone question this analysis, let me refer her to the expanding role of "risk management" by derivatives of higher powers.

For the purpose, I will introduce a powerful tool developed by the greatest of 19th century mathematicians, Karl Friedrich Gauss – modular congruence (GMC). Let no one feel intimidated. Our remote ancestors used modular congruence intuitively almost since Adam bit the apple. Rather than give every day on which the sun rose a different name, they used only seven names and started back to the first each time the seven cycle was completed. For biological, navigational and astronomical purposes they did the same with the modulus 30, and for seasonal activities with the modulus 365. That saved a lot of calculation. Take the square of a number expressed without and with congruence to modulus 7 or whatever: $(M+2)^2 = M^2 + 4M + 4$. If you equate all multiples of M, the modulus, to zero, you will find that instead of working this out for all three terms, you achieve the same result a lot more simply if you forget terms with M and just deal with the 2 and 4 remnants. Thus you could multiply, divide, add or subtract or raise to a higher power an expression eliminating the terms with M in it and just concentrating on the remnants left by extracting the modulus. If you apply the same idea to foreign trade, other things being equal, if you can reduce your foreign trade to what you cannot make at home, or where there is a great advantage in importing from a country with a natural advantage that brings costs down, and thereby eliminate a lot of mileage, pollution, spread of disease.

We can use GMC to circumvent the disinformation piled up by the perspective of the dominant revenue. In this policy operator, I apply exactly the procedure we learned in our first year algebra classes for solving two first-degree equations. We begin by multiplying one of the equations by a number that would render equal the coordinates of one of the two variables in both equations. Then we subtract one equation from the other to eliminate that variable. That gives us the value of one variable. Substitute that value in either equation to get the value of the second variable.

We choose a politically sensitive target, say the government treasury. The two variables determining whether it is balanced or in deficit or surplus will be its revenue and its spending. Our goal will be to by-pass the issue by choosing for our STEP ONE two measures of quantitatively equal but opposite effect on the treasury, that most people would prefer to see pointed downwards rather than upward. Say, in Canada, a reduction of the Goods and Service Tax, a Value Added Tax on most consumer goods and services. This the Liberal government promised to remove when elected, but it's still there in a big way. That would reduce the revenue of the government. To balance this revenue reduction, just enough federal debt would be shifted from the private banks to the central bank. Since the federal government is the single shareholder of the central bank that would increase the dividend reaching the government from the Bank. The immediate direct effect on the treasury would be a wash. In the US, though the Federal Reserve is owned by private banks, roughly the same proportion of its earnings are remitted to the government as happens in the case of the Bank of Canada. But the

rationale is different: it is by virtue of the ancestral sovereign's monopoly in coining precious metals (seigniorage) that has been largely assigned to the commercial banks.

Circumventing Pillboxes of Prejudice

STEP TWO is wholly passive. We would monitor the indirect effect of the two measures as they worked their way through the economy and back to the Treasury for a second-round effect. A lower end-cost of consumers' goods to the public by the reduction of the GST and a reduced interest expenditure by the government, would certainly perk up the private economy and lead to further income for the treasury. The removal of the GST would also help in the effort against perceived "inflation." Evidence of this should be in during the first year. With such confirmation of the positive effect of the policy, a second round of measures of balanced opposite effects would be in place.

STEP THREE. This could be of the same two items. The percentage of federal debt held by the Bank of Canada was some 22% in the mid 1970s and is less than 6% today. That provides plenty of elbowroom for shifting government debt to the central bank without running out of historical precedent. And by the time the old maximum is reached there will be enough data to guide us in pursuing the method still further. For the second and third helping of increased federal grants to the provincial governments for the restoration of health, social security and educational, and environmental programs could be addressed, with just enough further shift of federal debt to the central bank to cut the interest burden on the fisc sufficiently to pay for Step Three.

To present the measures in their true light, educational programs – reversing the steep increase of university fees – could be treated as a government investment and amortized, as all capital investments should be. Gaussian Modular Convergence techniques provides an effective way of doing so with all bases covered.

Since the subject of this paper is restructuring economic theory, we must allude to the genome of self-destruction of economic enquiry. The early economists were very concerned with establishing ties with the reality around them. Many of these founding fathers – from William Petty in the 17th century on – used a labour theory of value. Others devised a cost of production theory that added up cost columns to arrive at the value of a given product. A much-maligned figure of the period was Adam Smith, credited with an absolute belief in a free market. Smith in fact made use of not one but three different value theories depending on the angle of vision suitable to the problem at hand. Unconsciously what he was striving for was enough variables to match those in the problems before him – the Tinbergen Test long before Tinbergen. He was trying to capture the different factors underlying a given phenomenon in that early economy – precisely what systems theory is about. There was the theory of average labour that went into the production of a product, the theory of "embodied labour"; the theory of "commanded labour" – how much labour you could purchase with the proceeds of the sale of a product. On occasions he used a cost-of-production value concept. But all of them sought some tie with reality more basic than the last market price. You will note at once how tremendously Smith's "commanded labour" is today – in dealing with the trade between China today and the Western world, since its export prices at home command ten times the labour that they fetch in Japan. Any of these value theories was far more useful for warning economists of what cannot make sense than as a metric for precise calculations.

Smith's theory of commanded labour was useful for a later generation of economists like David Ricardo in challenging the wisdom of the Corn Laws that taxed food imports and thus had a powerful effect on the wages of industrial workers. But as industrial workers were fast learning how to read and write in mechanics' institutes, the labour theory of value became a free gift for the socialists advocating a more humane society. It became a dangerous indiscretion *devant les enfants*. In response those in power felt the need for a very different sort of value theory as a fig leaf for society's shameful parts.

That was met by marginal utility theory that saw price determined by the balance of supply and demand on a "pure and perfect market." It presented all classes from bankers to the unemployed workers as just traders busying themselves with the identical goal of maximizing their satisfactions. No room was left for social injustice. Those specifications were supported with a bit of calculus mistaken for science itself rather than a useful tool when properly applied. All that mathematics can do is shake out the implications of what we put into the premises of our propositions. And to use the differential calculus you must "assume that all actors on the "pure and perfect market" are of such infinitesimal size that nothing can do individually can affect price. It is enough to look around you and note the existence of Microsoft, Citicorp and General Electric to realize how inapt such premises are for an understanding our economy.

W. Krehm

1. Krehm, William (2002). *Towards a Post-Autistic Economy – A Place for Society at the Table*, p. 185. COMER Publications. From Bank of Canada statistics I compiled an "estimator" – the ratio of chartered bank assets to the cash held by them as a group. This rose from 11/1 in 1946 to 375/1 in June 2001.

2. "It has been argued…that inflation rates in the range of one to two per cent may be considered price stability for all practical purposes. Nonetheless, the move from an environment of low or moderate inflation to one of no inflation implies an important psychological shift" (Alexandre Lamfalussy, general manager of the BIS, in its 1991 annual report).

3. Krehm, William (ed.) (1999). *Meltdown: Money, Debt and the Wealth of Nations*, p. 205. COMER Publications.

4. (1966). *L'entreprise et l'économie du Xxe siècle*, p. 958. Paris: Presses Universitaires de France.

5. Krehm, William (1977). *Babel's Towers – The Dynamics of Economic Breakdown*. Chapter Four, "Fine-Tuning for the Heat-Death," p. 46. Toronto, and Krehm, William (1977 – #1). The Entropy Concept as a Tool of Economic Analysis, *Économie appliquée*. Genève: Librairie Droz.

6. Braudel, Fernand, *The Identity of France* (Vol. 2), pp. 415-7 (S. Reynolds, Trans.). Harper Collins. Braudel even notes the structural price change resulting from the shift of population from the countryside

to huge cities: "The prices of town-produced commodities began to rise, while farm prices slumped. The price 'scissors' effect operated in favour of the towns." The better economic historians have picked up the "social lien effect," but economists have been immune to historical evidence.

7. Krehm, William (May, 1970). La stabilité des prix et le secteur public, *Revue Economique*. Paris. Krehm, William (1975). *Price in a Mixed Economy – Our Record of Disaster* (Chapter 13). Toronto.

Imperial Banners Redesigned

THEY WHO CONTROL the credit of the nation direct the policy of governments, said Rt. Hon Reginald McKenna (1928) a former Chancellor of the Exchequer and one-time director of the Bank of England. Today, such a claim is highly relevant to the future relationship between Iraq and the United States – the world's only superpower. Having occupied Baghdad, one of the first actions of the United States was to encourage the Iraqis to exchange 2000 of their dinars for one American dollar.

The traditional method of exercising imperial power was through the acquisition of colonies and the imposition of taxation upon the subject people. This was the British imperial approach – most obvious in India. With the demise of the Soviet Union, the United States clearly became the great imperial power of the day (superpower). Typically, the United States extended and maintained its sphere of interest through monetary means; the military occupation of Iraq is quite uncharacteristic of the Americans. However, it is unlikely that the occupying troops will remain to be supported by locally imposed taxation. Financial and corporate control over the economy is much more effective – and much less obvious.

It can be taken that, in the name of democracy and the free market, American corporations will take control of the banking system and key elements of the Iraqi economy. There will be particular concern to gain privileged access to crude oil and to ensure priority in its refining. The Iraqis need not relinquish ownership of the oilfields but just as effective will be a requirement that royalties, and possibly all exports, be paid for with American dollars. In this circumstance, no matter how elected, any future government of Iraq will have to accept what is held to be monetary and economic reality.

The practical effect of the recommendations made at the Bretton Woods conference of 1944 was that each nation's credit system be underpinned by the American dollar. In practice, this meant that the availability of each nation's currency depended upon having adequate access to the world's master currency. The Cold War was won for a variety of reasons – not least of which was having the American dollar recognized as the world's reserve currency. The greenback had worldwide acceptability when paying for goods and services in ways not applicable to the rouble.

The requirement that a nation's currency depend on that nation's access to US dollars gave organizations like the IMF the means of dictating the policy of national governments. Of course, the greenbacks made available by the IMF and in circulation have all been created within the United States banking system – unrestrained by the size of the US current-account deficit.

However, what has endured for more than half a century is now threatening to unravel. There appears little doubt that the euro has the potential to rival the greenback as the world's master currency and the commensurate ability to exercise imperial power. In a rapidly changing world, the American corporate and banking takeover of Iraq is unlikely to experience the plain sailing that has been true for more than fifty years. Indeed, such means of exercising imperial power seem to have been recognized by those members of the European Union who opposed the war.

Furthermore, the decadence and unjustifiable inequity associated with the present international monetary system is increasingly being recognized. Protest is taking two forms. One is a mounting call for monetary reform. The other is based on religious grounds, primarily by those of the Muslim faith for whom the usurious nature of the system is of deep concern.

Les Hunter

Les Hunter is a member of the New Zealand Committee for Economic and Monetary Reform and author of the book Courage to Change – A case for Monetary Reform, *published by Harbourside Publications Ltd. and available at www.monetaryreform.co.nz.*

Gaussian Congruence as a Weapon Against Terrorism

ELSEWHERE IN THIS ISSUE I develop tools for dealing with the swarm of new menacing problems in our Globalized and Deregulated World, and in particular with Gaussian Modular calculus. Like Molière's hero who was astounded to learn that he had been talking prose all his life, our remotest ancestors used Gaussian modular reasoning. In naming the days to keep track of the working week they dropped all multiples of seven, and concentrated on the remainders. Instead of giving every new day since the Garden of Eden a new name, they started anew with Sunday. Were it not for that brilliant improvisation we would have had time for nothing else than keeping track of the teeming millions of day names, and devising new ones. To date our economists have been less wise and have concentrated on increasing such useless baggage, mileage and pollution. Moreover, the GDP is taken as a sign of increasing prosperity. But while I worked on that paper, the news of terrorism throughout much of the world continued relentlessly. That raised the challenge: can we use the same Gaussian modular to fashion a weapon of reconciliation between Islam and the Western world?

The guiding principle of the policy design model is circumventing the structured prejudice around some ideological preemption of a key institution – in the cited case the govern-ment treasury. The treasury is a key institution for such non-marketed objectives because it alone can fund the host of public services that are dismissed by conventional economists as "externalities." The strategy is to seek out paired measures crucial for our immediate target, one entailing increased government spending and the other a decrease in spending, and apply them in balanced dosages so that the initial joint direct effect on the treasury is zero. Next, we track their benign secondary effects as they work their way through the economy. When these effects have been confirmed, we can embark on a further dosage of two similar variables benignly pointed downwards and balancing to a zero immediate effect on the treasury.

The project will promote better mutual understanding and co-existence between the Islamic and non-Islamic worlds. This requires both enormous help in modernizing infrastructures without depending on aggressive Globalization and Deregulation to achieve the goal. It could lay the basis for a better understanding between the two worlds.

This will have to be carried out under the auspices of the United Nations, because the IMF and the World Bank have a regrettable record in using debt as a knuckle-duster. Substantial financing will be made available to impoverished Islamic countries for infrastructure development at rates just enough to cover administrative costs, expressed as far as possible in terms that will avoid the Islamic prohibition not only of usury but of interest as such.

This can be achieved by the developed countries using the facilities of their central banks. In return, the governments of the Islamic countries will introduce into their educational programs and make available in their libraries and government broadcasts a fair picture of Western culture, warts and virtues, emphasizing its very considerable progress towards not only religious and racial tolerance, but the existence of movements critical of usury and imperialism. In return, the Western governments will undertake similar obligations to explain Islam and its powerful feelings on usury and financial exploitation. Obviously, such a program will have to explain the nature of democracy, which, with all its imperfections, allows the coexistence of a variety of economic and other differences.

The financing of the Western effort will have to be done through the central banks because there is no other way in which governments can raise the amounts for this and other essential infrastructural projects, domestic or international. However, when the central government finances essential investments through its central bank, it is at a near-zero interest rate. In countries where the central bank has been nationalized – Canada, the UK, for example – are owned outright by the government, and the net income coming to the central bank from government debt held by it reverts to the government in the form of dividends.

But even privately owned central banks such as the Fed end up with a very similar amount of the interest they pay on their debt held by the central bank for another reason – it harks back to the ancestral monarch's monopoly on coining precious metals, now carried forward in assigning to the banks most credit creation – the only money in existence today.

Obviously, it would be a point of no small importance to the Muslim world to be assured that the financing of the reconciliation projects were free of anything that could be interpreted not only as usury but even as "riba" – interest. There will be no lack of imans who could work out the details of the arrangement – they could do so in approving business deals every day. In lieu of formal interest, the international fund would be granted a right to the eventual return of the principal plus a share of the "profits" that would return to the fund to be reinvested for similar purposes in impoverished lands.

What is not subject to special interpretation is the rejection of anything smacking of terrorism. And it is mostly here that the program would prove an important investment. Not only must a program against terrorism be taught in all schools of the world, but adequate policing provided to prevent it.

The use of the central banks for such financing will require the rejection of the notion of the "independence" of central banks from their government – a notion that has been much promoted in the last three decades. The material to dispose of such objections is to be found in a remarkable book, *The Central Banks*, by Marjorie Deane and Robert Pringle (London: Hamish Hamilton, 1994).

It is a highly critical work without anti-bank bias. Good enough evidence of the non-independence of central banks from their governments comes in the foreword written by no less an authority in central-bankdom than Paul Volcker. He writes, "[The authors] have correctly placed the emotive question of 'independence' in the context of the large political and market forces that inescapably impinge on, and set limits on autonomy."

It is noteworthy that most central banks have not done away with – just reduced their use of – the statutory reserves. They survive in the US and the UK (where they have been reduced to .35 of 1% of reservable deposits). Canada and New Zealand were the most prominent of the few countries pressured by the Bank for International Settlements to do away with their statutory reserves. The need for the refinancing of this reconciliation project will provide a good occasion for bringing back the statutory reserves where they have been completely done away with. Given the alarming deflationary dip in the world economy, adjustment to the needs of the reconciliation project will help the West quite as much as our Muslim neighbours.

William Krehm

Sorting Out the Good and Evil in Deregulation and Globalization

COULD IT BE that the Bush administration has fallen victim to its own rhetoric in its crusade to refashion the world according to its notions of absolute virtue? Even the suspicion that it may be so is so grave, that we are confining ourselves to the evidence of the US Justice Department.

The Wall Street Journal (23/04, "US Bribery Probe Looks at Mobil" by Steve LeVine) informs us: "Almaty, Kazakhstan – A US inquiry into oil deals in this Caspian Sea republic has turned into the largest investigation of possible bribery abroad since the US started prosecuting such cases a quarter of a century ago, experts say.

"The US is investigating whether Exxon Mobil Corp. participated in a scheme to route $78 million in payments from US and European oil companies to the Swiss bank accounts of Kazakhstan's president and others.

"A retired senior executive of the former Mobil Oil Corp. and a New York businessman have been indicted in federal court in Manhattan in the three-year investigation, participated in a scheme to route $78 million. Experts say it is far from inevitable that Exxon Mobil itself will be indicted under the 1977 US *Foreign Corrupt Practices Act*, which bars US companies from bribing foreign officials to obtain a deal. But, they say, the company will have to persuade prosecutors that its indicted former executive was a renegade, and that it did everything it could within reason to comply with the law.

"Prosecutions under the act are rare – just four dozen cases have been filed – because they usually require cooperation from the foreign country where the alleged violation occurred. In the Kazakhstan case, however, Switzerland tipped off the US Justice Department to what it considered suspect bank transactions, then provided documents that were used in the indictments, say persons familiar with the matter. In all, the US prosecutors obtained records for about 30 accounts in four Swiss banks.

"The two previous biggest cases under the act involved General Electric Co., which in 1992 paid $69 million in penalties after an employee bribed a former Israeli general, and Lockheed Martin Corp., which in 1995 paid a $24.8 million fine after an executive bribed an Egyptian politician. But in terms of the stature of the individuals cited, the size of the companies, and the sums at issue – the president of a country, four major US oil companies and almost $80 million – the Kazakhstan matter is the most far-reaching US bribery investigation ever, experts say." It is not always virtue that has the greatest growth in Washington's campaign to set the world straight.

"James H. Giffen, chairman of a New York merchant bank called Mercator Corp. was indicted on April 2 for allegedly directing the bribery scheme. Mr. Giffen negotiated some of Kazakhstan's biggest oil deals as a special adviser to the country's president, Nursultan Nazarbayev.

"A second indictment accuses J. Bryan Williams, a retired

senior vice president, of failing to pay taxes on an alleged $2 million kickback from Mr. Giffen for his role in Mobil's 1996 purchase of a 25% stake in Kazakhstan's Tengiz oil field on April 4. A federal prosecutor said in court that Exxon Mobil itself is a subject of the US investigation.

"Messers Giffen and Williams plead not guilty.

"Experts say prosecutors appear to be seeking to make an example of the 62-year-old Mr. Giffen. The charges against him carry a maximum penalty of 88 years in prison and $84.3 million in penalties, although experts say it is not likely the businessman would receive such a sentence if convicted. Until now the largest jail sentence for foreign bribery was seven years and $1.7 million received by GE executive Herbert Steindler in the Egyptian case."

It is not clear whether the motive of the prosecution was to defend the US dollar – such was the magnitude of the bribe to the foreign dignitaries – or pure morality.

"Though two of the six oil deals cited in the indictments involve consortia in which some of Europe's largest oil companies are members, there is almost no possibility that any of them will face similar investigations at home, experts say. That is because European anti-bribery statutes similar to the *Foreign Corrupt Practices Act* have been in force only since 1999, a year after the last transaction detailed in the US indictments.

"In one of the deals, prosecutors say six US and European oil companies paid $23 million into a Swiss escrow account as part of their 1997 purchase of rights to the offshore Kashagan field, which geologists describe as the world's largest oil find in three decades. Mr. Giffen allegedly transferred $5 million of that sum to a Swiss bank account belonging to President Nazarbayev, and $2.5 million to then-Prime Minister Nurlan Balgimbayev. The European companies that were part of the consortium are Total (Now TotalFina Elf SA), Royal Dutch/Shell Group, Eni Spa, BG Group Plc and Bp. The sole US Company was Mobil."

Here a word of warning is in place. Let no one lapse into the belief that what our oil corporations do in distant Kazakhstan is an "externality," and that what is done there does not affect our domestic way of life. To the extent that was ever true, it belonged to an age of innocence that was finally suppressed by G&D. What the marines did in Latin America in the 1920s helped bring home the bacon, but did not too seriously affect American democracy at home. In its most golden imperial age, Britain's tyranny in India hardly affected democracy in those sea-girt isles. That age is gone. The same high communication technology that made it possible to bombard Baghdad from distant seas, works two ways. What the United States does in Kazakhstan is no farther than our TV sets. Besides the mentors of President Bush have established him as the moral chief of humankind committed to lead its remotest tribes to democracy. Indeed, he has staked his credibility on that, since the prospects of the home economy are less inspiring. Willy-nilly G&D has blunted the cutting edge of the "externality" dodge. The oil titans' way of doing business in Kazakhstan will affect standards in the US as well. At least on that front some of those famous "externalities" will be internalized.

W.K.

The Debt Bomb

READERS OF *ER* are familiar with the problem of debt in our society. It is significant that the mainstream media is finally starting to pay attention. A recent article in *Barron's* (Jan 20, 2003) is well worth a look. Most of the stats here are from that article.

The raw data are amazing. Total US debt has zoomed from $4 trillion in 1980 (the approximate beginning of financial deregulation) to $31 trillion in 2002. Where total debt was less than 150% of GDP in the 1960s, it has doubled to almost 300% by 2003. Credit card charge-offs, mortgage defaults and personal bankruptcies have all escalated to new highs.

Of course debt must be balanced against assets. During the 90s the stock market bubble inflated the average net worth of US households to 6.3 times disposable income in 1999. The bear market has reduced that number to 4.9. Through US government debt as a percentage of GDP fell during the nineties to about 50%, President Bush's tax reductions, combined with huge increases in military spending, are projected to increase government debt by at least $5 trillion by 2010. Meanwhile the ratio of corporate revenues to corporate debt has been falling steadily, making it harder for corporations to service debt, especially given the climate of falling prices for their products.

The only part of the economy that is able to take on more debt is the housing sector. House prices have risen 50% in the past six years but consumers have tapped their increased equity by massive mortgage refinancing – $2.5 trillion in the past two years alone. The effect has been sharply reduced home equity – to 57% today compared with 85% in 1960. This use of homes as loan collateral is the only factor-keeping consumer spending going. If the housing bubble bursts, there is nothing left.

A collapse of the credit market has been predicted by a few financial analysts, notably Peter Warburton in his book Debt and Delusion. Such a collapse would directly impact our money supply, which is 96% credit, and precipitate us into a deflationary depression. This is what Japan has been experiencing for the past decade, and shows no signs of recovery.

Despite debt levels that now exceed those of 1929, our monetary authorities show no concern about deflation (or at least not in public). The Bank of Canada's recent tightening, citing concerns about inflation, is evidence that the old mindset of John Crow is still ascendant. There is little cause for optimism that our central banks will cope with deflation any better than did Japan.

David Gracey

Is the FCM Fiddling while Municipalities Get Burnt?

AT THE MEETING of the national board of the Federation of Canadian Municipalities (FCM) held on September 8, 2001, two resolutions were passed recommending that capital financing for municipalities be provided through the Bank of Canada; one came from the city of Kingston, Ontario, and the other from Squamish, BC. The FCM forwarded these resolutions to the federal government, but has received no response from the government other than to acknowledge receipt of the letters.

Since 1974 the government has not been using the Bank of Canada (BoC) to help finance public capital expenditures as it did in the previous 35 years. Instead, private banks and other private investors have been used exclusively for the purpose. As a result national and provincial debts have climbed to enormous heights. Interest paid by the three levels of government amounted to over $76 billion in 2000, $73 billion in 2001 and is expected to be over $70 billion in the current year in spite of lower interest rates. The share paid by local municipalities was $3.9 billion in 2000 and $3.2 billion in 2001.

Funds borrowed from the BoC by the federal government cost a fraction of 1%. The government could and should allow municipalities the same privilege or reimburse them for the interest they pay to the BoC minus the cost of administration. The cost of borrowing privately can double the cost of a project (depending on the rate and the term) because interest compounds over time. More than that, the amount budgeted for capital projects can be many times higher than if the projects were financed through the BoC and paid back over the expected useful life of the projects (e.g., a sewer's life might be 50 years or more).

For example, Kingston's current debt stands at $50 million, financed through 10-year debentures at an average interest rate of 7%. Principal payments amount to $7 million per year and interest is $3 million for a total of $10 million per year. On the other hand, if the estimated life of the city's projects was 50 years, and if these projects were financed at low interest through the BoC, the cost could be spread over the 50 years and reduced to $1 million per year plus the cost of administering the loan. Asked why the FCM was dragging its feet on pursuing the BoC option for financing municipal capital projects, John Burrett, Manager, Economic and Social Policy, Federation of Canadian Municipalities, in a letter dated January 7/03 offered the conclusions the FCM staff reached in researching the matter:

"The current legislation does not allow loans directly from the Bank of Canada, nor is Bank of Canada lending interest free. Moreover, an in-depth study by the City of Toronto, in 2001, says: 'Given that loans from the Bank of Canada are not interest-free and not available directly to municipalities under the *Bank Act*, we believe that the lowest cost of funds and most

flexible terms can be achieved in competitive capital markets without resorting to federal loans or programs that could have higher interest rates and restrict the City's future financing program.'"

The full report of the FCM staff contains a letter to Paul Martin, dated May 7/01, from the Toronto City Council's Policy and Finance (P&F) Committee, which recommended that:

(1) The Federal Minister of Finance, in conjunction with the Province of Ontario, be requested to provide low cost, below prime, long-term loans to municipalities, such as through the Bank of Canada; and (2) a copy of this request be forwarded to the Federation of Canadian Municipalities and the Association of Municipalities of Ontario.

This clause was adopted by the City of Toronto at its regular meeting held on April 23, 24, 25, 26, 27, 2001, and its special meeting held on April 30, May 1 and 2, 2001. At the same time, the P&F Committee submitted the report (February 14, 2001) of the Chief Financial Officer and Treasurer (CFO&T), Wanda Liczyk, entitled *Loans from the Bank of Canada*, which did not support getting loans from the BoC:

"(1) In response to an inquiry from the City in 1998 the BoC stated that 'according to the *Bank of Canada Act*, section 18 permits us to conduct monetary policy as set out in our mandate and we have told several cities that, under existing legislation, we are not authorized to loan funds to municipalities';

"(2) The Act is silent concerning the rate of interest to be charged (for loans under Section 18 j), but according to Bank of Canada staff, the bank rate could be used.

"Summary:

"Given that loans from the Bank of Canada are not interest-free and not available directly to municipalities under the *Bank Act* (*Bank of Canada Act?*), we believe that the lowest cost of funds and most flexible terms can be achieved in competitive capital markets without resorting to federal loans or programs that could have higher interest rates and restrict the City's future financing program."

It is interesting that Council adopted the P&F committee's recommendation and sent it to Paul Martin in spite of the CFO&T's report, but nothing has come of it. The arguments used in the CFO&T report are the same as used in an earlier letter from Ms. Liczyk to a COMER member to which William Krehm replied on September 28, 2000:

"…Section 18(c) (of the *Bank of Canada Act*) states that the Bank may 'buy and sell securities issued or guaranteed by Canada or any province.' That provides a means of handling the long-term financing of such projects (capital projects for municipalities) at less than market rates."

Regarding the second point, loans from the Bank of Canada to Canada are effectively interest-free:

"As sole shareholder of the Bank of Canada, the federal government receives the profits of the Bank (net of undistributed earnings) as dividends. Hence the interest rates that the Bank of Canada cited to you would end up (over 95%) with the federal government. Our proposal is that a portion of the money received by Ottawa from those municipal loans be returned to the municipality as a quid pro quo for its observing federal standards in the projects financed."

This information was sent to Mr. Burrett with the following comments:

Rates for the Government of Canada (after the dividend to the federal government as the Bank's one shareholder is taken into account) have been as low as 0.37%. Rates could and should be low for provinces and municipalities, too, if the government were of a mind to refund the interest paid less the cost of administration. Otherwise, provinces and municipalities would be subsidizing the federal government.

These issues or arguments are political in nature and need to be dealt with politically. Canada would have to take the initiative to provide guarantees for municipalities and/or encourage provinces to do the same. The same can be said for the interest charged. If, as BoC staff have said, "under existing legislation, (BoC staff) are not authorized to loan funds to municipalities," it is only a matter of political will to adjust the legislation or regulations.

Organizing municipalities to lobby the government to do this would appear to be a role the FCM could carry out.

The FCM has replied that it will consider BoC financing as an option in its current research on methods of municipal finance, that it will pass on our information to its consultants and will be issuing a report in September (2003) at an FCM-sponsored conference on municipal finance. This provides an opportunity for getting solid support for Bank of Canada financing for municipal capital projects. COMER members all across Canada should do several things:

(1) Write to John Burrett, FCM, at jburrett@fcm.ca, letting the FCM know that this is a question of great importance to Canadians because our municipalities are strapped for funds for infrastructure, that we object to paying unnecessary interest to the private sector when financing through the BoC could be effectively interest-free and that we want the FCM to recommend to all its member municipalities that they send letters to the Prime Minister, the Minister of Finance and all the leadership candidates recommending that the government allow municipalities to get financing through the BoC for capital projects;

(2) Write directly to the Prime Minister, the Minister of Finance and all the leadership candidates recommending that the government allow municipalities to get financing through the BoC for capital projects;

(3) Send copies of your letters to your MP, MPP, municipal council and media.

It is because BoC financing is so political that the FCM was asked to recommend to its members (about 1000 municipalities) to write individually to the government requesting that it implement whatever is required to enable municipalities to get BoC financing for capital projects. This is a good time, politically, to act on this. It might be the kind of thing that the Prime Minister would like to leave as part of his legacy, and federal leadership candidates are more inclined to listen to proposals from their constituents (especially 1000 municipalities).

Is the FCM is going to act on this or let the opportunity pass by?

Richard Priestman

With So Much Risk-Insurance, Why Are its Citizens So Scared?

THE WALL STREET JOURNAL (24/4, "Why Do Americans Feel That Danger Lurks Everywhere?") has tackled a problem as fundamental as any the ancient philosophers and dramatists had to face:

"Scott Jordan is not averse to risk. He has flown a small plane, tried bungee jumping and skied on glaciers.

"But terrorism and severe acute respiration syndrome have him worried. Mr. Jordan, chief executive of a small Chicago apparel company, is likely to cancel his business trip to South Korea next month. 'If I go and some crazy decides to bomb the Hyatt, I'm dead,' he says.

"Mr. Jordan may not be reading his risk rationally. Even in 2001, when more than 3,000 people died in a terrorist attack on the US, he was 12 times as likely to lose his life on a highway as at the hands of a hostile fanatic, but who can blame him?

"Today, thanks to research labs, tort law and media hype, danger seems to lurk in every corner of life, from children's toys to McDonald's coffee, anthrax to second-hand smoke, West Nile virus to SARS. Faced with a barrage of warnings – including the color-coded caveats of the new Homeland Security department – it's not surprising that in contemporary America, the safest society in recorded history, many people feel as though they have never been more at risk.

"Armed with scientific and technological breakthroughs, Americans have dramatically reduced their risk in virtually every area of life, resulting in life spans 60% longer in 2000 than in 1900. Many deadly infectious diseases were tamed, food and water purified, drugs and surgery helped forestall heart attacks, and thousands of safety devices – window guards, smoke detectors, circuit breakers, air bags – protected against every day mishaps. Even the risk of financial disaster was reduced by insurance, pensions and Social Security.

"The very safety of modern life in the US may amplify our sense of loss. To die prematurely today may mean losing 40 years of life instead of 10. And while humans have learned to control much of their environment, there are periodically new, catastrophic threats against which they feel helpless, at least initially, such as AIDS, SARS, and anthrax."

You have to grade fear in categories that relate to the different support envelopes that we depend upon. Will the risk that confronts you leave your world unshattered to your children, to your culture? The answer is yes even if you lose your life skiing on glaciers or bungee jumping. If it occurs to you to even try such a thing, it expresses your confidence in several such security envelopes. You believe in modern technology, you are reassured that you command a piece of it, even if it was not the piece you gambled and lost on. At least you feel that you will be seen by some as something of a hero to have staked all on what is recognized as an occupation worthy of a hero. When you take that risk, you are relatively in charge of things. You have simply gambled big in a gambling society. But there are risks with fangs that bite far deeper, and put a crimp in the framework of certainties in which you played out the drama of your existence. That stage itself suddenly goes up in smoke.

SARS, for example, has rattled our confidence in science, which filled us with the certainty that we were so much the dominant species in creation itself that we could practically pension off God Himself as a supernumerary. And here other creatures with a few genes in their constitution, manage to re-design themselves transiting from our god-like bodies to that of pigs and ducks, travel on our breath and our insolvent airlines to our very citadels to do their mischief. The very arrogance of our kind has been upstaged by life forms visible only through electronic microscopes.

Not so long ago we had the reassurance of insurance to help us over such life-bumps. Back to the *WSJ* article to see how we are faring on that front: "Many corporations now do formal risk assessments of their vulnerability both to financial disturbances and to physical attacks on their offices or employees."

But in the real world supreme Re corporations – firms that take on the riskiest tranche of the risk assumed by ordinary insurance companies – are themselves in trouble. Since risk management has risen to the point of just falling short of a revealed religion, there is a message there that is struggling to get out. Behind all risk management is the assumption of orthodox economic theory about the wisdom of the self-balancing market. And because of that no serious questioning of it has been permitted in our halls of learning. So we are left with the anomaly of a free market theory supported by the monopoly position of that theory maintained by all means fair or foul. That is something that warrants not only fear but terror. However, it is rarely brought into the open, and suppressed, unfocussed fears can be far more damaging since we are unable to do anything about them. The disastrous effects can only be compared with what the menace of SARS would be if all the information and research on its origins and possible cures were suppressed. That destroys all the safety envelopes that we depend upon.

Then the *WSJ* piece goes on: "Perhaps the most terrifying aspect of risk now is that humans are actually manufacturing it – with nuclear power plants, the ozone hole, toxic water, global warming, nuclear weapons, even terrorism. Most of these systems are so huge, complex and relatively new, that the possible consequences of them are largely unknown." Indeed, conventional economists keep them beyond understanding, by declaring anything that does not fit into the "pure and perfect market" of their dogma as "externalities"– something that we do not choose to know.

William Krehm

ER Mail Bag

Dear Bill Krehm,

Many thanks for forwarding a copy of your recent book "Towards a non-autistic economy: a place at the table for society." I have just begun reading it and am very impressed with what I have read thus far. Would you have any objection if I recommended its purchase (with details of how to obtain it) and reproduced the table of contents to subscribers of the ERA information network?

The preface is an excellent summary of the economic causes of global disharmony. Something like this would make a great article for our network, although I imagine copyright constraints would make this impossible.

Hope all is well.

Best regards,

John Hermann
Economic Reform Australia
Network coordinator

We have, of course, assured our sister organization in Australia that they are free to use all our published material as their own.

Stocktaking of Our Lone Superpower

IN THE WAKE of the Iraq war we are being inundated with releases on new weaponry of destruction that threatens humanity's survival. To evaluate the score of this race already run, we need disciplines that for some time now have been not only absent but proscribed. Let us begin with the raw evidence.

Military Might

The media have simply run out of superlatives for the American military pre-eminence. *The New York Times* (27/04, p. 41, "American Power Moves Beyond the Mere Super" by Gregg Eastbrook) sums things up: "Stealth drones, G.P.S. – guided smart munitions that hit precisely where aimed; antitank bombs that guide themselves; space-relayed data links that allow squad leaders to know exactly where American and opposition forces are during battle – the US military rolled out all this advanced technology, and more, in its lightning conquest of Iraq. For years to come, no other nation is likely even to try to rival American might." One of the purposes of the Iraq war had nothing to do with Saddam Hussein's weapons of destruction. It was to display to the run-up powers how far the US has left them behind. And to claim the privileges that go with such a rating.

That, however, raises more problems than it solves.

"The global arms race is over. Now, only a nuclear state, like, perhaps North Korea, has any military leverage against the winner. Paradoxically, the runaway American victory in the conventional arms race might inspire a new round of proliferation of atomic weapons. More countries may seek these to gain deterrence. If it becomes generally believed that possession of even a few nuclear munitions is enough to render N. Korea immune from American force, other nations may place renewed emphasis on building them. Iran is an obvious candidate.

"The extent of American military superiority has become almost impossible to overstate. The US sent five of its nine super-carrier battle groups to the region for the Iraq assault. A tenth Nimitz-class super-carrier is under construction. No other nation possesses so much as one super-carrier, let along nine battle groups guarded by cruisers and nuclear submarines.

"The former Soviet navy did preliminary work on a super-carrier, but abandoned the project in 1992. Britain and France have a few small aircraft carriers. China decided against building one last year. If another nation fielded a threatening vessel, American attack submarines would simply sink it in the first five minutes of any conflict. Knowing this, all other nations have conceded the seas to the US. The naval arms race – a principal aspect of great-power politics for centuries – is over.

"The US possesses three stealth aircraft (the B-1 and B-2 bombers and the F-117 fighter) with two more (the F-22 and F-35 fighters) developed and awaiting production funds. A few nations have small numbers of heavy bombers; the US has entire wings of heavy bombers.

"No other nation has air-to-air missiles or air-to-ground smart munitions of the accuracy or numbers of the US. This month, for example, in the second attempt to kill Saddam Hussein, just 12 minutes passed between when a B-1 received the target coordinates and when the bomber released the four smart bombs to land just 50 feet and a few second apart. All four hit where they were supposed to. American aerial might is so great that adversaries don't even try to fly. In recent fighting in Iraq, not a single Iraqi rose to oppose US planes."

Soon after WWII the crisis in the relations of the US with the next rank of democratic powers became evident. *The New York Times* (20/04, "Europe Finds No Counterweight to US Power" by Tony Judy) begins with an anecdote: "In November, 1956, at the height of the Suez crisis, PM Anthony Eden of Britain telephoned his French counterpart, Guy Mollet. Under intense pressure from Washington, he explained, Britain was withdrawing from the British-French force that had just invaded Egypt. France would have to do likewise.

"Mollet was stunned; the decision by the Americans and the British had been taken without his knowledge and would be especially humiliating for France, already facing an armed revolt in its Algerian colony.

"But Konrad Adenauer, the German chancellor, visiting him at the time, sought to lift his spirits by pointing to the prospects for a future European community of nations. 'Don't worry,' he assured him, 'Europe will be your revenge.'

"Forty-seven years later, after another Middle Eastern war, Europe has just signed a treaty in Athens celebrating the formal accession of 10 countries and 75 million new citizens. The European Union is now the largest and richest bloc of nation-states in the world, collaborating closely on an extensive range of economic, social and legal practices.

"Europe's influence should be boundless. But the war in Iraq has reminded Europe – France and Germany especially – of the difficulty of countering America's armed reach with so-called soft power alone."

Not only did the US bribe some of the new candidates to the European Union for small change to join its coalition in the Iraq war, but Defence Secretary Rumsfeld dubbed countries such as Latvia and Malta "New Europe." This was in contrast with the "Old Europe" states like France and Germany. That aroused a curiosity about the vulnerabilities of absolute power among the "Old Europeans." They know their history better than the Pentagon.

How immense these vulnerabilities are appears from the detail that they received no attention in the US press. Only months after you could read serious analyses on the subject from India and elsewhere were the implications of the immense US foreign debt broached even in *The New York Times* and *The Wall Street Journal*. As a perk of its preeminence, Washington has been able to produce at a token cost the dollars to pay for its vast unfavourable trade balance. As early as 1999 Saddam Hussein had instructed the UN to shift Iraq's blocked oil accounts from dollars to euros. And with the subsequent 40-odd percent rise in the euro value in dollar-terms that earned them a handsome profit. The effect was not lost on the Iranians. Eventually it may lead to patriotic US speculators, hand on heart, shorting the dollar. This is nothing that will contribute to the stock market revival on which President Bush depends to meet the bills for the reconstruction of his first two Muslim conquests. That bodes ill for Washington's ability to finance the future military adventures into which it seems headed.

The Wall Street Journal (20/04, "True Cost of Hegemony: Huge Debt" by Niall Ferguson) provides some relevant statistics. "'Is the US hooked on foreign capital'? The answer is yes. Foreign investors now hold about two-fifths of the federal debt in private hands – double the proportion they held 10 years ago. At a recent press conference, Kenneth S. Rogoff, chief economist of the International Monetary Fund, referred to American financial dependence on foreign investors, saying that he would be 'pretty concerned' about a developing country that had gaping current account deficits year after year of 5% or more. Of course, he hastily added 'the US is not an emerging market.'

"Yet serving as an engine of global growth, aspiring to be a liberal empire, and yet acting like an emerging market: it's quite a combination. Is it sustainable? When the US sought to exercise power by financial means with its dollar diplomacy of the 1920s, substantial American capital was exported to the rest of the world. From 1960 to 1976, the US ran balance of payment surpluses totaling nearly $60 billion." Today, the debt of the US to foreigners is in the $8 trillion magnitude – within hailing distance of an entire year's GDP ($11 trillion).

That has imparted a nasty competitive edge to the letting out of contracts for Iraq's reconstruction. A major contract for some early chores – repairing the damage to the oil fields – has been let to Bechtel, a huge American corporation with much experience of eye-gouging in the world's oil fields. As the world economy continues to sicken, and the impatience of Iraqis with their foreign liberators is on the rise, those Iraq contracts become all the more important. Washington will have to switch from its militant unilateralism to some multilateralism to attract foreign financing for even its own contracts in Iraq and Afghanistan.

Dangerous Temptations for a Military Superpower Shedding Financial Preeminence

The American political process is being reshaped around two poles – one a source of dazzling success and the other a sink of deepening failure. Inevitably, power tends to shift to the fount of triumphs and away from the one delivering defeats. The mantra of preemptive intervention in lands with undemocratic regimes leaves the president enough discretion to use his doctrine to fix what is broken in the US itself. We have seen enough of the consequences of intervention in both Afghani-

stan and Iraq to realize that there will be no lack of terrorism to legitimize such a course. Immediately after September 11th, the President had to pull his foot out of his mouth after referring to his proposed anti-terrorist campaign as a "crusade" – an uncheering word to Muslim ears. Now he is acting out that very verbal gaffe. The possibility of preemptive intervention to unseat a series of ugly regimes once befriended by Washington will not soon run out. Better than money in the bank that meanwhile is getting scarce. And after lightning military operations with slight casualties come the life-renewing reconstruction contracts. A sort of productive destruction that not even Joseph Schumpeter envisaged. Or Henry Ford's production lines applied to military adventures.

Couched in the language of idealism and security, such a program may initially seem manageable. Like the stock market scams, it was not in the original intention of those in charge to be villains. The dubious conditions for ongoing success simply left them no alternative. To the smart deal-makers of Wall St.'s glory days left dolefully unemployed, problems of that sort seem a golden cinch. Besides in the growing economic chaos, any half-year deferment is readily mistaken for a solution – especially with a key election in the offing.

Infrastructure for Military Schumpeterism

After the unpleasant surprises of Afghanistan, Iraq, and Wall St., the Pentagon has lost no time in setting up the world infrastructure for such a program.

The Wall Street Journal (27/05, "Pentagon Prepares to Scatter Soldiers in Remote Corners" by Greg Jaffe) relates, "Manas Air Field, Kyrghystan – At this long-abandoned Soviet bomber base, the future of the US military is taking shape. Kyrghystan allowed the US and its coalition partners to station jets here in December 2001 to fight the Afghan war. US forces aren't preparing to pull out. Last month, the Pentagon leased 750 acres of land now populated with shoeless shepherds and curious children who race past on horses without saddles.

"This summer the US will begin installing water and sewer lines on the property. Next year plans call for erecting mobile homes, temporary offices and maybe a swimming pool. Col. James Forrest, the base's deputy commander, acknowledges, 'this place is so deep into Central Asia you'd hate to lose it.'

"The US presence in Kyrghystan reflects a major change over the past 18 months in the US vision of who its enemies are and how to confront them. This shift is pushing the US forces into far more remote and dangerous corners of the world.

"At the outset of the Bush administration, Pentagon planners and national security thinkers assumed China was the threat the US would worry about for years to come, and the military was adjusting accordingly. The danger, it is now assumed, lies in what Pentagon officials call an 'arc of instability' that runs through the Caribbean Rim, Africa, the Caucasus, Central Asia, the Middle East, South Asia and North Korea. Worries about this arc of countries, largely cut off from economic globalization, increasingly are influencing how the military trains, what it buys and where it puts forces.

"The more thinly US forces are spread around the globe, the

less prepared they will be to fight a war against a major power. Some military officials fret about the US becoming embroiled in several simultaneous conflicts.

"In many of its fights the US could be reliant on new friends with poor human-rights records and far-different values.

"The more thinly US forces are spread around, the less prepared they will be to fight a war against a major power largely unknown to us. 'We will have to make them familiar,' says Andy Hoehn, the deputy assistant secretary of defense for strategy. Mr. Rumsfeld, chastened by the unprecedented power of terrorists and the threat of weapons of mass destruction falling into the wrong hands, is preparing US forces for a future that could involve a lot of small, dirty fights in remote and dangerous places. The new strategy assumes that the US is far more likely to send troops into countries disconnected from the global economy, either because they reject the whole concept or because they lack the resources to compete, says Thomas Barnett, a Defence Department analyst. 'Disconnectedness defines danger,' he says.

Thinning Out

"Mr. Rumsfeld is pushing US forces out of their big bases in the US, Germany and South Korea, three countries that typically host more than 80% of the 1.4 million US troops. Instead, he envisions a force that will rotate through a large number of bases scattered throughout the world in places including Kyrghystan, the Philippines, Singapore, the Horn of Africa and Eastern Europe. In some of these places the US might post a few dozen troops who would keep the base in good condition and maintain equipment for use by troops that occasionally arrive for training. In case of war, these bases could be used as launching pads for strikes elsewhere.

"For years the Army's annual computer-simulated war game has focused on fighting a major war. This year, however, the forces didn't face any single simulated enemy. Instead, they juggled military actions in the Middle East, South-east Asia, and the Caucasus, while monitoring unrest in Latin America and Africa.

"In the simulated Southeast Asia conflict, set in 2015, a radical Islamic separatist group, supported by funds from the Middle East and the drug trade, seized large parts of a country allied with the US. These parts became breeding grounds for terrorists. The US forces swooped in quickly. They appeared to drive the enemy from the country, and then mounted attacks on rebel strongholds elsewhere. As soon as the US troops left the capital, however, the rebels – many of whom had simply taken off their uniforms and melded into the city of five million – re-emerged to storm the parliament, the government television station and the airport. 'We were never able to set up conditions to make these disaffected people fewer in number. We won and then we found we owned this nightmarish place,' says retired Vice Adm. Lyle Bien, who played commander of the US forces in Asia.

"The experience left a few, such as Adm. Bien, believing that the best course of action should have been not intervening at all. 'We're developing a force that makes it almost too easy to intervene, 'he said. 'I am concerned about America pounding herself out.'"

What is emerging from all the confusion is a new system – a military-economic complex that is not without historic precedents. There have been empires that lived by conquests especially among nomads fleeing drought or other mishaps. The Germans learned from Napoleon to treat military expenditures as investments rather than as current spending. It was successful enough in 1871, when the gold and silver they brought out of French mattresses as reparations contributed to a French as well as a German boom. In World War I bookkeeping that treated war costs as an investment rather than an expenditure helped prepare that famous post-war German hyperinflation that still haunts the EU and the US today.

The military and civilian systems are like the poles of a huge battery. The flow is strictly one-directional. This not only takes the form of the initial armament needed for the destruction of much of the economy of the country whose turn has come for the villain role for its unacceptable "weapons of destruction." The successive wars of liberation are increasingly driven by the reconstruction contracts to keep the home economy churning. Not only do they perk up the economy in a way acceptable to the stock market – expenditures on health, the environment education could have served the same purpose but don't pass muster by the dominant revenue's creed. They are also a powerful means of discipline for the next chapter of anti-terrorist activity of the Pentagon. One of the beauties of the Bush-Rumsfeld doctrine is that there is an almost endless inventory of governments that could stand democratizing and deterrorizing as the need arises. At the moment they may be classified as Neo-European Democracies, but the files of the CIA will not be lacking in evidence of the tyranny of their regimes. Washington knows many of these regimes well enough, for many are their own creations. The case of Saddam Hussein was an instance. Thus there was a nigh-seamless transition long before even the beginnings of reconstruction in Afghanistan to move on to Iraq. And even before power and water were restored there, the campaign has been started against the Iran regime.

Meanwhile, there is no shilly-shallying with the contracts to be let out. Thus in *The Wall Street Journal* (27/05, "Core Principles for a Free Iraq") Defence Secretary Rumsfeld, in an oped piece, minces no words: "Whenever possible, contracts for work in Iraq will go to those who will use Iraqi workers and to countries that supported the Iraqi people's liberation." This will teach the blighters to rally to Washington's call promptly in the next round.

With the whip of future "reconstruction" contracts, the US is likely to discourage too much aggressiveness among those powers who aspire to join that privileged reserve currency club, or those powers who shift to these other aspiring reserve currencies.

But Washington will win no popularity contests if it relies too exclusively on its armament superiority. A study of world history should be made a requirement for presidential candidates. And for Secretaries of Defence.

William Krehm

249

A Most Significant World Heterodox Conference

FROM JUNE 5-7 I attended the first triennial conference of the International Confederations for Pluralism in Economics (ICAPE) organized by Texas Christian University at the University of Missouri, Kansas City. And a most notable gathering it was on several counts. To begin with the incredibly magnificent campus of the UMKC, and the number of questing, open-minded members in its economics faculty came as a surprise. 28 of the 80 papers were from participants from outside the US – Australia, Austria, Belgium, Brazil, Canada, France, Germany, Ireland, Italy, Japan, the Netherlands, Sweden, Taiwan, and the UK. The various papers emphasized "an interdisciplinary, pluralistic, anthropological and qualitative, multidimensional, multi-agent approaches," "deploying economic metaphors in social and cultural analysis," and the use of economic theories and concepts "to analyze artworks and other cultural artifacts"; an interest in "identifying which heterodox economic discourses within the official discipline are opposed, reformulated, or extended by academic noneconomists and economic activists; "evidence of a looming *crisis of basic concepts* in which the limits to modern theory and a *technological attitude* are exposed, and the axiomatic project begins to totter." Papers dealt with or made reference to new branches of economics that have emerged – "experimental economics," "super-realistic economics," "feminist economics," and much, much else.

What was hardly to the fore was the matter of money creation and the emergence of deregulated, globalized financial institutions as the new brazenly dominant power centre, driving the world economy towards exponential growth. My paper, carried in the June issue *ER*, alone raised the point. And yet all the impressive enquiry along the whole social field will be frustrated for "lack of funds," since all of these non-marketed concerns must be financed by the government. All the plump chickens have but a single neck that can thus be dealt with on the one chopping block – the preemption of money creation for Wall St.'s gambles.

18 of the approximately 80 papers read dealt explicitly with Marxist economic analysis. It would seem that the view may prevail in supreme spheres that because of the collapse of the Soviet Union, Karl Marx is a lesser menace than some things to be found in American history and even in legislation still on the books. Without the latter, the impressive researches on just everything else can be tolerated like kids playing in a sand-box.

However, lifting the world out of its current blood-soaked rut is going to require a whole spectrum of heroism of individuals and institutions. It was significant that most of the American participants hold teaching posts in some of the thousands of lesser US universities. And it must be left to those who take the risks to judge the exposure they can survive. Rather than criticize what was not covered in the conference, we must applaud what was. There was, for example James Galbraith, son of John Kenneth and professor at the Christian University of Texas, who announced his part in founding an organization of economists

against preemptive warfare. He also made the important point that the practical application of Keynesian theory was devised mostly in the United States.

Between the official conference sessions another equally valuable get-together took place. Participants, aware of what had not been dealt with adequately, exchanged views, references, and addresses.

ICAPE is only one of a bumper harvest of such conferences being held throughout the world. They are helping equip us for the trials ahead.

William Krehm

Standing on our Heads to Balance that Self-balancing Economy

THERE WOULD SEEM TO BE some persistent logic in standing on our heads to balance those unbalanceable self-balancing markets. A touch of super-salesmanship will have no difficulty in convincing you that up is down and down is up, and that you can valuate public companies into the billions of dollars on the share of the market they have conquered rather than by their non-existent earnings. To get over that road bump the Enrons got their auditors to declare the "times earning" accountancy "old hat." With some consistency, this happened, just as Rumsfeld was to declare Germany and France "Old Europe," overshadowed by New Europe – lands like Albania and Macedonia who hopped onto the war-wagon against Iraq. Once you stand on your head a lot of things fall into place – liabilities can become assets, and assets are either puffed up or hidden. There are some complications, however. Once you stand on your head things keep falling out of your pockets. There is no end of the mega scams that go on being discovered even though the Enron investigations have been going on for two years or more.

And there is no end to the upside-downside effect. *The Wall Street Journal* (2/5, "After Inflating Their Income Companies Want IRS Refunds" by Rebecca Blumenstein, Dennis K. Berman and Evan Perez) suggests that like Hollywood's sexiest stars of bygone generations, the big ex-stars of Wall St. simply won't stay out of the headlines: "A parade of big companies is under investigation for inflating their earnings during the stock market boom of the 1990s. Now some of them see an unusual silver lining: They want back the taxes they overpaid along the way.

"In the latest wrinkle in the unfolding series of corporate scandals, MCI and Enron Corp. are in the process of collecting or filing for tax refunds or credits from the Internal Revenue Service because of tax payments on billions of dollars they falsely claimed to have earned. Qwest Communications International Inc., which plans to restate $2.2 billion in revenue, also is likely to seek a refund. Embattled HealthSouth Corp., accused of overstating its earnings by more than $2 billion, said that it hasn't made a final decision to file for a refund but is considering it."

Busy Season for Ethics Experts

But meanwhile, we can draw a provisional conclusion. Part of the great surplus that President Bush gloried in was not only due to dubious profits that Wall St. firms had separated their trusting clients from with hyped-up analyses of the stocks they were peddling, but to the profits that weren't even there. So Washington is not only faced with returning refunds on yesterday's Wall St. killings to cover stock market losses of the last two years, but to hand back the taxes paid by companies convicted of cooking books to the public.

So it is busy season for the ethics specialists. "Fraud or not, the current tax code makes no distinctions. It is a basic tenet of tax laws – both for individuals and corporations – that those who overpay are entitled to a refund. With the number of corporate scandals and expected financial restatements at a historic high, no one knows just yet how much the federal government could forfeit on the refunds and credits. Even if such credits are ultimately lowered as part of settlements, observers believe that the federal government will probably be out hundreds of millions of dollars.

"Investigations into fraud at MCI, which recently changed its name from WorldCom Inc., have uncovered accounting irregularities expected to reach $11 billions. The fraud masked two years of losses at the country's second-largest long-distance company during the height of the telecommunications and technology boom of the late 1990s."

Meanwhile charges have been filed against principal actors of Enron. This is "part of an effort by prosecutors to bear down on former Enron Chairman Kenneth Lay and former CEO Jeffrey Skillings, who haven't yet been charged." The prosecution is approaching the biggest players as the US army hoped to nab Saddam Hussein, by doing deals with lieutenants that could produce evidence against the leader. The indictments name for the first time Joseph Hirko and Kenneth Rice, both former chief executives of Enron Broadband Services, the fiber-optic unit that was heavily hyped by company officials as a money-making breakthrough.

"The government said that Messers Rice and Hirko, as well as former EBS chief operating officer Kevin Hannon and two former senior vice presidents, Scott Yeager and Rex Shelby, engaged in a concerted plan to promote 'ground-breaking broadband technology' that the government says never existed.

"Dan Boyle, former vice president of global finance, was added to a previous indictment of Enron Chief Financial Officer, Andrew Fastow. Bill Rosch. Mr. Boyle's attorney, said that prosecuting his client was tantamount to 'prosecuting the piano-player in a whorehouse."

And that was a subject that inevitably had to come up. It was highly appropriate then that the papers of the same day should have reported the emergence of that blushing branch of the sagging economy in Australia. Habitually walking on their heads – by our limited geographical criteria – should make our Australian cousins more nimble in turning things upside down, doing with ethics what Wall St. did so effortlessly switching liabilities into assets and that sort of thing. The Toronto *Globe and Mail* (5/02, "Aussie IPO cashes in on naked greed"

by Sinclair Stewart) reports: "The world's first publicly traded brothel opened with a bang in its stock-market debut. The Daily Planet, which bills itself as the only 'six-star hotel' in Australia offers sex on its room-service menu, celebrated its listing with a promotional appearance of Heidi Fleis as the notorious Hollywood madam who once served a sentence for tax evasion. Given the state of international markets, analysts said small investors may have been lured by the staying power of the world's oldest profession.

"Room fees, which are payable to the Daily Planet are $115 per hour. Another charge of $115, called a ladies fee, goes directly to the individual sex worker. The company boasts that its hygiene levels are comparable to those of most hospitals. He might have made the point more aptly comparing its morality with that of the more conventional listings on the stock market. If the *Decalogue* were brought up to date as Secretary Rumsfeld has Europe (the New Decalogue superseding the Old) it is a moot point whether the combination of puritanic sex and licentious financial bookkeeping would rate higher or lower than puritanic bookkeeping and licentious sex." However, we will probably be offered a derivative covering you if your guess on the point was wrong. Or you might be able to offer St. Peter Daily Planet options for stretching the point. Thanks to our cousins in the Antipodes for offering us a new angle of vision on these ethical problems that would otherwise have us buffaloed.

William Krehm

A Suicide Bomber Abetted by Governments — Deflation

WE HEAR A GOOD DEAL of artfully disguised suicide bombers who work their way into crowded busses, dancing halls, and taverns to blow themselves up and kill innocent people. To unmask their real identify the Americans are employing every sort of technology, high and low. We applaud such precautions. For terrorism strikes at the very heart of democracy and even of plain survival. Nobody fails to see the connection when President Bush's marching plan for peace between Israel and the Palestinians is derailed because suicide bombers have moved in with successful strikes. The newspaper readers are not astonished when they read that one of the bombers owed his success to his disguise as an orthodox Jew. That is all part of the war game, and we mustn't be caught napping.

But on another front, governments of the anti-terror camp are actually abetting such disguises that could create more innocent victims in the same struggle.

Only now is talk beginning of deflation which is actually what is undermining economies throughout the world and leaving growing armies of desperate unemployed in its wake. Even today the talk by many economists and central banks is still of inflation, and how much of it can be allowed.

Listen to *The Wall Street Journal* (09/05, "In Shift, ECB Moves to Tackle Deflation Fears" by G. Thomas Sims): "Frankfurt – In a subtle yet significant shift, the European Central Bank (ECB) said that it will aim to keep inflation in the 12 nations that use the euro to 'close to 2%.' In the past the ECB said inflation should hover in a lower range of between zero and 2%. The announcement comes after a months-long internal review and still leaves the ECB one of the world's strictest central banks. The move disappointed critics who had hoped the ECB would tolerate higher inflation, but it allayed fears that the banks would keep such a tight lid on inflation that the euro-zone economy could inadvertently slip into a long period of falling prices."

But isn't that like fighting terror in Israel by prescribing the maximum length of the side locks of the suicide bombers disguised as orthodox Jews? Could you conduct a campaign against terrorism without even mentioning the word "terrorism"?

To get to the routes of such suicidal nonsense we must go back to a boner in elementary logic that would flunk a freshman in a philosophy or science course, but underlies many Ph.D. theses in economics departments. It is the assumption that because a proposition might be valid read from left to right, it is automatically right read backward. If a man holds a loaded pistol to his temple and pulls the trigger, he falls dead. But from that you can't conclude that if a man falls dead, a shot has been fired to his head.

Some propositions can, indeed be flipped over like pancakes in McDonald's. But whether they can or not depends on their structure. Such problems of structure occupied mathematicians of the 19th century more than any other – group theory, matrix theory. If you identified the same structure of symmetry and asymmetry in a problem of geometry and, in the most remote other field at the same time, you could solve both problems in one stroke. That in itself proved that there was nothing more basic in mathematical analysis than structure. It was nothing to be trifled with. But economists take a different approach. Other things being equal, if the demand for a certain commodity on a given market exceeds the available supply, its price will go up. But from that we cannot assume that if the price of the given commodity has gone up, it means that the demand for it has exceeded supply. It might be true, but part of the price rise or even all of it the price rise could be due entirely or in part to the fact that the government has raised taxes to combat terrorism, or SARS, or to fight a war in Iraq, or because the government has still not introduced serious accountancy into its books and when it invests money to educate more doctors or nurses, the cost of that is paid off in a single year and then carried on its books at zero value. Yet obviously the investment in such human capital will go on yielding important returns for decades and even generations.

So far the picture is pretty bad, but then it becomes still worse. A quarter of a century or so ago, higher interest rates were declared the only blunt tool at the disposal of our central banks to fight what was seen as "inflation." Obviously, higher interest rates will not make any of these major problems disappear.

The one or two percent of inflation that the Bundesbank will or won't allow is almost certainly not inflation – that is, an excess of demand over available supply, but is part of the increased layer of taxation in price raised to pay for essential public services. Not recognizing it as such is to mistake the terrorist suicidal bomber for a real orthodox Jew. You cannot have two entirely distinct and even contradictory factors designated by the same name unless you are out to confuse the problem rather than to solve it.

Cottbus Shrinks While the EU Fights "Inflation"

There is no need to wrestle with abstract theoretical concepts in dealing with the inflation-deflation ambiguity. Right under the nose of the German Government in Berlin, a mere couple of hours drive to the south is the ancient town of Cottbus. Its sad story symbolizes the highly non-inflationary future of much of Germany (*The Globe and Mail,* 20/05, "Barren city an ominous warning to the rest of the EU" by Doug Saunders): "At first glance Cottbus looks like an orderly and prosperous old German city, with cobblestone streets, and brightly painted 18th century buildings along a winding stretch of the river Spree. But as you stroll through the city's squares and laneways something begins to feel amiss. There are surprisingly few cafes, and a lot of buildings seem unoccupied. You begin to wonder where all the people are. Cottbus, in what used to be called East Germany, is a dramatic victim of what the Germans call shrinkage, a crisis of depopulation rooted in the declining birth rates afflicting all Europe. The city's population has dropped from 130,000 to little more than 100,000 a decade ago and is losing 7% each year. Most of the city's quaint but almost deserted historic center is maintained by the government at a cost of millions. Most of the residents live not in the fake 'centre city,' but in a wasteland of half-empty concrete apartment blocks on the outskirts of town. The government is spending millions reducing the infrastructure. The city is struggling to reduce the size of its sanitation and water system, whose pipes carry unused stagnant water. More than 5,000 apartment units are being taken apart piece by piece." Hardly an excess of demand here.

"The depopulation crisis is threatening to wreak havoc on the European Union as it expands to the Russian border over the next several months. The reduced population does not provide enough tax revenues to pay pensions for the aging. The Eastern European states have suffered the most acute population drop. Bulgaria's population fell by two million over the past 10 years.

"Across Europe, people fear their cities will become like Cottbus. So scholars from all from all the continent are coming there to study its depopulation at a conference entitled "Public Space in the Time of Shrinkage." Two weeks ago, a similar conference of civic administrators was held in a nearby town, attracting people from a half-dozen countries.

"Germany's fertility rate is 1.34 children per woman, far below the two needed to maintain a stable population without immigration. It is the second-lowest reproduction rate of Western European nations, beaten only by the Italians, with 1.23 children per woman. Across the European union the average is 1.47."

Given this, it shows how out of sync German monetary policy is in fighting inflation defined as an excess of demand. It should be employing its available workers to the fullest to prepare for their own retirement, as well as for the those who will precede them in leaving the work force.

William Krehm

The Missing Parts of our Jigsaw Puzzle

THE DEFINITION of a survival crisis? When you can find spread across the front page of your opinion-dictating newspaper what a few months ago you couldn't get published in a letter to the editor.

By that criterion a major crisis is on its way. *The Globe and Mail* (3/05, "Cutbacks fed SARS calamity, critics say" by Carolyn Abraham and Lisa Priest) minces no words: "Just 16 months before SARS hit Toronto, the Ontario government deemed the last of its leading scientists redundant and sent them packing as it scoffed at the prospect of any new disease threatening the province. The timing of government layoffs on October 18, 2001, left five top microbiologists in utter disbelief. Walkerton's tainted-water scandal was a fresh memory. Bioterror threats loomed after September 11 and the West Nile virus had made its Ontario debut.

"But the Ontario government declared that the province no longer needed their scientific expertise, insisting there were no new tests to develop: 'Do we want five people sitting around waiting for work to arrive?' said Gordon Haugh, a Health Ministry spokesman. 'It would be highly unlikely that we would find a new organism in Ontario.'

"This February, a new organism turned out to be just a plane flight away."

That is certainly an important missing part of our jigsaw puzzle. But you will not put the puzzle together with a single piece. Here are some other absent parts that somebody has cunningly dropped under the table: Why would the Ontario Health Ministry be so perverse in firing key scientific workers just not too long after the same government had been caught with its pants down in the Walkerton water contamination? Because the grants of the Ottawa government to the provinces had been slashed. And why would the federal government do such an thing? Because in 1991 the preceding Conservative government of Brian Mulroney had bailed out our banks from their speculative losses in oil, gas and real estate by doing away with the statutory reserves, a modest percent of the deposits it held from the public in chequing and short-term accounts that used to be put up with the central bank. These deposits earned them no interest. However, in return, the banks not only got periodic bailouts by the Bank of Canada (i.e., by its sole shareholder) as donor of the last resort. The reserves served two other important purposes: they gave the central bank an alternative to increasing the interest it charged the banks for short-term loans

to cool down the economy when supposedly needed. Elsewhere in this issue we give the details of this lurid tale.

Indirectly the federal government is as a result required to pay some $5 to $8 billion each year for borrowing from the money market what they used to get from the Bank of Canada at virtual zero rates. That ripped a huge hole in the federal budget. And here we have another key missing piece to our jigsaw. It was to plug the resulting deficit in its own accounts that the federal grants to the provinces were brutally and brainlessly cut. And that, amidst much else, led to the dismissal of the microbiologists now reported in screaming headlines.

To complete the picture, the real hero of that episode and hence of the shocking state of unpreparedness of the health authorities of Ontario was the Finance Minister of the then new Liberal government, Paul Martin. Taking his instructions from Bay St., he concentrated on "balancing the budget." It is for this achievement that he earned himself the gratitude of Bay St. and the funds for a cake-walk to the PM post.

More amazing still, immediately after this reverse bank heist, the banks were further deregulated so that they could acquire brokerages, and engage in all the high-jinx connected with the stock market.

The same gentleman was one of the promoters of Globalization and Deregulation without which SARS couldn't have happened. For that replaced subsistence agriculture in backward countries like China with production for the export market based on living and dying conditions that practically put livestock and peasants under the one roof. And all this a hop away from other continents. The promised efficiencies now turn out to have been largely for the cross breeding of viruses amongst swine, fowl, and humans.

And, of course, in terms of mileage, environmental pollution, and the undermining of non-commercial cultures, the consequences have long been evident. Paul Martin's boasted budget surpluses were as fraudulent as Enron's maximization of the shareholder's equity. To know how the budget was doing, you would have to include in your accountancy the consequences of dismantling vital public services like microbiological research. Meanwhile, looking ahead, we must consider the cross-breeding of the individual catastrophes. We still have to consider what might happen when SARS bounces off the unspeakable conditions in "liberated" Baghdad. where five million people are living week after week without potable water or power. This could well lead to the modern equivalent of the 14th century Black Death on a world-wide setting. Only when this is done, will we have an inkling of the extent of the problem before us.

It is time then that we started digging up the DNA chain of the policy disasters inflicted on the world by a failed economic system.

William Krehm

Teaching — A Tool

WHEN CHRISTOPHER COLOMBUS was searching for help to find a westerly and thereby a shorter route to China, the teaching in European schools was: Planet Earth is round and flat like a pancake, Planet Earth is huge, much bigger than any other body in the Universe, Planet Earth is the centre of the universe. Also, since Newton had not yet made his calculations, they taught the orbits to be perfect circles.

There was, however, a small number of scientist "teachers" who questioned the flat earth concept. Two of these were Copernicus and Galileo. Both were mathematicians and astronomers, and in studying the sun, the moon and the "lesser planets," they realized that the planets and the sun were spinning yet always presented a full circular "face." This observation led to the conclusion that these bodies had to be globular in shape. The obvious conclusion, to them, was that the planet earth is not an exception but also globular in shape; and in studying orbits, they realized that the sun, not planet earth is at the centre of our universe. Publishing this opinion led to excommunication for both these "teachers." In those days, that was very severe punishment.

Because of this challenge to their concept of a flat earth as the centre of the universe, that teaching system went on to cause the formation of the Flat Earth Society, whose primary purpose was to oppose the "heretic" teaching. That society grew tremendously and exists to this day, perpetuating and protecting those flat earth concepts.

Our present teaching system is an outgrowth of that European schooling system. Indeed we continue to use, in our daily lives, almost without a thought, the flat earth concept terms "sunrise: and "sunset." Both are false and deceptive, especially to young children, who have to relearn later the fact that the sun does not rise. Instead, the illusion is a result of the spin of the planet earth. How many other false concepts are being perpetuated is anybody's guess, but that influence must be found and eliminated. Our teaching needs to be completely separated from that 500 plus years old system.

Columbus rightly assumed and sailed southwest from Spain to avoid Iceland, Greenland and Vineland in his search for a shorter route to China. However, he mistakenly labelled the natives of the Caribbean Islands as Indians, because he wrongly assumed he had sailed too far south, missed China, and landed on an Indian island. But again our teaching system has failed, so far, to drop the "Indian" connotation of Native North Americans. Why can't we accept their own words? They are Mohawk, Cree, Iroquois, Cherokee, etc.

If the Flat Earth Society has managed to persist for over 500 years teaching their concepts and we the students have not, in that same time, been able to stop falsely calling our natives Indians, even with their efforts to correct us, what kind of teachers and students are we? What other false concepts are we accepting as valid and living with daily?

To me the success of the Flat Earth Society for such a long time is a good example of teaching, a tool being used successfully in a brainwashing process. There are many examples of brainwashing being used especially in religious cults – some small and some not so small. Two outstanding examples come to mind. One was that group which left the USA to reestablish itself in a northern South American country. Those poor souls committed mass suicide, on dictate from some leader, when confronted with an investigating group, which included USA government officials. The other dramatic cult death was in the south central USA, just a few years ago, although that deadly fire was of questionable origin.

Yes, we can and do learn a lot through our teaching system, but we cannot ignore the fact that this wonderful system can, has been over the millennia, and is today being used to establish and perpetuate falsehood, usually for the benefit of a rich, greedy, egotistic, power-hungry person or group.

Andrew Dwornick

REVIEW OF A BOOK BY MARJORIE DEANE
AND ROBERT T. PRINGLE, HAMISH HAMILTON,
LONDON, 1994

The Central Banks

THIS IS A REMARKABLE BOOK. Since it is in no way unfriendly to the central banking community, its revelation of the fragility of its claims to omniscience are all the more convincing. This feature turns up early in the introduction of Paul Volcker, the most aggressive of central bankers ever, who almost drove the world economy onto the rocks in the early 1980s with his final solution of the inflation problem: "It is a sobering fact that the prominence of central banks in this century has coincided with a general tendency towards more inflation, not less. By and large, if the overriding objective is price stability, we did better with the 19th century gold standard and passive central banks, with currency boards, or even with 'free banking.' The truly unique power of a central bank, after all, is the power to create money, and ultimately the power to create is the power to destroy."

No such sobering reflection was in the air in 1979 when newly appointed Governor Volcker hastily left an IMF meeting in Belgrade, with a stop-off at Hamburg, the home town of the German Chancellor, Helmut Schmidt. In Volcker's own words, "Schmidt, at his irascible worst, left his visitors in no doubt that 'his impatience with what he saw as American neglect and irresolution about the dollar had run out.' It was then that Volcker knew it was time to get back to his desk."

That not only gives you the measure of Washington' humiliation after Vietnam. Why the panicky adoption of the deflationary paranoia of the Germans that had brought them Hitler and WWII? Driving up the commercial rates into the 20% left no elbow-room for analysis of the new patterns of price inevitable under the mixed economy that had developed.

The 1923 hyperinflation, to be sure, had been a nightmare. It took wheelbarrowful of marks to buy a mug of beer. But it had been brought on by French army occupying the Ruhr, Germany's industrial heartland, to collect reparations. That unleashed a nation-wide strike supported by the entire nation from the

Communists to the future Nazis. In its most fateful economic decision the Fed in 1979 practically obeyed the diktat of the memory-haunted Bundesbank. Yet the US had not lost WWI and the French had not occupied Pittsburgh. It was just that central bankers acted as though they had and bamboozled governments and academics. Since the mid-1970s they warned that any rise in the price level no matter how slight would unleash a hyperinflation such as that of Germany in 1923. The implication was that if the German government had raised interest rates sufficiently there would have been by a retrospective miracle, no war, no occupation of the Ruhr, no virtual civil war.

Volcker's misadventure – handed down as a victory in central banking lore – left lasting damage. It gave big-time speculators a taste for blood, and left our bailed-out and deregulated banks turning their backs on their traditional banking business to gamble their heads off in every aspect of the stock market. It was a period when retired people spent an inordinate amount of time in search of highest short-term rates for the money that they had to put out. Overlooking that higher interest rates are a sure sign of higher risk, many lost their savings. Government-backed deposit insurance – real or supposed – was relied upon to shield them against losses. That, and bailing out banks every decade or so, became one of the few legitimate purposes of government recognized by conventional economists.

Leverage in speculation became, not only a virtue, but even a sign of genius if conducted on a big enough scale. So long as the investment did not end up in dust.

Concentrating on Short-term Rates

The book reports: "The Fed's previous focus on short-term-interest rates – specifically, the federal funds rate, the price at which American banks lend overnight to each other – was jettisoned for more direct control of money supply through a focus on bank reserves. In short, the Federal Reserve shifted from controlling the price of money to controlling its quantity.." This is of particular interest to Canadians since little more than a decade later their *Bank Act* was revised to do away with statutory reserves altogether. Volcker in fact adopted Milton Freeman's distrust of government control of financial institutions in any shape and form to let "the market decide."

Yet on page three of the book we read: "If a date is sought for when central banks started to come in from the cold, it must be put around 1980, or, more cautiously, in the second half of the 1970s. If was then that the major industrial powers retreated from the belief that economic policymaking should focus on the avoidance of unemployment by targeting specified growth rates of output. It was then that they turned instead to inflation control through the management of credit, interest rates and exchange rates." There is then a contradiction between the two versions of the change around 1980 – if you are focusing on the control of the money supply through reserves, the emphasis is not on interest rates. If however, as did the Fed, you are keeping the money supply relatively static and letting interest rates find their own level, you are simply ducking responsibility for shoving up interest rates to hysterical heights. That is a sample of the technique of both the Fed and the Bank of Canada. Never do

they openly and honestly abandon a failed policy. They just sidle out of it under a cloud of verbiage. It is a shortcoming of the book that this feature of central bank parlance is not examined.

In good time the disastrous nature of trying to flatten prices became clear. The Fed retired to short-term rates as its main method, though it did keep an eye on price indexes – with a 2% tolerance, and used the federal fund rates [the rate banks charge one another for overnight loans to meet their immediate obligations] as an active instrument. This however did not prevent the Bank for International Settlements from preaching zero inflation as the only means of preventing a recurrence of the German hyperinflation of 1923.

And while all this was going on, a vast campaign was underway for the recognition of the independence of the central banks from their government. It mattered little what the central bank charters might say. I remember receiving a letter from an academic economist, whose name I have charitably forgotten. Between us there had been no previous contact. He offered COMER the advice, that though we may question orthodox theory, that was still no reason for ignoring the "scientific finding" that independent central banks were more efficient than those dependent on government. "Science" on this occasion turned out to be a poll among academic economists on the matter. In any other academic discipline, such "science" would not even be used as a rag to wash the floor with.

The Deane and Pringle book, to its credit keeps a discreet distance from such science. Thus (p. 5): "Evidence (on the merits of independence of central banks) is mixed. "True, countries with 'strong' (i.e., largely independent central banks – America, Germany, Switzerland) – have done well in keeping inflation low or at least better than average. But so, too, has Japan whose central bank, although less under the thumbs of the finance ministry in practice than on paper, is still far from a free agent. Also France, with a central bank then totally controlled by the government and notoriously subject to political influence, has managed from time to time to get its inflation rate below Germany's. On the face of it, it is easier to make out a case *against* independence.... As we shall stress in later pages, if a central bank is given some freedom from government, it should be by way of a very specific mandate that puts its reputation on the line. It is imperative that the demarcation lines be very clear.

"The Deutsche Bundesbank saw in 1990 that its famed independence, mandated by law, offers it little protection against political forces on big questions. Disagreement with Chancellor Kohl over the financing of German reunification made the Bundesbank feel it had lost face and caused the central banking stage to lose one of its most colourful figures, Karl Otto Poehl, who resigned after the clash. In fact the US Fed is careful not to push its luck too far," and so forth.

But like the tip of a lady's petticoat, we catch a glimpse of the real fact behind the "independence" of the central banks. "To the extent that governments now look to the financial and capital markets for their borrowing needs, the objectives of state policy can be more effectively pursued if central banks appear independent.... Then the real power struggle could come into the open. Already it seems clear that giving monetary policy to central banks means also giving [them] priority over tax policy; in a conflict, monetary policy would prevail. And it wasn't just monetary policy that governments have given up, but all instruments for steering the economy.

"Governments, increasingly, were seen as just another group of borrowers competing with other borrowers and flaunting their wares to attract the all-powerful institutional investors. The state, increasingly, was simply being by-passed. Governments' authority over the markets steadily diminished. As Richard O'Brien, chief economist at American Express in London expressed it in a 1992 booklet: 'A truly global market knows no internal boundaries, and pays scant attention to national aspects. The nation becomes irrelevant, even though it will still exist.'

"The role of traditional banking – deposit-taking and lending – was declining. There was an increase in alternative forms of financing – notably through the issue of securities by firms and governments able to tap these markets. Meanwhile banks were pushed into higher-margin, higher-risk activities. The new markets were slippery, shadowy, hard to define and yet harder to control, full of pitfalls and strange devices. The globalization of services was led by banks, securities markets and other financial services companies. So firms everywhere had access to highly liquid international markets – both depositing money and borrowing, and availing themselves of the new products developed on the basis of 'derivatives' – such as options and futures…. Nobody could really say whether these markets had increased the risks of the financial system. It was reasonably clear that the markets had far greater resources than any government or central bank. That meant in turn that a return to fixed exchange rates was out of the question (except perhaps in clearly defined regional blocs)."

Practically never is there a reference to happenings in the real economy that may be contributing to changes in money supply and price levels. Thus (p. 83) "Average money supply growth in industrial countries was between 9 and 12% in every year of the 1970s except 1974. Then it dipped briefly to 7.8%. In some countries such as Britain, Italy, Spain, Ireland and Finland money growth exceeded 20% in one or more years as measured by growth of 'narrow' money. Even in Germany and France, the money supply in some years grew by 14-15 %. Prices rose steeply – in Britain prices rose by 24% in 1975, Even people who had previously denied there was any link between money and price started having second thoughts."

Second thoughts are fine and necessary things, but they should not be confined to seeking out unrecognized relationships between the two or three factors already recognized. There was the relationship between the velocity of money and the quantity of it and the average price of the volume of production. There was the high oil prices due to the oil embargo. But completely neglected was the amount of public capital investment which means immediate expenditures of investment capital that would not come back in finished goods for many years. That turns up as more government investment outlay (treated as current spending and covered by additional taxation). There is a second disregard of this investment when it turns up in the GDP not once but twice – once as government spending for materials and wages, and the second time in the layer of all taxation that directly or indirectly finds its way into the consumer national product. We have then a double *glitsch* – the one-year write-off of government investment that enters into the year's government spending covered by taxes or left as debt, and the second appearance of such government spending – when spent by the private sector in their tax payments. It just happens that the 1960s were years of unusually heavy capital investments of governments throughout the world and hence the double counting cum one-year writeoffs of government investments distorted the expansion figures far more than usual. This quite apart from the oil embargo and the added costs due to the high-interest rate response of the central banks.

There is no possibility of managing the money supply in a reasonably positive way, without understanding what goes on at the real product level in a mixed economy. Only after that has been done can the arguments on the role of money supply take on any serious relevance to our problems.

William Krehm

The Plight of the States

THE EFFECTS on junior levels of government of the collapse of Washington's "solid fundamentals" are ominous. For state rights have played a key role in the American saga from the Constitutional Congress through the Civil War to the Florida vote count in the last presidential election.

The Wall Street Journal (7/10, "Fiscal Crises Force States to Endure Painful Choices" by Russell Gold and Robert Gavin) writes: "Late last month, pharmacy cashier Janet Mata got some bad news from the Indiana Family and Social Services Administration. Her monthly $238 child-care voucher will end Oct. 20. If she can't find cheaper day-care for her 5-year-old son and two-year-old daughter, she'll need to quit her part-time job and go on welfare.

"In Massachusetts, cuts to the public health budget have left a Boston group that provides free flu shots with only 2,500 vaccines, half as many as two years ago." This was not in some war-torn African country, but in one of the founding states of the world's superpower.

"The public is feeling the pinch as state governments confront their worst fiscal crises in years. At least 46 states struggled to close a combined $37 billion deficit in their most recent year. And this year's gap is even wider: a combined $58 billion deficit. Most states, unlike the federal government, are required by law to balance their books at the end of their one or two-year budget cycles. That forces them to slash spending, raise taxes, or spend reserve funds.

"The last time states faced a budget crisis this deep was in 1983. That led to several years of higher taxes and cuts in health-care and other programs. But this time the pain is likely to be deeper and more widespread. The reason: State budgets play a larger role in funding education and social services than they did back then. It's a legacy of the Reagan administration, which championed sending money and power back to the state capitols. Congressional mandates have since reinforced the trend, requiring states to fund expanded medical assistance programs for the poor, while courts have required states to pick up a growing share of school costs." This was part of the Washington consensus that lost no time in blowing into Canada with killer effect.

"So far, states have opted mainly for draining their reserves and one-time fixes. Some have deferred maintenance projects or tapped some of the $208 billion the tobacco industry agreed in 1998 to pay for treating ill smokers." Gambling taxes have gone up as well. You wonder what would happen, were smokers to become more prudent, and gamblers more virtuous.

"With hope fading that a resurgent economy will replenish revenue anytime soon, states no longer can avoid deeper spending cuts or higher taxes. And that will weigh on the overall US economy. UBS Warburg estimates that closing the $58B gap could erase 0.6% from GDP.

"How did the states get into this mess?"

"In the 1990s the states grew accustomed to free-flowing revenue. It came from free-flowing capital gains, and other taxes inflated by stock-market gains and fat overtime checks which underwrote increases in consumption. Lawmakers responded by enacting popular spending programs and eliminating unpopular taxes. From 1995 to 2001, consumer prices rose an overall 16%, but the Indiana budget, for example, ballooned 48%. 'The assumption was that somehow the business cycle had been repealed,' says Indiana Chamber of Commerce President Kevin Brinegal.

"At the same time, states' tax bases kept shrinking. Internet shopping, for example, took off in the mid-nineties, but the federal courts prevented the states from collecting sales taxes on most [of such] purchases."

"None of this mattered until 2000, when a weakening economy started slowing revenue growth. By April this year personal income-tax receipts for all states had plunged 22% from a year earlier.

"In California, as the technology boom turned into a bust, state revenue swung from a 23% increase to a 14% drop.

"More than a dozen states are selling billions of dollars in future payments from the tobacco industry for a fraction of their face value in cash now. Bond-rating agencies aren't happy with states' reliance on reserve funds and non-recurring revenue such as the tobacco payments. The state and local government ratings at Standard & Poor's has lowered its outlook on nine states since January and downgraded the bond rating of three others. Aggregate state reserves are expected to drop to $13.2B this year from 31.5B just two years ago.

"Budget crises are putting a halt to expanding public payrolls. Iowa, Florida, Minnesota, Nebraska, Illinois and Ohio have all laid off state workers. Many other states have imposed hiring freezes. 'We're seeing an incredible reversal, including the closure of correctional facilities,' says Steven Kreisberg, associate research director at the American Federation of State, County and Municipalities.

"If so, it would spell the end of public payrolls as a source of

strength. Over the past 18 months or so, growth in federal, state and local government jobs has partially offset the drop in private payrolls. Since early 2001, the number of private non-farm jobs in the US has fallen, with more than two million job cuts. Government employment has grown by nearly 700,000 workers over the same 18-month span.

"Few states have been hit as hard as Indiana, partly because its manufacturing-heavy economy was hammered by the recession. In April 1999, with its manufacturing employment at a 20-year high, lawmakers used a $2 billion surplus to cut taxes by $1 billion, fund $800 million in projects such as university buildings and local roads and increase the reserve to a record $1.2B.

"Within a couple of months the budget began to unravel amid rising unemployment, the rapid disappearance of overtime pay and the loss of stock-market gains. In July 2001, Gov. Frank O'Bannon ordered state agencies to cut spending by 7%. In September he created a four-person 'freeze committee' to review every government job opening to determine whether it could remain unfilled. On Nov. 15 he laid out his plan to close a $1.3B budget gap. 'Our state is in fiscal crisis,' he said. 'We've cut the fat and even the muscle. More drastic cuts threaten the very backbone of state services – our public schools, our safety, our health.'

"He proposed making the temporary cuts permanent.

"Last month State Police Superintendent Melvin Carraway told the state's House and Way Committee, that his department has eliminated 250 jobs and is considering closing two trooper barracks."

This at a time when murderous violence, political and non-political, is spreading in the US. Surely there is something amiss when the levels of government closest to society's problems become warehouses for neglected needs, and elected officials can do nothing but wring their hands.

W.K.

A Textbook Case for Scrapping the Textbook

THE INCREDIBLE PREPOTENCE of American military might as show-cased in the Iraq war rules out any serious challenge of any combination of other military forces. A growing vulnerability, however, revolves around its huge foreign debt – a perk of the dollar as the world's main reserve currency. That has made it possible for the US to finance its insatiable dependence for foreign oil, and the vast imports of cheap consumer goods with currency of its own creation. However, several forces are undermining that position. The Afghan and Iraq wars have not been cost-free. That shows up in the increasingly stressed position of the dollar. The collapse of Wall St. in a miasma of scandals, the expansion of the European Union, and the spread of the Chinese currency as a reserve money in Eastern Asia are ominous.

That makes the contracts for the reconstruction of Iraq and any future "terrorist countries" of crucial importance. Undoubtedly that is a factor in the reorganization of US military to provide ready-made stations throughout the world.

Among the areas receiving special attention is Latin America where the collapse of the Wall St. boom has led to a negative flow of capital to the United States. It has brought about a decline in the activity of the maquiladoras, branch plants in Mexico along its border with the US and in Central America. Much of this has shifted to China that can offer far lower wages. The attack of September 11th, has put on hold the talks of liberalizing Mexican immigration to the US and thus increasing the flow of US dollars on which Mexico depends. And above all the drop of the US dollar has involved a large loss on the huge store of US dollars Mexico has built up. Meanwhile, the disaster of the Argentine has warned other countries of the perils of becoming too dependent on the US dollar, a policy long promoted from the US. It helps fend off competing reserve currencies.

That is what makes the article by Steve H. Hanke, professor at Johns Hopkins University, of interest. To promote the author's thesis, key details of Mexico's current monetary problems are provided, but in utter isolation from vital relationships.

The High Cost of Sopping Up the Remittances of Mexicans Working in the US

"Thanks in part to Mexico's economic malaise, almost a quarter of its labor force is now employed in the US. Its annual real GDP was solid during the 1996-2000 period [when the maquiladoras on a huge scale took over simpler manufacturing operations from the US]. It slumped from an annual rate of 3.6% to 6.8% in that period to -0.2% and 0.9% in 2001 and 2002. For a developing country, that is gross underperformance. A key culprit in the matter was monetary policy.

"Following the 1994-5 peso crisis, the Banco de Mexico rather than pegging the peso's rate to the dollar, as it had prior to the crisis, began targeting annual inflation.

"Consumer price inflation has come down to a tame 5% from 34.4% per year in 1996, and interest rates on 28-day treasury bills have fallen to less than 5% from 31.4% on the average in 1996. The peso has held its own in the foreign-exchange market over the same period, depreciating from around 10.3 to the dollar from 7.86. Yet, in recent years growth has been anemic.

"The trouble stems from the central bank's desire to maintain control of base money growth. For that it has to 'sterilize' dollar inflows. As dollars come into the country [largely from remittances from Mexicans in the US] the Banco issues new pesos in exchange. Simultaneously it issues debt to soak up the peso liquidity. Thus, dollars build up at the central bank but a flood of new pesos in circulation is avoided, and the exchange-rate is thus managed. Even though base money has increased to $23.43 billion from the equivalent of $10.63 billion in 1996, net foreign reserves have increased dramatically to $53.7 billion from $149 million in 1996.

"These operations, however, are not costless. The interest earned on foreign reserve holdings is less than the interest the bank must pay on the bond it issues. Sterilization also causes in-terest rates to rise above where they would otherwise be because the public's willingness to finance the government declines."

The Banco de Mexico has been issuing its own bonds known by the Spanish initials BREMS since August 2000, with coupons of about 6%. Such issues have ballooned to nearly 235 billion pesos, an amount that nearly equals the 241 billion pesos base money stock, and roughly 40% of the foreign reserves. The net result has been to impose losses on the central bank. The cash flows generated by the Banco's assets are less than those created by its liabilities.

"[To lessen this], effective May 2, the central bank will start auctioning off half the foreign reserves accumulated each quarter to domestic institutions. The real problem is the Banco de Mexico attempts to regulate base money in the face of foreign-reserve flows that overpower its domestic monetary policy instruments (hence the need to issue BREMS).

"With the peso's importance shrinking, it's time for Mexico to officially dollarize. By using $23.5 billion of its foreign exchange war chest, it could retire the peso. That would leave $30.2 billion in foreign reserves that would no longer be needed as a signalling device to scare away currency speculators and keep the rating agencies happy. Such a dollarization package would give Mexicans what they want (the dollar). It would eliminate the fiscal costs and higher interest rates associated with sterilization, and further boost Mexico's creditworthiness – and, yes, growth."

It is amazing that the learned academic did mention the Argentine, where the dollarization program led to disaster. Mexico is faced with the competition of China and other Asiatic countries even for the thin gruel of the US branch plants strung along their Northern borders without essential infrastructures. Once, "dollarized," Mexico would not have the recourse when needed to devaluating its currency. Moreover, since the United States is embarking on a new strategy of stretching its military forces over the whole world, its dollar is facing an uncertain future. Its losses against the euro in the past three years have already amounted to well over 40%. Threatened with the expanded Euro for the perks of owning the world reserve currency, the US is facing the likely need to earn more of the money to pay for its imports rather than just using computer entries for the purpose.

Prof. Hanke does not mention the most serious option open to Mexico: to use the sterilized dollars to finance a program for bringing in proper sewage, water systems, schools, roads, and civic amenities to Maquiladoraland. That will provide healthier growth, keep down the high crime, improve living conditions, and make it less necessary for a quarter of Mexico's population to seek a living by being smuggled into the United States. It is strange that Prof. Hanke should omit the special bond issues (tesobonos) that, though purchased with pesos, gave the holders the option of having them redeemed in dollars on maturity.

William Krehm

Precarious Footholds in a Derivative Economy

FOR THE PAST YEAR and more the one bright glimmer on the American economic horizon was the housing market. With interest rates in the US near historic lows, and the stock market comatose, people are rewriting their old mortgages and pulling cash out of their house equity. On the lending side, with the stock market and junk bonds so disastrous, investment is going into securitized housing mortgages. Now even this hope has been dented. We will quote from *The Wall Street Journal's* 10/6 front-page story: "Freddie Mac Ousts Top Officials As Regulators Prepare Inquiries"): "Freddie Mac, one of the nation's two huge government-sponsored mortgage finance firms, shoved aside its three top executives, questioned the 'cooperation and candor' of its chief financial officer and reiterated plans to restate three years' worth of earnings.

"[These] surprising developments sent investors fleeing from Freddie Mac's debt toward the security of US Treasury bonds. It also fanned the embers of a controversy over how adequately Freddie Mac and its sibling, Fannie Mae, are regulated. The market impact was muted, however, in part because Freddie said the restatement would make its profits and capital bigger than previously reported, not smaller.

"Still, the moves raise questions about Freddie's ability to continue to fuel the rapid growth of the mortgage market, an important force in an otherwise weak economy.

"Freddie Mac's board asked its longtime chairman and chief executive, Leland Brendsel, to step aside. The president and chief operating officer, David Glenn, was fired outright, and Chief Finance Officer Vaughan Clarke was pressured to resign."

So brutal a housecleaning of the top brass of one of the largest of world corporations may seem astounding for *understating* the profits and capital of the organization! Sounds crazy. But ours has become a "derivative" economy. "Derivative" is a term and a concept borrowed from infinitesimal calculus. It has to do not with the present value of a mathematical function, a corporation, or whatever is analyzed, but with its rate of growth, and the rate of growth of their rate of growth to higher orders. In the case of marginal utility theory – the very gene of the orthodox model for at least a century – all this supposed knowledge of the future growth rate is discounted for its *present* value and incorporated into the price of the corporation's stock. Hence, the great temptation of executives of listed corporations is to blow up this year's earnings, based on its rate of growth. It doesn't matter that the company hasn't earned a bean in its existence.

In many instances during the past boom, it was the growth of the market share that was used as the ersatz growth vehicle. But if the company share price fails to increase at the clip that has already been incorporated into price, that price will collapse. Hence the seemingly paradoxical scandal in Freddie Mac: part of earnings were deferred to future years, as was part of the increase in capital, so that the growth rate and hence the market price could be maintained. "Such a maneuver, sometimes known as 'cookie jar' accounting, has been used by companies experiencing strong earnings, but wanting to defer gains to a later date, when earnings may be weak. The SEC has settled with Microsoft Corp. and Xerox Corp., which were accused of setting up improper reserves." Cookie jar accountancy also defers taxes.

Cookie Jar Accounting Postpones the Dessert

Freddie Mac is the nation's fourth largest financial company with assets in 2002 of $722 billion. Along with its sibling Fannie Mae, Freddie Mac is in the business of buying home mortgages, thereby freeing up the resources of lenders to make new home loans. In turn it "securitizes" its own mortgage portfolio and sells pieces to other financial organizations. Its own shares are traded on the stock market and in recent years have done very well. But to quote The *WSJ* again, "The increasingly complex business compels the companies to use a bewildering array of derivatives and other hedging instruments to manage the immense risk that goes along with building up massive mortgage portfolios." For example, any shift in interest rates affects their business in multiple ways – through the demand for housing, but also via the market value of existing mortgages. At present with US interest rates headed downward, the equity in mortgages with a higher coupon will rise. But should the trend reverse, watch out!

"The company's regulator, the Office of Federal Housing Enterprise Oversight, has appointed a special investigation team to review Freddie Mac's 'management misjudgments' and 'employee misconduct.' Separately, the Securities and Exchange Commission is also looking into whether Freddie Mac's accountancy violated any security laws."

The dismissal of so much top brass sent shock waves throughout the financial system. "Treasury bonds rose and their yields fell as investors, rattled by Freddie's disclosures, sought safety. Yields on bonds issued by Freddie rose by a sizable six hundredths of percentage point relative to those on Treasurys, and those on Fannie by a lesser amount. It contributed to a down-day on the stock exchanges." The pillars of the temple of a sudden were leaning at a *risqué* angle.

"Freddie Mac and Fannie Mae between them own or guarantee about a third of all US residential mortgages. They help make mortgages affordable and available regardless of local financial conditions, in contrast to the time when savings and loans institutions dominated that scene. If the new disclosures fray investor confidence and impair Freddie's ability to borrow at a reasonable cost, that could undermine the mortgage and housing markets which have underpinned what little growth the economy now enjoys.

"Federal Reserve officials have long worried that investors may be complacent about the risk of owning Fannie Mae and Freddie Mac securities because they assume the federal government won't let them fail.

"The controversy may pass with no sustained impact on Freddie or the mortgage market, much as happened when Fannie roiled the market last fall by disclosing a sizable mismatch [in the terms of] its assets and liabilities. Nonetheless, the latest disclosures of Freddie Mac could lead lawmakers to consider changes hitherto unthinkable because of Freddie's and Fannie's political clout.

"One idea would require fuller public disclosure. Unlike other publicly traded companies, Freddie and Fannie aren't required to comply with all SEC rules. Under pressure from critics, they've recently agreed to file annual reports and register their shares. But they continue to resist formal registration of the mortgage-backed securities."

The disturbing fact is that increasingly the financial system is on a "too big to be allowed to fail" standard.

William Krehm

Tower of Babel on Mt. Olympus

FOR ALMOST a half century we were assured that parliament, governments, and of course the public should keep their noses out of the higher mysteries of monetary policy. These were best left to central banks, no matter what their charters might say. Declared independent, they seemingly get their wisdom from heaven – not directly, but via the Bank for International Settlements (BIS) That is a non-elected institution that has had more to do with the distribution of national incomes than elected parliaments.

The amazing story is to be found in *Meltdown, Money, Debt, and the Wealth of Nations,* COMER Publications, 1999, p. 15. "[Canadian] Prime Minister Kim Campbell has declined to explain just what she meant when she promised to make the Bank of Canada more independent" (*The Globe and Mail,* 8/4/93). Let us fill in that information gap. For the purpose, we will turn to a scholarly work that not surprisingly has been allowed to gather dust on library shelves: Henry H. Schloss, *The Bank for International Settlements* (New York University, 1970).

"BIS was set up in 1930 to manage the transfer of Germany's reparation payments to the victors of the First World War. BIS shareholders were to consist entirely of central banks, but because the US Federal Reserve was unwilling to participate, a syndicate of American commercial banks (J.P. Morgan & Company, the First National Bank of New York, and the First National Bank of Chicago) took up the US subscription.

"The shareholders of BIS are *central banks* rather than governments as are the members the International Monetary Fund and the World Bank founded at Bretton Woods towards the end of WWII.

"A further sign of BIS's dislike of anything smacking of democracy: voting rights are permanently reserved to the original members in the proportions to the shares *originally* subscribed by them, though they may subsequently have sold their shares. [Its shares can be bought on the Parisian stock exchange!]

"Quoting directly from Schloss: 'To safeguard the "independence" of BIS, a director of BIS shall not be an official of a government or a member of a legislative body, unless he is governor of the central bank. It is this provision that gives BIS its characteristic as a central bankers' organization. It has jealously guarded itself against the intrusion of government officials.'

"One of the major stigmas attached to the reputation of the Bank in the 1940s was a widespread feeling that it had been pro-German during the interwar period and collaborated in appeasing Germany in the 1930s and during the war. In fact, the charge of collaboration with the Axis was an important reason why the BIS was not transformed into the preeminent international monetary institution in the early postwar period and a new International Monetary Fund was created instead.

"These charges of collaboration by the Bank have been investigated in considerable detail by the author [Schloss]. The Bank may have been guilty of appeasement *in the late 1930s*. But the charges of pro-German conduct *during the war* are essentially unfounded." [More recently the question has been raised about BIS's role in handling gold extracted from the teeth of concentration camp victims during the war.]

At the Bretton Woods Conference Resolution Five was passed recommending the liquidation of the Bank at the earliest possible moment. But by 1951 the dissolution of BIS was a dead issue.

The Comeback Coup of the Banks

By then the commercial banks were well advanced towards recapturing the positions surrendered during the Depression. "In May 1951 President Truman assented to a negotiated settlement between the Treasury and the central bank agreeing to slightly higher rates of interest and granting minor flexibility to the Fed. Within two years, however, Fed officials claimed a more sweeping interpretation of the Treasury-Fed agreement. It was, they attested, a declaration of full independence for the central bank. By that point, the liberal Democrats were gone from the White House." Central banks on the comeback trail had need for an international bunker. BIS filled the bill.

It was at secret BIS sessions that much of the future of the world has been plotted. That appears from the annual report of the BIS General Manager Alexandre Lamfalussy of May 23, 1991.

"It has been argued that a quality bias in price level calculations implies that inflation in the range of 1-2% may be considered price stability for all practical purposes. Nonetheless, the move from an environment of low or moderate inflation to one of no inflation implies an important psychological shift. It has proved very difficult in recent decades to do better than achieve merely low inflation and to move to actual price stability, even in those countries with the best price performance. [This can only be seen as a reprimand to even super-achieving central bank heads such as John Crow in Canada who was brought in after an IMF career of bullying indebted Latin American governments. He ran up a good part of Canada's debt with interest rates four percentage points higher than of the US in his effort to obtain "zero inflation." In the article *Our Sunken Continents* in this *ER* issue you will learn that this elusive 1-2% of stubborn "inflation" that not even John Crow could eradicate was in fact not inflation but a reflection of the growing need of public infrastructures in a modern urbanized, high-tech economy.]

"From all this it must be clear why central banks – even if they enjoy full independence from government – find it difficult to pursue the objective of absolute price stability. An obvious condition is a sufficient degree of social consensus, since in a world in which unavoidable price increases need to be offset by price declines, the consequence will be felt very differently by different social groups."

Such then is the background needed to appreciate the sensational nature of a Dow Jones Newswire carried in *The Globe and Mail* (01/06, "Central Bankers, BIS at odds over degree of deflation risk" by Brian Blackstone and Antonio Ligie): "Central bankers from Europe played down the risks of deflation, even as the so-called central bank for central banks yesterday highlighted it's a growing risk.

"In an annual report that was sometimes quite blunt, the Bank for International Settlements backed US acceptance of a weaker dollar to stimulate the economy, arguing in essence that what's best for the US economy is best for the global economy that's facing deflationary risks.

"But an issue that received so much attention from the BIS, [deflation] got scant mention from central bankers gathered here for the annual meeting of the BIS.

"'Deflation isn't the main topic because there isn't any,' European Central Bank (ECB) President Wim Duisenberg said yesterday. Bank of France Governor Jean-Claude Trichet also underlined in his statements that deflation wasn't an issue in Europe.

"Central bankers do have a point. For now, Japan is the only major economy facing outright deflation. The US and euro zone have inflation rates above zero, conceded BIS general manager Malcolm Knight.

"But the US Federal Reserve Board has already signalled it considers a rapid fall in inflation a risk. And with annual inflation at one percent in June, Germany isn't far from price stability or an eventual fall in prices.

"History may explain the ECB's greater reluctance to identify deflation as a greater threat than the Fed's, BIS economic adviser William White said. He noted that the US economy's defining point in history was the deflationary great Depression. In contrast, Europe's defining moment was hyperinflation after the First World War."

It remains to ask why the Fed disregarded that "defining point" in the 1980s when chairman Paul Volcker, drove the Fed rate into mid-double digit levels – pushing commercial credit into the twenty-percent region, and in doing so almost wrecked the world economy.

"Defining points" (a new weasel expression) are no substitute for an economic theory that would tip us off on what was up and what was down, and what exists and what is fiction. What is lacking once more is the morality of a serious science. For that would begin by recognizing rather than covering up failures. That would help prevent the same faulty policies being repeated on a mounting scale because they seem to serve the interests of those in power. That has been the sorry record of the last three or four decades.

William Krehm

[SIDEBAR]
The Secret of Ponzi Pension Funds

The Wall Street Journal (1/07, "Firms help Keep Workers in Dark on Pension Status" by Ellen E. Schultz and Theo Francis) recounts a sordid tale: "For millions of American workers few

retirement issues are more vital than the health of their pension plans. Yet employees and retirees have no way to find out how sound their own pension plan currently is – in part because companies have long resisted attempts to let them have more up-to-date information. One source of pension information, company filings to the Securities and Exchange Commission, is of little use for employees. That's largely because most big companies have several different pension plans and lump them all together in their filings.

"Without access to accurate data, employees and retirees face two risks. One is that employers can mask the deteriorating health of a pension plan, and then take steps to cut benefits or kill the plan. Paradoxically, the other risk is that employers can exaggerate the ill-health of the pension plan to justify reduction in retirement benefits.

"Consider the fate of a pension plan for pilots at US Airways Group. On March 31, the airline, operating in bankruptcy protection, extinguished a plan covering more than 7,000 active and retired pilots. It said the plan was so underfunded that keeping it going would drive the airline into liquidation.

"Retired pilots suspected the airline was exaggerating the pension plan's ill health, and thus the need for future contributions to justify dumping it. But the pilots couldn't get their hands on the data needed to pursue this argument, even when the plan's life or death depended on it.

"A bankruptcy judge rejected the pilots' protest and let the airline kill the plan – citing, in part, the pilots' lack of current data about the plan's health."

Most of the US's legendary steel industry has been allowed to go into bankruptcy so that the assets could be sold to new companies – many foreign – free of responsibility for commitments to the pension funds of employees. Yet in the 1950s pensions were used by those corporations as a substitute for wage increases. Even in the "good old days" make-believe was an important ingredient in the soundness of the system.

"Last December, with US Airways pilots still assuming their pension plan was in tolerable health, agreed to the airline's request for another round of pension cuts. A few weeks later, to their dismay, US Airways stated that the pilots' pension plan was seriously underfunded. On Jan. 30, the airline filed with the bankruptcy court an intention to kill the plan. US Airways estimated it would have to put $1.7 billion into the plan over seven years, a burden that would force it into liquidation.

"Among those who took the airline's word were the creditors' committee: the Air Transportation Stabilization Board, which was poised to guarantee loans to the carrier; and the airline's main bankruptcy lender, Retirement Systems of Alabama, which stood to gain a large equity stake in US Airways if it emerged from Chapter 11. All acknowledge they didn't examine the health of the pension plan, didn't have up-to-date figures, and simply accepted US Airways' analysis. All nonetheless backed the request to kill the pension plan. Only the retired pilots questioned the company's estimate of how much it would have to contribute to keep the pension plan alive. But they said they had insufficient information.

"The information the pilots needed is in a form that

companies file to the Internal Revenue Service for each pension plan. This Form 5500 shows how much money is in the pension plan; how well the stocks or bonds it holds have performed over 12 months; and company contributions to the plan. Most important, it shows the plan's 'current liabilities.' This determines how much cash, if any, a company is required by law to contribute to the plan during the succeeding year. The problem is, this information remains inaccessible to most people until many months out of date.

"Hugh Greenwood, who retired in 1997, after dizzy spells suffered outside the cockpit, has lost a $2,000 monthly disability check that was supplementing the pension he took as a lump sum. Mr. Greenwood's wife has returned to work, and the former pilot, 67 years old, will likely do the same. Meantime, he is painting the house in Denver in case they have to put it up for sale."

Information – from the very heyday of some of our adventurous financial corporations to their present maneuvers on the brink of bankruptcy, is handled by those with power as a killer weapon.

Our Sunken Continents

T HOUGH MAN was the creation of a benign God, in another sense he is the ongoing product of a duel between the Lord and Satan. And one of the Devil's tricks is to harness man's greed to suppress what he learned through his God-given faculties. Accordingly it isn't enough to dig on dry land to recover much crucial work of the human mind. We must explore as well for continents sunk beneath the seas.

With a deep sense of the values of their past, the ancient Egyptians in their pyramids at least tried to preserve their pharaohs, in one piece if eviscerated. But it is not only in Greek mythology that we encounter cases of prophets hacked to pieces and flung to the beasts for a more thorough rubbing out. Loathed by the devil, resurrection is ever the labour of the Lord.

That is why economists must do their exploring in all the elements, on land and under water. Some of our findings, acknowledged in their day, were wiped out from official memory only a decade or two ago, but with a thoroughness that time alone could not achieve. For the purpose we frequently make pious visits to the stacks of our libraries, and even incur fines for overdue books that have beguiled us. Our reward is to share our rediscoveries with our readers.

Robert Eisner, a much respected, and once oft-quoted academic at North-Western University, picked a whole boneyard with the new Pieties in the 1980s. Today when the two great parties of our lone superpower talk of doing away the deficit and even of paying off the debt, nobody cites Robert Eisner when we need his wisdom most.

In this belated review we highlight some of the many strengths and a few weaknesses of his *How Real is the Federal Deficit*, published by The Free Press, a Division of Macmillan, Inc. in New York in 1986.

The preface begins with a wart, "While this work builds on the Keynesian model of the determinants of income and employment, it infuses that model with the traditional neo-classical emphasis on the role of real wealth and abhorrence of 'money illusion.' It is aimed at economists and non-economists of all schools and political persuasions" (p. xiii). Only 18 years after these lines were penned, they have a surrealistic aspect in an economy that has driven the money illusion to the point of replacing "earnings" in stock market evaluations goosed by financial derivatives.[1] Such criteria of corporative soundness have landed some of the world's largest accountancy firms in the defendants' docks charged with cooking their clients' books for handsome considerations. The neo-classic replacement of real wealth with a price derivative has been the very gene that has brought the world to its current plight.

The Real Sin is Bad Accountancy

"For most of the American public, debt and deficits are like sin: morally wrong, difficult to avoid, but not easy to keep track of. Our federal deficits have each year been adding huge $200 billion chunks to the 'national debt.' The sheer magnitude of that debt, currently approaching $2 trillion, suggests to some the danger of national bankruptcy." [It is around $8 trillion today.]

"Yet, election after election, from the early days of Franklin Roosevelt's presidency on, Republicans have traditionally cried out against budget deficit with little apparent success. Walter Mondale tried to reverse field and lead Democrats in a similar crusade in 1984. His failure is well-remembered.

"The Carter Administration, faced with seemingly explosive inflation, reacted sharply to the then supposedly large federal deficits believed responsible. It tightened fiscal policy and encouraged tight money as well. Carter thus further weakened a sluggish economy and contributed to his own demise.

"These Carter policies, we shall see, were based on false intelligence, misread by friend and foe alike. *In fact, we did not have real federal budget deficits from 1977 to 1980.*

"The new Reagan Administration in 1981, in the name of combatting inflation, continued the Carter policies – with sufficient dedication to bring on the worst recession since the Great Depression of the 1930s. Business investment and profits plummeted, and unemployment rose to a post-War World II record of 10.7% of the labor force. We counted almost ten million Americans unsuccessfully looking for jobs, and millions more too discouraged to look further, or only 'partially employed.'

"And then came an economic miracle. We began to run really huge budget deficits, and the economy recovered sharply. A new 'Reaganomics' and hitherto unheralded preachers of a 'supply-side' gospel claimed credit.

"But what really happened? Did the recovery take place despite the great move to very large deficits, as traditional budget balancers might insist?

"Because we have not measured deficits correctly, we have turned economic theory on its head. If we continue to act this way, we court future disaster.

"A deficit plays many tricks, and one of the biggest has been largely overlooked in the mounting rhetoric over budget deficits. *That trick, simply enough, is that as inflation wipes out the value of money, it also wipes out the value of debt.* As it does that, it profoundly alters the significance of conventional ways of measuring the deficits.

"Meaningful correction for inflation can cause a dramatic shift in understanding. Deficits which have appeared to be enormous can turn out to be moderate. Moderate deficits may even be corrected into surpluses!"

Here, however, we must recognize another wart or two.

In the process of "mismeasuring" the real debt and deficit, Eisner omits to mention what he cannot have been unaware of: rather than just a school-boy blunder, the mistakes transferred huge chunks of the national product from the working population to the lenders and financiers. In short it was very much a power-thing. Leave that out, and you cannot understand just what has gutted the economy.

The First Principle of Tailoring

The other wart is that Eisner uses the one term "inflation" to cover two very different things. The meaning of "inflation" in economic literature is an excess of aggregate demand over supply which tends to drive up prices across the board. But elsewhere Eisner has been one of the few pioneers to cotton onto something that I had based my analysis on since the latter 1960s: the growth of the public sector as a proportion of our mixed economy. That channels funds from the government to all non-market sectors and shows up in the price of marketed goods and services as a deeper layer of taxation of all sorts.[2] That obviously constitutes an important ingredient of what Eisner refers to as the "inflation" that gnaws away at the real value of government debt. But there is nothing pathological about that, as there is about a systematic excess over demand over supply. This I call *structural price rise*. That should be made clear. Otherwise you are making life too easy for those who are determined to suppress any serious analysis of what has hit the economy.

If we ignore it, we are unable to understand that never, ever, should the tailor cut the client to his cloth.

The Hide and Seek of Assets and Liabilities

But let us go on to the Eisner's next important point. "Inflation, however, is not the only source of our confusion about the deficit. The federal government has a strange accounting system. It differs not only from that of private business, but also from that of state and local governments. Every large corporation, just like the State of California under Ronald Reagan, distinguishes between current and capital expenditures. Every individual sensibly managing his own finances must so distinguish. Our official measures of the federal deficits do not.

"Why make the distinction? Because it makes a difference whether a family's outgo exceeds its income – a deficit – because of gambling losses in Las Vegas or due to the purchase of a new home. Business investment in excess of retained earnings is applauded as contributing to economic growth. But by federal government accounting practice, AT&T, General Motors, IBM, and many other companies would be guilty of 'deficit financing'" (p. 3).

"For every borrower there must be a lender. In other words, the federal deficit is someone else's surplus. If the government can be viewed as getting poorer by going into debt, then the individuals, businesses, and state and local governments that acquire the debt are getting richer. This has profound effects on private spending and saving and on the health of the economy…. With all the deficits, the general trend of real federal debt – the debt adjusted for inflation – has been downward. On a per capita basis it has indeed gone down very sharply over most of the last forty years. And the government's net worth, the difference between its assets – the financial and real – and its liabilities, has moved from red to black.

"Since federal deficits add to federal debt, which thus adds to private wealth, they can be expected to increase aggregate demand, or spending. If the economy is booming along at full employment of its resources, further increases in demand raise prices and encourage inflation. But if there is slack in the economy, deficit-induced demand stimulates output and employment. But for the deficits to matter they must be *real* deficits. A real deficit is one which increases the real net debt of the government to the public, and hence increases the public's perception of its own real wealth. Thus the vital importance of the inflation correction. For inflation in effect generates an 'inflation tax' eating away the value of the public's holdings of those Treasury notes, bills, and bonds, or the cash which they back" (p. 5).

"The less the *inflation-adjusted* surplus or the greater the deficit the data confirm, the greater the subsequent growth, or the less the decline, in real gross national product. With the major swing to a real federal deficit at the end of 1982, unemployment fell, in less than two years, from almost 11% to 7%.

"There has long been concern that federal deficits pass on our burden to future generations. What we really bequeath the future, however, is our physical and human capital. A 'deficit' which finances construction of our roads, bridges, harbors, and airports *is* an investment in the future. So are expenditures to preserve and enhance our natural resources or to educate our people and keep them healthy. Federal budgets which are balanced by running down our country's capital are real *national deficits*" (pp. 6-7).

"The market value of net debt varies with changes in interest rates, and a significant factor in such changes is changes in the rate of inflation. As inflation rises, it brings on expectations of higher inflation. Lenders demand higher rates of interest because they expect repayment of their loans to be in less valuable dollars. Borrowers are willing to pay higher rates of interest to finance the purchase of houses, automobiles, and business plant, equipment and inventories which they expect to rise in price.

"But in addition to the impact of *changes* in expected inflation on the market value of the debt via their effect on market rates of interest, inflation itself erodes the real value of any nominal market value. Unless individuals and businesses are guilty of 'money illusion,' it is the real value of their assets that should matter. *Hence it is the real value of the federal net debt that should matter"* (p. 17).

"The most remarkable differences between official and adjusted budget measures show up in the 1977-80 Carter years. The 1977 deficit of $26 billion is turned into a virtually balanced budget. The 1978 deficit of $29 billion is converted into an adjusted surplus of $33 billion. The 1979 deficit of $16 billion becomes an adjusted surplus of $32 billion. And the deficit of $61 billion becomes which caused so much consternation in 1980 now appears as an adjusted surplus of $7.6 billion.

Volcker's Only Game in Town!

"Looking at the official deficit figures, Carter Administration economists and their outside critics agreed that the economy was suffering from too much fiscal stimulus. Both the deficits and the stimulus had to be reduced to curb inflation.

"Yet there were nagging indications that the economy was sluggish rather than overheated. I recall asking Carter Economic Council Chairman Charles Schultz early in 1980, 'What's a nice guy like you doing trying to bring on a recession?' 'Yeah,' he quipped, 'but we're not even good at it!.' Nevertheless, unemployment, while below its peak two years later, was approaching 7%.

"Mesmerized by those official figures, most observers insisted that our fiscal policy was irresponsibly expansionary. That justified Federal Reserve Chairman Paul Volcker's tight money policy as 'the only game in town' to stop inflation.

"But the rising interest rates associated with escalating inflation reinforced by the restrictive monetary posture, had been driving down the market value of the public's holdings of federal debt. And the inflation itself was further reducing its real value. The purchasing power of the public was thus shrinking, not growing" (pp. 23 and 24).

All this points to the perils of number-crunching without even curiosity about what the numbers might mean. So many different influences are changing the real value of the numbers.

But equally important is a missing central piece of monetary policy that Washington used to finance WWII and the reconstruction and development of the world until at least the midsixties. It has been wiped out from economists' memories.

Thus Brian Milner in *The Globe and Mail* (23/03, "Those who watch Fed watchers fun to watch") alludes to the dilemma of Fed Reserve chairman Alan Greenspan, who has no elbow room to continue dropping the fed rate, even though the economy is already sinking into deeper deflation: "Mr. Greenspan first signalled that another rate deduction could be in the offing during congressional testimony a month ago and has dropped other hints since then. Dr. Opacity didn't actually say that he had his knife poised again. But he left no doubt that the Fed is concerned more about the economy's slowness to rebound than about the possible risks of stoking inflation.

"He said that because 'the cost of taking out insurance against deflation is so low…we can aggressively attack some of the underlying forces, which are essentially weak demand.'"

In short, after giving advice to the Japanese for over a decade on how to get out of their deflationary blind alley, Greenspan

finds himself stuck in the identical dilemma, having reduced the Fed rate to close to zero. (If you use either Eisner's adjustments or those of COMER which go further and include the *social lien*, the economy has long since passed into deflation.) That is a condition where producers are too frightened to borrow and lenders too scared to lend, Keynes's "liquidity trap." The only recourse left to policymakers is for the government to borrow substantially from the central bank to finance massive necessary public investments both in physical and human capital. That investment would provide activity for private enterprise and many unemployed. However, that facility of money creation central banks of the First World surrendered starting in the 1970s and climaxing in the bailout and deregulation of the banks in the early 1990s. If Greenspan has nowhere to turn, it is because he supported the destruction of the other great but less blunt tool that empowered the central bank to keep the economy on a relatively even keel. But let Eisner once more take over.

"A deficit need not imply borrowing from the public. It can be financed by 'printing money,' or by the current more sophisticated procedure which amounts to that, selling Treasury bills or bonds to the Federal Reserve. In fact, the Federal Reserve does not buy newly issued Treasury securities. It can and does accomplish the same thing by buying existing Treasury bills.

"We might try a brief explanation for those not up to the arcane process of money creation. First, we generally count as money the public's holdings of currency and its deposits in banks (or certain other 'depository institutions'). Thus, purchases of Treasury securities by the Fed create money when sellers deposit their Federal Reserve checks in *their* banks. They indeed provide 'high-powered money' as the banks take these checks and deposit them in *their* bank, the Federal Reserve Bank. These additional balances – or reserves – of the private banks then set off a further expansion of the 'money supply,' as banks with 'excess' reserves make loans, and the proceeds of those loans are deposited. This goes on until the growth of deposits subject to reserve requirements raised required reserves – currently 12% of deposits considered 'transactions balances' – to the new, higher level of actual reserves brought about by the Fed's purchase of securities.

The Marvels of the "Multiplier"

"If the Fed merely wanted to keep interest rates from *rising in the face of a deficit,* it need only buy Treasury securities equal to a fraction of the deficit. It could then rely upon the increased supply of money from the additional loans to generate public demand for that portion of additional Treasury securities outstanding which are not purchased by the Fed. Indeed, the banks might even use at least some of their excess reserves to buy Treasury securities themselves.

"It would therefore seem that conventional deficits need not raise interest rates and lower bonds and stock prices. It would also seem that federal budget deficits need not drain funds that would otherwise finance private borrowing and private investment."

On the contrary, if the private firms are too demoralized by deflationary forces to borrow, and banks are sitting on too great piles of dubious debt to seek out borrowers, all the government need do is borrow from the Fed – directly or indirectly – to fund any of the countless public investments that have been neglected in recent decades. That would provide contracts for private entrepreneurs and thus employment for the unemployed and turn the economy around. Unlike Canada, which abolished the statutory reserves that banks had to deposit with the central banks, statutory reserves still exist in the US at an average of about 3.5% of all banks' deposits from the public. But in other ways these have been emasculated. For example, the US Federal Reserve now counts the banks' operational cash in their tills as part of the statutory reserves, "sweep" accounts that switch cash deposits of the banks with the Fed into non-reservable accounts at the close of each business day, and back again into reservable accounts at the opening of the banks the next morning. The US's deflationary problem is of its own making. And the answer to it is to be found in the sunken continents of great economic writings in any university library. But all this is The Great Secret that Must Never Be Uttered. Suppressing the facts of money creation is like suppressing the facts of life under Queen Victoria. It made the English notorious for their prurience and perversions.

William Krehm

1. "Derivatives," a term borrowed from differential calculus, refers to the rate of growth in various powers. Thus the second derivative is the rate of growth of the rate of growth, or the acceleration of the growth, the third is the rate of growth of the acceleration, and so on to the infinite power. These are only two instances in human affairs of a function incorporating infinite powers of the growth rate – the exponential function where the first derivative always equals the value attained by the function itself, and hence all rates of growth to infinity do the same. This was "successfully "realized in the atomic bomb over Hiroshima, and not quite so successfully in the stock market sell-off of 1999-2000.

2. I quote some of Eisner's 1988 work on the subject in my *Towards a Non-Autistic Economy – A Place at the Table for Society*, COMER Publications, Toronto, 2002, p. 55.

Erratic Winters? — Worse to Come

EARLY LAST YEAR a notable Canadian climatologist expressed surprise at how warm the winter of 2001/2 was, especially when compared with the previous winter that he described as the longest on record. According to his definition, "Winter is snow on the ground: and during that winter 2000/1 we had snow for 104 continuous days. He went on to say that "Global warming had nothing to do with what's going on." Again late last fall, after a colder than normal October, our climatologists were projecting a warmer than usual December and January because of the pending El Niño effect. Well, it's obvious now how appropriate that forecast was.

However, these winters are not unusual and not surprising if we admit that the greenhouse effect and global warming do have an impact on our weather. When global warming started to creep into planet earth's climate, our climatologists had a rather long period of stable weather patterns and reasonable success with weather predictions. Then our atmospheric pollution began causing increases in the greenhouse effect and global warming. This in turn caused the weather patterns to change to where our climatologists, using the old patterns, are increasingly in error, especially in long-term forecasting. The weather patterns will continue to change; the distortions will continue to increase.

Weather patterns are changing because global temperature rise is not even. Generally, the temperature rise is greater in the hot parts of the planet than in the cold parts. And, as we all know, winds are created by the difference between hot and cold air masses. So, since the difference between hot and cold has increased, the resulting winds have to increase in both strength and duration. This includes the jet stream whose path is also subject to the position and size of the warm and cold air masses. These changes will continue for a long time, after all, it takes up to 50 years and more for some of our pollutants to get up into that part of the atmosphere where they do their damage, deteriorating the climate.

Here are some examples of what is happening:

1. In 1999 PEI had its normal amount of summer rainfall but considerably below their average potato crop. This was because the changing wind patterns produced a very dry spring and a very wet fall. Farmers had difficulty harvesting the poor crop in very muddy fields.

2. The current prolonged drought in Alberta and Saskatchewan is the result of a stronger than "normal" wind blowing the moisture clouds across Alberta and Saskatchewan into Manitoba. So Alberta and Saskatchewan lack enough rain and Manitoba is getting too much for their normal crops. Farmers are suffering in all three Prairie Provinces.

3. Watching the weather channel, it is obvious that both high and low temperatures are being exceeded almost every year. The old, long-standing records were mostly exceeded in the last 10 to 15 years. This is more evidence of the greenhouse effect, advancing global warming and changing weather patterns.

4. Recently in Southern Louisiana rain fell at the rate of 3 inches per hour for six hours continuously, for an accumulated total of 18 inches of water. The forecasters admitted that this tremendously exceeded their forecast of a "a strong storm with heavy rain expected" as it broke all non-hurricane records.

5. The massive 1993 Mississippi flood resulted in a lot of crop and property damage. So wisely some towns were moved out of the flood plain. That same spring, Ontario was blessed with 90 degree F plus for a high temperature all 15 days during the first half of April.

6. Last year one southern state had 50 recorded tornadoes in one 24 hour period. And about 10 years earlier a neighbouring state had a 71-tornado night. This is topped by a meteorologist comment "and the tornadoes are getting bigger."

7. In 1997 Chile's northern desert received 30 cm. of rain. That's more than the previous 30 years combined.

Admittedly, a pointed narrow view of each of these events individually can easily lead to attaching a label like "unusual," "once-in-a-lifetime," etc., event. However, taking these events as a broad comprehensive trend we must admit the impact of the greenhouse effect and global warming is real.

Climatologists! Good luck with your prognostications, especially if you stick to the old, long-standing weather patterns. In the meanwhile, weather distortions will continue to change in both frequency and strength. You think this is the worst? A lot worse is coming!

Andrew Dwornik

Andrew Dwornik is a high-school teacher in Welland, Ontario.

Economic Reform Mailbox

To Richard Priestman, Kingston, Ontario, from Andrew Jackson, Senior Economist, Canadian Labour Congress:

I was asked to reply to your letter in reference to the points made re: monetary policy.

We entirely agree that it is in the power of central banks to fund government deficits by buying government bonds. Indeed this is a very important policy tool. As you will have noted, even the Economist magazine and other conservative voices are now calling on the Bank of Japan to 'print money' to get the Japanese economy out of its current deflationary spiral. The US Federal Reserve recently signalled that it was prepared to take all necessary measures to prevent deflation by expanding the money supply.

Re: recent federal Budgets, in the mid-1990s the CLC supported calls for monetization of part of the federal deficit to avoid the need for crippling spending cuts.

Where we might differ is on the need for expansion of the Canadian money supply today. As you know, the federal government is no longer in deficit and, deflation is not in immediate prospect. There is certainly a case for expanding public spending much more than was the case in the federal Budget, but the recent Alternative Federal Budget of the CCPA (supported by the CLC) showed that a much larger spending program was possible using even the current fiscal base.

I do think it has to be borne in mind that bank lending in Canada has been expanding at a fairly healthy pace, so a non inflationary monetization of federal debt would likely require a squeeze on private credit.

To summarize, monetization of debt is an important policy tool, but we are not convinced it needs to be used right now.

Reply from Richard Priestman:

Thank you for replying to my earlier letter to President Georgetti.

You say we might differ on the need for expansion of the Canadian money supply (which was does not necessarily follow from use of the Bank of Canada – the BoC – to finance public projects) and you are also concerned that a non-inflationary monetization of federal debt would likely require a squeeze on private credit. The main point of my letter to President Georgetti is that our three levels of government spend over $70 billion a year on interest – an amount which more than covers the cost of improvements to or rebuilding of our social programs and other infrastructure. Furthermore, the interest is an unnecessary expense because we could finance public debt through the BoC at almost zero cost. William Krehm expands on this in *Towards a Non-Autistic Economy – A Place at the Table for Society* (pp. 165-169), *The Bank of Canada – A Power Unto Itself,* and in many other writings.

Public financing of public debt (government borrowing from the Bank of Canada) need not add one dollar to the money supply. It simply means that the government is borrowing from its own bank instead of from the private sector. If the government takes money from the private sector to finance a public project, that money is not available to the private sector to use in private projects. If, on the other hand, the government takes money from the BoC to finance the same public project, and curtails expansion of the money supply by requiring private banks to hold the same amount in reserve, that amount of money is not available to the private sector to use in private projects. So I don't see how a "non-inflationary monetization of federal debt would likely require a squeeze on private credit."

The argument put forward by the government for not supporting public health care, public housing, public infrastructure etc. boils down to "we can't afford it; we have too much debt and if we have a surplus we should use it to pay down the debt to lower our debt service charges." We can reduce those charges by monetizing the debt – rolling it over into the BoC in manageable amounts.

There is no good reason why Canadians should continue to spend over $70 billion a year on unnecessary interest. Canadians need the Bank of Canada to provide the financing for their public programs and infrastructure, and they need the Canadian Labour Congress to help them achieve this.

Bank Mergers to the Fore Again

THE GLOBE AND MAIL, 25/06, "Bank-Bidding Wars Expected" by Sinclair Stewart: "Ottawa's decision to block the first-mover advantage in bank merger proposals could spark a bidding war for smaller acquisitions targets, particularly Bank of Montreal, industry observers said yesterday."

Obviously the decision has been taken. Bank mergers are to be allowed without the most elementary public information of what is involved.

There is no lack of problems in our economy. Globalization and Deregulation have given us globalized terror, spreading joblessness and bloody warfare that lead to more of the same. Official economic theory has simply suppressed all alternatives, above all those that allowed us to finance WWII and finally pull the world into a quarter of a century of relative prosperity. "Deflation" that ruined millions of lives in the great depression of the thirties was even expunged from the vocabulary. In 1996 the then Governor of the Bank of Canada, Gordon Thiessen, actually expressed a timely concern about "deflation" to the House of Commons Finance Committee, but in a week he was back apologizing for having mentioned the "D" word. He assured the committee that he would regret uttering the word for the rest of his life. Moreover, in his expressed concern about deflation, he had been dead on. In those circles speaking a banned truth is more unforgivable than inventing a falsehood.

Within two years the monetary meltdown hit Eastern Asia and from there passed on to Russia and Latin America. Since then it is spreading over the world. However, the world's central banks, having high-jacked economic policy-making from their governments, have also reduced their own tools for that job to the "one blunt tool" of high interest rates. That leaves us clueless for dealing with deflation. Japan, sold a bill of goods by Western economists, has been trying to cope with a deflated economy when their official bank rate is already close to zero. Along that path, the next step would be for banks to pay the borrowers interest rather than receive it. Obviously, that reduces capitalism itself to nonsense.

The one problem that official-line economists recognized was inflation – rising prices which they equated with too much demand, too high wages, and too low interest rates. But today the number of unemployed is shooting up, commodity prices, continue to fall; the "fed rate" after the 13th reduction in little more than a couple of years stands at 1%. Along that path, there is nowhere to go.

Thus in yet another area the world has arrived clueless onto the lip of the precipice.

There used to be a simple way of handling such problems. Key parts of it are still to be found in the *Bank of Canada Act.* Until 1991 our private banks were obliged to redeposit with the Bank of Canada, a proportion of the deposits made by the public in cheque-writing and short-term accounts. On such redeposits with the central bank, they received no interest. The result: if the central bank raised the quota of such "statutory reserves," the banks could lend out only a lower multiple of the cash they held. Their drive to create more credit was thus reined

in if the reserve requirement was raised, and if it was lowered they were encouraged to ease their conditions for making loans. This enabled the central bank to gear the economy up or down without changing interest-rates. In short they had not one but two major tools for managing the economy. That meant that they did not have to rake the entire economy with deadly interest-rate fire. That was no small point, since the establishment price theory saw any increase in the price level a fatal sign of too much demand and not enough supply across the economy. In actual fact, it might very well be due to quite another cause inseparable from a rapidly urbanizing high-tech society – a need for ever more non-marketed services, like health, social security, public infrastructures that are covered by taxation. Inevitably that taxation shows up as a deepening layer of the price level. This I have called *structural price raise,* since it has a quite different cause than real market inflation. The world learned how to deal with real inflation under the great depression of the 1930s: the government made up for the lack of market demand by undertaking more capital investments. And then came the war. To finance it governments kept interest rates low and rigged.

Doing Away with the Roosevelt Bank Reforms

However, the great Roosevelt banking controls began being dismantled on the sly in 1951. The statutory reserves were used less and less and even completely done away in New Zealand and Canada. They continue, in enfeebled form in the US and the UK. In Brazil they are as high as 67%. Obviously there statutory reserves have been abused in Latin America to do much of the financing of the government without resorting to taxing the wealthy.

If you depend on higher interest rates to rein in inflation, you disturb just about everything in the economy. The economy in fact is reduced to what armies call *collateral damage:* The exchange value of the dollar goes up as foreign hot money floods in to profit by the higher rates, exports quoted in dollars become dearer, and hence find fewer customers abroad. Unemployment rises. Massive capital losses take place for those who hold previously issued long-term debt at lower rates, since their market prices sink below par. Such debt will not be renewed except for lesser amount at higher rates. And so forth. The government deficit rises. On the other hand, by leaving interest rates alone and just requiring banks to leave more of the credit they create with the central bank as reserves, they have less to lend out, and thus the restraint can be directed in a better focused way at those who actually are contributing to inflation. Meanwhile, the increase in the statutory reserves provides the central government with an interest-free source of credit with which it could undertake essential public investments to provide essential human and physical infrastructure.

As for the "structural price rise," recognizing its existence provided a whole menu of policy techniques. Elsewhere in this issue we deal with that very different problem.

The end of statutory reserves and the declaration of the debt of OECD countries to be risk-free requiring no additional bank capital for banks to acquire, empowered Canada's banks to load up with another $60 billion dollars of federal debt without putting up additional cash or capital. In addition they no longer had to provide reserves for some 473 billions of reservable deposits. All in all it amounted to an annual entitlement for the banks of some $5 to $8 billion dollars a year depending on how high the central bank had screwed up interest rates.

That left an ugly hole in the federal budget. And to cope with that, Ottawa slashed grants to the provincial governments and these eventually cut just about every social program – education, health, social security. That left the municipalities with the resulting social problems without the funds for dealing with them. In one form another that problem has spread throughout the world. All this is a by-product of governments and their central banks surrendering the basic powers of money creation to the private banks. Moreover, at the same time the private financial institutions have been deregulated to allow them to use these vastly extended powers of money creation in every aspect of speculative finance.

On all this there was a minimum of explanation or discussion.

Most of this was done in complete or semi-stealth, though a royal commission travelled across the country, as far as I could learn from appearing before it. Judging by the light it shed on what was underfoot, it could have saved the carfare and stayed at home. A central point in the banks' propaganda that looked into the matter, reiterated by the chairman of the commission, was that our banks could not possibly compete with the giant Japanese banks unless they merged. I pointed out to that commission something that has now become common knowledge. Several of those giant Japanese banks cited as models for our banks had already lost their entire capital in gambles on the euro-market and were making no further loans.

But there is a reason why after every financial crisis, a push for bank mergers comes to the fore.

This has little to do with their power to compete. After their last bailout and deregulation our banks – even without mergers – had managed to lose heavily in several countries of Latin America. At least a couple of them got mixed up in some of the most malodorous off-sheet balance partnerships of Enron. It hardly enhanced the fair name of Canada abroad, and was scarcely worth funding the banks to make such escapades possible. But nowhere has there been even the pretence of summing up the cost of the previous bailouts and mergers, before authorizing more of the same. We are instead experiencing a campaign to whip up enthusiasm for making our banks equal to the biggest and the best as though we were supporting the Canadian hockey team in a world contest. Little consideration is given to the effect of our bank legislation on the banks' services to our domestic economy.

A key reason why banks are given to singing their mating call so persistently stems from the very nature of banking. Banks, if they run their businesses properly, are able to lend out many times the amount of cash reserves they hold in their tills or with the central bank.

That is known as the *bank multiplier*. Banking arose historically when goldsmiths, large merchants, notaries in Britain who handled the sale of the Church properties that Henry VIII expropriated and resold, were left with substantial amounts of un-claimed cash until the new ownership was arranged. Merchants buying or selling goods to other parts of Europe in the Middle Ages, avoided risking the shipment of gold and silver to pay for them over the bad highways infested with robbers. Instead they arranged for a reputable money-changer in one center to release payment against a bill of lading when the goods arrived. Thus with a only a marginal shipment of gold and silver, accounts could be settled when the bills of lading were presented, or as new buyers were found for confiscated property, or court cases or estates were settled. Until then the money remained in the hands of goldsmiths or notaries. Those with whom it was left soon found that if they kept a discreet amount of that cash that was likely to be called for, they could put out the excess money for a return. On occasion they might even share what it earned as interest with its owner.

A Temptation More Powerful than Woman, Wine and Song

But the mere presence of idle money is an enormous temptation, far beyond that of women, wine or song. Indeed, it subsumes all such lesser temptations, since it makes it possible in theory or practice to indulge them And that is why so many the founders of banking went broke. This is why the deregulation of banks to allow them to engage in activities related to the stock market is madness. When it happens – and it is one of the defining follies of our age – it is a sure sign that speculative finance has become the dominant political power.

But for banks merging – no matter how few there may already be, and how large – merging is an irrepressible urge beyond anything that happens in, say, manufacturing.

It has to do with the mechanics of chequing accounts. A deposit-taking bank or other financial institution can lend out many times the cash it holds on hand to meet its obligations. When its depositors write cheques on their bank made out to someone who deposits the cheque in an account with another bank, the bank drawn on must surrender part of its cash reserves to the payee's bank. In that way it loses not only credit but base money that enabled it to write many times the loans of the amount of cash it pays to the other bank. However, if the depositor writes a cheque to another depositor of the same bank, his cheque in no way involves a surrender of cash or diminishes the bank's capacity to create further credit.

This leads to an indisputable conclusion. It is always in a bank's interest to merge with another bank, provided it does not over-pay.

However, such a monopolist bank would be completely against the interest of the community at large – even if our banks had not been deregulated to gamble on the market, in derivatives and countless other ways.

It is necessary that the public learn something about the basics of banking before it is too late. Unless they do, our politicians never will. The next lesson is that before we can authorize further mergers or further deregulation we need a competent objective report on the previous bailouts, mergers and deregulations.

William Krehm

Déja Vu with a Stutter

ON MAY 3, 2003, TV news-viewers saw a brilliant re-creation of an ancient Roman rite – the triumph of a returning general. Instead of the procession into the heart of the city by the general, his army, and the looted foreign treasures and noble captives in chains, this triumph featured the Commander-in-Chief of the world's biggest army landing on his aircraft carrier, the *Abraham Lincoln*. Dressed in his flight suit, as though fresh from the battle, the returning general emerged to the cheers of his assembled troops. Of course he changed to the imperial purple (the presidential business suit) for the next scene in which he addressed the world from a lectern set up on the deck.

It was PR heaven.

Moreover, instead of foreign slaves and looted gold, the Commander-in-Chief brought back real prizes – the secured oil fields of Iraq, and a new regime that will not sell oil for euros. Compared to this double triumph – maintaining the most profitable American export (the dollar) and securing the most vital import (oil) – a little looting by locals back in Iraq and the escape of the prime "noble slaves," Saddam and Osama, remained minor PR inconveniences.

Comparing modern United States with the behaviour of past empires offers illumination. For instance, when the US was pressing NATO into the Balkan war, readers of ancient history could hardly fail to consider the relations of 5th century Athens with the states of the Delian League. NATO and the Delian League were both created as defensive alliances to meet a threat on their eastern frontiers. Both saw themselves as defenders of "democracy" against an evil foreign tyrant.

What happened to the League is revealing. All members, large and small, undertook to make military or financial contributions towards their common defence. Athens made the biggest contribution and became increasingly the dominant partner. The Athenians transferred the treasury of the League from little Delos to Athens, where it was used to build Athenian ships, and to fortify and beautify the city. Member states who objected or who failed to make their contributions were suppressed, as Athens went on to use the League to further its own imperial interests. The city state which we still call "the cradle of democracy" had become an empire.

There is a caution in this tale, however. The Delian League, thus converted to the Athenian Empire, went on to shoot itself fatally in the foot by an ill-devised assault on the distant state of Syracuse, an ally of its nearby enemy, Sparta. Thucydides' *History of the Peloponnesian War* describes the catastrophic Sicilian campaign (415-414 BC) as an object lesson on the folly of reaching too far afield. The Sicilians' utter wipe-out of the Athenian army makes Custer's last stand sound like a tea party. Sparta, the great land power, biding its time, eventually defeated Athens.

But the US constitution was not modelled on Athenian democracy. In fact, right-wing apologists today point out that the US is not a "democracy" at all but a "republic." The model of the founding fathers was not Athens, but the Roman republic.

Washington's Roman Model

Like the US, the Roman republic was built on a successful revolt against a foreign monarch. So its institutions were designed to prevent the return of monarchy. The chief executive function was not lodged in one man, but in two consuls, who were elected annually. They shared the responsibility of governing, even to the extent, in war, of commanding the army on alternate days! That was a little too radical for the founders of the US, but they held the "separation of powers" to be a fundamental principle of the constitution, with power being divided among the two legislatures, the President, and the judiciary.

"Republic" derives from the early Roman state in which the *res publica* – public affairs – were handled by a classic see-saw of power between a patrician class, based in the Senate, and a democratic underclass, based in the plebeian assemblies. Julius Caesar was a leader of the latter. His former buddy and equally successful general, Gnaeus Pompey, cast his lot in with the senatorials – and lost. But the senatorials got Big Julie in the end on a sad day in March 44 BC, and by the time the dust had settled, Rome's republican quasi-democracy moved to a new stage – the empire.

With empire came wealth from abroad (including slaves) and for freemen at home, unemployment. The emperors kept the unemployed freemen placated with gifts of grain and entertainment, "bread and circuses." For the modern empire, of course, television supplies the mind-numbing violent entertainment, but it also has an important economic function – the creation of consumer demand, which is the life blood of our growth-addicted monetary system.

The slave element of the modern empire is supplied by foreign workers, who are encouraged to remain where they were born, and increasingly by the 1.2 million people in US jails, especially in the privatized working jails, where the prisoners are employed at modest wages.

The economics of empire, however, are tricky. The making of weapons of war – Athenian galleys, Roman swords, British battleships or American "smart" bombs – expands the GDP figures, and like other forms of wealth – houses, cars, clothing, foods – those products disappear from the net worth register when consumed. But the consumption of weapons of war involves a further calculus. In use, they consume other forms of wealth as well – buildings, vehicles, food stores, natural resources, physical infrastructure, and that form of wealth usually excluded from the simplistic calculation of GDP, able-bodied and educated people. So over the long term, empire may not be a good investment.

We wish our American friends well in their little conquests of smaller, weaker countries, but, as Canadians sharing a continent, and probably a fate, with them, we can only hope that a certain great land power, which we need not name, develops its own internal problems with democracy, and does not catch the great American Republic with its pants down on some distant field. We must so hope because there is no good reason to believe that an American empire will avoid the flaw which Aristotle identifies in Greek Tragedy as *hubris,* the overweening pride that precedes a fall.

Gordon Coggins

Coggins, a retired professor of Brock University, now resides in Windsor. As appears from his article, his mind admits no restrictions of space, time, or a lone discipline.

The Malignant Nodes of our Hyped Economy

ELSEWHERE we have set up diagrams of our mixed economy that show the interactions of its various subsystems in pursuit of their goals that allow the system as a whole to function. The market economy alone has as prime purpose earning a profit. The other subsystems – the government, the household economy, the environment, education, health, social security and so forth, get most of their money from the various levels of government. These in turn levy the taxation to cover their costs. It falls to the government to look after the creation of the infrastructures, physical and human, without which the economy could not operate. To achieve this governments must have lengthier time-horizons than the private sector.

Power has always been a key factor in any society. Privileged groups, whether a military elite, landowning classes, merchants, or bankers in various societies set the official ideology. Even the language helps predetermine how the national income is distributed. For the past three decades or so, that economic power has been largely in the hands of speculative finance. There is no lack of evidence on the point, starting with much in our law books that is disregarded.

Thus, in the very preamble of the *Bank of Canada Act*, the purpose of the Bank of Canada is given "to mitigate fluctuations in the general level of production, trade, prices and employment, so far as may be possible within the scope of monetary actions." That notwithstanding, in fact for at least forty years, the central bank has directed its efforts not to mitigate fluctuations but to keep unemployment high enough to provide enough unemployment to hold the price level flat. Even the word "deflation" disappeared from the vocabulary of the central bank. When its then Governor let a warning about the prospect of it slip out of his mouth before the Commons Finance Committee, he was back in eight days expressing regret for having uttered it. He even declared that he would probably regret having done so all his life. However, his warning about the danger of deflation was realized in Eastern Asia within two years and spread its devastation to Latin America and Russia, and now even to Canada and the United States. and Europe.

Moreover, our central bank like many throughout the world had abandoned the only effective means of dealing with deflation – a systemic lack of demand to take care of the over-supply of goods, services and willing workers. After WWII the widely expected depression was avoided by the central banks of the Western world taking on enough government debt to finance the huge backlog of neglect in infrastructures that had accumulated during a decade of depression and six years of war. The mechanism for this was simple, and was adequately described in the economic textbooks of the period. Because in countries like Canada and the United Kingdom, the sole shareholder of the central bank is the government, interest paid to the central bank on the debt of the government reverts to it substantially as dividends. But even where the central bank is owned by private banks as is the Federal Reserve in the US, roughly the same thing occurs by virtue of the monopoly of the ancestral monarch in coining precious metals. (This was known as *seigniorage* and has been largely assigned to the private banks.)

In 1991 an amendment to the Canadian *Bank Act* was slipped through Parliament without debate or press lease phasing out the statutory reserves. These were a modest proportion of the deposits deposited with them by the public that the banks had to leave – interest-free – with the central bank. They served a double purpose:

A Tool for Controlling both Inflation and Deflation

That provided a means of dealing with either inflation or deflation as the need arose, *without* being entirely dependent on interest rates. Instead, the amount of credit that the banks could create on a given deposit base could either be decreased (to restrain inflation) or increased (to combat deflation). Moreover, it allowed the government to target its goal, with a minimum of the collateral damage resulting from high interest rates. Our banks had at the time lost much or all of their capital in speculative loans in gas and oil and real estate plays, and the ending of the statutory reserves in 1991-3 had released the reserves to recapitalize them.

But those reserves had had another vital purpose. They allowed the central bank to make near-interest free loans to the Government within existing credit constraints. The mechanism was simple enough: the interest paid on the government debt held by the Bank of Canada found its way back to the government as dividends with the exception of administrative charges. Now that virtually free financing has been replaced by debt held by the commercial banks.

The Bank for International Settlements – a sort of central bankers's club whose sessions are not open to anybody connected with a government – issued its guidelines on risk-based capital requirements. Essentially these replaced cash reserves that had been abolished in a few countries like Canada and New Zealand and reduced to near irrelevance in most others including the US and the UK. Very little of the banks' capital is kept in cash because cash breeds no interest. It gets invested in stocks and bonds and derivatives, much of which, if at all, appear on the banks' books at their original purchase price.

Were the statutory reserves in place all that would be necessary in dealing with the deflation that is engulfing the world today would be to lower the reserve quota and have the government make essential infrastructural investments to fill the gap arising from the blue funk of the private sector. As in the 1930s idle physical and human resources for the purpose are gathering all around us.

There is talk of the Japanese Central Bank starting to buy government debt. That is good, but not enough. The private sector both in Japan and now in the US has been demoralized not only by the stock market crash but by the evidence still pouring out of the American courts of the massive fraud in some of the highest corporative circles.

A note of disbelief is replacing the awe that financial columnists used to show when the mighty Alan Greenspan, Governor of the US Federal Reserves, read the tea-leaves. Thus Brian Milner (*The Globe and Mail*, 23/6, "Those who watch Fed watchers fun to watch"): "[Greenspan] said that because 'the cost of taking out insurance against deflation is so low we can aggressively attack some of the underlying forces, which are essentially weak demand.' The only question then becomes how much to cut, and the answer hinges on how worried Mr. Greenspan and company are about the threat of deflation and how much ammunition they have left to fight it. Fed officials insist they have plenty of other arrows in their quiver, but outside observers are not so sure."

A Self-inflicted Dilemma

Those arrows were all shot at the moon in the great bailing out of the banks over a decade ago.

Were the statutory reserves still here and their use not proscribed by Wall St., all that Washington and Ottawa would need do is to lower the reserve requirement, and use the central bank to finance projects to renew and extend our defective infrastructures, health, education, social security.

The contracts for such work, of course, in most cases would be let to the private sector, and the lower reserve requirements would make available inexpensive financing for the private sector to step in to fill government contracts. That would set in motion the forces of economic recovery that are so clearly absent at present.

The Wall Street Journal (25/6, "The Fed Sharpens Rate-Cut Shears Again" by E.S. Browning pins down the prevailing business mood: "Some investors are…starting to look past the Fed news for signs of actual improvement in the economy and business performance. In some ways, they say, it matters relatively little how much the Fed cuts rates."

What really matters is whether the Fed's previous 12 rate cuts are starting to have impact. The Fed has suggested that this rate would be more of an insurance policy than anything else. (The 13th Fed rate-cut came in the next day at 1/4% bringing the Fed rate down to 1% the lowest since 1957.)

But clearly liquidity is not the problem. It is a sign how deeply all that was learned in the thirties has been buried, for it to take our political leaders so long to figure this out.

And the comparison of the present cut with an "insurance policy" could hardly have been more tactless. For the press is full of the scandal-tinged plight of the insurance industry.

The Globe and Mail (14/06, "Soaring Insurance, Outraged motorists" by Paul Waldie and Peter Cheney) writes: "Canada's auto-insurance industry is in crisis and governments across the country are scrambling to respond to pressure from outraged drivers who face soaring premiums.

"Rising injury costs, falling stock markets and a global slump in the insurance business since the September 11, 2001, terrorist attacks on the US have driven auto insurance beyond the reach of many Canadians. Industry officials said it is not uncommon for some drivers to be quoted premiums of up to $8,000 a year.

"Insurance companies say they are not making money. They cannot rely on stock market profits to keep premiums low, it costs them more to buy their own insurance known as reinsurance – to spread risks and they face skyrocketing claims. Undoubtedly the over-congested highways due to Globalization and Deregulation have contributed to this.

"A typical fender bender in Ontario can cost as much as $75,000 because of fees to lawyers, medical professionals and other. Only a small fraction of that money, they said, goes to the victim. Bob Smalley, a retired life-insurance executive in Florenceville, NB, saw his car insurance premium go up to $3,700 from $1,500 this year after he made two minor claims that cost his insurance company less than $1,200 after he had paid his deductible."

That introduces a fistful of factors from elsewhere in the economy. It makes it necessary for us to draw up a map of flows from one section of the economy to another, based not on what those connections should be, but what they have become under the stressful misdirections of exponential growth, globalization and deregulation, and the domination of financial capital.

There are definite nodal points in the economy where communications converge and where the economy is particularly exposed to serious ravaging by private interests. The term "node" is borrowed from mathematics, or more fully from biology (as in "lymphatic nodes") where malignant cells metastasize more rapidly throughout the body.

They are points of vulnerability that should be under constant attention from policy-makers. In general it is at such crossroads that much of society's capital pools are to be found, and can be most easily preyed on. One of these is the areas of money creation – the central banks and their control over commercial banking. Another is the insurance industry, where capital reserves are particularly important at a time like the present when an overstressed, world, at murderous odds with itself, raises risk to a fever pitch.

The notion of any insurance firm keeping its reserves on a hyped up stock market fingers an essential part of the trouble. For that compounds risks of our society rather than controls them. However, if you remove the firewalls that had been put in between insurance and banking, and the stock market, you are off to the races with a guaranteed ticket on the wrong horse. The trouble is that in its desperate need to keep its bubble in ascent, any pool of capital, no matter what its purpose, has been seized upon to keep the cauldron boiling.

The fact that bank holding companies were acquiring insurance companies and tapping their reserves to keep their favourite stocks looking well, was a cross-bred risk that no insurance company needed. Government debt is the proper investment for insurance reserves. The stock market itself in all its aspects is the node of nodes, where auditors are corrupted and lawyers become accustomed to a level of earnings that can only be explained by the black magic expected of them.

You can hardly open your newspaper any day of any week

without being confronted with something novel that qualifies disturbingly for this new concept of an economic node.

Investment Trusts — The Next Bubble

Today's *Globe and Mail* (June 27, "Banking on yield not a wise move – A Matter of Trust – The Booming Business of Investment Trusts" by Andres Willis and Rob Carrick) takes a hard look at the new fad of investment trusts intended to revive the drooping stock market: "Investing in trusts means embracing a contradiction. Trusts are bought for their yield, for the monthly income promised to trustholders. So doesn't it just make sense that the best trust boasts the highest yields?

"Not at all. Focusing exclusively on units that promise the highest income bang, is a strategy that's bound to backfire. The reality of today's market is trusts with the highest yields are the most likely to disappoint.

"More often than not, soaring yields signal a business is stumbling, and a trust's all-important distributions are about to be cut. The income trust hall of shame is rapidly filling with companies that boasted sweet double-digit yields before they took the axe to investors's income."

Unless of course, you believe in Santa Claus, and even if you did you would be at the wrong address unless you had control of stuffing the stockings. What you have there is the latest node to highjack income intended for other destinations. And the real trouble is that our economy re-engineered for dependence on a stock market that cannot function without such contrivances.

What we are encountering on all sides is a charter of inter-action between the different areas of the economy not as they logically should be, but as they have become. We are driven to think in term of nodal points where flows are intercepted and diverted to uses that have no call on them. The deregulated banks are one such, and we have alluded how the statutory reserves that provided both a control over the leverage of the banks' money creation and virtually free funds to the government, were preempted to serve as an annual entitlement for the deregulated banks' gambles. The deregulated banks themselves now in control of our stock markets and a growing interest in every capital pool tap money creation for speculation. That adds an unprecedented leverage to mega-gambles. Derivatives are another such nodal point combining insane leverage with a minimum of disclosure and endless possibilities for keeping things off the corporative books. Command of such nodes by speculative finance explains Governor Greenspan's plight with a single useless tool in his much-advertised kit. He has become a plumber called upon to fix a burst water pipe with a single toothpick in his tool kit.

William Krehm

Lessons from Norway for our Emerging World

*T*HE WALL STREET JOURNAL (30/6, "Norway Can Offer Lessons to Iraq on Redevelopment" by Bob Davis) has some powerful implicit advice for the Third World as well. But first what it can teach Iraq and its redevelopers:

"Norway is one of the few major oil producers to have made enduring economic gains since the 1970s. Among Middle Eastern oil producers, income per person actually *declined* during the past three decades after accounting for inflation, despite the run-up in oil prices.

"Saddam Hussein squandered Iraq's oil riches through war and Stalinist-type central planning. His neighbors were less venal but shared many of Iraq's vices. Oil wealth has been hoarded throughout the Mideast by corrupt leaders, who waste vast sums on inefficient state-run businesses, shut the borders to foreign competition and don't invest enough in education, especially of women.

"'Manna from heaven can be a mixed blessing,' says Thorvaludur Gulfason, a University of Iceland economist, who studied nations rich in natural resources.

"Compared with Iraq, Norway had many advantages. When Norway first pumped crude oil from the North Sea in 1975, it was a stable democracy, with honest civil servants, a well-established legal system and a large middle class. Median income trailed most of Western Europe, but was well above Iraq's. Also, Norway produces about three million barrels a day; before the war, Iraq was pumping out two million barrels.

"But, like other oil nouveaux riches, Norway was seduced by oil wealth. A generous welfare system was expanded. Today, Norwegians take 25 sick days annually, on average, and work only 26.5 hours a week. Investment poured into the oil sector, but Norwegian manufacturing languished as the currency appreciated. Mobile-communications firms prospered in Finland and Sweden, but Norway missed the high-tech boom and was tethered to the rise and fall of oil prices. The public sector became bloated, and exporters, outside of natural resources, suffered.

"Norway rebounded in the 1990s, largely by segregating the oil businesses from the rest of the economy. The Norwegians lessened its oil dependence, and the private sector diversified. Norway's growth has slowed since 2001, but many steps Oslo took are important for Baghdad, too.

"*Sharing the wealth.* Norwegian law makes clear that the oil resources are owned by the Norwegian people – not by a particular clique or geographic area. That wasn't the case in Mr. Hussein's Iraq, and it's still far from clear whether the Kurdish north and the Shiite south will make special claims to the oil fields there. 'If oil revenues have to be shared with everyone, you can't take the money, leave everyone poor, and spend it on nuclear weapons,' says Amy Jaffe, a senior analyst at Rice University's Baker Institute.

"*Separate Accounts.* Starting in 1990, Norway funnelled revenue from its state-owned oil business into a separate Government Petroleum Fund. Assets are expected to total 120 billion at year end – a huge sum for a country of 4.5 million. They are invested in foreign stock and bonds. (Investing in domestic companies would push the value of the currency too high, the government argues, and hook local companies on subsidies.)

"Norway uses only the *return* on the Fund's investments, estimated at 4% annually, to balance the non-oil budget. The oil revenue accumulates year after year, and is designed eventually for the retirement of Norwegian baby-boomers."

Since oil and gas are quickly fading resources, with price levels controlled by the enormously greater and lower-cost producers like Saudi Arabia, it would be wise for more oil producers in the Third and Emerging worlds to copy Norway's example. All or a large part of the country's oil revenues should be segregated in a similar fund and invested in a basket of foreign debt, and only the income from that fund be spent for current purposes. This will avoid the domestic price inflation during oil booms that imposes an impossible obstacle to the lasting improvement of the economy by making it impossible for young domestic consumer industries to compete with cheap imports. The difference with Norway, which already has modern infrastructures, is that these are very deficient in most Third World and emerging oil-producing countries. Consequently, it would be in the national interest that the accumulated capital from the oil fund should be carefully withdrawn from time to time to build schools, hospitals, and physical infrastructures, with an emphasis on getting as much of the necessary work and materials as are available at reasonable terms from domestic sources. That will provide for a more stable economy, less wholly dependent on the volatile oil and gas markets. It would give these countries a chance of working their way out of the oil trap.[1]

William Krehm

1. In *The Wall Street Journal* (9/07, p. A4, "[L. Paul] Bremer Says Iraq Will Depend on Oil to Finance New Budget," the occupying coalition's civil administrator of Iraq, "said he favors setting up an oil trust fund to fund pensions or pay yearly dividends to citizens like the system used in Alaska." For the masses of Third World oil producers, it would be better to have the fund capital earmarked for essential physical and social infrastructures, to increase the likelihood of such countries ever emerging from their Third World Status. Alaska, too, as a state of the American Union does not have the sovereign status that Third World producers must reinforce and protect by diminishing their economic dependence on the great oil-consuming powers.

Africa as a Corrective for our Segemented Economic Theory

MARGINAL THEORY reduces the world and its occurrences into just encounters of supply and demand on an idealized market of its dreams. The misfirings of this procedure are so teeming that there are days when even our bulkiest New York publications can hardly find the space for reporting the resulting disasters. This does have the occasional advantage of juxtaposing the real causes and effects in adjacent pages, reuniting what bumptious theories have parted.

Increasingly recognized as the mother continent of the human race, Africa has long been the deepest basket of its woes. On page A4 of *The Wall Street Journal* (9/07, "Drug Patents Draw Scrutiny as Bush Goes to Africa" by Michael Schroeder): "In a five-nation African tour this week, President Bush is trumpeting his $15 billion program to fight the continent's AIDS epidemic. But that program's gains could be undercut by a parallel US effort to impose strict patent protections that make AIDS drugs more expensive and harder to obtain.

"The Commerce Department is helping shape patent laws in countries such as Nigeria – that go beyond global standards in protecting drug makers. The US Trade Representative is seeking similar protections.

"Said Asia Russell, international policy coordinator at the Health Global Access Project, a non-governmental activist group, 'there are many ways that the Bush administration has contravened the letter and spirit' of global efforts to give needy countries better drug access. The drug companies are major bankrollers of his re-election effort.

"In 2000 the US Agency for International Development funded a $1.2 million technical-assistance program administered by the Commerce Department. It was aimed at helping Nigeria improve oversight of publicly financed projects, rework its regulatory functions – and rewrite patent laws.

"As part of the program, the Commerce Department sponsored some Nigerian officials, lawyers and lawmakers to attend patent-law writing conferences. Commerce Department letters and reports indicate 100 government officials and trade group representatives were invited, with the US picking up the airfare tab and total expenses of $940 each for about 20 attendees – the equivalent of three times Nigeria's annual per capita income.

"Non-government public-health representatives weren't invited, though after protests, they were allowed to attend. Olayide Akanni, a representative of the Treatment Action Group, an activist umbrella organization, presented an analysis of draft legislation saying its intellectual property protections exceeded those require by the World Trade Organization. Her points: The bill mandates a complex Nigerian court process to license cheaper generic-drug copies to treat serious diseases, instead of the simpler government procedure allowed by global rules. It adds a four-year waiting period for issuing drug licenses, when WTO rules in general have no waiting period. The bill would block non-government civil health organizations from applying for licences and would punish violators with criminal sanctions, instead of the more common civil sanctions.

"Nnamandi, the Commerce Department's commercial-development-program manager for Africa, says his group 'did not influence the process,' and Nigerian officials made the decisions about the legislation.

"But the US drug industry expressed concerns that relaxing patents beyond those for a limited list of epidemics would set a precedent leading to much broader erosion of intellectual-property rights. They cite industry fears that could spark an open season on lucrative drugs of little relevance to African public-health crises, citing Pfizer Inc.'s impotence remedy, Viagra, and products designed to prevent baldness."

Besides what is a mere four years wait for so great a benefaction as a drug to relieve the suffering AIDS?

For the answer we need only turn to page one of the same issue of the *WSJ* and another article, "In Africa, AIDS and Famine Now Go Hand in Hand" by Roger Thurow under a Swaziland dateline: "Their father died in 1999, their mother in 2000, both of them what social workers believe were complications from AIDS. Since then, Makhosazane Nkhambule, now 16 year old, has been caring for her four younger brothers and sisters in their one-room mud-brick shack.

"They sweep the floor of the house and the dirt yard with homemade straw brooms. They try to patch holes in the thatched roof and plug cracks in the mud walls. They fetch water from a well nearly a mile away. They scavenge wood for the fire. They go to school in a neighbor's house.

"Makhosazane says they can do everything, except feed themselves. 'I would like to plant corn and vegetables, but we have no money to buy seeds or tools. Her parents' cattle could have helped with the plowing, but they have died. The garden beside the hut and the two-acre field behind it haven't been planted since their mother died.

"For two years, the orphans scrounged what they could, asking neighbors for scraps of food and waiting for relatives in distant villages to bring something to eat. Last year, the United Nations' World Food Program came to Swaziland to distribute food to those suffering from the drought that has gripped southern Africa. Although the Nkhambule children had no crops to be killed by drought, they began receiving the food aid. So, too, did thousands of other households where the adults who had been tending the fields have died. According to government estimates HIV/AIDS infects more than one-third of adults in this tiny, hilly kingdom.

A New Variety of Famine

"The Nkhambule siblings, barefoot and wearing dirty, shabby clothes, embody what is being called an entirely new variety of famine. It breaks the historical mold of food crises. It isn't caused by weather, war, failed policy or crop disease. Rather this is a food shortage that kills the farmers themselves. Recovery won't come with weather improvement, new government policies, a peace treaty or improved hybrid crops. Once the farmers die, there is no rain that will make their empty fields grow.

"Across southern Africa, the region of the world hardest hit by AIDS, some seven million farmers have died from the epidemic, according to the estimates of governments and relief agencies. This has left many families with no means or experience to do the farming. The continuing AIDS crisis threatens to leave large populations 'reliant for their survival on a long-term program of international social welfare,' says Alex de Waal, of the UN Commission on Aids and governance in Africa.

"What is emerging in Swaziland has researchers ratcheting up the costs of AIDS. While nearby Botswana and South Africa have great mineral wealth and considerable industrial development, Swaziland is a largely agrarian country. AIDS and food shortages are combining to unravel societies and destabilize populations in new ways. 'A drought is usually in certain areas of a country, but AIDS is all over,' says Derek van Wissell, the national director of Swaziland's Emergency Response Council on HIV/AIDS.

"He notes that the percentage of women at prenatal clinics diagnosed with HIV skyrocketed to more than 38% in 2002 to just under 4% in 1992. Over the same period, per capital agricultural production fell by a third, even before the drought took over last year.

"In traditional famine, the first to die are usually the weakest, particularly children and the elderly. In the new variety, AIDS strikes at adults in the prime of life, leaving the children and elderly to cope. International aid organizations say that 10% of the nation's households are headed by children, and even more are headed by grandparents too old and too weak to work the fields."

W. Krehm

The Changing Sociology of Labour Relations

THE WALL STREET JOURNAL (1/07, "New Era for German Labor Movement?" by G. Thomas Sim and Christopher Rhoads) brings American readers tidings of novel German developments similar to those at home: "Germany's labor unions, once powerful enough to practically bring down the nation's leaders, have tumbled to their weakest position in the past half century.

"Over the weekend, one of Germany's largest unions threw in the towel in its fight for shorter working hours in former East Germany. The defeat came after four weeks of strikes and negotiations. It was the first time since 1954 that the IG Metall union of metalworkers and engineers failed to eke out even a minor victory.

"Other news showed Germany's hunger for reform as it tries to emerge from its second recession in two years. German Chancellor Gerhard Schroeder announced plans to accelerate tax cuts valued at 15.5 billion euros ($17.7 billion) in an attempt to inject new life into Germany, slashing the top tax rate to 42% from 48.5% next year instead of in 2005. The combined events prompted Bank of America yesterday to e-mail a note to clients titled 'A little German Revolution.'

"Martin Werding, head of social policies and labor markets

at Ifo Institute for Economic Research at the University of Munich, said the union's defeat reminds him of events in the UK in the 1980s. Margaret Thatcher swept to power in 1979 as Britons flinched during the 'Winter of Discontent.' Workers and employers lost sympathy for unions after prolonged strikes and high wage increases. Eventually, unemployment rose, unions lost their leverage and the government enacted legislation that stripped labor unions of their power."

The labor movement internationally and social-minded political leaders have still to open their eyes to the root causes of the serious decline of the labour movement over the past thirty years.

Picture the struggle for the distribution of the national product throughout the world as an ongoing war. Up to the 1970s on its main front, like the defences of Singapore in WWII, cannon were built to point in a single direction. This expressed the official doctrine that the only war that counted was between labour and industrial capital. The rules and scoring for that ongoing battle had been drawn up in the 1930s and 1950s. But since then another front has opened up. On it the challenger had enough firing power and mobility to encircle both industry *and* labour. The new contender diverted all available resources to its own ends. What remained to labour and industrial capital to scrap over was of dwindling importance. The main advantage of the new aggressor, speculative capital, was his command of the new magic of digital disinformation.

A good instance of this is the surreptitious appropriation of the pension funds for the new victor's own ends. Cast as a bone of contention between the unions and near bankrupt producing corporations in a setting of growing unemployment, there is really no way of enforcing the contracts that gave rise to the pension contracts. Steel companies, airlines or whatever, simply declare bankruptcy, and entertain offers for the sale of their physical assets rather than the companies that contracted to provide worker pensions.

"Particularly in its earlier history, the banks' power to get businesses started or stay afloat had been a steady source of pressure on politicians from those who want the government to make borrowing easier and cheaper. It was also the source of the popular desire to keep banking a local activity. Not unreasonably, people want their bank chartered locally, owned locally,

operated locally, and subject to pressure from the neighborhoods. The *McFadden Act* of 1926 and the Douglas Amendment to the *Bank Holding Company Act* of 1956, which narrowly restricted the deposit-taking offices a bank or a holding company could control, expressed the weight of the nation's experience. The *Community Reinvestment Act* of 1977 was only the most generalized and idealistic of many political efforts to make local banks and branches of distant banks lend their money where they got it" (Martin Mayer. *The Money Bazaars*. New York: E.P. Dutton, Inc., 1984, p. 323).

What then in this perspective, are we to say of the removal of the cash base raised in deposits locally, and the credit created under deregulated multipliers being sent not only to another state of the union, but into outer space? For such are the shenanigans that our deregulated banks engage in. Let us quote Martin Mayer again: "a Walter Wriston in New York [Citicorp] ran a phantasmagorical bank in which profits were merely reported and never earned; the loans never were and never would be repaid, and the borrowers could not afford to carry them. Increasingly, the interest on these foreign loans, which Citicorp reported as revenue, was merely another loan from the bank to the borrower, building reported assets faster than reported liabilities, but yielding no cash flow."

That is the key to many of the sterile confrontations between labour and industrial corporations. What they are disputing has already been high-jacked and gambled away. It is not there any more. Still worse, ever more frequently the same can be said of the jobs that were supposed to earn the workers those pensions on retirement.

Under Presidents Eisenhower and Kennedy, increased pensions were raised to the status of a substitute for immediate pay hikes, essentially to pseudo money supply. It was a trend highly approved and even sponsored by the government. As was the increased discretion of corporations to invest their workers' pension funds on the stock market rather than in government bonds.

The treatment of labor pensions contrasts strikingly with the quick response of the government, when confronted with a bank in trouble that is "too large to be allowed to fail." Workers and Industrialists of the World Wake Up!

William Krehm

Moral Stock-Taking

THERE ARE MANY THINGS that ail the world economy, but of these the most serious is the failure of morality. Morality not as an adornment of all other virtues, nor as an insider's nod to God to go on sending down His clearly addressed blessings, but rather morality as a basic requisite. Without it no social ties are possible. Even man's much-advertised genius for pursuing selfish ends takes a beating. Neither decalogues nor inhibitions of territoriality are left to prevent our species from ripping itself into extinction.

Evidence of that is overwhelming. The Enron scandal refuses to die. It is a hydra that does not run out of new heads. *The Globe and Mail* (5/08, "Roots run deep between Enron and CIBC" by Karen Howlett and Sinclair Stewart) reports: "In the summer of 1991, the London brokerage arm of Canadian Imperial Bank of Commerce was one [of several] firms selected to underwrite a £795 million financing for Teeside Power Ltd., the largest independent power project to date in Britain.

"The deal followed Prime Minister Margaret Thatcher's transformation of Britain. During her 11-year reign ending in 1990, her government sold the telephone service, the airlines and a host of other Crown companies. The electrical utilities in England and Wales were among the last privatized.

"The Teeside deal was pivotal for CIBC, which like many banks, was still coping with the fallout from the market crash of 1987, and the meltdown in commercial real estate in the early 1990s. The deal's importance was not its underwriting fees, much less the bragging rights that accompany a place in any large syndicate. Its real significance was that it helped the bank forge a relationship with Teeside's controlling shareholder – burgeoning energy concern Enron Corp.

"Those ties are now the source of considerable anguish for the bank, which last week was one of six financial institutions accused by the company's US court-appointed examiner, of 'aiding and abetting' some of Enron's officers in manipulating its now-infamous financial statements. The examiner concludes that Enron could not have pulled off the fraud without the help of Citicorp Inc., J.P. Morgan Chase & Co., Barclays Bank PLC, Deutsche Bank AG, CIBC, and Merrill Lynch & Co. Inc.

"CIBC has denied any wrong-doing. But Neal Batson, the examiner who wrote the more than 1,000-page report, highlights numerous transactions between CIBC and Enron that helped the energy trader conceal billions of dollars worth of debt and dupe unsuspecting investors. Although many of the big Canadian banks had some involvement with Enron, CIBC was the only one Mr. Batson singled out for aiding and abetting the fraud. CIBC had the people, the appetite and the ability to structure complex financing because of its aggressive move into the US investment banking scene in the mid-1990s. It was CIBC chairman John Hunkin who changed the mindset of the bank. The career banker was appointed to the helm of CIBC World Markets Inc. in 1990 shortly after the bank bought Wood Gundy.

"Mr. Hunkin became CIBC chairman in 1999, and led the push to reinvent CIBC World Markets as a leading North American investment banking house that could play in the same sandbox with the most powerful names on Wall St.

"CIBC began to develop a derivative team in 1994, after poaching a handful of notable professionals from Lehman Brothers Inc. The next year, the bank purchased Argosy Group LP, a merchant banking outfit that helped the bank and many of its employees earn a fortune on Global Crossing Ltd., the now-insolvent Bermuda fiber-optics company. 'It was all about financial engineering, and fancy off-balance-sheet transactions,' said a former CIBC official who was there at the time.

"The financial wizardry Enron applied to its balance sheet led to its collapse in December, 2001. The levels of profit it claimed between 1997 and 2001 had been inflated to the tune of $600 million (US)."

Canadian Bank Morality at Half Mast

"During an eight-day period in December, 1999, CIBC had completed staggering so-called FAS purported asset sales that were nothing more than disguised loans. CIBC the following June was elevated to one of Enron's 'Tier One' banks. One of the criteria for that was a bank's ability to underwrite a billion dollars in a short period, lead and/or structure complex deals and develop senior management contacts and distribution capabilities.

"In the aftermath of Enron's collapse, the Teeside plant, which was eventually built in 1993 and began supplying as much as 4% of the electricity requirements of England and Wales, was left stranded with a heavy debt and a worthless $500 million electricity purchase contract with Enron. It was sold earlier this year by Enron's receivers to SembCorp Utilities of Singapore for $187 million Canadian. The legacy of the Enron relationship is unfolding on a number of unpleasant fronts.

"The bank, along with several other financial institutions, is being sued by investors in a class-action suit. Legal experts say the banks' bargaining position could be undermined by Mr. Batson's damning report. That report pegs the bank's exposure as just under $500 million. CIBC is also confronted with possible regulatory actions by the US Securities and Exchange Commission.

"'Back in the mid-nineties, I think the ethics of these things were quite different,' explained a former senior executive at CIBC. "You were allowed to do these things. What the [client] was doing, so long as it wasn't overtly criminal, you didn't care why they were doing them. That didn't seem to be our issue."

That a Canadian bank official could make such a statement shows how deeply buried are the fatal steps that brought down

Canada's financial morality to half-mast.

Proof of that: some of our largest banks were chief actors in the Enron and other official investigations on corporative scandals under way in the US that have gone on for years. But to date there has not been even the pretence of a single similar Canadian enquiry. There is a reason for that.

The Dead Rat Under our Floor Boards

The bailout of our gambling banks in the early 1990s was more brazen and far-reaching than anything in the US. That is the Dead Rat under the Floor Boards that has tainted the atmosphere of our financial sector. It was just too scandalous to make public. The amendment of the *Bank Act* in 1991 that bailed out our banks from previous gambles in real estate, gas, oil and whatever, was slipped through Parliament without debate or press release. It is the Great Unmentionable in Canadian public life. Its consequences have changed the very nature of Canadian society.

The bail-out of our banks from the loss of their entire capital – as a group – was double-pronged. Prior to the 1991 decennial amendment of the *Bank Act,* the Bank of Canada had two main tools for stabilizing the economy: it could alter the rates charged banks for overnight loans to meet their net cheque-clearing obligations and the cash withdrawals of depositors. But it could also vary the proportion of the banks' deposits from the public that they had to redeposit with the central bank on a non-interest-paying basis. These were known as "statutory reserves." They gave the Canadian government – as sole shareholder of the Bank of Canada – the free use of that money – a modest return for the surrender to them of most of its powers of creating money. Today all money is credit, but the only legal tender is the credit of the federal government. When the central bank holds federal government debt, the interest paid on it comes back to the government almost entirely as dividends. For since 1938 the federal government has been the sole shareholder of the central bank: it bought out some 12,000 private shareholders at a good profit in 1938 after a 3-year hold of the shares since the central bank's founding in 1935.

Instead of using its interest rate for overnight lending to the banks to rein in an excessively booming economy or to revive a listless one, the BoC could leave that benchmark rate alone, instead changing the statutory reserve requirement. If this was raised, it lowered the amount of credit banks could create on a given cash base; if lowered, it would increase their leverage of money creation. However, the statutory reserves were phased out over a two year period under the 1991 *Bank Act* amendment.

A little earlier, to address the world-wide crisis of banks, the Bank for International Settlements – an international private central bankers' club in Basel, Switzerland, that does not even allow anyone other than central bankers in government employ at its sessions – introduced its *Risk-Based Capital Requirements.* These declared the debt of the industrialized (OECD) countries "risk-free" requiring no additional capital for banks to acquire. However, in its haste to save the banks, the BIS had not done its homework. Since under its guidance central banks had made higher interest rates *"the sole blunt tool to fight inflation,"* and

in the early and mid-1990s the Bank of Canada jacked interest rates well into the double-digit range, the government debt that the banks loaded up with was anything *but* "risk-free." When interest rates go up, the market prices of pre-existing bonds drop like stones. This was a key factor in the surreptitious introduction of capital budgeting (accrual accountancy) in the US in 1996 by taking account of the government investments of physical capital that had been ignored. Carried back some years, that disinterred some $1.3 trillion of assets that had been written off and carried on the US government's book at a token value. However, this was done under the false heading of "Savings." They were of course not "savings" but "investments" since they were not in cash. But the Clinton regime that made this amendment was seeking a single statistic that would get the government more favourable credit ratings to help bring down interest rates, but would not upset the "political center" with Keynesian talk of government "investment." With the additional load of government debt the banks had taken on, the old high-interest-rate policy would have bankrupted many of them.

Deregulation on Heels of Bailout

As a result of these two measures – the amendment of the *Bank Act* and the BIS *Risk-Based Capital Requirements* for banks, Canada's banks were able to quadruple their holdings of federal debt to some $80 billion. In addition they were released from the need to put up statutory reserves for some $470 billion dollars of deposits they already held. This was not a one-shot bailout, but an annual entitlement that refunded the banks each year. And most scandalous of all, having bailed out our banks on an ongoing basis, they were further deregulated to allow their holding companies to take over every sort of stock market activity – brokerages, merchant banking, underwriting, derivative boutiques, insurance. Such activities are incompatible with their banking function.

After the 1929 stock market crash when thousands of US banks closed their doors, Washington set up firewalls to separate banking from stock market activities, mortgages and insurance. This legislation became the model throughout the non-Communist world. Now these firewalls were torched. Bailing out the banks from their previous gambles at the public expense was bad enough. Doing so as a recurring entitlement was even worse. But what capped the incredible: the banks were further deregulated. Nothing in the banking tradition could justify this. It was a power shift of seismic proportions. The dominant revenue whose view of the world was official became that of speculative finance. The entire economy was reduced to a lemon for the banks to squeeze.

Similar changes throughout the world took place under the supervision of the Bank for International Settlements. Canada's financial coup was only an extreme case: along with New Zealand Canada did away with statutory reserves entirely. They are still on the books in the US and the UK, although reduced to near-insignificance.

This *coup d'etat* was unthinkable without an information blackout. The very language of economics in the text books was reworked for the purpose. The social effects were staggering. In

Canada the federal government's interest costs shot up by anywhere from $5 billion to $8 billion yearly, depending on what the Bank of Canada had screwed interest rates up to. The proportion of the federal debt held by the Bank of Canada, which had moved into the mid-twenty percent range in the1970s, now dropped to about 5%. The banks had piped into the government treasury.

A vast campaign of dumbing down the electorate became mandatory. Analysis which constantly reexamines the relationships within an ever more complex mixed and globalized economy was replaced by number-crunching – the identification of economic health with a few ill-defined statistics – "inflation," "debt" and "deficit," "productivity." It doesn't matter that statistics may leave out independent factors contributing to their movement and thus run up unacknowledged deficits in public health, the environment and all other non-market sectors. These were simply proclaimed "externalities." The public has been systematically misled to believe that such matters are beyond their grasp.

Yet few of the dodges devised by rogue corporations and their auditors were not anticipated by our governments in the management of their own affairs. Thus though a distinguished line of Auditors General had urged the adoption of capital budgeting, the government insisted on writing off its investments, direct or indirect, as current spending. This had the double effect of exaggerating the current deficit and the government debt. Converting liabilities into assets and assets into liabilities has played a key role as in the scams of Enron-like corporations.

After decades of pushing high interest rates into the sky to achieve "zero inflation" the governments and many central banks throughout the world, faced with a stalled economy, have recognized that a measure of inflation – "1% to 2%" – was "useful" to prevent the economy keeling into deflation. In actual fact that 1% or 2% of inflation was not due to an excess of demand over supply – the proper definition of inflation – but to two quite different factors: (1) the greater amount of public services necessary in a high-tech urbanized economy; (2) the increasing costs of the elimination of basic infrastructure maintenance – physical and social – that reflected the shift of government resources to the banks' new bailout entitlement. For the most part, government services are not priced and sold but paid by taxation which must find its way into the price level. The full implications of that for our policy-making must be pursued. Otherwise we will be handicapped by a terminology that applies the one term to problems of quite different causes. No scientist or engineer would wish to be caught dead committing such a gaffe. Only in official economics!

All this is clearly related to the sins of Enron – in cooking the books at any level of human endeavour there are just a limited number of arithmetical operations that can be thrown into reverse gear. But doing that systematically in the case of government policy deprives humanity of the possibility of learning from its errors. Since the inventory to be covered up grows bigger and bigger there is more effort spent in hiding what has failed than in devising what is likely to succeed. Along the path followed in recent years, there are few places left to go

apart from military adventures to get the economy out of the gutter. And, of course, fuelling the super-leveraged activities of the stock-market-driven economy, requires sourcing ever more low-skilled production in the most wretched Third World countries. The economic dimensions of the roots of world terrorism have not begun to be seriously explored.

Healing our economy will not happen through the recovery of a few questionable statistics. The last bubble was kept going for the systematic plundering of just about every capital pool available – this included the privatization of public services at a fraction of their value, seeking out of sources with the lowest labour standards to replace domestic production, the looting of pension funds and of the public treasury. Much of this could not have happened without the Wild Western profusion of derivatives. That makes urgent the regulation of derivatives – a measure long recommended by prominent pillars of the financial world itself, but resisted by central banks and the BIS. Without unregulated derivatives, most of the scams of Enron-like companies would have been impossible. Significantly, no study of that connection has made the headlines since the meltdown.

William Krehm

Suppressed Lessons of History

FERNAND BRAUDEL (1902-85) was a leading member of a school of French historians that shifted the focus of the discipline from "the froth of events" to underlying, geographical, economic and social factors. In this sense he and his distinguished colleagues of the publication *Annales d'histoire économique et sociale* – Marc Bloch, Lucien Febvre, the Belgian Henri Pirenne – were in headlong conflict with the "Sorbonne" of establishment historians. They were in a broad sense doing to historical research what a few of us in COMER have been attempting in economic theory – put it in the necessary context of other disciplines. Braudel's iconoclasm was rewarded with years in the wilderness. It was only at the age of 82 that he was accepted into the French Academy. Partly because of his long boycott by the French historical establishment, he spent long years in far-off climes like Algeria and Brazil. That only sharpened his insights into the interdependence of disciplines and of cultures. In the sixties the French *Annales* writings had a considerable influence on my attempts to broaden economics from the study of an idealized market to embrace the entire burgeoning mixed economy.[1]

Braudel's unfinished masterpiece on which he laboured with a team of researchers for some twenty years, *Civilisation, économie et capitalisme XVe-XVIIIe siècles* examines earlier attempts to reorganize the world into ever more embracing markets.

The Asymmetry of Trade

Basic to Braudel's thinking is the *asymmetrical* nature of trade. The trading city states of the past – Venice, Antwerp, Amsterdam – and even in the world-economy of today, have a unique function "as the logistic heart of its activity. News, merchandise, capital, credit, people, instructions, correspondence all flow into and out of the master city. Its powerful merchants lay down the law. At varying and respectful distances around the centre, will be found other towns, sometimes playing the role of associate or accomplice, but resigned to their second-class role. Their activities, governed by those of the metropolis, direct the flow of business toward it, redistribute or pass on the goods it sends them, live off its credit or suffer its rule. Any town of importance was a Noah's Ark. They were the scene of fantastic mixtures, whether London or Istanbul or Malacca, Surat or Calcutta. The colourful, cosmopolitan population had to coexist and work in peace. In Venice there was no inquisition in matters of faith. Perhaps the most distinctive characteristic of all of these super-cities was their pronounced social diversification. Patriciate and proletariat indeed grew farther apart as the rich became richer and the poor even poorer, for the besetting sin of these pulsating capitalist cities was *their high cost of living.* Constant inflation resulted from the intrinsic nature of the higher urban functions that led to the domination of adjacent economies."

Non-inflationary Price Rise

The reader of *ER* will be familiar with this notion from the world of today, but we do not use the term "inflation" in referring to the higher taxes in large urban centers resulting from the additional services that equips them to serve as world centers – such things as underground transport, huge airports, universities, cultural and educational institutions, etc. We have recognized this *structural* ingredient of price rise that is largely funded by the state, as a benign factor in the upward price gradient that has laws of its own. Only by recognizing them and designing policy around them can we curtail their price effect.

"Economic life flowed spontaneously towards the [city-state's] high prices. But caught in this high-tension system, the city and its economy ran the risk of being burned. In London and Amsterdam, the cost of living sometimes reached well-nigh intolerable levels, just as New York is losing firms and businesses, as they leave to escape the huge cost of local rates and taxes.

"Dominant cities did not dominate for ever; they replaced each other. When Amsterdam replaced Antwerp, when London took over from Amsterdam, or when about 1929, New York took over from London, it always meant a massive historical shift of forces. The whole circle of the world economy was affected by such changes, and the repercussions were never exclusively economic."

It is even more so when the dominant power is not just a city, but a more extensive power with a considerable territorial hinterland, or even a nation. Braudel goes on to analyze the growing asymmetries when territorial and national trading powers took over from virtual city states, and lone economic superpowers replaced contending national powers. There is no trace in history of benign symmetrical economic relationships that the current Deregulation and Globalization assumes. A key purpose of the increasing asymmetry in trade relationships is the destruction of the defences of the lesser trading partners, to prevent them from ever escaping their servitude.

A Whole Panoply of Power

"If we take the classic sequence of dominant cities of western Europe – Venice, Antwerp, Genoa, Amsterdam, London – it will be noted that the three first-named lacked a complete arsenal for economic domination. Venice at the end of the fourteenth was a booming merchant city; but possessed no more than the beginnings of an industrial sector. While she did have financial and banking institutions, this credit system operated only within the Venetian economy. Antwerp, with little shipping of her own, provided a haven for Europe's merchant capitalism; operating as a sort of "bring and buy" center for trade. Everything came to it from outside. When Genoa's turn came, it was really only because of her banking supremacy, similar to that of Florence in the thirteenth and fourteenth centuries. Her leading role she owed to the fact that her chief customer was the king of Spain, controller of the flow of bullion. By the time Amsterdam and London took over the stage, the world-cities possessed the whole panoply of economic power: they controlled everything, from shipping to commercial and industrial expansion, as well as the whole range of credit.

"Every world-economy is a sort of jigsaw puzzle, a juxtaposition of zones interconnected, but *at different levels.* At least three different categories can be distinguished: a narrow *core*, a fairly developed middle zone, and a vast *periphery*. The center or core contains everything most advanced and diversified. The next zone possesses only some of these benefits: it is the 'runner-up' zone. The huge periphery, with its scattered population, represents, on the contrary, backwardness, archaism, and exploitation by others." In the modern world, the pattern holds, but debt, with interest rates aggressively declared the sole instrument of adjustment, and free trade the imposed standard, leaves no possibility for this vast outer zone to ever shake off its enthrallment. Money has been transformed from a lubricant of commerce, to shackles that perpetuate the status quo.

All this is relevant to the increasing difficulties of the World Trade Organization in claiming even-handedness between the lone trading super-power and the emerging and Third World.

On the Discharge of the National Debt — Sole Economic Goal of Official Politics

Today the most basic issue of politicians in the developed countries is how fast we can cut and even pay off the national debt. That debt is proclaimed the ultimate of all evils. The national debt thus locks into the purpose and nature of money by which everything in our economies is weighed and judged. Let us then consult Braudel and history on some crucial great debates on these subjects.

"In 1560-1, Elizabeth I and her advisers, foremost among them the great Thomas Gresham, sat down to remedy the unspeakable chaos resulting from the Great Debasement, the phenomenal inflation from 1543 to 51. During these years, the silver content of the shilling and the penny had been excessively reduced. From $37/40$ of pure silver, the measure had fallen to only 1 part fine metal to 3 parts base metal. The Elizabethan reform consisted of a return to the ancient right standard of 11 ounces two pennyweights in every 12 ounces. The situation was one of extreme disorder, with the coins in circulation all of different weight and silver content, many of them clipped, yet with the same face value. They had become mere fiduciary currencies [i.e., with only the credit of the government to back them]. Prices had doubled or tripled in a few years, and the English exchange in Antwerp had deteriorated. England as a big cloth exporter was like a trading vessel moored to Europe: her entire economic life depended on the mooring-rope, the exchange rate on the Antwerp market.

"London hoped for two results: (1) that the exchange rate in Antwerp would improve, and (2) that prices at home would fall. Only the first of these hopes was fulfilled. The English people who had borne the cost of the operation (since the government had bought up coin in circulation at only a fraction of its face value) received no compensation in lower prices.

"The situation was rescued shortly afterwards by the influx of silver from America, which flowed into every country after the 1560s.

"In 1621 the stability of the pound was once more threatened. The English clothiers, suffering from surplus production, wanted a devaluation of the pound which would reduce their costs while improving their competitiveness abroad." England, however, rode out that storm largely thanks to a 1630 agreement with Spain: English ships were granted the monopoly of transporting the silver which financed the Spanish Netherlands. "A strange agreement which historians (with one exception) have ignored. The silver landed in England was minted in the Tower of London, and then re-exported to the Netherlands, but some remained in England."

Currency of Account — A Momentous Invention

That helped English credit, despite the Civil War. Throughout the remainder of the 17th century "the money in circulation in England consisted of very old silver coins, worn down, clipped and lightweight. Despite the intermittent sallies of pamphleteers, no one was seriously concerned." What was being birthed in England was the concept of a "currency of account" that had little to do with the coins in circulation. Indeed as the coins became more and more debased, they came to be regarded as mere *token*s of the government's credit, forerunners of paper bills. This explains an oddity of Britain: luxury goods – to emphasize their special category – are often priced not in pounds, but in guineas A guinea was never minted money, but *money of account* beyond the tooth of time. Indeed this "good" money that referred only to the excellent credit of the government benefited by a very small premium over real coin. [The reference in the name "golden guinea" was to Africa, the traditional source of gold for Europe.] The guinea was equated with 22 shillings rather than 20, but in the fullness of time it was brought down to 21.

All was well till a crisis in 1664, when bad harvests, involvement in wars on the continent with the need to export specie led to a crisis with the guinea touching 30 shillings. Currency and notes – including both those of the goldsmiths and the Bank of England, founded in 1694, were steeply discounted, with premiums as high as 40% for cash.

There was universal agreement that the silver coins had to be reminted. But were the new pounds to be issued at a devalued rate, adhering to the Elizabethan standard? The secretary of the Treasury favoured a 20% devaluation. But against him he had the prestige of the philosopher John Locke, for the immutability of sterling. "Let gold find its own level, but the pound must remain 'an invariable fundamental unit,'" Locke pontificated. Braudel observes: "Perhaps he had in mind not only the defence of a sound policy but also the rights of property-owners, the validity of contracts, the inviolability of funds lent to the state – in short the property of the minority ruling class.

"But why should the views of John Locke have prevailed over those of the Treasury? One reason no doubt was that the former Prince of Orange, now on the throne of England, had committed himself to a policy of loans and long-term debt, an unaccustomed policy in England. That inspired distrust on the part of many Englishmen, particularly since the new king was Dutch. An absolutely unassailable credit standing was necessary if the state was to pursue the still unpopular policy of large loans, and if the newly-created Bank of England was not to be placed in difficulties. This is probably the most satisfactory explanation for the adoption of the costly solution proposed by Locke." And it worked like a charm. The English with their cunning mixture of principle and expediency had bumbled into the right psychological and physical prerequisites for a strictly fiduciary currency. And for the next 234 years it served them as a charm.

Britain's Crowning Monetary Achievement Lies in Tatters

And when Britain restored the old high value to the pound in 1925 as though responding to the voice of John Locke from heaven, John Maynard Keynes wrote his devastating essay "The High Cost of Mr. Churchill." But Churchill, even then was harking back to the great if fading past glories of England. The crucial point, as Keynes was to experience with broken heart at Bretton Woods, was that Britain no longer held the baton of the new world orchestra. But one of her enduring achievements was to have brought to fruition the concept of the credit of the state backed by the talent, the tradition, morality, as well as the capital of the entire nation.

Today that crowning achievement of Britain's financial innovation lies in tatters. Rather than the mere word of the government, speaking for the nation and its full human and physical panoply serving as legal tender and money base, the pretence is that the government must borrow from banks at interest rates high enough to impose a flat price that in fact never existed. And the banks are declared by the government itself more trustworthy than the nation that has bailed them out at least once a decade. And yet the speculative malfeasance of some of these largest financial organizations is reported in the media on a near-daily basis. Gone are the days when the government could cover much of its financial needs – as it did in financing the Second World War – by borrowing from the central bank. When it did that the interest paid on the bonds held by the central bank came back to the government almost entirely as dividends in the UK and Canada, where the government is the sole shareholder of the central bank. Where it was not – as in the US – roughly the same proportion of the interest paid on the government debt held by the central bank returns to it by virtue of the monopoly of the ancestral monarch in coining precious metals. We are confronted then with the anomaly of the government borrowing at high interest rates from the private banks what they had received from the central bank at a nominal charge. Indeed, the new system was brought in as a form of bailout of those very banks from their unbuttoned speculations of the 1980s. Obviously, such an arrangement, that pipes private financial institutions into the public treasury, could not withstand the light of day. Hence it is the most militantly guarded secret in our public life.

Paying Off the Debt vs. Britain's Perpetual Bonds

In the days of William of Orange the final evidence of Britain's groping financial genius still lay ahead. "As she gradually moved towards the centre of the world, England, like Holland in her palmy days, had less need for precious metals. Easy, not to say automatic credit took care of her payments. Thus in 1774, on the eve of the American War of Independence, England did not interfere as gold and silver coins left the country. High-level circulation was now in the form of notes issued by the Bank of England or the private banks. It would hardly be an exaggeration to say that gold and silver had become lesser currencies. By dethroning Amsterdam, England had become the point of convergence of all the world's trade – the whole world settled its accounts in London.

"During the Napoleonic Wars, England's monetary problems were still growing: the war required the huge exports of immense quantities of specie to the continent, whose hostility to France had to be bought. With the deepest apprehension of the consequences of his action, the younger William Pitt, normally so sure of himself, persuaded Parliament to accept the short-term non-convertibility of Bank of England notes. And it was then that the final miracle took place: the *Bank Restriction Act* which laid down the compulsory exchange rate for notes, was supposed to last for a mere six weeks. Yet it remained in force for twenty-four years without a single breach. The bank notes, which had no guarantee whatever behind them, continued to circulate without losing value in relation to metal until at least 1809-10.

"Paper money's real guarantee was undoubtedly neither gold nor silver, but the huge output of the British Isles. It was with the goods created by British industry and profits from her trade that Britain paid out to her allies the fabulous subsidies that enabled her to defeat France, to maintain a fleet of fantastic proportions for the time, and the armies which fought in Spain and Portugal to turn the tables on Napoleon. It is as if in 1560 the English had had a revelation of the correct direction to take. And, of course, that is ridiculous. Perhaps then we should see sterling's history as the repeated result of the aggressive tension characteristic of a country fiercely conditioned by its insularity (as an island to be defended), by its efforts to break through to world status and by its clear identification of the enemy: today

Antwerp, tomorrow Amsterdam, the next day Paris. The stability of the pound was a weapon in this battle."

The National Debt — Something to be Paid Off or Nurtured in Perpetuity?

Who has not marvelled at the frequent reports of well-heeled individuals refused bank credit, because they have no record as debtors? For debt is the pulse of the modern economy. And a person without that heart-beat is declared dead as far as banks are concerned.

Britain's success is closely connected with its discovery that "the national debt was rooted in the security of its long-term or perpetual debt – a technical masterpiece. The English financial revolution required the prompt and regular discharge of the interest payable on the its *consols* in perpetuity.

"The feat is all the more remarkable in that English public opinion was overwhelmingly hostile to the national debt. England had of course borrowed money before 1688, but always on a short-term basis with high interest paid at irregular intervals.

"People distrusted 'these New Notions in Government,' wrote Jonathan Swift in 1713, 'to which the King, who had imbibed his Politics in his own Country, was thought to give too much way.' The Dutch idea that it was in the public's interest to be in debt might be true of Holland, but not of England" The "experts" which included eminences such as Defoe and David Hume, J.B. Say, expressed alarms familiar from contemporary utterances by the leaders of all major political parties.

"And yet all these rational observers were wrong. The national debt was the major reason for the British victory. It placed huge sums of money at England's disposal at the very moment when she required them. Isaac de Pinto wrote in 1771, "The scrupulous and inviolable exactitude with which this interest [on the national debt] has been paid, the idea of parliamentary guarantees, have established England's credit to the point where she has received loans that have astonished the rest of Europe. He regarded the English victory in the Seven Year's War as the natural consequence. France's weakness, he claimed, lay in her poor credit arrangements.

"It was only in the final decades of the 18th century that the truth of the matter was generally recognized and that Pitt could declare to the Commons that on the national debt depended the vigour and even the independence of the nation."

Surely this would make useful reading for our political leaders and central bankers, who are always chattering of reducing and even paying off the national debt. The obvious, if unanswered question, is with what? Undoubtedly with bills of a different colour. For the only legal tender since the early 1970s has been the credit of the federal government. No other real money exists.

William Krehm

1. The story of the long campaign of the *Annales* group against the French establishment is recounted in Fernand Braudel, *A History of Civilizations*, translated by Richard Mayne, Penguin Books, 1993.

A Derivative Market on Terrorism

CARL HULSE in *The New York Times* (29/07/03, "Pentagon Prepares a Future Market of Terror Attacks") brings us great tidings:

"Washington – The Pentagon office that proposed spying electronically on Americans to monitor potential terrorists has a new experiment: a futures trading market on which speculators would bet on terrorist attacks, assassination and coups. Traders bullish on a biological attack on Israel or bearish on the chances of a North Korean missile strike would have the opportunity to place their bets on such events on a new Internet site established by the Defense Advanced Projects Agency.

"The Pentagon called its latest idea a new way of predicting events and part of its search for the 'broadest possible set of new ways to prevent terrorist attacks.'

[However], "two Democratic senators who reported the plan called it morally repugnant and grotesque. The program fell under the control of Admiral John M. Poindexter, President Ronald Regan's national security adviser. Senator Byron L. Dorgan of N. Dakota, said the idea seemed so preposterous that he had trouble persuading people it was not a hoax. What if another country set up a betting parlor – sponsored by the government itself – for betting on the assassination of an American political figure?'"

No Bets on Abe Lincoln's Assassination!

Imagine the backward Americans of the day letting Lincoln's assassination pass without using it to enhance their personal fortunes and the national GNP!

Perhaps it should not be so surprising when lurid stories of billions of profits contrived by proactive speculators are still pouring out of sundry commissions of enquiry. At this rate the tale of Wall St.'s liabilities kept under the table, or entered on the books as assets, will become the dominant folklore of the land, filmed and set to music, and icons of East-coast culture to provide symmetry with the more staid epics of the Wild West. The heroes will be the Accountants who designed the scams, while the largest banks of the land laboured to find the credit to keep fictitious energy trades going. In such a setting, what would prevent a patriotic gambler, massaging the market for a decent profit, from organizing an assassination or two, going long instead of short on mayhem and murder, because it was the smart thing to do? The market, that can never be wrong, after all, is much of the time a spectral thing. Too many overachievers with an itch in some part of their anatomy make their own market and then modestly step back to hide the fact.

Such concerns seem to have trickled into the skulls of some high Republicans. *The New York Times* piece reports, "The decision to cancel government support for the efforts was announced by the Senate Armed Services Committee Chairman John Warner, a Virginia Republican. This followed a conversation with Tony Tether, head of the Department of Defense Advanced Research Agency, or Darpa, which was in charge of the project. Poindexter was fired within a few days.

"The project was a twist on a concept that has gained popularity in recent years. An April report by Credit Suisse Boston said that what are known as 'decision markets' had been 'proven to be uncannily accurate' in predicting every thing from election outcomes to Hollywood blockbusters. The key to their success, the market found, is that the markets' 'aggregate information across traders, allowing them to solve hard problems more effectively, than any individual can.'"

Undoubtedly that would include Florida electoral recounts.

"Still, Deputy Defense Secretary Paul Wolfowitz got an earful about the project when he showed up at the Senate yesterday. 'Darpa is brilliantly imaginative,' he said, 'in places where we want them to be imaginative. It sounds like maybe they got too imaginative in this area.'" That too, of course, could lend itself to a variety of interpretations. The criterion in distinguishing too much imagination from just the right amount is whether you can or can't get away with it.

We might in defence of the bizarre effort point out that this is only an extension of the basic official credo by which the economy has been run for at least three decades. "The market" is proclaimed all wise, rational, and better than anything else at solving society's problems. If the continents are beset with epidemics that were considered conquered, if pollution is changing the atmosphere we breathe into noxious fumes, or whatever, then all you need do is put a price on the problem, and those in eternal quest of bigger bucks will automatically come up with the solution.

Further growth, it doesn't seem to matter of what – profits, GDP, market share, or toe-nails – is the ultimate solution.

The Dangerous Gift of Abstraction

It is generally agreed by mathematicians and linguists that abstracting the concept of number from something concrete being counted – marked an enormous advance in human thinking. Before that, man's handling of numbers had been hobbled by his inability to achieve abstraction. Evidence of that is embedded in our language. Even the name of digital as in digital technology is a reminder that our ancestors at one time counted on their fingers and toes. Likewise expressions like two-score, four-score, or *quatre-vingt* in French. But if you passed from twenty (as in fingers plus toes) to larger numbers, there would probably have been be a switch from fingers to horses, or cows. But there was a limit to that, too: a point would be reached where the imaginary horses or cows necessary to support the concrete number would automatically introduce alien concerns – e.g., vast amount of pasture, and water to prevent the imaginary horses and sheep dying of famine or thirst as their numbers grew. That is why freeing the concept of number from its concrete physical embodiments was of such vast importance. You could count beyond 30 or 40 without being distracted by the problem of where the fodder to support them would come from. Otherwise your calculations would collapse.

But that gift for abstraction did not stop there. A capitalist economy itself is based on a not entirely dissimilar calculation. Karl Marx in his day pointed out that the concepts of interest or profit are eventually transformed from a clearly social arrangement and regarded as inherent traits of money itself. Interest and profit came to be seen as a derivative of money, an inherent attribute of it. And in our days such derivatives of useful products – their cost, their price, the increase of their price, the interest paid to finance the operation, or what could be gotten from lending out the proceeds of their sale – began living lives of their own. Precisely because it is an abstraction, and dealt with a rate of increase of something basic that really exists, this allowed you to vastly leverage up the scale of your speculation – say by two or three digits. If you won, you won big. And there were ways of ducking your responsibilities if you lost. That rate of growth of interest, itself was a "derivative" of the productive process. And in good time the increase in the rate of its growth becomes the important thing – the second derivative of profit. These value of these successive derivatives projected into the indefinite future are than discounted for their present value and incorporated into the prices of the stock market. Eventually it becomes more and more growth in the abstract. The more removed it is from its concrete social function – producing commodities that people really need – the more uninhibited its growth and the acceleration of the rate of growth.

But all that was not invented by Poindexter or Wolfowitz. It was directly copied from the economic model by which society has been run increasingly for the past three or more decades, and has given us the biggest speculative bubble and what might be the biggest bust on record. The Democratic senators who scotched the project on moral grounds, must not only be applauded but encouraged to pass on to a search for the roots of the Pentagon's inspiration.

William Krehm

Once More on Mutual Aid Projects with Muslim Lands

IN THE JUNE ISSUE OF *ER* we carried an article exploring the use of high-interest-free financing through our central banks of mutual aid projects with Muslim countries. Near-interest free loans through our central banks seem miraculously made to order to satisfy the Koran's prohibition on the charging of interest ("*riba*"). *Riba* is seen by Islamic scholars as taking place even where no money changes hands, but merely more of a commodity is repaid than was advanced.

Before dismissing this as hopelessly impractical, consider the following:

1. Our deregulated globalized financial system with its increasing use of derivatives elevates *riba* to higher powers and through the evaluation of stock market shares, puts it in supreme command. Structured on the concept of the interest-clock ticking 24 hours a day, from the pious Muslim's viewpoint it guarantees our being roasted for all eternity in hell-fire. Its effects on earth are hardly more benign.

The increase in the financial returns of a stock already

achieved is extrapolated into the future, as is the rate of growth of that rate of growth, and the rate of growth of all higher derivatives. The result is a compulsion towards the exponential growth of financial profit. It is the brazen nature of this monetization of the mere passage of time that underlies the meltdown not only of the stock market, but of economic morality as such. Putting Salvador Dali's famous painting on its head, everything *but* the clock gets melted down.

2. Venice, whose prosperity depended on its trade with Muslim lands, based much of her commercial enterprise on interest-free arrangements acceptable to Islam between passive financiers and active entrepreneurs....

The historian Fernand Braudel[1] observed "The Venetians very early accepted 'the legitimacy of credit operations according to the criteria of modern businessmen. Interest rates could be as high as 20% and such loans might be accompanied by pledges, which remained in the clutches of the lender. But the commercial loan, the *mutuo ad negotiandum* was another matter.... Nine times out of ten, this kind of loan was associated with a partnership or *colleganza* agreement. These made their first appearance in at least 1072-1073, and were soon to be found in two versions. There was the unilateral *colleganza*, whereby one party (known as the *socius stans* or stationary partner) advanced a sum of money to the *socius procertans* (or travelling partner). At the end of the voyage when the accounts were settled, the traveller, after repaying the sum originally advanced, kept one quarter of the profits, the rest going to the 'capitalist.' Alternatively, there was the bilateral *colleganza* whereby the lender put up only three-quarters of the sum required and the *socius procertans* contributed not only his work but one-quarter of the capital. In this case, the profits were split fifty-fifty.

"The entire Venetian population seems to have advanced money to the merchant venturers, thus perpetually creating and renewing a sort of commercial society embracing the whole town. This made it possible for merchants to operate alone or in temporary associations of two or three partners, without the need for the long-term companies with capital funds.

"Perhaps it is the very perfection and convenience of this organization that explains the limited nature of Venetian enterprise. The city's bankers, usually outsiders, were 'entirely taken up with the activity of the Venetian market and not at all tempted by foreign custom.' This undoubtedly required a massive outlay of capital. When the galleys sailed for Syria, the city was literally drained of specie. But the *turnover* of capital was quite rapid: six months or a year."

Today one of society's urgent needs it to muzzle speculative finance; for it has imposed unsustainable patterns of exponential growth.

Accordingly we have consulted the growing literature on Islamic Banking of collaborating Western and Islamic economists.[2]

Muslim scholars are concerned with the factor of causality. In the west, however, "growth" is the paramount concept – often it doesn't seem to matter of what in particular – whether of earnings, or of market share, the growth rate already attained gets incorporated into the price of shares. "Many [Muslim writers], however, argue that money is not a factor of production, and therefore cannot be valued as such. *Riba* is considered to occur even when money does not enter the picture, but more of a commodity than has been lent is paid back, measured by the passage of time.

"The borrower is required to pay back: (1) an amount of wheat equal to what he borrowed (principal, 100 kg), and (2) an extra amount as interest (10 kg). To simplify the argument, assume that the loan must be repaid within a single period of time (for example the end of the season) so that the time factor alone is not the basis of the reckoning, but the real factors of production. That is acceptable. The interest that the borrower is charged does not contribute to the productivity of the principal. The borrower, in accepting this contract, is relying on the hope that realized output will be sufficient to recover such a cost. He is, therefore, relying on change. [The deal] becomes a *gharar* (gamble)" (p. 18). That risk justifies his share of the profit.

To appreciate the chasm that separates the official economic dogma in the West from Islam, we need only refer to the "sweep" accounts brought into US banking in the mid-1990s. These automatically switch deposits from accounts that earn them no interest to accounts that do so overnight, and then switch them back at the beginning of business hours the next day. Moreover, for decades, higher interest rates has been "the one blunt tool" to fight the inevitable effects on the price level of the taxation needed to fund the various non-market investments of the public sector.

We in the West are going to have to deal with the dismantling of the many-tiered structure of parasitic finance that has arisen in recent decades. In doing so, a positive by-product of that will be the helpful collaboration that will become possible with the Muslim world.

Working Around Sources of Conflict

Here once more we can neutralize at least some the sources of the present conflicts by working around them. For example the ultimate source of the funding of such programs can be the central banks of the West, whose powers of money creation must be restored to what they were three decades ago. Until then banks had been required to redeposit 10% of the deposits made in chequing and other short-term accounts with the central bank where they earned no interest. By raising the statutory reserve and leaving interest rates alone, the amount of lending banks could do would be restricted. It also provided more elbow room for the central banks to take on more government debt, on a virtual interest-free basis for the government: as the sole shareholder of the central bank almost all the interest on government debt held by the central bank found its way back to the government as dividends. Indeed, even in countries like the USA where the Fed is owned by private banks, roughly the same amount of the interest on the debt held by the central bank reverts to the government – by a different rationale – by virtue of the ancestral monarch's monopoly right to coin precious metals. Today the only legal tender in the world is the creditworthiness of the government supported by its call on the productive resources of the nation.

A New Defence Against Terrorism

This will enable Western countries to bring to the table capital for essential physical and human infrastructures in the Muslim lands free of what to pious Muslims is the curse of *riba*. Even to lay-minded Muslims financing that will not lock them into the burden of servicing dollar-denominated debt will be a welcome innovation. In return either party would agree to introduce into its educational system unbiased information about the other, warts and all. Both parties would forswear engaging in terror and preemptive warfare. The capital made available to the Muslim countries would be earmarked for productive ends – water and power systems, health, education with emphasis on the education of women. From such investments modest profits will accrue to the Western parties. Part of such profits could be reinvested for an extension of the program to other Islamic and eventually non-Islamic countries.

Of particular interest are the joint studies of Muslim and western economists in appraising the outcome of banking arrangements based on such anti-*riba* principles. There is, for example a chapter entitled "Evidence on agency-contractual problems in *mudarabah* financing operations by Islamic banks" written by Abdel-Fasttah, A.A. Khalil, Colin Rickwood and Victor Murlinde. Under *mudarabah* contracts profit is distributed between the two parties in accordance with the ratio upon which they agree at the time of the contract. Financial loss is borne only by the financier. The entrepreneur's loss lies in not getting any reward for his services.

The authors find that the bank normally has no control over the assets employed in such contracts, particularly given the existence of the restriction to [against] collateralizing these assets. This will give rise to a high incidence of moral hazard problems due to the ability of the entrepreneur to hide information concerning his ability and background before contracting and to conceal actions after the contract is put in place. "It is therefore not surprising that banks place great emphasis on the agent's qualifications and reputation, given the need for compliance with Islamic rule (as a determinant factor to accept or reject such contracts)."

In short the contracting bank in such lending would rely greatly upon the piety and character of the entrepreneur who puts up none of the risk capital. This conforms, in fact, with the historical fact that bills of exchange originally became the most common form of credit in international trade because they would often be drawn up between the members of the same religious community – whether Jews, Huguenots, or Muslims.

This dependence on the individual trustworthiness echoed down the ages in banking until not so long ago. Your bank manager used to depend almost as much on the "character, character, character" of his borrower as on his collateral. In a world where the bubble of "securitized" debt has taken over to fuel exponential growth, we should not dismiss the old-fashioned reliance of Islamic bankers on reputation and community ties in managing their risks.

William Krehm

1. Braudel, Fernand (1984). *Civilization & Capitalism 15th-18th century, The Perspective of the World* (Vol. 3, p. 129). (S. Reynolds, Trans.). Fon-

tana Press, William Collins & Sons, Ltd. (Original published in 1979)

2. Thus *Islamic Banking and Finance – New Perspectives on Profit-Sharing and Risk*, edited by Munaware Iqbal, of the Islamic Development Bank, Saudi Arabia and David T. Llewellyn of Loughborough University, UK, published by Edward Elgar, Cheltenham UK, in association with the International Association of Islamic Economics, the Islamic Development Bank and the Islamic Foundation, 2002.

Tracking the Social Lien through the Economy

ONCE YOU RECOGNIZE the existence of a deepening layer of taxation in price – what I have called the Social Lien – the entire panorama of the economy appears in a different light. A growing stratum of taxation in the price level is the cost of essential, but unmarketed and hence unpriced public services.

These services, however, are delivered more abundantly in large cities than in the countryside. It is in fact such public services available mostly in large urban centres that led to a flowering of entire branches of private enterprise to an extent hardly feasible in the countryside and smaller centres. The largest cities are the locus of nodal activities of the economy, of arts and science. In this way much of the taxation that constitute a growing part of the national product and contributes substantially to the structural price ramp ends up as a disproportionate amount of our public services in our largest cities. That is increasingly the case when a growing portion of taxation has been shifted onto consumers.

Wealth, as well and economic, scientific and cultural facilities have since the earliest days of capitalism flourished in large urban centers. Fernand Braudel in his monumental *Civilization & Capitalism 15th-18th Century* arrived at the conclusions of a three-zone structure of all economic empires – the core, the subordinate centres and finally the periphery.

This has shifted a growing amount of taxes paid by the outlying areas for an increasing amount of services they do not directly receive. Conglomerate corporations, moreover, have developed to a fine art the bargaining for tax exemption and reductions as the price of setting up a plant in a given jurisdiction. One local administration is played off against another.

That trend is somewhat balanced by the subsidies to our farmers. But that tends to be treated as contravention of international free trade laws. Viewed in the above perspective, it may often be in fact an alleviation of an excess taxation of the non-urban consumers. There are, of course, other important reasons for preserving our domestic food production.

To sort out the combinations that are unfair to the countryside – traditionally condemned to the bruising end of the big stick – there must be a completely untrammelled freedom of analysis on taxation sources compared with the distribution pattern of public services. It is not enough to rely on historical precedent and the amount of political influence that each sector can muster. Ignoring the role of the social lien on the ratio of central government taxes paid by and services actually received by the periphery is certainly one of the key factors to be considered.

This asymmetry appears on a larger scale when we deal with the relationships between the first and emerging and Third World countries. But here discrepancy in the power wielded is heightened by the financial dependence of agriculture on the metropoles at home and abroad. And when debt of Third World countries is denominated in a strong foreign currency it can become as powerful a weapon of conquest as any army of occupation.

The very stresses imposed on the social structures of these Third World and emerging lands systems by the present international system guarantees that risk and hence interest rates there will stay high. And debt combined with free-trade commitments at those high interest rates is administered by the IMF and other international bodies to perpetuate the subject position of these sources of raw materials and cheap industrial labour. To roll over that debt they must agree to slashing their domestic social services, and increasing their exports – no matter how oversupplied the world market might be. *Export of raw and semi-manufactured products is often no longer a function of the supply-demand ratio – as academic orthodoxy holds – but of debt-servicing requirements.*

To reveal the extent of the misrepresentation of the model, you need to break up the notion of "inflation" to disclose the social lien component. There is a glimpse of this in the practice of most European countries to allow – in theory if not always in practice – in the restitution to tourists of the VAT they may have paid in the prices of goods they are taking out of the country.

Since they are not being consumed in the country where the purchase occurred, the tourist purchaser will not benefit in more than a minor way from the innumerable social services that VAT is supposed to fund. Ignoring the taxation layer in prices contributes greatly to the disarray taking over the world.

William Krehm

Insurance Industry's Crisis Defies Software

THE WALL STREET JOURNAL (23/07, "German Watchdog Says Insurers Fixed Prices" by Ulrike Sauer and G. Thomas Sims) has some dreadful news for an economy that stands sorely in need of insurance.

"Frankfurt – Germany's anti-trust regulator said it sent formal letters accusing Allianz AG and six other German insurers of fixing prices for industrial insurance. The move is the latest setback to Europe's strained insurance industry, which has taken a huge hit from the falling value of its stock-market holdings. The letters of accusation from Germany's Federal Cartel Office follow the watchdog's raids on nine insurance companies in July 2002. The office was alerted by an unnamed informant to possible price-fixing in the aftermath of the Sept.

11th terrorist attacks.

"Many industrial insurers, including those in the US, posted heavy losses in recent years because of mounting global competition, the slump of stocks, damage from terrorist attacks, flooding, and industrial accidents. After Sept. 11, some insurance rates rose sharply, in several cases doubling or even tripling. German insurers, however, have denied acting as a cartel. Fines for illegal price-fixing can be up to three times as much as the additional revenue stemming from the price fixing, according to the German anti-trust law."

The trouble is that both the insurance companies and the anti-competitive government watchdog have been sold some exceedingly bad software by official economists to hide the risks in the modern business world. And since selling protection against risks is the business of insurance companies, and they have been absorbed into a banking system that itself is deeply involved in stock market games, it was inevitable that they should be disoriented. Who then will insure the insurers?

But the problem goes farther back. The founding fathers of economics were serious folk who made an honest stab at understanding the economy. They came up with some very different answers, but in their respective ways they all strove to grasp the hard realities of the economy. That is why they were concerned with notions of value that ran deeper than the latest market prices. For market prices are notoriously subject to manipulation. The mercantilists of the 17th century felt it was the supply of precious metals that really counted, and hence concluded that governments should concentrate on preventing foreign traders from draining off the domestic supply of gold and silver. The Physiocrats in France, in the 18th century, believed it was the land and agriculture, that created the foodstuffs and fibres, that provided the raw materials for industry and thus were crucial. In early trading countries like Italy and Britain, more sophisticated theories arose to cover the more complicated relationships that developed. Adam Smith, a very different person than he is made out to be by official economists today, resorted not to one but to three theories of value, depending on the problem he was wrestling with. To lay bare basic principles, he harks back to "that early and rude state of society that precedes the accumulation of stock and the expropriation of land" to formulate a labour theory of value: "if it usually costs twice the labour to kill a beaver as to kill a deer, a beaver will usually sell for twice as much as a deer."

Elsewhere he draws on two other value theories. One is a cost-of-production theory that sees value as the sum of its components – wages, profit and rent – he therefore adds up cost columns much as our accountants do today in their better moments. In yet other instances he uses as a measure of value not "embodied labour," the amount of labour necessary to produce a commodity, but the amount of labour 'commanded' by a commodity, i.e., the amount of labour the proceeds of its sale could hire. This expressed the relative wage costs in a world that was being joined in trade. Prophetically, it has become of immense importance today when labour in China costs one tenth what it does in Japan, and less skilled manufacturing processes are being transferred to the squalor of the Third World.

These assorted value theories assured economics some relevance to the real world. By the mid-19th century, the tension between the classes in Europe and the US approached civil war. Any labour theory of value would prove a bonanza to the socialist and labour movements that had arisen with increasing literacy of the under-privileged. A great need was felt to cover up rather than expose society's shameful parts. In three different countries, quite independently, marginal utility theory was developed. In Austria and Britain (Karl Menger and Stanley Jevons), the new model appeared in the very year of the Paris Commune and its bloody repression (1871), and in France three years later came the more ambitious mathematical work of Leon Walras. The new theory saw price as eclipsing any other sense of value. All actors in society from bankers to unemployed workers, were presented as just "traders," striving to maximize their satisfactions. The workers compared the inconveniences of accepting work at the wages offered with the delights of leisure in their parlours. In this way in an idealized "pure and perfect market" all "traders" were of such negligible size that nothing they did or left undone individually could possibly affect price.

The Invisible Hand Sneaking into the Pockets of the Defenceless

It was left to the self-balancing market, also known as the "invisible hand," to mete out fair decisions on the division of the national product. There was simply no room left for social injustice.

In actual fact, the history of any period has been the record of the "invisible hand" sneaking its way into the pockets of the defenceless. Towards that end, the principal means is disinformation.

With a spot of misplaced differential calculus, marginalist theory has responded to every failure of the system by stepping up the dosage. Such mishaps are invariably diagnosed as evidence that the market has not been sufficiently deregulated, or in its lingo has not become sufficiently "pure and perfect." It is thus self-perpetuating. It violates the most elementary principles of mathematics on several counts. It assumes, because, other things being equal, an excess of demand over supply will push prices higher, it follows that when prices rise, it *means* that there is an excess of demand over supply. But it is an elementary principle of logic that you cannot turn any proposition around just because it is valid read in its original form When the price level goes up it might be due to an excess of demand, but it could also be because the role of the government sector has grown within the economy. For the government sector does not sell or even price most of its services, but pays for them largely out of taxation levied. Accordingly, as technology and urbanization creates the need for more public services, the layer of taxation in price, direct and indirect, deepens. And of course, in the age of Microsoft and General Electric, the infinitesimal calculus that assumes growth in infinitesimal degrees by infinitesimally small agents can't possibly have any relevance.

This is the software that prevents the insurance companies from protecting their clients against the growing risks of our world. What conventional economists mistake for a point of equilibrium crucial for estimating the risk of a given situation, is arrived at by a blunder that would flunk a freshman in any course of logic or mathematics. An equilibrium point in mathematics is a point where the rate of growth of a function becomes zero and either grows (or diminishes) whether it moves forward along the curve or retraces its steps. Such an *"extremum"* (a minimum or a maximum) assures us that the function will oscillate about the point. If you get that wrong you are programming for disaster. That holds for both the insurance industry or the economy as a whole. But that is only the beginning of our current quandary.

On Barefoot Bootmakers

The history of economic theory has been the record of the shift of control from the producers to high finance. Firms that produce useful goods and services have been systematically downgraded to mere dice for speculative gambles. The ultimate control was removed from the grunt and grime of physical work, as were the greater rewards. In economic theory this was translated into the association of wealth not with physical assets, but with the claim to the future growth of such assets. Mathematically this is expressed by the term "derivative." In mechanics the velocity of a function is its first derivative, the acceleration of its motion is the second derivative, and so forth to infinity. Increasingly, our financiers and the economists whose careers they make or break, deal with such higher derivatives. You can for, example, buy or sell a claim to any *increase* in the market value of a given currency, or of the rate of interest a security earns, instead of the underlying security or physical flow. One of the beauties of the arrangement is that it increases the leverage of your gambles without measure. And very often your obligations under your derivative contracts don't show up on your books. On top of that, the resulting deals are so complicated that that often those who use them, and even those who designed them, don't fully understand their consequences.

All this harks back to the way in which a corporation's shares are valued on the stock market. Whatever increase in the earnings of the company has been achieved is extrapolated into the unending future and, discounted for its present worth, is incorporated into price. This works wonders for keeping the stock market soaring while the fair weather lasts. But once the going gets tough the slightest failure to maintain this pace, brings down the whole house of marked cards.

That puts everything the CEOs learned in their distant Sunday school classes to an impossible test.

The Smell of Roses without their Thorns

The fact is that our economy has reached the point where it avoids real facts and real problems, to deal with fictions derived from them. It is concerned not with roses, but with the smell of roses. That avoids both the bother of growing them and their thorns.

In the insurance industry the proliferating veins of fantasy criss-cross and compound one another. Let us run through the incomplete list of these mentioned in the *WSJ* article: "Many industrial insurers including those in the US posted heavy losses in recent years because of mounting global competition, the slump in stocks, damage from terrorist attacks, flooding, and industrial accidents." Obviously, these disasters feed into one another. Needless mileage run up over congested airways, highways and seas, add to pollution, and provide and ideal setting for the agenda of terrorists. The collapse of morality on the world's stock markets has widened the spread between the rewards of financial adventurers and those of low-skilled labour to an unprecedented extent.

The desperation of the insurance industry gives us the measure of the crisis of our economy as a whole. In a version grandiose enough for Greek tragedy, it is a clear case of shoemakers and their kids running around barefoot.

William Krehm

China Talks Back

WITH A TOTAL DISREGARD of the historical record of overextended empires, Washington goes on bleeding itself of reserves that it will need for the challenges it has taken on. Today the only power that in the long run could seriously question the economic preeminence of the United States is China. Her wage levels are a tenth those of some of her main competitors. She has immense advantages of scale, and a highly motivated population.

To rein in China's conquest of world markets, the United States and Japan have been pressuring her to raise interest rates and thus strengthen the yuan's foreign exchange rate. That would slow down Chinese exports. That, however, is what China is determined not to do. From Japan's brilliant reconstruction after World War II, she learned that a low currency can be the best shooting iron in the trade war, and a means of turning around the Washington Consensus to goose the superpower. With a couple of hundred million reported unemployed and underemployed she feels impelled to conquer foreign markets. Exploiting Washington's need for Chinese diplomatic backing in the Near East and in North Korea, she has been bargaining successfully to obtain Western technology as the price of access to her vast, potential markets.

China Mentions the Unmentionable

In a most undiplomatic statement the People's Bank of China responded to a public statement of the US, the EU and Japan suggesting that the exchange value of the yuan be raised. The figure 40% was cited in the world press as the extent of the yuan's under-valuation. *The Wall Street Journal* of 25/08 reported the Chinese central bank's declaration that "the banks are sitting on too much liquidity." It blamed "inappropriate comments on the Chinese yuan exchange rate and unreasonable expectations of the yuan's appreciation among the international community" for the influx of hot money into China. "The central bank's comments were unusual both for their vigor and their acknowledgement that it has the tools to absorb foreign currency without having to adjust the value of the yuan."

As a sample of the alternatives open to it, Beijing announced that it will increase the percentage of deposits that commercial banks must hold on reserve to 7% from 6% as of September 21st. This means that Chinese banks will not be able to lend out as high a multiple of their cash reserves as in the past. They will therefore have to call in some of the loans already out. But even more than the strong language, the central bank's riposte seemed to flaunt the fact that it was applying the very tool that Washington and most Western central banks had renounced. In the early 1990s they proclaimed higher bank overnight rates the sole blunt tool against "inflation." That policy was the very core of the bailout of the their distressed banks in the early

nineteen nineties. Up to then governments had financed much of their needs through the central banks on a near-interest-free basis, since almost all the interest paid on their debt held by the central bank reverted to them. Today governments do almost all their financing through the private banks. The interest on government debt held by private banks does not come back to their government. Governments in general and Washington in particular are thus paying many billions in interest on debt that they had previously financed on a virtual interest-free basis.

Both the Nazis and the Allies used rates of interest rigged low to finance WWII – in the case of the US somewhere between 2% and 3%. Financing of government loans was done largely at quite nominal rates, and indirectly much of it through central banks. Without that the Allies may not have won, nor could they have carried out the post-war reconstruction with such dispatch.

It would be a tremendous disadvantage for Washington to continue using interest rates as its one blunt tool, while the Chinese followed the American example during WWII and the postwar period. Nor could Chinese not have been aware of the delicacy of the subject raised in their reply. The chances of the Fed daring to debate the matter publicly are low indeed.

Particularly notable is the detail that even the best-informed commentators in the media, either didn't know what was involved, or pretended such ignorance. Thus *The Wall Street Journal* repeatedly spoke of the Chinese requiring that the banks put up more *capital reserves* with the central bank. That would have been no effective weapon against inflation, since the banks' capital would include its bad investments. It is *cash reserves* that are involved.

High time that the West disinterred its own successful record in using its central banks in war and in peace. Of course, we prefer that it be done to make possible a productive, friendly collaboration amongst nations. However, what is likely to cut more ice in the world as it is spun these days is its ghastly relevance to financing wars.

William Krehm

Introspection Arrives in Washington

THE VICTORY couldn't have been more complete. Caesar and Alexander must have twisted in their graves. Entirely within budget, at undreamt speed, and with practically no casualties for his forces, Geo W. proved himself one of the great commanders of all times. So what if he's no great speaker, he dealt with terrorists and rogue nations as fast as a well-run barbershop: the chair was ready for the next customer to get a hair- and mustache-cut before the previous guy was out the door. The press releases didn't even have to be rewritten. We just change the name – that's got to be a big economy towards our tax-cuts. What worked so well with Iraq was already frightening the bejeezus out of Syria, and the Iranians know they we got'm in our sights if they don't smarten up, and realize who have everything needed for the job: the hardware, the software, and everything in between.

Of course, there are always the whiners, who will make a big issue of losing both legs, an arm, or their families, a small enough price for being liberated. Hell, who was that real famous guy that said liberty don't come cheap? And of course there was all the fuss about a few old pots pinched or smashed at that Baghdad museum – guys who don't realize that it's the new, the ultramodern that counts, stuff that can flatten a city with smart bombs directed from a ship hundreds of miles away, not old crockery. Just like those envious stick-in-the-muds of old Europe, France and Germany, who unlike the new Europe like Rumania and Bulgaria, don't know that a new age has dawned. And the smartie-pants commentators in New York who say that in spite of all that military glory that we don't have to share with the French, Germans, Russians and the Canucks, we still may have to let them in for their cuts of the reconstruction contracts. Otherwise they might refuse to share the reconstruction costs.

There's even buzz of their holding up getting the Iraq oil fields and the country in shape for marketing, if we don't. Somebody's always trying to stir up trouble. Like those geeks who go around saying if we hadn't done quite so fantastic a job of smashing up the country in no time at all, it would cost a lot less to put it together again. And we may be stuck with going it almost alone with Tony and Micronesia. And don't think it didn't cost a lot to put our great coalition together – but we are old hands at that in Washington, come budget time.

Embedding the Whiners in the Army or Concrete

And unless this is cleaned up soon, it could cost George W. the next election just like the economy did his old man. But deep down his father's buddies knew that Cheney and Rumsfeld are smarter than they are and will keep that White House until they finish their job on the planet.

One thing is clear. There are guys writing those smart-ass things in New York papers who should be embedded in something, if not the army, perhaps in concrete. What is all this unpatriotic stuff about the size of our debt to foreigners, and the talk of ungrateful Arabs pulling out of doing oil business in dollars, and shifting to the euro?

In a previous issue we carefully noted the references and in *The New York Times* of April 20 found the article "True Cost of Hegemony: Huge Debt" by Niall Ferguson. It almost covered the views that were coming out of remote places like India on the Internet some weeks before, that even the best US financial papers seemed to be avoiding. Perhaps until they could figure out the answers to the baffling questions raised.

"Can a global hyper-power also be a global hyper-debtor? Debates about the cost of occupying Iraq and reconstructing its burnt-out economy tend to duck this question. Having won the war on a shoestring ($79 billion is less than 1% of the annual output of the American economy), the administration apparently hoped that the reconstruction of Iraq will soon be paying for itself. A trifling $2.4 billion has been allocated to the postwar Office for Reconstruction and Humanitarian Assistance. Yet history strongly suggests that Iraq's reconstruction will require a kick-start of substantial foreign capital, particularly to modernize the antiquated oil industry.

"Can the US provide the necessary cash, even in the form of private-sector money? The answer is yes – so long as foreign countries are willing to lend it to the US. For the fact is that America is not only the world's biggest economy. It is also the world's biggest borrower. Its muscular power is underwritten by foreign capital."

When the Super-power was not a Super-debtor

"In the prime of the European empires, the dominant power was supposed to be a creditor, not a debtor, investing large chunks of its own savings in the development of its colonies. Hegemony also meant 'hegemoney.' Britain, the world's banker, before 1914, never had to worry about a run on the pound."

Whoa! the 19th century witnessed a series of crises during which Britain bled gold and – often surreptitiously – received temporary assistance from the continent. Take this random paragraph from the authoritative *A Financial History of Western Europe* of Charles P. Kindelberger (George Allen & Unwin, London, 1984, p. 281): "In 1825, when Britain was in trouble, the Bank of France swapped gold for silver. The Bank of England drew £800,000 in bills on Paris in 1836, and £2 million again in 1839, plus £900,000 more, partly against silver, on the Bank of Hamburg…. In the crisis of 1890 the BoE asked the Russian State Bank not to draw on its deposit with the Bank for the time being but, on the contrary, to lend it £800,000 in gold. It also drew £3 million in gold on the Bank of France – all this to meet the Baring crisis. In 1907 the Bank of France bought sterling bills with gold shipped to London, to help the BoE meet a drain from New York.

"These operations are discussed very little in banking literature, partly perhaps because they were felt to involve a loss of prestige on the part of the borrowing country, and for the system as a whole. Sensitivity of central banks and governments [was] also underlined by the BoE's prickly negative reaction to the Prussian National Bank's offer to help in 1873 by lending gold."

Karl Marx, supporting his family on the one pound note that Friedrich Engels sent him from Manchester each week, gloated over these great periodic financial panics. From them he forecast still direr things for capitalism. But these crises were episodic, and partly reflected the lack of an international facility to deal with them. The French, ever partial to a more planned capitalism, were actually suggesting an international lender of the last resort. An anticipation of the Bretton Woods institutions? Basically yes, but power – especially a surfeit of the dangerous stuff – has a way of converting the noble plans into apparatuses of enslavement – e.g., the IMF. The Americans during this period were defaulting first on some of their foreign loans to build canals, and then on even larger ones to build railways. A lot of the European capital lent for such purposes was never seen again. But that, too, is a chapter that American governments today are inclined to flit over.

But back to Niall Ferguson: "Today, as America overthrows 'rogue regimes' first in Afghanistan and now in Iraq, it is the world's biggest debtor. This could make for a fragile Pax Americana if foreign investors decide to reduce their stakes in the American economy, possibly trading their dollars for the increasingly vigorous euro.

"Foreign investors now have claims on the US amounting to about $8 trillion of its financial assets. That's the result of the ever-larger American balance-of-payments deficits – totalling nearly $3 trillion – since 1982.

"*The Wall Street Journal* recently asked: 'Is the US Hooked on Foreign Capital?' The answer is yes, and this applies to the government sector even more than the private sector. Foreign investors now hold about two-fifths of the federal debt in private hands – double the proportion 10 years ago.

"It is useful to contrast the present with the past, before WWII. American investors lent billions of dollars to foreign economies, particularly in Latin America and Central Europe. By 1938 the gross value of American assets abroad amounted to $11.5 billion. Having bankrolled both world wars, the US financed the peacetime reconstruction of the losers, as well. From 1960 to 1970, the US ran balance of payment surpluses totalling nearly $60 billion. Then things began to change, most noticeably in the Reagan years, through the 'current account deficits' – a measure of the net flow of goods and services between the US and the rest of the world.

"Some economists argue that this transformation from creditor to debtor is nothing to worry about. Capital flows into the US they say, simply because it is a great place to invest and foreigners simply want a piece of the action. That is the only way to explain why the US consistently receives higher investments abroad than it pays out to foreigners who have put their money into American assets."

Introducing George W. Bush to George W. Hegel

Not quite. In important part it reflects the world role the US has enjoyed since WWII as the world's reserve currency. Since the US and with it the world abandoned the gold standard even in theory – in 1971 – it has been on a pure credit standard with the US dollar the world's ultimate base money. The central banks of other countries held more American than other currencies as reserves for their foreign transactions. That meant that the US could pay in paper or computer entries at near zero cost to it for its vast imports necessary to allow the rest of the world the means of paying for their imports and net financial transactions in US dollars. But there is a rub. The German philosopher Hegel explained the reciprocal nature of many relationships. Having your currency function as reserve money requires you and your credit being accepted by other countries for that status. That will involve many hard-nosed calculations, but also some feeling for other people's sensitivities. Somebody should explain that to George W. Sin against that, handle your creditors too arrogantly, and your privileged position, already stressed, can vanish. Your creditors will not only foreclose on

you, but take a fiendish joy in the opportunity for doing so.

But meanwhile the US must create and put into the hands of the world enough American dollars to provide an adequate amount of reserve currency.

Since Washington has in recent years wiped out in its public life an understanding of how money creation works, governments are hardly equipped to use it wisely on an international scale. That is the very nub of our monetary confusion.

Complications have arisen as well from two other world programs the US is involved in. One is what is known as Globalization and Deregulation which pressures all countries to remove all barriers to the movement of goods and speculative money across frontiers. It also advances the goal of zero inflation, even though the world has an urgent need for more public services – environmental, educational, arising from changing technologies and population explosions. Such services, however, are paid for largely by taxation that makes up an ever deeper layer of price. Ignore that and try to flatten price and you are ruling out the funding of vital public services. Tagging them "externalities" indeed hints of this dirty secret. Trying to enforce this flat-price world with the one blunt tool of "higher interest rates" involves a screeching conflict of interest, since interest is the revenue of a group that needs no encouragement to become parasitic. Mixing all these dubious ingredients into a single witch's brew (the "Washington Consensus") and forcing it down the throats of the rest of the world disregards the sage observation of Hegel that has still to reach Texas. Someone should introduce George W. to Hegel.

The end result: deflation of the real economy, and compelling the Third, Second and First Worlds to cut their social programs and increase their exports to earn the foreign currency to service their growing debt. Such driven exports have reduced the price of staples like coffee far below their production costs. Internationally prices are no longer determined by the balance of supply and demand, but in the need of all debtors – except the US because of its reserve currency position – to service their debt. If they fail to, the IMF will be on their necks. In the developed countries it has brought on privatization of public services that had been entered on the government books at a token value. It has made possible the virtual give-away of public assets. And that added to the speculative money creation on the stock market. The collapse of that boom has contributed to the phenomenal rise of US indebtedness abroad. Dubious debt has become the cement that has held this world together. It is now financing its self-destruction.

The Musical Chairs of Banking

Even under the gold standard in its palmiest days, money creation had aspects of make-believe. The base money in the coffers of banks was never enough to pay off all depositors should they choose to withdraw their deposits at the same time. It was, if you wish, very much like a game of musical chairs when all the players tried sitting down simultaneously. But if everybody listened to the music when it played, it worked most of the time. Switching from gold to pure credit for the reserves required a tightening of the rules and discipline. Instead, Washington abolished restraints to give financial speculation a free playing ground. In the name of maximising shareholder value, the rate of growth of the earnings of corporations – real or imagined – were extrapolated into the remote future, and incorporated into price to serve as collateral for further financing. This was tantamount to money creation on a licentious stock market.

Meanwhile, much of the actual manufacturing has left America's shores. Toyota has for the first time pushed out one of the Big Three – Daimler-Chrysler – for car sales in the US itself. That means that the US is ever more dependent on its supremacy in technology. But for that its investment in education must be maintained and increased, as must its interest in keeping universities open to talented hard-working youngsters. But elsewhere in this issue you will read an article on the wilting of America's universities.

The terrorists of Islam seem to have a special flair for detecting these vulnerabilities. Remember, for Islam taking interest at any level will be punished by eternal hell-fire. Saddam Hussein switched his blocked accounts with the UN from dollars to Euros several years ago. Today whoever is conducting the terrorist attacks in Iraq seems to be counting on the US public's limited appetite for body-bags coming home.

As for the Chinese, they not only refuse to allow the value of their currency to rise to contain inflation, but have resorted to raising the statutory reserve to rein in the amount of capital creation the private banks can do rather than raising interest rates that would attract more hot money and create more real inflation. There could be no more wounding way of thumbing their noses at American monetary orthodoxy.

William Krehm

Robert G. ("Bob") Good, 1923–2000

BOB GOOD, one of the founding and key members of COMER, a truly eclectic and loyal gentleman, passed away on August 27. He succumbed to a cancer that returned after a remission of several years.

Bob came to his twin interests of farming and economics honestly. His father, William, had been the backbone of Canada's co-operative farm movement for the first half of the 20th century, holding the post of President of the Co-operative Union of Canada for a quarter of a century and representing that body in Parliament in the 1920s.

Bob was an active farmer in Puslinch, ON, and only recently, for health reasons, sought to sell his beloved family property. The planned move never did take place.

With the cancer in lengthy remission, Bob, with astonishing energy, decided to write an overview of economics, analyzing all aspects of this vast topic from Adam Smith, through John Maynard Keynes, to Canada's current problems. In it he distinguished between "free trade" and "forced trade." Recently, as he revised parts of his book, Bob grew more militant and contemplated using the term "economic terrorism" in the book's title as

US imperialism grew apace. Hopefully a publisher will be found for this original and challenging work.

In June this year the Good family held a splendid and well-attended 80th birthday party for Bob at the farm. It attracted the diverse strands of the family, including brother Alan who, at ninety still sketches the editorial cartoon for each issue of *Economic Reform* as he has done for many years. Bob's many farming friends from Puslinch were represented, as were personal friends, including members of the COMER Board. Bob was feted with cake, champagne and best wishes in the form of speeches and poems. It was a genuine celebration of life, much preferred to the stilted, often cliché-ridden eulogies offered upon a loved one's passing. Though we did not know it at the time, it was the last time many of us would see Bob, and it makes the event memorable. He will be missed.

Kurt Loeb

The Invisible Hand of Economics 101

AFTER A LONG SUMMER students have flocked back to the Canadian universities' sacred halls of learning. Many, as a sign of the times, are adding Economics 101 to their studies.

For anyone with an interest in economics this is good news. The bad news is, that when the hustle to find a seat in the overflowing auditoriums, what the students will be taught is not only a dogmatic version of neoclassical economics, one that often include a marked neo-conservative bias.

All economic phenomena are presented in a market-framed context. There is little place for government, which attempts to correct perceived market failures or social inequalities. Generally they are seen as just creating unintended inefficiencies.

For example, the following nugget of market fundamentalist reasoning from a textbook: "Driving slowly and careful is costly because is uses the drivers' time and energy. When deciding how safely to drive, rational people compare marginal benefits from safer driving to its marginal costs" (the latter being their own death). So, there we are. Government meddling, even in the form of seemingly innocuous traffic laws, are utterly superfluous when we have free markets and rational people thinking at the margin about their problems.

What neoclassical economics ignores is that all socio-economic situations arise as a result of path-dependent, evolutionary processes. Each society has its own content and reality that is not reducible to any simplistic model. Market institutions are a part of the evolutionary processes. The resultant distribution of opportunities and upholding of the "game rules" of property rights are not inherently equitable, as claimed by the libertarian philosophy underlying neo-conservatism. Instead, they are determined by a society's evolving economic asymmetries and institutionalization of power structures. For example, our society punishes theft quite harshly when the culprit is a common thief, but softly if it is a corporate stock manipulator.

Are Students Goosed by the Invisible Hand?

How the students form their understanding of the economy's larger questions will largely depend upon the presentation of microeconomics' basic framework. This is done by relying heavily on charts, graphics and mathematical equations. What is not easily detected by the unsuspecting students are the fundamental inconsistencies of this approach.

The markets supply and demand relations are shown by the well-known diagonal lines that cross each other at the supposed equilibrium point. After this, the students are initiated into the secrets of marginal schedules, which reveals to them how firms make decisions about prices and quantities. Firms are usually divided into four groups according to their market.

The first group are made up of small firms facing open, competitive markets, in which they are considered to have no ability to influence prices but only the quantities they supply. This makes their demand curve horizontal. The next group consists of firms in monopolistic competitive markets where competition is still strong but products are differentiated from each other. Therefore, direct price comparisons are not possible and demand curves starts to slope downwards, reflecting that demand now is responsive to firms' price decisions. Next again, oligopolistic markets are dominated by a small group of powerful firms, holding a pricing power that allow them to reap substantial monopolists surpluses. Finally, we have monopoly firms with an ability to manipulate prices and output to the point where the monopolists surplus is maximized.

In practice, though, no firms are likely to emerge in the two groups at the extremes. Instead, firms and households in today's societies confront each other in markets that are a mixture of monopolistic and oligopolistic competition. Therefore, when textbooks customarily show aggregate market conditions as projections of perfect competitive markets, it is a serious misrepresentation.

The fact is, that the markets in industrial societies have been characterized by a long term tendency toward oligopolistic concentrations. This is a result of the asymmetric factor accumulations mandated by industrial production. Consequently, a representative depiction of an aggregated average market is currently probably found somewhere in the lower range of the oligopolistic market sector. A reflection of this is the considerable market power the dominant firms wield in almost all modern market segments.

On the micro level, individual firms face conditions where many of their operative variables can be quantified reasonably well and by reduction assumed to occur in closed economic loops. Under such conditions, neoclassical marginal analysis can be a very useful technique. However, aggregate or macro situations are characterized by being open and influenced by constantly changing variables. Therefore, uncertainty and the blurring effect of complementarity perception in all social valuations now rise with a force that is an exponential function of time, scope and magnitude of aggregation. This renders the mechanical extrapolations of the neoclassical type a hazardous approach.

During the Keynesian epoch it was generally accepted that government had a role in dealing with problems such as negative externalities. Modern neoclassical economists have tried to outflank the troubling question this raises for their theories. Their counter is the Coase theorem, which claims that externalities can be solved by private bargaining if property rights are well defined and transaction cost zero. However, besides the unlikely condition of zero transaction costs, market power must also be non-existent. This contravenes the fact that today's average firm is found within a range of market conditions where market power is considerable. Furthermore, the theorem ignores the central question of how initial information is established. Detecting, for instance, industrial pollution is a task that requires highly specialized technical knowledge, which the accidental neighbour to a polluting firm is unlikely to possess.

When the students reach the topic of taxation, the stress is upon how government taxation create "deadweight losses." However, these "losses" do not end up in black holes in the economy. They comprise output and consumption that the taxes redirect to other parts of it. If we are talking, for instance, about green taxes this would be precisely the intention.

The conclusion is that Canadian students today are more likely than not to be taught a dogmatic, but incoherent, neoclassical interpretation of economics. Combined with the often added neo-conservative bias, this has evidently contributed to reinforce the prevalent materialistic and self-centered attitudes towards society. Such teaching has created a pseudo-scientific apologetics for individuals intent of avoiding contributions to society. This has stalled the development and maintenance of society's infrastructure.

Dix Sandbeck

CONFERENCE POSTER

Homage to Newton: For a Proper Use of Mathematics in Economics

WILLIAM KREHM presented a paper at the 2003 Economics for the Future Conference at Cambridge University, UK, September 17-19, 2003. He was one of 15 speakers who were asked to prepare a poster for the conference, the text of which follows.

The Committee for Monetary and Economic Reform (COMER) is an international think tank based in Toronto, Canada. It arose in the corridors of the Eastern American Economic Association, where its founders sought enlightenment on the ever more closely guarded mysteries of money creation. It was a subject never mentioned at plenary sessions.

Economic Reform, its monthly publication, is currently in its 16th year. Its website is www.comer.org. Its second video, *Toward a Non-Autistic Economy*, has just appeared.

In it we celebrate the partial dismantling in stealth by Washington and Ottawa of several great windmills that we have tilted against for decades: the introduction of physical capital budgeting both in the US and Canada – public investments in human capital are still out in the cold. No less remarkable is the belated discovery by the central banks of the US, Canada and the Bank for International Settlements that 1% or 2% of "inflation" might be beneficent.

But is that "last 1% or 2%" really inflation – or the deepening layer of taxation to pay for the growing essential public services required by a high-tech, rapidly urbanizing society? Plus the revenge of the many necessary public investments that should have been but were not made – SARS, Mad Cow disease, terrorism?

Will the Real Adam Smith Stand Up?

• Far from leaving all to the "invisible hand," Smith urged keeping it out of our pockets: "The mean rapacity of merchants and manufacturers who should not be the rulers of mankind."

• To keep in touch with the real world, he switched from one to another of three different value theories depending upon the problem he was tackling. He sought some deeper logic in the economy than the price of the latest trade.

• Two of these value theories were variants of the labour theory: "embodied labour," the amount of average labour that went to produce a commodity, and "commanded labour," the labour that could be purchased with the proceeds of its sale. Today, to understand the economic relations of China and the West, we go back to Smith's "commanded labour" – an hour's work in Japan would pay for 10 in China.

• At other times Smith used the cost of production theory of value which added up cost columns as our accountants in their better moments do today.

A Fig-leaf for Society's Shameful Parts

• The raw capitalism of mid-19th century felt a need to hide its shameful parts. That was answered by marginal utility theory that saw no value beyond the price of the latest trade of a commodity. It is no coincidence that this marginal value theory arose independently almost at the same time in three countries: Austria (Menger), Britain (Jevons), Walras (France). The first two were published in the year of the Paris Commune. The third three years later.

• It presented all classes in society as just traders seeking to maximize their satisfactions.

• If unemployment seemed to exist, it was just that the jobless worker had weighed the satisfaction of working at the wage offered against the delights of leisure in his parlour.

• To be able to make use of the prestigious differential calculus it was assumed that all actors in the economy were of such tiny size that nothing they did individually could affect prices. Obviously that is nonsense in the age of GE Corp. It violated the first principle of tailoring: "Never cut the client to the cloth."

Gene of Our Derivative Economy

• Marginal utility is the very gene of our current "derivatives economy." What really matters are rates of growth, whether, it seems, of earnings, market share or toe-nails. Some of them start almost flat and end up standing vertically, like a Viagra ad. Such a graph incorporates the higher powers of growth of whatever

is chosen. The transaction volume in financial derivatives now exceeds many times that in socially useful goods and services.

This makes possible fantastic leverage, ghostly counterparties, and great facilities for corporations to hide their more dubious involvements. Stock market prices so achieved are then extrapolated into the remote future, and incorporated into present prices.

• That, however, is a bargain with the devil. The Wall St. maker-shaker is promised everything he wishes in year one. But with a condition attached – that growth rate must be matched each future year or the structure craters.

• This produces stresses on morality hard to withstand. Every pool of savings and reserves that can be located is ransacked to maintain the achieved growth rate – pension funds, depreciation reserves, money-creating powers ceded by the government to the deregulated banks. The whole tends to exponential increase. It is the maths of the atomic bomb:

• The exponential function is designed so that each successive derivative of it remains the same as the previous one, and hence as the function itself. With every subsequent derivation each term in the base expression is replaced by the following one of the next derivative. The term lost on the left is regained on the right as the series moves one notch towards infinity unchanged. It is a sermon on the sin of worshipping unlimited growth.

The Important Relationship between the Price Level and its Marketed and Non-marketed, Unpriced Components

• This, however, is *terra incognita*, unexplored by economists. That appears from the current disagreement amongst central bankers on whether the current "1% to 2% of inflation" is a good thing, or the harbinger of the sort of "hyperinflation" that took over Germany in 1923.

We thought it was the German defeat in World War I, the reparations denominated in strong currencies that the Allies imposed, and the occupation of the Ruhr industrial heartland by the French army. Most of the national debt that preoccupies the American political leaders today was incurred with the high interest imposed to "lick" that inflation.

• In fact that 1% to 2% price climb isn't inflation at all. It is the deepening layer of taxation in prices that pays for the increased public services without which a modern society is unthinkable. Plus the needless costs and vulnerabilities produced by Globalization and Deregulation.

• But these vital services have been declared "externalities" – fancy word, but all it means is that – like Enron's liabilities – they have been kept off the books and under the table.

• If those needs are addressed, their costs show up in price as a greater stratum of taxes. I have called this "structural price increase" to distinguish it from market inflation caused by an excess of demand over available supply.

If not attended to, they become "stranded costs." Essential services not provided in the name of "efficiency" prepare surprises such as the power outage that left 50 million North Americans in the dark. The privatized power systems had neglected maintenance of their transmission lines, on occasion to gamble away their maintenance reserves in mergers. Schools and welfare facilities not provided will result in more penitentiaries, more crime and more terrorism.

An adequate sketch of our price system would show two upper non-market layers of the final price curve above the marketed layer (Figure 1). The first is the cost of the deepening layer of unpriced services that are not marketed and hence not priced. A second one above that is for "stranded debt" – as in the cost of getting rid of the spent fuel of decommissioned atomic generators.

Until recently in the US and Canada government investments were written off entirely in the year they were made, and carried on the government books at a token value.

• This distorted the balance sheet, drove up interest rates since it understated the government's assets. It led to a field day for privatization. Sold at a fraction of their real worth, such sales presented as a profit over book value. That was patriotically applied to "reducing the debt." The late stock market boom would have been inconceivable without the absence of serious accountancy in the public sector.

Beginning with January, 1996, capital budgeting was smuggled into the US public accounts as "government savings" rather than as the investments they were. "Savings" implies cash which is not depreciated. President Clinton had need of a statistic that would impress the bond rating agencies and bring down interest rates without alienating "the center" with talk of "government investment." That contributed to the largest stock market boom.

• But government investment in human capital is still totally ignored. In the 1960s Theodore Schultz won the Nobel Prize for Economics by assessing the rapid postwar recovery of Germany and Japan as proof that human capital is the most productive of all investments. But like the Vikings who discovered America long before Columbus, having no use for Schultz's finding, economists proceeded to lose it again.

Key Tools for Picking our Way through this Jungle

• **Tinbergen counting rule.** In our first-year high-school algebra classes we learned that to solve a linear equation with two independent variables, we need two equations. One won't do. Jan Tinbergen formulated that as his counting rule: to solve a problem with two independent variables, you need a solution with two such variables.

• Until the 1970s central banks used two variables for dealing with "inflation" – they raised the statutory reserves – the proportion of the deposits taken in from the public in chequing and short-term accounts; and/or raising interest rates on the overnight loans to banks to meet their net cheque clearing and the cash needs of their depositors. These reserves were abolished outright in New Zealand and Canada by the early 1990s, and rarely used in other countries. Interest rates became "the one blunt tool" against "inflation" that ran up most of the existing national debts and almost wrecked the world economy.

• The Tinbergen Test would have shown that the therapy of Volcker couldn't work.

• This sees the economy as a complex of subsystems, each with its own specific goal. For the system to function, each subsystem must be in working order. No subsystem must cannibalize another.

Systems Theory is Indispensable

Marginal theory on the other hand posits a self-balancing market (see Figure 2). D = demand; S = supply; P = price. The connecting semi-loops in our diagram are strictly directional, not quantified. An excess of demand over supply will drive up price and higher price will have a balancing reciprocal effect. A deficiency of demand will lower prices, and lower prices will increase demand. Likewise the relations between supply and price. The model is self-balancing.

• But from the 1930s and lesser depressions we know that if demand drops too drastically few people will increase their spending or make investments.

During the 1930s Keynes and others decided that government intervention was essential to start projects to get the economy out of the rut. This I have called the "Policy Shunt" or the "Keynesian Subsystem": aD = aggregate demand, aS = aggregate supply (Figure 3).

It not only serves the anti-cyclical purpose described, but funds all non-market subsystems – education, health, social security, environmental protection. As varied as these are, they all depend upon government funding. They are like chickens with a single neck, and that comes laid out on the one chopping block – the Policy Shunt. They can be blocked with the one rhetorical question: "Where is the money coming from?" That must be answered with another question: "Where did the money go?"

• One can't understand any economy otherwise than as a power play, and the "policy shunt" is a sort of strategic mountain pass, a Thermopylae savagely defended by those in power. The late French economist François Perroux focused on this with his concept of the "dominant revenue." In any given period, it is the volume of the revenue of those in power by which the well-

Figure 1

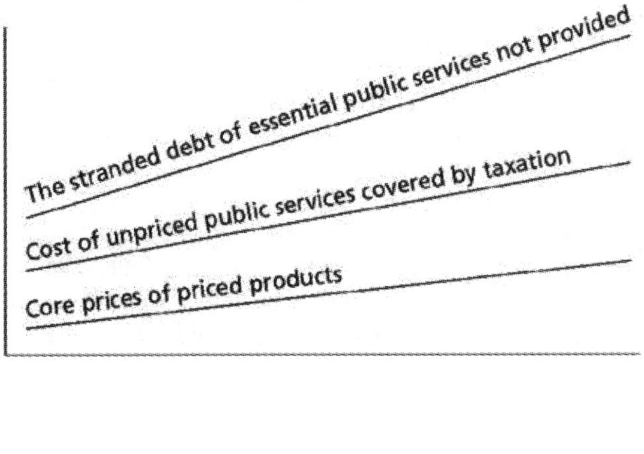

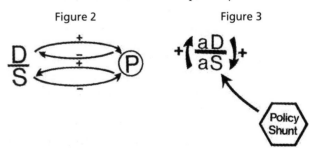

Figure 2   Figure 3

being of society as a whole is measured. In turn it has been the income of the large landowners, then of industrial capital, then under Roosevelt an alliance of government bureaucracy and a section of industrial capitalists, with the trade unions as junior partners, while the banks were in the doghouse. More recently it has been the winnings of speculative capital.

• **Is Bigger Really Better?** As unnecessary congestion and pollution are piled up by Globalization and Deregulation, the subsystems declared "externalities" are presenting us with the bills for their neglect. SARS, West Nile disease, Mad Cow, the revival of tuberculosis, syphilis, malaria and many others are instantaneously carried to our world centres over our bankrupt airlines.

Galileo observed that areas of similar figures vary as the square of their linear dimension. But the force that gravity exerts on them increases with their mass which usually varies as the third power of their linear dimension. Their power of resistance, however, is usually a function of their cross-section, e.g., the square of those linear dimensions. From that he laid down the general principle that if we tried building structures big enough, the nuts, bolts and beams would no longer hold together. Scientists from times of antiquity have worked on the assumption that if there were two alternative paths, nature will choose the shortest – *the principle of least action*. But economists, addicted to the GDP, have embraced a *law of most action*.

• The most important policy contribution of my paper may be an application of the modular calculus of Karl Friedrich Gauss, the greatest of 19th century mathematicians.

By eliminating the greatest multiple of a suitable modulus from a problem, Gauss simplified calculations enormously. Instinctively our remote ancestors applied modular calculus when, rather than giving every day since the Garden of Eden a special name, they adopted the modulus seven for the purpose and began with Sunday again after the seventh of these.

• Let us circumvent the pill-box of misinformation blocking any proposal for essential social programs by lifting the inevitable road-bar: "Where will the money come from?"

The state of the treasury depends on two variables – income and expenditures. To deal with these we choose two items that – other things being equal – most people prefer pointed downwards rather than upwards, e.g., lower consumer taxes and lower interest paid by the treasury.

These are chosen in dosages that directly would have a zero sum effect on the fisc. To make up the loss of revenue from lower consumer taxes, enough government debt could be shifted from the commercial banks to the central bank. For when the central bank holds debt of its government, over 95% of the interest on it will find its way back to the government as dividends where the central banks have a single shareholder – the government. And when it is owned by private shareholders – the case in the US – roughly the same portion of the interest on the debt held by it will revert to the government by the monopoly of the ancestral monarch in coining precious metals – *seigniorage*. The direct effect of our Step One will thus be neutral.

Step Two is passive. We monitor the indirect effect of reducing government spending and revenue as they work their way through the economy. Clearly the reduction of consumer taxes

and the net interest paid by the government will have a tonic effect on the economy. Once that is confirmed, a further dosage of the same two measures can be undertaken – or of a different pair. We will have contained either inflation or deflation, whichever is our problem. The same technique can be applied to a variety of problems – always keeping in mind the Tinbergen Counting Test, the admonitions of systems theory, and the prudence of Karl Friedrich Gauss. Economics could become again a science to be taken seriously.

Mail from New Zealand

Delivered by Les Hunter as an invited keynote speaker on Community Credit to the New Zealand Democrat annual conference held in Hawkestone Hotel, Wellington, August 2, 2003.

EVERYONE IN THIS ROOM can probably cite a local example of the requirement for investment in what may be broadly termed social assets – assets built to meet community, rather than commercial, needs. Individual home ownership must be included in this category, as must the property of the great number of incorporated societies that support a raft of sporting, recreational and community endeavours.

Community credit – that is, the creation of money by a government agency in response to community need, rather than by the multinational banks in the pursuit of profit – can provide much of the funding for social assets.

Some hundred and forty years ago, Abraham Lincoln said that meeting the nation's need for money was the government's greatest creative opportunity. Governments have created money in times of war and, today, the need is as great as ever. In association with a reformed monetary system, the use of community credit can alleviate the concerns about present rate revolts and the extent of taxation.

Every local authority in New Zealand is faced with the problem of funding infrastructure and environmental needs. Funding for roading, for example, is an ongoing issue in both Auckland and Tauranga. In the latter case, the Tauranga District Council – as a forerunner amongst New Zealand local authorities – has decided to toll a new highway rather than look to rates to provide funding.

On all New Zealand roads, an unnecessarily high accident rate and congestion with the related waste of time and fuel are evident. Moreover, there is a nationwide need to deal with the pollution of soil and waterways – the state of the Rotorua lakes has attracted recent attention. Those who look to central government to provide for education and health are desperately calling for additional investment in schools and hospitals – and in ways that do not involve increased taxation or user-pay charges. The same applies to providing adequate security, whether by the police or the armed forces.

The extension of community credit – also known as public or social credit – can provide the funding for social assets in ways that call for payment once only, rather than several times over because of interest charges. Repayment of the secured loan, plus a reasonable administrative charge and cover for risk, are all that is required.

In New Zealand, the idea of drawing upon community credit to fund social investment is not new. The first New Zealand Labour government funded the building of state houses by these means. At the same time, the Germans, Japanese and Italians built up a war machine for aggressive purposes. All of the participants in the Second World War added to the money created by the banks by utilizing what is generally known as reserve bank – that is, community – credit. The British economist JM Keynes provided theoretical justification for the particular policies. His recommendations came to be politically accepted in spite of the frantic opposition coming from those committed to classical economic doctrine and *laissez-faire.*

Every nation has to have a supply of money (with the ideal amount some 28 percent of the national income). Drawing upon community credit will add to the money supply, while the repayment of the principal of community credit advanced will reduce the money supply. In other words, the issuance (and retirement) of community credit can be used as a mechanism to optimize the money supply – of which over ninety percent is at present created as cheque money by the commercial banks. In the cashless society – if it ever eventuates – notes and coin will have been phased out and the money supply would consist simply of cheque money created by multinational banks – with horrendous implications.

When considering the use of community credit, it is essential to acknowledge what the term means.

The word credit implies trust and, in the context of community credit, cannot be divorced from a matching liability. The liability attached to the money created as the result of drawing upon community credit must be the nation's wealth of consumer goods – rather than a monetary reserve. When money is received as income there must be a matching value of consumer goods available to buy. In this context, there is nothing wrong with money being created as a debt – what matters is who owns that debt and the nature of the associated liability.

The debt associated with the extension of community credit must be interest-free and owned by the people of New Zealand. The New Zealand producers of consumer goods must accept the associated liability under conditions of private enterprise in a property-owning democracy. In this regard, profit must be the reward for producing appealing consumer goods, rather than the result of asset-stripping, speculation and money-lending – as presently applies.

Today, most of the world's economies are drowning in a sea of debt, with the effect that the rich are unnecessarily and inequitably becoming richer and the poor poorer. The debt of one person must be an asset to another – whether of a bank or simply a money-lender. At present, the most obnoxious form of debt is that imposed upon households. Credit-card debt in the order of billions is committed at interest rates that cannot be defined as anything but usurious. The amount of this debt is compounding at an alarming rate – as is household debt generally.

The responsible use of community credit can put a stop to compounding debt and the associated cost-inflationary pressures. However, drawing upon community credit cannot be reconciled with the conventional economic view that inflation-free investment can be funded only from savings or through some form of taxation. More generally, monetary reform policies cannot be formulated, promoted or applied unless underpinned by credible – but unorthodox – economic theory.

For some fourteen years as finance spokesman for Social Credit and the Democrats, I was held responsible for promoting the use of community credit but, always, the policy has been put down because of opposition from conventional economists.

In conclusion, I can but repeat Abraham Lincoln's contention that community credit provides each nation with its greatest creative opportunity. However, such a policy can be politically promoted only if underpinned by credible monetary and economic theory. After some twelve years of work, it is my fervent hope that I have made a significant contribution towards providing the required theory.

Les Hunter is a member of the Committee on Monetary and Economic Reform and author of the book Courage to Change – A case for monetary reform *(available in bookshops and at www. monetaryreform.co.nz).*

Editorial Comment

To put Les Hunter's mention of Keynes in proper perspective, Keynes was in some respects a late learner. There were accordingly several distinct Keyneses. As late as his A Treatise on Money (1930) he was still advocating lowering interest rates "a l'outrance" as a possible way of coping with the Depression…. He was condescending about what was best in Karl Marx – the analysis of Capitalism's mortal ailments ("non-scientific" in contrast the "science," we suppose, of marginal value theory). But when he did catch up with the world, he did so with a generosity, that is probably unique in the petty, eye-gouging universe of economic theory.

In his *General Theory* (1936), p. 32, he wrote: "The great puzzle of Effective Demand vanished from economic literature. It could only live on furtively in the underworlds of Karl Marx, Silvio Gesell or Major Douglas." On page 213 of the same work he tips his hat to the "labour theory of value," appropriately amended.

Keynes's mature views reach back to all these unconventional explanations of economic crises. Gesell emphasized the absence of adequate consumer purchasing power, and his chief policy recommendation was affixing a monthly stamp on currency to keep it valid, Gesell sought to remedy deflation by creating in its midst the phenomenon of a wasting currency usually associated with inflation. Douglas emphasized the "social heritage" and proposed among much else the humanistic and immensely practical vision of a social dividend to make it unnecessary "to build machine guns in order to be able to buy cabbages." Implicit in this was the need to encourage alternate life styles to rein in growth at the expense of the environment. Keynes grasped the key role of increased investment in keeping capitalism functioning. In his critique of capitalism, Karl Marx was far ahead of everybody. By contrast, in his complete ignoring the problems of socialism he was just another great prophet come out of the desert. Only now are we beginning to catch up with his analysis in Volume Three of *Capital* – of the fetishism of capital that sees it automatically and incessantly birthing interest.

The important point is not that one of these competing explanations of our periodic crises was right and the others wrong. Douglas and Marx were more complete than Gesell in emphasizing the key role of investment, rather than under-consumption. The concept of Douglas's common social heritage to justify a social dividend – the contribution of generations of inventors, scientists, martyrs, slaves, without which modern production could never have arisen. That will not only justify a "social dividend" to encourage less driven life styles, but could be taken alternately in adequate public services. The only limiting envelope is the available human and material resources. None of them could have anticipated the complete revolution in price patterns that arose with the development of urbanized mixed economies. Keynes died in 1946 before the price effects of his proposals and the necessary explosion of essential public services first appeared. He commands our reverence no matter how incomplete he left his reforms.

In its work on the very different components of the pluralistic price system of a mixed economy, COMER has taken the lead in addressing the resulting problems. See our Poster at the Cambridge University Conference in this issue.

William Krehm

REVIEW OF A BOOK BY MARTIN H. WOLFSON, 1994, M.E. SHARPE, ARMONK, NEW YORK

Financial Crises — Understanding the Postwar US Experience

W E CANNOT OPEN our financial pages of our paper without encountering a reference to something in the economy being cyclical. Wolfson reviews the record of financial crises to determine what was indeed systemic or, contrariwise, due to misfired policy.

"In the nineteenth and early twentieth centuries, financial crises occurred regularly in the US, with particularly severe episodes in 1873 and 1893. Later came the Panic of 1907 and the banking crises during the Great Depression of the 1930s. The severe trauma of the Great Depression led to major reforms in finance. The hope was that these would put an end to the dislocations of financial crises."

And indeed during, the period immediately following WWII, financial crises seemed a thing of the past. "Even mention of them disappeared from the literature. Nearly an entire generation of economists was trained without ever studying the origins and causes of financial crises.

"Accordingly, the 'credit crunch' of 1955 came as a shock."

Though the 1966 crisis was much less than the Panic of 1907 it was [disturbing] to observers who had thought financial crises were a thing of the past.

"Another crisis followed in 1970. Then the surprise bankruptcy of the Penn Central company threatened the commercial paper market and led to a 'flight to quality' (i.e., a preference for safe investments). As in 1966, prompt action by the Federal Reserve Board as lender of last resort, and appropriate monetary and fiscal policies prevented a full-scale panic.

"In May 1974 an even more serious financial crisis took place: the troubles of the Franklin National Bank, the twentieth largest bank in the US. Franklin had borrowed heavily in the Eurodollar interbank market and had engaged in substantial foreign-exchange speculation. Both of these markets were threatened by Franklin's difficulties.

"Again, government action prevented the situation from escalating.

"Silver speculation by the billionaire Hunt brothers again threatened a serious financial crisis in 1980. When the price of silver began to fall in January 1980, the Hunts borrowed on a massive scale – a total of nearly $1 billion from commercial banks to cover their losses. In September, 1982 fear of Mexico's default on its obligations to commercial banks aggravated the banks' problems, set off a capital flight, and required lender-of-the-last resort operations of international scope.

"Weakened by the bad loans they had purchased from Penn Square, both Continental Illinois and Seattle First National Banks were hit by a run on deposits by large investors. Only an unprecedented government bailout in the summer of 1984 prevented these difficulties from spreading throughout the banking and financial systems.

"During the summer of 1984, a run developed on the deposits of the American Savings and Loan Association, at the time the largest thrift in the US. Crises in state-insured thrifts in Ohio and Maryland produced the image of depositors waiting in long lines to withdraw their money – something not seen in the US since the Depression." Not only were financial crises becoming more shattering, but more frequent. Nothing routine there.

"In 1989 Congress passed the *Financial Institutions Reform, Recovery, and Enforcement Act* (FIRREA) providing bailouts for insolvent thrifts." And in September 1992 the European monetary system was rocked with devastating strikes by exchange speculators."

The Cyclical and the Random

Wolfson distinguishes between events of recurrent pattern and hence cyclical, and random ones.

"In general, the problems that borrowers and financial intermediaries had during the recession in 1982 continued on into the subsequent recovery and expansion. The severity of the 1981-2 recession, and its occurrence so soon after the 1980 recession, impaired the quality of loans. The combination of high interest rates, low inflation [that fails to erode the burden of debt], put further pressure on borrowers and made the usual cyclical improvement in credit quality more difficult.

"The failure of Penn Square Bank in 1982 played a major

role in the failures of Seattle First National Bank (Seafirst) in 1983 and Continental Illinois National Bank and Trust Company in 1984.

"Seaforth had enjoyed an excellent reputation. Its parent, Seafirst Corporation, was one of the largest bank holding companies in the country. In 1979 with energy prices expanding rapidly, lending to the energy industry seemed wise. Seafirst, however, was a relative newcomer to energy lending. As it moved out beyond its Pacific Northwest base, it found that it had to lend to relatively less creditworthy borrowers. It also discovered Penn Square in Oklahoma, which was making more loans than it could fund and was looking to sell loans to out-of-the-state banks."

The moral of the tale was that banks do not have to go global to get lost in unfamiliar jungles. They can manage it by moving into new industries or regions of their native land.

"In little more than two years before 1981, Seafirst's energy loan portfolio grew from $11 million to $300 million. In the last two months of 1981 Seafirst bought $350 million more energy loans from Penn Square and that portfolio went to $1.3 billion by the end of the first quarter of 1982."

"Penn Square's failure in July revealed the particularly poor quality of the loans Seafirst had purchased from it. [That illustrated the perils of banking by buying loans syndicated by others. It turned out a false efficiency having the purchasing bank avoid the costly drudgery of doing its own research and oversight.] Seaforth was required to set aside $125 million in June, 1982 for possible losses on its energy loans. That and the higher cost of money market funds resulted in a $56.2 million loss for the second quarter of 1982." The Federal Reserve Bank of New York organized assistance from other banks because of fear "that the failure of Seafirst would be a shock to the money market at home and abroad. The situation was resolved by the merging of Seafirst into the Bank of America Corporation on July 1, 1983, after emergency legislation was passed by the State of Washington to make this possible."

That should remind the Canadian public that bank mergers can serve to hide the difficulties that banks have gotten themselves into – a point that the Public Relations departments of the banks in question do not always emphasize.

But the punch-line of the wondrous tale of Continental Illinois and its losses is that both had become too big "to be merged into another bank" – $35 billion in assets in mid-1984, when it had already shrunk considerably.

"In 1976 Continental had decided to become, by 1981, one of the top three lenders to corporate business in the country. It embarked upon a program of rapid loan growth, especially in energy. Throughout 1978 its earnings and asset growth were higher than its peers,' and its loan losses lower. As energy prices rose sharply in 1979, Continental stepped up this program from 1979 to 1980 by an increase of nearly 100%. The next year brought an additional 50%. By 1981 they made up 47% of its business loans."

In the rush for growth, Continental began making loans on properties of uncertain potential. It increased the loans bought from Penn Square. There was no better formula for ready-made growth. These loans resulted in large losses, and Continental Illinois was obliged to set aside $262 million against possible losses. By the second quarter of 1982 had to set aside $383 million for possible bad loans.

Its net income for the quarter in the spring of 1982 was a negative $63 million. By the end of 1982 its bad loans had risen to $1,937 million. Penn Central had proved the "typhoid Mary" of banking.

Because of this unfavourable turn in its fortunes, it found its own funding on the domestic market increasingly difficult, and went offshore, paying a premium, to fill the gap. It sold its credit card business to help the problem. Banks in that position often end up by selling what is salable, i.e., profitable, and hanging onto what cannot be sold. By May, 1984 the rumours were that Continental was on the brink of bankruptcy. The bank had lost $9 billion of the offshore funding that it thought it had arranged. It took to borrowing heavily at the Federal Reserve discount window, from $850 million on May 8, 1984 to $4.7 billion on May 16.

A group of sixteen large banks headed by Morgan Guaranty Trust pledged a line of credit of $4.5 billion to rescue Continental Illinois. All that, however was ineffective to persuade depositors not to withdraw their money. Then the three regulators – the Comptroller of the Currency, Federal Deposit Insurance corporation, and the Federal Reserve Board – joined in an announcement of (1) a capital infusion of $2 billion; (2) continued access to the Fed's discount window, and (3) an increase in the line of credit from the banks to $5.5 billion. (4) a guarantee of the Federal Deposit Insurance that *all* depositors (not just those contractually insured) and other general creditors of Continental Illinois would be "fully protected."

The moral there is that once public distrust of financial institutions is aroused, deposit insurance cannot stop with the insured. If it does, the uninsured – those with deposits in excess of the insurance limit – will simply withdraw their funds, and bring down the wounded bank. With so much hidden in financial cupboards through deregulation, that is a powerful threat.

When Debtors Can Dictate the Bailout Terms

There is implicit in the Continental experience a sermon on the folly of encouraging or even allowing banks to grow ever bigger. There is the old adage about owing the bank a thousand and you are at its mercy. Owe it ten million and it is at your mercy. Well, on a vastly greater scale, it applies to banks in their relations with the government. When banks grow or merge beyond a certain magnitude, especially under deregulation and globalization, they have become involved with just about every gambling game on the world's stock markets. They might as well go to Las Vegas and save the carfare. No choice is left the government but to bail them out *on the debtors' terms.* The alternative is to countenance the folding of entire financial system world-wide.

In the case of the Continental the regulators took the course of action that they did, "because according to the Federal Deposit Insurance Corporation (FDIC) William M. Isaac, '2,300 small banks had nearly $6 billion at risk in Continental, 66 had more than their capital on the line, and another 113 had between 50 and 100%.'"

"The possibilities for a solution to the Continental crisis were narrowing: no bank holding company wanted to buy Continental. Thus a permanent assistance program was fashioned. A key concept in this program was the separation of the 'good bank' from the 'bad bank.' If Continental's bad loans were taken out of the bank, it was anticipated that the remnant of Continental would survive. The FDIC purchased loans from Continental with a book value of $4.5 billion; in exchange it agreed to pay $3.5 billion of Continental's borrowings from the Federal Reserve of Chicago. When the dust settled, the private stockholders were eliminated and FDIC was eligible for compensation by obtaining up to all of the remaining 40 million shares. In addition, "the guarantee by the FDIC, discount window support by the Federal Reserve and the $5.5 billion line of credit from the group of banks remained in place. Moreover, "the FDIC pledged, 'If for any reason the permanent financial assistance package proves insufficient, the FDIC will commit additional capital or other forms of assistance as may be required.'" Because of these provisions, many have claimed that Continental was "nationalized."

That format of bailout became a model for the periodic "rescue" of Mexico's banks by the government, as well as in the United States. It opened a new dimension for milking the public treasury.

"To an important extent, the story of the 1980s involves the growth, and subsequent collapse, of speculative lending and investment. Three of the most intensive arenas were commercial real estate, junk bonds, and the stock market. Banks in Texas and the Southwest searched for other profitable areas as lending to the oil industry soured. Real estate loans continued to grow even as oil lending declined. And it was more broadly based than oil. The share of commercial real estate loans grew rapidly from 1985 to 1990, even as the share of business loans in the banks' portfolios declined. This growth was encouraged by tax considerations. The *Economic Recovery Tax Act* of 1981 significantly increased depreciation allowances, which made real estate investment more rewarding. Banks continued to expand their commercial real estate lending. Developers continued to build, banks to finance downtown office buildings despite soaring vacancy rates.

"Commercial banks were not the only ones participating in this. Thrift institutions, whose areas of lending were considerably liberalized by state and national legislation in the early 1980s, also increased their interest in commercial mortgages – from $43.9 billion in 1982 (6.4% of their total assets) to $98.4 billions in 1985 (9.2% of total assets).

Other "non-traditional areas in which thrifts became engaged were high-yield securities, also known as 'junk bonds.' Their high yields, of course, were accompanied by corresponding high risks. Earlier in the decade, most junk bonds outstanding were 'fallen angels.' These had originally been investment-grade bonds, issued by companies whose financial condition had since deteriorated. However, increasingly in the 1980s, companies that were too new, too small, or too, risky for an investment-

grade rating were creating original-issue junk bonds.

"However, it was their use in the emerging market for corporate control, especially hostile takeovers, that really brought junk bonds into prominence. In a hostile takeover, the acquiring group or company typically makes a cash tender for the shares of the target company, against the wishes of its management. The ability to make such a tender offer was possible because of the mobilization of large amounts of cash through junk bonds. This radically transformed the nature of mergers and acquisitions. Prior to 1984, mergers or acquisitions of other companies were usually friendly, carried out through the exchange of stock. After junk bonds came to be used, the cash raised enabled the acquirer (or raider) to go directly to the stockholders, even if management was opposed to the deal."

Cash Raised by Junk Bonds Was Their Calling Card

Junk bonds might be the common ammunition in such battles. "Managements attempting to fend off hostile takeovers could also use junk bonds. By raising cash through junk bonds, management could buy the existing publicly held stock and "take the company private." Either way, the company was likely to end up overloaded with high-interest debt. Cutting staff to handle the situation was almost routine.

"The use of debt in corporate takeovers and LBOs was encouraged by favorable tax changes in the *Economic Recovery Act* of 1981 (ERTA), Law changes introduced accelerated cost recovery system (ACRS) of depreciation along with a more generous investment tax credit. This allowed an immediate increase of depreciation after merger or takeover.

"These helped put some companies in net operating losses (NOL) and tax credit carry-forwards (the ability to use tax credits to offset future income). Mergers with more profitable companies would enable those tax advantages to be utilized. The *Installment Sales Revision Act* of 1980 reduced the tax costs of asset sales. The pressure to use merger was especially great in an environment of high interest rates, which magnified the advantage of using the tax credit carryforwards as soon as possible." However, like the high interest rates that spurred the trend, it did nothing to help the public treasury.

The tax savings from substituting debt for equity can explain much of the premium paid to stockholders in takeovers. Researchers note the general trend: "There is clear evidence that the current American tax system subsidizes corporate restructurings and raises the premiums that acquirers can afford to pay for corporations" (Margaret Pickering, *A Review of Corporate Restructuring Activity*, 1980-90, "Staff Study 11, Board of Governors of the Federal Reserve, 1991"). Both the winners and losers in the struggle to take over a corporation make massive acquisitions of the stock, which drives up the price. In this bidding game both are likely to come out with a profit. Money made on the stock market is likely to stay in the stock market and become even more venturesome. Such winnings as those made with the leverage of junk bonds add to the supply of near-money. But the volatility of such winnings will increase with the interest rates involved, and the weakness of its links to the real economy.

William Krehm

The Perils of Number-Crunching

NUMBER-CRUNCHING is particularly dangerous because it has the appearance of utter accuracy – even high science – when it quite literally may not know what it is talking about. It was a grand moment in the earlier history of man when he separated number from what it was applied to. That was when man stopped counting on his fingers and toes. That he had not learned to make that separation is witnessed by our language – as in ten-score. In the name of our digital high technology, "digital," of course, referred to fingers, long before a keyboard existed.

However, liberation of the objects and activities that were tied to numbers was not without its perils. The founder of modern linguistics, Ferdinand de Saussure, distinguished similar contrasting effects in language itself. Language can take over our conversations and guide them according to its own *structure*. This de Saussure called the "structural" aspect of language. In a sense this is like employees carrying on private conversations on the boss's computer or telephone. In its well-behaved mode attending strictly to the boss's business, language is said to operate in a "functional" sense.

Number crunching, the practice that usurps the role of economic analysis is the source of many of its troubles. It creates illusions that contradict and even block reality. Thus in *The Wall Street Journal* (28/08, "Asians Snub Their Stock Rally") we read: "Asian economies are growing, the region's stock markets are soaring, and US investors are pouring money into Asian-Pacific mutual funds in a way not seen for years.

"Now if only Asians would buy their own stocks. Across the Pacific Rim, state-run funds and other big money managers are showing a notable reluctance to invest in local companies, even as foreigners flock to these highflying markets."

It may be that close up, you see more of the warts and the war-paint.

"In Taiwan, for example, foreign investors have bought 269 billion New Taiwan dollars of stock in Taipei since the beginning of June, while local investment trust have bought just NT$4 billion. In India, foreigners have purchased 79 billion rupees of shares, compared with local mutual funds buying a paltry 1.4 billion rupees. In South Korea, international investors have been net buyers of 6.9 trillion won of Korean stocks since May, while domestic institutions have been net *sellers* of 3.2 trillion won. The same trend applies to Japan."

Clearly, people are mistaking the numbers for what is being numbered. Possibly, fiction for fact. For surely investors on the spot must have the better picture of the local economy. Each of these markets is up more than 20% this year. "But with international investors notoriously fickle about Asia, many analysts say it would be difficult for the markets to maintain their gains without the hometown crowd."

"The reluctance of Asians to invest in their own markets reflects, in part, a lingering risk aversion from their experiences during the financial crisis of 1997 and 1998, which pommeled many portfolios. In addition, Asians exhibit a greater skepticism than Americans about the strength of the US economic recovery, which is crucial to the success of many of the region's companies.

"Domestic selling in the face of foreign buying is most pronounced in Japan, where companies traditionally have held small stakes in each other to cement business ties. In recent years, banks, insurance, and other companies have been unwinding those holdings so the cash can be invested more efficiently. Through mid-August they were net sellers of 2.5 trillion yen ($21.29 billion) of Japanese stock. Foreign investors, meanwhile, have been net buyers of 3.7 trillion yen of Japanese shares."

If ignorance of the pitfalls of shares grows more or less as the square of the distance from which they are admired, it follows that globalization must increase the hazard connected with what hype puts on the remote investor's plate.

"The story is similar throughout the region as investors eschew stocks for more conservative investments such as bonds or money-market funds. At the end of June, money held in bank deposits for Asia, excluding Japan, represented more than twice the region's stock-market capitalization. This is almost the same level as at the worst point of the Asian crisis even though rates are much lower. Much of the foreign interest in South Korea has been driven by a handful of stocks. Samsung Electronics, which makes up 22% of South Korea's market capitalization, has been the favorite. Close to 60% of its shares are owned by foreigners."

But local stocks are not without their pitfalls. "Local investors tend to gravitate towards banking stocks, which haven't done well lately as the banks deal with problems including growing write-offs of credit-card debt. Deposits into Korean investment-trust companies that buy stocks have fallen during the past four months, but deposits at trusts that buy money-market funds have risen by about 12 trillion won. Korean insurance and brokerage companies have been steadily shedding stocks since they got burned during the financial crisis."

The frailty of the "recovery" is deep and world-wide.

W.K.

All Circuits Backing Up!

IN MY RECENT BOOK[1] I draw on a variety of tools not only in economic theory, but from other disciplines to prove that Deregulation and Globalization are increasing the world's vulnerabilities.

Since then there has been an avalanche of confirmation by life itself. Not only have our ever more complex power circuits been collapsing from overload. Their capacity was drastically cut down in the pursuit of what passed for "sound fundamentals." The blackout of the electricity grids serving some 50 million people in the Northeastern part of the continent came as a jolt to Washington, that already had much more on its plate than it bargained for.

The supposedly greater "efficiencies" of G & D have brought

us new deadly microbes from Asia spawned by the virtual cohabitation of peasants with their livestock. As soon as they evolve, these are delivered into our midst over our bankrupt airlines. That is the story of SARS, and the West Nile virus. The eruption of new lethal diseases and the revival of others. like tuberculosis and malaria, believed under control, even grabbed the headlines away from the massive fraud of the world's largest financial corporations. At least two of Canada's largest banks have been mentioned by enquiries in the US financial scams as having not only financed, but designed and profited massively from them. Yet to date not a single such enquiry has been set up in Canada.

All Wall Street's Ploys Anticipated by Government Accountancy

There were few bookkeeping ploys perfected on Wall St. that were not anticipated by governments cooking their own books. Investments like buildings and education that would last for years were treated like outlays for floor wax or paper clips. They were written off as wholly consumed in the year of their completion. That had several grave consequences. Far more taxation was imposed than was really required – just as paying off your house mortgage in a single year requires a lot more cash. Enron and Global Crossing converted liabilities into assets, our government treated and, indeed, to a great degree still treats assets as liabilities. That could hardly be put down to ignorance of accountancy. For in Canada over the last forty years at least three royal commissions and a series of Auditors General recommended capital budgeting (technically known as "accrual accountancy"). Under capital budgeting investments are written off over their useful lives, and meanwhile the undepreciated portion of their cost remains on the books of the firm or government as an asset to set off against its debt.

The mirage of the deficit that resulted from such shenanigans was used to divert funds from vital public services to bailing out our banks from the previous gambling losses and funding their new financial frolics.

Worse still, those bogus deficits were the pretexts for privatizing key assets of the federal and provincial governments. Carried as they were on the government books at a token dollar, they could be sold to private promoters at many times their book value but still at a small portion of their real worth. Then the government can patriotically apply the proceeds to "reduce the debt." And the organizers of such scams inevitably go on to bigger things. Every pool of capital in sight – pension funds of their employees, reserve funds of insurance companies, money set aside for the maintenance of power grids, for example, used for buying out other companies to sustain the illusion of a heady growth rate that has already been embedded in its market price. The rate of growth already achieved for such a corporation is extrapolated into the indefinite future. In effect the ransacking of public assets has been monetized. For such shares can serve as collateral for new loans for ever more highly leveraged gambles.

That is why the distinction between capital expenditure and current spending is so crucial.

Yet too many activist organizations have declared it too difficult for the public to understand. However, dumbing down the public is playing the game of those in power. There is nothing more complicated in distinguishing government investment from current spending, than in understanding the mortgage just about everybody takes on to buy a home.

It is true that politics is the art of compromise. However, there is a crucial dividing line between what you may compromise on, and what would be tantamount to surrender. No politician can straddle that line and stay honest.

The process of educating the public is a complicated one. Not every voter may be able to grasp all the details of government accountancy or economic policy. However, university teachers and university students will certainly have no difficulty with that sort of thing. If high school students cannot, our aspiring political reformers must campaign for adequate consumer credit courses in our high schools. For in these days when some of the world's largest banks have lost much of their capital and their good name on the stock market, they are rushing to recoup their losses in "retail credit" and even "sub-prime" debt. Sub-prime debt is the exploitation of people who don't have banking accounts, and don't know enough to ask what rate of interest is being charged them. They just ask whether they can get the money before their next pay-day, and how much they will have to pay each week or month. Rarely for how long. Would-be reformers must stress the instruction that must be made available to the electorate, rather than what the public is allegedly too dumb to learn. But that requires adequate government funding of our universities to guarantee their freedom to study alternatives to the orthodoxies that clearly aren't working.

But aren't we banging our heads against a brick wall?

Recent furtive measures by governments indicate that some of the things that we urged decades ago, are being introduced in stealth. Thus the governments of both the US and Canada have brought in a considerable measure of capital budgeting without letting the public know what they were up to. They had a powerful reason for doing so.

When the BIS Goofed

The last time the banks were bailed out – in the early 1990s – it was by discontinuing the need for them to deposit with the central bank a modest part of the deposits they received from the public. At the same time the Bank for International Settlements (BIS) declared that the debt of the industrialized powers was risk-free, requiring no extra capital of the banks to acquire. As a result Canadian banks quadrupled their holdings of federal debt to $80 billion. Banks throughout the world did something similar. That was the gimmick at the heart of the bailout. But in its haste to rescue insolvent banks, the BIS overlooked a detail: whenever the central bank raises interest rates – and by its own doing it was the only blunt tool left to fight "inflation" – pre-existing bonds drop in price like rocks. When that started happening, the governments were shocked to see that the banks were losing their capital once again – by the very workings of the bailout.

Hence the United States, starting with its Business Statistics of January 1996 found $1.3 trillion of assets previously ignored. But rather than calling it investment, it called it "savings." But the assets discovered were not really "savings," since they weren't kept as cash. However, all the Clinton administration wanted was a single statistic that would show a surplus instead of a deficit. That would convince the bond-rating agencies to raise their credit rating of the government and bring down the interest it paid on its bonds. That started the greatest boom on record, which has led in turn to one of the largest busts.

Some in COMER had raised the matter of the disregarded government investment more than a quarter of a century earlier. However, there are larger activist organizations who avoid even mentioning the point. Through their silence on such issues, they became accomplices in the prevailing information blackout. And this, moreover, is when the greater part of the job – the recognition of the investment by governments in *human capital* – is still to be done.

Another front where the results of years of effort have begun to appear. Today the world is rapidly sinking into deflation, a word that central bank governors were not even allowed to utter not so long ago. Today even the central banks of both Canada and the US have declared themselves for a degree of "inflation" of from one to two percent as necessary to keep the economy functioning. But is that one or two percent really "inflation"? For almost four decades I have identified part of the price rise as the growing layer of taxation that covers the cost of the growing volume of unpriced public services in our Gross Domestic Product. That has nothing to do with the ratio of total demand to supply.

In the 1960s the price climb started, and the evidence had not yet been seriously contaminated with the "cure" of high interest rates. Accordingly this tie was obvious to the naked eye. By the 1960s the baby-boomer generation was approaching post-secondary school age, and new high schools, and university campuses were springing up like mushrooms across the land. Obviously this accelerated the inching up of price. But Bank for International Settlements dictated that only zero inflation was acceptable, and by the 1980s our central bank gave us commercial interest rates in the twenty-percent region. As a result, our debt more than decupled. That was the main factor in pushing real short-term interest rates in Canada by 1990 to 10.9% compared to 4.7% in the US. To really understand what was happening, it was necessary to distinguish the rise in price reflecting the growth of the public sector within the economy, and that really due to an excess of demand. To use the same term for the results of distinct causes is to guarantee confusion. That is why I coined the term "social lien" as label for the structural price rise which was caused by the changing proportions of public to private sectors.

Economics' "Terra Incognita"

That space between the total national output and the product of the priced, marketed sector remains *terra incognita* for economists. Fearing to fall off the flat earth of their dreams. they have never explored it. Today in fact it is no longer enough to divide the national product into the priced output net of the tax overlay and the part representing the total tax layer in price.

To understand what is now happening, it has become necessary to break up the price of the national product into three rather than just two components. The first represents the core price of the market economy, the second, the layer of taxation paying for unpriced public services. The third represents the essential public spending *that should have been, but was not made.* The latter must be booked as a debit in the current year, and a "stranded capital debt" over the years. Our ever greater power blackouts, the pollution of our water supplies, certainly a part of the global warming, our overcrowded prisons, and even part of the terrorism across the world are the fruits of the decade-long struggle to balance a budget that avoided serious accountancy. Overloading our circuits is not an efficiency, but a guarantee of ever bigger breakdowns.

When the Lord created man and beast, He might have farmed out their design to a profit-oriented archangel. And the saintly contractor would undoubtedly have planned us with a single eye, one kidney and one lung. For certainly life – under normal conditions – could manage with that and leave a greater profit margin. But in His wisdom, He saw that the extra lung, eye and kidney were not inefficiencies, but reserve circuits. They would allow life to go on, if one of these twin organs were disabled. We can start there in helping the ordinary citizen to understand the need for urgent public investment at a time when ever more clawing and shooting are taking over throughout the world.

William Krehm

1. *Towards a Non-Autistic Economy – A Place at the Table for Society.* Toronto: COMER Publications, 2002.

Germany's Messed-up Reunification

WHENEVER ideologues present social transitions as zero-sum games where the good knight unhorses the evil one to deliver his head on a platter, there is trouble ahead. That proved so in Central America where the civil wars stirred up by Washington lasted as long as Europe's Thirty Years War and took as great a relative toll in human lives. It was so in post-Soviet Russia. When the Berlin Wall came down, it was an occasion to celebrate, but it was no reason to let the other super-ideology take over. Because the Soviets collapsed under the weight of their incompetent dogma, that did not prove the ideologies of the Western right can survive the burden of their unzipped faith.

That much is surfacing in Germany, 13 years after the Wall came down. *The Wall Street Journal* (5/08, "A Big Bet on Land in the East Haunts German Banks" by Marcus Walker) tells a weird tale.

"Schoenfeld, Germany – Of all the problems hobbling Germany's efforts to climb out of recession, one of the most persistent stems from land, such as the overgrown fields outside this village south of Berlin."

The three hundred acres had been the property of a potato farmer, Friedrich-Wilhelm Ziedrich and his cousin, who were too old to farm it themselves. So when after the Wall came down, the Bayerische Hypo-Bank, a shrewd eye on the rundown airport serving East Berlin, approached the owners to buy it for a mere $65 million. Ziedrich had defected to the West in 1953 and had spent long years working in the Mercedes-Benz plant in Duesseldorf. Ziedrich turned out more astute than the mighty bank – the second largest in Germany. He insisted on getting his money up front, even if it meant a lesser price than the one originally offered. He had no stomach for speculation.

It turned out that he would have made a better banker, and that the heads of Germany's second largest bank would have been more suitable for growing potatoes. But in all fairness, it was not just the banks that had been swept away by the conviction that with the Wall down, everything else would go straight up. The Chancellor Helmut Kohl promising "blossoming landscapes" offered investors that 50% of the value invested in the East could be taken off their tax-bill. "The Eastern currency was absorbed into the Western at four times its black market quotation. Hypo-Bank made other further land purchases with much patriotism injected into the purchase price. At Grosskugel, a dilapidated farming hamlet around a crumbling church, the bank financed land acquisition to the tune of $50B for 360 acres of fields for a new town of 8,000 people with a large office park and shopping mall. Other loans made possible lighting, water, and electricity connections and streets. Trillions of dollars have been poured by the government that made possible gleaming office towers. Autobahns that hadn't been improved since the

Nazis built them in the 1930s were brought up to contemporary standards, or higher. Real estate peaked out in 1993, and in 1996 went into a tailspin. In 2000 Hypo's partner in the Grosskugel venture, a large Heidelberg developer went bankrupt because of his East German losses."

Scenes enacted were familiar to Americans from the follies of the Savings and Loans in the 1980s – at a pitch a full octave higher. Today on the east side of the proposed village, new brick-inlayed residential roads are flanked by new street lamps with driveways running off them at right angles, The only things that are missing are houses. Only years later was the extent of the financial catastrophe exposed and led to seven Hypo executives resigning. What leases had been negotiated even at glamorous Berlin locations had to be renegotiated, or rented at far less than the scheduled rents.

The position of some of the largest German banks is not unlike that of some leading Japanese institutions who are clogged with non-productive real estate loans. The first inkling of the extent of the bank's difficulties appeared in 1999 when it merged with another Munich bank specializing in real estate loans and is known as HypoVereinsbank.

By last fall, HVB's stock had fallen so low that, on paper, shareholders could earn twice as much if the bank were broken up and its assets sold, than if it stayed together.

A plan was adopted to spin off $64 billion of risk-weighted property assets to shareholders in a new company. That in effect ended the bank's real estate business, which dated from the years following Germany's first unification in 1871.

W.K.

Our Visit to the Cambridge Conference

IN RESPONSE to more than a single great need, conferences on Heterodox Economics are becoming a world-wide phenomenon. To the point in fact where their heterodoxy has begun developing a disquieting orthodoxy of its own. Universities on all continents are feeling the pinch of budgetary downsizing, and transforming the current disrepute of economics into a source of income is a brilliant if delicate operation. Franchises by their very nature exclude as much as they include.

And what university the world over has a vaster franchise than Cambridge that nurtured Newton and Keynes? Newton's glory remains safe, and by the sheer force of personality Keynes goes on dazzling as during his lifetime. It is a grandiose doghouse to which he has been committed today by those who hold our economy in a throttling grip. The policies that won both the war and a good stretch of the peace are today decried by all major parties on both sides of the great waters. At the Cambridge Conference the way to Keynes's office was clearly marked, but less evident were the rebellious stands that made Keynes Keynes: his recognition of the need for government investment not only to keep capitalism churning, but in the process of doing so producing a more just and durable society. And there was his ability – rare enough in the eye-gouging profession of economics – of scrapping previous certainties and admitting his debt to those whom he had dismissed as "unscientific" just a few years before: Marx, Gesell, Major Douglas.

Unfortunately, pressure from academic peers led Keynes to do his most basic thinking in a private manner, much as a gentleman does his ablutions. In the words of G.L.S. Shackle, "Keynes spared his readers, even in the deliberately provocative *General Theory* of 1936, the ultimate force of his conclusion uttered in speech, 'Equilibrium is blither.'"

On reading the proofs of *The General Theory*, Roy Harrod, his future biographer, had offered this advice: "[Your] effectiveness is diminished if you try to eradicate every deep-rooted habit of thought unnecessarily. I am not thinking of the aged and fossilized, but of the younger generation. It is doing a great violation to their fundamental groundwork of thought, if you tell them that two independent demand and supply variables won't jointly determine price and quantity. Tell them that we don't know the supply function. Tell them that the *ceteribus paribus* clause is inadmissible and that we can discover more important relationships governing price and quantity in this case which render the s. and d. analysis nugatory. But don't impugn the analysis itself."

Despite such advice, there are in *The General Theory* the two most significant and least-quoted passages of his entire output. One we referred to above.[1] "The great puzzle of Effective Demand vanished from economic literature. You will not find it mentioned once in the whole of the works of Marshall, Edgeworth, and Professor Pigou. It could only live on furtively in the worlds of Karl Marx, Silvio Gesell or Major Douglas."

On page viii of the introduction there is a passage that must have been the fruit of much anguished rethinking, but no Keynesian seems to have read: "I sympathize, therefore, with the pre-classical doctrine that *everything is produced by labour....* It is preferable to regard labour, including, of course, the personal service of the entrepreneur and his assistants, as the sole factor of production, operating in a given environment of technique, natural resources, capital equipment, and effective demand."

There is the nugget that would not only equip economics for dealing with the problems of deflation, which were foremost when it was written, but to the new ones of today. Ours has become a two-tiered world economy that brutally deflates the markets for real production to make space for the unbridled speculations of high finance. It diverts our attention from the root production for human needs to remote derivatives of them, i.e., the growth rates of the profits wrung out of their deflation. Incorporated into share prices, these commit our security markets to exponential growth. Since by definition these are as unsustainable as the atomic bomb, inevitably they crash.

That ignored observation at the very gateway to *The General Theory* might have warned us against the fate that has befallen our world. Instead the "pure and perfect market" where supply and demand dance around equilibrium points has taken over. Everything else – all aspects of public investment in material and human capital have been declared "externalities," not depreciated over their useful life but treated as current spending. This leaves no depreciated asset to balance against the debt incurred for their creation.

Keynes Continues Bemusing the World for Lesser Reasons

The phenomenon of Keynes bestrode the world; his wisdom played a key role in mobilizing the Western world against the Nazis. Yet his fate is surely one of the most paradoxical in recent human history. His teachings were completely wiped out of official and even academic memories, but the man himself has continued bemusing the world, as though it were troubled by the injustice it had done to both Keynes and to itself. Biographies continue appearing, but the obsession is with the personality both in his Bloomsbury and Cambridge contexts, rather than his theories. Of the first volume of Sidelsky's three-volume effort in the field, Keynes's brother remarked – "Sidelsky took his entire first book to let us know that my brother was a bugger." His economic views, however, Sidelsky took little pain to understand.

That format of reverence was in evidence at the Cambridge Conference. The essence of his mature theory as transmitted in the above quotes did not show up at the sessions I managed to attend. Instead a far greater bias against mathematics as such turned up than against illiterately misused mathematics. One academic, whom I leave charitably unnamed, even referred to chemistry as a science "free of mathematics" that might be a possible model for economics. That disposes of molecular weights, isotopes, and indeed Mendeleieff's table.

Few who read papers or discussed those of others disrupted the conventional view of the economy as a market surrounded by "externalities." These included activities like the household economy, the public sector, the environment, investment in human capital, social security, that are not driven by the search for maximized profits. All the greater surprise then, that Victoria Chick should have read a paper on systems theory, a subject that is quite the exact inverse of "externalities." For it brings these areas of the economy out from the cold and ceases treating them as mere food chain for the market. Recognized as essential for the system as a whole, they assume the status of subsystems. Of course, they must really be indispensable for the proper functioning of the entire socio-economic system. That requires a discipline for monitoring their reserve resources.

Entropy as in Niagara Falls

In the natural sciences such reserve resources are known as "negentropy," and if they are drained by another subsystem, "entropy" ensues. In the physical world, energy is always present in matter, but it can be harnessed only where a difference of potential – negentropy – exists. In the natural sciences too, there is a precise mathematical equivalence between the different forms of negentropy – chemical, thermal, electro-magnetic, nuclear. Between the negentropies of the different social-economic subsystems, that is not the case. There the notion of negentropy is essentially a metaphor, but a very essential one. Although the "fuels" or "food chains" of the various subsystems are very different, they do have some common factors. One of these is funding, that almost invariably comes from the government. Another such common need is an economic theory that sees everything indispensable to society as subsystems rather than externalities, that concentrates on the doughnut rather than on the hole.

That is what caused conventional economists to shun the very idea of systems theory that had become familiar among engineers and scientists. The compliment was returned by the systems theory people. Except for a brief period in the early 1970s when Jay W. Forrester and his colleague Meadows did a study on the subject for the Club of Rome, economists have been notable for their absence at conferences of the systems people. The attempt of Howard T. Odum and Elisabeth C. Odum, "to equate the flow of money with that of energy in an equal-value loop" as "the way human beings recognized that the flows are of equal value" is an echo of the equilibrium model of economics. It is unlikely that the total energy consumption in Shakespeare's London was as great as that of a modern urban slum, and yet legacy that it left to human survival today is proof that no such equivalence exists.

The title of Victoria Chick's paper was "The Future is Open"

and from that resulted a discussion of whether the future as seen through the lense of systems theory is open or closed. At the same time, from the floor came the statement, "Keynesianism has failed." I don't know whether the person who expressed that view was from Cambridge or not, but no one from Cambridge rose to dispute it.

I attempted to find an answer by combining the two questions. Keynes had died in 1946, before the price effects of his policies could possibly emerge and hence could not have been addressed by him. Price controls were still in effect. And in 1951, a serious event took place in Washington. At this point Dr. Chick almost in unison with me gave that a name – the Treasury-Fed Accord: behind President Truman's back proclaimed the independence of the Federal Reserve from the government, and gravely disturbed monetary creation. And in the 1960s immense public investments had to be made not only to catch up with the backlog of ten years of depression and six of war, but to introduce any number of new technologies. This caused a great need for additional public investment as we moved into a mixed economy. Thus the economic system is continually changing adding and altering subsystems, to benign or malignant effect.

Dr. Chick was good enough to recommend attention to my "efforts to recruit economists" to some of the points I raised in my paper. I was delighted to have possibly contributed to a deeper appreciation of Keynes in Cambridge. For elsewhere in the conference I had heard more of the flatulences of Lord Kaldor than of Keynes's deeper doubts about conventional economics.

A Rating for Economic Conferences?

In what tiny portion of the great gathering that I was able to attend, another closely related theme emerged that has been central in my writings of the past 35 years. Isabel Salavisa of Lisbon, Portugal, read a paper on the economic role of the state and its future, that reached the conclusion: "It seems to me that this trend [towards the growth of public expenditure in advanced countries in the 20th century] is connected with the erosion of the external environment of capitalism, be it through the spread of capitalist relations across the world economy, be it through the progressive demolition of non-capitalist institutions in advanced societies. From the point of view of a systems approach, at the end of this process [the] capitalist system would turn into an isolated system. However, every system needs to pursue its exchanges with the exterior, under the form of matter, energy or information. And this is, in my view, the role of the state in advanced countries, and the fundamental explanation for its stubborn growth, against all recommendations, expectations and attempts. The state has become the main externality of capitalism, ruled as it is by non-transactional principles, or at least by non-market principles. The magnitude of resources allocated through public agencies deserves careful examination. That is not the case. Rather it is treated as a black box, a quasi-isolated sub-system, a subject for control and manipulation. Opening that black box seems to me an urgent task."

Open that black box and such phenomena will jump out at you as non-inflationary price rise that merely reflects the increased taxation to pay for the spreading responsibilities of the state, the treatment of the growing investments of the state as current expenditure, and the resulting deficits that are largely the products of bad accountancy and of a freebooting private sector. Notable, too, is the fact that systems theory is the only means of dealing with our key problems.

On the whole the conference, ranked very high amongst the many I have attended. I propose in a future issue to draw up a list of ratings of heterodox economic conferences that I have recently attended. Such ratings are routine in the bond market. They are no less important in what claims to be the science of economics.

William Krehm

1. *The General Theory*, page 32.

Chameleon Bank

MANY are the prerogatives of power. If you have enough of it, you own the theatre, choose the repertory, decide who is cast as hero, and when the curtain drops. Remember when the banks sold the politicians and the public their new program of one-stop banking? To save us shoe-leather they were going to put credit cards, mortgages, sub-prime debt, derivative boutiques, underwriting, stock brokerages, insurance and just about everything else at a single address. But before we knew what had happened, we found ourselves dealing with an ATM machine out in the cold. It was hard explaining to it that character, character and character, as the bank once assured us, decided whether we got a loan or not.

The protean aspect of banking has not stopped developing since then. When they get burned gambling big-time and are bailed out by the government once again, they simply remake their persona.

At this game, some are smarter than others. You may have the impression that to be rewarded with all those options and bonuses the top executives have only to close down bank branches and dismiss enough staff. But apparently that's no longer always the case.

A More Successful Bank that Does Some Things Differently

Let's consult a front-page story of *The Wall Street Journal* (23/9, "Royal Bank's Road to Riches: Stay Divided, Conquer…. It Defies Industry practice and Juggles Rival Brands" by Erik Portanger): "London – On New Bridge St. near the Thames, two bank branches are backed in a fierce battle for customers. Royal Bank of Scotland [not to be confused with Royal Bank of Canada] woos them with a floating credit-card rate averaging a competitive 16.9%. A few steps away, National Westminster offers a flat 17.4%. Royal touts itself to students by offering an interest-free line of credit; NatWest does the same but throws in a $65 cash gift.

"Behind this rivalry is an odd fact: both banks are owned by the same company. Royal Bank of Scotland Group PLC bought NatWest 3.5 years ago. Since then it has turned one of the most commonly held tenets of banking on its head. Where once large banks have studiously built 'financial super-markets' around a single brand – slashing away at their combined operations to reduce overhead – Royal Bank has bought myriad brands and left them to duke it out.

"With that stealth strategy, Royal has built a many-tentacled empire in the UK and the US, where it has expanded through 24 acquisitions in the past decade or so. It now has more branches than Chase Manhattan. Twenty years ago the banks did little more than provide basic lending and deposits to Scots. Today, it is the world's fifth-largest bank by market value, ahead of J.P. Morgan Chase & Co. Its net profit in 2002 totaled about $3.2 billion, compared with about $17.4 million in 1992.

"For years, banks have been scrambling for the right formula to keep their profits growing in a rapidly maturing industry."

We should pause here to establish what "rapidly maturing" might mean. As used in the growing up of humans, it includes developing a sense of what is realistic and responsible, at the very time that physical growth stops. In banking, however, this no longer seems to hold. For the *WSJ* goes on: "Some [banks] have pushed into high-risk, high-reward markets such as investment banking. Others have focused on squeezing out costs. At the same time, many have bet heavily on a strategy to extract more money out of existing customers by offering them everything from credit cards to mutual fund products under a single roof." Nor is it unusual for that one roof to be leaking.

"So far, though, this supermarket approach hasn't lived up to its billing. 'For most banks it's still an unrealized dream,' says James McCormick, president of First Manhattan Consulting Group in New York."

Royal Bank of Scotland is on a different route – one that could offer US banks an alternative path to growth. Rather than trying to be all things to all people in one place, like a Wal-Mart, the Scottish bank operates more like a shopping-mall. It presents a variety of products under multiple brands – letting customers choose what they like, but profiting from whatever choice they make. It makes the strategy work by combining back-office operations to save on costs while benefiting from the exposure of its different brands to the public.

"So rather than kill brands, Edinburgh-based Royal Bank collects them. Its current total is 22. [The bank] then makes them compete for customers, many of whom never know they're ultimately dealing with the same institution. The logic: If the bank's own units don't provide effective competition for each other, other financial institutions will." In a sense it seems to work on the theory of give the customer the sense that he is running away, while making sure that he has fewer refuges to run to, and is kept in the dark as to where they might be.

An Acknowledgement that Bailouts-cum-deregulation hasn't Helped Banking's Image

"Running these businesses separately and under different brand names allows you to be different things for different people,' says Fred Goodwin, Royal Bank's CEO. It also avoids turning off customers wary of dealing with conglomerates." In one sense then RBC's strategy is an acknowledgement that the speculative mad-house that the last bailout-cum-further-deregulation has made of banking has done little for its image.

"Royal Bank's approach is fueling rapid growth while many of its UK rivals such as Barclay's PLC and Lloyds TSB Group PLC, which just a few years ago were much larger, increasingly find themselves in a strategic straitjacket. UK regulators have effectively barred any more mega-mergers because of anti-trust concerns. Expanding significantly in Europe remains troublesome for UK banks because national regulators and politicians there aren't welcoming to foreign intrusion. The US banking landscape is littered with the failed ambitions of UK banks, including NatWest and Lloyds.

"There are drawbacks to Royal Bank's low corporate profile, chiefly in attracting new investors and talented recruits. 'You go to graduates and ask them, "Do you want to join RBS?"', says Mr. Goodwin, and they respond, 'No I'd rather join a big bank like Barclays, [actually] a smaller UK bank. Later this year, it will make a concession to global branding by affixing a tiny, barely visible version of its "snowflake" logo to some of its materials.'

"In theory, maintaining multiple brands is costly and inefficient. But what customers don't see is that behind the bank's many facades lies a massive, centralized technology and purchasing infrastructure that handles everything from cleaning toilets to tracking purchases. The bank's chief executive of manufacturing, for example drives hard bargains by purchasing 17 million checkbooks a year for NatWest, Royal Bank of Scotland, Coutts and other UK brands. According to its most recent results, Royal Bank's cost-to-income ratio – its expenses as a percentage of profit – stood at 43%, a full 11% points lower than Barclay's.

"In the US, Royal Bank hasn't been able to pursue the same multibrand strategy. All of Royal Bank's acquisitions carry the Citizens' Financial name, the legacy of a 1988 purchase of Citizens Financial Corp. in Providence, RI. In some cases, such as the purchase of Pittsburgh-based Mellon Financial Corp.'s retail network, the name wasn't for sale. In others, the name was considered more of a liability than an asset. Yesterday, Citizens Financial agreed to acquire Philadelphia-based Thistle Group Holdings, the holding company of Roxborough Manayunk Bank, for $136M in cash.

Instead of Just Copying the Yanks, the Scots Innovate

"Royal Bank was founded in 1727. A year later it claims to have invented the bank overdraft – a standing line of credit attached to a checking account. It also was the first bank to print multicolored and double-sided banknotes in a bid to combat fraud. But until the 1980s, it remained little known outside Scotland. One ground-breaking idea was the 1985 creation of Direct Line, a car-insurance unit that promised to keep costs low by serving customers entirely by telephone. It attracted 250,000 customers in three years, and Royal Bank soon began offering household and other insurance under the Direct Line banner. In 1997 the bank launched a joint venture, Tesco Personal Finance, with British supermarket chain Tesco PLC. The venture offers banking and insurance products that compete directly with Royal Bank's own offering and those of other units such as Direct Line.

"In 1999, Royal Bank took its biggest leap yet, with a $40 billion hostile bid for NatWest, a record for British banking at the time. Not only did Royal Bank preserve the NatWest brand and others under the NatWest umbrella, it didn't close any of NatWest's 1,790 branches around the UK, as many others have done after a merger.

"Royal Bank also looked for other ways to expand into complementary businesses. It was buying so many cars for its corporate fleet that it decided to buy the seller, Dixon Motors."

Keeping open the branches of other banks acquired is an interesting departure from the Canadian model, where banks bailed out by the government and decontrolled to engage in even bolder speculations, shut down hundreds of the branches acquired as an "efficiency." Undoubtedly that helps cover some of their losses in their new non-banking speculations. And, of course, it has contributed to our baffling high-tech wonder – our "jobless recovery."

And, of course, there is an unspoken and unspeakable advantage that goes with any bank merger: the amount of cash reserves to cover negative net balances in the daily cheque clearances goes down. I don't refer to the statutory reserves that banks must hold with the central bank as a percentage of the short-term and chequing deposits they take in from the public. Such reserves were abolished in Canada by 1993, and have been reduced in the UK to .35 of one percent. I refer to the cash voluntarily kept in the till to honour cheques drawn on one bank by a customer of another of the two banks that merge. Depending on the size of the banks acquired and their location, this can amount to an important net gain. Here, too, once more, the advantage is that they end up more frequently dealing with themselves.

These are interesting details of banking, that our political leaders would be well-advised to study. However, still another key point that emerges from the *WSJ* article, must not be passed over: its net profit from US$17.4 million in 1992 to $3.2 billion in 2002. That's an increase of almost 2,000%. Whether due to acquisitions or other sheer market speculations, such growth rate gets extrapolated into the indefinite future and incorporated into the stock-market price of its stock. That means that they must continue to grow at that rate or face a price collapse. And that has a whip-lash effect on the economy as a whole. There are not enough banks to go on acquiring to continue supporting the price of the stock.

The result is, despite its best intentions, and in spite of the morality that its CEO may have been taught at Sunday school, the bank will be pushed ever more into speculative and morally questionable adventures. The alternative is simply not an option open to banks showing such growth. That is why banks are always feeling the mating itch. Governments should consider whether deregulation that puts banks on such a course of exponential growth is in the nation's interest.

William Krehm

Mass Migration in Reverse

NEVER EVER had such soul-searching overtaken the US before. Let us bring in *The Wall Street Journal* (8/10, "Capital Journal" by Gerald F. Seib): "The blow to the doctrine of pre-emptive strikes is the Iraq aftershock with the greatest reach, well surpassing any of today's political repercussions. The Bush goal in ousting Saddam Hussein wasn't merely to remake Iraq and the Middle East but to change the principles the US would use for protecting itself for decades to come.

"The idea is now imperiled, at least it is being challenged from outside the US – most notably by United Nations Secretary General Kofi Annan, who spoke out again yesterday against the idea of pre-emptive action – and by Bush critics within. Make no mistake; these critiques wouldn't hit home if piles of chemical and biological weapons were being found in Iraq…. [That was intended to enshrine pre-emptive] action as a doctrine of US security strategy, akin to the doctrine of containing the Soviet Union that shaped strategy for a generation."

The Domino Theory Predecessor of the George W. Doctrine of Pre-emptive Strikes

However, as eloquent and well-directed as Seib's comment is, it misses a central point. The Weapons of Mass Destruction in Iraq that stubbornly refuse to be found had their precedent: the Domino Theory practised under President Eisenhower and openly advanced as a doctrine under Reagan. It warned Americans that unless democratic revolutions in Central America were suppressed free institutions would keel over seriatim like dominoes on edge right into Texas and keep falling until they reached the Canadian border. By the light of the Domino Theory the perfectly democratically elected government in Guatemala of Jacobo Arbenz – in the second democratic election in a row – was overthrown not by an American-backed coup, but by the Americans themselves. When a counter-revolutionary Guatemalan force that had been trained on a Honduran property of the United Fruit Company invaded the country and was stopped by the Guatemalan army, the CIA brought in planes from Nicaragua to drop dynamite sticks on the capital, while their radio in Honduras spread false reports of a mass rebel army moving on the capital. Much the same thing happened throughout the isthmus. What followed in Guatemala and El Salvador was a murderous civil war that lasted longer than Europe's Thirty Years War of the seventeenth century and led to as numerous deaths in proportion to the population. This not only included the extermination of entirely villages of Indians in Guatemala, but Catholic archbishops, and many American missionaries. All in the name of the "Domino Theory" that was disproved by the collapse of the Soviet Union due to its own corruption and incompetence. Who mentions it in connection with the blind-alley Washington has gotten itself into today?

Yet domino or no domino, the policy of preemptive suppression of democratic rights moved on into the most developed countries in South America – Chile, the Argentine, Brazil, leaving very little undisturbed in between. The atrocities of murderous military regimes brought to power with American backing can match anything that Saddam Hussein contrived – hundreds of victims dropped into the ocean from planes.

Economics, too, was much to the fore. As though for increased efficiency the Secretary of State, Foster Dulles, was an ex-solicitor for the United Fruit Company, 94,354 of whose 2,210,000 hectares of land – of which all but 56,000 lay fallow – had been expropriated by the Arbenz government for distribution amongst landless peasants. Moreover, Arbenz's plans to build highways threatened the transport monopoly of United Fruit's railways from the capital to both oceans. Though the recent war had been fought in the name of democracy, and the promise of a bright new world had been broadcast, these important projects sealed Arbenz's fate.[1]

When US intervention throughout the isthmus had run its course, the brave new world of Globalization and Deregulation was ushered in. The small Central American countries had throughout their history made efforts to establish common internal markets to allow a modest degree of industrialization to lessen their dependence on agricultural exports like coffee and bananas. The 2001 report of the Economic Commission for Latin America and the Caribbean reporting that poverty and unemployment throughout Latin America are the highest in twenty years, with 44% of the population living in poverty as the gap between rich and poor widens. "The Central American countries saw their growth rates slacken, as external problems were exacerbated by a widespread drought that caused heavy losses in agriculture and by low prices for these nations' traditional exports." About half the population of El Salvador, Honduras and Nicaragua earn less than US$2 a day.

The industrialization under Deregulation and Globalization fall into two categories:

(1) *maquiladoras* that transfer to the poorest countries the lowest tech manufacturing operations done mostly by women and rationalized as "supplementary family income." At the slightest attempt at unionization or demands for increased wages, the firms can move on to still cheaper countries in Asia.

(2) Vast proposed engineering projects geared to facilitating exports industries – electricity grids, hydroelectric dams and super-highways. These would provide lucrative contracts for US conglomerates, and throw open the gates widely for large foreign controlled enterprises. Many of the projects would invade the Mesoamerican Biological Corridor – a protected areas where some of the globe's largest bio-diverse eco-systems exist.

The dismal future of the region under D&G is apparent from the massive migration of Latin Americans not only to the US, but to Europe.

Somewhere around 1200 BC Europe underwent a violent change of population. Due in part to traumatic changes in climate, in deepest Asia, in part to technological innovations of the invaders – horses, improved harnesses, metallurgical discoveries that gave them bronze and eventually iron, improved ships for the purpose, they eventually replaced the earlier populations. Surprisingly enough, the invaders included the Greeks, the Celts and other peoples identified by their Indo-European speech – were amongst these relatively recent arrivals to Europe. By the shape and size of their skulls we can tell where they are likely to have come from. And they all bear witness to a mass influx that did not stop short of total elimination of the preceding inhabitants.

Something similar is occurring with the exodus of Latin Americans, driven by hunger and US high policy from their homelands. The contrasting demographics of Europe and Latin America and the tightening rules of entry into the US brought on by the terrorism threat have contributed to the trend.

The Wall Street Journal (12/09, "Europe Becomes new Destination for Latino Workers"): "Madrid – An old US problem is hitting Europe as a new wave of illegal immigrants from Latin America sweeps across the Atlantic.

"Europe's population of Latin illegals surged in the past decade and especially since the Sept. 11 terror attacks. It could rise as high as three million this year – half the number now in the US. The immigrants are pushed by poverty at home, pulled by demand for workers overseas, aided by porous borders and abetted by forged documents.

"Latinos represent the fastest-growing immigrant community in Italy, Switzerland, Spain and Britain. Switzerland, once a trilingual society, has as many residents who speak Spanish, including long-term guests from Spain and new arrivals from Latin America. Spanish is about to pass Italian as the country's third most-spoken language, after German and French.

"Europe has become an easier destination than the US and in some ways a more attractive one. Since the Sept. 11 attacks, the US has tightened its borders against would-be entrants. Washington wants to thwart Muslim terrorists by reducing all immigration. Some Europeans follow a different logic, arguing that drawing labor from a new source may slow the tide of illegal arrivals from Muslim lands."

The Brave New World Ground Under Heel

The ideal of "One World" is being further ground under heel.

"In addition, the European Union until recently granted open access to Latin Americans arriving as tourists. A united Europe offers Latin Americans who land anywhere in the EU an open door to labor markets in the 15 member states and even to countries not part of the EU.

"The vast migrations from the wretched of Europe to the New World has swung into reverse."

Like the endless sequence of invasions from Asia in remote millennia, this invasion, too, echoes natural and human catastrophes far to the rear.

"A surge in remittances from immigrants to their home countries underscores the trend. In March, Washington's Inter-American Development Banks reported that cash remittances from Europe to Latin America doubled between 2000 and 2002 to $2 billion a year.

"Spain is the most popular portal for Latin immigrants. Its population of legal Ecuadorian immigrants has surged from just 7,000 in 1999 to more than 200,000 – and at least that many illegals. Spain for years granted a special status to Latin Americans. Spanish citizenship can be available after 24 months of residence. There's also a burgeoning black market in Spanish birth certificates and passports. And since 1996, Spain has been one of the fastest growing economies in Europe. Madrid's leading daily, *El Pais,* reported that 550,000 Latin Americans entered Spain as tourists in 2002, but only 86,000 left. How many stay in Spain or move on to another European country is unknown."

Human Import Substitution

"Efforts to control the influx come up against economic and cultural forces. Many Europeans are happy to employ the new immigrants because they tend to work for less money than the earlier transient laborers.

"'It's import substitution,' says Ricard Zapata at Barcelona's University Pompeu Fabra. 'The government wants Christians and it wants Spanish speakers. The cost of integration is so much lower, so why not?'

"Latin America, where birth rates remain high, is a beneficiary of Europe's plummeting fertility. The Continent is facing a dearth of workers, especially those catering to the old and infirm.

"Spain began recruiting women from the Dominican Republic in the 1990s as domestics. Eventually the new arrivals replaced Spanish migrants who once flocked north for jobs in richer countries such as England and Germany. As Spain prospered fewer of its own workers went abroad, creating further opportunities for Latin Americans in the rest of Europe.

"Hundreds of illegal immigrants ride the rails from Spain or Portugal up to the French Alps, then slip into Switzerland. Lausanne, a quaint city of 150,000, has one of Europe's fastest growing Latino enclaves, with one of every ten residents a recent arrival from Latin America. That's a Latino share of population exceeding that of Boston, Philadelphia or Atlanta."

William Krehm

1. The only eyewitness account of the original Guatemalan and Salvadoran revolutions, *Democracies and Tyrannies of the Caribbean*, by William Krehm, is available in English or Spanish from COMER.

Kyoto Comes to Europe

FROM A NOBLE ABSTRACTION, environmental protection will shortly be translated in Europe to costly, direct obligations of corporations, some of them US corporations operating in the EU. The US itself, of course, has not committed itself to supporting the Kyoto decisions. *The Wall Street Journal* (10/10, "In Europe, Clues to Kyoto's Impact" by Jeffery Ball) lays out the facts.

"Paris – Big industry is about to get its clearest sign yet of how global warming will hit its bottom line.

"Over the next several months, governments throughout Europe are expected to release lists showing how much carbon dioxide they will allow thousands of individual factories and power plants within their borders to emit, starting in 2005. Until now, the governments that have ratified the proposed Kyoto Protocol on global warming have agreed only to nationwide caps on the amounts of carbon dioxide and other 'greenhouse gases' they emit. Now comes the hard part: slapping limits on the industrial sites that produce nearly half the EU's output of these gases, typically by burning fossil fuel such as coal."

As a result, a notable step taken on a national and hence somewhat abstract basis, is moving on to the point where it affects the bottom line of the individual corporation. Predictably, the result will be a surge of lobbying in all its less lovely aspects: arm-twisting and/or seduction of politicians.

"Which companies – and which industries in which countries – will lose won't be obvious until March 31. That is when the 15 EU countries, all of which have ratified the Kyoto Treaty, are due to propose to the EU how they would allocate their emissions allowances. All additional 10 European nations that have ratified the treaty must submit their lists to Brussels by May 1, when they join the EU."

Leaving the Air You Breathe to the Wisdom of the Market?

"Despite questions about whether Russia will ratify Kyoto – as it must if it is to go into effect – EU officials plan to proceed with their caps. Europe's system offers an early look at the impact on the industry. Although the Bush administration has rejected the Kyoto treaty, saying the proposed emissions cuts would cripple the world's largest economy, plenty of US companies have factories in the EU that will be hit with the limits.

"Initially, the European caps will apply only to highly energy-intensive industries such as steel, oil, cement and paper, as well as to fossil-fuel-powered electricity plants with output above 20 megawatts. Together, these industrial sites account for about 45% of the carbon-dioxide emissions in the EU."

"Under the new EU rules, each country will let each site emit a certain number of tons of carbon dioxide. A company whose sites collectively emit more than they are allocated will face a choice. It could spend lots of money to reduce those emissions – say, by switching from coal to natural gas – or buy extra emissions allowances from companies that stay below their limit. The result is a nascent market in these allowances across the EU. Ultimately, particularly if the Kyoto Protocol takes effect, trading could go global."

The trouble there, is that surplus polluting rights could be sold by a company in a less vulnerable area – either as far as the ecology or the local population are concerned – into an area that is extremely vulnerable in one or the other or both these respects. Leaving it all to the wisdom of the market that has failed us so many times is less than wise.

"Steve Drummon, managing director of London-based emissions broker CO2e.com, estimates the average one-ton emission allowance will be trading at about US$17.75 by 2005, when the EU caps take effect. The fight is particularly intense within the German electricity industry. For certain German power companies, what their government decides could be 'a question of 200 million or 300 million euros per year,' says Per Lekander, a consultant with McKinsey & Co. in Paris. 'Not an insignificant amount of money.'"

W.K.

China Teaching Technology to the US?

THE UNITED STATES is being tested on several fronts. At the heart of its problem is the clash between a financial sector driven to an exponential voracity for the maintenance of its market valuations, and the responsibilities of an imperial power. Promoting Globalization and Deregulation allows an ever freer field for reshuffling the playing cards and disposing of those that don't serve its game. This would, of course, include the disregard of its own protectionist traditions and those of all evolving industrial powers.

The one exception was Britain that got there first. Contrast that with knocking down all cultural barriers, even the right of traumatically disadvantaged nations to their cultural identity. At times it seems that the US is extending its brusque internal assimilation of immigrant cultures in a campaign to market its own huckster style throughout the world.

Contrast that with the Roman empire that not only acknowledged the existence of other cultures, but in some instances even bowed to their superiority. That was notably the case with Greek letters and philosophy. Compare that with the pushy American insistence on removing a degree of protection of Canada's sickly magazine efforts. One trouble with this bias is that it precludes alternate ways of looking at problems. Herodotus tells us that the rulers of ancient Persia before adopting an important policy paused to consider it in two different ways – once in a sober state, and again when they were drunk. Too often, we get the impression that Washington examines its foreign policies only once – when drunk with its sense of limitless power.

At bottom the struggle is to rig the trade terms to favour the imperial power over the provinces acquired. The Romans managed that with sweeping military operations that at times reduced much of the population to slavery. Those who retained some freedom were often placated by the respect shown their culture, and even their puppet kings and their gods. The United States seeks to achieve much the same goal with debt. No matter how unconditionally its universities teach the virtues of the free market where supply and demand on the margin determine price, the reality is that Third World export prices are set not by supply-demand but by the IMF's pressure to service debt denominated in foreign currencies. Production for export becomes a function of the diktat to increase exports even though they may already be below costs.

To grasp all the important factors in the terrorism that is sweeping Islam, you cannot ignore the collision of this backbone item of the Washington Consensus, and the Koran that considers interest in any form as a sin damnable with eternal hell-fire. You might think that the advisers of President Bush would have recognized this in their efforts to track down the roots of terrorism. Yet I have yet to see a reference to it in the flood of research on terrorism out of Washington.

Meanwhile the superpower position has brought the United States a bonus: the role of its currency to serve as by far the largest reserve currency – supplying 60% of the total in the world's central bank reserves. Since the gold standard was abandoned in 1971, that is tantamount to creating the money with which it settles its huge import surplus with a mark-up that approaches 100%. A credit-based reserve rather than one based on gold, increases the seignorage – the spread between its nominal value and the cost of producing it physically.

And deregulating the banks shortly after their massive bailout of the early 1990s gives us the measure of the power that goes with such a position. This contrast between the debt-determined export prices of the underdeveloped lands and the US's near-costless imports paid for with its own paper dollars, is bound to be paid in blood. It is an indulgence that neither the US nor the rest of the world can afford.

Enter China, Great Turner of Tables

What makes China the one really formidable eventual challenger of the US is not only its immense population, its powerful cultural tradition, but its long experience in contriving defences against invasions by land and sea. This extends from the building of the Great Wall against the invaders from the north to the closing of the land routes to the West, the Boxer rebellion against the barbarians arriving from the East, the nationalist uprising of the 1920s against extra-territoriality, to the Communist revolution itself. China's pioneering technology reaches back to their invention of paper, gunpowder, paper money, and much else. Their failure to profit from their own great inventions haunts them today. It is certainly a factor in their hard-nosed bargaining for Western technology as a condition for opening its markets to world trade. Their own resources for coming to the fore in the modern world have been vastly enriched by the Diaspora during the Cold War accepted and encouraged by the United States itself.

Western-trained scientists and engineers returning to a somewhat freer China are producing surprising results in many fields. And one positive thing that they brought out of the Communist period is a sensitivity to the vulnerabilities of Western capitalism.

As the United States becomes more entangled in its preemptive invasion of countries fallen out of its favour, it is turning more frequently to the good offices of Chinese diplomacy. That is becoming a distinct asset for Beijing's insistence that it be given access to higher technology in return for entry into the potentially huge Chinese market.

This context lends special interest to the article in *The Wall Street Journal* (11/09, "Invisible Supplier has Penney's Shirts all Buttoned up" by Gabriel Kahn): "On a Saturday afternoon in August, Carolyin Thurmond walked into a J.C. Penney store in Atlanta's Mall and bought a white Stafford wrinkle-free dress shirt for her husband, size 17 neck, 34/35 sleeves.

"On Monday morning, a computer technician in Hong Kong downloaded a record of the sale. By Wednesday afternoon, a factory worker in Taiwan had packed an identical replacement shirt into a bundle to be shipped back to the Atlanta store."

"This speedy process, part of a stream-lined supply chain and production system for dress shirts that was years in the making, has put Penney at the forefront of the US retailing revolution. In an industry where the goal is speedy turnaround of merchandise, Penney stores now hold almost no extra inventory of house-brand dress shirts. Less than a decade ago, Penney would have had thousands of them warehoused across the US, tying up capital and slowly going out of style.

"The new process is one from which Penney [itself] is conspicuously absent. The entire program is designed and operated by TAL Apparel Ltd., a closely held Hong Kong shirt maker. TAL collects point-of-sale data for Penney's shirts from its stores in North America, then runs the numbers straight through a computer model it designed. The Hong Kong company then decides how many shirts to make, and in what styles, colours and sizes. The manufacturer sends the shirts directly to each Penney store, by-passing the retailer's warehouses – and corporate decision makers.

"TAL is a no-name giant, the maker of one in eight dress shirts sold in the US. Its close partnership with US retailers is part of a power shift in global manufacturing. As retailers strive to cut costs and keep pace with consumer tastes, they are coming to depend more on suppliers that respond swiftly to changing needs. This opens opportunities for savvy manufacturers, and TAL has rushed in, even starting to take over such critical areas as sales forecasting and inventory management.

"On the week-end Mrs. Thurmond made her purchase, the same Atlanta store sold two sage-colored shirts of similar size but of another Penney house brand, Crazy Horse. That left none of this size and color in stock at the store. Based on past sales data, TAL's computers determined that the ideal inventory level for that brand, style, color and size at that particular store was two. Without consulting Penney, a TAL factory in Taiwan made two new shirts. It sent one by ship, but to get one to the store quickly, it dispatched one by air. TAL paid the shipping, but sent a bill for the shirts to Penney."

The Chinese Tell the Americans What They have Just Bought

"'Instead of asking Penney what it would like to buy, I tell them how many shirts they have just bought,' says Harry Lee, TAL's managing director.

"TAL was born in 1947 after Chinese border guards blocked Mr. Lee's uncle, C.C. Lee, from importing state-of-the art weaving machines to Shanghai for fear they would hurt the local industry. So he set up shop in Hong Kong, then under British rule. With low-cost Asian manufacturing, TAL thrived. It supplies labels such as J. Crew, Calvin Klein, Banana Republic, Tommy Hilfiger, Liz Clairborne, Ralph Lauren and Brooks Brothers. Mr. Lee, 60 years old, joined the family business 30 years ago after earning a Ph.D. in electrical engineering in the US and serving a stint in Bell Labs.

"Now TAL is negotiating a deal to manage Brooks Brothers' shirt inventory the same way it does Penney's. For Lands' End TAL stitches made-to-measure pants in Malaysia and flies them straight to US customers, with a shipping invoice that carries the Land's End logo.

"These retailers have been willing to cede some functions

once seen as central because TAL can do them better and more cheaply. Before it started working with TAL a decade ago, Penney would hold up to six months of inventory in its warehouses, and three months in its stores. Now, for the Stafford and Crazy Horse shirt lines that TAL handles, 'it's zero.'"

US-inspired High Interest Policy Made US Business Vulnerable

Let us note that it was the high interest rates at the core of "leaving all to the market" that gave the Chinese their missionary edge in introducing "delivery as needed" to the West. Now on a larger scale the same enthronement of interest rates is leading to the surrender of core strategy control, with unlimited possibilities of the US relinquishing its technological lead. There is nothing basically wrong or bad about that. At every stage of history whether in Greece, the Renaissance or in recent centuries, states have succeeded one another in leading roles. It is just that with its fixation on imposing its blind dogma on the rest of the world and backing it up with military adventures, Washington risks doing more and more damage to its own people.

The Chinese have reached the stage of not begging for technology but of producing it themselves. In the process they are taking over command of a vital part of the planning and management of sectors of the US economy. Washington's lint-witted involvement in preemptive military intervention can only accelerate this process.

William Krehm

Vignette on Why They Hate the West

MORE IS INVOLVED than just theological prejudices of Muslims against debt and interest. The point is conveyed by a vignette from late 19th century Egypt after the cotton boom brought on by the US Civil War and the building of the Suez canal.

"To extricate himself from bankruptcy [Sultan] Ismail conducted a losing battle against European bondholders, 'unofficial' government officials, commissions of inquiry, and consuls general. In a pretense at constitutional government Nubar Pasha was installed as prime minister, Mr. Rivers Wilson as finance minister, and M. de Blignières as minister of public works. Threats of action on the part of Bismarck in 1879 led England and France to join in obtaining the Ottoman Porte's deposition of Ismail in favor of his son Tawfik.

"The controllers could attend cabinet meetings, demand information, give advice, and report to their diplomatic representatives in the event advice was ignored. They became the real rulers of Egypt. On the findings of the International Commission of Liquidation (British, French, German, Austria, and Italian), the *Law of Liquidation* was enacted, squeezing the debt down to £85 million and reserving £4M of the annual government income for the budget. All excess income, then estimated at £4M, was to be employed to retire the debt. Unfortunately for the future development of Egypt, expanding revenues resulting from increased productivity and hard work or from inflation would not benefit Egyptians or improve government services. Since the controllers were duty bound to guard the revenue and pay off the debt, they could hardly fail to be unpopular with Egyptians.

"Establishment of the mixed courts frustrated the operation of the government. As part of the Ottoman Empire Egypt was subject to the Capitulatory Treaties with other states, chiefly European. The treaties practically assured that law cases were settled by diplomatic pressure rather than on the basis of merit or justice [a foretaste of 'globalization'?]. In 1873, a conference in Istanbul authorized mixed courts, judges, Egyptian and foreign, appointed by the khedive, although foreigners were nominated by participating governments which agreed to recognize judgments of these courts. Inaugurated in 1875, the courts had a majority of foreign judges, used French as their language, and employed a code based on French law."[1]

1. Fisher, Sydney Nettleton (1971). *The Middle East – A History*, pp. 288, 289. London: Routledge & Kegan Paul.

The Right and the Wrong in US Investigations of High Finance

BARRIE McKENNA (*The Globe and Mail*, 5/09, "Spitzer's spotlight shows fund risks") points a finger in the right direction, but fails to pick up the ultimate significance of the evidence.

"It's a safe bet that most of the millions of mutual fund investors don't have a clue of what really happens to their money. And how could they?

"New York Attorney General Eliot Spitzer blew the lid this week on some of the dirty little secrets in the mutual fund business, including rampant conflicts of interest, secret backroom deals and hidden fees.

"In a 44-page complaint filed in a New York court Wednesday, Mr. Spitzer alleges that Canary Capital Partners LLC, an obscure New Jersey-based hedge fund, had agreements with 30 different mutual fund companies to engage in inappropriate after-hour trading in fund units. The deals allegedly allowed Canary to reap enormous profits by securing privileged access to mutual funds at a better price than the rest of us get, enabling taboo practices known as 'timing' and 'late trading.'

"Without admitting wrongdoing, Canary and its owner agreed to pay a $40 million (US) penalty and to get out of the fund managing business for a decade.

"But it's the role played by the 30 mutual fund groups, only four of which Mr. Spitzer identified – Bank of America, Bank One, Janus and Strong – that is most intriguing. Mr. Spitzer lays out a damning portrait of an industry greedily looking for ways to generate fees without regard for the interests of their investors.

"Mr. Spitzer conceded that he doesn't yet know how widespread the scam was, or how much it may have cost investors. The suggestion is that Canary is just the tip of the iceberg."

The Deep Rot of Mutual Funds

"But if Canary's relationship with one of them – Bank of America – is any indication, the industry has a colossal problem on its hands. Not the least of the industry's troubles is that many mutual funds are not disclosing to their investors an increasingly complex web of relationships with other financial intermediaries. An ordinary investor, for example, would have no way of knowing about Bank of America's ties to Canary because it isn't mentioned anywhere in the fund's prospectus.

"Far from being duped by Canary, Bank of America is cast by Mr. Spitzer as a willing partner in an illegal scheme. Starting in 2001, Bank of America's fund unit reportedly installed state-of-the-art software at Canary that allowed the hedge fund to do so-called late trades in its mutual funds. And it allegedly loaned Canary the funds for the dubious transactions, extending a line of credit that grew to $300 million.

"In the process, Canary became one of Bank of America's largest customers, the plaint alleges. Canary made tens of million through late trading and timing, while various parts of Bank of America that serviced Canary made millions themselves."

If Gang Crimes Enjoyed the Silk Stocking Treatment of Wall St.

"Like Mr. Spitzer, the US Securities and Exchange Commission has grown increasingly concerned about what investors aren't being told. Among the suspect practices, the SEC is probing so-called "directed brokerage" in which a mutual fund agrees to do its trades with a particular brokerage in exchange for distribution of its products. Some funds also share revenue with brokers to get the same results. Then, there are 'soft dollars' or barter arrangements, that mutual funds offer to brokers – all apparently to help push its products."

Even the terminology is the same as in politics!

"The problem for investors is that these arrangements eat into a fund's overall return, while providing no benefit to existing fund holders. These so-called trading costs can more than double the real expense ratio of many funds, sapping the long-term returns that should flow to investors."

And amazingly Mr. McKenna, as good a reporter as they come, overlooks that these arrangements direct the fund manager for selfish reasons to investments that he may not have bought but for the kick-back from the brokerage house with which he has such a deal. The chain of under-the-table motivations compound one another.

Then comes the remarkable passage that is almost routine in the reports of "successful" US investigations: "Without admitting wrongdoing, Canary and its owner agreed to pay a $40 million penalty and to get out of the fund-managing business for a decade" To appraise the moral message of such settlements, you need only transfer them to blue-collar crime. Suppose somebody who robbed a bank with gun in hand, killing a teller or two

en route, would be required to surrender to the state, say 25% of the loot without a judgment of guilt. Then he could write that off as a "cost of doing business," and afford a ten-year holiday. Or labour in another vineyard, for a decade, before coming back to bank robbery, if that were his career choice.

Morality, then becomes largely a matter of public relations, politicians' problems in buying prime TV time, and how many influential political friends you can afford.

Should the state and federal investigators not get together and investigate the root question: What is there about our financial system that drives our financial institutions and their auditors to delve into crookery that makes a blue-collared criminal appear an innocent? Could it be the system that requires embellishing an original scam year after year because the profits from that knavery have been extrapolated into the indefinite future, and incorporated into the share price? That means that unless you continue with mounting skullduggery, your shares will crash on the market. The supreme virtue then is how much you can get away with. And on such contrivances – indirectly – the government depends for its success in running a budgetary surplus or a deficit. And that has been identified as the one virtue in the political arena.

These are the ultimate "dirty little secrets" that need to be brought into the daylight.

Let Canada's Government Cast No Stone

And let no condescending thought cross a Canadian mind, that here there are few or no investigations of crime in our financial circles. That is only because the cover-up is almost absolute.

Especially, on the victims of brokerages in modest margin accounts. Try contacting the Ontario Security Commission to complain about your bank-broker having taken the crudest advantage of you in your margin account, and you will get a voice message: "If you have a complaint against your broker, contact a lawyer." They know and the bank knows that a lawyer will cost you more than your not inconsiderable loss. Margin accounts – the field of the little guy – are open game for banks especially when they themselves are in trouble.

But then perhaps you should not have been in the stock market on margin?

But isn't our financial system – particularly the bank-broker-underwriters-derivative boutiques itself on margin? Currently at a leverage of about 380 to one.

William Krehm

Greenspan in a New Light

THE CANADIANS might feel a bit beaten up by their free-trading neighbour in the matter of softwood lumber, steel, grain and a host of other things. To the point that we are left at times wondering, whether this is really free trade, or just the price that Canada is paying for having given Washington some invaluable if ignored advice on its Iraq policy. Yet it should come as a consolation that the spirit of a great disappeared Canadian has come to hover over the US Federal Reserve – Marshall McLuhan, our native prophet who coined that great, unpatented reading of the future "the medium is the message."[1] For the recent powwow of the Fed high brass suggests that the great astuteness of Chairman Alan is not what he says, but his virtuosity in not letting you know what it is he is saying. "Keep'em guessing what is really going on in them thar tents" as the circus barkers used to say, when they took time off for a beer.

That is the burden of *The Wall Street Journal's* report (2/09, "Greenspan Confronts Criticism of Fed Decision-Making Methods" by Greg Ip): "Federal Reserve Chairman Alan Greenspan regularly gets praised for his deft interest-rate decisions and criticized for how he explains them. That criticism reached a crescendo in recent months as investors blamed conflicting signals from the Fed for taking the bond market on a roller coaster ride at a delicate time for the economy.

"In his speech to the Kansas City's annual symposium in this mountain resort Mr. Greenspan called the combination of analysis and judgment by which the Fed operates 'risk management.' He said when the Fed sets interest rates, it considers not just the most probable forecast of the economy's growth, but also improbable outcomes with big consequences – such as deflation or a financial collapse. For example, the Fed recently cut rates more than conventional forecasts would recommend because of the slight chance that low inflation could become 'pernicious' deflation, in which falling prices undermine heavily indebted consumers and businesses and weaken the Fed's control.

"'Some critics have argued that such an approach to policy is too undisciplined – judgmental, seemingly discretionary, and difficult to explain,' Mr. Greenspan said. These critics think that the Fed should tie its actions solely to the prescriptions of a formal policy rule.

"The rules would inevitably fail, because of the 'complexity of a world economy whose underlying linkages appear to be in a continual state of flux.'"

But if that is so, it is all the more important to understand both the points of departure of these fluxes and their nature. And if we ask what the schools taught Mr. Greenspan to help him intuit about these things, the answer is the self-balancing nature of the "pure and perfect market" in which all actors are of such negligible size that nothing they do can affect prices. That is not the message that is coming out of New York Attorney General Mr. Spitzer's investigations of countless huge firms who conspired with their mammoth bankers and their auditors not only to fix prices, but to pretty-up the books to the point where assets became liabilities and vice versa. Cooking the books goes far beyond just influencing prices.

That was the reality that Mr. Greenspan wrestles with and the heart of his "risk management." It sounds so grand but means so little. Just look at the state of our insurance industry whose business it is to manage risk on "no kidding" terms. Or the Long Term Capital Hedge Fund that required a standby credit of $50 billion, if our memory doesn't deceive us, from central bankers and governments to prevent it bringing down the world banking system. The methodology of that "analysis" was to find the equilibrium points and build your certainties around them. The trouble was that there never ever were such equilibrium points, and since Globalization and Deregulation there's still less chance that they might have arisen. For even a blind man by now should be aware that G&D has had the effect of increasing the size of and decreasing the number of big hitters. It thus takes us ever farther away from equilibrium points and Nirvana.

Our Stranded Costs — A Good Look in the Mirror

And as for paying attention to "improbable outcomes with big consequences like deflation and or a financial collapse" why doesn't Mr. Greenspan consider the very great "likelihood" that the "low inflation" is not inflation at all but "deflation"? Price levels have been rising over decades not only due to an excess of demand over supply but for two other reasons: (1) the huge increase in public services *that have actually been provided* within our mixed economy. The cost of these is covered by taxation, and that taxation does not disappear, but makes up an ever deeper layer in price; (2) those essential services – more schools and universities and many others – *that should be but are not being provided* – mean far higher costs down the line for more penitentiaries, more crime, more power breakdowns, more outbreaks of diseases never known before or considered conquered, that will result. This growing component of "stranded costs" must be posted as a debit. Of course it would unbalance our budget. That, however, would be an invaluable warning signal. The cost of polluted water due to "economies" in scientific controls, SARS, the spread of West Nile disease, and much of the terrorism that afflicts the world today are samples of such "stranded costs."

In short Mr. Greenspan has a great deal of contemplation on the point of departure for his fluxes, and on the nature of the fluxes themselves. Just striking the pose of Rodin's thinker and talking in ambiguities, makes double-talk the medium, which according to McLuhan becomes the message. Oh boy! has our Marshall been hitting homers these days!

On the "Absence of Inflation" Standard

The article continues: "Indeed, Mr. Greenspan's recent troubles stem not from his preference for risk management over rules, but rather his perceived failure to communicate how he weighs risks. In May and June, he repeatedly said the odds of deflation were low but the Fed still wanted insurance against it because the cost of that insurance – in terms of possible inflation later – was so low." We thought that legal tender was money, not the absence of inflation. But lo! This seems to have changed. The next time your auto insurance jumps, just ask your insurance company to switch the billing into units of the absence of inflation!

I knew that good tidings must be in the offing. We have heard a lot about sky-high insurance rates and of insolvent and near bankrupt insurance and re-insurance companies, of soaring auto and life insurance rates, but nary a word about low insurance rates. When the supreme monetary authority of the lone superpower cannot say with certainty whether we are in a state of inflation or deflation, shouldn't we be taking out insurance against bum economic theory? And how would those risks be appraised? We would recommend to Mr. Greenspan that he step up his reading of history so that he can tell us when living costs in large cities were not far higher than in the countryside and small cities – not only because of the costlier logistics, but reflecting the wealth of additional services huge cities must provide. From there he will only have to check the number of cities of one million and more that have sprung up throughout the world, and vast unbroken urban areas of thirty-five million people and more like the Federal district of Mexico, the north-Eastern US seaboard and the Tokyo-Yokohama area of Japan. No individual moving from Vermont to New York City, is foolish enough to expect his cost-of-living to remain the same. How can Mr. Greenspan expect the price level to stay flat when humanity makes just such a move? That is not the entire message, but enough of it to show that Mr. Greenspan's real risk is that he might not know what he is talking about.

William Krehm

1. To be fair to McLuhan, he emphasized that he was not advocating this sort of communication in blank messages, but was merely telling it as it was.

Fur Flies as an Astrophysicist Gets into the Energy Trading Fold

IN A SENSE Enron and other energy traders who have been in the bankruptcy court news in past months have done a sort of Einstein in reverse, demoting time to an even humbler status than before relativity amazed the world. Amongst energy traders, Enron was the first to be exposed for doodling around with the time parameters of a deal – booking at once the income from a deal not closing for a year, or two or ten as a profit, while leaving the liability incurred for the product sold until the actual closing date. Now, however, it is emerging that with minor variations other traders did much the same thing. Rather than an aberration, it turns out to be a culture. And those who spread that culture, and even helped create it, were some of the nation's foremost auditors, who were supposed to ensure that morality as transparent as a June morn would illumine firms' doings. The unpleasant fact is that we are separated from the future by barriers of risk and uncertainty, of interest accumulating at change-

able rates, and by double-entry bookkeeping that requires that the two entries refer to the same time span.

That is why the case of Williams Companies, a leading energy trader now in distress, illustrates the point.

But let *The New York Times* tell the tale (2/06, "A collision on Risks on Energy Trading" by Neela Banerjee): "Jones Murphy might not have noticed what his colleagues at the Williams companies were doing if they had not been gloating.

"Mr. Murphy, previously a Wall St. executive, was trained as an astrophysicist at the California Institute of Technology." That makes a difference: astrophysicists must bring the astronauts back to this planet. Energy traders are under no such constraints.

"Murphy had recently been hired at Williams's Tulsa headquarters to help manage trading risks. He was on the trading floor when he heard a commotion at the desk of Blake Herndon, director of risk management. 'I went over to ask what was going on,' Mr. Murphy recalled of that day in December 2000. Blake laughed and said they were going to corner the market for natural gas and run it up for December closing, which means delivery in January.

"Williams is the second-largest owner of natural gas pipelines in the country, and Mr. Murphy, who is no longer with the company, says that an examination of trading records would show that the company drove up natural gas prices in California.

"Williams executives dismissed the allegation as impossible. Mr. Herndon said, 'It is comical to think that anyone could corner the gas market in California. These are just not cornerable markets.'

"Mr. Murphy said he was told by Mr. Herndon that Williams probably made hundreds of millions of dollars from its strategy. It was at the top of its game."

"But now Williams is teetering. Its share price has plummeted 71% from its high of $48.77 three years ago. It is scrambling to pare its $13 billion of debt and announced last week that it plans to sell as much as $1.5 billion in equity and $3 billion in assets over the next year. Adding to its woes are several regulatory investigations, including one by the Security and Exchange Commission, and an accusation by creditors of the communications spin-off, the Williams Communications Group, that Williams loaded up the new company with excess debt.

"E-mail messages sent months before Mr. Murphy was dismissed show that he and other employees repeatedly warned Williams executives that the company had to reduce its trading risks, especially with shaky counterparties like Enron. Blinkered by arrogance and an ignorance of the financial sophistication required to trade electricity, critics say, Williams executives thought the company and the deregulated power sector would thrive uninterrupted. Reducing risks, or hedging, takes away from the bottom line, critics added.

"'Not hedging properly is the same as inflating profits,' said James Chanos, president of Kynikos Associates, a New York short seller, because hedging has a cost.

"Electricity trading is a riddle to outsiders, given its complexity and the proprietary models that each company uses for its trades. But as investors have come to realize that the mark-to-market style of accounting used for trading gives companies great leeway to inflate profits and that trading may actually be a money loser.

"That question is crucial to Williams because energy trading is such a big part of its business. In the first quarter, marketing and trading contributed $271 million to Williams's operating income, or 42%, before one-time charges and taxes the most of any business unit. But a close look at its cash-flow statement shows that energy marketing and trading did not generate cash; Williams, however, said it did.

"The paradox stems from the fact that the cash Williams expects from those contracts might arrive 10 or 20 years in the future, but the profits are booked to the bottom line now, under the mark-to-market accounting that Williams and other energy companies use for their trading operations.

"Another accounting approach that Williams used was the so-called competitive deal basis, Mr. Murphy and others said. Future prices for power would be set according to deals competitors were striking or even discussing. It was immaterial if the transactions actually occurred, as long as the forecast could show that Williams could immediately book a substantial paper profit, Mr. Murphy and others said.

"'They were so entrenched in their ways, that it went against their egos to surrender the power to take care of these risks.'

"Those risks were alarming. In September 2000, Mr. Williams noticed that Williams had bet on a fall in interest rates and did not hedge, or set up counterbalancing contracts to neutralize risk, in case rates did not drop. Interest rates did fall, and Williams made huge profits. But Mr. Murphy tried, unsuccessfully, to convince Williams that it could not have a position on the direction interest rates would go without mitigating the risk that they might move the opposite way.

"In the early fall of 1999, Mr. Murphy said, he also warned the company about the rapidly deteriorating finances of the California utilities to which it had sold power, the Pacific Gas and Electric unit of Edison International. Pacific Gas has since gone bankrupt. Mr. Murphy saw that the utilities' debts to Williams were growing, and he thought that Williams should hedge against the risk of their bankruptcy. 'But the contention of the higher-ups was that they would get it back. They were too big, they said, to fail.' They did get a big part of it of the $800 million back eventually. But the interest costs incurred by then amounted to some $50 million. 'I could have hedged that debt for a lot less than that, honest.'"

In a less arcane field than power trading such stubborn blundering would have been judged plain incompetence. But a freebooting business of that sort has its own rules of conduct.

William Krehm

A Letter to the Editor

I FIND your September issue particularly informative and recommend it to my friends who can read it on the COMER website. I have learned much from COMER these many years and have a question.

The states of the USA have a common money, the US dollar. Private banks are allowed to multiply that amount subject to restrictions by the Fed. In Canada a similar system exists.

It seems to me that the move in Europe to have a common money is a step forward. The US Constitution established the first Common Market when the 13 colonies became the USA. It took a hundred years to get a central bank and a regulated bank system.

I read how the nations using the Euro are subject to a limit on their deficit and France is under pressure to reduce it or be penalized. In the USA our states struggle to balance their budgets – no deficit spending is allowed. The Fed does not make loans to states as the Bank of Canada is allowed. Congress subsidizes corporations and farmers but not our states.

My question is how are Euros created and put into circulation? Is there a Euro Central Bank which manages the creation and distribution of new Euros? Do the nations using the Euro each have central banks which can print new Euros or create credit through loans like our private banks? I read about how the hard-nosed German Central Bank "fights inflation" and challenges its government's fiscal policy.

It seems to me that having a common money is necessary for common market. But then must there not be one central control?

Thanks so much for COMER.

Robert W. Zimmerer, Longmont, CO

Dear Mr. Zimmerer:

Thank you for your words of encouragement.

It is true that the Bank of Canada is still able to make loans to the provinces, or to corporations under guarantee of a provincial or the federal government. But that has not been done for many decades. The space for it is still in the central bank's accounts, but has been an empty pew for many years. If may be a somewhat hollow consolation for you that while Canada under our former PM Brian Mulroney abolished the statutory reserves that permitted the central bank to restrain what they took to be "inflation" without raising interest rates, you still have statutory reserves. However, that power has been reduced to practical disuse. To begin with the operational cash needed by the banks for their dealing with the public and for the daily clearances are now counted as part of these statutory reserves. And at the end of each working day what reserves are actually put up with the Fed are shifted to non-reservable "sweep accounts," only to be brought back to the reservable accounts the next morning. In that way the use of the funds interest-free by the federal government (within the restrictions in force) is denied it.

This absence of financing to the junior levels of government has thus made them particularly vulnerable to the present recession. Increasingly they depend for revenue on the avails of stock market booms, when they exist, the fines that have been levied on tobacco companies, and the privatization of their assets.

The EU Central Bank creates its own money and this reserve currency is being used by an increasing number of foreign central banks to replace the dollar. The present system is expected to accept another 12 countries as EU members, but accepting the euro is a separate decision. If they choose to accept the euro as their currency they will still have their own central "national bank" but it will not issue its own currency but use the Euro as its reserve currency. Thrusting less developed countries defenceless into the EU would leave them without the necessary defences for their interests. That was very much the case with US banking, and that is why so many branches were set up in the Federal Reserve system. Farming states feared that with a single Fed bank the deposits received from their people would end up in New York where more exciting games were always played. The former head of the European Central Bank argues national central banks will not reintroduce the "national element" into their decision making. The countries in the EU and even more so those expected to join it shortly represent a wide range of development, and if they are going to move towards EU standards they will have to look after their special development needs. From the information obtained from the ECB's website it appears that the national central banks' governors will have a minimum of one voting right on the governing Council of the ECB, but their vote will correspond to a "reasonable area of the Euro territory."

W.K.

The Efficiency of Britain's Private Schools

BRITISH PRIVATE SCHOOLS certainly rank among the most prestigious in the world. Since privatization is being pushed on this continent as a way of making our education more efficient, it may be useful to see how it is faring in public esteem in the UK.

Our source is the *Sunday Times* of London (21/09, "Are Parents getting what they pay for or are they being ripped off?" by Jonathan Calvert and Robert Winnett). *The Times* is a journal of renowned Conservative convictions.

"Robert and Penelope Bottomley have saved for more than 20 years because they believe in giving their children the best education that money can buy.

"Although relatively affluent, the couple from Wetherby, North Yorkshire, still struggle to meet the costs and do not take expensive foreign holidays. They choose to spend their money on sending their sons, aged 13 and 14, to Winchester College, one of the country's foremost independent schools.

"But they are growing concerned about the cost. Fees rose by 9% this year, bringing the annual bill to £42,000 (CA$95,000)."

"'When we decided to send the boys to the prep schools five years ago, we budgeted to spend £12,000 each a year, but the fee rises have been crippling,' said Bottomley, who owns a small business selling car-care parts. 'We may have to sell our house, because we simply can't afford it.'

"Already they have mortgaged their house, but they now wonder whether they really need to pay quite so much. Like others they have been shocked to find that Winchester is one of the schools being investigated by the Office of Fair Trading (OFT) for allegedly fixing fees with its competitors to its own advantage.

"The OFT's inquiry – triggered by a *Sunday Times* investigation – is only three months old but it already seems clear that scores of schools have broken competition laws by sharing sensitive information about pricing.

"Last week the Independent Schools' Bursars' Association (ISBA) admitted its members had broken the law. Almost simultaneously Tommy Cookson, headmaster of Winchester, told parents that sharing of information had been going on for years. It was, he said, an innocent activity. As a charity, he argued, there is no incentive for the school to charge parents more than is necessary. 'There has been no profiteering.'

"Nevertheless, it begs the question: why have the fees risen much more than inflation, and where has the money gone?

"Almost uniformly, independent schools argued that the rise was unavoidable because of government changes to teachers' pensions and National Insurance (NI). But there was another factor, too. Schools were quietly comparing not only costs but also the level of increases in their fees.

"The main national groups that meet regularly are headed by three schools: Eton, Rugby, and Haileybury. Fees within the groups are remarkably close.

"The exchange of information came to light when a *Sunday Times* investigation in April reported evidence of cartel-like behaviour. Transcripts of interviews with bursars were passed to the OFT. The schools initially responded to the investigation with a stony silence, but further damaging information leaked out. Copies of e-mails, sent in February by Julian Patrick, bursar of Seven Oaks school surfaced. A note attached said, 'Confidential please, so we aren't accused of being a cartel.'"

Breeding the Spirit of the School Necktie

"Despite the evidence the schools insist that it is an innocent mistake and one that will now stop. Competition law never crossed our minds.

"That is perhaps surprising since among the schools' governors are leading company executives, judges and high-ranking civil servants. None of the governors contacted by the *Sunday Times* would comment publicly although one, a high-profile public figure, did agree to discuss the matter off the record. "We are surprised that the OFT is looking into this,' he said. "We are charities who like to keep fees as low as possible. Nobody thought that this law was for the people who don't make a profit.'

"Certainly there does not seem to be any evidence that anyone is lining their pockets. But critics say that the cozy system does nothing to encourage competition. Dr. Eamonn Butler of the Adam Smith Institute which has studied the private sector system said, "A lot of the schools generate all this money in fees and don't know what to do with it. They keep spending on capital projects such as buildings which may or may not be necessary."

They simply like the feel of money passing through their hands. Like having friends in highest society.

"In recent years schools have spent millions building luxury facilities such as riding schools, swimming pools, and concert venues. A survey of 378 independent schools obtained by *The Sunday Times* revealed that capital spending has more than doubled from £107 million annually in 1998 to £247 million last year. Neil McIntosh from the Centre for British Teachers, an education consultancy, said, 'People are no longer paying simply for education. They are paying for country-club luxury that competes to provide unnecessary facilities. They are offering a status symbol.

"Higher fees are also providing a comfortable life for those who are working in the schools. While many teachers in the state sector struggle to afford to buy homes near their schools, independent school teachers often have the benefit of a free house. At Eton most of the housemasters are given the use of a substantial family home worth at least £500,000.

"Soaring fees raise an important issue. If schools are spending not merely on education, but also on luxury facilities for the better off, should they retain charitable status? Ministers are now examining whether to draw a more narrow definition of charitable status so that it includes only educational spending – arguably in the public good. Facilities such as sports centres and theatres might become taxable if the schools failed to make them available to the local community."∾

The Serendipity of Page Make-up

IT IS A SIGN OF OUR TIMES that often the sheer chance of page-make up in many of our leading newspapers can tell us more about the world we live in than their editorial columns.

Thus *The Wall Street Journal* (11/08) carries on a front page one over the beginnings of two articles "For Iraq Oil, Signs of Progress Mix with a Glut of Problems" by Chip Cummins and "As Taxes Fall, Dividends Rise – and Executives Reap Big Gains" by Ken Brown. The second carries some big, cheerful tidings: "The federal tax cut, which slashed the tax rate on dividends and prompted many companies to increase their pay-outs, is proving a boon for some corporate executives who are reaping millions in after-tax gains. Charles Schwab, chairman of discount brokerage firm Charles Schwab Corp., picks up an additional $5.4 million. Leslie Wexner of retailer Limited Brands Inc. will get $9.3 million extra."

The first article from Iraq might have come from another planet. It tells of the trials and discontents of the Iraqi technical personnel in getting the battered and looted oil fields running again. "After oil fields are shut down, it can take weeks or longer just to start pumping. Engineers must spend long hours re-inspecting pipes and pumps before spigots are reopened. Wells that have been shut off can also suffer from temporary shifts in the underground pressure that nudges oil to the surface.... At another production site at Kirkuk, Fadil Awad Abdullah was recently monitoring the flow of 13 wells. His crumbling control room, built in the 1940s doesn't have a single electronic control or working gauge. But Mr. Abdullah and his colleagues got the field up and running cranking the valves open and shut across the three-acre site by hand. 'We have experience, so we can feel how much to turn, Mr. Abdullah said, as he pointed to a jumble of pipes with more than 90 rusting hand wheels. 'We know them like we know our names.'

"Even as the engineers make headway, a third challenge looms: tensions between the Iraqis and their new bosses. Iraqi oilmen are proud of having kept their industry running on a shoe-string under Saddam Hussein – until the US invasion triggered the system's breakdown Perhaps inevitably, Iraqis grumble that Americans are slow to deliver spare parts."

But more characteristic of Washington's dunderheadedness in handling delicate foreign situations is the following: "Tempers flared when coalition authorities slashed salaries for the Ministry of Oil's 55,000 full-time employees. The move dropped seasoned engineers into the same pay scale as new hires. Some engineers have stopped showing up at work and staged protests, posing the threat of more serious strikes.

"Omar Jassim, an assistant technical supervisor at North Jambur, stayed on the job, but he is seething over the pay cut. His salary is now about $44 a month, down from $75 before the war. 'We are graduates from institutes and now they put us on the same grade as cleaners,' he said."

In view of the fact that Americans at home are awaiting the resumption of Iraqi oil shipments to bring down fuel prices closer to where they were, the juxtaposition of these two bits of news – the bonanza tax cuts for high executives and the reduction of skilled Iraqi oil personnel to a Chinese level or below, makes one wonder whether Washington's Warriors know what they are doing. Or care.

W.K.

Further Chapters in Ongoing Tobacco Drama

BASIC to the enthralment of young and old by tobacco is that it seems to fill in many of life's painful vacuums: the absence of a mother's consoling breast, what to do with our hands and mouths at critical moments, the seductive curl of smoke that offers whatever you read into it. Add to that the finger-in-the-eye politics of lobbying and you have an ongoing drama that can hold its own with the Borgia popes – the wealth of principalities, slow death by poison, incestuous beddings of piety with murder. No tale for telling in a single chapter.

In our May issue ("Returning to Tobacco for Currency"),

hitch-hiking on *The Wall Street Journal's* reporting, I pondered the sudden reversal in attitude towards the tobacco companies of American states starved for revenue by the Wall St. crash: "Once Tobacco's Foe, States are Hooked on Settlement Cash." An Illinois judge ordered that Philip Morris post a $12 billion bond to appeal a massive defeat in a class-action lawsuit. But states were counting on the proceeds of that victory to help them with their budgets over the next 25 years, and now the size of the bond to be posted threatened to drive the tobacco giant into bankruptcy. That would spell disaster for the states in question, and it sent them scurrying to switch sides and ask that a far smaller bond be accepted. That, of course, raises the ethical issue whether the pimp living on the avails of his hookers has a better shot at slipping through the pearly gates than the hard-working gals themselves. Once government abandons its age-long monopoly of money creation, just about anything can follow. Not only may it not make sense: it *cannot* make sense. And obviously the nonsense would not be complete without some trading in futures. Thus New York state, which hopes to sell bonds based on future tobacco-settlement payments, has enacted one of the nation's toughest laws restricting smoking in public places.

But on to more recent chapters. *The Wall Street Journal* (23/09, "New Leaf – Why Philip Morris Decided to make Friends with FDA") reports: "Philip Morris lobbyist John Scraggs journeyed from his office here to a Kentucky warehouse in March 2002 to meet with tobacco farmers. His mission: persuade them to back a plan for the Food and Drug Administration (FDA) to regulate the cigarette industry. He knew it would be a hard sell when he saw several farmers sporting baseball caps with the legend 'Keep FDA off the Farm!' – hats that Philip Morris had given them a few years ago.

"After years of rallying farmers, sympathetic politicians and other friends to oppose government regulation of cigarettes, Philip Morris had switched sides. Now 18 months later after Mr. Scrugg's tour, Philip Morris's wooing of the tobacco farmers might be on the verge of paying off. A bill headed for the senate would put the industry under the purview of the FDA – with new marketing and manufacturing rules, such as more disclosure of harmful ingredients and more visible health warnings in ads and packaging. The FDA could require that nicotine levels be reduced, even to zero."

To get to this point, "a motley collection of interest groups managed to find common ground, tobacco executives and anti-smoking advocates, northeastern legislators and tobacco state politicians, farmers and urban liberals."

William Krehm

Does Washington Really Need More Servility from its Northern Neighbour?

I AM JUST BACK from a visit to Japan, Germany and the United Kingdom. What impressed me deeply was the outspoken disgust in the press of these lands with Washington's preemptive strike policy as applied in Iraq, and, budgetary deficits permitting, with Iran and other targets in the offing. That is why I was shocked to read (*The Globe and Mail*, 30/10, "Ottawa urged to expand military, improve US ties" by Kim Lunman) of a report, compiled by the Canadian Defence and Foreign Affairs Institute, recommending that "Canada be more strategic and selective in openly expressing differences with the United States than in the recent past and that it should restrict those differences to issues that directly threaten Canadian interests."

Are we to conclude that we can only express our friendship for our neighbour through servility? That, however, would not only be an insult to the US, where the leading press could hardly be more critical of a policy that has garnered hatred throughout the world. A friend in need is a friend indeed; but bootlickers to the mighty are never in short supply.

There is really little novel about the current "pre-emptive strike" course. Under the name of the "Domino Theory," it was pursued in Vietnam right to shameful disaster. That split the American nation for at least a generation. Historically, Canada proved her friendship for what was best in American tradition, not by denying entry to the blacks rescued over the Underground Railway, nor to the thousands of Americans who refused to serve in Vietnam. Though the labels are distinct, there was much in common between the Domino and Preemptive Strike. doctrines. Applied in Central and South America the Domino Theory held that if a democratic non-communist regime were not overthrown by the American secret service, the Communists would take over not only Texas but Northern Dakota in no time flat. Would Canada have been a better friend to the US if it had sent a few thousand troops to spread lethal gas (à la Saddam Hussein) on Vietnamese villages? Instead, it gave Washington advice that, though not taken, has been vindicated by history.

Martin's Old Tricks

It was characteristic of our government's contempt for its electors, that its new course appeared as advice from a supposedly independent think-tank which presumably had pondered alternatives. In fact, when the above-cited report was issued, the veering of policy *vis-à-vis* Washington had already been decided. This way of doing things has characterized Paul Martin's way with democratic process right from his ascension to office.

Immediately upon the defeat of the Mulroney government a decade or so ago, as new Finance Minister he spent a lot of taxpayers' money in a gigantic show in a downtown Toronto hotel. All right-thinking economists of the land were brought in supposedly to "consult," but in fact to applaud the Martin budget-balancing line in an allotted three-minutes a piece. Meanwhile those who had some independent counsel to offer, cooled their heels outside. There, too, the deed had been done and the Little Red Book that helped win the election by promising such things as the abolition of the Goods and Service Tax, was forgotten.

Just 9 days later (*The Globe and Mail*, 8/11/03, "Just 'doing what's good for me'" by Drew Fagan) high personnel of Foreign Affairs had already been replaced for the implementation of the newly recommended policy. Thus Canada's Ambassador to the UN, Paul Heinbecker, in this article announces "ending a 38-year career in the diplomatic service and accepting an academic posting. Deputy minister of the Department of Foreign Affairs Peter Harder, who took over in June, has ruffled feathers by suggesting to diplomatic staff that some may need to refocus their thinking to give Canadian-US relations greater priority. That message is roughly in tandem with a speech of Mr. Martin in April, emphasizing that Canada had to take a 'far more sophisticated' approach to ties with the US, and said pointedly that 'multilateralism…is a means not an end.'" What he meant, of course, was that it is a pretence, not a reality. There you have on a surgeon's scalpel the lily-liver of our national policy as it will be under Paul Martin.

"Mr. Heinbecker had gained national notice last March when he tried without success to broker a compromise at the UN Security Council over Iraq. Last summer there was even speculation that Mr. Heinbecker's posting might be cut short by a Martin government, especially after Mr. Martin did not meet with Mr. Heinbecker during a trip to New York."

To put matters into perspective, Mr. Heinbecker is no flaming radical in foreign affairs. "He was once a speechwriter for Brian Mulroney, in addition to having had numerous diplomatic posts including ambassador to Germany."

A Time for Cool Heads — The Hard Facts are Alarming Enough without Embroidering

The stresses generated by terrorism throughout the world do not make for cool heads. That goes both for wild anti-Washington rumours, and for obsequiousness to the lone superpower on its power trip.

Thus as pendant to the quaintly timed veering of Canadian foreign policy, there are the irresponsible theories being spread about the Rumsfeld-Bush group having itself blown up the Twin Towers. Thus the following report was e-mailed by *New Global Free Press* on 03/10/02: "Berlin – The first sign of the appeal of the new theory among people for whom it should have none was a standing-room-only meeting in June at Humboldt

University of Berlin, one of Germany's premier institutions of higher learning. More than 700 people enthusiastically greeted speakers whose argument was that the terror attacks of Sept. 11/01, were not carried out by the young Islamic militants identified by the FBI. That, the argument went, is one of many lies and distortions perpetrated by something vaguely called 'the media' and by the US administration of President George W. Bush.

"Who, then, did carry out the attacks? The answer was not clear, but the implication was: It was either allowed to happen or supported by the US itself, or the US actually organized the attacks to give it a pretext to send troops to Iraq, and, more generally, to dominate the world.

"Since the meeting at the university, the Sept. 11 conspiracy theory mania has grown in strength in Germany. At least four books are on the market here. One of them *The CIA and Sept. 11: International Terror and the Role of the Secret Service*, by Andreas von Buelow, who was Germany's federal research minister from 1980-82.

"Von Buelow's book, which has been as high as No. 3 on the best-seller list in Germany, is, as the magazine *Der Spiegel* put it, 'full of the subjunctive 'would have,' 'could have,' 'may have.' He does not directly accuse Washington of anything, but he writes that the planes hijacked on Sept. 11 had been secretly fitted with equipment allowing them to be guided from the ground.

"Most unsettling, perhaps, in a poll first published by the newspaper *Die Zeit* in April and published again two weeks ago by *Der Spiegel*, roughly one in five Germans agreed with this statement: 'Do you believe that the attacks were carried out by the US government itself?'"

Serious people, no matter what their suspicions, will keep them on a tight leash until the evidence is on hand. And that evidence has now appeared to link three fanatical Muslim groups in responsibility for the Twin Towers outrage. Notably, it has come to light far sooner than Bush's Weapons of Mass Destruction.

Confirmation from Terrorist Sophisticated Propaganda Shops

Der Spiegel, Germany's prestigious weekly magazine, in its 44/03 issue, carries a 15-page lead article entitled: "The Confession. What the wire-pullers of the terror attacks of 11/9 confessed after their capture to the US Investigators." It is not entirely based on the confessions released by the US government. The source of much of it is broadcasts and videos of various terrorist groups. For these run very sophisticated propaganda shops.

Let us quote briefly from this massive release of information – most of it above reproach.

"Operation Holy Tuesday – Both chief planners of September 11th have confessed. And the record of their hearings provides a clear picture of the events leading up to that great strike. Their testimony reveals how Osama Bin Laden himself chose the pilots for the coup from candidates in Hamburg.

"Just when he heard these words and in which of the many hideouts in the Afghan-Pakistan mountains, the prisoner can

no longer say. But this remark of Osama Bin Laden had etched itself into his memory. Uttered in a velvety soft voice, it was to prove the death sentence for some 3000 people: 'Why use an axe, when you can apply a bulldozer?'

"The word 'axe,' as the Pakistani Chalid Sheik Mohammed told American cross-examiners, referred to his own plan submitted in 1996 to hire a small chartered plane, fill it up with explosives and drive it into the central headquarters of the CIA. But Bin Laden had chosen a 'bulldozer.' Trusted underlings would hijack several passenger jets and direct them as flying bombs to their goals.

"Since his arrest in March of this year, the heavy-set Sheik repeatedly astounded his interrogators with such inside snapshots of the Quaeda Network. Since his chief assistant Ramzi Binalshibh, picked up in September 2002, had told his own life story, it was possible for the first time to reconstruct the genesis of the most spectacular act of terrorism.

"Their statements prove that the Quaeda leadership had for years been planning the coup." Surely, if the FBI were cooking up evidence, they would not have omitted a prominent presence of Saddam Hussein, so necessary to restore President Bush's credibility.

What is wrong with a little fantasy to combat the Bush-Rumsfeld clique? Everything. It trivializes the lies and exaggerations of the very people you wish to combat. And, secondly, you discredit the fight against them by adding to the confusion. Well-sifted truth is our best weapon.

William Krehm

Letters to the Editor

Dear John Riddell:

Ian Woods suggested that William Krehm would be able to answer the following question for me about the Bank of Canada. He himself didn't know the answer.

According to section 17(2) of the *Bank of Canada Act*, it appears that the Queen of England owns the Bank of Canada. Is this understanding correct?

Todd Smith

Dear Mr. Smith:

Section 17(2) of the *Bank of Canada Act* explicitly says that the shares of the BoC shall be held on behalf of Her Majesty in right of Canada.

It does happen that the Queen of the United Kingdom and the Queen of Canada are the same person. Under our constitution, however, the Crown is a purely ceremonial post.

Bill Krehm

Dear COMER:

You might find interesting this comment by MIT professor Norbert Wiener on the abuse of mathematics by economists. The quotation is from his final book written for the lay public *God & Golem, Inc.* (1964): "From the very beginning of my interest in cybernetics, I have been well aware that the considerations of control and of communication which I found applicable in engineering and physiology were also applicable in sociology and in economics. However, I have deliberately refrained from emphasizing these fields, as much as the others. Cybernetics is nothing if not mathematical, if not *in esse* then *in posse*. I have found mathematical sociology and mathematical economics or econometrics suffering under a misapprehension of what is to be expected from mathematical techniques.

"Mathematical physics has come to be one of the great triumphs of modern times. It is only during this century, however, that the task of the mathematical physicist has come to be properly understood. The observer has ceased to be an innocent registrar of his objective observations but has, rather, come to take an active participation in the experiment.

"The success of mathematical physics led the social scientist to be jealous of its power without quite understanding the intellectual attitudes that had contributed to this power. Just as primitive peoples adopt Western modes of denationalized clothing and of parliamentarianism out of a vague feeling that these magic rites and vestments will at once put them abreast of modern culture and technique, so the economists have developed the habit of dressing up their rather imprecise ideas in the language of the infinitesimal calculus."

Robert W. Zimmerer, Longmont, Colorado

We are much indebted to Mr. Zimmerer for the quotation. We have been trying to say that for decades.

The Editor

Hello Bill,

I'm the Australian fellow you met recently at the Economics for the Future Conference at Cambridge. I've been reading some of your book and the two issues of COMER you gave me. Very interesting – you are a rare and wise man with a great amount of knowledge.

I promised you I would write something for COMER about the need to make the transition away from growth to qualitative improvement (development). I used the analogy of a human being whose growth between the ages 0-20 is an early phase in one's development process – that one need not have to keep growing to develop. I will send something in the near future. The trip was wonderful but, as always, you return with a pile of work to catch up on. Anyway I look forward to reading the remainder of your book.

Best wishes,

Dr. Philip Lawn, Lecturer, School of Economics,
Flinders University of Southern Australia

I read in your NEWcomer section that the Bank of Canada creates only 5% of the national money supply. Does this 5% consist entirely and exclusively of bank notes?

Can you tell me anything about the magnitude of coinage in the Canadian money stock as a general rule? Where is such information available from official sources?

Thank you for providing the informative site. I look forward to receiving you answers to these ancillary questions.

Keith Wilde

Dear Keith Wilde:

Our base money no longer consists of anything but Bank of Canada credit which is indirect debt of the central bank's one shareholder, the government of Canada. It is the only legal tender in the land. "Legal tender" indicates that it must be accepted in payment of any debt. The coins and the bills that you refer to are mere tokens, of less or no intrinsic value – i.e., the metal in the coins or the paper in the bills. The bulk of the money creation in the country was transferred to the private banks to bail them out of their bad-loan losses in real estate and gas and oil in the 1980s.

The difference between the face value of the government-created money and the intrinsic value of the metal in the coin, or the paper in the bills. or the ink and power spent to provide the computer entries, is known as "seigniorage" – referring to this spread when the monarch had the sole right to coin precious metals. Obviously the seigniorage has increased enormously since money actually consisted of coined silver or gold – even though the monarch would periodically call in the old coins to replace them with coins of less precious metal content.

You will find the data on the coins and bills and credits held by the commercial banks with the Bank of Canada in the *Bank of Canada Review*, section C1, series B403 for Bank of Canada notes and coin, and Series B404 for Bank of Canada deposits of the chartered banks. You can get the review in your library (depending on where you are located), or on the Internet.

It is necessary to emphasize that the banks were deregulated further after their surreptitious bailout in 1991-3 by doing away with the statutory reserves they had to hold with the Bank of Canada that earned them no interest. These consisted of the redeposit with the Bank of Canada of a modest amount of the deposits they held from the public. These reserves had provided a powerful tool in the hands of the central bank to combat any perceived inflation without raising interest rates. All they had to do was increase the reserves, or in the case of a recession lower them without directly changing the bank rate – which hits everything throughout the economy. Today the banks control most financial institutions – starting with the stock market – and that is where the bulk of the money creation takes place. We have compiled a ratio of the assets to legal tender held by the chartered banks (now transformed into holding companies of a great variety of financial institutions). In 1946 it was 11:1. Currently it is around 380:1.

Go about your study of the subject step by step. For step one I would suggest two little books W.F. Hixson's *It's Your Money* published by COMER and W. Krehm, *The Bank of Canada, a Power Unto Itself* (published by Stoddard). We will make them available to seriously interested students at our handling and postage costs (we don't even know what part of Canada you are in) – $10 to cover both. In addition we would recommend our website at www.comer.org. And either or both of our two videos available on DVD as well at $15 each.

Sincerely,

William Krehm

Doodling Around with CEO Pensions

EVER NEW SCAMS are coming to light in the United States in the conduct of public companies, even as the old ones are in some manner dealt with. Nor is the detail taken into consideration that executive recompense covering the last boom was based on earnings that weren't always really there. And no matter what legislation is brought in against specific abuses, the established distribution of income between high executives and other corporation employees seems to undergo little change. It is too firmly grounded in the power structure and even in the economic theory of recent decades.

The notion that the reward of a large corporation head must be 40 or 50 times that of its average worker was replaced some twenty years ago with a ratio of closer to 1,000 to one, and in instances perhaps 10 times that. Even higher, if one takes in foreign labour's share in the manufacturing outsourced to emerging lands like Mexico and China. Such ratios have come to be seen as well established as the fact that a Roman emperor may have needed, say at least 100 slaves to ply the oars of his pleasure galley. That is why as one abusive over-payment of high corporate brass is outlawed, another has already sprung up to replace it.

And don't for a moment believe that because Canadians are mere spectators of this incredible unfolding in the United States, that corporate governance in Canada is any cleaner. Proof of that is the fact that two or three of our banks have been disclosed to have participated in planning some of the shadiest crookeries of Enron and other US mega-scams.

The difference between Canada and the US is that our government have turned a glass eye on such goings-on. No politician has made a great political career here by unmasking financial malfeasance.

Preserving the Distribution Spread between CEOs and Hoi Polloi

So while old rogueries get tracked down or collapse under their own weight, new ones arise to preserve the established reward-ratio between those who produce wealth and those who gamble with its shadow.

Thus in *The Globe and Mail* (3/11, "Firms quietly boosting executive pensions" by Janet McFarland) we read: "Canadian companies are quietly padding executive pension plans with millions of dollars of future obligations, a practice one expert describes as the 'new stealth weapon' in boosting pay.

"Critics say pension plan adjustments can be a low-profile way to enhance compensation for executives.

"That's because compensation costs must be disclosed annually for top executives in a company's proxy circular, but it is difficult for shareholders to calculate the value of any changes made to a CEO's pension plan.

"'I think this is the new stealth weapon for inflation of executive compensation,' says David Beatty, managing director of the Canadian Coalition for Good Governance, which represents major institutional shareholders."

Note the use of the term "stealth weapon," one that COMER has made much use of to describe the abolition of statutory reserves that banks had to put up on an interest-free basis with the central banks. That bailed out our banks from their huge gambling losses in the 1980s. More than any single measure that changed the ratio of rewards of high finance compared with that of productive labour. In Canada and New Zealand these reserves were done away with wholly in the early 1990s. In the US and most other leading countries they remain on the books, but in emasculated form. What contributed still further to multiplying the ratio of CEO income to that of lowly workers was the incredible further deregulation of the banks after their costly rescue at the taxpayers' expense. That sequence of deregulation after bankruptcy merits a judicial enquiry.

"Mr. Beatty says people were shocked to learn about the retirement payments owed to New York Stock Exchange chairman Richard Grasso, which topped $187.5 million (US).

"Last year, Shaw Communications Inc. in Canada disclosed that it had created a new defined benefit pension plan for its top executives. The proxy circular did not identify its cost.

"But in the pension footnote in its year-end financial statements, Shaw said the projected benefit, based on the past service of its executives, is $30.54 million (Canadian).

"'Pensions are not disclosed in the same way that salaries, bonuses and options would be,' said Michel Magnan, an accounting professor at Concordia University. 'They do not want to give a CEO too many stock options because it would look bad, so giving a bigger pension is a neat way to hide the magnitude of what is granted.' Although companies disclose some details about the basis for paying executive pensions, an investor has to have a sophisticated understanding of pensions to figure out future costs, especially of a specific amendment to a plan.

"Fiona Macdonald, head of the executive compensation practice at Towers Perrin in Canada, says she expects executive pension costs to become a new area where regulators will require more detailed disclosure for shareholders.

"John Hughes, manager of continuous disclosure at the Ontario Securities Commission, says the *Ontario Securities Act* requires public companies to disclose pension information, including the 'estimated annual benefits payable upon retirement,' There is no requirement to separately identify the value of new pension enhancements. Such benefits are enhanced for executives in a wide variety of ways not typical for other employees.

Elastic Choice of Years for Basing CEO Pension Rewards

"Companies, for example, can change the years of compensation to be based on the annual average of the best five consecutive years of salary in the 10 years prior to retirement, plus any of the best five years of bonuses in the past 10 years. Unlike the salary, the bonus years don't have to be consecutive.

"Prof. Magnan argues that allowing CEOs to receive pensions based on an assortment of their best years shelters them from the impact of weak performance.

"A striking example Michael Sabia, CEO of BCE. Mr. Sabia was hired at Bell Canada International and negotiated 6.5 years of pension credit when he joined the company. He moved on to parent BCE and negotiated another nine years of pension credit when he became CEO in 2002. He also earns 1.5 years of credit for each year he works.

"Toronto-Dominion Bank toughened some of its pension details last year, but the bank exempted chairman Charles Baillie, who retired at the end of 2002.

"The bank's supplementary pension for executives are based on the average annual salary and bonus in the five years before retirement, except for Mr. Baillie. His supplementary pension used the best five consecutive years within the past 10 years, up to a maximum.

"Mr. Baillie got no bonus in 2002 when the bank took a huge hit on bad loans to telecommunications companies. But he had some large bonus years prior to 2002. By choosing his best five-year period, he can avoid taking a hit from his last poor year prior to 2002.

"Ashley Witts, an actuary and consultant at Towers Perrin in Vancouver, says that if more detailed disclosure of CEO's pension costs were to become mandatory, there would have to be a consistent methodology used. Otherwise, he warns the costs might not be comparable between companies."

This is in striking contrast to workers losing their pensions that in industries such as steel in the US were given workers as early as the 1950s in lieu of pay increases. Under the lash of the foreign competition of countries like Brazil and China, such industries chose bankruptcy that allows them to sell the assets clear of pension obligations rather than the companies that would retain such liabilities. And the workers, of course, are robbed of their retirement funds. That widens the gap between the high-shooters in the financial sector and the average wages in the firms that serve them as dice in their games.

And Now the Specialists' Scams

On the same day that *The Globe and Mail* carried the piece cited above, *The Wall Street Journal* (3/11, "SEC Blasts Big Board Oversight of 'Specialist' Trading Firms" by Deborah Solomon and Suzanne Craig) reported another major dodge helps create the widening reward-spread between the drones and the honey-makers.

"The Securities and Exchange Commission, in a confidential report, blasted the New York Stock Exchange for failing to police its elite floor trading firms and for ignoring blatant violations by which investors were shortchanged by millions of dollars in trades over the past three years.

"The 40-page report, dated Oct. 10, is a severe rebuke of both the floor-trading firms known as 'specialists,' and the self-regulatory structure that monitors the Big Board floor. It paints a picture of a floor-trading system riddled with abuses, with firms routinely placing their own trades ahead of those by customers and keeping flawed records of their own behavior – and an in-house regulator either ill-equipped or too worried about increasing its work-load to care. When the NYSE does act on investor abuses, the exchange offers little more than admon-

ish the specialists, who are charged with assuring their trading is orderly for specific stocks, or slap them on the wrist with a light fine.

"It all amounts to a big black mark for the exchange, that cuts to the heart of public trust in the 211-year-old exchange – the world's biggest and one of the last that still matches buyers and sellers with human traders."

These and innumerable other irregularities continue to widen further the discrepancy of rewards between exploiters and exploited. That is well on the way to devastating our society.

William Krehm

General Electric and the Plagues of Egypt

THE EXPLODING HORRORS that assail us today seem to come from every point of the compass. That is because we are treating them as unrelated, as though an angry God had decided upon reenactment in technicolor of Sodom and Gomorrah, but in which not even the righteous are spared. New York state and the SEC hog the headlines with the billion-dollar settlements of Wall Street malefactors. The police futilely try closing in on growing crime. President Bush goes on seeking Bin Laden, though the persistence of terrorism is clearly giving him some second thoughts on extending his preemptive strikes to further countries. The states within the superpower are reduced to living on the indirect avails of the killer tobacco industry. California has devised a script that might be a box-office hit on the screen, but in real life requires undoing just about everything wrought by the founding fathers. Piety in this setting assumes increasingly bizarre forms.

It is reaching the point where no matter what the party in power, it is impossible for it to find the time or understanding to address all these multiplying afflictions. And it does call for gobs of money to bribe and shoot up the world. We are coming to envy the fortunate Pharaoh who had only 10 plagues to cope with.

We are then forced to seek a string of common causality that connects all of our major problems beyond a call for "more growth." The past decades in fact have in many respects witnessed more growth – benign or malignant – than any other period of the human record. Is it not astounding then that heads of state should be calling for more and ever more of the same? Moreover, it is not specified just what is supposed to be doing the "growing." The GDP? But that is a hybrid statistic thrown together of the most diverse things, good and bad.

The most direct way of grasping what underlies this swelling flood of disaster, is how our economy has become structured. Whatever contributes to the current increase in earnings, real or imagined, is at once extrapolated into the indefinite future and incorporated into the price of the corporation's stock *The rate of increase* in those earnings is brought into the market price of corporate shares. The obligation is thus incurred that it go on growing at that rate. Especially during a boom, you will find such graphs in the financial pages of your newspapers, starting horizontal and before you know it, standing tall. If there are no earnings – any substitute for earnings will do, so long as the semblance of growth is created. This makes for incredible profits, but so iffy that the knowing folk – including many of the executives who achieve this lucrative effect – rarely lose time in selling their options. To attain such growth the stock price is under pressure to conform to the mathematics of the atomic bomb – growth rates to the infinite power. The rate of growth, the rate of growth of the rate of growth, and continued growth rates of higher order to infinity. Such a rate of growth is by definition unsustainable. Hiroshima and Nagasaki are there to prove it. So much for the blind concentration of growth without enquiring for what, of what.

That message is being delivered once again in the fate of a foremost corporate star. Under its previous CEO, Jack Welch, no corporation approached GE as a success model. He was accorded all the trappings of the wisest, most successful executive on the block. His book on how he managed such achievement, became a best seller. Even his divorce, closely following his retirement, was accorded all the respectful publicity of a royal wedding. GE was noted for bringing under its palatial roof the most disparate unrelated industries, but all of them as steady as the Rock of Gibraltar.

Now, however, we read in *The Wall Street Journal* (13/10, "GE's Immelt Faces Hurdles After Acquisitions" by Ken Brown and Kathryn Kranhold): "While Jeff Immelt (Welch's successor as CEO of GE) is pedalling as fast as he can, reality is starting to catch up to General Electric.

"In three days last week, the industrial and financial conglomerate reached agreement or closed on more than $25 billion in acquisitions, a massive spending spree that included two of the biggest deals in the 111-year history of GE.

"On Wednesday, the company signed a definitive agreement to buy Vivendi Universal's film and television assets, in a complicated deal valued at about $14 billion. On Thursday its $2.3 billion deal to buy Finnish medical-device maker Instrumentarium. "On Friday, GE said it would pay $9.5 billion for Amersham, a British medical diagnostic and bioscience company, in the second-biggest GE acquisition ever, behind Vivendi.

"All of the transactions crystallize an important shift for the conglomerate away from the steady industrial businesses that have dominated it for decades, into riskier, high-growth new areas that executives hope will redefine the company.

"Why Mr. Immelt is in such a rush was explained in part by GE's earnings, which met expectations Friday but thrilled no one." But thrill has long been embodied into price.

"The rest of the year is looking dim as well, and analysts aren't expecting much for 2004.

"GE stock fell nearly 3% Friday and is down nearly 9% from its 52-week high in mid-September.

"In the near term, two concerns are weighing on investors. First, GE's cyclical businesses, which should rebound as the economy picks up steam, are fairly flat. Second, investors seem to realize that Power Systems and its commercial and consum-er-finance unit – the two engines that drove GE's growth during the 1990's, other than its serial acquisitions – aren't going to help anytime soon.

"Operating profit from Power Systems was down 31% the third quarter. and 40% for the year, even though 2002 wasn't so great either. And its finance business, while growing rapidly, already accounts for one half of GE's earnings. GE which trades at nearly 21, slightly above the broad market, risks being valued as a financial stock, where Price to Earning Ratios in the middle teens are more the norm. Mr. Immelt has said that the financial group, mostly commercial and consumer, will eventually make up less than 45% of the company's earnings.

"For two years since taking over GE, Mr. Immelt has been working to make over GE, looking to scrap some of its industrial businesses like industrial diamonds and pushing to high-tech and high-growth businesses."

It is prisoner of its commitment – through its price multiple – to continue its growth rate and the growth rates to higher derivatives of the growth rate already attained. That is the Deal with the Devil for its past successes: a growth rate, once achieved, must be maintained into all higher derivative-powers.

"With Amersham, Mr. Immelt is signalling that health care, with $10 billion in revenue this year, will become an even bigger part of the $132 billion behemoth, and that it is willing to pay up – and shake up GE's management.

"The Instrumentarium deal boosts GE's presence in hospitals, where it is trying to build information technology systems. While this is a growing area, hospitals are having a harder time coming up with the capital to invest." Balancing the government's budget is undercutting the very growth rate that it is supposed to be stimulating.

"The Vivendi deal is by most accounts a good one financially for GE, and the company has done well running NBC. The question remains, though, whether GE's strong management style will work at a movie studio and a chain of theme parks.

"GE has been working with Amersham on new agents that can target diseased cells and illuminate cell activity when scanned. With Amersham, GE will now manufacture the agents, as well as embark on a new specialty – the protein-separation business. Amersham is the major supplier of instruments and agents to pharmaceutical companies developing genetically bio-engineered protein drugs used to treat diseases.

"Analysts also note that GE is willing to use its own stock as currency for the deal, even though its valuation is below its average for the past few years. On top of that, GE paid 800 pence ($13.32) a share for Amersham, a 45% premium based on Amersham's closing stock price before rumors of a deal." While chasing growth, GE in several ways is actually moving away from it. Its past successes return to haunt it.

What the economy needs is the equivalent of Amersham's desired "new agents that can target diseased cells when scanned." That would reveal the perils of embedding exponential growth of no matter what aspect of society's future.

William Krehm

On the Atomic Bomb of Exponential Growth

OUR UNIVERSITIES are undergoing a round of self-searching to make ends meet. That is particularly the case with economics departments that are increasingly verging on business schools in their curricula and personnel. I was going to say "soul-searching" rather than self-searching, because "soul" seems the main victim of the process. It has to do with narrowing budgets, the sting of growth and the lack of funds to even properly pay the staff for those ever grander bits of real estate in which they are coming to be housed.

Were I to have a voice in the proposed "enrichment" of the curricula, and indeed for all curricula on social subjects, my suggestion would be a brief mathematics course for freshmen on the implications of the exponential curve. This, almost sixty years after Hiroshima, is still being used by otherwise literate people as a synonym for "huge," "egregious", "monstrous." But that is to trivialize the notion of exponential growth. It is a very special function designed so that as its value increases, its rate of growth (known as the first derivative) keeps pace with that value, as does the rate of growth of the rate of growth (a.k.a. the acceleration), and as a result so do all successive higher rates of growth (or derivatives) to infinity. It is the mathematics of the atomic bomb. And anyone who adopts it as a model for economic policy is without conscience, or victim of mental sloth.

To fill in the picture, we must note that the mathematics of exponential function are closely related to the mathematics of equilibrium economics, that assumes a "pure and perfect market" defined so that all actors are of such infinitesimal size that nothing they do individually or leave undone can possibly affect prices. In this way equilibrium points are guaranteed to exist so that the first derivative that we have met in the previous paragraph returns to zero to create a path that retraces its steps and gets us back to where we came from. A further detail is that the fatal array of rates of growth to ever higher powers has been applied in the world of high finance where attention is shifted from products useful for human existence, to the their prices, and then to the increase of their prices and then the rate of change of an aspect of the value of the company, and then of the financial holding company that issues the securities, and then to the change in the currency of the security and its market value, and so forth to every high rating of the rate of growth of an ever more abstract aspects of a financial item. Hedging and trading in these "derivatives" is known as risk management. But where is the risk of such gambles expected to go? Rocketed to another planet? Clearly it can only be unloaded on innocents or rogues still on the planet earth. Eventually it must share the fate of anything connected with exponential growth.

China's Exponential Industrial Sucesses

All this is adds up to rather seismic reflections on reading an article on China (*The Wall Street Journal*, 13/11, "Behind China's Export Boom, Heated Battle Among Factories") by Peter Wonacott): "Shajing, China – Under the corrugated-metal roof of China Hai Electric Works Co., hundreds of workers toil in six plants to meet orders for millions of small appliances. Inside one factory, ex-farmers bend over a clanging converter belt where they turn squid-shaped hunks of steel and wiring into electric fans. The fans cost about $4 wholesale and eventually will retail in the US for $15 to $40 through such online stores as Amazon.com.

"This is the kind of picture US politicians might conjure up when tapping the hot-button issue of American jobs lost to the flood of Chinese exports. But China's smaller manufacturers themselves face brutal new competition right at home.

"China, one of the world's busiest factory floors, increasingly suffers from a production glut, and the big overseas retailers such as Wal-Mart Stores Inc. that soak up China's exports have been quick to capitalize. They're demanding rock-bottom prices and forcing factory bosses to cut costs any way they can to remain in contention for export orders. The average wholesale price for Ching Hai's fans has tumbled to $4 from $7 a decade ago, according to company executives.

"At Ching Hai, manager David Liu has cut his labor force in half, to 1,500 workers, even while maintaining the same level of orders. The company's starting salary of about $20 a month is some 40% less than the local minimum wage. Many workers put in 18-hour days with minimal training and constant pressure to boost output. Ching Hai, which has a high rate of accidents involving fingers severed by machinery, has been investigated by the local labor bureau for possible violations.

"The lure of low costs has been attracting new plants to China from around Asia for the past decade. Easy credit and expanding know-how has caused the number of local manufacturing operations to mushroom. The trade liberalization undertaken since China's entry into the World Trade Organization two years ago drew another raft of foreign manufacturers. Shajing, alone, a city of 600,000, boasts about 1,200 factories.

"Buyers are moving aggressively to play one factor against another. 'As things get more competitive, the pressure that comes along with that, yeah, we try to take advantage of it,' says Gary Meyers, a vice president in global procurement at Wal-Mart.

Two Giants in Confrontation China and Wal-Mart

"A decade ago, Chairman Ji Maosong, 64, saw that Ching Hai, then based in Taiwan, wouldn't survive paying Taiwanese workers $15 a day to assemble fans in competition with labor costs as low as $1 a day in China. He shifted much of his manufacturing to China and asked Mr. Liu to serve as general manager for a no-frills electric-fan factory the company built for $10 million in Shajing, outside the southeastern city of Shenzhen.

"At first, Chin Hai was successful, enjoying a 20% profit margin on exported fans. But then scores of factories, mostly from Taiwan, Hong Kong and South Korea rushed in to take advantage of China's cheap labor. Migrant workers from other provinces would come to outnumber town residents 10-to-1.

"Multinationals were buying from China in bulk. While impressed by the size of Wal-Mart's huge order for electric fans, Mr. Liu recalls being distressed by the low price demanded.

Other encounters with big-name retailers rang alarm bells at Ching Hai. They saw Chinese competitors accepting astonishingly low bids.

"Small savings in materials couldn't offset the slide of product prices. Profit margins have narrowed to 5% currently from 20% a decade ago.

"Though the city's minimum wage is about $56 a month, Ching Hai starts recruits at the $32 level and promises subsidies for food and lodging.

"As abuses come to light, many multinationals are enforcing codes of conduct for supplies. [They read well in the US.] Wal-Mart's *Standards for Suppliers* demands that factories comply with local laws for wages and work hours. Wal-Mart also forbids forced labor and child labor, and promotes proper training, safety, and clean restrooms. But Chinese labor experts say enforcing standards would increase costs, deter investment and undermine local development. "

William Krehm

Heterodox Conference Ratings

IT IS A GOOD thirty-five years since I began attending economic conferences. The late John Hotson, on introducing me into the world of academic economists, warned me about their eye-gouging tendencies. It was in the corridors of the Eastern Amerian Economic Association rather than at its formal sessions that a group of us improved our knowledge of the technicalities of money creation. As the years went by, the few papers read on the subject seemed to come from specialists from ever more modest universities – working in that vineyard was clearly no way of advancing an academic career. The very subject had begun reeking of sulphur and barricades. Meanwhile, formidable speakers like Paul Volcker thundered away in the plenary sessions on the danger of rising prices in any degree.

In time our group moved from the corridors of the Association to sessions of our own. There was far more freedom then for discussing such matters than today. Proof of that was that Hotson around 1977 was able to arrange for me to read a paper on the theme of my second book (*Babel's Tower – The Dynamics of Economic Breakdown*) at the sole plenary session of the Canadian Economic Association's conference at Fredericton New Brunswick. It dealt not only with non-inflationary price rise, but with systems theory that would end the "externality" treatment of the environment, health, and all other non-marketed areas of the economy. My referee on the occasion, R. Lipsey, author of a successful textbook, devoted two sentences to my effort, pleading a previous engagement, but assuring the audience that if the present policies continued not working for another four years, economists would address the problems I raised. Many times four years have passed, and we have not heard from Mr. Lipsey on the subject.

However, in recent months the current wisdom of the US Fed is that a couple percent of "inflation," rather than bringing on hyperinflation as in Germany of 1923 as had for years been claimed by the central banks of the world, is actually beneficent. Like good and bad cholesterol, it would seem. The possibility that the desirable 2% of price rise might not be inflation at all – i.e., due to an excess of demand over supply – has still escaped them. Instead, it might merely reflect the growing layer of taxation in price that paid for the world-wide higher technology and urbanization, and the ever more costly human and physical infrastructures. Capital budgeting (accrual accountancy), when it was brought in to cover physical investments by governments, was done so in complete stealth (in the US in 1996) or without adequate explanation (in Canada in 1999 to 2003).

Capitalizing the Disrepute of Economics

Given the financial straits of universities, it would seem inevitable that the very ill repute of economists can make of conferences on heterodox economics an appealing source of revenue. As a result, such conferences are developing an orthodoxy of their own. They are coming to be seen as a franchise; but not to the point of alienating the corporations whose endowments are important to pay the bills.

Thus a couple of years ago I attended a heterodox conference in Calgary that took place within the orthodox conference of the Canadian Economic Association. You bought a ticket to the big conference and that allowed entry, should you wish it, to the little heterodox economics conference held in its bowels. That, I suppose, helped puff up the statistics of the waning attendance at these traditional association conferences and provided a bit of extra income. On the walls of the huge building where it took place were the names of the corporations that contributed to the university rather than those of Aristotle, Newton and Adam Smith who apparently had failed to do so. Clearly, in such a setting, there was no mingling between those who attended the Canadian Economic Association proper, and those who came to its heterodox sub-tenant.

All this leads to a demand in certain delicate areas for talents that can create the semblance of unrestricted enquiry, while enforcing the unwritten boundaries that confine it.

At several of these gatherings I attended – among them that of the Levy Institute held in New York City almost a decade ago and later at the Laurentian University in Sudbury – a banker-economist from West Palm Springs, Florida, bankrolled the expenses of out-of-towners who observed the rules of this game. On two such occasions I had been told that my expenses would be paid, but clearly I violated that condition. In Sudbury the charming Finnish-speaking Moroccan academic who organized the conference took me aside and with some embarrassment told me that they had run out of funds. and were unable to cover my expenses. Without my suggesting it, however, he had taken the trouble to provide a receipt for tax purposes for books I had contributed to the university. The good man was sympathetic enough to attend a COMER conference some months later. I understand that the Levy Institute broke up on just such issues.

At the Sudbury Conference I had written figures on the blackboard to show the leverage of Canadian banks to their cash reserves that had risen from 11 to one to approaching

400:1, since 1946 and this led to a dispute between me and the patron economist-banker. At the very peak of the stock market boom I predicted a meltdown of the credit system. He disputed that, pointed to the modest stock of short-term government paper our banks held as a reserve against this danger. Much of this, however, is needed for routine bank operations. Rumour has it that the good man himself may have turned out a bit over-extended in Russia and elsewhere. In any case, I have missed his commanding presence at recent conferences.

The Spirit Lives On

However, here and there his spirit lives on. At the New York City Levy Institute Conference the person in charge of the conference, whom we shall refer to as MF, had developed an artful way of handling me, but when I offered to make a gift to the Institute of several copies of Bill Hixson's superb little book *It's Your Money* just published by COMER, in a flash of open hostility he spurned the offer.

Last June, I attended a Heterodox Economics Conference at the Kansas City campus of the University of Missouri, sponsored by that university and the Christian University of Texas. To my surprise MF turned up very much in charge and greeted me like a long-lost friend. Perhaps by coincidence he also chaired the session where I read my paper. He introduced me with fulsome praise, and spoke of the original ideas he had been surprised to hear from me in the northern regions of Canada. Then he placed the three people with papers to read. The other two faced the audience, me with my back to it. And when the papers were read, each of the other two got ample time for questions and answers taken in sequence, but there was not a minute left for a question or answer on mine. MF had pulled another of his coups.

Conferences on heterodox economics can thus be a mixed bag. However, they do minister somewhat to society's great need for a fundamental rethinking of what passes for economic science. Particularly at Kansas City and at Cambridge an interest in systems theory was in evidence for the first time in three decades. This technique, long recognized in science and engineering, identifies the subsystems, each of which observes its own rules but whose continued functioning is essential for the performance of the entire system. If a single subsystem fails, it brings down the entire system with it. Consequently, the reciprocal effects of all subsystems must be carefully monitored to ensure that none of them infringes the supreme constraint on subsystems: "Thou shalt not eat another subsystem's breakfast."

Systems Theory is Incompatible with Equilibrium Economics

There is then no way of seriously introducing systems theory into economics so long as it goes on treating the environment, the household economy, public investment in human capital and much else as "externalities." That means restructuring the entire conventional doctrine that regards any increase of the price index as inflationary, indicating an excess of demand over supply. In fact it might merely signal that more essential government investment has been made in non-market subsystems. Thirty-five years ago,[1] I distinguished this growing layer of taxation in the price level from real market inflation and termed it the *social lien*.

Over the past few months, the US Federal Reserve and the Bank for International Settlements have suddenly made the distinction between beneficial "inflation," and "bad" inflation which had to be exterminated with high interest rates. That, however, is not analysis but cover-up.

To introduce systems theory we must end the disallowance of the main source of revenue of all non-market subsystems – public financing – as "inflationary." Responding to the inevitable structural rise of the price level by raising interest rates is to cannibalize the non-market subsystems in a double way – not only disallowing their funding by the state, but choosing higher interest rates as the means of doing so. If heterodox economics conferences are to be serious about systems theory, rethinking the conventional dogma of a flat price index is essential.

Investors are guided by bond-rating agencies in grading bonds. There is a similar reason for rating our heterodox economic conferences. For in their oft unsteady hands rests much of society's ability to learn from past errors. Such conferences can be graded on several counts. (1) The range of the subjects dealt with, and how well these are interlinked as required by systems theory; (2) the fairness in the time allotment to the various contributors of papers; (3) the breadth of curiosity of the audience; and (4) the extent to which that curiosity could be expressed and satisfied. (5) Other merits – this item not quantified.

Grading these over a scale 1 to 4 to indicate an ascending value, here is how I would rank some of the more recent heterodox economics conferences I have recently attended.

World Conference on the Future of Heterodox Economics of University of Missouri, Kansas City, and the Christian University of Texas, ICAPE, June 5-7, 2003. Range of subjects dealt with and how well they were interlinked – rating: 2.

Fairness in time allotment to these subjects – rating: 1.

The breadth and depth of interest amongst participants – rating: 4

Extent to which that curiosity could be satisfied – rating 2.

Other merit: the high point of the conference was the announcement by James Galbraith, son of John Kenneth and professor at the Christian University of Texas, of his part in an organization of economists against preemptive warfare. The high breadth and interest of the participants was proved by the response to the issue of *Economic Reform* containing the paper I read. It was snatched up and most favorably commented on by people unknown to me.

Economics of the Future conference at Cambridge University, UK, September 17-19, 2003. Range of subjects dealt with and how well they were interlinked – rating: 3.

Fairness in time allotted to these – rating: 3.

Breadth of interests among participants – rating: 2.

Extent to which that interest could be satisfied – rating: 3.

Other merit: a demerit was the reluctance at many sessions of participants to challenge some most outrageous statements made by at least one author in defence of their papers. In one instance it was argued that economists could and should follow the example of chemistry that makes little or no use of mathematics. That of course would exclude molecular weights, the Mendeleiev table, isotopes, entropy, and in fact the atomic bomb. In the house of Isaac Newton (who did, however, have his alchemist side) I alone challenged this. Undoubtedly, British good manners had taken over.

What also played an obvious role in this amazing incident, was the leaning of some leaders of the original Post-Autistic Parisian movement against mathematics per se. There seemed to be a weary desire of troubled folks teaching an absurdly misapplied version of mathematics simply to get rid of the bothersome stuff.

JSPE Annual Conference, "Political Economy Now – Marxist Reappraisal," Tokyo, October 18-19, 2003. On a purely statistical basis, a review of the agenda of heterodox economic conferences, since the collapse of the Soviet Union, Marxist economic theory seems to have lost its old position at the head of the outlawed to money creation. That is unfortunate insofar as money creation, is concerned. On the other hand, whatever the enormous gaps in Marx's critical analysis of socialism, his work on speculative finance and the fetishism of capital is amazingly relevant today. I attended the English-language at Mushasi University in a suburb of Tokyo that was a new experiment, and a rewarding one with a handful of papers read by Americans, Canadians, Koreans, Chinese and Japanese.

Range of subjects dealt with and how well they were interlinked – rating: 3.

Fairness of time allotted to these – rating: 4.

Breadth of interest among participants – rating: 3

Extent to which interest could be satisfied – rating: 3.

The Bromsgrove Group, UK. This a broad group of nonprofessional and professional economists, all of whom are monetary reformists, with a broad representation of Greens. Over the past four years I have attended two of their sessions, and this year my effort to do so was frustrated by airline snafu.

Range of subjects dealt with and how well they were interlinked – rating: 3.

Fairness of time allotted– rating: 4.

Breadth of interest amongst participants – rating: 2.

Extent to which interest could be satisfied – rating: 3.

We hope to continue our grading of heterodox economics conferences.

William Krehm

1. Krehm, William (May 1970). *Revue Économique*, "La stabilité des prix et le secteur public." Paris.

A Stock-Taking of Two Decades of Effort

COMER'S origins are lost in the distant murk of the latter 1960s That was when I met John Hotson, economics professor at Waterloo University. About that time I had a lengthy paper published in the then leading French economic publication. Significantly, that publication has since disappeared from the living as the nature and purpose of economic theory were rejigged. Essentially economics has been reduced to a shill for our banks turned stock market gamblers. *Economic Reform,* COMER's publication, began appearing in the fall of 1988, and soon became a regular monthly to meet the challenge of John Crow, governor of the Bank of Canada, who declared 'zero inflation' the one goal of central banking. That was the party line of the Bank for International Settlements, a non-elected international body in Switzerland. "Inflation" was defined for the purpose as any persistent increase of the price index. And the BIS argued that the slightest amount of such "inflation," unless suppressed with higher interest rates, would become hyperinflation as in 1923 Germany and lead the world to ruin. The counted academics who persisted in resisting that nonsense soon found their academic careers at a dead end.

My entry into the lists was determined by a significant observation I had made in handling my personal affairs. Having been blacklisted (as *Time* correspondent) for my coverage of the initial democratic Central American revolutions[1] I had to win economic independence to pursue my interests – essentially to understand why society tended to become malfunctional. In the process of doing so, I became a modest house-builder and developer. Having little capital, my main asset was having identified an upward price ramp unrelated to any excess of demand. This reflected the huge growth of public services to accommodate one of the greatest mass migrations in history after WWII, the introduction of new technologies, and unprecedented urbanization. The deepening layer of taxation in price that resulted I call the *social lien.* Economists have never made use of this readily available statistic. But my business depended on observing what immense government investments – unrecognized as such – were being made that could only tilt this price ramp further. As a result, more often than not, I was able to foresee rightly rather than wrongly what the economy would be doing.

Lessons in the Rough-and-Tumble Business World

In the rough-and-tumble world of business you would have to be blind to overlook the interdependence of the public and private sectors. Or to believe for a moment the academic fiction that if prices go up in one industry, then a healthy "non-inflationary" economy requires that they go down to the same extent in another so that the general price level might stay flat. Those in the industry required to lower its prices to compensate for the increase in prices for its suppliers, to say nothing of those of its butchers, bakers, and landlords, would go bankrupt, and their bankruptcies would spread with woeful certainty throughout the economy. And if higher interest were chosen – as it was for 30 years – to enforce this "non-inflationary economy," there would be a surrender of economic power to the most parasitic financial interests.

That led me to seize the concepts of system theory when I was introduced to it by a close friend of my youth, Sam Madras. Madras had been dean of the Science Faculty at Sir George William College in Montreal and subsequently had studied under Jay W. Forrester, one of the great pioneers of systems theory. He wrote an appendix to my work on systems theory published in 1977 – *Babel's Tower: The Dynamics of Economic Breakdown*. That little opus has stood up well over the years. You cannot get very far applying systems theory to economics, if you do not break up the secular rise of price into its two subsystems with completely different causes and trace their respective effects throughout society.

But to systems theory the economics profession for three decades turned a deaf ear. The official model of a "self-balancing, pure and perfect market" was in fact the very antithesis of systems theory. Rather than studying the mutual interrelations of all subsystems of the economy, it declared all the non-market subsystems – such as the public sector, the household economy, the environment, human investment – "externalities" – i.e., pushed them out the back door. Moreover, public investment including investment in human capital such as health, education and, welfare, was disregarded; the money spent on it was written off as a current expense while the debt incurred appeared on the government balance sheet without the capital assets that it had paid for. Obviously this utterly distorted the government balance-sheet and justified the cannibalizing of the non-market subsystems by the financial subsector.

A Balance Sheet with Anonymous Credits

Since I have mentioned balance sheets, the question inevitably presents itself: has all the effort gone into COMER over the quarter of a century of its existence proved justified? To assess that properly we must keep in mind the official restraints that have been tightened on economic thinking. Just about everything society learned in getting out of the Depression and in financing WWII and the postwar reconstruction has been buried. That results in a weirdly inverted metric for measuring the success of any unorthodox view, particularly *because* it is based on the dearly bought lessons of our history. Economics theory is no innocent sport: it is closely connected with the distribution of the nation's income and the keys to power. We cannot therefore define success by personal recognition or reward when what dissidents have fought for comes to be finally adopted by officialdom. Increasingly, this is happening in garbled, conspiratorial form because no alternative is left to it.

The Dominant Revenue that Won't Step Down

The French economist François Perroux summed this up in his "dominant revenue" concept. Under any economic regime, the revenue of a particular group is regarded in its volume and rate of return, as the measure of the welfare of society as a whole. This is in fact so, as it appears through the eye of those in power. But if power passes to another group, it is no longer so. The dominant revenue has thus passed from the large landowners to the industrialists and then in the latter 1930s to an alliance of the trade open-minded industrialists and the state, with trade unions as a junior partner. The angle of vision of the dominant revenue is in effect a powerful weapon in maintaining the domination of the given ruling group, and when that view is challenged, restrictions are tightened like a hangman's noose. In a sense then the degree to which they are barred from the media and the universities can serve as a sort of inverse scale for measuring the achievement of the challengers. Eventually, of course, when the discrepancy between the dominant revenue and the reality becomes too great, those militant defences collapse. Obviously such blockage of society's ability to learn from its current mistakes, is a wasteful way of conducting our affairs.

In 1996 the United States in near-complete stealth, and in 1999 Canada in semi-stealth, adopted capital budgeting for their physical investments. That was the main factor in producing a budgetary surplus and lowering interest rates. Why the near-secrecy for a laudable if tardy move? Because bringing it into the open would disclose the non-accountancy on which an engineered shift of power from the productive economy to speculative finance was based.

More recently, the US Fed and the Bank for International Settlements have taken the position that 2% of inflation is benign rather than harmful and is even needed to keep the wheels of commerce spinning. This is a sensational departure from the "zero inflation" position taken by the Fed for many years that drove interest rates into the 20% range, and ruined millions of people. Instead of reviewing those two decades of programmed disaster, with no explanation of why 2% inflation was a mortal menace calling for preemptive warfare for many years, but is now suddenly considered desirable.

And after turning a deaf ear to the need for systems theory to understand the complex interweavings of the subsystems of a mixed economy, we are now confronted with the beginnings of an interest in systems theory.

This has not as yet worked its way to the official level. But is has become a feature in conferences organized by economists who are restive under enforced dogma. Systems theory, however, is the opposite of money-crunching. Instead of setting "good" figures against "bad" ones, it deals with the entire constellation of interactions of all subsystems. For that you must not only attach a distinctive tag to a newly recognized factor, but explore its interactions with all other subsystems of the economy, and indeed of society. That means a critical reexamination of the price theory which determines the very quantification that economists are so wholly engrossed in.

William Krehm

1. Krehm, William (1999). *Democracies and Tyrannies of the Caribbean in the 1940s*. Toronto: second English edition. Innumerable Spanish editions, pirated and authorized, have appeared since 1949.

Can Marx Help Us Understand the Russian Mess?

FOR ALL its endless muddling, Russia is becoming a very key country for the continued supremacy of the United States. For its oil wealth, evenly partly put into shape, already amounts to some 8 million barrels a day, nudging Saudi Arabia for first place in the world. The Saudis, moreover, have more than casual links both as targets and accomplices with the fanatical Islamic terror, that may blow its potential as supplier sky-high. Russia, too, is the source of much of the natural gas for Western Europe. The Lord was kinder in creating the geology of that vast land than its institutions. And that is why the new chapter in the incredible tale of the "oligarchs" – the fabulous barons who literally picked up the nation's greatest assets for kopeks – has so rattled the Western world.

The oligarchs are like a mythical race of Titans, but sprung not from heaven, but from humble ranks of Russian society. They profited fabulously from the disarray when the Soviet regime collapsed. American pressure to denationalize on the quick and bring in capitalism at a fast-food tempo contributed to the corruption that engulfed the country after that breakdown. Since there were no capitalists around to take over, the assets of the state were left to Communist heavies and speculative adventurers. The official American view took over that every human was created by the Lord as a potential Wall St. grabber and mega-crook. The Western experts who pocketed a significant part of the loans of the US government earned themselves a reputation back home as wizards for the execrable advice they handed out. But they had little curiosity about what made the Russian economy tick.

The whole transformation was conceived as power play rather than in social terms. There was, for example, a complete failure to recognize that in many instances those government firms they urged the instantaneous liquidation of, provided the infrastructure of the areas in which they operated – the schools, the roadways, the power, the food supply. Treated as mere "externalities," they soon disappeared. Shares were distributed to the population for the privatized concerns, but what would an underfed, underpaid Soviet citizen know about company stock, and where would he find the rubles to take advantage of these sudden "opportunities"? Especially since there was no reliable stock market – even by American terms – for the transactions?

The result: a few keen-minded operators with black-market background acquired or improvised the semblance of banks, went in for currency speculation in a grand way, made killings in imports, acquired radio, TV stations or newspapers to fawn on politicians who were following not dissimilar improvisations in clambering up giddy political ladders. The result: billions of dollars of assets in oil and gas wells, and mines were acquired for a song. Not infrequently, the new multi-billionaires had to dodge the bullets of gangsters; some of them ended up fleeing to Israel, Italy or Britain.

Nor was it wholly breaking the laws, for on many of these matters there simply were no relevant laws. And when the oligarchs achieved wealth running into 11 US digits, a need was felt for legal infrastructure that protected the new wealth and restrained the powers of the parallel political improvisation – the state. It all ended in a stand-off between the alumni of the dreaded Soviet secret service, and the new oligarchs whose wealth threatened to dwarf the financial fortunes of the West.

It had its precedent in what Marx called the "primitive accumulation of capital," where the British amassed fabulous fortunes by their rapine in India and other colonies, in the Chinese opium trade and the opium war, in slave traffic, to say nothing of the commons enclosures at home. There, too, the looting was punctuated with at least one sensational trial – of Warren Hastings – in which the established legal bureaucracy – non-existent in post-Soviet Russia – tried to rein in the marauding of the proto-capitalists. However, the good fortune of the British that made possible their reputation for high morality, was that much of the pillage took place far from home in Asia and North America, and on the high seas.

The Russians had the added bad luck that the constellation of world power placed in the hands of Washington and Wall Street the design of this "Great Transformation" of Russian society. That has been a major cause of the drastic drop in the longevity and actual population in Russia since US-inspired "democracy" took over.

Nor is the "primitive accumulation of capital" in Russia without parallel in recent years in the West itself. The effects on the distribution of wealth and political power in the bail-out and subsequent deregulation of the world's commercial banks is hardly of lesser dimensions than "oligarch" pillage of Russia. The take-over of the Western economy by finance capital with the abolition or downgrading of statutory reserves as a an alternative tool against real inflation, and the elevation of short-term interest rates to the role of sole "stabilizer" of the economy, had far-reaching effects throughout the world. Without it the oligarchs would have had a tougher time achieving their incredible wealth in Russia.

What was in the process of becoming a partnership of Western oil and gas conglomerates and the Russian oligarchs has now been shaken. A neglected aspect is that the Russian state is still in control of the pipelines built and to be built, and apparently has in mind to recover some of the wealth the oligarchs stole by upping pipeline rates to painful levels. That could undermine Washington's reliance on Russian oil to replace its excessive dependence on Arab sources. That is a serious complication. It is bound to give rise to some bizarre alliances in the Russian madhouse.

A Clash of Rival Power Centres

Mark Mackinnon in *The Globe and Mail* (1/11/03, "Yukos CEO, politics a volatile mix") tells a strange tale. "Putin's government, Mikhail Khodorkovsky broke protocol. The gathering was supposed to be a cordial chat about what was going right and wrong in the business world, but Mr. Khodorkovsky went on the attack, directly criticizing the President and suggesting his administration was corrupt. Mr. Putin, unused to be so openly chastised, gave Khodorkovsky his trademark steely gaze before responding. 'If the people at the table were to start criticizing each other,' he warned obliquely, 'I, too, can criticize.'

"Many now see these as the opening shots in a very personal war that has rocked Russia's business world and landed Mr. Khodorkovsky and other top Yukos shareholders behind bars.

"What drove the billionaire tycoon to step out of the shadows to confront the President is not known. His supporters say he grew tired of watching the creeping return of authoritarianism in Russia, and decided to use his resources to fight it, buying a newspaper, funding opposition parties and making a campaign-style speaking tour of the country.

"His detractors say that a man who had bought so much else thought that he could buy Russian democracy, too, and that he was cynically trying to use his billions to ensure Yukos' interests would be well represented in the next parliament." What emerges is a struggle between the political power center, much of its personnel originating in the secret service of the old Soviet state, and the new oligarchs. That melds many of the aspects of primitive capital accumulation achieved centuries ago in the West with the contemporary preeminence of bank holding companies in the West.

William Krehm

Japanese Private/State Partnerships on the Rise

JAPAN once again is proving its genius for innovation in economic management. *The Wall Street Journal* (5/11, "Japan's Cost Cutter: Ministry of Toyota" by Todd Zaun) recounts: "Japan has developed a new technology to control runaway government spending. It's called Toyota.

"The auto-maker is leading a remarkable public-private partnership created to manage the construction of an international airport outside the nation's fourth-largest city, Nagoya. The partly completed Central Japan International Airport, is a feat of engineering, built on an artificial island in Ise Bay and connected to Nagoya by high-speed rail and highway.

"Even more striking, it is on track to become completed on time and under budget. If it succeeds, it could serve as a template for future projects, keeping them efficient and affordable. Japan's outstanding government debt has ballooned to 150% of GDP, by far the biggest proportion in the Group of Seven nations."

However, it is nothing compared with what a similar statistic would have looked like when Japan came out of WWII devastated by defeat and two atomic bombs. Nevertheless Japan charted and fulfilled a brilliant course of recovery probably with few parallels in human affairs.

"Toyota Motor Corp., together with a group of Japanese companies, is putting up half of the money to build the airport – and lending its management expertise to make sure the funds are well spent. Toyota's vehicle production system is built on a relentless drive to eliminate waste and make continuous small

improvements to cut costs. Those lessons are being applied to trim construction costs.

"The project leader is a former Toyota executive, Yukihiso Hirano. His management team includes executives from other private investors, such as banking group UFJ Holdings Inc.

"It is important to keep a lid on construction costs, because the less money it takes to build the airport, the less the group will have to charge airlines to use it. Mr. Hirano learned how to get a big operation off the ground in the early 1990s as head of Toyota's first large-scale vehicle plant in Europe.

"'For the airport to thrive,' said Mr. Hirano, 'it will need to draw traffic from other international airports, such as Narita Airport, outside Tokyo.'

"The undertaking outside Nagoya is the first major Japanese public-works project in recent memory in which private investors have played such an important role. Japanese government officials say that an effective partnership of government and companies at Nagoya could set a precedent for big public works projects in Japan. The project comes at a time when the government is trying to control spending through greater use of public-private partnerships to provide services such as university research and subsidized housing.

"For Toyota and many of the more than 700 investing companies that jointly own 50% of the project (the Japanese government holds 40% and prefecture and local governments 10%), the new airport will offer more convenient transport to their rapidly growing operations in China. The airport is expected to be Japan's third busiest airport, with China its main destination. Toyota, which like the four other biggest corporate investors holds a 2.8% stake, has its headquarters a short distance from the new airport.

"'We also believe that this airport will serve as the key to the development of the central Japan area,' says a Toyota spokeswoman.

"Mr. Hirano's team has so far trimmed 106 billion yen ($900 million) from the airport. This includes some 60 billion yen trimmed in the island-building phase. Instead of first building up the island to a uniform height and then digging out the sites for the terminal building, hangars and warehouses, the island construction team left holes where the buildings would go. It had that much less soil to haul in to form the island and didn't waste money re-excavating buildings sites."

A Neglected Advantage of Public Land Ownership

That could be a highly useful model for public-private partnerships throughout the world – but with a couple of conditions: (1) the government stake in such investments be inalienable, i.e., not subject to sale to private parties for any reasons whatsoever. (2) the private holdings may be sold, but with the right of the government to approve the buying firm as possessing the technical skills that would replace those of the departing private partner. The reasons are obvious: the private parties' role is to provide the technical expertise and motivation, and the public interest – above all since it is less than a controlling participation, it must guarantee that the public interest is observed, and that long-term capital gains accrue to the nation.

Far less promising, however, is the application of a competitive format to Japanese universities. The *Asahi Shinbun* (20/10, "Competitive Universities") reports: "National universities, which will become corporate entities for administrative purposes next spring, have developed drafts of their mid-term goals and programs. The mid-term goals address academic focus, research objectives and administration for six years, and the programs describe specific approaches to be taken to achieve these targets. Together, they represent a new approach for national universities as independent entities, and the targets and plans are, in their way, something like political manifestos in terms of pledging what they intend to achieve.

"Universities will be held up to public scrutiny in terms of whether they achieve their objectives and carry out their plans, and *the money they receive from the central government coffers will depend upon such assessments* [our italics]. This is the first opportunity to show what they plan to do as they attain independence.

We wonder whether Einstein, had he found an academic post while working on special relativity, would have passed muster under such competitive criteria to have his salary extended. Certainly the necessary reconsideration of what has come to pass for economic theory might not.

William Krehm

INDEX

Mulroney, Brian 84, 120, 170
Musgrave, Richard 99
Muskin, Selma 54
Muslim 284
mutual funds, deep rot 314

N

NAFTA 109
Napoleon 19
National Auditing Office 158
Nixon, Richard 71
non-core items 213
NORAD 32
Norway 273

O

Obsidian Hedge Fund 108
Ontario Hydro 158
    privatization 2, 86
Ontario Security Commission
    89, 107
Ontario Teachers' Pension 7
Orwell, George 16
Ostry, Sylvia 109

P

Panama 18
Pavlov 58
pension funds, ponzi 262
pensions, CEO 324
Peron, Juan 19
Perroux, François 72, 95, 98, 213
    dominant revenue 95
Peters, Douglas 212
Petty, William 239
Pew Charitable Trusts 147
pluralism 95
Popper, Karl 201, 211
pre-emptive strike doctrine 309
price-earning ratio 81
Priestman, Richard 222, 245, 267
principle of least action 296
privatization 2, 156
    wholesale 20
Project Alpha 64
purchase accountancy.
    See accounting

Q

Quality of Life Indicators 86
Qwest Communications 108

R

Rabinovitch, Robert 10
Rae, Bob 78
Railtrack PLC 158
railways in France, Switzerland,
    Italy, Spain, Hungary, Austria
    and Hungary 123
reduction to absurdity 94
reserves
    misused 101
    statutory 96, 201
reunderwriting 73
Rice, Condolezza 66
Rich, Bruce 121, 132
Risk-Based Capital Requirements
    guidelines. *See* Bank for
    International Settlements
Rockefeller Foundation 147
Romanow Commission 54
Romanow, Roy 42
Rosenwald, Julius 147
Rowbotham, Michael 171
Russia 215
Rymes, Thomas 31

S

Sabia, Michael 87
Saint-Simon, Claude-Henri 123
Sandbeck, Dix 212, 293
Sarbanes-Oxley Act 202
Sarbanes, Sen. Paul 98
SARS 302
Saudi Arabia 223
Sawyer, Malcolm 5
Say, J.B. 123
Scholes, Myron 92
Schultz, Theodore 54

shareholder equity 1
silver speculation 298
Singapore 178
Singapore Technology Telemedia
    Pte. 125
Skilling, Jeffrey 16, 30, 92
Smith, Adam 93, 123
socialisme 123
Schloss, Henry 261
Schmidt, Helmut 254
social lien 237, 286
South Korea 301
sovereign debt 23
Spain 310
Spitzer, Eliot 88
Sprint Corp. 63, 125
steel industry legacy 70
stock options 91
Stradivarius violins 214
subprime 17, 200
swaps 181
systems theory 155, 295, 329

T

Taft, Robert 132
tax bonding 164
telecoms 63
The New Republic 9
"There Is No Alternative" 109
Thiessen, Gordon 126, 154, 170
Tellier, Paul 14, 88, 158
Thatcher, Margaret 157
Thorsell, William 126
Time magazine 330
Time Warner 88
Tinbergen, Jan 94, 233
    counting rule 94, 163, 233, 295
tobacco 224
tobacco as currency 224, 319
Towers, Graham 169
Toyota 333
Trudeau, Pierre 170
trust companies 11
Tyco International 108

U

ul Haq, Mahub 86
underground. *See* London
United Steelworkers of America 71
University of Waterloo 330

V

Venetian republic 229
Vietnam 109
Vivaldi, Antonio 229
Volcker, Paul 98, 255

W

Wal-Mart 327
Walras, Leon 93
Waste Management Inc. 8
wealth, negative 16
Weber, Max 133
West Nile virus 302
Wilmeth, Harvey 236
Wolfson, Martin 298
Wood, Robert 20
World Bank 134, 205
WorldCom 101, 108, 113
World Trade Organization 205

X

Xerox Corp. 100

Y

Yugoslavia 214

Z

Zimmerer, Robert 317, 323
Zoellick, Robert 14
Zola, Emile 93